UNITED STATES ARMY IN THE WORLD WAR
1917-1919

REPORTS OF
COMMANDER-IN-CHIEF, A. E. F..
STAFF SECTIONS AND SERVICES

HISTORICAL DIVISION
DEPARTMENT OF THE ARMY
WASHINGTON, D. C., 1948

For sale by the Superintendent of Documents, U. S. Government Printing Office
Washington 25, D. C. — Price $2.75

CONTENTS

	Page
A. C. of S., G-3, G. H. Q., A. E. F.	1
A. C. of S., G-4, G. H. Q., A. E. F., and TRANSPORTATION CORPS	61
A. C. of S., G-5, G. H. Q., A. E. F., and SCHOOLS	289

ILLUSTRATIONS

No. Maps

3 - Military Training Centers, A. E. F. 300

Note: Documents herein are reproduced as found without editorial correction of spellings or other grammatical errors in text.

ASSISTANT CHIEF OF STAFF, G - 3, GHQ, AEF

C-in-C Rept. File: Fldr. 88: Report

Final Report of G-3

3d Section, General Staff   GENERAL HEADQUARTERS, A. E. F.,

Chaumont, Haute Marne, July 2, 1919.

From: The Assistant Chief of Staff, G-3.

To: The Chief of Staff.

    1. Herewith is the report of this section to include June 30, 1919. * * *
    2. In submitting this report I desire to invite attention to the hearty cooperation which this section has always received from the other sections of the General Staff and from the Staff Departments at these headquarters. It must, I think, be evident to all that, considering the difficulties encountered, the staff work at these headquarters has been most successfully accomplished.
    In my judgment this success has been due:
        (a) To the control vested in the General Staff by the Commander-in-Chief;
        (b) To the method followed by the Commander-in-Chief of enunciating general policies and then leaving all details to be executed by the responsible staff officers;
        (c) To the willingness of the several sections of the General Staff to exercise their initiative and to accept responsibility;
        (d) To the teamwork which has existed in the General Staff and between the General Staff and the Adjutant General. This teamwork has been due to the fact that, with the exception of G-1, the Assistant Chiefs of Staff and the Adjutant General were men of about the same age and who had been trained in the same school.
    This gave assurance of similar habits of thought and of a personal touch which is most essential.
    3. The thanks of the Chief of Section are due to the officers, field clerks, and soldiers who have been on duty with the section. Their loyalty and ability made possible such success as the section achieved. My estimate of the ability of each officer of the section has been given in reports already submitted.

                                              FOX CONNER,
                        Brigadier General, General Staff,
                             Asst. Chief of Staff, G-3.

REPORT ON OPERATIONS

1. REVIEW OF GENERAL SITUATION UP TO JUNE, 1917

NECESSITY OF REVIEW

[Extract]

A summary review of the general situation as it existed upon our entry into the war is necessary to appreciate at its true value the American effort and in order fully to understand many important decisions reached in the early days of the American Expeditionary Forces.

YEAR OF 1914

Although the German onslaught of 1914 failed in its primary purpose of crushing France, yet German arms had, before the close of 1914, realized successes which had a decisive influence on the future course of the war. On December 31, 1914, German armies stretched from Switzerland to the English Channel. Her forces were within 48 miles of Paris, and Germany retained the initiative. With her own resources intact and secure, Germany was in full possession of all the resources of Belgium. German armies exploited the richest industrial provinces of France, provinces which contained 7.4% of France's population, 78% of her iron, and 65% of her coal. In the east the rapidity of the Russian mobilization had come as a surprise, and Germany had been forced, before the battle of the Marne, to meet the Russian menace against East Prussia. By the close of 1914, however, the Russian armies had been driven out of East Prussia, while farther south they had been thrown back on Warsaw. Neither France nor Russia was ever able fully to make good the losses of 1914.

The entry of Turkey (November) into the war created a most delicate situation for the Allies in the Near East. Not only did the declaration of war by Turkey have a great moral effect on the Moslem world, but, equally prejudicial to the Allies, their communications with the east were at once endangered. The attempt to counteract this prejudicial moral effect and to relieve the danger to the Allied communications finally resulted in the ill-fated Dardanelles Expedition. Throughout the remainder of the war the southern fronts absorbed many thousands of Allied soldiers who were so often badly needed on the western front.

YEAR OF 1915

Looking back on 1915 it is easy to see that Germany planned for that year a strict defensive on the western front, while she directed her main effort against Russia in the east and toward aiding German allies in southeastern Europe. The entry of Italy (May) into the war on the side of the Allies offset the addition of Turkey to the German side and definitely drew approximately one-half of Austria's strength from the eastern and southeastern theaters of war.

In the west the French and English launched several offensives against the German front. The Allied attacks were, however, so limited in extent and in objectives that they were foredoomed to failure.

Against Russia, German arms achieved a remarkable series of successes: Second Battle of the Mazurian Lakes; Mackensen in Galicia; fall of Warsaw; fall of Brest-Litovsk; fall of Vilna. In the southeast the Central Powers, joined by Bulgaria (October), overran Servia and Montenegro. The Allied Dardanelles Expedition was wrecked and was withdrawn in January, 1916. In Mesopotamia, Allied interests went from bad to worse.

The British Fleet held the mastery of the sea, but on February 18 Germany had established the so-called submarine blockade, which constantly developed its menace to the Allies.

YEAR OF 1916

The developments of 1916 leave no doubt but that Germany, satisfied that Russia would remain quiet, decided before the close of 1915 upon a decisive offensive in the west as the task of 1916. The great German offensive against Verdun was accordingly begun on February 21, 1916.

French heroism and the expenditure of British blood on the Somme were, perhaps, not the only causes of the failure of German plans in the west. Russia again astonished the world by her powers of recuperation, and, at the beginning of June, Brussiloff had commenced the great offensive which was virtually to destroy the Austrian Army of Galicia and menace the very existence of Austria. Austria was powerless to meet this threat. Her difficulties were still further increased when her armies in Italy were defeated, the Italians taking Gorizia on August 9, and when Roumania entered the war on August 26 and at once undertook a promising offensive against her. Once again it was essential to Germany that she rescue Austria. So quickly did the German Great General Staff abandon the offensive and assume the defensive in the west, that, on September 15, Hindenburg was able to begin the great eastern offensive which was the beginning of the end for Russia. By October, Mackensen and Falkenhayn had been furnished the forces with which they eliminated Roumania before the close of 1916.

FIRST HALF OF 1917

Germany evidently concluded to remain on the defensive in the west, to keep in the east the forces which she deemed necessary for the final conquest of Russia, and to lend a hand to Austria in an effort to crush Italy. So successful were these plans with reference to the eastern front that, aided by the Russian revolution, by midsummer 1917 the end of Russia was in sight.

In the west the Allies had at last decided to undertake an offensive on a scale large enough to obtain results in the event of success. The Allied attacks were launched during April. Heavy losses were suffered and no great results were accomplished. The French attack at Chemin-des-Dames was particularly unfortunate in its reaction on the French morale. In this attack the French are said to have lost 25,000 killed and 95,000 wounded.

Following the Chemin-des-Dames failure, unrest and accusations of all kinds increased by leaps and bounds not only among French civilians but in the Government and the army itself. At the end of April, when General Pétain succeeded General Nivelle in command of the French armies, the state of morale of the soldiers was to the last degree alarming. Naturally every effort was made at the time to prevent these conditions from becoming widely known, but in 1918 the French press was allowed to publish statements showing the extent to which disaffection had spread in the army. (See French Senate Report and *Révue des Causes Célèbres* of July 28, 1918, *et seq.*)

On May 4 the heads of the British and French Governments and armies held a conference at the Quai d'Orsay in Paris. After considerable discussion it was decided to resume the offensive on a large scale but all attempts at an extensive and combined offensive soon ceased.

Germany began unrestricted submarine warfare on February 1, 1917, and the extent of this peril is shown by the fact that by June 30, 1917, more than three and one-quarter million tons of shipping had been sunk.

RESUME OF THE SITUATION IN JUNE, 1917

During the nearly three years which had elapsed since the beginning of the war, Germany had seen practically all her offensives crowned with great success. Her battle lines were on foreign soil, her own resources untouched, and wherever she had assumed the defensive she had inflicted crushing reverses to every Allied attack. Naturally the German morale was high, while the Allied morale, especially the French after the Chemin-des-Dames, was low. French statesmen and great newspaper owners were suspected of aiding in the campaign of defeatism, even when they were not more or less openly accused of dealing with the enemy. This condition is well described in the following quotation from a French source: The suspension of the offensive in the last week of April has thrown a veritable wave of defeatism over the country and over the French army. (French Senate Report.)

Certainly as early as June, 1917, the German Great General Staff could look forward to the early elimination of Russia, the possibility of eliminating Italy before the end of the year, and finally to the great campaign of 1918, which was to crush the French and English and make good the cry of *Deutschland über alles*. Moreover, leaving aside for a moment the new factor of America, it cannot be said that these German ideas of final victory were extravagant, either in June, 1917, or, in the light of history, at the present time. Italy still had men, but her finances and supplies were in the most serious difficulties, and the occurrences of the fall of 1917 were to show that serious deficiencies existed in her armies. France had sacrificed much of her best blood, discouragement ran like wildfire through her civil population as well as among her soldiers, many of her leaders were distrusted, and her people had begun to complain of the vast sums that France had expended. Although she rang true to her traditions with her back to the wall, England was, except perhaps for morale, scarcely in any better condition than was France. England, too, had spent her best blood and had endangered her dominant position in the financial world; but, worst of all, the submarine war had brought about critical conditions of food and other shortages, so that the very existence of England seemed to be threatened. The French and English superiority on the western front during the last half of 1916 and the first half of 1917 had proven totally insufficient to break down the German defense. Now in June, 1917, it was hopeless to expect that the French and British could increase their armed strength, and it was doubtful if they could maintain that strength. On the other hand, Germany, with the end of Russia in sight and with the possibility of eliminating Italy, could look forward to bringing her whole weight against France and England. The Allied prospects were very black except for America.

Such was, in brief, the situation when the Commander-in-Chief reached France on June 13, 1917.

2. PRELIMINARY WORK OF GENERAL HEADQUARTERS, AMERICAN EXPEDITIONARY FORCES.

NECESSARY MILITARY EFFORT

At the time the Commander-in-Chief left America neither the Headquarters, A. E. F., nor the War Department had formulated any definite conclusions as to the military effort required of America. The first and most important duty was, therefore, to get into touch with the existing military situation and, after duly considering the possibilities of transport, supply, and other factors, to make intelligent recommendations as to the necessary military effort. Within thirty days after reaching France the Commander-in-Chief cabled, July 6, 1917: Plans should contemplate sending over at least 100,000 men by next May. The events of 1918 justified this recommendation.

GENERAL ORGANIZATION PROJECT

Prior to our entry into the war the United States had no complete and permanent organization larger than the regiment. Moreover, it was recognized that neither the internal organization of the infantry regiment nor the theoretical organization of larger units was suitable for the character of the war in which we were to engage. The Commander-in-Chief was, therefore, charged, upon leaving America, with reporting upon the entire question of organization. Immediately upon reaching Europe, G-3 began the necessary studies. In the meantime the War Department had sent a board of officers to Europe, and upon the completion of the G-3 studies the Commander-in-Chief called a conference of his staff and the members of the War Department Board to consider the plan proposed by G-3. With minor modifications the plan prepared by G-3 was adopted by the conference, and, after approval by the Commander-in-Chief, came to be known as the General Organization Project. This project was extremely important since it formed the basis of our entire organization. The satisfactory character of the project is shown by the fact that at the end of the war it had undergone no radical modification.

A quotation from this project, which is dated July 10, 1917, shows the effort believed necessary at the time on the part of America.

> It is evident that a force of about 1,000,000 is the smallest unit which in modern war will be a complete, well-balanced and independent fighting organization. However, it must be equally clear that the adoption of this size force as a basis of study should not be construed as representing the maximum force which should be sent to or which will be needed in France. It is taken as the force which may be expected to reach France in time for an offensive in 1918, and as a unit and basis of organization. Plans for the future should be based, especially with reference to manufacture, etc., of artillery, aviation and other material, on three times this force, i. e., at least 3,000,000 men. Such a program of construction should be completed within two years.

The year 1918 also justified the correctness of this opinion and recommendation.

SERVICE OF THE REAR PROJECT

The General Organization Project provided certain supply troops which necessarily form an integral part of the larger combat units, but did not include the large numbers of troops which would be needed at the ports and depots, on the railroads and roads, and in the forests, if we were to develop and supply an American army in France. Studies as to the classes of troops and number required were undertaken, and in September, 1917, the Commander-in-Chief approved the Service of the Rear Project. This project listed item by item the troops considered necessary for the Services of Supply.

The Service of the Rear Project gave the Services of Supply a strength equal to about 26% of the total American Expeditionary Forces, but, due to conditions noticed later, the Services of Supply never received the troops provided for it in the project. The soundness of the project is shown, however, by the difficulties, due to lack of personnel, encountered by the S. O. S., and by the fact that no considerable change had been made in the project at the time of the cessation of hostilities.

SCHEDULE OF PRIORITY OF SHIPMENTS

Beginning on July 6, 1917, a series of cables was sent to the War Department fixing the order in which troops should arrive to meet existing conditions. It was evident, however, that a comprehensive statement covering the order in which a force of at least twenty combat divisions should arrive was necessary. The Priority Schedule was accordingly drawn up, approved by the Commander-in-Chief, and forwarded to the War Department on October 9, 1917.

The importance of the three documents (General Organization Project, The Service of the Rear Project, and The Schedule of Priority of Shipments) above mentioned can hardly be overestimated. Taken together, they formed the basic plan on which all our efforts in France were founded. It is a matter of great pride that the fundamental principles of these projects, drawn up as they were under great pressure, were shown to be sound by the critical tests of 1918.

EVENTUAL AMERICAN SECTOR

Before the Commander-in-Chief left Washington certain features as to the part of the western battle front on which the American Forces should be employed had been discussed. But no decision other than that our troops were to be employed in closer relation to the French than to the British front had been reached.

Naturally, the selection of the region in which the American Expeditionary Forces should be built up and operate, and the choice of lines of communication as well, was largely dependent upon the plans as to the size of those forces and as to whether or not they should be developed under their own flag. A small force could be employed anywhere along the front, and no distinctly American zone was necessary if our troops were, as they arrived, to be turned over to our Allies. The Commander-in-Chief's original instructions had directed him to keep in view that the forces of the United States are a separate and distinct component of the combined forces, the identity of which must be preserved. Before arriving in France the Commander-in-Chief had decided that a very large American force would be required, and his first observations after landing confirmed his view that all plans must be based upon the employment of several million Americans in France.

The primary considerations in the choice of the region in which we should operate were then that we should be able to develop and employ a force numbered by millions and that conditions should favor the retention of the identity of our forces.

Now the course of the war, as fixed by the operations of 1914, had kept the masses of both sides in Northern France and Belgium. Paris was all-important to the French as were the Channel ports to the British. It was manifest that our Allies must keep their masses in northern France and Belgium as long as the German chose to keep his masses in those regions. It was equally clear that the French must command the armies which covered the approaches to Paris and that the British must command the armies covering the Channel ports. Both on account of the masses already there and because of the difficulties which it was evident must be encountered in preserving our identity, it appeared undesirable, therefore, to consider organizing and employing our forces in northern France.

On the other hand, Lorraine was occupied by comparatively few troops. This had long been a quiet sector and was, therefore, favorable for undertaking the training and development of a new army. The French had proposed that our first troops go to Lorraine for training and it was desirable that we agree at once to that proposal. But it was not likely that the French had made their proposals in view of the employment of millions of Americans as a distinctive American force. The Commander-in-Chief, therefore, at once (June 21) sent staff officers to Lorraine and studied the suitability of this as a region in which not only to develop but to employ a great American army in a decisive offensive. From this visit and these studies the Commander-in-Chief decided that Lorraine satisfied both conditions. So far as concerned the possibilities of an offensive in this region it is sufficient to point out that the Briey iron basin to the west of Metz, the coal regions to the east of Metz, the vital railroad communications in the same regions, and the fortress itself were at least as important to the Germans as were Paris and the Channel ports to the French and British.

Such were the considerations on which the Commander-in-Chief decided, prior to July 1, to choose Lorraine for the development and employment of the American forces.

But the studies undertaken led to the further conclusion that the first operation to be undertaken by the first American army to be formed should be the reduction of the St-Mihiel salient. In the face of difficulties of all kinds this plan was ultimately realized. It is certain that the early decision upon the general region in which our troops were to operate, and, above all, the constant determination of the Commander-in-Chief to unite all American troops under their own flag, were indispensable factors in the realization of the Allied victory.

LINES OF COMMUNICATION

But while the considerations outlined in the preceding paragraph pointed to Lorraine as our eventual sector, the possibilities of supplying in that region forces of the size contemplated were dependent upon the availability and suitability of ports, railroads, and other facilities. Thus the choice of the immediate theater of operations and that of lines of communication were inseparable. The necessary studies were, therefore, carried on concurrently, and these studies required the closest cooperation between the various sections of the Commander-in-Chief's Staff as well as with the French.

So far as ports were concerned, the question was simple, since the only ports which could be developed to meet the necessities of an army of several millions were those of southwestern France: Brest, St-Nazaire, La Pallice, and Bordeaux.

The choice of a region within which interior depots and other facilities could be located was more complicated. Existing rail facilities had to be considered. It was necessary to avoid crossing important supply lines used by our Allies. Finally, while the region of interior depots must be primarily located with a view to supplying our troops in Lorraine, our depots must allow considerable latitude in the location of our troops, since eventualities of battle might require changes in plans. The regions around Tours, Bourges and Nevers satisfied these conditions. In short, all considerations pointed to the development and employment of our forces in Lorraine, the use of the ports of southwestern France, and the utilization of the rail lines leading from those ports through Tours, Bourges and Nevers toward Epinal and Toul. * * * After having personally discussed the questions involved with General Pétain, the Commander-in-Chief cabled, on July 1, 1917, the basic plan for the employment of our troops and that on which the Services of Supply developed.

No material change was made in this plan, and when the Armistice was signed the Services of Supply projects had materialized to meet the needs of nearly 2,000,000 men, while further expansions for an additional 2,000,000 men were possible and were under way.

LOCATION OF TRAINING AREAS

The same studies which pointed to the reduction of the St-Mihiel salient as the first operation to be undertaken by a purely American Army also pointed to the desirability of grouping our training areas around Chaumont. To secure this, the cooperation of the French was necessary, and conversations were at once begun. Relations between Headquarters, A. E. F., and both General Foch's and General Pétain's Headquarters were necessary. General Foch, as Chief of Staff in the Ministry of War, controlled many matter in the Zone of the Interior. General Pétain, as Commander-in-Chief of the Armies of the North and Northeast, was supreme in the French Zone of the Armies.

The ultimate result was the acquisition by the A. E. F. of training areas. With but few exceptions each of these areas was capable of accommodating a division. But these training areas were not suitable, on account of the number of villages, for extensive firing for field artillery, and this fact had been recognized by Officers of the Operations Section who visited the region in June 1917. Consequently officers of the Operations Section undertook to secure suitable artillery ranges from the French, with the result that during June and July the camps of Le Valdahon, Coëtquidan, Meucon and Souge were placed at our disposal. Later additional camps were secured at La Courtine, Le Corneau, Clermont-Ferrand, Montmorillon and, for railroad artillery, at Mailly.

EQUIPMENT AND ARTILLERY

The negligible quantity of war material possessed by the United States upon our entry into the war gave the Commander-in-Chief much concern, especially in the matter of artillery, the manufacture of which requires months or years. Consequently while still on shipboard en route to Europe he directed officers of the Operations Section and of the Ordnance Department to study this question. As a result of this study it was decided to attempt to secure artillery matériel from the French. Upon landing in France negotiations were at once opened to this end, and on June 27, the Commander-in-Chief was able to cable that he already had promises for more than 1,000 75-millimeter guns and more than 300 155-millimeter howitzers. Later, arrangements were made for a total of more than 2,800 75's and more than 1,400 155's. The wisdom of this early decision to adopt the French types of artillery, and to secure as many guns as possible from the French, is shown by the fact that at the date of the Armistice not one American-made gun corresponding to the 75-millimeter gun or the 155-milimeter howitzer had appeared on the battle line.

DIFFICULTIES ENCOUNTERED IN AND IMPORTANCE OF PRELIMINARY WORK

In the above résumé of the preliminary work of the General Headquarters, A. E. F., only those matters in which the Operations Section was directly concerned have been mentioned. Many other matters of equal importance were, of course, taken up and decided. No mere outline can give an adequate idea of the amount of work involved in the studies necessary in reaching a decision and securing an agreement with the French on the matters considered. Nor can anyone, not a part of General Headquarters during the first three months of its existence, realize the extent to which the staff was hampered by lack of adequate personnel and facilities. But in spite of all difficulties the work was accomplished, and, within the first three months of the History of the American Expeditionary Forces, all basic plans had been formulated. The importance of these plans has already been mentioned, but too much stress cannot be laid upon the fact that the successful conclusion of the war was due to the farseeing vision of the Commander-in-Chief in enunciating general policies, and to the sound basic plans to carry out those policies which were formulated by the General Staff in the overcrowded rooms at the first headquarters in Rue Constantine, Paris.

MOVEMENT OF GENERAL HEADQUARTERS

As the original staff was increased it became necessary to secure additional accommodations. At the same time the work with the War Ministry in Paris had so advanced that at the end of August it was possible as well as desirable to locate the General Headquarters conveniently to our training areas and to the region within which the Commander-in-Chief had determined to bring together the American forces. Chaumont, in the Department of Haute Marne, was determined upon as a suitable location, and on September 1, 1917, General Headquarters moved to that place.

3. SECOND HALF OF 1917

ALLIED PLANS AND EFFORTS

As has been stated above, the Quai d'Orsay Conference had resulted in a decision to continue the offensive on the western front. The principal reasons for this decision were the conclusion that if the enemy were not attacked in the west he would attack either Russia or Italy, and the belief that neither Russia nor Italy were in condition to withstand a German attack. In carrying out the adopted policy the British carried on offensives throughout the months from June to November, inclusive. Thus on June 7 the British attacked at Messines, while the third battle of Ypres, beginning on July 31, only terminated on November 10 with the capture of Passchendaele. On November 20 the British attacked at Cambrai, and the battle continued with varying fortunes until December 7.

Although the battle of Cambrai was not a decided Allied victory, it was important for several reasons. First, it clearly demonstrated the value of surprise. Second, this battle was the first Allied demonstration of the possibility of a break through. Finally, the lesson was clearly shown that the difficulties in the offense were rather after than during the breaking through of the first hostile positions. To Americans the battle of Cambrai is of special interest since it was the first battle in which American troops, 11th Engineers, participated and suffered casualties.

French troops assisted the British in some of the Passchendaele attacks, and the French attacked and captured Le Mort Homme on August 20 and succeeded in an offensive at Malmaison on October 23. These actions were local in character and marked the extent to which the French armies felt capable of undertaking the offensive in the last half of 1917.

The incessant British attacks undoubtedly used up many German troops and may have had some effect in hampering the execution of German plans. On the other hand these attacks were limited as to objectives and extent of front involved and consequently did not secure decisive results. The British losses were extremely severe, so that at the end of the year the army was reported to be at a low ebb both as to training and numbers. (Haig's Dispatch, July 20, 1918.) The exhaustion of British manpower was largely responsible for the decision to reduce the infantry component of British divisions from 12 to 9 combat battalions.

The failure of the Allied offensives in the west to accomplish the relief of Russia or Italy sought by the Quai d'Orsay Conference was marked by the collapse of Russia, fall of Riga, September 3, and the near collapse suffered by Italy after her defeat at Caporetto, October 24.

ENEMY PLANS AND EFFORTS

As early as the spring of 1917 the German Great General Staff had formulated the plan which the enemy afterwards followed in his attempt to win a decisive victory over the entire world. The outline of this plan involved the completion of the downfall of Russia, first by aiding the elements of disorder in Russia and later by destroying the remannts of the Russian army. Next was to come the elimination of Italy. Finally, the destruction of the British and French armies was to be accomplished during 1918. After Riga the first aim might be considered completely attained. At Caporetto the extent of the German success was marked not only by the territory gained but by the fact that it is estimated that during the month following the opening of the battle of Caporetto the Italians lost 300,000 men, 600,000 rifles, and 3,000 guns, in addition to enormous stores of all kinds (Mott's* final report). So serious was the Italian situation that a number of French and British divisions were sent to Italy in the effort to render that front secure.

Under these favorable auspices Germany began, as early as November 1917, the movement from east to west of the divisions she needed to give her the superiority for the spring offensive. The German efforts in the fall of 1917 to obtain a peace through secret negotiations may have been indicative of a lack of absolute confidence in the complete success of the proposed operations. These negotiations, however, were not allowed to interfere in any way with the military preparations.

OPINIONS AS TO POSSIBLE AMERICAN HELP

In May of 1917 it is probable that the Allies did not dare hope for the aid of a large American army. Even the idea of as many as 500,000 Americans in France must, in the early spring, have appeared to the British and French as a dream. Thus, at the Quai d'Orsay Conference Mr. Lloyd George is said to have remarked:

> It is upon the shoulders of France and Great Britain that the whole burden of the war rests. . . . America is still an unknown. We must not count upon her aid in a military way for a long time to come. Five hundred thousand Americans brought to this side of the water would be useful to us, if the war lasts so long, but we must live while awaiting them and we do not know whether we will have next year the tonnage necessary to maintain such considerable forces transported from the other side of the Atlantic. (French Senate Report.)

However, the increasing fear as to the future of Russia, the farreaching plans of the Commander-in-Chief, and the optimism which from the beginning was made a matter of duty with every member of the Headquarters American Expeditionary Forces, soon brought about a temporary change in the expectations of the Allies in the matter of American aid. This change is indicated by Cable S-69, giving a summary of a conference held in Paris on July 26 between the Commander-in-Chief, the British and French Chiefs of Staff, and the French and Italian Commadners-in-Chief. The following extract is taken from this cable:

> General conclusions reached were: Necessity for adoption of purely defensive attitude on all secondary fronts and withdrawing surplus troops for duty on western front. By thus strengthening western front believed Allies could hold until American forces arrive in numbers sufficient to gain ascendancy.

The same cable shows that the conference urged the immediate study of the tonnage situation with a view to accelerating the arrival of American troops and also shows that the conference placed little reliance on further military assistance on a large scale from Russia. The conference went so far as to urge that steps be taken to avoid extreme eventualities in that country.

Until early summer of 1918 the Germans were, to all appearances, frankly scornful of America's ability to exercise any real military influence in the war. The German idea appeared to be: First, that America could not create a large army; second, that

---

* [*Col. T. Bentley Mott, Chief Liaison Officer of Commander-in-Chief, A. E. F., at Allied General Headquarters.*]

even if we could organize a large army we could not transport such a force to Europe; third, that even if we did succeed in transporting a large force to Europe it would not fight.

ARRIVAL AND EMPLOYMENT OF AMERICAN TROOPS

During the visit of the Viviani-Joffre Mission to the United States immediately following our declaration of war, Marshal Joffre made a special request that a combat division be among the very first American troops sent to France. As a result of this request, the 1st Division was formed under a provisional organization, pending final decision on organization, and dispatched to France; divisional headquarters landing at St-Nazaire on June 26, 1917. The arrival of this division and the parade of certain of its elements in Paris on July 4 caused great enthusiasm among the people and, for the time being, was of the greatest benefit to French morale.

On July 14, the 1st Division (less artillery) moved to Gondrecourt and began its training. Finally, on October 20, part of the division moved into the Lunéville sector, where battalions, under command of their own officers, were incorporated in French regiments for a first tour on duty in the trenches. The division continued the progressive training of battalions in sector during the remainder of October and during November. Meanwhile, other troops were arriving. The 26th Division landed in October, the 42d in November, while the 2d completed its arrival in January. These three divisions were promptly dispatched from the base ports to the 2d, 5th, and 3d training areas, respectively, with headquarters at Neufchâteau, Vaucouleurs, and Bourmont. By the end of 1917 the infantry of the 41st Division had also debarked in France but as this had been designated in the United States as a replacement division it was not sent to a training area but was held in an area near St-Aignan on the lines of communication.

The experience gained in the training of the first few divisions enabled the Training Section to perfect the general plan of training which had been formulated in the summer of 1917. This plan will be reported upon by the Training Section, but it is desirable to note in this report that the situation resulting from the German offensive in March 1918, prevented the realization of the training program in its entirety. In fact, although the program was adhered to as closely as possible throughout the war, it may be said that the 1st Division was the only division which and an opportunity to complete the course of training.

The total number of American troops in France on December 31, 1917, was 176,655. As will appear later, this total was very disappointing to our Allies. But still more disappointing was the fact that no American combat troops, other than the 1st Division, had appeared upon the firing line even though more than eight months had elapsed since our declaration of war.

EFFORTS OF FRENCH AND BRITISH TO SECURE AMERICAN TROOPS FOR THEIR UNITS

The Allied depression resulting from the Russian collapse and the Caporetto disaster was deepened by the slowness of arrival of American forces and because so few American units had appeared upon the front. By November, it was generally accepted that the Germans would undertake a decisive offensive in the spring of 1918. This belief and the realization of previous lack of coordination in the Allied efforts were largely responsible for the elevation of M. Clémenceau to the French Premiership and the creation of the Supreme War Council in November, 1917. Since M. Clémenceau was the most prominent French exponent of the fight to a finish policy, it may be assumed that his appointment as Prime Minister indicated that, notwithstanding the disillusionment as to the immediate assistance which the popular mind expected from America, the French morale was better in November than it had been in May and June.

But while the French morale had improved and the British had obtained sufficient success in their fall offensives to enable them to bear their heavy losses, there were no illusions among the Allies as to the serious situation which they would face in the coming spring. By December of 1917, British and French authorities began to urge the more rapid entry of American troops into the line and to suggest in one way or another the amalgamation of our troops with their own. In anticipation of some such action and on account of the serious situation resulting from the Caporetto disaster, the Commander-in-Chief had, in November, directed the Operations Section to prepare certain studies under various assumptions. The net conclusion of these studies was that although the probabilities were that the Germans would attack in the spring, only the most untoward combination of circumstances could give the enemy a decisive victory, provided the Allies held firm and secured unity of action. It was recognized that a situation might arise which would necessitate the utilization of all American troops in the units of our Allies. But it was considered that such a course was a last and desperate resort and that nothing in the situation existing in November 1917, justified either the curtailing of the instruction of our troops or the relinquishment of our plans to form our own army under our own flag.

There was nothing new in the British and French suggestions that our troops be amalgamated with theirs. When, in April, of 1917, the British and French Missions visited the United States, General Bridges, the senior officer with the British Mission, in a written proposal to the War Department, urged the drafting of America's manhood into British battalions. The French Mission did not make such a proposal, but it is understood that their refraining from such action may have resulted from the unfavorable answers given to diplomatic inquiries made by the French military attaché prior to the arrival of the French Mission. The reason for these early proposals is probably to be found in a sincere belief that it would be impossible for America to form her own army in time to plan an effective part in the war. Later on, other motives entered and the British and French desire to employ American troops in their own units never abated. The military motives which principally influenced the French and British efforts in this direction in December were the anticipation of the German offensive and the failing manpower of France and Great Britain.

On December 23 the French Commander-in-Chief made verbal proposals concerning American troops to the Commander-in-Chief, and on December 28 repeated these proposals, in more detail, in writing. General Pétain set forth the fact that the general military situation had been entirely changed through the defection of Russia and the recent events in Italy. The changed military situation carried with it the menace of an imminent and large scale hostile offensive on the French front which, in General Pétain's opinion, obliged the French command to contemplate the utilization of all resources, not omitting the support of the American forces. General Pétain observed that the American methods of training would delay the entry of American troops on the front and that any delay would have an unfortunate reaction on opinion in France and more especially on the morale of the armies then in action. General Pétain made certain definite proposals, the net result of which, if accepted, would have been the incorporation for an indefinite time of our troops in French divisions. Such a solution was unacceptable, but our own observation had also led us to the conclusion that an early appearance of American units on the front would be most beneficial to French morale. The Commander-in-Chief, therefore, decided to accept so much of General Pétain's proposal as concerned a more rapid appearance of American units in the line.

But the question of incorporating American troops under other flags was not urged in Europe alone. On December 25, the War Department cabled (558-R) that both England and France were pressing upon the President of the United States their desire to have our forces amalgamated with theirs, by regiments and companies, on account of their belief in an impending heavy drive by the Germans somewhere along the western front.

In answer to this cable, the Commander-in-Chief cabled (433-S) to the effect that no emergency then existed which would warrant putting our companies or battalions into British or French units and that he would not do so except in a grave crisis.

All these questions were most delicate. On the one hand the Commander-in-Chief recognized the justness of the contention of the Allies that the early appearance of our troops on the line was necessary for reasons of morale. On the other hand America could not humble herself as no other nation in history had done by consenting to draft American manhood under a foreign flag. The Allied cause itself demanded that we should not sacrifice the identity of our forces but that the best use be made of those forces by training and employing them in conformity with our national characteristics. Both the French and British believed their own methods best and did not hesitate to criticize each other accordingly. Although we had taken what seemed to us best in each of their methods, we did not feel that either the French or British systems were suited to the best utilization of our troops.

Then, too, the matter of shipping played a part in these questions. Beginning in July, when the Commander-in-Chief had cabled that plans should contemplate sending over at least 1,000,000 men by next May, a series of cables had urged the importance of increasing our shipping. Now, in December, the Commander-in-Chief believed that the British might be able to furnish additional shipping and, although he could not accept proposals to incorporate American companies and battalions in British divisions, he opened negotiations, to be noted later, with the British authorities which were ultimately to result in an enormous increase in the rate of arrival of American troops.

RESUME OF SITUATION, DECEMBER 1917

The elimination of Russia made it possible for Germany to reduce her forces in the east to a minimum and these could safely be composed of inferior troops. The disaster suffered by Italy at Caporetto made it possible for Germany to withdraw not only her own but Austrian divisions from the Italian front.

These and many other considerations convinced all concerned that in the spring the Germans would probably attack on the western front. In November the Operations Section had believed that the chances were in favor of the enemy's blow falling in eastern France, but by December an uncertainty developed, which was to continue in all the Allied Headquarters until late in February.

The Allied morale was better than it had been in May and June, but the shortage of British and French manpower and the disappointment over the slow arrival of American troops gave the governments and the high commands much concern. In brief, the state of feeling in the governments and armies as well as among the civil population of France and England my be summed up as one of uncertainty and uneasiness.

4. JANUARY 1 to MARCH 21, 1918

MATTERS AFFECTING RATE OF ARRIVAL OF AMERICAN TROOPS; THE 6-DIVISION PLAN

The uneasiness existing in December 1917 continued to increase during January. The Supreme War Council, during the latter part of January, indicated its estimate of the general situation by approving Joint Note Number Twelve, submitted to the council by its military representatives. The note concluded that France (i. e., the western front) would be safe only under certain conditions. Among the more important of these conditions was: That the French and British forces in France are continuously maintained at their present total aggregate strength, and receive the expected reinforcement of not less than two American divisions a month.

Prior to the date of Joint Note Number Twelve, conversations were going on between the Commander-in-Chief and the British authorities. On January 10, 1918, the Commander-in-Chief had an interview (reported in Cable 487-S) with Sir William Robertson during which the latter requested, on behalf of the British Government, that American battalions be brought over for service in British divisions. The British desired 150 infantry battalions without any auxiliary troops whatever, three of our infantry battalions to be assigned to each of fifty British divisions in order that those divisions might be maintained at a strength of 12 infantry combat battalions per division. General Robertson stated that England would not only supply these troops but that she would also undertake to divert sufficient commercial shipping to assure the transport of the American battalions to France without interference with our own program. The condition that these American battalions serve in British divisions for a minimum period of four or five months, and the failure of the proposal to include arrangements for bringing over such auxiliaries as medical units, artillery, etc., made the British plan unacceptable, but the opportunity to obtain additional shipping was too great to be lost. Consequently, negotiations were continued with the result that on January 30 the Commander-in-Chief cabled (555-S) an agreement between the British authorities and himself.

* * * * * *

This arrangement secured the transport of six divisions and the agreement subsequently became known as the 6-Division Plan.

Following this 6-Division Plan, officers of G-3 and G-5 were sent to British Headquarters to arrange certain details. It was made perfectly clear to the British that the troops affected by the plan were ultimately to unite as divisions and would be employed in an American sector. It was agreed that the period of training with the British should cover a period of about ten weeks; these and other details were cabled the War Department in 596-S.

For purposes of supervising the administration and training of the six divisions involved, the II Corps Staff was created without at first a Commanding General but with Lieutenant Colonel George S. Simonds as Chief of Staff.

EMPLOYMENT OF AMERICAN COMBAT TROOPS

The request of General Petain (December 23 and 28) concerning the use of American troops, and the Commander-in-Chief's view that, for reasons of morale, the appearance of our troops upon the front should be hastened, have already been mentioned. The Commander-in-Chief's determination to avoid the incorporation indefinitely of our units under another flag prevailed and finally agreement was reached as to the immediate use of American troops. Under this agreement the 1st Division had, by January 19, 1918, relieved the French Moroccan Division in sector north of Toul; Major General R. L. Bullard, Commanding the 1st Division with headquarters at Menil-la-Tour, assumed full command of his sector on January 30, 1918. The appearance of the 1st Division in the line as a complete division marked an important step in the development of the American Expeditionary Forces. The Allied morale was benefited as soon as it became known that at last a large, entirely American unit was on the front.

Steps were also taken to advance the date of the entry of the 26th and 42d Divisions into the line for preliminary training. On February 8, the 26th Division left its training area for a month's tour of duty with French units in the Chemin-des-Dames sector, while the 42d Division was sent into the line on February 21 with the French near Luneville. On March 18 the 2d Division was also brigaded with the French in the

Verdun---St-Mihiel region. Meanwhile our combat forces had been increased by the arrival of the 32d Division, the headquarters of which debarked at Le Havre on February 20.

On March 21, when the first German offensive was launched, America had three divisions in the line. Of these the 1st held its own sector north of Toul, the 42d was with the French near Lunéville, and the 2d was with the French in the region of St-Mihiel---Verdun. The 26th Division had just returned to an area after having served with the French in the region of Soissons. * * * On March 21, 1918, the total number of American troops that had reached France was approximately 287,500.

QUESTIONS OF AN AMERICAN SECTOR
AND ORGANIZATION OF I CORPS HEADQUARTERS

The early conclusion that the reduction of the St-Mihiel salient should be looked forward to as the first offensive operation of the American forces has been mentioned. By December of 1917 it was necessary, in order to insure the proper location of installations, to notify all concerned as to our eventual sector. Accordingly, on December 15, the Commander-in-Chief informed the chiefs of all the General Staff sections that his plans contemplated establishing an American sector immediately west of Pont-à-Mousson and conducting a limited offensive in that region in 1918.

On January 20, 1918, the I Corps, General Hunter Liggett commanding, came into existence and an important step toward the realization of a distinctive American force was thus taken.

The Commander-in-Chief had frequently verbally discussed the matter of an American sector with General Pétain and there was a tentative understanding between the two commanders that eventually we should take over the Woëvre sector. As time went on, and especially after December 15, 1917, preparations and plans were continued to this end but without any formal agreement with the French. The desirability of having such an agreement became more and more evident for several reasons. On February 6, 1918, the Commander-in-Chief informed the Chief of the French Mission at General Headquarters of his desire to extend the front of the 1st Division, then in the Ménil-la-Tour sector, by putting other American divisions in the line to the left of the 1st Division. At the same time the Commander-in-Chief informed the Chief of the French Mission that he desired that June 1 be fixed as the date upon which a purely American sector north of Toul should be effective. The French at first suggested a joint staff study of these proposals and later made a counterproposal that the front of the 1st Division be extended by placing more troops of that division in the front line without placing other American divisions alongside the 1st. This unsatisfactory and unsettled condition of the question still existed when the March 21 offensive opened. However, General Headquarters continued to look on the Woëvre as an eventual American sector and our resources were, so far as possible, utilized with that end in view.

5. GERMAN OFFENSIVES FROM MARCH 21 TO JULY 18, 1918

ANTICIPATION OF GERMAN ATTACK
AND RELATIVE FORCES ON WESTERN FRONT DURING MARCH

In January it was considered quite probable that the British front would be involved in at least a secondary attack in the coming great hostile offensive. By the middle of February the enemy's preparation for a great offensive had become so evident that doubt no longer existed as to the enemy's intention. It was not until the end of February, however, that it became certain that at least one of the enemy's principal blows would be directed against the British front. But so general had been the enemy's offensive preparations in the way of improving railroads and roads and increasing ammunition and supply depots that it was difficult to localize his probable front of attack and even on March 21 some doubt existed as to whether or not a main attack was imminent in Champagne. (Haig's* Report; Hubbard's letters.) Actually it was not until hostile divisions from the Champagne were identified on the Somme front that all fear of an immediate attack in Champagne subsided.

Sufficient data are not yet available to justify accurate calculations as to the relative strength of the Allies and enemy on March 21. Aside from this lack of data such comparisons are difficult because of differences in the several armies in the method of calculating strength. In numbers of actual fighting men and guns the enemy undoubtedly had a superiority but, whatever this numerical superiority, it was of much less importance than the advantages which the enemy possessed in morale, in his experience and training in mobile warfare, and in unity of command.

In any event the German army on the western front was, on March 21, 1918, by far the most formidable force which the world had ever seen. This force had been gathering and training, since the Italian defeat at Caporetto, for the grand offensive intended to end the war before the armies from America could arrive in sufficient strength to influence the result. Germany's best troops, her most successful generals, and all the experience gained in three years were mobilized in a supreme effort. Against this effort the Allies were handicapped by the lack of unity of command and by a doubting spirit which, even though it did not extend to the High Command, was yet serious on account of its being widespread among all other ranks.

SOMME OFFENSIVE, MARCH 21 to APRIL 5

This first great offensive of 1918 was preceded by a brief but violent artillery bombardment which involved practically the whole of the front between Lille and Verdun. The actual attack was launched on a front of more than 80 kilometers extending from Oppy to La Fère; the Cambrai salient was not, however, subjected to infantry assault. Favored by ideal weather conditions and by the weakness of the British troops, who had only taken over in January a part of the front attacked, the enemy, in the initial period of his attack, overran all resistance. Within eight days the enemy had completely crossed the old Somme battlefield and had swept everything before him to a maximum depth of 56 kilometers. The German onrush was finally stopped * * *.

Failure of supply arrangements to keep pace with the rapid advance was probably of no less importance in stopping the hostile onslaught than was the effective use finally made of the British and French reserves.

The results obtained by the enemy were: The cutting of one of the four railroads leading into Amiens from the south; the serious interruption of all other railroad and all road traffic through Amiens; the fact that the Allies must hold a longer front with forces diminished by the heaviest casualties; the lowered Allied morale and the increased morale of the enemy. But important as were the results obtained by the German, he had for a moment been upon the point of obtaining a still greater success. In fact, there is good reason to believe that the fall of Amiens, which for a couple of days seemed imminent, he would have been an all but fatal blow to the Allied cause. To add to the general confusion, to the Allied uncertainty and depression, the enemy began his long-range bombardment of Paris on March 23.

---

*[Maj. Samuel T. Hubbard, on duty in G-2 at G. H. Q., A. E. F.]

LYS OFFENSIVE, APRIL 9 to 26

The battle line in the vicinity of Amiens had hardly stabilized when, on April 9, the Germans broke through the British lines on a front of some 35 kilometers in the vicinity of Armentieres and along the Lys River. It seems probable that the initial success of this offensive was greater than the enemy expected. At any rate efforts to exploit did not seem to be as well coordinated as was usual with the German and these efforts proved very costly to him. However, the drive was not stopped until Mt. Kemmel and Merville had fallen and a deep wedge had been driven into the British front. As a result of its being included in a salient formed by the German advance, Passchendaele, the capture of which had cost so dearly in 1917, was abandoned by the British on April 17.

Although the advantages gained by Germany on the Lys were not so great as those secured on the Somme, still a position had been won which threatened the important ports of Dunkerque and Calais. A portion of the coal fields around Bethund had been taken, and German artillery was in position to interfere with production in a still larger portion of this important coal field. Still more important to the enemy, the ability to break through the elaborate trench systems had again been demonstrated, and German morale had been raised while that of the Allies had been lowered.

On the Somme the enemy attack had been made on the extreme right of the British front and the French had helped to meet the threat by the extension of their front to the left. French divisions also assisted in meeting the Lys attack, but in this case they were incorporated in the British armies.

AISNE OFFENSIVE, MAY 27 to JUNE 4

Following the stabilization of the lines after the Lys offensive it was considered a foregone conclusion that Germany would again attack. Great uncertainty and much speculation existed, however, among the Allies as to exactly where the next blow would fall. The general belief was that it would come somewhere on the British front. As between the sectors of the British front the Amiens-Arras sector seemed the most probable. Consequently, when the German attack was launched between the Oise and Berry-au-Bac, on a front of about 35 kilometers, it came as a complete surprise. The first suggestion of a possible attack in this region came from questioning prisoners taken on the night of May 25/26. The attack fell upon one French corps and one British corps, the latter being in this sector for rest after hard fighting in the battles to the north.

The initial Aisne drive met remarkable success. In four days the German armies had advanced no less than 50 kilometers and had reached the Marne. Using that river as a defensive flank, the enemy changed direction toward Paris, with the result that during the first two or three days of June something akin to panic seized that city. But, on June 4, when the German was only 70 kilometers from Paris, his advance was stopped.

This German offensive cut the main Paris-Nancy railroad and seriously threatened Paris. It is estimated that one million people left Paris during the spring of 1918.

MONTDIDIER-NOYON OFFENSIVE, JUNE 9 TO 13

The first three German offensives had made three large pockets in the Allied line. Since the two largest of these, that on the Somme and that on the Marne, were not far apart and since, by the success of the Aisne offensive, the enemy was, for the time being, more or less committed to another effort toward Paris, it seemed logical to expect the Germans to strike against the front which connected these two pockets. The

French command, therefore, took the necessary measures to meet, and devoted especial care to noting all indications of, the anticipated attack in the region Montdidier-Noyon.

The attack was not long delayed, and on June 9 - five days after the Aisne attack had been stopped - the Germans advanced on a front of over 30 kilometers between Montdidier and Noyon. On June 12 a secondary attack was launched on a front of nearly 20 kilometers west of Soissons.

Both the main and secondary attacks were stopped by the French with but comparatively little loss of ground. To add to the French success, it was believed that the German losses were unusually heavy.

The failure of the Germans to make a clean breakthrough had a very beneficial effect on the Allied morale, which for more than two months had sadly needed stimulation.

It is worthy of note that the first yperite gas shells fired by the Allies were used by the French against the German Montdidier-Noyon offensive.

CHAMPAGNE-MARNE OFFENSIVE, JULY 15 TO 18

Although the German army had seriously failed in its Montdidier-Noyon offensive, the enemy still retained the initiative and it was believed that he would make another great offensive effort. The result of the Montdidier-Noyon attack, and the rapid increase of the Allied forces, due to the arrival of American troops, gave the Allies confidence, with the approach of mid-July, in their ability to sustain another German effort.

This final German offensive was carefully prepared and was freely advertised to the German soldiers as the final battle which would result in a German peace. The allied information as to the place of attack was perfect and, although in the early days of July the attack was expected before the middle of the month, the final information as to the time of attack was equally exact. The Allied dispositions (made by the French High Command) to meet the attack were completed a week before it was launched.

The actual attack started on July 15 and involved practically the entire front from just east of Chateau-Thierry to Tahure just west of the Argonne. In Champagne the French command knew the hour and minute at which the attack was scheduled to begin and in this region it was stopped almost at the outset and with heavy losses. Southwest of Reims and on the Marne the Germans were at first somewhat successful. The Marne was crossed east of Mezy and progress was made up the Marne Valley. However, the Allied counterattack on July 18 on the west face of the Marne salient turned the tide and marked the end of all German offensive efforts here as elsewhere.

SUMMARY REVIEW OF RESULTS OF GERMAN OFFENSIVES

Germany held absolute initiative from January 1, 1918, until the breakdown of her attack of July 15. At least two of her offensives, the Somme and the Aisne, had all but attained results from which the Allies could have recovered only with the greatest difficulty, if at all. A few of the straits of the Allies at different periods of Germany's powerful effort will be referred to later. But whatever the Allied difficulties, Germany failed in her purpose, and on July 18 the Allies regained the initiative which they retained to the end. Germany not only held more and more to a strict defensive but, due in large part to a vastly increased shipping program for American troops, the enemy's final break-up came with a rapidity that, before the middle of July, would have seemed incredible.

Certain features of the strategy of the German offensives of 1918 will probably always remain subjects of controversy. For example, when Germany once began her attack against the British and continued this first blow by an attack, still farther north, it was assumed by many that the enemy's primary purpose was to crush the British and gain access to the sea. Whether or not this was the real plan - and if it was, why it was changed - may yet be subjects for discussion. It is well, however, to remember in such discussion that attacks of the extent and success of that on the Aisne are not prepared in a few hours.

6. EMPLOYMENT OF AMERICAN TROOPS DURING PERIOD OF GERMAN OFFENSIVES (MARCH 21 JULY 18)

ENGINEERS WITH THE BRITISH ON THE SOMME

On March 21, when the German attack was launched, elements of the 6th, 12th, and 14th Engineers, serving with the British, were employed in rear of the battlefront. All these units rendered valuable service, several of them, notably two companies of the 6th Engineers with Carey's Force, taking an active part in actual combat. (Haig's 21 October Dispatch, cable 938-S.)

GENERAL DECISIONS AS TO USE OF AMERICAN TROOPS AND ARRANGEMENTS WITH FRENCH HIGH COMMAND

As soon as the grave crisis brought about by the March 21 offensive became apparent, the Commander-in-Chief decided that every available American unit must be put into the line and that all other considerations must be secondary to that of meeting the series of emergencies which must inevitably arise. But while this was to be the primary consideration, the Commander-in-Chief was equally determined, while meeting any particular necessity, to bring our forces together whenever and wherever such a result could be accomplished. * * * On March 23 the Chief of the French Mission at General Headquarters made certain proposals with reference to the use of American troops and on March 25 the Commander-in-Chief had an interview on the same subject with General Pétain at the latter's headquarters. The Commander-in-Chief informed General Pétain of his desire to use American troops wherever needed, at the same time continuing, as it became possible, to unite these troops into larger units. The two Commanders-in-Chief discussed the matter at some length with the result that it was finally decided that the 1st division should remain in sector north of Toul; that the 26th Division, en route to a training area after a first tour of duty in the trenches, should go into sector near the 1st Division; that the 2d Division should remain in the region north of St-Mihiel, eventually being concentrated as a division; that the 42d Division, which was in the vicinity of Lunéville, just having been withdrawn from its first tour in the trenches, should take over a sector in the region of Baccarat.

On March 25 it was also determined to equip with 8-inch howitzers provisional batteries to be formed from Railway Artillery personnel at Mailly. The six batteries thus organized ultimately became the 44th Artillery.

Orders in consequence of the above decisions were given and in addition the I Corps was directed to establish an Advanced Headquarters near the French corps commander of the Toul sector, the object being to prepare to take over this sector as an American sector, provided events should permit concentrating more American troops in that region. On March 29, however, these plans were modified due to a request of the French High Command, made through the Chief of the French Mission at General Headquarters, that the 1st Division be made available for the battle. The Commander-in-

Chief believed that the moral effect of the appearance of American troops on the battlefront was of supreme importance and orders were at once given for the relief of the 1st Division by the 26th Division and for placing the 1st Division entirely at the disposition of the French.

EMPLOYMENT OF 1st DIVISION NEAR MONTDIDIER

After its relief (April 3) by the 26th Division the 1st Division moved to the northwest of Paris for rest and training prior to entering the battle line.

On April 25 the 1st Division took over a sector west of Montdidier, under command of the VI Corps (afterwards the X Corps) of the French First Army.

For the first time a large American unit faced the enemy in an active sector of the battle front and although the 1st Division met every hope that had been founded on it, it is well to recall the significant fact that after America's declaration of war more than a year had elapsed before there was a single American division on an active front. Moreover, the enormous expansion which the American army had undergone had left even the 1st Division below the standards of experience, training, and discipline which should be attained before men are called upon to submit to the ordeal of modern battle.

In the latter part of May, the 1st Division carried out an operation which, although of minor importance within itself, was of the greatest possible value in that it demonstrated to our Allies and to the enemy the value of American troops in the offensive.

This operation was the capture of Cantigny. This village, which lies a few kilometers northwest of Montdidier, and the surrounding terrain was important to the enemy in that it furnished him valuable observation stations. Not only was it desirable to wrest these stations from the enemy, but, due to the configuration of the terrain, these same stations would be of the greatest importance to the 1st Division and the French corps and army as well, once they were in our hands.

On May 20 preliminary orders were issued and, after detailed rehearsals, May 28 was selected as the day of attack.

After a violent artillery preparation of one hour, the 28th Infantry launched the assault at 6:45 a. m. Artillery, loaned by the French, assured an enormous preponderance of artillery and this, together with the assistance of French tanks and flamethrowers, greatly aided in so completely smothering all resistance that such Germans as were left in Cantigny quickly surrendered and the occupation of the town was complete at 7:25 a. m.

But if the capture of the village had been accomplished without great difficulty, holding the ground gained was to prove another matter. It seemed as if the Germans were determined at all costs to counteract any moral effect which an American success, coming just at the first moment of Allied depression over the enemy's great success on the Aisne, might have. For three days guns of all calibers were concentrated on Cantigny and, beginning at 7:30 a. m. May 28, the Germans launched counterattack on counterattack against the positions which the 28th Infantry had taken. The enemy's attacks all broke down and gradually his efforts relaxed and the normal state of an exceedingly active sector returned.

No American divisions other than the 1st participated in the defense against the German Somme offensive and the 1st did not arrive until after the German advance had been stopped.

EMPLOYMENT OF THE 2d AND 3d DIVISIONS NEAR CHATEAU-THIERRY

On May 1 the French General Headquarters, through the French Mission at General Headquarters, A. E. F., proposed to send to the battlefront the 26th Division, then in sector north of Toul, relieving it by a French division which it was thought would be available within a week or ten days.

But this proposal was not satisfactory to us for several reasons. First of all, as we had no American divisions to relieve the 26th Division we would, in a sense, hav to abandon our purpose of building up an American sector north of Toul. This purpose had been adhered to for nearly a year and the few special units available had been employed in work which was consistently directed toward preparing for an eventual American operation intended to reduce the St-Mihiel salient. Moreover, it was believed that either the 2d or the 42d Division should be sent to the battle before the 26th Division.

These views were presented to the French authorities and it was finally agreed that the 2d Division should be relieved by the available French division. In accordance with this arrangement, the 2d Division was relieved between May 9 and May 16, and, after being concentrated around and to the west of Bar-le-Duc, was sent (May 19) to the Pontoise area, north of Paris, preliminary to taking a sector in the Picardy battleline. The German Aisne-Marne drive, however, completely upset these plans and as the few immediately available French reinforcements were successively swept out of the German road to Paris every nerve had to be strained toward saving that Capital. Among the troops called upon for that purpose was the 2d Division.

The infantry of the division was moved on May 31 by French camions to the vicinity of Meaux, where, after debussing, the regiments were sent forward in the direction of Château-Thierry. Early on the morning of June 1, the 2d Division was deployed across the Château-Thierry---Paris Road near Montreuil-aux-Lions and the German advance was stopped. The 2d Division remained in this sector until it was relieved by the 26th Division July 4 to July 10. Throughout this period the sector was extremely active, and the enemy made special efforts to prevent the American troops from securing any success. But Bouresches, Belleau Wood, and Vaux were taken by the 2d Division, and the reports of the stubborn fighting in these places had an invaluable moral effect on the Allies and depressed the enemy.

The 3d Division arrived in France during April. Prior to the German Aisne-Marne offensive it had been planned to use the 3d to relieve, in conjunction with a French division, the 26th Division. The 26th was in sector north of Toul, and after its relief, about June 1, this division was to be prepared to go to the battlefront. Arrangements to this end were completed with the French May 23 to May 25, but the German May 27 offensive caused a change in these decisions. On the afternoon of May 28 the French asked that the 3d Division be held ready to go to the Vosges and that the 26th Division be left in sector north of Toul, thus allowing the French division, which, with the 3d, was to relieve the 26th, to be sent into the new battle. This was promptly accepted and necessary orders given. But, in the morning of May 29, when the full extent of the German success on the Aisne was realized, it was again necessary to change the plans. On the 29th the Chief of the French Mission at General Headquarters, A. E. F., stated the difficulties of the French High Command in securing troops to meet the German threat and expressed the uneasiness felt concerning the possibility of stopping the Germans on the line of the Marne. The Chief of the French Mission asked that the 3d Division be placed at the disposal of the French High Command for employment in holding the crossings of the Marne. This was at once done.

The 7th Machine Gun Battalion, motorized, preceded the remainder of the division and, on May 31, after a run of 24 hours, went into action with French units at the critical river crossing at Château-Thierry. On the morning of June 1, a company of the 9th Machine Gun Battalion also reached Château-Thierry, and on the same day the Germans began attacks which for more than three days were constantly renewed in a desperate effort to secure the crossing.

The French commander of this sector and French General Headquarters gave credit to these machine-gun units for the part played by them in stopping the German advance.

The remainder of the division followed close behind the machine-gun elements and, after being distributed at first among French units, was gradually concentrated until by the end of June the division held the sector extending from Château-Thierry to about 2 kilometers east of Mezy.

On the morning of July 15 following ten hours' artillery preparation, the Germans attempted to secure crossings in front of the 3d Division as a part of their grand final offensive. On the right of the 3d Division the French were forced back a considerable distance and this, together with the violence of the attack on its own front made the task of the 3d Division a difficult one.

The following quotation is taken from the 3d Division report:

> Although the rush of German troops overwhelmed some of the front line positions causing the infantry and machine gun companies to suffer in some cases a 50% loss, no German soldier crossed the main road from Fossoy to Crézancy, except as a prisoner of war, and by noon of the following day there were no Germans in the foreground of the 3d Division sector except the dead.

IMPORTANCE OF THE CONDUCT OF THE 1st, 2d, and 3d DIVISIONS

The action of these three divisions prior to July 18 has been given at considerable length because of the very great importance attached to the conduce of these first American divisions to participate in active battle. Important as was the material aid rendered the Allied cause by these troops, the moral effect of their superb conduct was of far greater importance. They had shown the fighting qualities of the American soldier and the capacity of American staffs to handle divisional units. By the conduct of these three units our Allies judged the possibilities in the Americans who were now arriving in greatly increased numbers. That the hope thus founded on America should reach the British and French peoples and soldiers was insured by widespread publicity given to most encouraging statements by high British and French officials.

While the conduct of the 1st, 2d, and 3d Divisions was thus a powerful aid to the morale of the Allies, the reverse was the effect on the enemy. The German Great General Staff could no longer conceal the importance of America's effort. Too many German soldiers had tested the fighting qualities of the American and the disillusionment had begun which, before August 6, was to be completed by the conduct in attack of these same three and numerous other American divisions.

EMPLOYMENT OF 32d AND 5th DIVISIONS IN THE VOSGES

When the 32d Division arrived in France there was a critical shortage of personnel in the Services of Supply. This division had been designated in the United States as a replacement division, and on its arrival in France a large part of it was used to relieve this shortage as well as to supply replacements to combat divisions. In consequence the 32d Division had been much reduced in strength, and, when the German March 21 offensive began, there remained in the divisional area but one regiment whose companies numbered only about 55 men each.

In conformity with the Commander-in-Chief's instructions of March 29 that every available man should be put into the line at the earliest possible date, efforts were at once begun to assemble and equip the 32d Division. But in addition to the fact that the division was scattered and reduced in strength, there was also at this period a critical shortage in our supplies. Consequently, it was not until May 17 that the movement of the division to the front began. On May 21 the division entered the line near Belfort, remaining in line until July 20, when it was withdrawn for transfer to the Chateau-Thierry battlefront.

It was at first intended that the service of the 32d Division as a combat division should be temporary and that as soon as the emergency passed it would revert to its status as a replacement division. The emergency never passed, however, and the 32d continued throughout the war as a combat division.

On May 23 the French authorities were informed that the Commander in Chief hoped to place the 5th Division in a quiet sector not later than June 20. The American plan was to use the 5th Division to extend the sector north of Toul then occupied by the 26th Division. After the proposed relief of the 26th by the 3d Division it was planned to give the I Corps Headquarters command of the 3d and 5th Divisions, thus inaugurating an American corps sector. These plans were in conformity with an agreement reached by the Commander-in-Chief with General Pétain at Chantilly on May 19.

The German May 27 offensive was again to delay the grouping of our forces, and on May 29 the Commander-in-Chief agreed to send the 5th Division to the Vosges. This was upon the request of the French and because of their uneasiness for the safety of that front. However, one regiment was detached from the 5th Division and sent to the 26th Division because of the extent of front the latter division occupied and because it had been subjected to heavy raids.

SENDING THE 26th AND 42d DIVISIONS TO THE BATTLEFRONT

Early in May the Commander-in-Chief had decided that the 42d and 26th Divisions should be relieved from the sectors they were then holding and that, after such training as might be practicable, both divisions should be sent to the battlefront, if conditions required such action.

On May 22 and 23 the French were informed of this by letters which were in confirmation of previous conversation.

Arrangements for the relief of the 26th Division and its concentration in a training and rest area were in progress when the German Aisne-Marne offensive upset this as well as so many other plans, and it was necessary to leave the 26th Division in sector north of Toul for the time being. On June 25 however, the 82d Division, brigaded with a French division, began the relief of the 26th. The 82d had been brought from the British front as will be noticed later. After being relieved (June 28) the 26th was moved to the vicinity of Meaux and almost immediately began the relief of the 2d Division, this being completed on July 10.

On June 21 the 42d Division was relieved in the Baccarat sector by the 77th Division brigaded with a French division. The 77th had also been brought from the British front.

On June 23 the 42d Division was moved to the Champagne, which was already considered as a possible scene of the next German offensive. On the morning of July 15 the Division was holding the second line, but before July 18 more than five battalions of infantry in addition to the artillery had been engaged in the repulse of the final German attack.

MOVEMENT OF AMERICAN DIVISIONS FROM THE BRITISH FRONT TO THE FRENCH FRONT

After the March 21 offensive and prior to May 27 the French had extended their front from the Oise to a point just east of Amiens, a distance of about 93 kilometers. During the Lys offensive (April 9-26) the French had sent reinforcements to that theater until, on May 6, 18 French divisions were behind the British front. By June 2 the French front had been further increased by approximately 36 kilometers as a result of the pocket made by the German Aisne-Marne offensive. Due to this extension of front and to the fact that a number of French divisions were not in condition to be used, the French reserves were extremely low. To meet this situation the Allied Commander-in-Chief proposed on June 2 that a certain number of American divisions then training with the British be moved to the French front.

The Commander-in-Chief agreed at once, and, although the British were not certain that a further attack on their front was not imminent, the British Commander-in-Chief also agreed when the matter was presented to him on the morning of June 3. Selection of divisions to move and details of the movement were arranged at a conference of American, British, and French staff officers held at French General Headquarters on June 3. The divisions selected were the 4th, 28th, 35th, 77th, and 82d. The 4th and 28th Divisions were brought to the region of Meaux and Château-Thierry as reserves; and before July 18 both these divisions had units in the front line, brigaded either with the French or with our own troops. The 35th Division was sent to the Vosges and on June 30 went into the line brigaded with a French division. The 77th Division was sent to Lorraine where, as already noted, it relieved the 42d Division on June 21. The 82d was brought to the region of Toul, and on June 28 relieved the 26th Division in sector north of that place.

ORGANIZATION OF ADDITIONAL CORPS HEADQUARTERS AND PLANS FOR

TACTICAL EMPLOYMENT OF ARMY CORPS

On May 16 the III and, on June 21, the IV Corps Headquarters were organized. Constant progress was, therefore, being made toward obtaining the necessary higher staffs for the operations of an American force. So far, however, none of our plans for the grouping of our divisions under the actual tactical command of an American corps headquarters had materialized. The plans to this end agreed upon at the Chantilly Conference on May 19, and the reasons for their failure to materialize, have been mentioned. But with the movement of the divisions from the British front and with the concentration of a number of American divisions around Château-Thierry it became possible again to look forward to the formation of a tactical command for an American corps headquarters. Under date of June 6 General Pétain, in a letter expressing his appreciation of the aid which the Commander-in-Chief was furnishing in the existing crises, agreed to the formation of an American corps in the region of Château-Thierry. On June 13 the Commanding General, I Corps, was directed to proceed to that region and to be ready to assume a tactical command when opportunity should offer. Since the Commander-in-Chief was not willing to abandon the plan of an American sector in the Woëvre, all matters affecting American troops in the Woëvre region were taken over by the Chief of Staff of the IV Corps (there being no corps commander as yet named); Colonel Stuart Heintzelman had been designated on June 25 as Chief of Staff of that corps. The Chief of Staff of the IV Corps also exercised administrative control over all American troops in the territory of the French Eighth Army.

On June 28 the French proposed to change the plan of forming an American corps in the Chateau-Thierry region. They now proposed that the 26th Division be sent to relieve the 1st Division in Picardy and that at some later date the 42d Division be placed alongside the 26th. This proposal was unacceptable for two reasons: First, it continued the process of dispersing American troops, and, second, it again postponed the formation of an American corps. The French were at once so informed.

The final outcome was that on July 4, at 10:00 a. m., the I Corps took over the tactical command of the sector occupied by the French 167th and American 26th Divisions. On July 7 orders were issued, in accordance with proposals of the French, for the III corps staff to proceed to the region in which the 1st and 2d Divisions were to be concentrated as a reserve at the disposition of General Pétain. This region had not been definitely chosen but was to be either the region of Beauvais or that of Meaux.

When the III Corps Headquarters were relieved from duty in connection with the American troops in the French Seventh Army, instructions were issued looking to the organization of the V Corps Headquarters which were to take over this duty from the III Corps.

PART PLAYED BY AND DIFFICULTIES ATTENDING EMPLOYMENT

OF AMERICAN TROOPS DURING GERMAN OFFENSIVE

Throughout the period of the German offensives the Commander-in-Chief freely placed American units at the disposition of the Allies. Nine divisions, the 1st, 2d, 3d, 5th, 32d, 35th, 42d, 77th, and 82d, were employed in the line as divisions; the 1st, 2d, and 3d holding most active sectors. The four regiments of the 93d (colored) were in French divisions where they remained until after the Armistice. In addition, parts of five other divisions, the 4th, 28th, 27th, 30th, and 33d, the latter three with the British, had entered the line for training purposes. As American divisions were twice the size of those of the Allies the material assistance rendered by America in resisting the German efforts was of great importance. Still more important was the moral effect, for the appearance of our troops in every quarter, from Switzerland to the sea, had given the Allied soldiers confidence in the ultimate arrival of America.

But while the free employment of our troops with our Allies was necessary under the situation, and while the dispersion of our units along the entire front was of the utmost benefit, problems of a most difficult and delicate nature were created thereby. On many occasions the French assumed that troops placed under their command for a specific purpose were thereby incorporated in the French army. Under this theory, which was merely the adherence to the original policy of drafting our men in French and British units, and on account of the rapid decisions necessitated by the situation, the French frequently moved our units from one region to a widely separated one without notification to our General Headquarters. Not only did this make more difficult the execution of the Commander-in-Chief's policy of bringing our forces together whenever opportunity offered, but the supply and control of our troops was often rendered all but impossible. Although this state of affairs began in May it was not until July 31 that the difficulties were finally adjusted.

RESUME OF DISPOSITION OF TROOPS ON JULY 18 AND STRENGTH

OF AMERICAN EXPEDITIONARY FORCES ON SAME DATE

On July 18 the American divisions were disposed as follows:
The 27th, 30th, and 33d were with the British, each having elements in the line for training. The 78th and 80th were in training areas. The 1st and 2d Divisions had been transferred as divisions to the French XX Corps, French Tenth Army, and had taken their

places in line south of Soissons ready for the counterattack. South of the French Tenth Army the 4th Division, brigaded with the French in the French Sixth Army, was ready for the attack. At the southern part of the Marne salient was the 26th Division in line as such, supported on its right by the 3d Division. Elements of the 28th Division were in line with the 3d Division and with the French division on the 3d Division's right. Farther east in Champagne serving with the French Fourth Army was the 42d Division in the second position. The four colored regiments of the 93d Division were in the Argonne, and the 82d Division, brigaded with the French, was in sector east of St-Mihiel. In Alsace were the 5th, 32d, 35th, and 77th Divisions, brigaded with the French. The 29th Division was moving to the relief of the 32d at this moment. In the training areas were the 37th, 89th, 90th, 91st, and 92d Divisions, and the 41st and 83d Depot Divisions were at St-Aignan and Le Mans, respectively. By July 18 the arrival of troops had been so increased that more than one million Americans had landed in France.

7. IMPORTANT CONFERENCES AND DECISIONS AFFECTING THE AMERICAN EFFORT DURING PERIOD OF GERMAN OFFENSIVE

REASONS CONFERENCES AND DECISIONS WERE ESPECIALLY IMPORTANT TO AMERICA

Prior to March 21, 1918, the methods and experience of nearly four years had led to a popular belief that the deep trench systems were so nearly impregnable that a breakthrough on a large front was out of the question and that the war must be fought on the existing front lines. While military opinion was, perhaps, somewhat better informed, the lessons of Riga and Cambrai had been appreciated by only a small percentage of officers, and even of these very few had imagined the possibility of such complete success and so rapid an advance as the Germans achieved on March 21 and during the first few days thereafter.

The situation created by the Somme offensive was, therefore, all the more grave because the possibilities of the anticipated enemy attack had not been foreseen. The Allied conferences and decisions which immediately followed, continuing until the final German attack, are especiall important to America because she was the last remaining potential resource of the Allies.

DESIGNATION OF AN ALLIED COMMANDER-IN-CHIEF

The difficulties arising from the lack of a Supreme Commander on the western front were apparent upon the arrival of the Commander-in-Chief in France. Naturally, these difficulties must have been even more apparent to our Allies, but for one reason or another no single chief had been designated. The appointment of a Supreme War Council during November of 1917 was due to the necessity which was felt of coordinating the action of the several armies on the western front, as well as to the necessity of coordinating Allied efforts on all the fronts.

The great German offensive of March 21 falling as it did just to the north of the junction of the British and French armies, brought the necessity of an Allied Commander-in-Chief strikingly to the attention of the governments.

On March 26 the British and French Governments agreed to place the supreme control of operations in the hands of General Foch, who had previously been Chief of Staff in the French War Ministry. On March 25 the Commander-in-Chief had expressed to General Pétain his desire to utilize American troops to the utmost in the emergency, and on March 28 he expressed the same desire to General Foch. This action of the Commander-in-Chief at this crisis made a deep impression on the French and British Governments and

High Commanders, and when, on March 30, the press was informed, the enthusiasm created among the people at large served in some measure to relieve the depression resulting from the threat to AMIENS and the British armies.

At first General Foch was not formally announced as Allied Commander-in-Chief and, in fact, while it had been arranged that he was to be supreme enough to coordinate, it was agreed that he should not be called Supreme Commander. However, it soon became known that Foch actually exercised Allied Command, and on April 16 the President of the United States approved for the United States the designation of General Foch as Commander-in-Chief of the Allied Armies in France. (820-S, 923-S, 1113-R, Haig's Dispatches.)

* * * * * *

8. JULY 18 TO SEPTEMBER 12, 1918

SUMMARY OF SITUATION AND GENERAL PLAN OF ALLIED JULY 18 ATTACK

In the first days of July 1918, it became apparent that the Germans would be unable to launch more than one other great offensive. It was not considered certain that the enemy would again attack, but towards the 10th of the month, it was believed that if he did the blow would, without doubt, fall in CHAMPAGNE. Thanks to the arrival of American troops, the Allied reserves were now sufficiently numerous to justify a counteroffensive, and if, as every High Command was confident, the CHAMPAGNE front could hold with the troops already allotted to it, the Allied Command retained complete freedom in the selection of the front upon which the counteroffensive should be made. The selection by the Germans of Champagne and the eastern face of the Marne salient was fortunate for the Allies; for this decision allowed an Allied counteroffensive which, while affording immediate relief to the enemy's thrust, would also obtain other advantages for the Allied cause. Paris is still France, and the approach of the German lines along the Marne toward Paris had caused apprehension throughout France; it was essential that the threat on Paris be relieved at the earliest possible moment. Aside from reasons of morale, material reasons also demanded the reduction of the Marne salient as the first task of the Allies when the offensive should pass to their hands. Paris contained a multitude of essential war industries, and, so long as the Germans maintained their lines, these industries were seriously interfered with and production reduced by the constant long range bombardments and air raids. The great east and west railroad through Chateau-Thierry must also be regained by the Allies as a first necessity in the troop movements required in any general offensive.

With each day there came increased certainty that the Allied counteroffensive could be properly launched to the north of Chateau-Thierry, and the French armies on that front began, by July 10, to plan accordingly. But the Allied resources were not sufficiently great to permit a final decision until after the actual launching of the hostile attack. It thus happened that only on the 16th could many of the actual preparations be commenced.

* * * * * *

The general plan for the Allied counteroffensive of July 18 involved the entire west face of the Marne salient. This main attack was at first to pivot on Chateau-Thierry; later the Allies in the region of Chateau-Thierry were to push the attack. The Allies were also to attack that part of the German salient south of the Marne and to the southwest of Reims. The plan then really involved attacking the entire Marne salient, the principal blow falling at first on the west face, with the critical point, at which eventual success or failure would be determined, southwest of Soissons.

OUTLINE OF AMERICAN PARTICIPATION IN THE COUNTERATTACK

The three divisions selected to break the most sensitive part of the German line were the American 2d, the French Moroccan 1st, and the American 1st. If these three divisions could seize and hold the heights south of Soissons the German position in the salient proper became untenable and its ultimate reduction was assured.

At 4:35 a. m., July 18, after some of the American infantry had double-timed into line and when some of their guns had barely gotten into position, the American 1st and 2d Divisions and the Moroccan 1st Division jumped off. Notwithstanding their desperate resistance the Germans were driven back, and the results upon which ultimate success depended were secured. The 2d Division advanced 8 kilometers in tne first 26 hours, took about 3,000 prisoners, 2 batteries of 150-millimeter guns, 66 light guns, and 15,000 rounds of 77-millimeter ammunition, besides much other matériel. This division suffered some 4,000 casualties and, as it had made exhausting marches to reach the battlefield after having recently been withdrawn from its desperate fighting at Château-Thierry, the division was relieved after the second day.

The 1st Division suffered some 7,000 casualties, of whom it is believed that not one was a prisoner. Sixty per cent of its infantry officers were killed or wounded. In the 16th and 18th Infantry all field officers were casualties except the colonels, and in the 26th Infantry all field officers, including the colonel, were casualties. Notwithstanding its losses the 1st Division, by constant attacks throughout four days and nights, broke through the entrenchments in the German pivot to a depth of 11 kilometers and captured 68 field guns and quantities of other matériel. In addition, the 1st Division took 3,500 prisoners from the seven separate German divisions which had been thrown against it in the enemy's desperate effort to hold ground essential to his retaining the Marne salient.

From this time on the fighting qualities of the American soldier could not be questioned.

But while the work of the 1st Division and 2d Division attracted most attention because of the special importance of their attack, they were not the only American divisions to participate in the July 18 offensive. A little to the south of the 2d Division the 4th Division was in line with the French, and the 4th Division joined in the attack and continued to advance until July 22 when it was assembled and, as a division, relieved the 42d Division on August 3. The 26th Division was just northwest of Château-Thierry and, together with the French 167th Division, formed the American I Corps. This was the first American corps to exercise tactical command. The I Corps acted as a pivot in the beginning, and later had to advance under peculiarly difficult conditions. For the 26th Division, maneuver was much complicated in order that the front of the division might conform to the general plan. Before its relief the division had advanced more than 17 kilometers against determined enemy resistance, and had captured large quantities of enemy matériel. On July 25/26, after having had some 5,300 casualties, the 26th Division was relieved by the 42d Division which, after having taken some part in the successful resistance to the German attack of July 15 in Champagne, had been brought round to the Château-Thierry region.

Just east of Château-Thierry and south of the Marne, the 3d Division had broken up all efforts made against it on July 15. Now, on July 20, the 3d Division received orders to join in the counterattack. By skillful work of the command and staff the division had gotten well across the Marne by the 22d without having encountered serious resistance. From the 22d to 25th the division was engaged in bitter fighting on the wooded slopes leading up to the village of Le Charmel, which was taken on the evening of July 25. Constantly fighting its way forward, the division took Ronchères, and finally, on July 30, was relieved by the 32d Division after having suffered a total loss, in the defense of the Marne and in crushing the German resistance, of about 7,900. It will be remembered that the 32d Division had been in the line near Belfort on July 15. In the meantime this division had been relieved by the 29th Division and brought to Château-Thierry.

The 28th Division also had elements with French and American divisions during the attack, and won great credit.

As has been mentioned, the 42d Division relieved the 26th Division on July 25. On the next day the 42d Division attacked, and by the 28th it had crossed the Ourcq and taken Sergy. Here the enemy offered desperate resistance, launching counterattack after counterattack, the village of Sergy changing hands four times. But the 42d Division definitely occupied Sergy on the morning of July 29 and continued to press forward until August 2 when the enemy withdrew. The 4th Division now relieved the 42d, and on August 6 the operation of the reduction of the Marne salient terminated and the battlefront stabilized on the line of the Vesle, our 4th and 32d Divisions being in line. The 42d Division had lost some 5,500 officers and men.

RESULTS OF THE JULY 18 COUNTERATTACK

In the hard fighting of July 18 to August 6 all objectives had been gained; the Paris-Nancy Railroad freed; the threat on Paris removed; and, most important, the Allies had gained their first victory of the year and had regained the initiative which they were never to lose.

* * * Summed up in words, it may be said that the 2d and 3d Divisions had played a conspicuous part in stopping the May 27 offensive, and now eight American divisions (the 1st, 2d, 3d, 4th, 26th, 28, 32d, and 42d) had been of indispensable assistance in the reduction of the Marne salient. American losses were over 30,000. But the value of the American soldier, first demonstrated by the 1st, 2d, and 3d Divisions, had been confirmed by the conduct of five other divisions.

SOMME OFFENSIVE OF AUGUST 8, 1918

In accordance with the general plan of operations discussed at the July 24 conference, the British and French - the French First Army being under the command of the British Commander-in-Chief for this operation - launched, on August 8, the offensive which was intended to free the railroads around Amiens. This attack was a marked success from the beginning, and within five days the important center of Amiens was entirely freed. America was represented in this offensive by the 131st Infantry of the 33d Division. On August 9 this regiment attacked the enemy in Gressaire Wood and on Chipilly Ridge. The attack was successful, and the 131st captured some 700 prisoners and considerable matériel.

Previously, on July 4, parts of the 131st and of the 132d Infantry had also participated with the British in the attack on Hamel.

The British continued the pressure begun on the Somme by attacking on August 21 in the region of Bapaume.

THE OISE-AISNE OFFENSIVE OF AUGUST 18

Following the success of the British and French attack on the Somme, the French, on August 18, undertook an offensive between Reims and the Oise. In this offensive the American Expeditionary Forces furnished three divisions - the 28th, 32d, and 77th.

When the attack was launched, the 28th Division was in the line along the Vesle in the region of Fismes, and the 77th was on the left of the 28th. The III Corps had relieved the I Corps and the 77th Division was under the tactical command of the III Corps. The III Corps also exercised administrative control over the 28th and 32d Divisions. The 32d Division was in reserve, having been withdrawn after having captured Fismes on August 7.

The 28th Division participated in the action until it was relieved on September 8 by a French division and sent to the Argonne. The 77th remained in the line until September 15 when it was relieved by the Italian 8th Division and also sent to the Argonne. * * *

On the night August 27/28, the 32d Division, which had been moved up from reserve south of the Vesle, entered the line north of Soissons under the command of the French XXX Corps, French Tenth Army. The 32d Division attacked on August 29, 30, and 31, taking the important position of Juvigny and finally reaching the Chauny-Soissons Road after having broken the German front to a depth of 4 kilometers. * * *

During these attacks the casualties of the division amounted to nearly 3,000. The 32d Division was almost constantly in advance of its French neighbors on either flank. On the night of September 1 and 2, the 32d Division was relieved by the Moroccan 1st Division and was sent to a training area prior to participation in the Meuse-Argonne offensive.

RESUME OF EFFORTS TO ORGANIZE AN AMERICAN SECTOR AND FINAL

DECISION TO ORGANIZE THE FIRST AMERICAN ARMY FOR THE ST-MIHIEL OPERATION

The early adoption by the Commander-in-Chief of the policy looking to the employment of our forces in Lorraine, and the conclusion soon after his arrival in France that logically the first operation to be undertaken by an American army was the reduction of the St-Mihiel salient, have been mentioned. But in actually assembling our forces and taking over a sector, it was necessary to agree with the French, and later with the British, since it was behind their fronts that our troops were arriving and being trained. The plan of organizing an American corps sector in the Woëvre was, as we have seen, approaching realization when it was interrupted by the imperative necessity of meeting the several succeeding crises which began on March 21. This interruption did not mean the abandonment of our original plans, and the Commander-in-Chief, in accepting the principle that our troops go wherever they might best assist in meeting the emergency, fixed the policy of working toward assembling our troops in larger units wherever and whenever the emergency permitted. Our Allies were, however, inclined to consider that all plans to organize an American army were abandoned and that they were free to allot American troops as they saw fit. This idea complicated an already difficult problem. The Commander-in-Chief made his views fully known in the various conferences and insisted that the principle involved be acknowledged. Thus, the London Agreement, cabled April 24, contained the clause:

> That it is contemplated American divisions and corps, when trained and organized, shall be utilized under the American Commander-in-Chief in an American group.

The London Agreement did not suit the French and, as already stated, the discussion at the Abbeville Conference largely centered around the Allied view that American troops were to be allotted in small units to the Allies. The Commander-in-Chief could not be driven from his position, however, and in the end the Abbeville Conference stated as a principle:

> It is the opinion of the Supreme War Council that, in order to carry the war to a successful conclusion, an American army should be formed as early as possible under its own commander and under its own flag.

* * * * * *

On June 6, General Pétain agreed to the organization of an American corps sector in the Château-Thierry region, and on July 4 the I Corps assumed tactical command of a sector in that region. But this result was by no means fully satisfactory since only one American division was under command of the I Corps, while on July 4 the American Expeditionary Forces had eight divisions (1st, 2d, 3d, 5th, 32d, 35th, 77th, and 82d) in front line, one (42d) in second line, and no less than thirteen others (4th, 26th, 27th, 28th, 29th, 30th, 33d, 37th, 78th, 80th, 89th, 90th, and 92d) which had been in the line or were in training areas and might soon be expected to be equipped for entry into the line. Thus, although placing the I Corps Headquarters in command of a sector was a distinct success, and an important step in the struggle to organize an American force, yet so much remained to be done that, by comparison, it seemed that nothing had been accomplished. The matter was all the more important in view of the rapidity of American arrivals and the great dispersion of our troops which made proper supply and control all but impossible.

In the July 10 conference, therefore, the Commander-in-Chief urged, in the strongest terms, upon General Foch the necessity of bringing American troops together and creating an American sector. General Foch finally accepted the principle and stated it in his own words as follows:

> Today when there are a million Americans in France, America must have her place in the war. America has the right to have her army organized as such; the American army must be an accomplished fact. Moreover, the cause of the Allies will be better served by an American army under its own Chief than by an American army with its units dispersed. Therefore, it is necessary at the earliest possible date to constitute, side by side with the British and French armies, the American army; and it is necessary to make this American army as large as possible.

In urging his views on July 10, the Commander-in-Chief expressed the opinion that the American army should be formed in the Toul region. Upon objection by General Foch, however, the Commander-in-Chief expressed his entire willingness to group all his available forces in the Château-Thierry region and General Foch accepted this solution *en principe*.

Although the Commander-in-Chief had once more secured an acceptance of principle, nothing was really accomplished because it was impossible to obtain any agreement upon a definite date for the creation of an American sector, nor could any final action be agreed upon looking to the organization of such a sector. Moreover, it was clearly apparent from the July 10 conference that General Foch was inclined to postpone the assembly of American forces. On the other hand the Commander-in-Chief felt that under the existing situations he could not, in the common good, insist upon immediate action. By July 21, however, after the breakdown of the German final attack and when the July 18 counteroffensive had already gained a decided Allied advantage, the Commander-in-Chief discussed with General Pétain the question of the immediate grouping of American forces. During this discussion the Commander-in-Chief stated his intention, which he had long held, of assuming command in person of the first army to be formed, and expressed his willingness to operate under the immediate command of General Petain. Not only did General Pétain agree to the organization of the First Army in the Chateau-Thierry region, but he also agreed to the gradual creation of a purely American sector extending from Nomeny to north of St-Mihiel. Having reached an agreement, the two Commanders-in-Chief went, on the same day, July 21, to General Foch's Headquarters and discussed with him the plan they had formed. By letter dated July 22, General Foch agreed to this plan, although this letter and another of the same date indicated a desire to utilize one of the American divisions, the 32d, which had been intended for the American First Army, with the French Tenth Army. During the July 24 conference an agreement was reached that on July 25 movements of troops would be begun for the purpose of grouping in the Château-Thierry region the troops to form the American First Army; the army was to have two corps of three divisions each; a corps to have two divisions in front line and one in reserve. On July 26 a complete plan for gradually concentrating in the Toul region the American troops not intended for the First Army was presented to the French, and by letter dated July 28 General Foch also accepted this plan *en principe*.

In the meantime, events were moving rapidly, and it appeared to American General Headquarters that the time would soon be opportune for the St-Mihiel operation. During the first two or three days of August it became evident that the reduction of the Marne salient was practically complete, and that the line in the region of the Vesle would soon stabilize. After studying the availability of staffs and divisions, it was decided that if we were to undertake the St-Mihiel operation at a comparatively early date, we must form our First Army at St-Mihiel and reduce our forces in the Château-Thierry region to a minimum.

Up to this time there had been nothing more definite on the St-Mihiel operation than the decision that the American army would undertake such an operation when conditions permitted. On August 8, however, the Commander-in-Chief decided that, in view of the fact that the situation on the Vesle had stabilized, for the time being at least, the plan of forming the First Army in the region of the Vesle should be abandoned and that all American energies should at once be directed toward the reduction of the St-Mihiel salient. On August 9, the Commander-in-Chief presented his views to Marshal Foch at Sarcus (Foch was appointed a Marshal of France on August 6). At this conference Marshal Foch expressed himself as in full agreement with the Commander-in-Chief's views but considered that four American divisions should be left on the Vesle. Marshal Foch ended by leaving all details to be arranged between the Commander-in-Chief and General Pétain. The Commander-in-Chief discussed the question with General Pétain on the night of August 9 and complete agreement was reached. General Pétain further agreed to reduce the number of divisions left on the Vesle from four to three.

SITUATION OF AMERICAN TROOPS ON AUGUST 9

When the decision of August 9 was taken, the American troops were * * * dispersed along the entire front from Switzerland to the English Channel.

The First Army Staff was at La Ferté-sous-Jouarre, where it had been organized late in July. On August 10, the First Army was nominally organized on the Vesle in accordance with the agreements of July 21 and later. The assumption of command was nominal only, and was given publicity with the object of keeping secret the plan of August 9.

The three corps headquarters designated to participate in the St-Mihiel attack were the I, IV, V. Of these the I was on the Vesle, the IV was at Toul, while the V Corps Headquarters was not formally organized until August 19, 1918.

On August 9 the total number of American troops in France was a little more than 1,275,000. This number was more than sufficient to furnish the forces needed to undertake the reduction of the St-Mihiel salient. But on account of the priority which had been given to infantry and machine gunners the American Expeditionary Forces were not balanced and were woefully deficient in artillery, aviation, transport, and other essential arms and services. All these deficiencies were supplied by the French, and the British also cooperated with the assistance of the Royal Independent Air Force which was at the time operating from the region south of Toul.

COMPLICATED NATURE OF STAFF WORK

To assemble our dispersed troops and to undertake a major operation with staffs so recently organized was in itself an extraordinary task. In addition, it was necessary to secure assistance from our Allies in artillery, aviation, and countless other ways. In addition also to the question of units required by the American forces it was necessary to coordinate the action of French and American armies and regulate questions concerning territorial command. These questions could only be solved in the brief time available by a further complication of staff work. The solution was presented to Marshal Foch by the Commander-in-Chief's letter dated August 15, 1918, from which the following extract is taken:

> That in all that concerns the operations I deal directly with the Commander-in-Chief, Armies of the North and Northeast.
> That in all that concerns territorial command and other matters under the direct control of the Commanding General of the Group of Armies of the East, I deal directly with General de Castelnau.

Another possible source of complications was the fact that the Commander-in-Chief had two staffs to deal with, he haveing assuming personal command of the First Army. In addition to the above complexities of staff work, a certain limited amount of cooperation with British General Headquarters was necessary as certain troops were to be moved from the British to the American front.

To sum up, the higher staffs involved in carrying out the August 9 decision were: General Headquarters, A. E. F.; Headquarters, First Army; Allied General Headquarters; French General Headquarters; Headquarters, French Group of Armies of the East; British General Headquarters.

No work at cross purposes of serious importance resulted from the exceedingly complex nature of staff relations indicated by the above outline.

So far as concerns G-3 it is believed that successful cooperation was largely due to the fact that the Chief of Staff, First Army (General Drum), and two of the members of G-3, First Army (Colonels Marshall and Grant), had, prior to the organization of the First Army, been members of G-3, General Headquarters, and were thoroughly familiar with all staff work at these headquarters. While with G-3, General Headquarters, these three officers had also made special studies of the operation which the First Army was about to undertake.

ORIGINAL PLANS FOR THE REDUCTION OF THE St-MIHIEL SALIENT

Prior to the decision of August 9, members of the Commander-in-Chief's staff and of Marshal Foch's staff had discussed the general features of the proposed reduction of the St-Mihiel salient. No difference of opinion existed among any of the staffs concerned as to these features, nor could such differences well exist. Any study of the St-Mihiel salient inevitably led to the conclusion that its reduction involved a nutcracker operation involving two attacks - one against the south face and one against the west face - to pinch out the salient. But while the general features of the operation were so plainly indicated, many variations in the actual plans were possible, depending upon the extent to which the drive was to be pushed. Actually the First Army had to prepare several plans to meet the situation presented by varying decisions.

On August 11 the First Army Staff began moving to Neufchateau and immediately began preparing plans for the operation. On August 28, the First Army Headquarters moved to Ligny-en-Barrois. On August 16, General Headquarters sent a letter to the Chief of Staff, First Army, in which the ultimate objective of the operation was defined by the general line: Marieulles (east of the Moselle)---heights south of Gorze---Mars-la-Tour---Etain. This letter of August 16 contemplated that the attack on the west face would be made by three or four divisions and indicated the efforts that were being made to have the left of this secondary attack supported by an attack of the French Second Army in the direction of Etain.

By letter dated August 17, received and transmitted to the First Army August 18, Marshal Foch stressed the desirability of striking the heaviest possible blow, and directed an attack by four to five divisions of the French Second Army in support of the American attack on the west face, which Marshal Foch considered should be delivered with a force of five American divisions. The objective contemplated by Marshal Foch was virtually that contemplated by the American General Headquarters' letter of August 16. On August 18, the First Army received direct from General Petain instructions which, in effect, repeated those contained in Marshal Foch's letter of August 17.

The action of the First Army staff and the general features of the proposed attack are summed up in the following quotation from the First Army report:

> With the foregoing instructions as a basis, the original First Army Plan, known as the August Plan, was perfected and approved by General Pershing and General Petain by August 20. However, the attack of the French Second Army north of Watronville was so closely related to the American attack that General Petain decided to place all the French troops involved in the Woëvre attack under General Pershing as commander of the First Army, A. E. F. The French troops in the attack north of Watronville were to comprise six divisions formed into two army corps under the French Second Army. The whole attack contemplated the employment of twenty-five divisions.
>
> This attack, is successful, would, first, cut off the salient, second, pierce the Hindenburg Line and, third, threaten the Metz and Briey defenses.

MODIFICATIONS IN PLAN FOR REDUCTION OF St-MIHIEL SALIENT

The August Plan of the First Army had its origin, of course, in the decision of July 24. In the conference of July 24 it had been considered that the reduction of salients and the release of certain important railroads and ports would consume the remainder of the year. More extensive operations were, therefore, thought of as belonging to 1919. A general discussion of plans for 1919 had taken place between the Commander-in-Chief and Marshal Foch during the conference of July 10. At that time Marshal Foch had expressed himself in favor of an offensive between the Argonne and Arras, with the American army between the Argonne Forest and Reims.

But by the end of August 1918 the reduction of salients had so far advanced and had been attended by such success that it was evident that the offensive during 1918 could be continued far beyond the plans developed during the July 24 conference.

As a result of this change in the situation, Marshal Foch prepared a note, under date of August 30, and on the same date came to see the Commander-in-Chief at his First Army Headquarters at Ligny-en-Barrois.

* * * * * *

9. REDUCTION OF St-MIHIEL SALIENT

HISTORY OF SALIENT PRIOR TO AMERICAN OPERATIONS

The necessity of meeting the German attacks of August and early September 1914, had caused the French to draw troops from the south of Verdun to such an extent that von Strantz found it easy on September 20, 1914, to occupy the plateau of Hattonchatel. In the next few days the Germans took St-Mihiel and the nearby forts of the Meuse. But, by September 26, the joint action of the French commanders at Toul and Verdun contained the German advance practically to the lines which for the next four years marked the St-Mihiel salient.

During February and April 1915, the French made a serious attempt to force the enemy from his threatening position. In this effort two attacks were launched; one against the west face, and one against the south face of the salient. The western attack was successful in that the French took and occupied the village of Les Eparges and a part of the neighboring heights. The southern offensive was launched down the Moselle and the French succeeded in occupying most of the Bois-le-Pretre. But the final result of the 1915 offensives was local success only, and the Germans retained the salient practically intact.

CHARACTER AND IMPORTANCE OF THE ST-MIHIEL SALIENT

The primary strength of the St-Mihiel salient lay in the natural defensive features of the terrain. The western face ran along the eastern heights of the Meuse, north of St-Mihiel, and constituted the exceedingly strong position, dominating both banks of the Meuse. These heights of the Meuse were generally wooded, and the more important open spaces---such as those around Spada and St-Remy---were in valleys or on the lower hills which were dominated by the surrounding heights. On the southern face, the heights of the Meuse around the Fort du Camp-des-Romains were continued to the east by the offshoots of Loupmont Ridge and Montsec. These heights not only constituted so strong a position as to offer the greatest security against attack, but afforded the enemy observation stations of unusual importance. On a clear day practically the whole of the Woëvre was visible to the hostile observers on Montsec.

Woëvre is the name by which the region lying between the heights of the Moselle and the heights of the Meuse is known. The southern face of the salient, therefore, crossed the Woëvre and the greater part of the enemy's position on this face lay in the so-called plain of the Woëvre.

That part of the Woëvre which was crossed by the front lines is not really a plain except that it is dominated on either side by the peculiar heights lying along the Moselle and the Meuse. This southern portion of the Woëvre is, for the most part, a region of low-lying hills, many of which are wooded, separated by meadow land, and dotted with small ponds or lakes with marshy borders. Farther north, towards the base of the salient, the terrain is flatter but woods and ponds are still found. A number of small streams cross the region and some of these, particularly the Rupt-de-Mad, form in places serious military obstacles. Due to peculiarities of the terrain and its soil the Woëvre is very difficult ground in rainy weather.

But in spite of the great natural strength of the St-Mihiel salient it had the weakness of all salients in that it might be attacked on both flanks and pinched out. Consequently the Germans had, throughout four years, strengthened the salient by a great mass and variety of artificial works, the main feature of which was an elaborate system of wiring. This wiring was found not only in the front lines but was encountered to a depth of ten to twelve kilometers in rear of the forward positions.

The offensive value of the salient to the Germans lay chiefly in the fact that it interrupted French communications in an east and west direction on the main Paris-Nancy Railroad, while constantly threatening the entire region between Nancy and Bar-le-Duc, as well as that between Bar-le-Duc and Verdun. The principal defensive value of the salient from the German point of view was that it covered the strategic center of Metz and the Briey iron basin. It must be reduced before any general offensive against these two vital points or father east could be contemplated. Its reduction was also extremely desirable, if not indispensable, as a preliminary to any extensive operations between the Meuse and the Argonne.

GENERAL PLAN OF ATTACK

The plan of attack drawn up by the First Army after the decision of September 2 provided: A main attack against the south face, through and on both flanks of the wooded area south of Thiaucourt; a secondary attack against the west face between Les Eparges and Mouilly towards Hannonville-sous-les-Cotes and Hattonville; follow-up and holding attacks around the apex of the salient.

The main attack was to be made by the I and IV Corps, the secondary attack by the V Corps, and the holding and follow-up attacks by the French II Colonial Corps, which had passed to the First Army when that army assumed command of the sector from Port-sur-Seille to Watronville at 4 p. m., August 30.

CONCENTRATION OF TROOPS

The St-Mihiel operation involved more than half a million American troops and some 150,000 French troops. When on August 9, the operation was decided upon, the greater part of the American troops to participate in the offensive were, as has been mentioned, dispersed along the battlefront. The concentration of these troops on the St-Mihiel battlefront was a problem of no small magnitude.

The movements into the actual theater of operations began on August 28, and the final movements, which had to be made at night, were completed on September 11. Roads were none too plentiful and the First Army staff was further handicapped by our dependence upon the French in many matters of supply as well as for special services.

The problems involved were all successfully solved and, on the night of September 11/12, the First Army stood ready to attack. * * *

BATTLE ORDER OF THE FIRST ARMY

I Corps---Port-sur-Seille to Limey
    82d, 90th, 5th, 2d Divisions in line (82d Division merely to follow up the
       attack on both banks of the Moselle).
    78th Division in reserve.
IV Corps---Limey to Richecourt
    89th, 42d, and 1st Divisions in line.
    3d Division in reserve.
French II Colonial Corps---Richecourt to Mouilly
    39th Division, 26th Division, and 2d Dismounted Cavalry Division (all French).
    No division in reserve, as this corps made only follow-up attacks.
V Corps---Mouilly to Watronville.
    26th Division, French 15th Colonial Division, and part of 4th Division in line.
    Part of 4th Division in reserve.
    (The attack to be made by the 26th and 15th Divisions.)

The army reserves were the 35th Division, at Liverdun, and the 91st Division, at Sorcy-sur-Meuse. The 80th Division at Tronville, and the 33d Division west of Verdun, had not been designated as army reserve but were available in emergency.

HOSTILE SITUATION NIGHT OF SEPTEMBER 11/12

The enemy occupied the general line in front of Rouves, Cheminot, Regniéville-en-Haye, St-Baussant, Apremont, Fort du Camp-des-Romains, St-Mihiel, Chauvoncourt, Spada, Seuzey, Combres, Trésauvaux, and Ville-en-Woëvre. The strength and depth of the enemy's work, especially of wire, have been mentioned. The enemy units in line amounted to eight divisions and two separate brigades. These forces were distributed in great depth in accordance with the accepted principles of defensive tactics.

Documents captured in June 1918 had shown that the enemy planned the evacuation of the salient in case of a threatened heavy attack. This plan, however, was based upon a methodical retirement extending over a long period. For several days prior to September 12 the statements of prisoners, and abnormal activity noted by observers, tended to indicate that the enemy had begun to move his artillery and other matériel out of the salient. Information obtained after the attack verified the enemy's intentions to withdraw and pointed to the conclusion that he had anticipated the September attack, but at a later date. In any event the attack was a tactical surprise.

BRIEF DESCRIPTION OF THE ATTACK

The infantry attack was preceded by an artillery fire of destruction which began at 1:00 a. m., September 12. Through reinforcements of French artillery the First Army had at its disposal 2,971 guns. The American and French artillery completely dominated the hostile artillery, the reaction from which was very light.

On the south face the six American divisions, in line from the center of the Bois-le-Prêtre (the scene of the desperate fighting of 1915) to Xivray-et-Marvoisin, were launched in the infantry assault at 5 a. m. The advance proceeded like clockwork, and wire proved but a small obstacle to the American infantry, notwithstanding the fact that the infantry soldier was, for the most part, dependent upon his own resources in crossing the wire. By midnight September 12/13, the southern attack had advanced until our lines were beyond Viéville-en-Haye, Jaulny, Thiaucourt, Nonsard, and the success of the whole operation was assured. On the western face the artillery preparation continued until 8 a. m., when the infantry assault was launched. By midnight of September 12/13, the western attack had passed beyond Dompierre-aux-Bois and Dommartin-la-Montagne.

But while the main and secondary attacks were progressing so satisfactorily, the situation of the enemy is all that part of the salient to the southwest of Vigneulles was not accurately known. Reports of observers indicated the enemy's withdrawal from the region of St-Mihiel toward and beyond Vigneulles but, on the other hand, the raids undertaken by the French on either side of St-Mihiel met with little success. However, the Commander-in-Chief (commanding the First Army) directed the IV and V Corps to push detachments to the region of Vigneulles during the night of September 12/13. These detachments, from the 1st and 26th Divisions, met near Hattonchâtel and Vigneulles early on the morning of September 13. The enemy's main forces had, however, succeeded in withdrawing beyond Vigneulles during the afternoon and night of the 12th.

On September 13 the occupation of the limited objective decided upon at the conference of September 2 was practically completed and the process of stabilization begun. Deep raids and a few local operations, especially on the right where the advance was pushed until the whole of the Bois-des-Rappes was occupied, continued until September 16 when the operation may be said to have terminated.

- 37 -

RESULTS OF THE ST-MIHIEL OPERATION

The material objectives of the attack were completely secured; the threat of the St-Mihiel salient was removed and the railroads freed. The captures included 15,000 prisoners and 257 guns. (Report of Commanding General, First Army.) The First Army had developed a sense of power that was very essential to overcoming the more difficult tasks awaiting it; American staffs had shown their ability to control large masses; the enemy saw America entering the war capable of organizing and employing her millions as a distinct National Army.

St-Mihiel was also a demonstration to the Allies that, in the existing state of the German armies, good troops could successfully attack the most elaborate trench systems. Before St-Mihiel the Allied successes of 1918 had been against German positions won by the enemy during his great offensives, and the assaults were, therefore, not made against elaborately organized trench systems.

Perhaps the most important result of all was the fact that the American infantryman had learned that wire without fire was no obstacle and that, given a superiority of fire, he could, with his own resources, cross any wire however deep and thick. The fact that the American infantryman had so crossed the elaborate system of wire at St-Mihiel was published by French General Headquarters in the following order:

GENERAL HEADQUARTERS OF THE ARMIES OF THE NORTH AND OF THE NORTHEAST
GENERAL STAFF
3d Bureau   General Headquarters,
No. 26,074   September 18, 1918.

For the: General Commanding the Group of Armies of the Center;
General Commanding the Group of Armies of the East;
General Commanding American First Army.

It is desirable for a certain number of French officers, non-commissioned officers and soldiers to visit the terrain so that they can fully understand the manner in which the American infantry has been able, during the last attacks carried out by the American First Army, to overcome the obstacles encountered during the advance and not destroyed by artillery or by tanks.

The American units have cut themselves a passage with wire-cutters through the thick bands of wire or they have walked over these wire entanglements with much address, rapidity, and decision. It is interesting that our infantry soldiers should see for themselves the nature of the difficulties thus overcome and that they should persuade themselves that they also are capable of doing as much on occasion.

To this end visits will be organized as soon as possible by an understanding between the Group of Armies of the Center and the Group of Armies of the East on the one hand and the American First Army on the other hand, with a view to showing to our troops on the battlefield of the Woëvre the places which are interesting from the point of view above set forth. Advantage will be taken of the location of French divisions within a reasonable distance of the battlefield in order to transport, by motor trucks, detachments comprising, in principle, an officer, a noncommissioned officer, and one or two soldiers for each battalion. The detachments will be conducted over the terrain by selected officers who have previously reconnoitered the interesting itineraries and who are capable of furnishing necessary information concerning the development of the attack.

By order: Chief of Staff.

BUAT

The American battle casualties were approximately 11,000.*

The light losses and the evident disorder of the enemy justified the belief that very much greater successes would have been obtained had not the operations been limited by the decisions made during the period August 30 to September 2. Great disappointment existed that we could not push our initial success in accordance with the August Plan. The Allied Commander-in-Chief had decided, however, that the American army must be employed in the Meuse-Argonne attack, and the American masses had to begin the movements to that theater even before the completed stabilization of the Woëvre front. Viewed after the event, there is no reasonable doubt but that the continuation of the St-Mihiel offensive would have broken the Hindenburg Line. Whether or not even greater successes might have been attained is an interesting subject for speculation

10. FRENCH AND BRITISH OPERATIONS OF AUGUST AND SEPTEMBER 1918

The French attack northwest of Soissons and the British and French attacks of August 8 near Amiens have been mentioned. The Allied attacks in these regions were continued and a steady pressure on the enemy was kept up on other parts of the front. On certain parts of the front, too, the Germans began, as early as August 8, a withdrawal not immediately forced by the Allied attacks. As a consequence of the Allied action and the German withdrawals, the enemy's line in the north was, on September 26, almost identical with that of March 21; in fact, the only material difference on the entire western front was that resulting from the reduction of the St-Mihiel salient.

11. GENERAL PLAN OF THE COMBINED ALLIED OPERATIONS

Although many of the important points in the general plan under which all the Allies operated have been mentioned, it may be well to trace the development of this plan before taking up the Meuse-Argonne operation.

During the July 10 conference Marshal Foch discussed a plan which he was then formulating with the Commander-in-Chief. This tentative plan was to be executed in 1919, and, in outline, contemplated an attack on the front ARRAS-ARGONNE Forest. There was to be no attack east of the ARGONNE Forest and the American army was to be placed between that forest and REIMS.

The note drawn up as a result of the July 24 conference, after enumerating the operations of reducing salients, continued:

> How far the different operations planned above will carry us in space and time it is impossible to foresee now. However, if the results which they have in view are achieved before the season is too far advanced, it is advisable to plan at this time an important offensive for the end of the summer or for the autumn, the nature of which should increase our advantages and give no respite to the enemy.
>
> It is now too soon to determine its nature in a more precise manner.

Thus, on July 24, the success of the counterattacks begun July 18 had already brought the hope that before the end of the year something might be done that theretofore had been considered as impossible of execution before 1919.

On August 9 the initial success of the FRENCH and ENGLISH attacks near AMIENS and the completion of the reduction of the MARNE Salient brought the decision to begin immediately the preparations for reducing the St-MIHIEL Salient.

The Final Report of the Commander-in-Chief places the casualties at less than 7,000.

Finally, on August 30, Marshal Foch drew up the Note which contained the definite decision to execute the attack planned for 1919 during 1918; the front of attack was now now extended to the MEUSE.

* * * * * *

The discussions concerning the August 30 Note and the final decision that the First Army should undertake the attack on the Meuse-Argonne Forest were mentioned. It is well to record that, although the grand offensive which was to end the war in November, was fully outlined on August 30, no one dared on that date to express the opinion that the final victory could be won in 1918. Thus, on August 31, General Pétain did not hope that the Meuse-Argonne attack could be pushed much beyond Montfaucon before winter stopped the great offensive.

12. THE MEUSE-ARGONNE OPERATIONS

HISTORY OF THE MEUSE-ARGONNE REGION PRIOR TO AMERICAN ATTACK

By the end of August 1914, the German armies had reached the line of the Meuse north of Verdun, and the heights just north of the city became the pivot of the great wheel of the German armies. Although it was at one time practically entirely surrounded, the fortress of Verdun held. By September 5 this wheel had placed the center of the German armies well south of the Marne, while von Kluck, sweeping down from Brussels, had passed just beyond range of the outer forts of Paris and stood with his army on both banks of the Marne at Meaux. The French armies which, toward the end of August, had stood along the Meuse north of Verdun had been forced back until, on September 5, their battle line ran southwest from Verdun to Revigny. The battle of the Marne (Ourcq) began on September 6, and by September 12, 1914, the German lines between the Meuse and the Western edge of the Argonne were practically those against which the American First Army launched its attack on September 26, 1918. Although the great German offensive in 1916 and the French counterattacks of 1916-1917 had witnessed fluctuations of the lines around Avocourt, Malancourt, Forges, Le Mort Homme, Esnes (all of which were points of direction either within or beyond our jumping-off line of September 26), neither French nor Germans had been able to force the other back materially. The net result of the four years' struggle was that in September 1918, the German defenses were unusually deep and strong, while "No-Man's-Land" was as worthy of all that the name implies as any spot on the western front.

CHARACTER AND IMPORTANCE OF GERMAN POSITION

All supplies and evacuations of the German armies in northern France were dependent upon two great railway systems; one, in the north, passing through LIEGE, while the other, in the south, with tracks coming from LUXEMBURG, THIONVILLE and METZ, had as its vital section the line CARIGNAN---SEDAN---MEZIERES. * * * Neither of these systems alone could supply the huge German forces in northern France and no other important lines were available to the enemy because the mountainous masses of the ARDENNES had forbidden the construction of east and west lines through that region. In addition to his dependence upon it for supply, the line CARIGNAN---SEDAN---MEZIERES was essential to the German for movements of his troops. Should this southern system be cut by the Allies, the ruin of the German armies would be complete. From the MEUSE-ARGONNE front as it existed on September 26, 1918, the perpendicular distance to the CARIGNAN-MEZIERES Railroad Line was about 50 kilometers. This region then formed the pivot of all German operations in northern France, and the vital necessity of covering the great railroad resulted in the convergence on the MEUSE-ARGONNE front of the several enemy defensive positions which farther west were separated by 30 or even 60 kilometers. In fact, although in the northern part of the sector the works were not so complete, the German defenses on the MEUSE-ARGONNE front consisted of trenches, wire, etc., one series behind another, to a depth of 20 kilometers or more. In thus preparing to hold a region which was so vital to him that utter ruin must follow its loss, the German was greatly aided by the natural features of the terrain.

East of the MEUSE, the dominating heights not only secured the enemy's left but gave him positions in which powerful artillery could be installed to bring an oblique fire on the western bank. Batteries located in the elaborately fortified ARGONNE Forest secured the right flank and could even cross their fire with those of the guns on the east bank of the MEUSE. Midway between the MEUSE and the ARGONNE the heights of MONTFAUCON afforded the enemy perfect observation and formed a strong natural position which he had elaborately fortified. But while these were the most prominent features, the east and west ridges, abutting on the MEUSE and AIRE Valleys, affording as they did perfect machine-gun positions, were, perhaps, the natural features which most favored the desperate defense which the enemy of necessity would have to make. North of Montfaucon, wooded heights such as those west of Romagne and south of Barricourt constituted natural features which were most favorable to the defense and unfavorable to the offense.

Even though the attack of the First Army would have to be made against so strong a natural position, to strengthen which the resources of Germany had been lavished for four years, it was, nevertheless, a sector in which the fighting could be forced. Thus, by compelling the enemy to draw in reinforcements, the advance of our Allies farther west could be best assisted. Above all, if the American army could but win victory in this sector the end of the war would be in sight.

GENERAL PLAN OF ATTACK

The attack of the First Army was to be coordinated with the attack of the French Fourth Army west of the Argonne. By this coordination it was expected that the advance of one army would facilitate the advance of the other. General Pétain was charged with the high direction of the attack of the American First Army as well as that of the French armies farther west. General Pétain issued his original orders for the attack under date of September 6; these orignnal orders were slightly modified on September 16.

Under these orders the task of the First Army was to break through the enemy's successive fortified zones to include the Hindenburg Line on the front Brieulles---Romagne-sous-Montfaucon---Grandpré and thereafter by developing pressure toward Mézières to insure the fall of the Hindenburg position along the Aisne in front of the French Fourth Army. The penetration required to reach the Hindenburg Line was about 15 kilometers and the defenses were virtually continuous throughout that depth.

The orders of General Pétain provided for leaving French troops on the front until the last moment and for the cooperation of the French Second Army staff with the First Army staff in troop movements and other preliminary work.

The essential part of the orders issued by the First Army contemplated the capture of Montfaucon and the complete penetration, on a broad front, of the enemy's second position, running roughly east and west through Montfaucon, on the first day. Orders for further advances were to be issued after attaining this objective.

CONCENTRATION OF TROOPS

When, on September 2, the decision to attack on the Meuse-Argonne front was reached, the First Army was engaged in the preparation of the St-Mihiel drive. A portion of the staff was withdrawn from the St-Mihiel operation, however, and plans were begun for initiating the new operation.

The original concentration for the Meuse-Argonne operation was to include fifteen divisions. Of these the 1st, 3d, 4th, 35th, 80th, 82d, and 91st were involved in the pending St-Mihiel drive; the 29th, 37th, and 92d were in sector in the Vosges; the 28th, 32d, and 77th were in the neighborhood of Soissons; the 79th Division was in one of our own training areas; and the 33d was near Bar-le-Duc. Practically all the artillery, air service, and other auxiliaries which could be found for the new operation, were committed to the St-Mihiel drive and could only be moved after it was completed.

Arrangements to move all units not to be employed in the St-Mihiel fight were begun at once, and on the second day (September 13) of that fight, reserve divisions and army artillery units began moving toward the Meuse-Argonne front. Other artillery and tanks followed and finally some of the divisions which had been in first line in the St-Mihiel attack were withdrawn and joined the forces moving to the new scene of action. To insure secrecy, all movements had to be made at night, and as only three routes were available, the roads were jammed to utmost capacity. The movement of the masses involved was one of the most delicate and difficult problems of the war and its successful accomplishment is a tribute to the willingness and spirit of the whole First Army.

On September 22 the command of the front from east of the Meuse to the western edge of the Argonne passed to the First Army, with headquarters at Souilly; the French XVII Corps, with three divisions, passed to the command of the First Army, and the army front now extended from east of the Moselle to the western edge of the Argonne. The Meuse-Argonne front had been taken over from the French Second Army, which had rendered much assistance in routing troops, filling dumps, etc., etc. Finally, the First Army stood, on the night of September 25/26, ready for the attack. * * *

FIRST ARMY BATTLE ORDER

On the night of September 25/26 the battle order of the First Army from right to left on the sector of attack was as follows:

III Corps:
    33d, 80th, and 4th Divisions in line;
    3d Division in reserve.

V Corps:
    79th, 37th, and 91st Divisions in line;
    32d Division in reserve.

I Corps:
    35th, 28th and 77th Divisions in line;
    92d Division in reserve.

In army reserve were the 1st, 29th, and 82d Divisions, in rear respectively of the III, V, and I Corps; the French 5th Cavalry Division was also in army reserve.

Due to the fact that artillery organizations had not yet arrived for much of the infantry shipped over in the great troop movements of May, June, and July, many of the divisions were not served by their own artillery brigades. The 33d, 37th, 79th, and 91st Divisions were supported by brigades not belonging to these organizations, while the 3d, 32d, 92d, and 29th Divisions, in reserve, had no artillery brigades with them. The shortage in artillery matériel was largely made up by the assistance given by the

French Command, who made ample French artillery units available for use in the operation, so that a total of 2,775 guns supported the attacks.

In addition, the appropriate corps and army troops were available. These included 189 small tanks, of which 142 were manned by Americans and the remainder by French; and 821 airplanes, 604 manned by Americans and the remainder by French.

* * * * * *

HOSTILE SITUATION

On the night of September 25/26 the enemy had ten divisions in line and ten in reserve on the front Fresnes-en-Woëvre---Argonne Forest. After St-Mihiel the Germans had naturally expected a further American effort, but successful ruses east of the line of the Meuse, extending as far south as Lunéville, had deceived the enemy and, as a consequence, the actual attack came as a tactical surprise. The surprise feature had also been assisted by arrangements under which a screen of French troops covered our first line until the last possible movement before launching the attack.

DIVISION OF MEUSE-ARGONNE OPERATIONS INTO PHASES

The operations in the Meuse-Argonne region, though forming a continuous whole, were extended over so long a period of constant battle and were so complicated, that they are properly divided into phases the number of which depends upon the amount of detail to be considered. Thus, the First Army Report logically recognizes three distinct operations, with five phases making up the first operation. For the present purpose it seems sufficient to divide from September 26 to November 11 into two phases, the first of which closed with the end of October.

FIRST PHASE---SEPTEMBER 26 TO OCTOBER 31

At 11:30 p. m., September 25, the First Army artillery opened fire on the enemy's roads and other communications. At 2:30 a. m., September 26, the artillery fire was increased, and a general and intense artillery preparation began all along the front. At 5:30 a. m., the infantry advanced to the assault following the usual rolling barrage.

The necessity for securing surprise had forbidden a long artillery preparation, and tanks had been unable to precede the infantry in the initial jump-off. The infantry was, therefore, practically dependent on its own resources for cutting through the elaborate system of wire. Under these conditions and owing to the natural difficulties of the terrain, the infantry advance was slow. But the progress was steady and no special difficulties were encountered except before Montfaucon. The early overrunning of the enemy's first positions led to the hope that the French 5th Cavalry Division in army reserve might be pushed through the line to exploit the success in the direction of Grandpré. However, blocked roads and other causes prevented the cavalry from getting through before the enemy reorganized his defense. The cavalry did not reach Varennes and the French 5th Cavalry Division took no further part in the fight.

The success of the initial assault having been assured, the important problem became the movement of artillery and ammunition across the trackless "No-Man's-Land" to support the continued progression of the troops. The strong point of Montfaucon, which had not fallen on the 26th, at first interfered with moving guns forward; but at about noon on September 27, the 79th Division captured Montfaucon, and the center of the line, which had fallen behind flanks, went forward. The right had made a splendid advance into the woods south of Brieulles-sur-Meuse, but the extreme left was meeting strong resistance in the Argonne. Day and night the attack continued without interruption, and the enemy, recognizing his danger, threw six new divisions into line before September 29, developed a powerful machine-gun defense supported by heavy artillery fire, and made frequent counterattacks with fresh troops, particularly on the fronts of the 28th and 35th Divisions.

By nightfall of the 29th the First Army line was approximately Bois-de-la-Côte-Lemont---Nantillois---Apremont---southwest across the Argonne. Some of the divisions had suffered severely. Units had become intermingled - a consequence both of their inexperience and of the difficult nature of the ground over which they had attacked and the fog or darkness which had covered them. Relief of these divisions had, therefore, to be made before another coordinate general attack could be launched. Consequently, on the night of the 29th, the 37th and 79th Divisions were relieved by the 32d and 3d Divisions, respectively, and on the following night the 1st Division relieved the 35th Division.

At 5:30 a. m. on October 4, the general attack was renewed. The order of battle of first line divisions and corps from right to left was as follows:

III Corps:
    33d, 4th, and 80th Divisions.

V Corps:
    3d and 32d Divisions.

I Corps:
    1st, 28th, and 77th Divisions.

The number of enemy divisions on the front from Fresnes-en-Woëvre to the Argonne had increased from 20 to 23 in line and in reserve, and included some of his best divisions. The resistance was desperate, and only small advances were realized, except by the 1st Division on the right of the I Corps. By evening of October 5 the line was approximately Bois-de-la-Côte-Lemont---Bois-du-Fays---Gesnes---Hill 240---Fleville-Chéhéry---south west through the Argonne.

The battle was now extended to the east of the Meuse to obtain relief from artillery fire from that bank and in pursuance of a plan to increase the extent of the battle front and thus to involve more German divisions. On October 8, the French XVII Corps made a general attack on the front east of the Meuse with the following divisions in line from right to left: French 26th Division, French 18th Division, American 29th and 33d Divisions. This attack fell on the exact point on which the enemy's armies must pivot to effect an orderly withdrawal from northern France, and our troops encountered elaborate fortifications and desperate resistance. Although the attack progressed until the 10th, the advance realized was not sufficient completely to relieve troops west of the Meuse from enfilade artillery fire from the east bank.

In the meantime, on October 7, the I Corps launched the 82d Division in an attack, northwest toward Cornay, to outflank the Germans in the Argonne and to free the 28th and 1st Divisions from enfilade fire from the eastern edge of the forest. The success of the 82d Division and of the simultaneous action of the 28th Division was marked, and did much to break down resistance in the Argonne.

On October 9 the V Corps attacked, with the 1st Division reinforced by one infantry brigade of the 91st Division, and with the 32d Division. The stubbornest defense was encountered, and the fighting was desperate, but an advance was made. On the 10th the Argonne was cleared, and on the night of the 11th the line was approximately Bois d'Ormont (north of Verdun)---Molléville Farm---Sivry-sur-Meuse---Bois-de-la-Côte-Lemont---Bois-de-Foret---Cunel---Romagne---Sommerance---Aire river west to Grandpré.

The Meuse-Argonne fighting up to October 9 had been desperate, and there was every indication of the enemy's intention to contest in this region every foot of ground, while by more rapid retirements farther west he endeavored to withdraw his masses from northern France before disaster, which would follow cutting the railroad line through Sedan, should overtake him.

On our own side, we were confronted with the situation of having a number of exhausted divisions and an insufficiency of replacements. Our combat units required some 90,000 replacements, while not more than 45,000, at most, would be available before November 1 for these and other vacancies. On October 9 also America had the 2d, 6th, 36th, 81st, and 88th Divisions with the French, and the 27th and 30th with the British. These and other conditions demanded a definite decision as to a policy covering a considerable period. On the night of October 9/10 the Commander-in-Chief reviewed the entire situation, not only the tactical situation of the First Army, but the strategical situation on the entire western front, and, as well, the question of our resources in men for the next two months. In brief, the Commander-in-Chief decided that the general situation demanded that the attack on the First Army front, and that of the Allies farther west, should be pushed to the limit. But if the First Army was to continue its pounding, this action must be coordinated with that of the Allies, and we must not only bring our divisions then with the French to the First Army, but we must break up incoming divisions to furnish, in part at least, the replacements so urgently needed. On October 10, therefore, the Commander-in-Chief sent the Chief of Staff, A. E. F., and the Assistant Chief of Staff, G-3, A. E. F., both to Allied and French General Headquarters, to present his views and to make certain arrangements of details. Marshal Foch expressed his appreciation of the fact that the First Army was striking the pivot of the German withdrawal and announced his view that the Allied attacks should continue as then conducted.

At French General Headquarters General Buat (Chief of Staff) at once agreed with the view that the American divisions with the French were essential to us if we were to keep up the battle against the German pivot. The French were, however, straining every nerve to keep up their own attacks, and they were only able to release our divisions by degrees. Before the last of the divisions above mentioned had been relieved (on November 4) two other divisions (37th and 91st) were sent to the French in Flanders.

At this time also it became apparent that the organization of another army was necessary. On October 10, therefore, the Second Army was created, and on October 12 Major General Robert L. Bullard was assigned to command it. The St-Mihiel front, extending from Port-sur-Seille to Fresnes-en-Woëvre was taken from the First Army and assigned to the Second Army. On October 12, the Commander-in-Chief assigned Major General Hunter Liggett to command the First Army and, establishing his own Advanced Headquarters at Ligny-en-Barrois, assumed command of the Group of Armies formed by the American First and Second Armies. (But while his Advanced Headquarters were at Ligny-en-Barrois, the Commander-in-Chief actually spent the major portion of his time on his train at Souilly, the headquarters of the First Army.)

* * * * * *

In the meantime, the struggle went on. On the night of the 11th/12th the 1st Division was relieved by the 42d Division and the 80th Division by the 5th Division, both relieving divisions coming from the St-Mihiel front. Local attacks continued on October 12/13 preparatory to a general assault, which on October 14 was delivered on the front from north of Verdun to St-Juvin. The order of battle in line on the front of attack from right to left was:

794888 O - 50 - 4

French XVII Corps:
: French 10th Colonial Division, French 26th Division, French 18th Division, 29th and 33d Divisions.

III Corps:
: 4th, 3d, and 5th Divisions.

V Corps:
: 32d and 42d Divisions.

I Corps:
: 82d and 77th Divisions.

Stubborn resistance was encountered everywhere, and on most of the front only small advances were realized. Nevertheless, La Cote-Dame-Marie fell, and the Kriemhilde Line of defense was broken.

On October 18 there was heavy fighting east of the Meuse, and the dogged offensive continued everywhere by local operations. On October 23, the III and V Corps pushed northward as far as Bantheville. It was now necessary to relieve certain troops, consolidate positions, and generally to get forces and supplies in hand before attempting another general attack. The remaining days of October (or to the end of the period we have called the first phase) were, therefore, devoted to preparing for the great attack to be launched November 1.

The material results which had been obtained by the First Army up to the end of October may be summarized as follows: The enemy's most elaborately prepared positions had been broken through; all of the Argonne Forest was in our hands; 18,600 prisoners, 370 cannon, 1,000 machine guns, and countless materiel of all sorts captured; an increasing number of German divisions, rising from 20 in line and reserve on September 26 to 31 on October 31, had been drawn into the fight; the great railway artery through Carignan and Sedan was seriously threatened.

The American soldier had shown an unrivalled fortitude in enduring incessant efforts and all the hardships due to constant bad weather and never-ceasing battle. The army had developed into a powerful and smooth-running machine and everyone, from the Commander-in-Chief to the last arrival in France, was supremely confident of the ability of the American soldier to carry through any task. On the other hand, the enemy's morale had been reduced until his will to resist had reached the breaking point, and he was ripe for the disaster which was soon to overtake him.

SECOND PHASE---NOVEMBER 1 TO NOVEMBER 11

On October 19, Marshal Foch issued general instructions for the continuation of the offensive on the entire front west of the Meuse. Under these instructions the French and Belgians in Flanders were to march on Brussels, while the British, together with the French First Army, were to march toward the region north of Givet. The mission of the First Army and that of the French Fourth Army remained unchanged, i. e., to reach the region of Sedan-Mezieres.

On October 21, the Commander-in-Chief directed the First Army to prepare to carry out its part of the above plan by being ready to launch a general attack on October 28. But the French Fourth Army, as well as our First Army, had felt the need of a period of comparative inactivity, so that the troops might be reorganized and supplies accumulated for another concerted attack. It was, of course, desirable that the attack of the First Army and that of the French Fourth Army should be simultaneous. As a result of conferences with French General Headquarters and Marshal Foch's Headquarters, and between the First Army and the French Fourth Army, November 1 was finally selected as the day of attack.

The primary purpose of the attack of the First Army and the French Fourth Army was, of course, to cut the great Carignan---Sedan---Mezieres railroad. The first and immediate objectives of the First Army were Buzancy and the heights of Barricourt, the turning of the wooded region north of the Aire (in reality a continuation of the Argonne Forest), and establishing contact with the French Fourth Army Boult-aux-Bois.

The line on the night of October 31/November 1 ran approximately as follows: The Meuse river---Clery-le-Grand---north of Bantheville---northern edge of the Bois-de-Bantheville---south of St-Georges---north of St-Juvin---north of Grandpre. The order of battle west of the Meuse from right to left was as follows:

III Corps:
    5th and 90th Divisions in line;
    3d Division in reserve.

V Corps:
    89th and 2d Divisions in line;
    1st and 42d Divisions in reserve.

I Corps:
    80th, 77th, and 78th Divisions in line;
    82d Division in reserve.

The 32d Division was in army reserve.

* * * * * *

The attack was preceded by two hours' violent artillery preparation. By continuous effort all available artillery had been moved forward to suitable positions to cover the infantry advance, and was well coordinated in a tremendous preparation. The enemy was overwhelmed and broke before the determined infantry. The III Corps took Andevanne, and the V Corps pushed forward most rapidly and drove the enemy from the heights of the Bois de Barricourt, a formidable natural obstacle which had blocked the way to Sedan.

On November 2, the I Corps pushed rapidly forward and occupied Buzancy. On the 3d, the entire line advanced, and by night the III Corps had taken Beauclair, the V Corps had reached the southern edge of the densely wooded region south of Beaumont, and the I Corps had taken St-Pierremont and Vierrieres. On the night of November 3, the 3d Brigade of the 2d Division penetrated the entire wooded region south of Beaumont and, by daylight of the 4th, established itself overlooking Beaumont, thus reversing the rôle which the Germans had played in 1870 in this historic spot. By the morning of November 4, the enemy's line of November 1 had been penetrated to a distance of 20 kilometers, and selected heavy batteries were being hurried forward to fire on the important railroad lines through MONTMEDY. The ultimate object of more than a month's continuous and desperate battle was now within reach.

On November 4, the pursuit was continued and the operations were extended to the heights east of the MEUSE at and south of DUN-sur-MEUSE. By nightfall of November 4, the III corps of the First Army held all the left bank of the MEUSE as far north as STENAY, and on November 5 this occupation of the river line was extended to the north by the right of the V Corps, while on the left the I Corps reached an east and west line north of STONNE. On November 5 also, the 5th Division of the III Corps had crossed to the east bank of the MEUSE and had driven the enemy over two kilometers to the east of BRIEULLES and DUN-sur-MEUSE.

Seeing the early completion of the operations then in progress, the Commander-in-Chief, on November 5, issued instructions for future operations as indicated in the following extracts from a letter signed by himself:

* * * * * *

2. The First and Second Armies will at once prepare to undertake operations with the ultimate purpose of destroying the enemy's organization and driving him beyond the existing frontier in the region of BRIEY and LONGWY.

3. As preliminaries of this offensive, the First Army will:

(a) Complete the occupation of the region between the MEUSE and the BAR.

(b) Complete the present operation of driving the enemy from the heights of the MEUSE north of VERDUN and south of the FORET-de-WOEVRE.

(c) Conduct an offensive with the object of driving the enemy beyond the THEINTE and the CHIERS.

The operation ordered in (c) will be begun at once by establishing a footing on the east bank of the MEUSE in the region of STENAY-MOUZON.

4. The Second Army will:

(a) Conduct raids and local operations in accordance with verbal instructions already given.

(b) Advance its line between the MOSELLE and ETANG LACHAUSSEE toward GORZE and CHAMBLEY.

(c) Prepare plans for an attack in the direction of BRIEY along the axis FRESNES---CONFLANS---BRIEY.

In submitting plans under (c), recommendations will be made as to the necessary extension of the present Second Army front toward the northwest.

On November 6, the occupation of the left bank of the Meuse was complete as far north as Allicourt, the great railway through Sedan was within two kilometers of our line, and farther to the west our troops were within easy light-gun range of the center of Sedan itself.

On November 6, then, the great railway artery was definitely cut and a continuation of our efforts and those of our Allies farther north meant the end of all the German armies in northern France.

Since October 7, a date which coincides with that on which it became certain that the German could not wrest from the First Army its initial success in breaking the Meuse-Argonne Line, the German Government had sought, through the President of the United States, to secure an armistice which, needless to say, would, in the German mind, be acceptable to Germany. Several exchanges of notes between the German Government and the President took place, until finally, on November 5, the President informed Germany that the question of an armistice must be taken up with Marshal Foch for a conference. Two such coincidences are not the result of chance, and are, themselves, sufficient proof that the American soldier had borne his share in securing victory.

The German representatives met Marshal Foch on the night of November 7/8 and asked for an immediate cessation of hostilities. In anticipation of an eventual request for an armistice, Marshal Foch had, on October 25, discussed the principles on which the armistice should be based with the several Commanders-in-Chief; since that date the Marshal had drawn up armistice terms in collaboration with the Supreme War Council. In answer to the German request for an armistice, the Marshal presented the enemy representatives with the terms already prepared and gave the Germans 72 hours in which to sign or reject those terms. While awaiting the expiration of the 72 hours all the Allies were ordered to continue the attack.

On November 7, 8, and 9, the German forces southeast of Stenay were pushed into the plain of the Woevre.

On November 9 at 9 p. m., appropriate orders were sent to the First and Second Armies in accordance with the following telegram from the Allied Commander-in-Chief:*
From Chief of Staff Bacon to
> General Headquarters (for General Petain)
> Chaumont Military Mission (for General Pershing)
> Ytres (sic) Mission (for Marshal Haig)
> Conde (for General Degoutte)

The enemy, disorganized by our repeated attacks, is retreating along the entire front.

It is paramount that we maintain and relentlessly push our efforts. I appeal to the energy and initiative of the Commanders-in-Chief and their armies to render decisive the results thus far obtained.

Marshal FOCH.

The attack of the First Army had now been directed towar Carignan. The I Corps sector was, in accordance with orders issued on November 7, taken over by the French Fourth Army, and, on November 10, the I Corps passed to the reserve.

On November 10, the V Corps forced a crossing over the Meuse south of Mouzon, and the III Corps occupied practically the whole of the forest of the Woëvre and reached the outskirts of Stenay from the south.

On the morning of November 11, the V Corps enlarged its bridgehead south of Mouzon and, crossing the river at Stenay, joined up with the III Corps in completing the occupation of that place. But, early on the morning of November 11, orders were received that the Armistice had been signed to take effect at 11 a. m. The armies were at once notified, and they in turn transmitted the order through the corps headquarters to the troops. The advance of our troops had been so rapid, however, that communication beyond corps headquarters was uncertain, and in at least one case one of our small detachments took prisoners after 11 a. m.

RESULTS OF THE MEUSE-ARGONNE

From September 26 to November 11, twenty-two American (1st, 2d, 3d, 4th, 5th, 26th, 28th, 29th, 32d, 33d, 35th, 37th, 42d, 77th, 78th, 79th, 80th, 81st, 82d, 89th, 90th, and 91st), and four French (10th Colonial, 15th Colonial, 18th, and 26th) divisions had, on the front Fresnes-en-Woëvre---Argonne, engaged and decisively beaten forty-six different German divisions. Of these German divisions, twenty had been drawn from the French and one from the British front. Of the twenty-two American divisions, twelve (2d, 26th, 28th, 33d, 37th, 42d, 78th, 79th, 81st, 89th, 90th, and 91st) had, at different times during the period September 26 November 11, been engaged on fronts other than that of the First Army between Fresnes-en-Woëvre---Argonne.

Forty-six divisions represented 25% of the enemy's entire divisional strength on the western front, and these divisions probably represented a still higher percentage of fighting value.

The First Army reported the capture during the Meuse-Argonne operation of approximately 26,000 prisoners, 874 cannon, over 3,000 machine guns, and a large amount of materiel of all kinds.

---

* *(Translation made from Foch correspondence.)*

The First Army reported that its own losses amounted to about 117,000. The resistance of the enemy during the month and a half's battle had been determined. We had completely broken down the enemy's desperate defense of the region which for more than four years had been the pivot of all his offensive and defensive action in northern France; and which was still more vital to him in endeavoring to carry out his intention, evidently formed by mid-September, of saving his army by a withdrawal to the vicinity of the Belgian-German---Belgian-Luxemburg frontier. Considering all these circumstances, our losses were remarkably light.

13. ORGANIZATION AND OPERATIONS OF SECOND ARMY, INCLUDING PROPOSED CHATEAU-SALINS OPERATION

As mentioned, the American Second Army was organized on October 10, and on October 12 began to function under its own commander, Major General Bullard.

The prospect, which became more and more of a certainty, of forcing an early conclusion of the war made it essential to keep all troops in line to the utmost limit of their powers of endurance, and forbade the rest to which the tired divisions were richly entitled. Divisions which could no longer remain in the active battlefront were, therefore, often sent to the calmer sector of the Second Army. The spirit in which the Headquarters of the Second Army accepted what, by comparison, was a secondary role, and the ability and activity of the Second Army staff, are worthy of all commendation. This spirit, ability, and activity were destined to reap their reward by a great success when all offensive movements were stopped by the Armistice on November 11.

The Commander-in-Chief's order of November 5, under which the Second Army was preparing for an offensive toward Briey, was mentioned.

On the same day (November 5) that the Commander-in-Chief wrote his instructions concerning the future operations of the First and Second Armies, Marshal Foch dated a letter in which he asked that six American division be held in readiness to assist in an attack which the French were preparing in the region of Chateau-Salins. Such an operation had long been favored by the Commander-in-Chief, and in fact had been studied by General Headquarters as early as September, 1917. Upon receipt, on November 6, of Marshal Foch's letter the Commander-in-Chief, therefore, at once concurred in the general idea and directed that arrangements be made to secure the necessary number of divisions. The 3d, 4th, 28th, 29th, 35th, and 36th Divisions were designated, and the Commander-in-Chief planned that they should be employed under the Second Army staff. At first the French desired that these divisions be placed as divisions at the disposition of General Mangin who was charged, under General de Castlenau, with the conduct of the French attack. The commander-in-Chief insisted that these divisions be not dispersed, and on November 10 sent a staff officer to the headquarters of General de Castlenau, General Mangin, and of the Second Army to make arrangements accordingly. The result of this visit was an agreement that the 6 divisions were to be employed on the right of the Second Army, that the Commanding General, Second Army, was to cover the left of the French attack and that, to insure this, he should conform to the wishes of General Mangin.

The movement of the six divisions was under way, the French having tentatively scheduled the attack for November 14, when it was stopped by the signing of the Armistice.

14. OPERATIONS OF AMERICAN UNITS WITH THE ALLIES AFTER SEPTEMBER 12, 1918

DIVISIONS WITH THE BRITISH

Of the ten American divisions in the British area (4th, 27th, 28th, 30th, 33d, 35th, 77th, 78th, 80th, and 82d), all but the 27th and 30th had been brought to the American or French fronts by September 12, the date of the first American offensive. The American II Corps, with the 27th and 30th Divisions, remained with the British until after the Armistice. These two divisions, under the II Corps staff, played an important part, with the Australians, in breaking the Hindenburg Line near Le Catelet on September 29, and, when the Armistice was signed, they had taken nearly 6,000 prisoners, 44 guns, and over 400 machine guns. * * *

DIVISIONS WITH THE FRENCH IN THE VOSGES

Between September 12 and November 4, six American divisions (6th, 29th, 37th, 81st, 88th, and 92d) held sectors at different times in the Vosges; until September 16 four divisions were in the Vosges; and until October 16 three divisions were constantly in that region.

THE 2d AND 36th DIVISIONS IN CHAMPAGNE

On September 30, the 2d Division entered the line of the French Fourth Army in Champagne, and October 3 attacked the very strong position of Blanc Mont near Somme-Py. The line was broken through to a depth of 4 1/2 kilometers on the first day, enabling the French on the left to advance. The 2d Division made further progress, breaking down all enemy resistance until it was relieved on October 10 by the 36th Division. The 2d Division losses in this sector were 4,975 officers and men. Its successes included 2,296 prisoners and a large quantity of matériel, but most important of all was the assistance rendered the French by its great initial success and by holding all ground gained. This was exploited by the 36th Division, which in two days advanced with the French a distance of 21 kilometers to the Aisne. The 36th remained in line on the Aisne with the French Fourth Army until October 28. * * *

DIVISIONS IN FLANDERS

In October, while we were so heavily engaged in the Meuse-Argonne, the Commander-in-Chief received a call from Marshal Foch for two American divisions to help the French Sixth Army and the Belgians who were attacking in the extreme north. In answer to this call the 37th and 91st Division (the 91st being accompanied by the artillery of the 28th Division) were sent. On October 30, these divisions entered the line and methodically overcame the enemy's resistance until they were relieved on November 4. On November 10, they again entered the line and were there when the Armistice was signed.

TROOPS IN ITALY

During the Abbeville Conference, the Italian Prime Minister asked that American troops be sent to Italy. This was reported to the War Department by cable 844-S. It appeared that the Italian representatives in Washington were making similar proposals, and, after a series of cables, the War Department directed the Commander-in-Chief, by cable 1560-R, June 19, 1918, to send one regiment of infantry to Italy. The 332d Infantry of the 83d Division was designated for this service and, accompanied by necessary hospital and other units, was sent to Italy during July. During the Austrian retreat in the fall of 1918, parts of the 332d Infantry saw active service.

MURMANSK EXPEDITION

During the London Conference, in April 1918, the Commander-in-Chief received information that the War Office had urged on Washington, through Lord Reading, American participation in the Murmansk Expedition. By cable 1757-R (received July 23, 1918) the Commander-in-Chief was directed to furnish 3 battalions of infantry to the Murmansk Expedition, and also 3 companies of engineers, provided the latter could be spared. In accordance with these instructions the 339th Infantry of the 85th Division and the 1st Battalion, 310th Engineers, were designated. The Commander-in-Chief decided that these troops should have American medical attention and accordingly designated the 337th Field Hospital and the 337th Ambulance Company to accompany the expedition. These troops sailed from Castle, England, August 26 and became a part of the Allied Expeditionary Force in North Russia which was under British command. The regiment was spread over a large extent of territory and was engaged from time to time with Bolshevik forces.

THE 93d DIVISION

The four infantry regiments (369th, 370th, 371st, and 372d) of the 93d Division were attached to French divisions upon their arrival in France. These regiments remained with French units throughout their service in France.

OTHER AMERICAN TROOPS WITH ALLIES

In addition to the units above mentioned, a large number of other units were, at different times throughout our participation in the war, placed at the disposition of our Allies. These units included engineers, aviation, mechanics, chauffeurs, medical service, etc., etc.

15. SPECIAL DIFFICULTIES AFFECTING OPERATIONS

REPLACEMENTS

Throughout our active participation in the war the question of replacements caused much trouble.

The General Organization project which the Commander-in-Chief submitted to Washington early in July of 1917 assumed the necessity of having in France a supply of replacements equal to 50% of the infantry of combat divisions and 25% of the other arms. The same project also invited attention to the necessity of preparing at home to assure the steady flow of additional replacements to France. The estimate as to the number of replacements to be maintained in France had as its basis the creation of a sufficient reservoir of personnel to enable us to carry out two principles which were assumed as fundamental:

(a) All losses of combat troops should be promptly replaced, not only in order to keep up fighting strength in actual numbers, but to maintain the morale of the organizations. This principle had been clearly shown to be fundamental by the experience of all our wars:

(b) Sick and wounded should, on their recovery, be returned to their own units.

The replacement organization in France, as originally contemplated (General Organization Project), included a so-called depot division and a so-called replacement division for each army corps of four combat divisions. These two divisions were to have a full complement of infantry, but one half of their artillery and other auxiliaries were to be utilized as corps and army troops. The organization thus provided the 50% reservoir of infantry and 25% of other arms considered necessary to insure carrying out the two fundamental principles mentioned above. Experience more than justified the stress which the Commander-in-Chief so early placed on the importance of replacements, and fully justified the early estimates of the numbers required. The German March 21 and following offensives created conditions, however, which, coupled with other reasons, prevented the functioning of the replacement system as originally planned. Some of the reasons for this failure were as follows:

(a) The situation required our troops to be spread over France.

(b) During May, June, and July 1918, every possible division had to be put into line; hence it was necessary to reduce the number of replacement divisions from two out of six to one out of six.

(c) During September, October, and the first ten days in November, it was necessary to utilize all troops to the limit of their endurance; hence the proportion of time spent in the line was greater than had been anticipated, and battle casualties and sickness as well were increased.

(d) The number of replacements required never reached France.

(e) It became essential to fill up certain divisions on account of tactical necessities, and since the shortage of replacements was at the time acute, sick and wounded returning to duty were sometimes necessarily sent to such divisions without regard to whether or not the soldier originally belonged to the division to be filled.

Our shortage of replacements became acute early in September, and by October 1 the situation was desperate. Only one recourse was possible---to utilize incoming divisions for replacements, holding the cadres to be reconstituted whenever replacements in adequate numbers should be received from home; the 34th, 38th, 84th, and 86th were so used. Even this action did not suffice to bring our 29 fighting divisions to full strength, but we were able, by a judicious use of the soldiers thus obtained, to maintain a reasonable strength in the divisions at the most critical points of attack. There is no doubt but that this decision to break up divisions contributed in a large degree to concluding the war in 1918.

CORPS AND ARMY TROOPS

The various decisions to give priority of shipment to infantry and machine-gun troops left us woefully short in the necessary corps and army troops. This condition was never corrected, and it was necessary to the end of active operations to arrange with the French for a great part of the corps and army artillery, aviation, and other services required for the American armies. The French High Command always responded most generously to our requests and we conducted all our attacks with a dominating force of artillery and of aviation.

HORSES

The horse situation was always acute. Due to the large amount of tonnage required in bringing horses from America, the Commander-in-Chief began, in February of 1918, intensive efforts to obtain the necessary animals in Europe. The French agreed to furnish the animals required, but the Government was unable to deliver horses as rapidly as they were needed.

The allowance of animals was reduced to the barest necessities, and even then it was found impossible to keep pace with the arrival of troops.

FIELD ARTILLERY

The field artillery of divisions, as well as corps and army artillery, was delayed on account of the various priority agreements. The effect of this, together with the shortage of horses and the difficulties of securing equipment, may be summarized as follows:

(a) On September 12 there were 25 divisions in or ready to go in the line, but artillery brigades for 8 of them were not yet ready.

(b) On September 26 there was a shortage of 6 artillery brigades.

(c) On November 1 there was a shortage of 7 artillery brigades.

This shortage of artillery brigades was met not only by the assistance given by the French but by leaving our own brigades in the line when the divisions they were serving were withdrawn. This was necessary but was unsatisfactory, in that it interfered with the establishing of the close relations which must exist between the infantry and its artillery. The artillery also lost the opportunity, which it would otherwise have had, for rest, training, and reequipping.

ARTILLERY AMMUNITION

In addition to our dependence up to the Armistice upon the French, and to a less extent upon the British, for all artillery materiel, we were also dependent upon them for artillery ammunition, practically none of our own manufacture, other than shrapnel, having reached the front by November 11.

Fortunately the French were able to supply our actual needs, but at times the French reserves of ammunition were so periously low as seriously to affect operations. The following data are believed to be approximately correct and are interesting in this connection:

On March 21, 1918, the 75-millimeter reserve under control of the French Commander-in-Chief was 21,987,000 rounds; on October 11, this reserve had sunk to 2,394,000 rounds. The daily production during this period was about 200,000 rounds of 75-millimeter.

In the nine days July 15-23, 5,200,000 rounds of 75-millimeter and 1,000,000 rounds of 155-millimeter howitzer ammunition were fired. The total expenditure of 75-millimeter ammunition on the western front on certain dates was as indicated below:

Date	Rounds
September 26	1,842,000
September 30	853,000
October 1	300,000
October 2	288,000
October 3	330,000
October 4	491,000
October 5	353,000
October 6	275,000
October 7	223,000
October 8	446,000
October 9	320,000
October 10	244,000

16. GENERAL SITUATION ON NOVEMBER 11, 1918

* * * The status of divisions on this date, using the same system for determining whether or not a division (Allied or enemy) should be classed as tired or fresh, is shown by the following table:

STATUS OF DIVISIONS ON THE WESTERN FRONT

(November 11, 1918)

ARMIES	IN LINE			IN RESERVE			TOTAL AVAILABLE DIVISIONS
	FRESH	TIRED	TOTAL	FRESH	TIRED	TOTAL	
U. S.	4*	12	16*	3	11	14	30*
French	19	17	36	19	53	72	108
British	5	24	29	6	29	35	64
Belgian	3	1	4	2	1	3	7
Italian	1	0	1	0	1	1	2
Portuguese	0	0	0	2	0	2	2
TOTAL ALLIES	32	54	86	32	95	127	213
GERMAN	47	97	144	2	39	41	185

*This includes the 93d Division, comprising 4 colored infantry regiments serving with the French.

IMPORTANT NOTE: U. S. divisions approximately twice as large as other divisions.

The map and the above table, taken together, tell the whole story of the German willingness to accept the severe terms of the Armistice. The American forces had broken down the enemy's defenses at the pivot of his withdrawal and had cut his great southern railroad system before he was able to complete the retreat of his masses from northern France and western Belgium. The table shows that, whereas the Allies had, on November 11, 127 divisions in reserve, of which 32 were fresh, the Germans had, on the same date, a total of only 41 divisions in reserve, of which only 2 were fresh.

The shrinking of German manpower is further shown by the fact that between July 15, 1918, the date upon which the last enemy offensive was launched, and November 11, no less than 26 German divisions were broken up.

But in considering the reduction of German manpower and the comparatively few divisions Germany had in reserve, it must be remembered that had the enemy succeeded in withdrawing his masses in northern France and Belgium to his lines through Liége and Marche and Neufchâteau, he would have shortened his front by more than 150 kilometers and would have stood, with his own country intact, behind the most difficult part of the Ardennes. With his front so shortened, and in such a position, there was no military reason why, as Sir Douglas Haig pointed out at the conference of the Allied Commanders-in-Chief on October 25, the German could not still make a very effective stand. The principal military factor which forced the German to accept the Armistice on November 11 was the decisive American victory resulting in cutting the railroad through Sedan and his consequent inability to succeed in the further withdrawal of his masses under the Allied attacks.

17. THE THIRD ARMY AND THE ADVANCE INTO AND OCCUPATION OF GERMANY

In accordance with the terms of the Armistice, the Allies were to occupy all German territory west of the Rhine with bridgeheads of 30 kilometer radius at Cologne, Coblenz, and Mayence.

The zone assigned the American Command was the bridgehead of Coblenz and the district of Treves. This territory was to be occupied by an American army with its reserves held between the Moselle-Meuse Rivers and the Luxemburg frontier.

The instructions of Marshal Foch, issued on November 16, contemplated that two French infantry divisions and one cavalry division would be included in the French forces which were to occupy the Mayence bridgehead. This would have created mixed commands, which, in the work to be undertaken, might have easily led to unnecessary complications. The Commander-in-Chief, therefore, represented to Marshal Foch the desirability of giving each nation a well-defined territory of occupation and of using within such territory no troops other than those of the commander responsible for the particular zone. Marshal Foch did not consent at first to this view, and considerable correspondence followed, but finally, by letter dated December 9, the Marshal accepted the principle of preserving the entity of command and troops. In doing this, however, the Marshal reduced the bridgehead, proper, entrusted to America by about one half and added the part taken away from the Coblenz bridgehead to the French command at Mayence.

Various reasons made it undesirable to employ either the First or Second Army as the Army of Occupation. Plans had already been made to organize a Third Army Headquarters, and, on November 14, this army, with Major General J. T. Dickman as Commander, was designated as the Army of Occupation. The III and IV Army Corps, staffs and troops, less artillery, and the 1st, 2d, 3d, 4th, 32d, and 42d Divisions were assigned to the Third Army. This force was later increased by the addition of the VII Corps and the 33d, 89th, and 90th Divisions. The 33d Division was, however, subsequently assigned to the Second Army.

The advance toward German territory began on November 17 at 5 a.m., six days after signing the Armistice. All of the Allied forces from the North Sea to the Swiss border moved forward simultaneously in the wake of the retreating German army. At first the Germans had a lead of six days upon the Allied forces, but inasmuch as it developed that certain disorders were occurring in Allied territory and in Luxemburg, through which the Germans were passing, the Allied forces were ordered to accelerate their march so as to maintain a distance of ten kilometers only between their advance elements and the rear elements of the German forces.

The Third Army advanced with four divisions in the first line and two in the second, following the first line at a maximum distance of two marches. Upon arrival at the German frontier, a halt was made for several days, until December 1, when the leading elements of all Allied Armies crossed the line into Germany.

The arrival of our troops was watched with unfeigned interest by the inhabitants, and without any manifestation of hostility. The Third Army headquarters were established at Coblenz, and the troops were disposed so that the III Corps, comprising the 1st, 2d, and 32d Divisions, occupied the bridgehead, the IV Corps in close support with the 3d, 4th, and 42d Divisions, and the VII Corps, 89th and 90th Divisions, occupied the territory down to the Luxemburg-German frontier. An advance General Headquarters was established at Treves.

Steps were immediately taken to organize the bridgehead for defense, and dispositions of troops were so made that, should hostilities be renewed, an immediate offensive could be resumed.

Efforts were next directed toward establishing the troops in comfortable quarters, reequipping the command, and providing the necessary amusements and recreation to keep up their morale and to counteract any tendency toward homesickness. The latter provisions were very important, inasmuch as military considerations made it necessary to refrain from fraternizing with the inhabitants.

18. THE OCCUPATION OF LUXEMBURG

The zone of march of our troops into Germany, and the lines of communication of the Third Army after reaching the territory to be occupied, lay through Luxemburg. It was, therefore, necessary for our forces not only to cross Luxemburg but to occupy a portion of that Grand Duchy. Upon entering this country, the Commander-in-Chief published a proclamation assuring the people that American troops entered Luxemburg solely on account of military necessities, that we respected their neutrality, and that we would not interfere with their internal affairs.

After the passage of the Third Army, the occupation of Luxemburg for the purpose of guarding our lines of communication was intrusted to the 5th and 33d Divisions of the Second Army. The Luxemburg people were not only tranquil but they welcomed the Americans and assisted them in every way. The whole of Luxemburg, however, was not in the American zone as fixed by Marshal Foch. Moreover, the city of Luxemburg, though lying in the American zone and the principal point on our lines of communication, was excluded from our control. Garrisoned by French troops, this city was designated as the Allied Commander-in-Chief's Advanced Headquarters. These arrangements created a dual control. The situation was further complicated by a note dated December 14 in which Marshal Foch gave the French General de Latour, Commandant d'Armees in the city of Luxemburg, control of all troops in the Grand Duchy insofar as concerned a Decree, issued by the Marshal on December 9, regarding the Administration of the Grand Duchy of Luxemburg. Thus a French general was to control American troops in administering certain affairs within a neutral state. The decree itself contained minute and apparently, in view of the attitude of the people, unnecessary restrictions on the inhabitants. Our troops were promptly directed to take no orders from General de Latour, and Marshal Foch was notified that the Commander-in-Chief did not recognize the necessity for the decree and did not accept it.

The entire Luxemburg situation was most delicate. There was reason to believe that certain French elements were intriguing to create a sentiment in Luxemburg for annexation to France and that the Belgians were anxious to undertake the same thing with reference to annexation to Belgium.

After the Commander-in-Chief declined to allow American troops to pass under the Commandant d'Armees' authority, Marshal Foch endeavored to obtain our acceptance of the principle involved by modifications of detail. Much correspondence and several conferences followed, but the Commander-in-Chief stood firm on his policy of noninterference in the affairs of Luxemburg, and finally, on January 25, 1919, Marshal Foch agreed to include the entire Duchy in the American zone.

19. RETURN OF TROOPS TO THE UNITED STATES

The Commander-in-Chief cabled, on the day the Armistice was signed, suggesting that the return of troops be studied at both ends of the line. On November 15, four days after the Armistice was signed, the Commander-in-Chief cabled (1897-S): It is now certain that resumption of hostilities of character heretofore the rule is impossible. The cable then recommended the adoption of a policy of sending home certain auxiliaries and stated that, if the policy was approved, we could, without delay, begin to utilize all available shipping in the withdrawal of our troops. The policy involved was approved by the War Department, by cable dated November 16. On the same date the Commander-in-Chief issued instructions under which 30 divisions, with a minimum of corps and army troops were held, and all other combat troops were released for return to the United States. By cable 1905-S, the Commander-in-Chief informed the War Department of his plan of reducing at once to 30 divisions with but few auxiliaries, and added: . . . present prospects of restoration of order in Europe make it possible to hope for reduction even of the thirty divisions which I have recommended be held in Europe for the present.

As our troops entered Germany, the Commander-in-Chief became more and more certain that order would prevail in that country, and he at once adopted the policy of keeping every ship returning to the United States filled with returning soldiers. It soon became evident that, in order to carry out this policy, we must send home some of the 30 combat divisions which were temporarily being held under the decision of November 16. The reduction of our forces, decided upon November 16, had been consented to by Marshal Foch, but in further reductions the Commander-in-Chief at once encountered the opposition of the Marshal. This opposition was based on the Marshal's view that a state of war still existed, and was complicated by the French desire, expressed by Marshal Foch in a letter dated November 23, that the American troops assist in the labor of restoring the devastated regions.

The question of using the labor of our troops was soon settled, but the difference of opinion as to military necessities resulted in conferences and correspondence which only ceased with the signing of peace. The A. E. F. view throughout this period is well summed up in the following quotation from a letter dated December 11, 1918, from the Commander-in-Chief to Marshal Foch:

> As there is little possibility of resumption of hostilities, I cannot see the necessity of retaining a greater number than 29 divisions even now, and the need of troops will grow less and less in the near future, when I shall recommend further withdrawals.

In spite of all difficulties, agreements were reached and our ships kept filled by reductions which, by May 19, 1919, had resulted in all combat divisions, except the 1st, 2d, and 3d of the Third Army, being placed under orders to proceed to ports of embarkation. On that date the President of the United States gave the Commander-in-Chief information which made it appear advisable not to reduce the Third Army below five divisions. Orders were, therefore, issued, cancelling the movements of the 4th and 5th Divisions. The 5th Division was stationed in Luxemburg, which became a part of the Third Army territory on February 6. But even without the 4th and 5th Divisions, sufficient troops were found to assure filling to capacity all available shipping to include June 30.

The treaty of peace was signed on June 28, and orders were at once issued for the release of the 4th and 5th Divisions.

All the Commander-in-Chief's recommendations since the Armistice had been against leaving American troops in Europe, but on May 19 he was informed by the President of the United States that it would be necessary to leave a regiment in occupied Germany. Under date of May 26, the Commander-in-Chief approved a memorandum which gave a tentative list of auxiliaries necessary to make the American force to be left an independent unit. No action by the President was obtained until June 25, when the basic principles of the May 26 memorandum were submitted to him in a letter from General Bliss. But, while the President approved the recommendations of the May 26 memorandum, he informed the Commander-in-Chief on June 27 that it would probably be necessary to leave several divisions in occupied Germany until the military terms of the treaty had been executed. The final decision was left to be decided by the Commander-in-Chief after conference with Marshal Foch. This conference was held on June 30, and agreement was reached as indicated by the following quotation from cable 2800-S:

> By direction of President, I have discussed with Marshal Foch question of forces to be left on the Rhine. Following agreed upon: The 4th and 5th Divisions will be sent to base ports immediately, the 2d Divisions will be commence moving to base ports on July 15, and the 3d Division on August 15. Date of relief of 1st Division will be decided later. Agreement contemplates that after compliance by Germany with military conditions to be completed within first three months after German ratification of treaty, American force will be reduced to one regiment of infantry and certain auxiliaries. Request President be informed of agreement.

The location of troops and the difficulties indicated above made it necessary in the beginning to return troops without particular reference to the length of time they had been in France. But the policy was at once adopted, other things being equal, of first to come first to go, and, as time went on, it was possible to give more and more attention to length of service in designating units to go home. Regular divisions were necessarily excepted from the provisions of this policy.

In reviewing the return of our troops to the United States, one feature stands out: It was the early adoption by the Commander-in-Chief of the simple policy. Keep every returning ship filled, and the determined adherence to that policy, in spite of all obstacles, that made possible the wonderful record in the repatriation of the American Expeditionary Forces.

20. INFLUENCE OF THE MILITARY EFFORT OF THE UNITED STATES UPON THE WAR

In a war so stupendous as this, it is manifestly absurd to pretend that any one nation, much less any one army, arm, or individual, won the war. Without the *poilu* of France, without the sacrifices of Belgium, without the fleet of England and the fighting spirit of her armies in 1916 and 1917, without the great Russian efforts of 1914, 1915, and 1916, without the aid of Italy, the effort of the United States would have been utterly impotent. Nevertheless, the United States played a decisive part in the final victory. Certain features of our participation in the war stand out with such dramatic distinctness that they alone are sufficient to recount as evidencing the fact that America's effort was worthy of her traditions and institutions:

First, our declaration of war gave the Allies new hope at a time when hope was bitterly needed;

Second, our adoption of the principle of universal service and the beginning of plans for an army, numbered by the millions, gave our Allies further encouragement and enabled them to face the defection of Russia;

Third, the great troop movements of the spring of 1918 and the fortunate availability of our units in the first days of June saved, in the popular mind, Paris, and brought firmness, renewed strength, and even enthusiasm at a most critical period;

Fourth, the reserves furnished by America enabled the Allies to undertake the July 18 offensive and to regain the initiative which was essential to victory;

Fifth, America made it certain that victory would be attained in 1919, and it was the American soldier alone, particularly in his great attack of November 1, who made victory possible in 1918.

21. MILITARY LESSONS OF THE WAR

The tactical lessons to be gained from the war are infinite, and even though it were possible it is not desirable to attempt their enumeration here. Their study is rather a matter for the future, and in such study we should avoid the error of assuming that our experiences, within themselves, rather than logical deductions from them and other experiences, are the lessons which we seek.

But our experience taught one great lesson that, while it stood out so prominently to the General Headquarters, is likely to be soon forgotten. That lesson is: The unprepared nation is helpless in a great war unless it can depend upon other nations to shield it while it prepares. Every scrap of the history of the American Expeditionary Forces bears this lesson, but it is only necessary to justify it by remembering a few of the facts brought out in this report.

More than a year elapsed after our declaration of war before we were able to undertake an offensive action and then only one regiment of infantry was actually engaged;

Not one American-made gun of the most essential calibers appeared upon the battle front in the 18 months from our declaration of war to the Armistice.

First the necessity of saving a defeat and, next, the possibility of winning the war in 1918, thereby saving American lives as well as the suffering of the world, required putting the American soldier into battle without the training, discipline, and leadership which he deserved.

22. RECORD OF THE AMERICAN SOLDIER

In spite of, or perhaps on account of, all the handicaps under which he struggled, volumes could, and will, be written on the American soldier's part in the war. Without doubt, many mistakes were made and many units might have accomplished more. But, in a large sense, only a brief statement of fact is necessary to establish for the American soldier a record to which no other nation can lay claim; In the defense no American division lost ground intrusted to it, except locally, and then only for a few hours, and no American division failed in attack.

* * * * * *

C-in-C Report File: Fldr. 90:

Final Report of Assistant Chief of Staff, G-4

GENERAL HEADQUARTERS, A. E. F.,

Washington, D. C. April 5, 1920.

To: THE COMMANDER-IN-CHIEF, AMERICAN EXPEDITIONARY FROCES.

SIR: I have the honor to submit herewith a report of the operations of the Fourth Section of the General Staff.

PART I

ORGANIZATION AND DEVELOPMENT OF THE FOURTH

SECTION OF THE GENERAL STAFF

The most important problem for solution following America's decision to send an expedition to France was the organization of a military machine abroad, properly controlled and coordinated by a suitable staff - an organization which could take an orderly and strategic setting in France and into which the men and munitions coming from America, as well as the material purchased abroad, could be logically absorbed. At home it had never been possible to have an orderly military establishment constructed on the best principles. Political consideration too often took precedence over military requirements. The various military establishments built up were not fitted to meet the emergency of war. They were generally peace organizations, pure and simple. In France, on the contrary, we had the advantage of starting with a clean slate in a position isolated from America by the conditions of the war. Most important also, we were, from the outset, generously supported by a loyal people and by the administration which represented them.

Before the Commander-in-Chief embarked on the steamship Baltic, a tentative organization had been drawn up and these plans were worked over on shipboard and at headquarters in PARIS until July 5, 1917, when the first organization was announced. This order [G. O. No. 8, A. E. F., 1917] provided for a General Staff divided into three major sections designated respectively, Intelligence Section, Operations Section, and Administrative Section, and an administrative, technical, and supply staff consisting of a Judge Advocate, Inspector General, Chief Quartermaster, Adjutant General, Chief Engineer, Chief Ordnance Officer, Chief Surgeon, Chief Signal Officer and Aviation Officer. The purpose of this order was to establish coordinated action between the several staff departments of the whole command.

At the outset, the Commander-in-Chief made the important announcement that there was to be general staff control and coordination throughout. The fact that this announcement was made from the outset and strictly adhered to accounts largely for the success we had. It meant that the military machine of the American Expeditionary Forces was to grow and develop in an orderly, balanced manner. No one arm, bureau, or department, was to be developed in advance of its needs or at the expense of other. It meant, in effect, that the personal interest in the case of each chief of an important subdivision was a personal interest in the welfare of the whole military establishment abroad rather than in his own part alone. This principle was maintained to the last and as a result there was developed a loyal and efficient group of commanders and staff officers

794888 O - 50 - 5

united upon the accomplishment of a single mission in a manner which America had never witnessed before.

The Intelligence Section was charged with gathering from all sources the information in reference to the enemy and this section controlled or was in liaison with all agencies from which this information could be secured. The Operation Section had to do with all matters connected with the employment of our combat units against the enemy. In its initial organization also, it was charged with training, equipment, and organization. The Administrative Section had to do with general administration and supply policies and it was also charged with coordinating the line of communications with the field forces. The Coordination Section of the General Staff (G-4 as it was designated later) did not come into existence until August 14, 1917, when a revision of the original plan of organization was published creating two new sections of the General Staff, namely, Training and Coordination. The Coordination Section took over many of the duties previously devolving upon the Administrative Section. The order described the duties of this new section as follows:

> The Coordination Section may be considered the connecting link between the General Staff and the regular Supply and Staff Departments and the Line of Communications Service. Its function in maintaining intimate relations between the office of the Chief of Staff and these various services will be both executive and advisory. It will keep on hand the latest information regarding supplies, state of construction, efficiency of rail transportation and will study and frequently report upon the practical working of all staff and supply departments.

This revision provided also three new agencies, destined to play an important part in our services of supply. These were a General Purchasing Agent, and associated with him, a General Purchasing Board; a Department of Transportation with a Director General of Transportation at its head; and a Commanding General, Line of Communications. These were equal in rank, and coordinate with each other and with the chiefs of the previously existing supply bureaus, and divested the latter of some of the duties devolving upon them under the previously existing organization.

The General Purchasing Board was in fact a directorate of purchases. It was organized to purchase all supplies requisitioned from European sources by the various departments, to effect liaison and cooperation with French and British authorities with a view to preventing competition between the Allies in the same market, to provide cooperation between the various supply bureaus of the American Expeditionary Forces, and to forestall competition between them. Its function was to consolidate orders for articles of the same class and to secure thereby the advantage of low prices for purchases in bulk. It was in effect a purchasing agency organized on the basis of commodities rather than on that of the staff bureaus which were responsible for their distribution or employment.

The Transportation Department was charged with the operation, maintenance, and construction of all railways and canals under American control; with the construction and maintenance of roads and wharves and of shops and other buildings for railway purposes; with the procurement of railway supplies; with the control of telephone and telegraph for railway purposes; with railway personnel; with liaison with French authorities in matters of transportation; and with the investigation and compilation of claims and indebtedness incurred in transporting American materials or troops over French railways.

Troops continued to arrive from the United States in ever increasing numbers and their arrival in divisional training areas brought to the front new questions of administration, particularly with reference to our relationship with the French government and the French military authorities. Conferences with these officials were held from time to time and our supply system began to take shape. The Coordination Section of the General Staff enlarged its scope and necessarily supervised more and more closely the activities of the various supply bureaus with a view of balancing effort and keeping all estsblishments on a corresponding footing. As the problems increased in number and complexity it developed that the division of duties and responsibilities between the Coordination and Administration Sections was not fully understood outside of the sections themselves. This was clarified in instructions issued November 19, 1917, in which the duties of the Administrative and Coordination Sections were carefully defined. The same order decentralized and simplified staff methods of administration. This order indicated the direction in which the Coordination Section was developing and defined its duties as follows:

> All questions concerning supply and transportation in France. Operations of the technical services, except the Red Cross, Y. M. C. A., and other similar agencies, the General Purchasing Board, War Risk Bureau, Auditors and Field Ambulance Service. Operations of the Line of Communications and the Transportation Department. Statistics concerning supply, construction, and transportation. Supply and transportation arrangement for combat. Assignments of labor and labor troops. Location of railway and supply establishments. Hospitalization and evacuation of sick and wounded. Orders for assignment of new units.

In the meantime studies were continually in progress as to the British and French systems of staff organization as well as our own and eventually a method of staff coordination and control of the important services of construction, transportation, and supply was evolved. It resulted in the Coordination Section restricting its jurisdiction to questions of supply within the American Expeditionary Forces, leaving to the Administration Section the supervision of the procurement from the United States, of the allotment of tonnage and the arrangements for transportation to France.

Specifically, the Coordination Section continued to deal with questions of supply and transportation in France, embracing operations of the technical and supply services, operations on the Line of Communications and of the Transportation Department. It compiled statistics concerning the most important articles of supply and the status of construction and transportation. It maintained records of progress of construction work and made assignment of the necessary labor in conformity with a priority of construction which was established by this section in anticipation of the needs of the service. Studies and recommendations for the location and character of railway and establishments required for the transportation and service of our troops came to this section for approval. The same was true with regard to all hospitalization projects including the location and distribution of hospitals and the number of beds. Arrangements for the evacuation of sick and wounded and orders for the original assignment of troops arriving in France were also made in this section, though in the course of time, as the armies began to take shape, the procedure involved in such assignment became practically automatic.

The whole machine was shaping itself so as to function properly in the active field operations which were to follow. The Commander-in-Chief could control the whole plant through the chiefs of his General Staff sections. Based on the information furnished him by the Intelligence Section, the Commander-in-Chief could communicate his orders to the Chiefs of the Third and Fourth Sections through whom all the operations of the combat armies were coordinated and controlled as well as all the agencies for their transportation and supply. Thus, the system enabled the Commander-in-Chief to direct the whole situation without divulging confidential plans and orders, except to the Chiefs of his General Staff sections. Chiefs of the Operations and Coordination Sections could then allot specific tasks for performance without explaining to all subordinates concerned the whole plan. Naturally, at first, there was a tendency on the part of subordinates to run directly to the Commander-in-Chief or his Chief of Staff in a desire to get their orders direct and to be informed on the whole situation. But the powers of the Chiefs of the General Staff sections were built up and augmented from time to time so that they could give final decisions in practically all questions arising in the activities assigned them. The supply of troops in France was divided into three phases, viz: The procurement of supplies, their care and storage, and their transportation. The responsibility for the first was vested in the chiefs of the various supply bureaus while the Commanding General, Line of Communications, was responsible for the care and storage of supplies, material, and equipment and for the construction, maintenance, and repair of all agencies necessary to accomplish these purposes. He was responsible that supplies were distributed among the several departments in accordance with approved plans for military operations. The Director General of Transportation, under whose control the Army transport Service had also been placed, was charged with unloading freight and troops from ships arriving at our ports and for the transportation by rail to points designated by higher authority. He was also made responsible for construction, maintenance, and operation of such railroad lines and rolling stock as came into American control. The general supervision of all these activities was exercised by the General Staff, General Headquarters, and, as a rule, through the Coordination Section.

While the number of troops in France was comparatively small and the work incidental to their administration and supply was correspondingly limited, the control centered at General Headquarters. At these Headquarters were located the various sections of the General Staff and also the main offices of the various administrative, technical, and supply staff bureaus. With the expansion of the Expeditionary Forces, this extreme centralization of control became unwieldy and not conductive to the best interests of the expedition. Certain weaknesses in the scheme of organization had also developed and required rectification.

Accordingly a careful analysis of the situation was made with a view to effecting necessary improvements. It was found that great diversity of opinion and practice existed among the different chiefs of services with respect to the degree of personal responsibility assumed and methods employed in details of supply. It appeared that, in decentralizing to secure a distribution of the heavy burdens of administration and the execution of the incidental tasks, an undesirable division of responsibility and authority had also been brought about which induced uncertainty and hesitancy and which might prove disastrous in an emergency. The analysis also indicated the immediate necessity for providing a single and direct line of responsibility for all matters of supply while at the same time utilizing to the fullest possible extent the services of the experienced and able chiefs of the various administrative and supply departments. This situation led to a rather radical revision of the system of supply which was promulgated February 16, 1918 [G. O. No. 31, A. E. F., 1918].

Under this order the line of communications as reorganized was designated the Service of the Rear. This title was almost immediately changed to the services of supply, abbreviated S. O. S., and under this name it continued to function to the end. In accordance with this latest order, the chiefs of the supply services exercised all of their functions in matters of procurement, transportation, and supply under the direction of the Commanding General, Services of Supply, by whom their activities were coordinated. Their principal officer were moved to TOURS, which had become the headquarters of the Services of Supply.

The names of the five sections of the General Staff were altered to a numerical designation which incidentally corresponded very closely to that of the French and facilitated the transaction of business with the French staff; thus the Administration Section become the First Section, the Intelligence Section became the Second Section, and the Operations, Coordination, and Training Sections became respectively the Third, Fourth, and Fifth Sections of the General Staff. The officers at the heads of these various sections became know as Assistant Chiefs of Staff and for convenience the names of the Sections were abbreviated to G-1, G-2, and so forth. The whole system became quite generally known as the G-system of staff organization.

In a very short time the readjustments necessary to put this order into effect had been accomplished. The transaction of business soon crystallized into an orderly and almost automatic procedure which greatly assisted in fixing responsibility and was conductive to that expedition of deicision and action vital to the efficiency of our operations in the field. Under this form of organization the Commander-in-Chief and the staff at General Headquarters were relieved from consideration of much time-consuming detail and were left free to devote their energies to the preparation of plans for the movements of our combat forces on a large scale.

Somewhat later, to confirm practice already instituted by letters and oral instructions, orders were issued (August 6, 1918) G. O. No. 130, A. E. F., 1918 enunciating the basic principles covering the development of the Services of Supply. Under this order, the Commanding General, Services of Supply, was charged with all matters relating to automatic supply from the United States to the Services of Supply in accordance with policies proved by the Commander-in-Chief. His duties embraced the handling of requisitions initiated by the supply departments and the direction of purchases through the General Purchasing Board; the discharge and transportation of supplies by rail and water; the chartering and requisition of vessels; the necessary construction of facilities for these various purposes and the procurement from the United States of personnel necessary to the administration of all activities under his control in accordance with further letters of instruction issued to him from time to time. He was also charged with the development of port facilities, storage facilities, railroad transportation, and the allotment of tonnage.

The General Staff at General Headquarters concerned itself with the broader phases of policy, including those relating to new troops and new scales of equipment, and excepting only those pertaining to the troops in the Services of Supply. General Headquarters also retained immediate control of military transportation and supply in the Zone of the Armies and the determination and control of war material required in the conduct of military operations against the enemy. Thus, for example, the Deputy Director of General Transportation in charge of railway transportation in the Advance Zone became the chief of that subsection of G-4 which dealt with transportation matters; and again, the senior medical officer on duty in the medical subsection of G-4 served as Deputy Chief Surgeon and in that capacity controlled all agencies of hospitalization and evacuation in the Advance Zone. So also G-4 acted directly on all questions relating to the assignment of motor transportation and the allotment and distribution of ammunition and engineer materials and equipment required by combat forces in the field. General policies governing all these matters in the Services of Supply were also handled in the Fourth Section and communicated to the Commanding General, Services of Supply.

The precise duties of the Section, as outlined by the final instructions were as follows:

Supervises: Supply, construction, and transportation in France, including location of railways and supply establishments.
Analyzes: Statistics concerning the above.
Guarantees: Supply and transportation arrangements for combat.
Supervises: Hospitalization and evacuation of the sick and wounded.
Makes Assignment Of all new units arriving in France.
Of all labor and labor troops.

The plans for future operations of the Allies were communicated only to the Commander-in-Chief and by him to a small number of the higher staff officers under his immediate command. Arrangements for the employment of American troops in conformity therewith were necessarily made at General Headquarters, and G-4 being responsible for supply and transportation arrangements for combat was therefore obliged to keep in close touch with the primary activities of the Services of Supply. Projects of any importance, especially those involving the location of facilities, were examined by this section of the General Staff to assure their harmonizing with the general scheme.

PART II

AGENCIES OF THE FOURTH SECTION OF THE GENERAL STAFF

The Fourth Section was intimately concerned with the question and development of the Services of Supply, the great reservoir of munitions and personnel in France. It handled for the Commander-in-Chief all matters of general policy concerning the Services of Supply. This enabled it to control the growth and development of that great organization along proper strategic lines in such a way that the machine thus built up was flexible and always able to conform to the ever changing conditions at the front. Charged as it was with the distribution of supplies to the armies, the Fourth Section was in a position to coordinate the activities of the Service of Supply so that the needs of the armies at the front could be met at all times.

The outlets of this great reservoir to the front were the regulating stations. These were networks of railway sidings through which trains for the front were passed or where they were made over into new trains containing supplies called for by each unit. The regulating officer who completely controlled the station was a member of the Fourth Section of the General Staff.

The Fourth Section also maintained an office at French General Headquarters and later at the Headquarters of the Allied Commander-in-Chief. This gave us a direct line for arranging all matters with the French in which the Fourth Section was concerned. Liaison was also maintained with the Assistant Chiefs of Staff of the armies for the settling of matters of established policy.

To sum up then, the Chief of Fourth Section had ample authority to enable him to carry on the duties with which he was charged - a direct line to the Commanding General, Services of Supply, in matters of general policy and operations, a direct control over all regulating stations through which our supplies and personnel were forwarded to the front and evacuated to the rear, and a direct line to his representative at the Headquarters of the Allied Commander-in-Chief, over which to secure direct and prompt action on request made on French authorities for transportation, supplies, and facilities which we found necessary to obtain from them.

1. Regulating Stations: The mobility demanded of combat units precludes the possibility of their being burdened with even a single day's stores over and above their standard authorized reserves. This can readily be understood when one realizes that a single division requires the equivalent of twenty-five French railway cars for its normal daily consumption.

The supply distribution system must, therefore, be so modeled that it can turn over to each division, with absolute regularity, the supplies that it requires for its daily consumption at a point on the front from which distribution to the smaller units can easily be made by its motor or horse-drawn transport, whether the division be in the line, on the march, or in rest area.

Only in this way can the tactical command be left entirely free to shift, concentrate, or otherwise maneuver the troops with a maximum degree of battle effectiveness, at the same time deriving the full benefits from absolute secrecy of movement. Elaborate preparations in advance of a contemplated movement must be made unnecessary, and the final disposition of troops must not be divulged until the last moment.

This high degree of elasticity and adaptability of the supply system is assured and maintained by an instrumentalith which has grown out of the necessities of this war - the Regulating Station, the nerve center of the supply and transportation systems in the Zone of the

Armies. It is the connecting link between the armies and the services of the rear, coordinating them with the railroads that tie them together. The regulating officer is answerable and responsible directly to the Assistant Chief of Staff, G-4, General Headquarters.

On the regulating station falls the responsibility that the regularity of supply is maintained, that troop movements and evacuation proceed smoothly, that congestion is prevented at railheads, and that cars of supplies, men, horses, etc., reach their proper unit without delay, even though the unit in question be moving. The physical requirements of a regulating station are simple, merely one or more large railroad yards, preferably situated at or near a junction point of several lines leading from the various interior depots and centers of production from which supplies are drawn and with two or more separate lines leadingtto the front served by it, to insure against interruption of traffic should one line be cut by bombing or shellfire or blocked by a wreck. The regulating officer was kept informed of the number of mouths to be fed in the army depending upon his station as well as the number of animals and pieces of artillery to receive their daily rations. Likewise each motor vehicle was allotted an average amount of gas and oil, and this gave a total which had to reach the army every day. The supply of such articles was made automatic. To accomplish this, regulating officers were authorized to draw direct on designated depots put at their disposal for the purpose and in this way they established an automatic flow of supplies through their regulating stations to the troops in the area assigned them. Supplies which were only called for as needed and for which a daily rate of supply and consumption could [not?] be fixed, were kept in dumps and depots in the army and these stocks were kept filled up with requisitions on designated depots in rear of the regulating station.

The regulating officer was a most important personage in the working of the whole system. He knew the capacity of his station in cars. Strict orders required that no trains be forwarded to him except on his call or as released by him. It took a long time to get this practice established. The automatic supply had to flow, as far as most articles were concerned, whether the army was engaged or not. The remaining capacity of the regulating station was devoted to things needed at the moment by the army. This might be clothing and equipment one day for divisions refitting behind the line, a rush of munitions the next for divisions in preparation for attack, replacements during and after battle, or important engineer material during an advance. But priority was ordered in each case. An army must have what it needs each day. There is never 100% equipment and supplies. There is never sufficient transportation to forward 100% of everything even if we had it. The problem is then to deliver promptly those things which are vital to success. Such articles must arrive on schedule time and they must not be blocked by nonessentials.

It was sometimes argued that the control exercised by the Chief of the Fourth Section of the General Staff stood in the way of the Chiefs of the supply and technical services who had their own responsibility in supplying the army; that each such chiefs should be allowed to ship directly to troops what he believed they needed. We tried this once with a very small army in '98 and the result forms one of the saddest pages in our national military history. Tracks were blocked for miles and still the troops were not supplied. In the campaign just concluded in France the General Staff control led. We had teamwork, and for the first time in our military history our supply and technical services finished the war with great credit and success in practically every case.

Regulating stations were of two general types. One type had large storage facilities connected with it. At such a station the supplies and munitions for an army could be actually loaded into cars, these cars made up in groups or trains for the division, and these dispatched at the proper time to the front. Such a regulating station involved enormous construction with a great outlay of money, and it could not be placed very near the front where it might be jepardized by a reverse on the part of our troops. I had the advantage that in the event of an advance it could be made to serve as an advance depot.

The second type of regulating station is called a regulating station of movement only. Here loaded cars and trains are received from depots in the rear. They are switched into proper groups or trains and dispatched to railheads at the front. Only small stores are kept at such a station. These small stores enable the regulating officer to balance calls for rations in the small items and to meet emergency calls for such articles as small arm ammunition, clothing, and gas masks.

From the outset the regulating officer was a general staff officer and a member of a Fourth Section at General Headquarters. If there was to be only one army to supply there might not be great objection to having the one regulating officer a member of the army commander's staff, as all supplies on hand would be intended for a single army, but just as soon as additional detachments are added or additional tactical units come into existence not included in the one army, there must be an allotment and an apportioning of supplies and some superior authority must decide who is to have priority in such cases. Thus, troops in active combat get first priority, while troops in quiet positions have second priority, and troops in training third.

In order to increase the authority of these regulating officers they were later invested with all the powers of the commanding officer. This was necessary, particularly during active operations involving all manner of emergencies. At such times things have to move. There must be action. There is no precedent and the regulating officer charged with the great responsibility must be in a position to command everybody and everything necessary for the successful functioning of his station. The old line regular army man, who rises up at such a time to quote precedent or old established methods, as well as the technical man, who would insist on all the requirements of civil practice, must be made to get results along lines altogether new or improvised for the emergency and results must come in a minimum of time. The operation of this system gave the maximum degree of flexibility. As divisions were shifted from place to place along the front it was not difficult to arrange for their supply. This was accomplished, when the shift was in the area of a single regulating station, by giving the division a new railhead from time to time. If the division made a long move and was transferred to another army, the regulating officer was instructed by the Fourth Section of the General Staff to be prepared to drop the division on a certain date and the regulating officer of the new area was informed to be prepared to supply the division beginning with a certain date. Each regulating officer made suitable modifications in their calls on the depots supporting them so that the flow of supplies was made to conform to the movements of the division.

A most striking example of the mobility and efficiency attained by the operation of a regulating station is that presented by the 1st and 2d Divisions during their movements immediately preceding and during their memorable counterattack south of SOISSONS in July, 1918. These two units were withdrawn from the lines, moved rapidly by march and motor truck, so that they each had seven different railheads in eight days, and yet the supply train from the regulating station at Le BOURGET (SEINE) arrived each day at the required spot. So complete was the secrecy of this movement that only the Supreme Command knew what the final disposition of these troops was to be, and to the fact that it was so entirely unexpected was the success of this attack largely due. Later, when these divisions were transferred to the east in the formation of the First Army, the flow of supplies through Le BOURGET was cut off altogether and transferred to their new regulating station, St-DIZIER.

Only two regulating stations were actually constructed by us in France---IS-sur-TILLE (COTE d'OR) and LIFFOL-le-GRAND (VOSGES)---and of these the second was not completed until after the signing of the Armistice, when it served for the march to the RHINE and for the Army of Occupation. On all other portions of the front where American troops were engaged the existing French facilities were found to be sufficient to meet our requirements, rendering further construction unnecessary, except such construction as might be needed for housing the regulating personnel. In some cases we increased the storage facilities and built additional sidings. The French stations of CREIL, MANTES, le BOURGET, NOISY-le-SEC, St-DIZIER, GRAY, and DUNKERQUE were used by us at various times.

On August 30, 1918, IS-sur-TILLE was actually supplying over one million men. Approximately seven hundred and fifty thousand were Americans, the remainder French. Similarly during the MEUSE-ARGONNE operations supplies for over one million were being regulated through St-DIZIER.

2. Railheads: A railhead, as the name indicates, was merely a point on the railroad where the supplies were unloaded and turned over to the supply trains of the divisions or other army units. It should be as centrally located in the divisional or other unit area as the railroad facilities permit in order to reduce to a minimum the animal or motor transport required in distribution. Railheads were under the control of the regulating officer.

Railheads fall logically into two general categories: (1) temporary; (2) permanent or semipermanent. The former, used often for one day only for troops on the march or advancing or retreating, and changing to meet the varying conditions of the battle, requires no construction or modification. A side track with a road or unloading platform capable of handling one or two daily *rames** is all that is required. No storage space is necessary as all the supplies are supposed to be carried away by the divisional trains before nightfall. During the battle of CHATEAU-THIERRY and the march to the RHINE, practically all railheads used fell in this category, almost any railroad station with a reasonable yard being selected, the important factor being one of location rather than of facilities. In fact, during the march of the Third Army into Germany, the terms of the Armistice made thorough reconnaissonce in advance of the marching troops impossible, and many railheads had to be selected on the basis of prewar maps and information.

The railheads of the St-MIHIEL and ARGONNE-MEUSE sectors, on the other hand, fell into the second category. The front here had been comparatively stable for four years and most of the railheads, conveniently situated for the supply of troops in the line, in support, or in reserve, were developed to a considerable degree by the construction of additional sidings, unloading tracks, and building for storage. In fact, each of the important railheads in these areas resembled more or less a small depot where a limited reserve of supplies of different classes was maintained. The proximity of the front precluded the maintenance of large stockages as practically all of the advance railheads were within the range of shellfire. In preparation for our big offensives, however, the normal stockages were greatly increased.

3. Office at French G. H. Q., Headquarters Allied Commander-in-Chief: The Fourth Section maintained an office at French G. H. Q. up to the time Marshal Foch was made Commander-in-Chief of the Allied Armies when this office was moved to his Headquarters. This placed the Fourth Section in direct touch with Allied Headquarters and avoided the delay incident to tryping to do business through the French Mission at American Headquarters and the American Mission at French General Headquarters. Thus, in dealing with French Headquarters and the Allied Commander-in-Chief, the Chief of the Fourth Section dealt through his own office using men thoroughly familiar with the subject, directly

---

*Ramè: A cut of cars, that is, a group of freight cars less than a complete train. A French freight train might be made up of two or more rames.

interested in the success of each case, and who were themselves held directly responsible for accomplishment. Similarly, when French Headquarters or officials at the Headquarters of the Allied Commander-in-Chief desired to deal with the Chief of the Fourth Section of the American General Staff they used his representative stationed at their headquarters. This gave direct methods, direct responsibility, and action when action was needed. From the outset the corresponding sections of the of the American and French armies worked in the greatest harmony. Supplies and facilities were made interchangeable from the outset. Thus, during combat or periods of emergency, we could go to the French for assistance and generally get it at once as a result of a conversation over the telephone, and likewise they could make requests upon us and we would divide with them anything we had.

4. Advance Offices: During the operations of the First and Second Armies a small advance office was established and maintained at LIGNY-en-BARROIS. This put a limited number of staff officers of the Fourth Section in closer touch with operations and it was the means of detecting promptly any failures in our plans. Later a similar office was established at TRIER to supervise our operations in German territory.

5. The Fourth Section of the General Staff in the Armies: The staff of each army corresponded with that of G. H. Q. All important matters were communicated to army commanders, but this having been done, a direct liaison was established with the Assistant Chief of Staff, G-4, of each army in working out the details of established policies. It is important that staff officers understand this procedure and not impose upon it. Subordinate commanders must be held responsible and orders and instructions must be communicated to them or through them and not along many parallel lines connecting corresponding staff sections.

PART III

MISCELLANEOUS ACTIVITIES OF THE FOURTH SECTION OF THE GENERAL STAFF

1. Locating Facilities for Supply and Transportation: Numerous conferences were held with the French, dating from the time of our arrival to study the question of regulating stations along the entire front. It was always a question whether or not these stations had the proper strategical setting and whether or not their total capacity was sufficient to supply all the armies at the front and which were to be ac the front. As a result of one of these first meetings IS-sur-TILLE was built. It was intended primarily to serve the army while in the training areas. Later when the army went on the line it would become an advance depot or a regulating station of the second line. It was also decided to build a regulating station at LIFFOL-le-GRAND. This part of the front was not properly covered by a regulating station and one was needed in that vicinity, regardless of whether it was finally to be used by American or French troops.

The location of each important facility of our line of communications was determined at these headquarters, for only here were the plans for the employment of our army known. Each depot or facility was placed so as to enable it to function with the maximum amount of flexibility in serving armies wherever they might be placed in the line. Local conditions might cause a concentration of effort at one point, but the general scheme remained the same.

The acquisition of a location for a depot or facility on the line of communications was quite a complicated problem. After having decided for ourselves where we wished the establishment constructed, it was generally necessary to present the question to the French Staff and obtain their approval. Often a desirable location would have to be abandoned on account of a congested railway situation in the vicinity of the point selected. This was exemplified in the case of DIJON where congestion, due to movements of troops to Italy, prevented the establishment of any large facilities.

It was very interesting to observe how the morale of the French and their true estimate of the tactical and strategical situation was reflected in the formal discussions which took place with the Allied representatives. When Paris was under long-range artillery fire and we did not know how long we could continue to use the railway belts around that city, and when the German offensive was progressing towards CHATEAU-THIERRY, the regulating stations on the line GRAY, IS-sur-TILLE, CHATILLON-sur-SEINE, MONTARGIS, ORLEANS, and Le MANS looked very attractive and well-placed and decisions were made accordingly. But before construction proceeded very far the situation changed, thanks largely to the fighting quality of the individual American soldier, and the regulating stations on the line described were found to be too far back to serve, except as regulating stations of the second order, or depots served by regulating stations of movement placed far to the front. When the German line rolled back we heard criticism that our small depot at LIEUSAINT, 40 kilometers southeast of PARIS, was too far back, but it was forgotten that when we selected that depot the French had little hope of holding PARIS, and LIEUSAINT was as far forward as the Allied High Command would permit us to place our stocks.

The location of an advance depot is not always a simple question. It must fit properly into the railway system. It must be well forward and yet must not become involved in the minor fluctuations of the line. The location of a large American depot had to be such that a flow of supplies from it could be changed in direction to meet the changes in the position of our troops. Often our division made long moves by the flank, even while the line was stable. Depots, however, cannot be changed on a moment's notice. The strategy involved in a system of supply must be sound at the outset, for after a depot takes root, it cannot be transplanted on short notice, while divisions and corps, wrongly placed, can often be moved to their right positions by a simple command. A depot may be well placed, when construction begins, but the army may leave it high and dry, by maneuvering away, during the period of its construction.

The old front was served by a chain of regulating stations, SOTTEVILLE-lès-ROUEN, CREIL, les BOURGET, NOISY-le-SEC, CONNANTRE, St-DIZIER, IS-sur-TILLE, and GRAY. These in turn were backed up by a series of advance depots. All of these regulating stations, with the exception of IS-sur-TILLE and GRAY, were in a position to be threatened by a further enemy advance, and as the Allies were still on the defensive, the possibility of a further advance rendering CREIL, le BOURGET, NOISY-le-SEC, CONNANTRE, and St-DIZIER useless as regulating stations, was not beyond the range or possibility. Their loss would have completely disorganized the Allied supply system, and to provide against such a contingency, the development of a series of so-called regulating stations of the second line was considered, and detailed studies were made as to their proper placing. After discarding the possibility of satisfactorily utilizing the existing French facilities at Le MANS, MANTES, and Les AUBRAIS, the minimum combined requirements of the French and American armies were determined to be four new regulating stations, of which two, POINSON and CHILLEUR-aux-BOIS, were to be constructed by the Americans, and La LOUPE and CONCHES were to be undertaken by the French. It was felt that these, together with IS-sur-TILLE, would enable the Allied forces to successfully continue the struggle even should their existing facilities be lost. Then, suddenly beginning with the memorable counterattack south of SOISSONS by American and French Colonial troops on July 18, 1918, the whole aspect changed. All work on these second line regulating stations was abandoned and the construction of the regulating station at LIFFOL-le-GRAND, which had been stopped at the moment of the German advance, was ordered ahead full blast. Thus in less than two weeks, from a defensive position with attention directed towards the development of facilities along a general line running east and west, south of PARIS, we had passed to the offensive, with our attention now directed to the extension forward of our lines of communication to keep pace with the advance that was being made on all fronts.

2. Equipping of Divisions: There were several very perplexing and difficult problems presented in equipping troops upon their arrival in training areas from the United States. Although every division was fully equipped before sailing from the United States, except for certain ordnance items that were being furnished by the French, they arrived in the training areas woefully short of many things. This was due to the fact that the property of a regiment, for example, would be loaded on a different transport from the one on which the regiment was embarked, and in some cases it was scattered over several ships. More often the ships, carrying the property, would arrive in France long after the organization had left the port for its training area, or the ship or ships might go to entirely different ports than the ones at which the organizations had debarked. Even in cases where the property was loaded on the same ship as the regiment to which it belonged, it frequently happened that it was so mixed with other property or so buried under all kinds of other supplies that it was not accessible to the unit before it was ordered to leave the port for its training area. The troops could not be held at the ports, because of the need of space for the steadily increasing flow of newcomers. Upon arriving in the training areas, it was imperative that the divisions begin their training immediately and to do so they needed to have their lost equipment quickly replaced. Some of the essential items were either not on hand in France at all or only in limited quantities for it had been contemplated that the troops would arrive fully equipped. To meet this situation, available stocks were often drawn down to a point below the margin of safety, and emergency purchases in Eurpoe were resorted to. This resulted in a great waste of equipment as organizations were issued equipment in the training areas when they had similar equipment en route to them somewhere between their former station in the United States and the training area in France. To correct this, it was arranged, with the home authorities, to strip troops of all their equipment, except that carried on the person of the individual, before they started on their journey to France. All their other equipment was turned in and thus became immediately available for reissue in the United States or for shipment in bulk to France without reference to any particular organization. It was thus handled as any other bulk equipment of its same kind. This new policy met, very satisfactorily, the peculiar conditions with which we were confronted at the time. It would not have done, however, for the normal case when troops were to be employed tactically after disembarking.

3. Organization of the PARIS Group and TOUL Group: When the 1st Division was engaged at MONTDIDIER (SOMME) and the 2d Division was sent to relieve it, the question was raised as to whether or not we should be prepared to supply a large force in the vicinity of PARIS as this would necessitate the construction of an advance depot to serve that region. A negative answer was received. Notwithstanding this, within less than ten days, the success of the German drive on PARIS had so changed the situation that every available American soldier was rushed to this point. Within a few days it was necessary to arrange for the supply of 180,000 troops. This figure rapidly mounted to over 300,000. IS-sur-TILLE was not well located to supply troops in the vicinity of PARIS. To use IS-sur-TILLE involved shipments across the front. In an emergency the French could be called upon to supply our divisions, but this they would which to do only temporarily and there were certain articles peculiar to our system that they could not supply at all.

The Fourth Section had been organizing corps and army staffs in anticipation of the organization of our own armies. The divisions had to be supplied under a proper system whether they were organized into American armies or not. It was to meet this emergency (June 11, 1918) that the American divisions operating around PARIS and those operating on the extreme eastern wing of the front were organized and grouped for supply into two groups called the PARIS Group and the TOUL Group.

The TOUL Group of divisions was based on IS-sur-TILLE and this advance depot dropped all responsibility for the supply of the divisions in the PARIS Group. An American regulating officer and staff were sent to Le BOURGET, a regulating station on the eastern outskirts of PARIS, and the great intermediate depot of GIEVRES, which was due south of PARIS, and connected by a direct railway, was put at his disposal. This, with a small advance depot which was organized near the front, solved the situation. When the formation of the First Army was ordered a regulating officer and staff were installed at St-DIZIER. The great depot of GIEVRES also supplied this regulating station. As divisions left the PARIS Group for the First Army it was only necessary to direct the flow of supplies to St-DIZIER at the proper time instead of to le BOURGET.

4. Supply of Troops serving with the French and British: The final training of our first few divisions to arrive in France was effected in conjunction with French units. The finishing touches of this training, in the case of the 1st Division, had been accomplished by a tour of front line duty, a battalion at a time, with the French troops in the region of TOUL. This lay in what was ultimately to be our sector and as our depots and regulating station at IS-sur-TILLE were designed to serve troops in this area, no difficult supply question presented itself. A railhead was established at TOUL, with a refilling point at MESNIL-la-TOUR on the one-meter gauge, supplied by the regulating station at IS-sur-TILLE and the troops received the full American ration drawn from our own depots.

An entirely different situation presented itself in the case of the 26th Division which, instead of being employed in the so-called American zone, was ordered late in January to join the French Sixth Army then holding a sector along the CHEMIN-des-DAMES and the AISNE River.

This was our first experience in moving a complete division with full equipment by rail and yet this movement was accomplished without a hitch. Beginning February 3 and ending February 6, the fifty-five trains required were all unloaded in and around SOISSONS whence the division moved into the line.

This movement raised an interesting and difficult problem of supply. A complete division far removed from the American zone operating in a sector where there existed no American installations, created a situation without precedent. The first thought had been to leave the matter of supply entirely up to the French, but it was at once realized that while the French ration was satisfactory to the French soldier, it was not suitable for American troops. The wine and spirit components were not desired, and the ration did not contain a sufficient quantity of meat, coffee, sugar, etc., things which the American soldier was in the habit of getting.

The solution finally reached was along the following general lines: That all such articles as were common to both French and American rations were to be supplied from French sources in the quantities called for by the American ration; that such articles as were peculiar to the American ration alone were to be supplied from American sources as far as might be possible. This compromise solution was necessary as the supply of one division was not sufficient to warrant complete trainload shipments from our American base ports or depots and only by such trainload shipments could regularity of supply be maintained.

The results of this arrangement were most carefully watched by both the French and American commands. It was inevitable that tactical organizations of two or more Allies would be drawing supplies through the same regulating station and some solution had to be devised so that facilities for supply could be made to serve any Ally or two or more simultaneously.

As the machinery for working out details and putting into effect this combined method of supply an American regulating station was established at CREIL (OISE) in conjunction with the French regulating station at that point which was supplying the French Sixth Army. The American regulating officer called upon the French regulating officer for such supplies as were required from French sources each day for the supply of the American division. To the rame containing these supplies were added such cars of American supplementary rations or other supplies which had arrived at the regulating station from American sources. All shipments for the various units of the division were made to the regulating station as first destination and were forwarded from this point with the daily supply rame. As time went on more and more elements of the ration were supplied from American sources and the calls on the French correspondingly reduced.

It was realized that if French and American troops were to be used indiscriminately at any point on the front the supply systems of the two armies must correspond in principle. By continuing to work along the lines inaugurated at CREIL in February, 1918, the American regulating system was extended so that at various times isolated American divisions were supplied without difficulty from practically all of the French regulating stations by merely installing an American regulating personnel alongside of the existing French organization

The success of this so-called pooling of supplies was of inestimable value to the Interallied High Command in that it enable the divisions of the several Allies to be grouped indiscriminately according to the dictates of the strategic situation without restriction from the standpoint of supply. The most striking illustration of this was presented in the case of the RHEIMS---CHATEAU-THIERRY advance when at one time English, French, American, and Italian divisions were engaged in a very small sector served from one regulating station and yet no break in the supply of any of these units resulted.

During the St-MIHIEL and ARGONNE-MEUSE Offensives, both French and American troops were supplied by the regulating station at St-DIZIER, and all supplies that could be pooled were used indiscriminately by either army, as for example bread, potatoes, vegetables, hay, oats, and fuel. This pooling greatly simplified the railroad switching problems and enabled full advantage to be taken of each classification.

So much applies to units equalling a division or more serving in French armies. At various times, however, small American units, a regiment or less, were grouped with French divisions. In these cases the straight French ration was supplied supplemented by periodic shipments from American depots of special American components not available from French sources. It was impossible, however, to maintain any degree of regularity in this supply of supplemental American components, and the results following the detaching of small units, from the supply standpoint, were not entirely satisfactory.

'Early in 1918, the Commander-in-Chief entered into an agreement with Field Marshal Sir Douglas Haig, Commander-in-Chief of the British forces in France, for the transportation from America in British bottoms of six American divisions. The scheme contemplated that the division, less artillery and ammunition trains, would train in the British theater of operations for a period of from ten weeks to three months and would then be transferred to an American army. With the success of the German spring offensives the need of man power became so imperative that the original program of six divisions was increased, with the result that, at one time, ten American divisions, less artillery and ammunition trains, amounting to over 200,000 men, were included in the arrangement. For the purpose of coordination and administration of this force, the American II Corps Headquarters was organized previous to the arrival of the divisions and located near the British General Headquarters. Lieutenant-Colonel (now Brigadier-General) George S. Simonds, General Staff, was appointed Chief of Staff of this corps and continued in that capacity throughout. Until June, 1918, when Major General George W. Read was assigned as Commanding General, Colonel Simonds carried on the work of the corps and the negotiations with the British in the name of the Commander-in-Chief. It had been agreed in general terms that the British army would supply the American divisions, but the working out of the numerous and important details of the arrangements fell to Colonel Simonds.

The American troops were to arrive with Equipment C except transportation, automatic rifles, Stokes mortars and 37-mm. guns. These latter articles with the exception of the 37-mm. guns were to be supplied by the British. Our Ordnance Department supplied the 37-mm. guns, obtaining them from the French. Certain items received from the British were to be kept permanently by us, such as wagons and animals, Stokes mortars, etc.; other items were for use only during the period that the units remained with the British, such as motor transportation, Vickers and Lewis guns, etc. The British rifle and rifle ammunition were to be substituted for the American, the latter being stored at suitable places and held for return to the organizations when they left the British area. The British were to furnish the necessary mounts and mounted equipment and provide for the transportation of ammunition in the absence of the divisional ammunition train. The British ration was to be supplied throughout except that rum was to be omitted and coffee substituted for tea. All articles of clothing, except caps, coats, and breeches, which distinguished the soldier as American, were also to be supplied by the British army. In general, the divisions were to depend entirely upon the British sources of supply and to call on us only in case of failure on the part of the British or where the item involved was peculiarly American.

The arrangements above indicated were worked out in conferences held from time to time. Because of the constantly changing conditions and the divergences in the needs of the units, it was not possible to formulate an all-embracing agreement at any one time to cover the whole subject. In September, 1918, however, a formal contract was drawn up to confirm the informal agreements and to provide a method of payment by the United States Government to the British Government for the supplies furnished and services rendered. This contract became known as the Capitation Agreement because of the provision contained therein that the payment should be worked out on a per capita basis. It was not finally signed by both parties until after the Armistice.

As our divisions arrived in the British training areas from America, they were immediately affiliated with skeletonized British divisions for training and administrative purposes. British methods of supply were forthwith inaugurated under the direction of the affiliated staff and continued in this manner until the American staffs and supply units had become thoroughly familiar with the system. The British system of supply did not differ fundamentably from our own, except that greater dependence was placed on the daily *rame*, supplies not being accumulated at or in advance of the railheads.

Such difficulties as were encountered from the point of view of supply were due either to the fact that the British found themselves short of equipment that they had promised, owing to large losses during the successful German advance on AMIENS, or to the fact that American organization was different in many respects from the British and our tables of allowances much more liberal. Thus, in the British army in the field there is no organization corresponding to the regiment, and therefore the British found it difficult to supply the regimental headquasters and headquarters company. The administrative unit for them is the battalion. As a matter of fact, with the exception of the 27th and 30th Divisions, none of the ten divisions sent into the British area remained there to complete their training. The situation in the months of June and July required the early withdrawal of these divisions from the British area and their use eleswhere. The 27th and 30th Divisions, however, remained with the British until after the Armistice and took their part with them in the great offensives of September and October. In these divisions adjustments were made to conform to some extent to British organization by making the battalion more of an administrative unit, but the general principles of American organization were not departed from. A minor difficulty encountered at first was the inability of our cooks to make the most out of the British ration with the result that the soldiers felt that they were not being fed as well as their comrades supplied by our own system, but instruction in cooking and experience remedied this situation without the necessity of changing the ration to any great extent.

To take care of such items as were to be supplied by us, small depots of clothing and ordnance were established at CALAIS and DANNES. At first, requirements were filled from the excess equipment turned in by the divisions upon their arrival.

5. Supply Situation, June, 1918: What promised to be a very critical problem in supply of food was presented in May and June, 1918. During the last week in May troop arrivals had reached the approximate figure of 600,000. Previous to this time the freight tonnage available had been large enough to permit the building up of a reserve of supplies in France, although the goal of a 90-day reserve had not been attained. When the 600,000 mark was reached in troop arrivals, however, the available American tonnage was just sufficient to meet the current needs but did not allow for the continued building up of the reserve. We had, so to speak, reached the point of equilibrium. With the assistance given by the British in supporting ten divisions, as a result of the ABBEVILLE Agreement, this point of equilibrium was raised to approximately 800,000 men, or in other words, the available American tonnage could supply 600,000 men and British resources could take care of 200,000, making it possible for us to have a total of 800,000 men in France. The ten American divisions (less artillery) with the British were to be supplied for a period of about three months only from British sources. The return of these divisions to the American army would suddenly increase the calls on the American supply system by approximately 200,000 daily rations in addition to large demands for transport and equipment or, in other words, with British assistance cut off, the point of equilibrium would be reduced from the 800,000 point to a point somewhere above 600,000 but considerably below 800,000. The reason why the equilibrium point would not fall back to the original figure of 600,000 was that available tonnage was expected to increase at the rate of about 37,500 tons a month. The increment, however, would not reach the point to which the British assistance had raised the point of equilibrium until the middle of September and, consequently, the sudden withdrawal of British assistance would have meant that our reserve of supplies would be drawn upon until the middle of September. The above assumes that troop arrivals would be stopped at the 800,000 mark. As a matter of fact, it was planned to continue to rush troops to France. The need of men was too imperative to permit of a cutting off of diminution in the flow. Thus, with new troops arriving in ever increasing numbers, with the tactical situation requiring the withdrawal and placing on American resources of all but two of ten divisions temporarily with the British, and with no immediate promise of ocean tonnage being increased sufficiently to meet the needs, we were confronted with the dire prospect of not only failing to receive supplies commensurate with consumption but also of completely exhausting our reserves by about September 1.

There was only one solution of this problem possible. The military situation was too serious to admit of restricting the troops arrival program to the number that could be safely supplied by the available ocean tonnage. The only answer was to secure more tonnage. As time went on some relief was furnished by the delay in the ordnance production program in the United States, which permitted the assignment to the Quartermaster Corps of tonnage allotted to the Ordnance Department. Cables urging that more ocean tonnage be assigned to army use, even though sacrifices were involved, and that every effort be made at home to increase shipbuilding, brought the real relief that was needed.

6. Animal-drawn Transportation, Motor Transportation, Light Railways: Throughout the war there was a shortage of animal-drawn transportation. This was due to our failure to obtain animals in sufficient numbers either from the United States, from France, or from Spain. At the signing of the Armistice, the armies were short over 106,000 animals, notwithstanding the fact that the number of animals authorized for a division had been greatly reduced directly and also by motorizing artillery regiments. This situation was particularly serious, for, at the same time, we were short about half of our authorized motor vehicles.

On the other hand, we had ample light railway material and where it could be used it rendered very satisfactory service in taking part of the burden off other means of transportation in advance of our railheads.

When hostilities ended there were under American army control 2,240 kilometers of 60-centimeter lines, of which about 300 kilometers had originally been constructed by the French but rehabilitated by the American Expeditionary Forces, 200 kilometers had been constructed outright by the American Expeditionary Forces, and 1,740 kilometers had been taken from the Germans, the latter figure comprising 900 kilometers south of the battle line of November 11, 1918, and 840 kilometers just in front of it.

Animal-drawn transportation, motor transportation, and light railways when operating in the zone of the armies are all army means of transportation for distributing personnel and ammunition throughout the army areas and they should never be viewed as part of the railway transportation department for the distribution of supplies from railheads.

7. Hospitalization and Evacuation: As far as possible, hospitals were located on our main lines of railways for the purposes of supply, and also so situated that evacuations of sick and wounded from the front could be made to them in hospital trains routed over secondary lines. Plans for an attack included notification to the medical authorities of the number of beds which were to be made available by a certain date in a certain forward area. These beds were generally obtained by evacuating patients from forward hospitals to those in the interior, by putting up additional hospital facilities, and in some cases by taking over hospitals from the French. A medical member of the staff of the regulating officer handled evacuations from the front. A certain number of hospital trains were placed at his disposal and garaged at convenient sidings. A certain number of beds in hospitals were put to his credit each day. He was in direct telephonic communication with the Chief Sergeon of the Army his regulating station was supplying. When the Chief Surgeon reported a trainload of cases ready for evacuation at the evacuation hospital, the regulating officer ordered forward a hospital train, received the patients, and despatched the train to a hospital in the rear where the reported credits showed there was room for the patients.

By November 11, 1918, we had constructed hospitals with a normal capacity of 171,830 and a total emergency capcity of 233,092. A total of 271,455 American patients had been evacuated through the five regulating stations of CONNANTRE, CREIL, DUNKERQUE, Le BOURGET, and St-DIZIER. Of these, 154,898 were evacuated by the regulating officer of St-DIZIER between September 26 and November 11, On November 12, there were actually 193,026 patients in hospital.

8. Supply and Evacuation Via the Rhine: With the signing of the Armistice there incurred congestion throughout the French railway system due to the demands for transportation to meet the needs of the civilian population. This situation had made it very difficult to supply the Third Army during its advance to the RHINE. To obviate this difficulty and also to put ourselves in a position to supply the Third Army when all our facilities in France had been withdrawn, negotiations were opened at the HAGUE with the Netherlands Government during the month of January, 1919, which finally resulted in our obtaining authority to build up an organization by which we could supply the Third

Army via ROTTERDAM and ANTWERP and evacuate troops and munitions via the same route. With this effected we were able to proceed to evacuate our men completely from France and dispose of our entire establishment in French territory.

9. Food Supply for Civilian Population in the American Zone of the Occupied Area: The Interallied plan of organization for supplying the civilian population in the occupied area was premised on the assumption that the food supply for the left bank of the RHINE was to be furnished from the Hoover stock by the Permanent Supply Commission at ROTTERDAM and ANTWERP. For various reasons, principally the delay of the Central German Government in perfecting the financial arrangements with the Hoover Commission, there seemed to be little immediate prospect of deliveries. Meanwhile, the situation in the American zone became more and more acute, especially so as the French and British authorities had made temporary arrangements to meet the situations in their own zones. To meet this emergency, G-4 withdrew stocks which had been sold to the Hoover Commission and supplied the civilian population in the American area directly. Theses stocks were figured on a ration basis and sold to the German authorities and by them distributed under strict supervision of the American military authorities.

10. Control of Transportation: During our participation in the war it was repeatedly argued that railway transportation should be handled independently of all other services; that it was a cut and dried problem of moving an article, a human being, or a remount from one place to another, from the base at home to the wire entanglements; in other words, that peacetime railway methods should govern. This is true to a limited degree, but success in war results when all arms, services, and bureaus are cooperating in a loyal team, forming an organism entirely devoted to the single mission of defeating the enemy. Every service can present a strong argument showing why it should be independent. In peace such arguments often make good, and the disorganization which we have often had in our peace establishment has resulted largely from the fact that, instead of the army being a properly balanced coordinated machine, it has been, instead, a loosely moulded confederation of different arms and different bureaus, all with their conflicting interests.

In a war involving the dispatching of an expeditionary force, railway operations may be divided into two or three general zones. In the home country, the railways can continue functioning largely with civilian personnel in direction and control, provided only that certain results are obtained. If these results are not obtained or if the military situation overburdens the railways at home, making coordination necessary, then their direction and control must be in the hands of the government. If the theater of operations ms in an Allied country, the railways behind the line of regulating stations may be operated largely as they are operated in time of peace, but subject to absolute military direction and control. But when we get to the zone of the armies, the system must be such that the army can be supplied without the Director General of Transportation knowing where the army is. Technical rules ordinarily governing peacetime railway operations must often be violated in order to obtain the results necessary. The gist of the problem is in the General Staff properly using the transportation department to carry out its plans as far as railway transportation is concerned and in the absolute willingness of the transportation department to subordinate any or all of its strictly technical ideas in order to secure results that suffice, at least for the time being.

11. Extension of the Automatic System of Supply: As our operations progressed the system of automatic supply was extended and simplified. This was accomplished by establishing within the armies, dumps, parks, and depots where limited stocks were kept which were within a short motor journey of the troops. The armies were also given certain credits at ammunition depots and engineer depots outside the army jurisdiction and these credits could be drawn upon without reference to higher authority. At stated times the credits could be renewed. This [not only] gave us a check on the rate of

expenditures of our stocks but [also] simplified issues and reduced paper work.

The foregoing is a summary of the reports submitted by the Fourth Section of the General Staff. Whatever was accomplished was due, on the one hand, to the untiring and efficient service accorded the Assistant Chief of Staff, G-4, by a loyal and faithful crew and, on the other, to the absolute support and never-failing encouragement which the chief of the section received at all times from a great commander.

Respectfully submitted,

GEO. VAN HORN MOSELEY,
Brigadier General, U. S. Army,
Asst. Chief of Staff, G - 4.

C-in-C Report File: Fldr. 92: Report

Appendix A [Ordnance]

4th Section, G. S.   GENERAL HEADQUARTERS, A. E. F.,

(Ordnance) G-4-A   *Chaumont, Haute-Marne, December 24, 1918.*

From: G-4-A.

To: Asst. Chief of Staff, G-4.

Subject: Ordnance Activities of G-4-A.

    1. In accordance with memorandum dated November 27, 1918, the following report is submitted. This report will necessarily have to be of a more or less general nature as this office does not keep detailed records as to quantities of ordnance material under procurement, quantities received in France, or quantities issued. A complete report covering these matters in detail will undoubtedly be made by the Chief Ordnance Officer, A. E. F., and the Chief of Ordnance.

GENERAL STATEMENT OF ORDNANCE ACTIVITIES

    (a) At the date of entrance of the United States into the war, there was comparatively little ordnance material on hand, and manufacturing facilities were not developed for producing this material. A great deal of ordnance material requires a considerable time to develop manufacturing capacity and a considerable time to manufacture the material itself. After our entry into the war, important decisions had to be made in regard to some of this material before manufacture could start. On account of our having to fight in a foreign country thousands of of miles from our base of supplies, with large Allied forces in the field already well equipped with artillery and small arms equipment different from that with which our army was equipped, it was necessary to decide just how our large forces to be organized should be equipped. In deciding these questions consideration had to be given to the matter of supply of our forces while developing our production capacity, and also the question of supplying our troops in France, having in view the shortage of ocean tonnage.

(b) In view of the above considerations, it seemed advisable to so arrange our equipment as to take advantage, as much as possible, of the production capacity in Europe; also to adopt, where possible, calibers of ammunition used by our Allies so that interchangeability of ammunition could be had.

(c) To this end most of the calibers of artillery were adopted so as to use either French or British ammunition. The caliber of our field gun was three inches but in order to utilize French ammunition and French artillery material the caliber was changed to 75-mm. The three-inch material which we already had on hand was used in training camps in the States and our troops were equipped in France with 75-mm. material and ammunition upon their arrival. In the meantime, manufacture was started in the United States of 75-mm. ammunition and 75-mm. guns and carriages of the French type and at the same time our new model field gun (model of 1916) which had been designed as a 3-inch gun was changed to 75-mm. caliber and manufacture continued. In a similar manner, other calibers, either French or British, were adopted.

(d) After decision was arrived at in regard to type and caliber of artillery to be used it was necessary to get detailed drawings of the material befor manufacture could commence in the States. Comparatively very little manufacturing capacity for artillery material had ever been developed in America and it was necessary to develope this capacity. Artillery material requires great care in manufacture, and plants taking up this manufacture for the first time usually run into many difficulties which cause delays. It was inevitable, under these conditions, that there should be a considerable time before the manufacturing capacity of the country would be able to take care of the needs of our forces. This was foreseen and, as our Allies desired our troops in France as early as possible, arrangements were made with them for supplying our needs in artillery material and ammunition until such time as we should be able to take care of our own needs.

(e) Under this arrangement, artillery organizations came to France without artillery material and were supplied with it at our training camps after arrival. There was some difficulty at that time in getting material to them in time as, on account of the military situation, the French were unwilling to allow us to keep a stock of this material on hand for supplying our troops, but would only deliver it to the organizations after they were informed as to the name of the organization and the camp to which it was to go and, at first, only after they had received notice that the organization had arrived. This necessarily caused delay; on account of the rapid arrival of artillery organizations, the scarcity of training camps and the delay in receiving information, it frequently happened that an organization would arrive at its camp before its equipment could be delivered. This sometimes caused more or less delay in their training but, as a whole, organizations were equipped within a reasonable time and it is thought that there were no organizations kept out of action for lack of artillery material or ammunition.

(f) In preparing to take care of the ordnance matters of the A. E. F., it was necessary at first to study the experiences of our Allies, the French and the British, and, from the beginning, such ordnance personnel as was available was sent to study the French and British systems of ordnance supply and maintenance and to gather as much information as possible from their experiences. On account of the great distance from our base of supplies, it was considered necessary to maintain larger reserves in France than was the case for the French or British and it was decided to keep 90 days' reserve supply in France for all our troops in France. Storage facilities were therefore provided on this basis. Building programs had to be modified from time to time on account of the necessity for bringing troops to France at a more rapid rate than was at first thought necessary.

(g) The 90 days' reserve supply was supposed to be distributed; 45 days in the Base Section of the S. O. S., 30 days in the Intermediate Section, and 15 days in the Advance Section. Storage was therefore provided at base ports and in the Intermediate and Advance Sections to take care of these supplies.

(h) As it was considered necessary to have an automatic flow of supplies from the States, an automatic supply list was made up based on the best experience obtainable from the French and the British. This automatic supply list consisted of the necessary replacement of supplies for 25,000 men per month and was modified from time to time as experience indicated advisable. * * *

(i) Ordnance material may be divided into several classes and for the purpose of this report will be classed under the following heads:

        Artillery materiel
        Tractors and other motor vehicles
        Small arms, automatic arms, and machine guns
        Personal equipment
        Ammunition

The artillery material may be further subdivided into:

        Railroad artillery
        Heavy artillery
        Field artillery
        Trench artillery

ARTILLERY MATERIEL

(a) Railroad Artillery: Most of the railroad artillery materiel used by our forces was loaned to us by the French and is to be returned to them. The following materiel was loaned by the French for use by our troops:

      2 340-mm. guns
      4 400-mm. howitzers
    12 32-cm. guns
    32 19-cm. guns
    24 24-cm. guns

In addition to the above there were a number of 14-inch 50-caliber navy guns which were mounted on railway mounts. The navy had these guns available and mounted five of them on railway mounts and sent them to France manned by naval personnel. 22 additional guns were later turned over to the Ordnance Department for this purpose. Some of these were to be mounted on the navy type mount and the others on a type which was developed by the Ordnance Department in France. Altogether only eight of these guns and mounts were received in France, these being the five manned by the navy and the three manned by the artillery. A number of 8-inch, 10-inch, and 12-inch seacoast guns were withdrawn from the fortifications in the United States for the purpose of mounting on railway mounts. Three of the 8-inch mounts were received in France but not in time to be used.

(b) Heavy Artillery: Included in this class are the heavy types of artillery which travel by road and are used as corps and army artillery:

        240-mm. howitzers
        9.2-inch howitzers
        8-inch howitzers
        155-mm. gun (G. P. F.)
        4.7-inch gun
        6-inch gun
        5-inch gun

The largest mobile artillery in our army before our entrance into the war was the 6-inch howitzer and the 4.7-inch gun. The Ordnance Department, however, had worked on a design of larger caliber and had under construction pilot guns and carriages of new model 6-inch howitzer, new model 4.7-inch gun, new model 7.6-inch howitzer, and new model 12-inch howitzer. However, no production capacity had been developed for any of these upon our entrance into the war. It was, therefore, necessary to adopt certain calibers used by the French and the British. A new design of 240-mm. howitzers was adopted and manufacture commenced. Inasmuch as it would take some time to obtain production on this, a number of 8-inch howitzers and 9.2-inch howitzers were obtained from England; also a certain number of 8-inch howitzers were manufactured in the United States as these howitzers were being manufactured there for England.

At the time of the signing of the Armistice we had in France 212 8-inch howitzers, 88 of which had been shipped from the United States and 124 were received from England. Of these 124 received from England, 88 were Mark VI and 36 were Mark VII. We also had 40 9.2-inch howitzers, also received from England; 24 were Mark 8 and 16 were Mark II.

To equip our corps artillery regiments a number of 155-mm. guns (G. P. F.) were obtained from the French and manufacture of these guns and carriages was also commenced in the United States. At the time of the signing of the Armistice, however, 16 of these, without recuperators, had been received from the States and 232 had been received from the French; of these 232, 96 were issued to organizations which took part in activities at the front and the remainder had been issued to organizations in training camps. In addition to these G. P. F. guns, 64 4.7-inch guns were received from the United States and issued to troops.

On account of the shortage of this class of gun, a number of 5-inch and 6-inch seacoast guns were withdrawn from the seacoast fortifications in the United States and mounted on improvised mounts and sent to France for use as substitutes for the 155-mm. gun and the 4.7-inch gun. 26 5-inch guns and 72 6-inch guns were received in France but none of the organizations equipped with these got into active service.

As it was contemplated that, even with all of these guns, there would be a shortage of this type for equipping our troops, steps had therefore been taken to obtain some 6-inch guns from the British but none of these had been obtained at the time of the signing of the Armistice. It is probable, however, that a number of these 6-inch guns together with other calibers which were being obtained on contract with the French and the British will have to be accepted under the contract.

In addition to the different types of heavy artillery mentioned above, all of which were hauled over road by tractors, there was being developed a type of heavy artillery designated as caterpillar artillery. This is a type of mount mounted upon a self-propelled vehicle with caterpillar treads. The French had made certain experiments with this type of mount with a 220-mm. howitzer. As it appeared that this type of mount might be very useful on account of its ability to cross difficult terrain off the prepared roads, this design was taken up and a manufacturing program started in the United States. Mounts were being prepared for the 155-mm. gun, 194-mm. gun, and 240-mm. howitzer. Some of these were to be of electrically driven type in which the generator outfit was on separate vehicle from the gun mount. This was the type developed by the St-Chamond Co. in France. However, only a small number of this type were to be built in the United States, the greater number were to be of the type in which the entire propelling mechanism would be on the same vehicle and probably of the gasoline engine type. It was contemplated that a number of these caterpillar mounts would have been available for operation in France in the spring of 1919.

(c) Field Artillery: Included in this class are the calibers used by divisional artillery, i. e., the 75-mm. field gun and the 155-mm. howitzer. Previous to our entry into the war, our army was equipped with 3-inch field gun, model 1902, but the Ordnance Department had been working for several years on a design of a new 3-inch field gun. This design had been practically completed and pilot gun and carriage had been manufactured and tested. However, no production capacity had been developed. In order to obtain the large quantity of field guns that would be required by our forces in France, it was necessary to obtain 75-mm. guns from the French and the French agreed to equip our troops with these guns as rapidly as they were sent to France and until our own production could take care of our needs. Manufacture was started in the United States of the French type of 75-mm. gun (model of 1897) and also the production was developed of the new model American field gun which had been changed to 75-mm. At the time of the signing of the Armistice 1,862 75-mm. guns had been delivered by the French to our troops. None of the French 75-mm. guns under manufacture in the States had been delivered in France at this time. However, 32 of the American type 75-mm. gun (model of 1916) had been delivered in France and some of these have been issued to an artillery organization for test.

As it was considered that there might be a shortage of field guns and certain manufacturing plants in the United States had been making the British type of field gun and carriage for the British, arrangements were made with the company for making a certain number of this British type of carriage but of 75-mm. caliber. 124 of these guns and carriages were received in France and issued to various artillery training camps for instruction purposes.

The 6-inch howitzer was in use in our army before our entrance into the war, but as very few were on hand, it was necessary to obtain from the French the 155-mm. howitzer to equip our troops. 821 of these were received from the French.

As mentioned above, a new design of 6-inch howitzer had been under way in the United States and the pilot gun and carriage was under construction at the time of our entrance into the war. However, this type howitzer was not completed in time to start production for our forces. Manufacture of the French type 155-mm. howitzer was commenced in the United States but none of these were received in France before the signing of the Armistice.

There is one other type of gun which will be mentioned here, although it is not considered as field artillery and is not manned by artillery personnel. This is the 37-mm. gun which is used by the infantry. Our army had no equipment of this type before the war and guns of this type were, therefore, obtained from the French.

In addition to the types mentioned, there is another type which, while not strictly field artillery, will be classed here; that is the antiaircraft artillery.

We had no antiaircraft artillery at the beginning of the war but had designed a mount to take the 3-inch 15-pounder seacoast gun and had several under manufacture. This was for fixed emplacement and was not designed for field work. In order to provide quickly additional protection of this kind, an improvised mount was designed for taking our 3-inch field gun which was changed to take the French 75-mm. ammunition. 50 of these mounts were manufactured and delivered in France where 75-mm. guns were furnished for them by the French. There were also manufactured 51 antiaircraft truck mounts and 38 of these were received in France. Some antiaircraft material was also furnished our troops by the French. A 3-inch antiaircraft trailer mount of greater power than the 75-mm. had been designed and a number were under manufacture. At the time of the Armistice none had been received in France.

* * * * * *

(d) Trench Artillery: This trench artillery, so-called, includes the 3-inch trench mortar, 58-mm. trench mortar, 6-inch trench mortar, and 240-mm. trench mortar. These are all types developed by the war and all of them were, therefore, obtained from either the French or the British. The 3-inch trench mortar used was the 3-inch Stokes which was obtained from the British. This mortar was manned by the infantry personnel. While it was developed as a trench warfare weapon it was later found to be useful in open warfare. However, as originally designed, it was not sufficiently mobile for use in open warfare and experiments were made with a view of obtaining a cart for hauling it around in order to make it more mobile. This experiment had not been completed at the time of the signing of the Armistice.

A medium-sized trench mortar manned by divisional artillery was the 58-mm. trench mortar type and the 6-inch Newton trench mortar type (British). The first six divisions arriving in France were originally equipped with the 58-mm. mortars and it was then decided to equip the remaining divisions with the 6-inch Newton as this was considered a better weapon. However, at the time the other divisions were to be equipped the English had a shortage of ammunition for the 6-inch Newton and it was necessary to equip the 2d, 26th, 42d, 32d, and 41st Divisions with the 58-mm. mortar. The remaining divisions were equipped with the 6-inch Newton and, at the time of the signing of the Armistice, arrangements were being made for exchanging the 6-inch Newton for the 58-mm. mortars in the divisions which had been so equipped.

The French had developed a better type of mortar - the Fabry 159-mm. mortar. This was more accurate and of greater range than the 58-mm. mortar. A battery of these had been ordered from the French but had not been delivered at the time of the signing of the Armistice.

The heavy type of French mortar adopted was the 240-mm. trench mortar, French type.

TRACTORS AND OTHER MOTOR VEHICLES

Before our entrance into the war, a number of experiments and tests had been conducted by the Field Artillery Board which had been convened for the purpose of determining the different types of motor vehicles necessary for the motorization of artillery. The result was [that] a number of different sizes of tractors and types of motor vehicles and trailers were developed:

(a) Tractors:

1. The 2 1/2-ton tractor, used for towing the regimental and battalion reel and cart.

2. The 5-ton tractor, used in connection with the motorization of 155-mm., 9.2-inch and 240-mm. howitzers.

3. The 10-ton tractor, used in connection with the motorization of 155-mm. G. P. F. guns. This tractor is to replace the 75-h.p. and 120-h.p. Holt caterpillar tractors that are commercial vehicles and used as temporary equipment for heavy guns and howitzers.

(b) Trucks:

1. The artillery repair truck is a small machine shop on wheels and was developed by the Ordnance Department to be furnished as part of the mobile repair facilities in line organizations.

2. The artillery supply truck is used as a companion truck of the artillery repair truck and also replaces the battery and store wagon when regiments of artillery are motorized.

3. The equipment repair truck forms part of the Mobile Ordnance Repair Shop and is used as repair facilities for small and automatic arms and soldiers' ordnance equipment.

4. The light repair truck is supplied to all line organizations where the Ordnance Department is charged with the repair of material.

5. The ammunition truck was a result of a recommendation of the Field Artillery Board and was supplied in two sizes;
    (a) The two-ton truck as divisional equipment,
    (b) A three-ton truck as corps and army equipment.

The ammunition truck in both these sizes is used as a personnel truck, tank truck, wireless truck, telephone truck, and for carrying supplies, spare parts, etc., in the Mobile Ordance Repair Shops and regiments of artillery.

6. The White truck, with an antiaircraft gun mounted on the chassis was developed and delivered in France in limited quantities as improvised substitutes for the trailer type of mount.

7. The machine-gun truck was developed as equipment for the motorized divisional machine gun battalions and antiaircraft machine gun battalions.

(c) Trailers:
    1. The antiaircraft trailer was developed for carrying an antiaircraft mount (the gun being fired from the trailer).
    2. The 3-inch field gun trailer was developed as a means of carrying a 75-mm. gun and limber, which enabled rapid movement of material, and was supplied to 75-mm. regiments of field artillery when used as army artillery.
    3. The 4-ton trailer was developed in order to carry the firing platform and accessories of the 240-mm. howitzer.
    4. The 10-ton trailer was developed as a means of transport for the Renault type tank.

(d) Motor Vehicles:
    1. The reconnaissance car is a special type supplied to artillery organizations and was developed on recommendation of the Field Artillery Board.
    2. The staff observation car was an outcome of a similar action of this board.

The experiments conducted by the Field Artillery Board revealed the fact that the commercial types of vehicles were unsuitable in many instances for artillery purposes, more prominently so in connection with the tractors, but not until after the outbreak of the war did the Ordnance Department have the proper authority or means of developing these special vehicles. Therefore, in order to meet the requirements of the troops in France, a limited quantity of Holt 75-h.p. and 120-h.p. caterpillar tractors were supplied as the most suitable commercial vehicles for heavy howitzers and guns. The commercial types of tractors were to be weeded out as they became disabled and the 10-ton furnished. The Ordnance Department had anticipated the motorization of the 155-mm. howitzer and had under way a suitable type of tractor developed before the plan of motorization of the 155-mm. howitzer was actually approved.

The result of this foresight was the dovelopment of the 5-ton tractor. This action can be readily appreciated when it is known that the only suitable types of commercial tractor that could be provided were those manufactured by the Holt company. These vehicles weighed between 11 and 12 tons and had a maximum speed of 3 miles and hour, whereas the 5-ton tractor weighed between 5 and 6 tons and had a maximum speed of 8 miles an hour. In addition, the 5-ton tractor did not have the usual guiding wheel out in the front part of the machine, which hinders the traversing on any terrain where shell holes or other obstacles are to be encountered.

It is a well known fact that the securing of tonnage to float this class of material was very difficult. Therefore, the Ordnance Department only initiated the floating of certain types of vehicles that were essential to its repair system and tractors that could not be obtained in Europe. This, of course, demanded the most careful kind of a distribution of the vehicles actually received and required placing motor equipment in Class IV supplies.

The method of issuing and handling this material was the same as with all other ordnance material. However, it became necessary, on account of the large volume of vehicles to be handled, that a separate depot and repair shop be established, namely Doulaincourt. This depot was situated centrally between the 4th and 18th areas and in close proximity to the line. The 18th area was used by the motorized regiment of corps and army artillery and the 4th area by motorized regiments of divisional artillery.

The scarcity of material prevented completely equipping regiments of artillery in the S. O. S. area and caused the issue to Organization and Training Centers and to other places of training a certain portion suitable for training purposes; the balance of shipments went to Doulaincourt where it could be used as replacement for organizations in the line, depending therefore upon additional shipments to arrive from the States in order to equip organizations training in the S. O. S. If the shipment did not arrive to effect this plan the material at Doulaincourt was withdrawn and supplied to the organization when it moved into the advance area. Then, a portion of the next shipment arriving from the States would be forwarded to Doulaincourt. In this manner the result was accomplished of equipping units in the S. O. S. and, at all times, having sufficient reserve at Doulaincourt in order to supply the requisitions from the army.

The spare parts for tractors were forwarded direct from base ports to Doulaincourt so that they could be distributed to organizations going into the line and fill army requisitions from this point. The quantity of spare parts was limited and the issue was controlled as a Class IV supply. Cable information from the States indicated that great quantities of spare parts for all ordnance vehicles were available at the seaboard and the Ordnance Department secured ample tonnage in order to have these parts floated. However, the parts did not arrive in sufficient quantities in order to allow the removal from a Class IV supply.

Equitable distribution of tractors and other ordnance motor equipment required the submitting of improvised allowances to organizations entitled to these special vehicles. These improvised allowances were submitted to the chiefs of services concerned and the Operation Section of the General Staff, these headquarters, for approval. The issue to division Mobile Ordnance Repair Shops of artillery repair, supply, and light repair trucks was such that all shops actually in the line had been supplied with a sufficient portion of their equipment to allow the proper functioning of the shop in addition to the distribution of certain quantities of these vehicles to corps parks and heavy artillery mobile ordnance repair shops.

The Ordnance Department compiled and issued to all concerned complete motor equipment tables, instruction books, and such pamphlets as would enable the operators to know how vehicles should be equipped, as well as furnish information regarding maintenance, operation, and care. In addition, the Ordnance Department had recruited and brought to France a commissioned and enlisted personnel that was detailed to various training centers where line organizations were trained and assisted in the instruction of the operation, care, and maintenance of this motor material.

There was procured from the French in connection with G. P. F. gun material complete motor equipment, excepting touring cars and motorcycles, for seven groups and, in addition, 20 Renault tractors were procured to effect the motorization of 240-mm. St-Chamond material. From the British source of supply the Ordnance Department had secured the motor material for 3 batteries of 9.2-inch and 13 batteries of 8-inch howitzers, which consisted of tractor, trucks, touring cars, and motorcycles. Because of the delay and disappointment that might arise in the delivery of tractors from America, a purchase order was placed with the British for 104 caterpillar tractors. Only a portion of this order was actually delivered up to the signing of the Armistice.

At present, there is sufficient ordnance motor equipment and tractors actually in France to equip 29 regiments of divisional howitzers on an improvised motor equipment allowance, together with full allowance of ordnance motor vehicles for the 66th, 166th and 151st Brigades of corps artillery. In addition, an ample reserve has now been created by the release of material from regiments of army artillery now turning in their material in the 18th Area.

1. At the time of the Armistice there were in the A. E. F.

    1   2 1/2-ton tractor
  220   5-ton tractors
  563   10-ton tractors
  437   15-ton tractors
   81   20-ton tractors

On this same date therewere assigned and actually in hands of troops:

    0   2 1/2-ton tractors
  144   5-ton tractors (comprising an emergency equipment of 6 155-mm. howitzer regiments)
  210   10-ton tractors
  437   15-ton tractors
   81   20-ton tractors

The balance of the tractors were at base ports or in intermediate and army depots, pending assignment to troops.

2. Since the Armistice, large numbers of 5-and 10-ton tractors have been received and issued to troops, and at date of writing this memorandum, the status of artillery tractors in the A. E. F. is as follows:

Total tractors delivered in A. E. F.:

    5   2 1/2-ton
 1018   5-ton
  933   10-ton
  451   15-ton
   91   20-ton

Of these tractors, actual issues to troops are as follows:

    5   2 1/2-ton tractors
  848   5-ton tractors
  648   10-ton tractors
   31   15-ton tractors
    7   20-ton tractors

The balance of tractors are in reserve at depots, base ports, or in ordnance shops, with the exception of 113 10-ton tractors which have been returned to the United States and 7 20-ton tractors likewise returned to the United States.

3. Among some of the novel uses to which the 5 and 10-ton tractors have been put, may be mentioned the following:

During excessive road congestion at the front, tractors were quite frequently used for clearing up road congestion. They were at times used to drag disabled trucks from the road and move other heavy vehicles which had broken down, causing a tie-up of traffic.

Tractors have also been issued to a number of motor transport parks for the purpose of hauling motor trucks out of mud holes in and around these parks.

Tractors have also been issued in considerable numbers to the engineers for hauling wood out of forests. Quite a number of the large commercial 15-ton tractors have been issued for this purpose.

Since the Armistice, issues of 5-ton tractors have been made to caisson companies of ammunition trains for drawing the caissons in place of horses. This use was in a way experimental, but if hostilities had continued, it was the intention to use the 2 1/2-ton tractor extensively for this purpose. On account of the shortage of 2 1/2-ton tractors, the next largest size, namely the 5-ton, has been used in the Third Army.

During winter conditions, tractors were stationed along the line of communication to the Third Army, particularly adjacent to certain steep hills, to assist heavily laden motor trucks up slippery grades.

Shortly before the Armistice, plans were under way to motorize a number of 75-mm. battalions. It was the intention to use 2 1/2-ton tractors for this purpose to the extent which these tractors could be obtained. In addition, it was contemplated to use the Ford tanks as a substitute for 2 1/2-ton tractors. These Ford tanks, although not ideal for tractor purposes, have been tried out at Le Valdahon and have proved fairly satisfactory in connection with the drawing of 75-mm. battalions. Ten of these Ford tanks are now at Le Valdahon.

4. The use of trailers in the A. E. F. has not been extensive, due to delay in deliveries. It was planned to utilize 3-inch field gun trailers to transport rapidly, from one place to another, 75-mm. guns and caissons. The guns and caissons are placed upon the trailer and the latter are drawn by motor truck.

5. It was also contemplated to use 10-ton trailers for the transportation of tanks over the roads when quick movements were desired; it was also intended to use 10-ton trailers for the salvaging of the 5 and 10-ton tractors which had been put out of commission in the advance area. As explained above, the use of these trailers was not extensive, due to the small number on hand in the A. E. F.

SMALL ARMS, AUTOMATIC ARMS, AND MACHINE GUNS

Included under this heading come rifles, pistols and revolvers, automatic rifles, and machine guns. At the beginning of the war, our army was equipped with the Springfield rifle, model of 1903. Manufacturing capacity for this rifle, however, was contained in two of the United States arsenals and was not nearly sufficient to take care of the forces to be organized. Considerable manufacturing capacity had, however, been developed by the Allied governments and large quantities of rifles had been manufactured for the British government. In view of this fact, it was decided to utilize this capacity and, therefore, the model 1917 rifle, which was the British rifle changed to caliber .30, was adopted. At the same time the manufacturing capacity of the two arsenals manufacturing Springfield rifles increased to the fullest capacity. This provided ample supply of rifles for our forces. At the beginning, there was some shortage of rifles for the training camps and it was necessary to use several hundred thousands of the old Krag rifles, which had been held in reserve when they were superseded by the Springfield rifle. However, our forces in Europe always had sufficient rifles.

The change of the British rifles to caliber .30 enabled our already existing large capacity for the manufacturing of caliber .30 ammunition to be utilized.

Our forces were equipped with the caliber .45 automatic pistol. Our tables of organization called for much larger percentage of pistols than that of any other of the Allied forces. There was not sufficient manufacturing capacity available for manufacturing all the pistols required and it was, therefore, necessary to use the caliber .45 revolver and utilize such manufacturing capacity which existed for manufacturing revolvers. In order to use the same ammunition for the pistol as for the revolver, the revolver was adapted to loading by means of a small clip holding three cartridges; the empty shells were ejected by means of the ejector.

Even by utilizing the manufacturing capacity for both pistol and revolver, sufficient pistols were never received in France to meet the needs. One reason for this was that very few of these weapons were received back in salvage. This is a weapon which everyone desires and it is thought that many unauthorized persons equipped themselves with these weapons from salvage.

Previous to our entrance into the war, our troops were armed with the automatic machine rifle, caliber .30, model of 1909. As result of comparative tests, however, the Vickers machine gun had just been adopted and a number of these were under manufacture. As the machine-gun manufacturing capacity was, however, quite limited, it was necessary to obtain large number of machine guns from the French to take care of the equipment of our divisions until manufacturing capacity could be developed. Our troops were therefore armed with machine guns and automatic rifles after their arrival in France. The machine gun used was the Hotchkiss 8-mm., and the automatic rifle, the Chauchat 8-mm. There was also developed in France a caliber .30 Chauchat; a number of these were manufactured in France and several divisions were armed with them. In the meantime, considerable number of caliber .30 Vickers machine guns were manufactured in the United States and a number of divisions were armed with them.

Just before our entrance into the war, a new machine gun and a new automatic rifle had been developed in the United States. These were the Browning machine gun and the Browning automatic rifle. These gave such successful tests that they were adopted as the standard weapons of these types for our army and large production capacity was developed for their manufacture. At the time of the signing of the Armistice a number of divisions coming from the States had been equipped with Browning machine guns and Browning sutomatic rifles and all other divisions then coming were so equipped. Also a considerable number of these machine guns and automatic rifles had been shipped to France and steps were beginning to be taken to equip divisions already here, which had been previously equipped with Hotchkiss or Bickers machine guns and with Chauchat automatic rifles, with Browning machine guns and Browning automatic rifles.

Fire control equipment for machine guns had not been thoroughly developed and manufacture of the Browning gun enabled the department to develop this important line of equipment to correspond with the standard gun. The entire line of fire control equipment was, therefore, designed and manufactured after the entry of the United States into the war.

The whole system is in mils and consists of:

The so-called Browning tripod. This tripod is far superior to any similar item in use by our Allies but it did not meet all of our requirements and another tripod, the model 1918, was designed. This tripod is suitable for all purposes, including antiaircraft firing.

The rear sight of the Browning with deflections in mils and sight elevating slide in mils.

The Lensatic compass with alidade protractor and luminous dial in mils.

The machine-gun clinometer.

The angle-of-site instrument.

The Corselli's graphs for 8-mm. and caliber .30.

The machine-gun protractor. (Note; A new complete map fire director will supersede the protractor.)

The machine-gun panoramic sight and various incidental items.

Our Allies after four years of war have only begun to develop their fire-control equipment.

In addition, many new articles in the machine-gun line have not only been developed but are actually being manufactured; amongst these is the .50-caliber Browning for aircraft and antiaircraft firing, for armor-piercing use against tanks, and for long range incendiary purposes.

From all reports received from divisions who had the Browning automatic rifles and machine guns in action, they gave very satisfactory service and it is considered that they are the best weapons of this type so far developed.

Large quantities of automatic rifles and machine guns were required for our Air Service and for this purpose large quantities of Lewis, Marlin, and Vickers machine guns were used. At the time of the signing of the Armistice the production of the Browning aircraft machine gun was beginning and delivery of these had begun to be received.

A detailed report covering the supply of small arms and automatic arms and machine guns including their maintenance has been made by Colonel A. E. Phillips, Chief Inspector, Machine Guns and Automatic Arms.

PERSONAL EQUIPMENT

Included in this class are such articles of general ordnance equipment as have not been covered in other classes already mentioned. There is nothing particlar to report on this, other than one or two items which may be of interest, such as helmets and trench knives.

The helmet had never been previously used by our forces. The British helmet had much greater resisting qualities than the French and was, therfore, adopted for the use of our troops. A large number of these were obtained from the British and a large number were also manufactured in the United States. It was thought advisable, however, to have a distinctive American type helmet and considerable experimenting was done by the Ordnance Department in France to develop such a helmet. At the time of the signing of the Armistice, a helmet had been designed and this had been approved by G-1 at General Headquarters, and an order for manufacturing several thousands had been placed in France. These were to have been tested by our troops in service before larger orders were to be placed.

In a similar manner the trench knife had been developed and a quantity were under manufacture to be issued for trial.

Considerable investigation had also been made of other types, their special equipment and the equipment of all the different Allied Armies and captured enemy material was studied with a view of developing such articles for our forces. This included such articles as body armor, sniperscopes, periscopes, pack carriers of various kinds, etc.

AMMUNITION

As mentioned previously, it was found necessary, on account of supplying our troops so far from their base of supplies, to adopt certain calibers of ammunition as were already used by the French and the British. Owing to the necessity of obtaining detailed drawings and developing manufacturing capacity for this ammunition, it was necessary to obtain practically all our ammunition from the beginning from the French and the English. As our Allies had a large manufacturing capacity developed, they were able to do this and agreed to take care of our needs in this regard until our manufacturing capacity could be developed. It was contemplated that they would be required to take care of most of our needs until the end of 1918. At the time of the signing of the Armistice, production of ammunition on a large scale had been developed in the United States and large shipments of ammunition were beginning to arrive. We have been able to supply all the caliber .30 ammunition required by our forces for their rifles and such caliber .30 automatic rifles and machine guns as were in use. Also large quantities of 8-mm. ammunition had been manufactured in the United States and shipped here for use in the

Hotchkiss machine guns and Chauchat automatic rifles. All the necessary ammunition for the pistols and revolvers had also been furnished. Considerable shipments of 75-mm. shrapnel and high explosive shells had also begun to arrive. Also some ammunition for the 4.7-inch guns. Up to this time, however, practically all the ammunition used by our forces for the following calibers had been obtained from the French and the English: All the French railway artillery loaned to our forces; ammunition for 9.2-inch howitzers, 8-inch howitzers, 155-mm. guns, 155-mm. howitzers, 75-mm. guns, 37-mm. guns, 3-inch Stokes mortars, 58-mm. trench mortars, 6-inch Newton mortars, and 240-mm. mortars.

A detailed report showing the system of ammunition supply, has been compiled by Captain D. H. Maring, Ord. Dept.

GENERAL SYSTEM OF SUPPLY

The general system of supply of ordnance material to troops is covered in general orders, A. E. F. In the beginning, troops were supplied from Advance Ordnance Depot No. 2, this latter depot being used as an advance depot when troops were operating in Chateau-Thierry district. It was found that supplying the troops from depots as far back as these caused great delay in getting supplies to the troops. This was on account of length of time required in getting requisitions to depots and inadequate shipping facilities. It was, therefore, found necessary to establish a system of army depots under the control of the chief ordnance officers of the armies. Under this system each army established one or more general depots and one or more automatic arms centers and certain artillery repair centers. This system was just getting into operation at the time of the signing of the Armistice and it is thought would have worked out very well. Under this system each army would have been allowed credits of different classes of material and would have controlled the issue to troops from their depots, thus allowing trainload shipments to be made to these depots from the S. O. S. depots in the rear and cutting out small shipments from S. O. S. depots to organizations. On account of inadequate shipping facilities, it was found almost impossible to get small shipments delivered promptly to organizations in the line. By having army depots to which trainload shipments could be made the organizations could obtain necessary equipment on a very short notice.

Under this system, however, it is thought that it would have been necessary to have frequent and rigid inspections by competent and accredited inspectors for the purpose of seeing that equipment was properly cared for and that only such equipment as was actually required was obtained. Under a system which made it easy for organizations to obtain supplies, it is thought that, unless organizations know they will be checked up and held rigidly responsible for the efficient handling of these supplies, there is great tendency for them to be careless in handling their equipment, so that the supply department would never be able to keep up with the demand. This was instanced in a number of cases where divisions came out of action and requisitioned for large quantities of equipment in excess of what their casualty list would indicate would have been necessary. Of course, in many cases the loss of equipment may have been unavoidable but if troops know that they can easily obtain additional equipment in case they lose that which they have and that no questions will be asked, there is a great tendency for them to discard their equipment when going forward instead of being burdened with it as they advance.

A. F. CASAD,
Colonel, Ord. Dept.,
Deputy of Chief Ordnance Officer.

C-in-C Report File: Fldr. 101: Report

Appendix B [Medical]

4th Section, (Medical) General Staff.   GENERAL HEADQUARTERS, A. E. F.,

Chaumont, Haute-Marne, December 31, 1918.

From: Chief of Group

To: A. C. of S., G-4, G. H. Q., A. E. F.

PART I

I. INTRODUCTION

In compliance with your verbal instructions the following report on the operations, observations, and methods of functioning of this group is submitted.

As the supervision now exercised by G-4 over hospitalization and evacuation was not clearly defined before, and the Medical Group of G-4 did not come into existence until the publication of G. O. 31 on Feburary 16, 1918, no report on the status of hospitalization and evacuation of the A. E. F. as it existed upon the cessation of hostilities on November 11, 1918, would be complete without briefly reviewing these subjects from their inception.

In this narrative, criticism of a constructive character has been freely introduced. Should we fail to profit by and avoid in the future the mistaken policies that have hitherto been followed, all the lessons learned in this war would prove useless. Under every subject discussed therein will be found certain recommendations for improvement. These conclusive recommendations are proposed as policies on which any future organization plans should be based.

The important guideposts or factors leading up to or facilitating the establishment of our hospitalization and evacuation service or a substantial basis were as follows:

     1. May 26, 1917: Creation of the A. E. F. with an Administrative Staff and Headquarters at PARIS (G. O. 1, A. E. F., 1917).

     2. July 5, 1917: Definition of staff duties. The coordination of policies for the A. E. F. placed under general staff control. Evacuation of sick and wounded supervised by the Administrative Section (later G-1) of the General Staff, and procurement of hospitals, particularly construction, supervised by the Coordination Section (later G-4) General Staff (G. O. 8, A. E. F., 1917).

     3. July 20, 1917: Red Cross hospitalization under military control recognized (G. O. 17, A. E. F., 1917).

     4. July 21, 1917: As an evacuation measure, authority was granted to purchase standard vestibuled hospital trains in England for use of the A. E. F.

     5. July 23, 1917: Chief Surgeon, A. E. F., submitted to the Chief of Staff an estimate of sanitary personnel required for the Medical Department, A. E. F., including all grades and other services functioning under the Medical Department, representing a total of 14.5% of the entire A. E. F. strength in Europe. As finally approved by the General Staff, A. E. F., this ratio was reduced to 7.65% * * *

     6. Aug. 2, 1917: Chief Surgeon, A. E. F., recommended steps be immediately taken to provide 125,000 beds to meet needs of 500,000 men in France, and that barrack hospital construction of our own be inaugurated.

7. Aug. 13, 1917: General Staff, A. E. F., authorized establishment of 73,000 beds on the then Line of Communications to meet needs of 300,000 men.

8. Aug. 13, 1917: Organization of the Line of Communications effected; headquarters at PARIS; limits of Advance, Intermediate, and Base Sections outlined (G. O. 20, A. E. F., 1917).

9. Sept. 1, 1917: Separation between G. H. Q. and Headquarters, L. O. C., the former moving to CHAUMONT.

10. Sept. 17, 1917: Chief Surgeon, A. E. F., submitted approved plan of type A Base Hospital Unit, prepared in his office; this to provide a barrack hospital of our own construction, with a normal capacity of 1,000 beds and a crisis capacity of 2,000 beds by use of tentage.

11. Sept. 30, 1917: Chief Surgeon, A. E. F., submitted approved plan of Type B Camp Hospital Unit, prepared in his office; this to provide a barrack hospital of our own construction, with a normal capacity of 300 beds and a crisis capacity fo 500 beds by use of tentage. This hospital was particularly designed for training areas and to meet local needs of isolated commands.

12. Oct. 10, 1917: Scarcity of construction material necessitated curtailment of resources and assignment of definite allowances of floor space in hospitals, etc. (G. O. 46, A. E. F., 1917).

13. Oct. 16, 1917: Administrative Section of General Staff materially reduced our hospitalization allowances and placed them on a phase basis. For normal hospitalization there was allowed 10% on all troops, and to provide for combat conditions an additional 10% on the strictly combatant troops.

14. Oct. 20, 1917: Joint Franco-American conference at French Mission attached to these headquarters, in which method to be followed in procuring hospital accommodations for the A. E. F. was prescribed.

15. Dec. 18, 1917: Joint Franco-American conference held in office of French Minister of war, PARIS, in which agreement was mutually adopted whereby in emergency American patients would be received in French hospitals, and vice versa, French patients in American hospitals.

16. Jan. 15, 1918: Headquarters, L. O. C., moved from PARIS to TOURS.

17. Feb. 16, 1918: Reorganization of A. E. F. General Staff; division into five sections, G-4 supervising all hospitalization and evacuation matters. Provision for Medical Department representation in various sections of the General Staff. Assignment of medical officers to G-4. Transfer of Chiefs of Administrative and Technical Staff Services to Headquarters, S. O. S., TOURS, leaving behind here representatives on the General Staff, with authority of deputy (G. O. 31, A. E. F., 1918). Under this reorganization scheme, supervision of Red Cross activities was left under G-1.

18. May 6, 1918: Adoption by the A. E. F. of mobile hospitals and mobile surgical units; new departures in our organization (G. O. 70, A. E. F., 1918).

19. June 1, 1918: Hospitalization placed on a new basis. Medical Department authorized to maintain an actual current bed status aggregating 15% of total troops in Europe. This allowance to concern fixed hospitalization only. To overcome delays in acquirement incident to construction, additional credits also authorized.

20. June 4. 1918: Joint Franco-American conference held at the office of the French Minister of War, PARIS, at which arrangements were perfected for the interchange of statistical data regarding American patients in French hospitals and French patients in American hospitals.

21. Aug. 29, 1918: Promulgation of regulations concerning operation of hospital trains.

II. GENERAL STAFF SUPERVISION

Before proceeding with a discussion of hospitalization and evacuation, the functions of G-4 in relation thereto must be described. G-4, G. H. Q., exercises supervision over matters relating chiefly, but not exclusively, to procurement and location of hospitalization and evacuation resources and their coordination with other activities. G-4 directs policies; the S. O. S. or other agencies execute them. Under our present scheme of organization at these headquarters, it has become the custom to refer all Medical Department matters presented to any subdivision of the General Staff to this section for study and recommendation.

Prior to February 16, 1918, when General Orders 31, these headquarters, became operative, representatives of the Chief Surgeon's Office took up directly with the various sections of the General Staff concerned all Medical Department matters requiring their execution or coordination. As the Chief Surgeon was then at these headquarters, and in close liaison with the General Staff and other administrative and technical services, the more important policies were usually placed on record and then verbally discussed with those concerned. Accordingly, the Hospitalization Section of the Chief Surgeon's Office, since the organization of the A. E. F., had been dealing directly with G-4 in matters relating to the procurement of hospitals. When the Chief Surgeon removed to TOURS, he left behind as his representatives with G-4 two medical officers who had been associated with the hospitalization program from its inception. Under the new reorganization, the A. C. of S., G-4, proceeded to establish the Medical, or B Group of G-4, and it immediately began to function as an integral part of the section under the chief of that section. The Chief Surgeon also left a representative with G-1 to handle the tonnage and supply matters arising in that section, and another representative in G-5 who handled training matters.

With this separation of the Chief Surgeon's Office from Headquarters, A. E. F., his relations with the combat forces virtually ceased, and as his deputy, the senior medical officer in G-4-B supervised all the combat activities of the Medical Department in the Zone of the Armies. The demands upon the medical group of G-4 constantly grew, and from the beginning of our A. E. F. combat activities it was called upon to meet the daily emergencies of battle conditions as they arose.

The composition of the group varied according to circumstances, but on the average included four medical officers of field rank and two officers of the Sanitary Corps for office management, with a large clerical force. Two of these officers were eventually detailed on the General Staff. Two officers were almost constantly in the field, representing G-4 in the coordination of hospitalization and evacuation.

In addition to the Medical Department personnel composing B group of G-4, one medical officer was attached to G-1. In actual practice, this officer functioned as a member of this group but was placed with G-1 to handle certain specific duties. Such a detail was found to be necessary for the reason that all questions of ocean tonnage were treated in the latter section of the General Staff. It was essential, therefore, that there should be a medical officer on the General Staff thoroughly conversant with the Medical Department supply problem and the method of getting these supplies shipped to France.

Lieutenant Colonel A. P. Clark, G. S., (M. C.), the officer who held this detail, discharged his duties in a most able and conscientious manner. * * * It is very largely due to this officer's far-sighted vision that the difficulties of procurement of supplies, transportation overseas, and the placing of the whole question on an automatic basis were successfully solved.

With the growth of the organization, the group soon became the center to which all matters affecting the Medical Department arising at these headquarters were referred for recommendation or suitable action. No important questions of policy were decided without first submitting the proposition to this group. All actions initiated in the group were of course executed over the signature of the Assistant Chief of Staff of the Section, G-4. This system was followed even with questions involving another section. In this case a memorandum was usually prepared for the other sections of the General Staff involved and transmitted to it through the A. C. of S., G-4.

Aside from the many questions which arose and involved hospitalization and evacuation policies in the S. O. S., the greater part of the time of this group was taken up with questions concerning operations and policies connected with combat activities at the front. The chief of section kept the members of this group informed as to impending combat plans, and, through advance notice so furnished, the medical group was able to keep in touch with the chief surgeons of the various armies, corps, and divisions concerned, as to their facilities for meeting forthcoming obligations, and permitted prompt assistance when and where it was needed.

The Chief Surgeon was granted the privilege of having a medical representative on each section of the General Staff. At the time no officer was detailed to G-2 (Intelligence) or G-3 (Operations), largely because of the very great shortage of Medical Department personnel.

It soon became evident that the medical representation of G-2 was unnecessary, but as to G-3 it appeared desirable that there should be such representation in order that Medical Department plans might be coordinated with combat operations in general.

As events developed and American troops began actual participation in the war it was soon apparent that no military operations could be planned or undertaken without consultation and fullest cooperation with General Moseley, the A. C. of S., G-4. It has been a policy of this officer to consistently take the medical representative of his section into his confidence. The wisdon of so doing has been amply demonstrated; it has been equally as well demonstrated that without this harmonious cooperation the Medical Department would have been doomed to failure. General Moseley's stand in this matter is particularly to be remarked for the reason that a number of officers of high rank were convinced that the Medical Department should not be advised in advance of impending combat activities. It is believed that in the light of the experiences of the recent past the most skeptical has been convinced that military objects can be attained only by considering the military machine as composed of numerous reciprocating parts, each striving towards a common end.

Prior to the creation of A. E. F. army and corps formations, there devolved upon this group the necessity of functioning in the dual capacity of an army or corps surgeon, as there was at that time no other agency through which the higher coordinative functions could be exercised.

Until the Chief Surgeon, First Army, was designated in July, 1918, the duties of chief surgeon of our divisions in combat, including all of the early military activities of the A. E. F., were discharged by this group. This of course was not contemplated in the organization of the General Staff, but through force of necessity it became a duty which was, and could be, discharged in no other way. This placed a very heavy burden of responsibility on this group, which its organization had not provided for and which it was not contemplated should be provided for. With the appointment of corps and army surgeons in the summer of 1918, the group was relieved of this part of its duties. Even after the formation of corps and armies, very careful supervision was exercised by this group over medical department activities at the front.

The hospitalization and evacuation plans for the St-MIHIEL and ARGONNE-MEUSE offensives, as far as procurement and evacuation were concerned, were largely prepared in this section and placed into effective operation through personal consultation with the Chief Surgeons of the First and Second Armies. The battle casualties to be cared for were carefully estimated and every available resource drawn upon to properly meet them. Owing to the limited resources, it frequently became necessary to move sanitary formations and resources from one place to another. As a part of G-4, controlling all transportation resources, the affiliation materially assisted in these movements. All changes of station of army units were accomplished on orders issued by G-3, based on recommendations prepared in this group for the signature of the A. C. of S., G-4. Therefore, from a practical standpoint, G-4-B made battle disposition of sanitary units as dictated by military necessity and thus discharged the superlative functions of a chief surgeon of a group of armies.

The geographical location of G. H. Q. permitted of maintaining close and immediate contact with division, corps, and army headquarters. It was not only possible for a member of this group to reach rapidly almost any part of the front occupied by American troops, but a splended system of telephone and telegraph communication enabled the office to know exactly the conditions to be met at any and all times. It was due largely to this fact that the Medical Department was able to meet the daily problems created by the lack of authorized personnel, sanitary units, and equipment. By means of this rapid system of communication, casual personnel, operating teams, and sanitary units (ambulance companies, field, evacuation, and mobile hospitals) were moved on orders initiated by this group from one sector of the front to another. Without this machinery for coordination of effort and consolidation of resources, failure to care for, evacuate, and hospitalize battle casualties would have been certain.

In retrospect, the members of the group believe that without this elasticity of control, as reflected in the authority of the A. C. of S., G-4, serious embarrassment to the Medical Department would surely have resulted. This elasticity permitted us to utilize our limited resources to a maximum degree of advantage.

The present method of providing for medical department representation on and with the General Staff is ideal, and is favored over all other previous propositions. Medical department representation on the General Staff as conceived by the A. C. of S., G-4, more nearly approaches the ideal of organization than any other plan which has been proposed. It is hoped that the policy inaugurated by the chief of this section in this respect will have demonstrated its value, and will be perpetuated in any future reorganization of the General Staff. It is also hoped that the results obtained by this section of the General Staff have amply demonstrated the wisdom of having adequate medical department representation on the General Staff.

[The next several paragraphs of the report discuss medical representation on the General Staff and describes briefly the practice in the French army.]

* * * * * *

III. HOSPITALIZATION

This subject must be discussed under two headings:
1. Fixed establishments
2. Mobile sanitary formations accompanying the armies in the field.

FIXED ESTABLISHMENTS

These included:
1. Base hospitals.
2. Camp hospitals.
3. Convalescent camps.
4. American Red Cross military hospitals.
5. American Red Cross hospitals.
6. American Red Cross convalescent homes.

G-4 controlled the allowances, decided on the location of hospitalization on the L. O. C., ordered new construction, and coordinated these projects with other activities.

Base and Camp Hospitals: The first A. E. F. troops to arrive in France in any considerable number landed at St-NAZAIRE in June, 1917. Hospitalization obligations at that time, and for several months thereafter, were confined solely to meeting the local needs of our troops in a fairly restricted area. Obviously, it was impossible to construct hospitals in time to meet the immediate needs; therefore, the French were called upon and willingly relinquished to us hospital accommodations, such as they had, wherever they were needed.

This process of acquiring hospitals from the French, or through their agency of obtaining buildings suitable for hospital purposes, continued over a period of many months. As our needs increased and our troops became located over a gradually expanding area, it became necessary, even in meeting normal needs, to increase these demands on the French. The hospitalization acquired through these means comprised French hospitals taken over intact, hotels, barracks, schools, and even stables. When the training areas selected for our troops in the foot hills of the VOSGES were designated, we were confronted with a new problem, as the French did not have in those areas sufficient hospitalization available to meet our needs. This made necessary the immediate construction of our own hospitals, the needs being met by the establishment of one of our Type B 300-bed camp hospitals in each of those areas where hospitalization did not exist. Thus was born our first construction program.

Coincident with the monthly arrival of large numbers of troops from the United States, the acquisition of existing buildings for hospital purposes was pushed to the utmost. Many of these when taken over required alterations, additions, and repairs to render them suitable for occupancy as hospitals. However, it was realized that a limit soon would be reached beyond which the French could not safely go without seriously jeopardizing the sufficiency of their own hospital service.

In this connection, it is well to direct attention to the fact that the available buildings in France at this time which could answer the purpose of providing hospital facilities were very limited. The French Government had had first choice in the early days of the war. Later the British, Belgian, and Italian Governments had established hospitals in France, and there were also a large number of hospitals maintained by volunteer aid societies from different parts of the world. The result was that at the time the United States embarked on its hospitalization program the available resources in this direction had been almost completely exhausted. Those buildings which were obtained were generally of a most unsatisfactory character, very expensive to maintain, difficult to administer, and usually required an excessive number of personnel to properly operate them.

School buildings were among the first placed at our disposal by the French Government. These were almost invariably unsatisfactory. Few of them had running water, sewer connections, or toilet facilities. Under French law when school buildings are requisitioned for military purposes the teaching personnel must be allowed to retain their living quarters in the school. The result was that in the same building there would be wards for patients, quarters for personnel, and living quarters for French civilians.

The first American military hospital established in France was located in a school building in St-NAZAIRE. Under one roof there was an A. E. F. hospital, a school for young boys, and living quarters for the American medical personnel and the French teaching staff with their families. All were hopelessly intermingled, and at one time there was under treatment in this hospital measles, mumps, scarlet fever, and cerebro-spinal meningitis. Proper isolation of these contagious cases became a difficult matter.

In this comment there is no criticism either intended or implied. The French gave freely and generously of the best of their hospitals. While the French had to submit to the same conditions regarding the use of schools, they were not confronted by the barrier of language between hospital and school personnel or the countless petty misunderstandings engendered thereby.

In utilizing hotels as hospitals the objections to these buildings, while serious, rested on other grounds. As shown above, practically all the good buildings obtainable had been taken over by the Allied Governments. Those remaining were very largely summer hotels without heating facilities, insufficient water, and very limited plumbing. In addition, when private buildings are taken possession of for military purposes the owner is allowed by law to reserve certain parts of the buildings, and the law also requires that they shall be returned to the owner in the same condition as when taken out of his control. The latter provision necessitates refurnishing such buildings at tremendous cost and removing all improvements or additions which may have been installed. In spite of these many disadvantages inherent in leasing or requisitioning private buildings no other course was open. Building was out of the question until an organization could be secured and personnel and equipment, including saw mills, transported to France. As the available supply of buildings, unsuitable and expensive as they were, was soon exhausted it became necessary to institute a building program on a large scale.

A type A 1,000-bed barrack unit was adopted as the model for this program. Our first large venture on the construction of these base hospital types was located at BAZOILLES-sur-MEUSE, centering on our training areas and ideally situated as regards lines of communication and prospective combat activities. Five units, or a total of 5,000 beds normal capacity, were authorized for that place in September, 1917.

Up to the fall of 1917 no definite policy had been announced as to what sector of the fighting front the American troops would eventually occupy. The absence of this definite information rendered it extremely difficult to map out a comprehensive hospitalization program. However, as we were expecting combat activity, and delay could not be countenanced, it was necessary to proceed on the assumption that our principal bases must be St-NAZAIRE and BORDEAUX and our sector in the proximity of the training areas in which we were already placing our troops. This afforded us a fairly well-defined line of communication, and as events later proved, our early conjectures as to the sector on which our maximum combat efforts would be put forth proved to be reliable.

The decision was soon reached to hospitalize along those lines of communication, adhering as far as possible to a distribution of hospital facilities which would approximately provide for 15% of our total beds in the Advance Section, 60% in the Intermediate Section, and 25% in the Base Sections. Every possible means of acquiring existing buildings, in order that accommodations for meeting the needs of incoming troops could be assured, was used, and at the time construction programs looking far into the future were pushed to the limit of our capabilities. Following our initial effort at BAZOILLES, sites were early selected and construction ordered at the following places: RIMAUCOURT, BORDEAUX, BEAUNE, ALLEREY, MARS, MESVES, LIMOGES, PERIGUEUX, NANTES, etc., on a progressive scale. The monthly status of total beds made available for the year 1918, and during the height of our combat activities, are shown in the following table:

1918	Total Beds Normal	*Emergency	Total patients in hospital	Approximate strength, A. E. F.
Jan. 31	9,377	----	5,091	215,788
Feb. 28	10,694	----	4,960	251,889
Mar. 31	22,125	----	10,723	318,621
Apr. 30	28,090	----	11,115	439,659
May 31	33,077	37,086	15,336	651,284
June 30	39,713	42,815	22,905	873,691
July 31	58,687	75,793	42,740	1,169,072
Aug. 31	90,204	102,144	54,485	1,415,128
Sept. 30	110,953	148,596	79,580	1,705,392
Oct. 31	166,534	221,421	163,767	1,807,143
Nov. 11	171,830	233,092	169,235	1,870,257

* Emergency includes normal.

* * * * * *

The Process of Realizing a Construction Program. [Discusses routine procedure in selection of sites and construction or acquisition of hospitals.]

* * * * * *

Hotels: Due to the inability to construct hospitals rapidly enough to meet our needs it became necessary to lease a considerable number of hotels for hospital purposes. These buildings generally were very expensive, not only because of the high rate of rental, but because of the necessity of replacing them in the condition in which they were taken over, when no longer needed by the A. E. F. The acquisition of this class of property was postponed as long as possible and was resorted to only as a measure of absolute necessity. Seldom was a hotel found which could be utilized in its present condition for hospital purposes. Removal of many partitions and modifications in plumbing, sewage, etc., to render it habitable as a hospital necessitated not only the original monetary outlay, but a second outlay in restoring the building to its original condition when evacuated for the purpose of returning it to the owner. A considerable number of these hotels were built for summer use only. It was necessary of course to use them during the winter, and this entailed a certain additional expense through the absence of heating appliances and the constant freezing of plumbing.

Origin and Development of Base Hospital Units: The development of A. E. F. hospitalization in its broader aspects is of interest. The War Department had made no provision for fixed hospitalization prior to the declaration of war. The need for base hospital units, both personnel and matériel, was very clearly understood. It had been forcibly brought home to the Surgeon General's Office by the observation of eminent civilian medical men who had served as volunteers with the French during the early days of the war.

The idea of the base hospital unit was first given publicity by Major Karl Connel, M. C., New York National Guard, who had brought the Whitney Unit to France in the fall of 1914. The necessity of organizing such units in the United States was urged upon the War Department. The absolute lack of funds which could be used for such a purpose threatened for a time to prevent any steps in this direction. At the request of the Surgeon General, the National Red Cross Society agreed to lend its aid. Colonel J. R. Kean, M. C., U. S. A., was detailed for duty with the Red Cross and, with the influence and money of that organization, he was able to make progress. Public minded citizens donated the money for the equipment, and the personnel was recruited from the surgeons, nurses, and other employees of the big metropolitan civil hospitals.

These base hospital units were organized on the basis of 500 beds each. The equipment was the best obtainable and was complete in every detail. The very cream of the medical and surgical profession of the United States made up the commissioned personnel.

When the United States came into the war, a considerable number of these units had already been orgsnized and equipped. They were Red Cross organizations until called into the government service, when they were given a military designation and became army sanitary formations. Due to this foresight and the splendid assistance furnished by the Red Cross a sufficient number of these units were ready to be transported to France almost immediately after war was declared. As a matter of fact, six of these units were sent to England on short notice for service with the British army, and these units were the first organized forces of the United States to be sent to France. To Base Hospital No. 4, American Army, organized at the Lakeside Hospital, Cleveland, Ohio, fell the honor of being first in Europe.

As stated above, the base hospital was organized on a 500-bed basis. As soon as the allowance of sanitary personnel was fixed by the General Staff, A. E. F. (July, 1917), it was apparent that the Medical Department could not function unless the personnel overhead was reduced to the absolute minimum by adopting a unit with larger bed capacity. It has generally been accepted that in the armies of civilized countries the sanitary personnel must be at least 10% of the strength of the forces. The Secretary of War had decided in June, 1917, that the enlisted personnel of the sanitary service should be 10% of the total forces. The figure finally fixed by the General Staff, A. E. F., for total sanitary personnel - officers, nurses, and enlisted men - was 7.65%.

A hospital of 10-bed capacity will require a total medical personnel of not less than 20 people, but a hospital of 1,000 beds can be administered with a personnel of 330; in time of emergency the latter can be increased for a short period to 2,000 beds with the same personnel. The quality of work done and the amount of care and attention given patients will, however, steadily deteriorate because of the necessity of working personnel continuously both day and night.

Because of the above considerations a standard base hospital was modified to provide capacity for 1,000 beds, to be doubled in time of emergency by so-called crisis expansion under tentage. The details of this type hospital and the considerations which require its adoption in the form finally approved will be found elsewhere in this report.

Having arrived at this point, it was a natural development to group these hospitals into hospital centers with a capacity of from ten to twenty thousand patients each. The advantages of such grouping are pointed out below. In making the decision to adopt the principles outlined above the personnel situation was the controlling factor, although other very important advantages followed naturally. In passing, it is desired to record here that without such a centralization of resources, both of personnel and materiel, the care of the great numbers of battle casualties which were suddenly thrown upon the Medical Department in the summer and fall of 1918 could never have been provided.

This paragraph should not be closed without a word of tribute to tnese base hospital units. All of them arrived in France with no previous military experience. The regular medical officer assigned to command the unit had in practically every case to be relieved for some other more pressing task. The work of the hospital was continued by a commanding officer fresh from civil life and unaccustomed to military administrative details. Under such conditions it is not to be wondered at that there were a few failures; the astonishing thing is that so large a percentage were able to conduct successfully and efficiently a great military hospital of from one to three thousand beds. Always there was the shortage of personnel of all grades to complete administration.

It is unfortunate, but certain, that the army and people at large will never be able to realize the debt of gratitude which they owe to the splendid and self sacrificing personnel of these units. Owing to the chronic shortage of sanitary personnel for duty at advanced sanitary formations (evacuation and mobile hospitals), it was necessary in times of active operations to draw upon the base hospitals. It was at just these periods that the burden carried by the base hospitals was heaviest and personnel could least well be spared. Surgeons and nurses literally dropped at the operating tables from fatugue but complaints were almost never heard. It was a splendid manifestation of magnificent devotion to duty.

Centralization of Hospitals: Wherever suitable sites could be obtained, it was believed, as stated above, to be in the interests of economy in personnel, materiel, and other resources to establish large centers, which virtually became hospital cities. For example, adjoining the small villages of BEAUNE, ALLEREY, MARS, and MESVES construction was well along towards the establishment of ten large base hospitals in one group at each of those places. For BORDEAUX, one of our principal base ports, twenty base hospitals were provided for. This necessitated the building of roads, railroad sidings for supplies and hospital trains, and water and lighting systems on a very large scale. This aggregation of hospitals into large groups materially simplified evacuation problems and enabled the Medical Department to establish in these centers all the specialties needed to maintain a well-balanced hospitalization; one hospital received fracture cases, another chest cases, others psychiatric, contagious, abdominal, etc. Battle casualties, or those sick requiring special treatment, could be sent to one of these centers on any of our hospital trains and find there all the specialized facilities required. The scheme also permitted of a rotation or elasticity of service which could not have otherwise been provided. By this grouping, not only was the cost of our hospitalization materially reduced but it permitted the insufficient personnel available to accomplish a task which would have been impossible had we located our units in widely separated localities. Another very important advantage of this system arose in the fact that a recently arrived inexperienced unit had an opportunity to be guided and profit by the earlier experience of the older units in these centers. It also engendered a spirit of helpful rivalry among the various units that accrued to the general efficiency of the center as a whole. * * *

Strategic Fixed Hospitalization: In locating hospital centers, the guiding principle should be establishment on or immediately off the main arteries of railway traffic, and preferably radiating from a regulating station serving the forces at the front. In the Advance Section, our hospitalization was well located with reference to the regulating stations of IS-sur-TILLE and St-DIZIER.

Unexpected combat activities of American troops on the PARIS front found us facing a difficult evacuation and hospitalization problem. This was due not only to the fact that we had insufficient hospital facilities on the lines radiating from the regulating stations established there, but to the necessity of cutting across the lines of communication serving Allied Armies, in order that our hospital trains might be sent to places where we had adequate A. E. F. hospitalization. Despite the recommendation of the Medical Department, hospitalization in the PARIS region, except for the Red Cross military hospitals in the city of PARIS itself, was denied the A. E. F. To evacuate to our available hospitalization from the regulating stations established at le BOURGET and CREIL during the MARNE operations necessitated considerable cross movements on railroad lines, that slowed up our evacuation and seriously interfered with the trains supplying and evacuating other armies. In future operations, tentative regulating stations in the theater of operations should early be indicated by the General Staff, G-4, and the hospitalization for the forces mapped out on lines in the rear radiating from those stations. Without this provision, an excessive number of hospital trains will always be needed and unwarranted congestion of traffic lines result.

In locating base hospitals, from a railroad standpoint, it is as stated above preferable to establish them on a branch line, slightly off the main line of traffic. However, our hospital trains were so large that this factor had to be taken into consideration in selecting sites. Instances arose where an excellent site was available but could not be utilized because a bridge on the branch line to it did not possess sufficient strength to sustain a heavily loaded train.

From a strategic standpoint, the geographical location of base hospitals in France was not always ideal. The demands for hospital accommodations were constantly so pressing that it became necessary to accept any facilities that were available. This accounts for the fact that a fairly good proportion of our hospitalization was established in remote regions, yet still accessible to the main lines of traffic by long hauls for hospital trains over branch lines.

Wherever hospitsls cannot be ideally located from the strategic standpoint, the only remedy lies in the provision of a sufficient number of well equipped vestibuled hospital trains to permit of wounded receiving every necessary care en route over the long hauls involved. During the latter part of our combat activities properly equipped hospital trains to meet all the needs were not available, but by using American trains for the long hauls and the more seriously wounded, and borrowing from the French some of their trains for the short hauls and the moderately wounded, the situation was met in a fairly satisfactory manner.

Base Hospital Allowance: The accepted shipping schedule called for the despatch to France of four base hospitals for each division in France. Those first to arrive were organized and equipped in the U. S. on a 500-bed basis. It soon became evident that this was not an economical organization with which to meet the problem presented in caring for the large number of sick and wounded certain to arise among our troops. Accordingly, recommendation was made early to the War Department that they be organized and equipped on a 1,000-bed basis. After the lapse of several months, this increase in size was adopted for all incoming units. For some reason not yet explained, our shipping schedule for base hospitals did not progress smoothly. Units failed to arrive, frequently being displaced by combat troops, and often when they did arrive their equipment was not received for many months afterwards. This created a very serious situation, as at no time was our hospitalization maintained on a safe margin. Our depots in France had been depleted and during our final combat operations there were over twenty base hospitals in France with complete personnel but no equipment for them. Repeated cablegrams to the War Department during the entire period of our operations here failed to bring about the desired result of placing us on a safe hospitalization basis.

As a matter of much interest, and to preserve historical accuracy, it should be pointed out that had hostilities continued much longer and casualties occurred at the same rate as in the concluding weeks of our activities, the A. E. F. would have been confronted with a situation of having on its hands more patients than could possibly have been hospitalized.

This was due to a number of causes, the most important of which were:

First, the original estimate of sanitary personnel requirements was placed by the General Staff, A. E. F., at a figure far below the actual needs. Second, failure to get to France the limited authorized personnel and equipment provided for in shipping schedules. Third, our own construction projects had been permitted to progress too slowly, and some of the work on them was of such a makeshift character that the buildings could be utilized only temporarily and would have become uninhabitable during the winter months.

As it was, it became necessary to shelter thousands of our wounded in unfloored and unheated tents. The general situation, from the standpoint of hospital accommodations in the fall of 1918 was fraught with great anxiety to those responsible for providing adequate accommodations for our constantly increasing battle casualties.

The above is not offered in a spirit of criticism, but merely as a plain statement of fact and for future guidance.

Camp Hospitals: These play an important role in the hospitalization of an army. They are recognized in the Manual for the Medical Department, but not in the tables of organization as prepared by the War Department. To conserve our resources and provide a limited amount of hospitalization, local for large commands, and for smaller commands in remote regions where base hospitals were not available, these camp hospitals were established wherever needed throughout the area of activities occupied by our troops. The establishment of these hospitals, which were absolutely necessary, was a factor which seriously depleted our limited Medical Department personnel and equipment. To man them it was necessary to withdraw personnel and equipment from base hospitals and other authorized organizations.

As early as July, 1917, the Chief Surgeon attempted to secure authorization for personnel for these important units but this recommendation was disapproved, on the ground that personnel from the divisional sanitary trains would be available to fill this need. Experience has shown that such a view is based on a misconception of the problem presented. To employ the sanitary train personnel in this way prevents the training in preparation for combat, which is just as essential for sanitary units as for those of the line. Moreover, divisions were constantly changing from one area to another and to have followed the plan proposed by the General Staff, A. E. F., would have resulted in abandoning these excellently equipped sanitary formations until the next division chanced into the same area.

The necessity of providing and authorizing sanitary personnel for the camp hospitals is one of the outstanding lessons of the experience gained in this war. These hospitals when established in buildings taken over for this purpose had a capacity varying from 100 to 500 beds, depending upon local facilities and needs. Those of our own construction, in the training areas, had a normal capacity of 300 beds and a crisis capacity with tentage of 500 beds. Of necessity, the personnel of all these units was obtained from base hospitals and by detaching some from combat troops already insufficiently supplied.

Hospitalization Programs: (Bed allowance). As far as the adequate provision for fixed hospitalization is concerned, the mere inclusion in any approved shipping schedule for a certain ratio of hospital unit personnel and equipment to accompany or precede troops sent overseas will always fail to meet the current situation. The hospitals to be administered by incoming units must be ready for occupancy prior to their arrival. Where construction is necessary it should be inaugurated far in advance of the arrival of the troops that it is intended to accommodate. The director of the hospitalization division of the Chief Surgeon's Office should be a futurist in the truest sense of the word. His work at all times should be centered on anticipatory requirements. In January he must plan for the contemplated requirements of July, and so on.

The adoption of any hospitalization program is merely an attempt to assure that adequate and timely provision shall be made to care for the sick and wounded. In authorizing facilities and directing procedure to meet the needs, allowances should be based in terms of beds and not in terms of hospital units. The morbidity expectations for the forces can always be estimated with a fair degree of accuracy. If we can provide a sick or wounded soldier with a bed in a hospital it is safe to assume that the other necessary hospital appurtenances, in the form of operating, messing, clinical, and other features, are always at hand in commensurate proportions. To base the needs of an army in the terms of units would eventually lead to errors, as in many instances, depending largely upon local conditions, a unit may occupy buildings that will permit it to administer a hospital with twice the number of beds contained by a neighboring hospital. This difference in bed capacity of the various hospitals established in France was very marked, particularly where it became necessary to take over existing

French hospitals or to acquire existing buildings and alter tham for hospital purposes. In those of our own construction the capacity was stwndardized.

The first comprehensive hospitalization program prepared for the A. E. F. was submitted by the Chief Surgeon as early as August 2, 1917, to the General Staff for consideration. As a result of his recommendation, the General Staff on August 13, 1917, authorized the establishment of 73,000 beds on the then Line of Communications to meet the needs of 300,000 men. This program or, as it was often referred to, approved policy, continued in force until October, 1917, when hospitalization was definitely placed on a percentage basis. The method of computing our hospitalization allowance under this percentage decision as prescribed by the General Staff did not prove satisfactory. The phase basis, or that of authorizing hospitalization only coincident with the arrival of troops and making no provision for the long delays incident to constructing hospitals of our own, proved wholly impracticable and would not have withstood the test of time.

An analytical study of hospitalization resources and defects in the then existing method of authorizing construction was presented in a paper prepared by a member of this group (Colonel A. D. Tuttle) on March 31, 1918, and submitted for the consideration of the General Staff. Approval for the automatic bed allowance therein proposed was not forthcoming and between that period and June 1, 1918, when a new policy was announced, it became necessary for the Medical Department to take up direct with the General Staff any new project for which authorization was believed to be necessary. On May 17, 1918, the outlook with regard to the future of hospitalization became so grave as to prompt the Chief Surgeon to recommend that a program embodying provision for future needs be authorized by the General Staff. This recommendation of the Chief Surgeon was referred to this section for study and recommendation.

The new policy, or program, as prepared by this group and authorized by the A. C. of S., G-4, on June 1, 1918, was in force on the date of the Armistice and provided as follows:

> As the basis of an approved hospitalization program, the Medical Department is hereby authorized to maintain an actual current bed status aggregating 15% to be computed on the total A. E. F. strength of troops in Europe. The establishment of this flat rate will tend to avoid any future conflict of opinion as to the ratio between combat and other troops. Moreover, this percentage is practically that stated in the Chief Surgeon's letter.
>
> This numerical bed allowance will include the accommodations provided in all fixed hospitals, irrespective of type, as well as convalescent camps The computation is to be made on the basis of ordinary bed capacity; temporary increases in capacity by the use of tentage in fixed formations or the temporary hospitalization provided in mobile sanitary formations will not be included.
>
> It is well recognized that projectd involving new construction will not be available for occupancy before the lapse of at least six months and that the provision of adequate hospital accommodations must keep pace with the arrival of troops. Therefore, in order that the Medical Department may make timely provision in anticipation of its future needs, it is hereby authorized to utilize, until further orders from these headquarters, an additional credit of 90,000 beds over the 15% flat rate authorized in paragraph 2 above. In utilizing this credit, it should preferably be written off in monthly allotments of approximately 15,000 beds each.
>
> Convalescent camps as herein recommended are authorized as part of this hospitalization project.
>
> As heretofore required, all matters of hospitalization involving new projects will be referred to these headquarters for consideration, with a view of their coordination with other activities as regards location and supply.

Matters concerning the expansion of existing hospitals or hospital centers or the construction of camp hospitals, need not be so referred.

* * * * * *

Convalescent Camps: With the speeding up of troop movements, early in the summer of 1918, it was soon realized that fixed hospitalization, as its acquisition was then progressing, could not keep pace with the arrival of troops. To meet this situation it was decided to provide convalescent camps in the vicinity of, and as part of, large hospital centers to which men not yet fit for duty but who no longer required careful hospital treatment, could be sent pending their fitness for return to duty. In these camps they were provided with shelter, with limited bed space, but good food, and given a certain amount of work and exercise to fit them for their forthcoming duty. G-4, in a letter dated June 1, 1918, authorized the construction or establishment by tentage of these convalescent camps, on the ratio of 20% of our total bed capacity. Many of these camps were in operation upon the conclusion of hostilities on November 11, 1918, and it was through their operation only that we were able to provide accommodations for the battle casualties occurring during the summer and fall of 1918.

Aside from the necessity of providing in these convalescent camps adequate shelter, food, etc., the essential points to be borne in mind in establishing them are:

First, they must be Medical Department units. Second, the necessity of removing men who are almost well and face early return to combat duty, from the atmosphere of the hospital at the earliest possible moment. Third, the most careful selection of medical officers qualified to carry on mental and physical reconstruction of men who have once been subjected to the nervous shock and physical damage wrought by combat. Fourth, there unquestionably being a psychological element in the reconstruction of these men, the assignment of bands and other means of providing music and entertainment at these convalescent camps must be recognized. It has been the experience of our Allies, extending over a much longer period than our own, that a good band is of the first importance in restoring the moral fibre in a man who has been shaken by the ordeal of battle.

American Red Cross Military Hospitals: The establishment of these hospitals might properly be characterized as camouflage A. E. F. hospitalization. The designation of these hospitals was one of necessity. During our operations in France there were certain regions where hospitalization was absolutely essential from a strategical standpoint. In these areas we were denied by the French authorities the privilege of establishing A. E. F. hospitalization, but on account of its affiliation with and the great assistance rendered by it to the French nation, the American Red Cross was given this privilege.

[The report here takes up the subject of leases or accommodations available to the Red Cross but not available to the army, whereby hospitals were established by the Red Cross but operated with military personnel.]

* * * * * *

American Red Cross Hospitals and Convalescent Homes: These facilities provided by the Red Cross were an asset in the hospitalization scheme of the A. E. F. and were operated on our recommendation. They provided for civilian hospitalization, and at the same time wherever located were available to us for emergency military hospitalization. The convalescent homes were established in watering places and mountain resorts. To them we were able to send our convalescents for recuperation, thus greatly expediting their return to Class A combat condition. They served a very useful purpose and, as a military asset, their establishment should always be encouraged.

Detailed Narrative of American Red Cross Hospitalization and Related Activities of that Society in the A. E. F.: During the early period of the development of the A. E. F. American Red Cross hospitals played a very important part in the care of our sick and wounded. For that reason, and also that there may be a record of the very valuable assistance rendered by the Red Cross, this subject is treated below in some detail.

From the beginning of the war the American Red Cross had rendered vital aid to the French War Department. The scope of its work became very greatly augmented upon the entrance of the United States in the war.

One of its first endeavors at this time was the taking over of the American Ambulance. As has been explained elsewhere, this institution was organized by the American Colony in PARIS shortly after the beginning of the war. The French Government furnished the building, a partially completed school located at NEUILLY, a suburb of PARIS. The equipment and maintenance of this ambulance or hospital was assured by voluntary contributions from the American people. The professional personnel was composed of eminent American surgeons who served without compensation. The hospital developed into a splendid institution, capable of accommodating 1,000 patients. It received only French wounded. Without doubt, there was not a better institution of its kind in Europe at the time the Headquarters of the A. E. F. arrived in France. The hospital was not only perfectly equipped, but it had provided in addition an efficient ambulance service and the most complete hospital train at the service of the French Government.

In July, 1917, the Red Cross began negotiations for the taking over of the support and management of the hospital. On July 20, 1917, G. O. 17, A. E. F., accepted the hospital from the Red Cross and its designation became American Red Cross Military Hospital No. 1. It had, however, been stipulated in this transfer of control that it should continue to receive only French soldiers. The hospital was placed under command of an officer of the Medical Corps of the army and gradually the volunteer personnel was replaced, very largely by officers, nurses, and enlisted men of the army.

In preparing a hospitalization program for the A. E. F. the Chief Surgeon was instructed by the C-in-C that no A. E. F. hospitals should be located in PARIS. This was apparently due to the desire of the C-in-C to reduce the number of Americans in PARIS to the absolute minimum, and also to the belief that the American sector of the line would be so far to the east that hospitals in PARIS would not be needed. In spite of the intention to maintain only a very small garrison in and about PARIS, it early became evident that a very considerable number of men would always be stationed there. At first, arrangements were made with the French to hospitalize our sick in French military hospitals. The differences in standards of hospital care, the barrier of language, and the inability to get accurate records of cases admitted produced a most unsatisfactory situation. Owing to the prohibition mentioned above, no A. E. F. hospitals could be established in PARIS and it, therefore, became necessary to appeal to the Red Cross to provide additional hospital facilities. This was done and a number of so-called Red Cross military hospitals were opened under that designation, although the personnel of the various staffs was almost entirely furnished by the army.

In the meantime the provision of A. E. F. hospitals progressed according to the approved program. These hospitals were located at the base ports, along the Line of Communications, and in the advanced area in the general vicinity of the TOUL and VERDUN sectors.

Early in the spring of 1918 the 26th Division was sent into the trenches in the SOISSONS area. This part of the front was so far removed from that which it was considered would become the American sector that it became necessary to make provision for the hospitalization of our sick and wounded in an area where no A. E. F. hospitals existed. In this emergency the French were appealed to and permission was given by them to send our patients to Red Cross Military Hospital No. 1 in PARIS. This was a most generous act on the part of the French, inasmuch as it closed to them the best equipped hospital in France. It also relieved the A. E. F. and the Red Cross of the obligation entered into with the French of maintaining this hospital exclusively for French patients. The French *Service de Sante* took the broad ground that inasmuch as the 26th Division was going into the line as part of a French corps it was their duty to provide the necessary hospitalization. While this was made as a temporary arrangement, it may be noted that this hospital from this time on, to the close of the war, received almost exclusively American patients.

The German offensive of March 21, 1918, had indirectly a far reaching influence on the hospitalization program of the A. E. F. Following this offensive, the American divisions available were placed by the C-in-C at the disposition of the French. In the next few months, A. E. F. divisions were serving with French armies all along the western front. The French had agreed to assume the care of all battle casualties. The A. E. F. divisional sanitary formations under this agreement were to evacuate directly to French evacuation hospitals, from which evacuation would be made by French hospital trains to French hospitals in the Zone of the Interior.

It fell to the lot of the 1st Division to operate first under this agreement. In April, 1918, this division was moved from the eastern part of the line to CHAUMONT-en-VEXIN. A little later it went into line north of BEAUVAIS and northwest of MONTDIDIER, and on May 28, 1918, the successful operation known as the CANTIGNY fight took place. During this operation, the divisional field hospitals were well installed and well equipped and fulfilled their functions in an excellent manner. From that point on difficulties began to occur. The wounded were very much dissatisfied with the care received in French hospitals. The difference in language caused friction, and evacuation in the wretchedly equipped French hospital trains caused further hardship. A very serious administrative difficulty arose through the fact that French hospital trains were distributing American patients to French hospitals from one end of the country to the other. These patients were lost sight of for months at a time. Deaths occurred which were not reported for excessively long periods of time. Nothing but an emergency of the gravest nature could justify the continuance of such a method.

With a view to remedying this condition, permission was requested of the French to install an A. E. F. evacuation hospital at BEAUVAIS. The A. E. F. had no such hospital available at this time. Instead of having the two per division allowed by tables of organization there was less than one quarter of one such hospital for each division in France. However, more such units were expected daily from the United States and it was hoped one or more would arrive in time to meet our needs. Temporarily, the whole question was taken out of our hands by the French decision that no A. E. F. hospital could be established in the rear of this, the 1st Division. At the time, this decision appeared to be arbitrary and unfair. Investigation showed, however, that it was an unavoidable conclusion on the part of the French. It was purely a question of railroad transportation. An evacuation hospital at BEAUVAIS would have meant American hospital trains for moving patients from that hospital to the base hospitals in the interior. Such trains would have set up cross currents of travel and would have required practically a separate line of communication for the service of a single division, comprising only a single element of a French army. This was clearly impossible. The French made a counter-proposition to permit the Red Cross to establish a hospital in BEAUVAIS, this hospital to receive only Americsn patients, but to have a French officer in command and to be evacuated by French hospital trains. This proposition was accepted as offering the only possible solution. While it did not permit the collection of American patients in American base hospitals, it did ensure that the first surgical care was obtained in an American hospital with American personnel. Later an agreement was made whereby all French hospital trains with A. E. F. patients were stopped near PARIS and these patients removed and transported by ambulances to our PARIS hospitals.

This militarized Red Cross hospital at BEAUVAIS was the first institution of the kind established in the Zone of the Army. Its personnel was very largely made up of officers and enlisted men of the Medical Department. It served to fill a very urgent need and did splendid work. Because the establishment of so-called Red Cross hospitals in the Zone of the Army was a radical departure from the generally accepted sphere of usefulness of such institutions, the circumstances surrounding the inauguration of such a policy have been given at some length. As has been shown, the two impelling motives for adopting this solution were, first, that the French railway transportation lines would not permit of having two parallel systems of evacuation going on over the same railway line, particularly on an active front, and, second, the failure of arrival in France of the authorized evacuation hospitals and the shortage of personnel and matériel caused thereby. (It may be added here that never up to the time of the Armistice was there more than 25% of the authorized allowance of these units.)

The end of March and the months of April and May were dark days for the Allied cause. The German lines were steadily nearing PARIS. American divisions were being concentrated both to the north and east of PARIS, but the larger number to the northeast of that city. This was a cause of grave uneasiness for the reason as stated above that no hospitals had been provided in PARIS except the militarized Red Cross ones. As early as April 8, 1918, a member of this section (Colonel Sanford H. Wadhams, G. S.) went to PARIS and assembled the commanding officers of these hospitals in conference with Major James H. Perkins, Q. M. C., Red Cross Commissioner for Europe, and pointed out to these officers the possibility that the PARIS hospitals might have to serve as evacuation hospitals, in which case they would receive wounded directly from the battlefield by ambulance.

Instructions were given to expand each hospital to its maximum, or crisis, capacity and to so organize it that it could receive, operate, and evacuate up to the limit of its possibilities.

The Red Cross was also asked to put up a large tent hospital on the Auteuil Race Course, in the Bois, PARIS. This was agreed to by Major Perkins and work was commenced as soon as the necessary permission to occupy the ground could be obtained from the French authorities.

On May 30, 1918, the 2d Division was being assembled at CHAUMONT-en-VEXIN, northwest of PARIS, and received orders on that day to be prepared to move into line the next day, ostensibly to relieve the 1st Division at CANTIGNY. In the meantime, the situation created by the German advance to the MARNE at CHATEAU-THIERRY produced a most critical situation. The orders of the 2d Division were hastily changed on that day, directing this division to proceed with all haste to MEAUX, to the east of PARIS, and to take position across the CHATEAU-THIERRY---MEAUX road. By June 2 this division was heavily engaged and casualties were occurring in large numbers. The French, who under the agreement referred to above were to hospitalize and evacuate our wounded, found that they were in no position to do so. Their army in that sector had been forced back and the finest evacuation hospitals they possessed, totaling some 45,000 beds, had fallen into the hands of the enemy. Evacuation by hospital train was out of the question because of the congested condition of the railways, incident to supplying the forces engaged. The result was that evacuation by ambulances into the city of PARIS offered the only possibility of clearing the battlefield.

Fortunately, there was a small hospital at JUILLY, about half-way between PARIS and the front. This hospital had been organized and supported by Mrs. Payne Whitney, of New York, and functioned only for French patients. In our extremity, it was taken possession of and the Red Cross were appealed to enlarge it by means of tents as rapidly as possible. A limited amount of additional personnel was provided and this formation was designated for the reception of the most seriously wounded. Its personnel performed prodigies in the next few days, but not more than 25% of the number needed could be furnished.

Ambulances were very scarce. Every available vehicle in the A. E. F., including trucks, were put to work. All the Red Cross ambulances in PARIS were secured, and a few French, and for a week these vehicles were running night and day between the front and PARIS in the effort to keep the battlefield cleared. The distance involved in the round trip was about eighty miles. Half of the distance was over rough cobbled roads. The hospitals in PARIS were poorly adapted to meet this emergency, yet in some way each convoy of wounded was absorbed, operated, and rapidly evacuated by hospital trains into the interior. Medical officers, nurses, and enlisted men worked continuously for 72 hours without sleep, and with but very little food. All in all, it was one of the most remarkable achievements of the war. There was no doubt but that wounded lacked in some respects the care which they should have received. Also, there is no doubt that the long ambulance trip from the front destroyed or reduced the chances of recovery in some of the more serious cases. It could not have been otherwise when the lack of personnel and equipment (ambulances and evacuation hospitals) is considered. The point to be emphasized at this time is that the only hospitals which could be reached were the Red Cross hospitals of PARIS. Without them, it is difficult to conceive how the situation could have been handled.

While the 2d Division was first holding the enemy and later on, in this first week of June, driving him back foot by foot towards CHATEAU-THIERRY, other A. E. F. divisions were being brought into this sector. It was absolutely essential that hospitalization should be provided in this area. There were not sufficient evacuation hospitsls available in France to meet the needs of this and other sectors, so again the Red Cross was called upon and again help was obtained. A French hospital at JOUY-sur-MORIN, south of CHATEAU-THIERRY, was obtained and by the addition of tentage a very complete and well equipped unit was rapidly installed. The personnel was mixed, that is, both army and Red Cross. As was the case in all these hospitals of this type, an officer of the Army Medical Corps was in command and all of the commissioned personnel were of the Medical Corps. This particular hospital was first called Militarized Red Cross Hospital No. 114 and later, with practically the same personnel and equipment, became Evacuation Hospital No. 114.

Fortunately, about this time a few evacuation hospitals arrived from the United States. The first to reach this sector was No. 7, under command of Lieutenant Colonel W. H. Tafft, M. C. A site for it on the grounds of a château in the outskirts of COULOMMIERS was secured and, with the addition of Mobile Hospital No. 1, also just become available, it began to receive patients about June 13. In the next six weeks these two units, combined and functioning as one, handled and evacuated 27,000 casualties--- an achievement probably not surpassed by any similar unit during the war.

Later, or during the latter part of July, one more militarized Red Cross hospital for the advanced area was organized in this same sector. This hospital was known as No. 110. Both of these units were later moved to the west [east], one participating in both the St-MIHIEL and ARGONNE-MEUSE offensives, and the other in the latter. Both functioned as evacuation hospitals and both did most excellent work.

As more and more A. E. F. divisions became engaged the problem of adequate hospitalization and evacuation became increasingly difficult. Evacuation hospitals, while never adequate, began to arrive and every effort was made to provide units of this kind for duty eith the different divisions engaged.

The A. E. F. divisions placed at the disposition of the French were moved here and there with little or no advance notice furnished these headquarters. The necessity of secrecy was also a factor in complicating the problem of providing adequate evacuation hospital facilities. This was particularly true of the Allied offensive beginning July 18, 1918, when surprise was depended upon to play a most important part. Neither the French nor the A. E. F. Medical Service was prepared to meet the situation created at this time.

Criticisms were many regarding the lack of proper care of wounded and slowness in evacuation. There was no doubt as to the truth of these charges but a thorough investigation made by the Inspector General's Department showed conclusively that this condition was not due to Medical Department failure, but to other causes entirely outside of its control or power to remedy. The principal factor in contributing to the creation of this situation was the lack of advance information from the French as to the movements of A. E. F. divisions. After the experience mentioned above, attending the resumption of the offensive by the Allies on July 18, serious Medical Department breakdown was narrowly averted on several occasions and this by good luck rather than by good coordination.

This situation had become so acute that, under date of August 31, the C-in-C informed the French by letter that in the future he must be furnished information regarding the movements of A. E. F. divisions, in order that suitable arrangements for the care of and evacuation of battle casualties might be ensured. From this time on the care and evacuation of our wounded was very good and worked smoothly. While a little later the A. E. F. was given a definite sector, a number of divisions continued to operate exclusively with our Allies. Because of the very great shortage of personnel and evacuation hospitals, this distribution of A. E. F. divisions along the whole western front very seriously complicated the problem of this section. Nevertheless, the situation was met and with a very considerable degree of success.

In the Zone of the Interior the Red Cross organized a very considerable number of hospitals, convalescent homes, homes for nurses on sick or convalescent leave, and dispensaries. In addition, large quantities of medical supplies, consisting of drugs, instruments, hospital equipment, etc., were supplied the A. E. F. Under an agreement made between the Chief Surgeon and the Red Cross a factory was established by the Red Cross which manufactured the thousands upon thousands of splints used by the army, and a second factory was provided for the manufacture of oxygen and nitrous oxide gasses.

Through the acceptance by newspaper correspondents and writers in general of the term Red Cross as indicating all personnel and equipment which is employed in the care of sick and wounded, an erroneous impression has grown up that the Red Cross Society has had complete charge of all medical work, including hospitalization and evacuation of battle casualties. This is to be deplored. The work of the Red Cross has been so splendidly conceived and executed that only harm can result through forcing upon this society credit for lines of endeavor which were outside its sphere of activity. It was only natural perhaps that the newspaper correspondent seeing the Red Cross markings on medical department ambulances, hospital trains, etc., should conclude that they were agencies of the Red Cross Society. It has been unavoidable, therefore, that adverse criticism developed. The Red Cross activities have been of far-reaching scope and of the greatest service in alleviating the suffering of our sick and wounded and the society should not be humiliated by the extravagant claims of misguided publicists.

[The next paragraphs pay tribute to Red Cross personnel and make mention of difficulties under which the Red Cross functioned.]

* * * * * *

MOBILE SANITARY FORMATIONS ACCOMPANYING THE ARMIES IN THE FIELD

These included:

1. Field hospitals.
2. Mobile hospitals.
3. Evacuation hospitals.
4. Red Cross hospitals.

Field Hospitals. There are four (three motorized and one animal-drawn) for each division, equipped and organized according to existing tables, as part of the divisional sanitary train.

Each corps sanitary train has three motorized field hospital companies, provided by withdrawing them from depot and replacement divisions.

The army sanitary train has four motorized companies, shipped direct from the United States as army troops.

Owing to shortage of equipment and transportation, many of the corps and army field hospitals did not become available for use until the concluding phase of our combat activities.

The location of the division field hospitals devolved upon the division surgeon, of the corps field hospitals upon the corps surgeon in consultation with the army surgeon, and of the army field hospitals, the army surgeon.

In each group of four field hospitals, two of them were operated as previously equipped. To one of the field hospitals it was necessary to add extra bedding and a mobile surgical unit in order to provide proper hospitalization for the wounded who could not, without endangering their lives, withstand transportation to other formations in the rear. It is conservatively estimated that this provision of a division field hospital for nontransportable cases resulted in a saving of the lives of 50% of those properly belonging to this category.

It also became necessary to meet another requirement of modern warfare by providing the remaining field hospital in the divisional train with matériel for the treatment of gas casualties. Shower baths, new clothing, and requisite chemicals were provided for these hospitals.

The subject of *triage* and specialization of services, as conducted in these hospitals, is a strictly professional matter and does not require description in this report.

The efficiency of our field hospitals, particularly those belonging to the corps and army trains, was seriously impaired through lack of motor transportation prescribed for them in the tables of organization. The so-called method of pooling transportation resources reacted to the great disadvantage of the wounded, in that the Medical Department, under it, did not possess the mobility to quickly meet the changing conditions of combat activities. In future operations, if it is deemed impracticable to assign to the Medical Department the full allowance of transportation needed by it to function properly, a minimum Medical Department pool, under its exclusive jurisdiction and sufficient to provide for the movement of at least one complete company in a sanitary train, should be allowed.

The field hospital has justified its existence and while its equipment needs some modifications in the light of our recent war experience, its general organization and functions have been found to rest on sound military principles.

If the use of lethal gasses is to be sanctioned in future wars, provision must be made for modification in the equipment of one of the field hospitals to meet this special requirement.

The increasing use of high explosive projectiles, and the mutilating character of the wounds produced by them, will also necessitate the addition to the equipment of one of the field hospitals of extra surgical materiel to care properly for the strictly nontransportable cases.

Mobile Hospitals: The mobile hospital is a new type of unit in our service and was adopted by the Medical Department as a result of the experience of our Allies in this war. These units were designed in order that facilities for competent and immediate surgical aid to the seriously wounded might be brought to the patient close to the battle line, instead of removing any chance of recovery that the nontransportable man might have by conveying him an uncertain distance to a hospital in the rear. It was moved by truck transportation, and with its complete equipment provided a modern surgical hospital of 120 beds. The operating features provided modern facilities for six surgical teams. The special type of tentage and matériel needed for the equipment of these units was obtained in France through contracts placed with the French. It was our aim to provide these hospitals on the ratio of one for each combat division. Upon the conclusion of hostilities we had in operation twelve complete units. These were army units and utilized wherever needed by the chief surgeon of the army concerned. These mobile hospitals, through the results achieved in their operation, have fully justified their existence and should be provided for in future tables of organization as filling a very important role in combat hospitalization.

Mobile Surgical Unit: The adoption of this unit was also the outgrowth of our experience during the present war. This formation enabled us to provide portable sterilizing, X-ray, electric-lighting facilities, and a small operating room for divisional, corps, or army field hospitals, thus enabling them to carry on their surgical operations on the nontransportable wounded. They should also be retained in our equipment manuals and transportation provided for them in the tables of organization, on the basis of one per division.

Evacuation Hospitals. These hospitals are the backbone of all combat hospitalization. Previous to our operations here, existing regulations prescribed that they should be operated as L. O. C. formations. This provision was soon recognized as a tactical mistake and under orders issued by G-4 these headquarters they were divorced from S. O. S. control and made army units.

If they are to function properly, the location of these hospitals is a matter of the utmost importance. Their primary function is indicated by their name. Aside from the small percentage of very seriously wounded who must be hospitalized in them because they cannot withstand transportation to the rear, evacuation hospitals are merely relay or clearing stations in the hospitalization and evacuation chain of an army. Accordingly, they must be located on, or near, standard guage railroad sidings, readily accessible to hospital trains. This permits of a steady stream of evacuation from them to the base hospitals in the rear, which are designed for the definitive treatment of wounded.

In estimating total bed resources, the temporary accommodations provided in evacuation hospitals should never be included. A patient admitted to, and occupying a bed in, an evacuation hospital in the morning may, and probably will, be evacuated by hospital train to a base hospital in the rear and occupy a bed there on the night of the same day.

During extensive operations, the location of evacuation hospitals away from railheads is a tactical blunder. Even when troops are moving forward, from a practical standpoint, much more efficient results are achieved by retaining an evacuation hospital at the railhead and transporting the wounded even a great distance to that hospital, than by moving the evacuation hospital, thus separating it from sources of supply and necessitating evacuation of post-operative cases to railheads by ambulance.

According to the shipping schedule these hospitals were to be provided automatically at the rate of two for each division. This program was never realized and at no time during combat activities did we have at hand a sufficient number of these important hospitals equipped and efficiently functioning. As prescribed by tables of organization, each provided a bed capacity of 432. To meet the varying conditions of static and mobile warfare, it was recognized early in our operations here that they should be organized on a 1,000-bed basis.

Another factor in actuating this increase in the capacity of the evacuation hospitals was their failure to arrive, as provided for in the shipping schedule, and the urgent necessity of more than doubling the capacity of each hospital. In no other way was it possible to care for and evacuate battle casualties. Eventually, this organization was adopted for units arriving from the United States, as a result of cabled representations made from this side. This 1,000-bed capacity was tentatively divided into two sections; first, a mobile section of 500 beds capacity, consisting only of the essential equipment and providing folding cots; second, a demi-fixed section containing beds, mattresses, and a more liberal hospitalization equipment for a similar number of beds. The mobile section was provided with tentage and whenever transportation was available could be quickly located wherever needed. The fixed section was usually installed in such buildings as could be found for shelter, being moved to take its place alongside of the tented mobile section when transportation by rail or truck became available.

Annexes of these evacuation hospitals were operated for special treatment of gas, neurological, contagious, and other cases.

Red Cross Hospitals: These hospitals were permitted to function in the Zone of Armies only through urgent necessity. The Medical Department was at all times so short of matériel that it became necessary in emergencies to call upon the Red Cross to furnish tentage, equipment, and some personnel to meet our needs. These hospitals functioned in the same manner as our own evacuation hospitals and under the command of an officer of the Medical Department. They rendered exceptionally efficient service. Two of them were utilized during the CHATEAU-THIERRY operations, and two during the St-MIHIEL---ARGONNE offensives.

IV. OTHER AGENCIES, RELATING TO HOSPITALIZATION OR EVACUATION, ESTABLISHED OR ORGANIZED IN THE ZONE OF THE ARMIES FOR THE SERVICE OF AN ARMY OR GROUP OF ARMIES

Medical Department Concentration Area: (JOINVILLE, HAUTE-MARNE.) The establishment of these areas is an important link in meeting hospitalization and evacuation demands incident to combat activities. Under conditions existing during operations in France the Medical Department mobile formations belonging to the armies were landed at base ports and dispersed to various localities in the S. O. S. for the purpose of securing equipment. After being equipped, there arose the problem of securing transportation to, and a location for them in, the combat area. To bridge this gap we soon faced an urgent need for the selection and designation of a place properly located in the Zone of the Armies, to which incoming sanitary formations, particularly evacuation and mobile hospitals, ambulance companies, surgical teams, and other auxiliary personnel and equipment for front line work could be sent for the purpose of mobilization, equipment, training, and assignment.

Accordingly, upon our recommendation, and with the approval of the French, a medical department concentration area was designated and set aside at JOINVILLE for the exclusive use of sanitary formations. This area comprised approximately twenty-five square miles, and contained nine villages which afforded billeting capacity for about 500 officers and nurses and 10,000 enlisted men. From it good roads led to all parts of the American front and the distance was such that any sector could be reached by motor transport in only a few hours. In addition, it was located on several railroads which admirably served for the purpose of assembling the units arriving from base ports and their distribution by rail to the remoter parts of the front if the need should arise.

Prior to the establishment of our concentration area at JOINVILLE we lacked the means of providing for reserve units and keeping in close supply liaison with the armies. None of the sanitary formations temporarily kept there were established for the purpose of receiving patients. It was our aim, however, to have one of each type of unit set up from time to time in adjoining fields for purposes of demonstration and training. In order that trained units so held in reserve might be thrown in behind any part of the line, as dictated by the necessity of the military situation, geographic proximity and good roads with adequate railroad facilities are important factors in determining the location of a concentration area of this character.

The operation of these areas is somewhat as follows: The personnel of all army and corps mobile sanitary formations upon arrival at a base port are sent directly to the area. A supply depot is established in the area with sufficient matériel on hand at all times to equip these units fully as they arrive. After equipment has been turned over to the unit, the personnel is given a quick course of training in the demonstration hospital established there. In other words, they are given a working view of the equipment and functions of the various types of hospitals they are to operate in the field. Being established at a central but advanced point immediately behind the Zone of Operations, these mobile formations, by use of truck transportation, can be quickly moved to any part of the line to meet emergencies.

These areas also provide for rest periods for the personnel of mobile formations engaged in active operations and afford an opportunity for overhauling and repair of equipment. Overworked personnel can be sent back to the area for needed rest, being replaced by fresh personnel from the area, without requiring any changes in transportation or equipment.

The value of these areas was so amply demonstrated, even during the brief period in which the JOINVILLE area was operated, that the necessary overhead for their establishment in future wars should be authorized in the tables of organization.

Convalescent Depots: The need for these units in an army, as part of an army organization, had long been recognized, but owing to the scarcity of personnel and matériel it was impossible to proceed with their establishment until the concluding phase of our combat activities. When the Armistice was declared the Medical Department was in the process of establishing one of these large depots at REVIGNY for use of the First Army.

These convalescent depots must not be confused with convalescent camps operating in conjunction with the large hospital centers in the rear, or S. O. S. A constant and serious strain was thrown upon our evacuation service, as represented in hospital trains, through the fact that in our efforts to keep sufficient beds available in evacuation hospitals it became necessary to evacuate to distant points in the rear the slightly wounded as well as sick, even though they showed a reasonable expectancy of returning to duty within a few days.

[The report here discusses the need for convalescent depots in conjunction with evacuation hospitals and the importance of their location well forward.]

* * * * * *

V. GENERAL REVIEW OF MOBILE (COMBAT) HOSPITALIZATION AND EVACUATION EARLY PERIOD---TRAINING IN TRENCH WARFARE

This embraced the period of training in the trenches, with our troops usually brigaded with the French. Because of the peculiar geographical, tactical, and organizational conditions, the direction of this phase of hospitalization and evacuation devolved upon G-4, through its Medical Group. There was gracually evolved a situation whereby the functions of the S. O. S., (Chief Surgeon, A. E. F.), with reference to the mobile sanitary formations operating in the Zone of the Armies, resolved themselves into those of procurement, supply, and transportation to the forward areas.

In providing for battle casualties, main reliance was placed on evacuation hospitals. As above stated, for each division sent to France, the shipping schedule called for the coincident despatch of two evacuation hospitals. For some reason not yet known here, and despite repeated appeals by cable to the War Department, this automatic supply was never realized and shortage of evacuation hospital personnel and equipment was one of the principal factors in creating perpetual and well warranted anxiety as to our ability to meet the forthcoming combat obligations.

In the early period of A. E. F. activities, this shortage did not cause any grave concern. With the stage set up, as it were, in the form of fixed hospitalization, in the rear, fairly well established, the problem of finding adequate hospitalization to meet the needs of our forces engaged in training for trench warfare was easily solved. Static conditions prevailed. This situation of immobilization had existed sufficiently long to permit the French to establish well-organized and equipped hut evacuation hospitals behind their trenches, or in lieu of complete construction, they had taken over and altered existing buildings for these purposes. These French formations offered every facility for carrying on the treatment of the wounded along modern lines. Coincident with the arrival of one of our divisions in the trenches it was arranged with the French to have them relinquish to us on a temporary or a permanent status one or more of these hospitals. Many of the hospitals taken over by us from the French in this manner were transferred with full equipment. In these cases it only became necessary to send in our medical personnel and immediately begin functioning as an American hospital and caring for our own cases. However, this very desirable mutual cooperation existed only in fairly restricted sections, notably in the TOUL, LUNEVILLE, and BACCARAT regions, where the greater part of our early training in trench warfare was conducted. In the remoter regions, to which it was sometimes necessary to send our divisions for training purposes or to relieve French organizations in quite sectors of the line, we were not accorded this privilege of taking over French hospitals, sick and wounded of our forces being sent to nearby French hospitals administered with French personnel.

[The next paragraphs discuss the difficulties encountered in the treatment of casualties hospitalized by the French and in providing strictly American hospitalization.]

* * * * * *

The German offensive of March 21, 1918, created an entirely new situation on all parts of the Allied front. Up to that time hospitalization had been comparatively a simple matter. This German offensive caused a reversion from static or trench warfare to mobile or open warfare. Incident to the changes daily taking place in the surging battle lines, the stationary hutted evacuation hospital became relatively useless and, for purposes of immediate combat hospitalization, a thing of the past.

To maintain hospitalization abreast of the lines, the utilization of tentage and such existing buildings as could be found and were habitable became necessary. Prior to this era, motor transportation played a relatively unimportant role. With its advent, adequate transportation facilities became a crying necessity. As is well known, so far as the A. E. F. was concerned, these resources were woefully lacking.

As the Medical Department did not have at hand the mobile hospitalization provided for in the shipping schedule, this shortage, combined with limited transportation facilities, seriously increased our operating handicaps. Prior to the German offensive of March 21, 1918, we always knew sufficiently in advance where our divisions were to be placed in training in the front line and had ample time to prepare to meet their needs. Quickly following in the train of this offensive, the locations of our divisions on any part of the front were governed solely by existing military exigencies. Thus commenced our first virtual hospitalization and evacuation problem. In quick succession these problems became manifold. Facing a critical shortage in personnel, equipment, transportation, and many other essentials, the summer of 1918 became a period pregnant with anxiety and deep concern to the Medical Department of these forces. A division was here today, away tomorrow, and thrown into the battle line next day, perhaps on some distant front. The only local combat occurring during this period that threw any strain upon our hospitalization resources was the action at SEICHEPREY on April 20. In this, the 26th Division became engaged and confronted us with our first real evacuation task. We had already taken over from the French existing hospitals in the TOUL and AULNOIS regions which provided hospitalization sufficient to permit of excellent care being given all wounded from the action.

BATTLE OF PICARDY; OPERATIONS AT CANTIGNY

The pioneer movement in our divorce from the satisfactory conditions of static warfare to the anxious moments of mobile warfare devolved upon the 1st Division. As previously mentioned, this division was hurriedly withdrawn from the TOUL sector and placed at the disposition of the French in reserve behind the MONTDIDIER salient. We possessed no hospitalization in that region short of PARIS. As the division was placed under the French the responsibility for hospitalizing the sick and wounded devolved upon and was assumed by the French. As above stated, this obligation was in keeping with the ruling previously adopted during our period of trench warfare instruction. In orders prepared by the French, and directing the despatch of the division to the new front, it was specified that all hospitalization (except that furnished by divisional field hospitals) and evacuation of our forces would be provided by them. These orders also prescribed the liaison to be established between our own field hospitals and the French formations further to the rear. This order was received by us with considerable apprehension. Facing not only a most serious shortage in personnel and equipment for army sanitary units and the frankly stated objection of the French to the establishment of A. E. F. evacuation hospitals in the rear of divisions operating with the French, it was, nevertheless, very early recognized that every effort must be made to provide for the hospitalization and evacuation of our own wounded.

On May 28 the 1st Division participated in the battle of CANTIGNY. We had notice of the impending attack to be made by this division and preceding its execution sent a member of this group to that front for the purpose of arranging for the hospitalization facilities to be provided.

Repeated efforts were made to secure permission from the French to establish at BEAUVAIS at least one American evacuation hospital in the rear of the division. These requests were disapproved by the French on the grounds that a dual hospitalization and evacuation service in that region would, in view of existing traffic conditions, result only in confusion.

At the request of this section, the American Red Cross appealed to the French for permission to establish a hospital at BEAUVAIS to serve this division. The growing dissatisfaction as to the treatment being received by our wounded in the French formations made it necessary to leave no effort unmade to remedy this condition. The permission of the French to establish a Red Cross hospital was obtained on condition that it should be known as a French military hospital, with a French medical officer in command. Thus arose the necessity of permitting the Red Cross to enter the zone of the Armies to assist the Medical Department in its scheme of hospitalization.

A suitable building was obtained and with a mixed army and Red Cross personnel, the hospital was equipped and rendered excellent service. The French medical officer in command was insisted upon by the French authorities for the reason that by keeping it a French hospital they could control its evacuation. This was accomplished by French hospital trains, as no permission could be obtained to utilize A. E. F. trains for this purpose. The objections of the French were, without doubt, well grounded and this condition is not detailed here in a spirit of criticism, but merely to set forth the difficulties surrounding the hospitalization and evacuation of battle casualties wherever American divisions were operating under French command. While this arrangement had many advantages, it was still far from perfect for the reason that the patients after receiving primary care in the so-called Red Cross hospital were evacuated on French trains and were distributed in French hospitals all over France. After a long delay, attended with many conferences and much negotiation, authority was ultimately obtained to remove, at a station in the vicinity of PARIS, all American patients passing through on French trains. A small detail of sanitary personnel was placed at this station with sufficient ambulances to evacuate our battle casualties to American hospitals in PARIS. Under the conditions as outlined above, it is unavoidable that there should have been criticism of the care given our wounded. It is true, however, that no effort was spared to better these conditions.

It was in the operations about CANTIGNY that this group first started the system of sending out a member of the section to represent it in all important field operations. Very effective coordination resulted from this action. Our representative had the freedom of action and latitude that could not otherwise have been exercised by an officer attached to the operating forces He kept in close touch with this office by telephone or telegraph, wnd also with the officers in charge of the hospitalization reservoirs to which he directed evacuations. With hospital trains operating under G-4, his liaison with this service also proved most advantageous. During quiet periods he automatically returned to and resumed his duties in this office. The office force itself from March on habitually worked far into the night and was able to keep in constant touch with field operations and its representatives there.

Following the CANTIGNY battle, the 2d Division was also removed from the comparatively quiet LORRAINE sector to a place in reserve near MONTDIDIER.

SECOND BATTLE OF THE MARNE

With the beginning of the Germans' AISNE offensive, the latter part of May, 1918, it became necessary to throw in other American divisions hurriedly on the enemy's front before PARIS. The first American divisions to be utilized in the repulse of this offensive were the 2d and 3d. At the height of our MARNE activities we had nine divisions intermittently engaged. This created a new hospitalization problem. As in their retreat the French had lost all of their evacuation hospitals in that region, they were not in a position to assume the additional burden of caring for our casualties. Unfortunately, this condition was not admitted by the French as soon as it should have been.

For the first time, the French not only permitted, but assisted us in every way to begin the establishment of our own chain of hospitalization behind our divisions and evacuation from them by means of our own hospital trains to fixed American formations in the rear. However, our initial efforts met with almost insuperable obstacles. Behind the 2d Division the best hospitalization that we could provide under the circumstances was established at MEAUX and UUILLY-DAMMARTIN. The rapid German advance had so demoralized the evacuation service that it was impossible to operate hospital trains. Consequently, evacuation by ambulance, and in lieu of ambulance, by truck, from 40 to 100 kilometers into our hospitals at PARIS was at first necessary. By concentrating all our available resources and borrowing from the French, we were able to provide 200 ambulances for the 2d Division, which were barely sufficient to meet the needs, owing to the great length of our evacuation avenue. For the immediate evacuation of PARIS, another 100 ambulances had to be brought into service. As the other divisions in rapid succession were concentrated on the MARNE, our activities upon that salient extended in a semicircle, of which CHATEAU-THIERRY was the pivot. All available mobile hospitalization, in the form of evacuation and mobile hospitals, was concentrated on that front. As far as possible, buildings were utilized, but in this new phase of open warfare our main reliance for shelter frequently had to be provided by the use of tentage. The early phase of the battle found us confronted with transportation difficulties and shortage of personnel, hospital equipment, and ambulances. The evacuation into PARIS, our nearest hospital center, which was gradually expanded for and during the emergency to a capacity of 10,000 beds, was continued by ambulance, until the railroad situation permitted the use of hospital trains, which we had garaged there to meet this emergency.

Our evacuation hospitals, which were gradually brought up, did not possess the mobility that was necessary to meet the changing military conditions existing at that time. The shortage of motor transportation was primarily responsible. Divisions were hurriedly withdrawn from one part of the line and thrown into another part alongside of the French without advance notice to the medical representatives in the field and at times evidently without due notice being furnished the tactical headquarters of the PARIS Group, then established at la FERTE-sous-JOUARRE, under which title all American divisions operating in that region functioned.

This condition of affairs created a situation on the SOISSONS front that evoked considerable unjustifiable criticism of the Medical Department. The 1st and 2d Divisions were thrown into battle there without advising the American Headquarters, and as we had no hospitalization established in that sector the heavy casualties sustained were not promptly and well cared for. As it developed, moreover, the French were no better prepared to meet the hospitalization obligations that this new situation imposed upon them. This incident was regrettable, in that we had, packed and available for quick transportation, a mobile and an evacuation hospital to meet an emergency of this nature. Had we had notice of this impending tactical change, we could have established hospitalization of our own behind the troops engaged on the SOISSONS front. The French Medical Department was greatly embarassed by the large number of wounded that flowed into their organizations from our two divisions engaged there and while the responsibility for the care of our sick and wounded devolved upon them, events showed that they were woefully unprepared to receive them. The evacuation of our own men from that sector was eventually carried out under the direction of our G-4 representative on our own trains, hurriedly sent up on his call. This situation, which is purposely dwelt upon at some length, eventually rendered it necessary for these headquarters to inform the French that thereafter, when American divisions were brigaded with them, due notice of impending movements must be furnished to the proper American authorities in order that American hospitalization and evacuation facilities could be provided for them, and that the French designate in their battle order suitable sites for the location of American Evacuation Hospitals.

With the massing of our troops on the true CHATEAU-THIERRY salient, we were able to utilize our limited hospitalization and evacuation facilities to maximum advantage, but only be carefully husbanding our inadequate resources and working our insufficient personnel to the limit of human endurance.

In marked contrast to the chaotic conditions that obtained on the SOISSONS front were the smoothness and precision with which operations on and evacuation of thousands of American wounded flowing into our American hospital formations from our divisions engaged on the CHATEAU-THIERRY front were handled. For example, on the ninth day of the offensive and counteroffensive, operations and evacuations had carried through with a regularity that still left us with 3,800 vacant beds in our evacuation hospital chain there. Here our forces were operating with the French Sixth Army and we were given unrestricted opportunity to conduct our own hospitalization and evacuation. The work carried on there under most trying circumstances challenged any criticism.

The ambulance shortage was so acute that trucks had to be utilized in the transportation of the wounded. By working the personnel day and night, oftentimes without adequate rest, and operating our hospital train and ambulance evacuations to maximum possibilities, we were barely able to meet our requirements. Reserve personnel and hospitalization were withdrawn from wherever they could be spared and sent there for duty.

One evacuation hospital, urgently needed, through lack of motor transport had to be ordered up by rail. It was four days en route from BAZOILLES-sur-MEUSE to COULOMMIERS. Personnel in the region of LANGRES, also urgently needed, could not be provided transportation until the French were appealed to and furnished us with motor camions for the movement.

When the maximum combat activities of our troops developed, provision of and supervision over hospitalization and evacuation provided for them centralized in the Medical

Group attached to G-4 at these headquarters. One or more representatives of this group was constantly in the field during the more important operations on the MARNE, submitting recommendations for coordination by these headquarters, and, at times, actively directing the operations of the service at the front. One of the G-4 B representatives sent to the CHATEAU-THIERRY front acted as and was assigned as chief surgeon of the PARIS Group (Colonel Paul C. Hutton, M. C.). At the height of our activities there the hospitalization provided for our forces was six evacuation hospitals, two American Red Cross hospitals, and two mobile hospitals, with a total bed capacity of approximately 7,000. These were successively located at MEAUX, JUILLY, JOUY-sur-MORIN, COULOMMIERS, la FERTE-sous-JOUARRE, SERY-MAGNEVAL, CHATEAU-THIERRY, VILLERS-COTERETS, CREZANCY, and COINCY. Evacuations, which were first regulated from the station at CREIL and then transferred to the more centralized station at le BOURGET, were largely carried on through the operation of American hospital trains garaged at PANTIN, PARIS. We frequently had to borrow trains from the French, but during the height of activities we had sixteen trains of our own in operation there. * * *

CHAMPAGNE DEFENSIVE

During this period one of our divisions (42d) was detached for service with the French army operating east of RHEIMS for the purpose of resisting the German offensive of July 15 in that region. From a hospitalization and evacuation standpoint, this division operated remote from our resources. However, the first time, and overcoming the objections of the French, active steps were taken to provide the sick and wounded of a division operating under French control with our own hospitalization. An evacuation hospital and a mobile hospital were established behind their line, in the region of CHALONS-sur-MARNE, and handled all the battle casualties occurring in that division. These formations were evacuated by our own trains to base hospitals in the rear, and evacuation of slightly wounded was made by ambulances and trucks to our camp hospital at MAILLY. When the 42d Division was moved to the CHATEAU-THIERRY front these formations were transported with the division on trucks borrowed from the French. * * *

ST-MIHIEL---ARGONNE-MEUSE OFFENSIVES

As the operations of the American First Army are covered in statistical detail in the report of the chief surgeon of that army (Colonel Alexander N. Stark, M. C.), a copy of his report has been obtained. * * * The hospitalization and evacuation resources, largely procured through the agency of G-4 and placed at the disposition of the First Army, are set forth in detail in that report. As a reference or guide, its annexation will serve a useful purpose and permit us to restrict and confine our remarks to generalities. * * *

In the interim between the reduction of the MARNE salient, with gradually lessening American participation there, and our preparations for the battle of St-MIHIEL, shipments of materiel from the States had somewhat, although far from satisfactorily, relieved our critical shortages. In other words, medical department personnel and materiel were constantly arriving but not in proportion to meet initial shortages and at the same time keep pace with the increased needs resulting from augmentation in arrival of combatant troops.

The Medical Department, through its G-4 representatives, immediately took steps to cooperate with the chief surgeon of the First Army in providing, as far as possible, adequate hospitalization for the large number of casualties expected to occur in the forthcoming battle of St-MIHIEL. As the number of casualties apprehended happily were not realized, we found ourselves for the first time facing a conforting situation of over-hospitalization. Had the number of casualties that we had every reason to expect actually developed, the Medical Department would again have found itself short in resources and embarrassed in meeting its obligations. Even at this time our critical shortages were personnel, hospital equipment, ambulances, and hospital trains. The shortage in personnel was particularly acute and as we had already withdrawn from base hospitals all the personnel that could be spared without seriously jeopardizing their efficiency, to help out in this emergency, it was necessary to secure authority for the assignment of 1,200 men of the line from the Orthopedic Training Battalion to our mobile sanitary formations. These men suffered from flat feet or other joint infirmities, but their acquisition at this critical time tided us over another difficulty.

Our borrowing resources were exercised to the utmost possibilities. Ambulances and hospital trains were borrowed from the French. The situation seemed so acute that it was necessary to detach fifteen ambulance sections sent to Italy direct from the United States for the Italian Government and bring them up for our use in the battle.

Following the reduction of the St-MIHIEL salient, the greatly augmented American First Army began to prepare for further, and what proved to be final, combat activities in the ARGONNE-MEUSE offensive. This was divided into a first, second, and final phase, leading up to the declaration of the Armistice. This, the first time that the American forces acted as a unit on a broad scale, found the Medical Department still facing critical shortages in equipment, personnel, hospitalization, and ambulances. During the entire operations of these offensives, a representative of the Medical Group, G-4 (Lieutenant Colonel Leon C. Garcia, M. C.), remained at Headquarters of the First Army, SOUILLY, for the purpose of coordinating medical department activities, and the other representatives were frequently at the front.

OPERATIONS OF AMERICAN DIVISIONS WITH FRENCH NORTH OF

CHALONS-sur-MARNE, OCTOBER, 1918

During the ARGONNE-MEUSE offensive it became necessary to detach two American divisions from the First Army and assign them to the French Fourth Army, engaged in the offensive taking place to our immediate left. These divisions were the 2d and 36th. They were not used by the French simultaneously, one division being held in reserve while the other was in the line. The 2d Division relieved a French division on the front line near SOMME-PY on Seotember 30. On the night of October 9/10 it was relieved by the 36th Division. After its withdrawal on October 10, the 2d Division gradually moved back to a position in the neighborhood of Ste-MENEHOULD, arriving there about October 25 and again rejoining the American First Army. The 36th Division was relieved on October 28 and also proceeded, on October 30, to the Ste-MENEHOULD region for return to the control of the American First Army. While on this detached service with the French Fourth Army these divisions naturally became separated from the administrative and supply control of the American First Army. Accordingly, it devolved upon this section to arrange for the hospitalization, supply, and evacuation of these divisions during their period of separation from the American army. Evacuation Hospitals No. 3 and No. 5, Mobile Hospital No. 7, Evacuation Ambulance Companies No. 5 and No. 7, and a medical supply dump were withdrawn from the army and assigned to positions at Mt-FRENET and La VEUVE, in the rear of the American divisions, and north of CHALONS-sur-MARNE. These sanitary units were located entirely under tentage on two French sidings which were installed for serving French evacuation hospitals at that point, and were entirely self-sustaining in every detail.

As these divisions became engaged in action in rotation only, the hospitalization provided for them was entirely adequate and cared for the comparatively heavy casualties sustained by them with creditable efficiency and despatch. This was one of the operations carried out with the French where the disposition of sanitary units, even before casualties occurred, left us with a feeling of assurance that every conceivable contingency had been provided for. The evacuation of these American hospitals was carried out in this territory under French control by American hospital trains furnished through our St-DIZIER regulating station, and immediately regulated by our G-4 representative stationed at the subsidiary regulating station at CONNANTRE.

OPERATIONS OF THE II CORPS

This corps comprised American divisions attached to the British Expeditionary Forces. They arrived via England and, under the ABBEVILLE Agreement, the Medical Department organizations attached to them were furnished British equipment. All the hospitalization was provided and exclusively supervised, as far as this office was concerned, by the British authorities. There was a provision, however, in the ABBEVILLE Agreement which proved to be of inestimable advantage to the A. E. F. Medical Department. We refer to the provision whereby the British requested that we limit the sanitary train personnel attached to those divisions to one-half of the complement authorized in the tables of organization. It seems that this was necessitated through shortage of British equipment and the fact that a well-organized overhead in British hospitalization and evacuation resources was always locally available for the use of these divisions. Consequently, approximately the personnel of two field hospitals and two ambulance companies of each of the ten divisions brigaded with the British were sent to France on A. E. F. shipping and concentrated in the 17th Training Area. As there was little likelihood that this sanitary personnel would ever be called for while the divisions continued to operate with the British Expeditionary Forces, this personnel, in the form of ambulance companies and field hospitals, in the 17th Area, and despite their total lack of equipment, practically saved the day for us during the operations of the summer. In consultation with G-3, these headquarters, an arrangement was made whereby this personnel could be utilized wherever their services were most needed. They were thrown in behind the line to augment depleted Medical Department establishments, and some of the ambulance companies were utilized to good advantage at base ports in rapidly assembling and forwarding incoming ambulances so urgently needed at the front. This reserve, that so fortunately came to hand in this manner in our hour of need, was one of the most important factors that enabled us to carry on and discharge our weighty obligations at that time.

OPERATIONS ON THE BELGIAN FRONT

During the final phase of our combat activities, two divisions (37th and 91st) were detached from the First Army and sent to Belgium to cooperate with the French and Belgian forces in the offensive then taking place on that front. For these divisions, a regulating station was established at Dunkerque. An evacuation hospital and a mobile hospital and two evacuation ambulance companies were sent there by rail and established behind the divisions to care for our own sick and wounded. The casualties were relatively few, although approximately 4,000 were handled by these units in a brief compass of time. The entire medical department activities were supervised by a medical representative from G-4 (Lieutenant Colonel Leon C. Garcia, M. C.), sent there for that purpose.

OPERATIONS ON THE ITALIAN FRONT

Our activities here were practically nil. One regiment of infantry (332d) was detached from the 83d Division and sent there. With this regiment we sent a fully equipped field hospital, with such additional X-ray and other surgical facilities as might be needed. Extra surgical personnel was also attached to this hospital. As we were so short of ambulances, the Chief of the United States Army Ambulance Service attached to the Italian army was directed to provide the necessary ambulance facilities to meet the needs of this regiment. A base hospital (102) was sent to Italy direct from the United States for the purpose of assisting the Italian Medical Department in the hospitalization of their casualties. With the arrival of our small force in Italy, authority was obtained from the Italian Government to admit to Base Hospital No. 102 such Americans as could not be hospitalized in the field hospital referred to. G-4 kep in close touch with the senior medical officer on duty with this regiment, with a view to meeting his supply and other needs. A small medical supply dump was established in Italy. To reinforce their surgical facilities, arrangements had been made with the American Red Cross to provide the medical organization on duty with that regiment a mobile hospital, then at the disposition of the Red Cross in Italy. However, the combat activities of our troops there were so slight that it was not necessary to take advantage of this loan.

OPERATIONS IN RUSSIA

While passing through England, one regiment of infantry (339th) and the 1st Battalion of the 310th Engineers were detached from the 85th Division and sent with the Allied Expeditionary Forces to western Russia. None of the details of the hospitalization of that force was handled in this office. One field hospital and one ambulance company (337th) accompanied those forces to Russia. From reports received, it seems that these medical units furnished all the hospitalization that was required throughout their operations there.

VI. MISCELLANEOUS TOPICS

MEDICAL REPRESENTATION AT REGULATING STATIONS

Regulating stations are established and administered by the A. C. of S., G-4, G. H. Q.

These stations are the funnel through which our sick and wounded are evacuated from our mobile sanitary formations at the front to our base hospitals in the rear.

Early in our regulating experience the necessity of assigning to the staff of the regulating officer a member of the Medical Department who could supervise the operation of hospital trains, became evident. Up to the period of the second battle of the MARNE, in the summer of 1918, no great strain had been thrown in our evacuation facilities. At that time, we were fairly well along toward the completion of the delivery of the first ter hospital trains for which an order had been placed in England in the fall of 1917. The large number of casualties occurring in the MARNE battle were evacuated through the regulating station at Le BOURGET. At that place there was stationed an officer of the Sanitary Corps (Medical Department) who directed the movements of our hospital trains for the regulating officer. As the evacuation requirements increased, it became evident that there should be organized in each regulating station a Medical Group to handle the evacuation records and movements of hospital trains. The results achieved by this Medical Group at regulating stations have been so uniformly satisfactory that the staff of no regulating officer in the future should be considered complete without one.

During extensive operations, the efficiency of the Medical Department reposes in the stability of our evacuation service, as represented in the proper coordination of hospital train movements. Hospital trains are assigned to regulating stations on the order of the A. C. of S., G-4, at these headquarters. For example, when plans for the St-MIHIEL offensive were perfected, it was estimated that it would be necessary to place at the disposition of the regulating officers at St-DIZIER and IS-sur-TILLE at least sixty hospital trains. Less than twenty of our own trains were at hand at that time and it was necessary to borrow from the French the additional number needed. As the activities of these regulating stations are described in reports to be rendered to you by the regulating officers, it is not deemed necessary to enter into further details on this subject in this report. It is presumed that a report of the regulating officer will also clearly show the method by which hospital trains are handled and how G-4-B arranged to provide them daily with a sufficient number of bed credits in formations in the rear, to which trains could be despatched.

* * * * * *

HOSPITAL TRAINS

It was recognized, in the formative period of the organization of the A. E. F., that we would need, with our long lines of communication, an unusually large number of hospital trains.

It developed that the British on the Continent and in England were using a standard type of vestibuled hospital train, which, with a few modifications, would admirably serve the purpose of the A. E. F. In the fall of 1917 authority was granted by the C-in-C for the purchase of fifteen of these trains. Upon the conclusion of hostilities a total of thirty-eight of these trains had been ordered, and nineteen were on hand. We also had two hospital trains of French type, turned over to us on a rental basis. With the exception of the latter two mentioned French trains, these trains consisted of sixteen coaches, provided accommodations for 360 lying cases and approximately 600 sitting cases.

Borrowed French hospital trains, by which a considerable portion of our wounded were evacuated, were required to stop at intervals en route for meals, examination of cases, and sometimes removal from the train of dangerously ill patients.

In the English type of train, as adopted by the A. E. F., the vestibuled arrangements, kitchen, operating, staff, supply, and ward cars provided practically a complete rolling hospital which permitted of serving of meals and surgical attention en route, without interruption in transit of the train. * * *

EVACUATION OF BATTLE CASUALTIES FROM THE FRONT
LINE, WITH SPECIAL REFERENCE TO DELAY SOMETIMES
OCCURRING IN ACCOMPLISHING SAME

[This part of the report brings out the difficulties encountered in evacuating battle casualties from the front lines in both trench and open warfare, recounts in some detail routine procedure, mentions the danger of gas gangrene, and places the average time it took a wounded man to reach a triage or sorting station in open warfare at 5 hours and to reach an evacuation hospital at 10 hours.]

UNITED STATES ARMY AMBULANCE SERVICE

The United States Army Ambulance Service was created by General Order No. 75, War Department, 1917. It provided for the organization of a large number of ambulance sections for duty with the French army. In the formation of these units, the organization adopted by the French army was very closely followed. The basis of this system is that the French Ambulance Service is charged only with the transportation of the sick and wounded, and has no dressing station or litter bearer sections, as with us.

[The report here discusses the ambulance sections which were equipped in the spring of 1917 by voluntary contributions from the people of the United States for service with the French army and, based on these units, recommends a modification of American divisional ambulance companies.]

* * * * * *

LIAISON OF THE A. E. F. MEDICAL SERVICE WITH
THAT OF THE ALLIES

The necessity of a close working connection between the Medical Department of the A. E. F. and the same Department of the Allied Armies was early apparent. This was particularly true of our association with the French. At the beginning, the A. E. F. was entirely dependent on the French for the hospitals necessary to care for the sick who began to arrive in France on the first transport and have continued to arrive ever since.

Fortunately, a member of this section (Colonel S. H. Wadhams, G. S. M. C.), had been in France on duty as medical observer for a number of months prior to the entrance of the United States into the war. Before the arrival of Headquarters, A. E. F., the question of hospitalization had been taken up with the French Minister of War. With French officers detailed for that purpose, all the Atlantic ports were visited and inspected as to existing facilities. Work on a camp hospital at the principal debarkation port was begun by the French, and existing French hospitals in the vicinity were vacated and prepared for transfer to the A. E. F. at the earliest moment that personnel should become available.

From this time on the development of the A. E. F. hospitalization program was so intimately associated with the French War Ministry that close contact between the two services was absolutely essential. Moreover, French bureaucratic methods are such that progress in the transaction of business can be made only through the utilization of authorized agents. An officer of this group (Colonel S. H. Wadhams) was, therefore, designated officially as American Liaison Officer with the Office of the *Sous Secretaire d'Etat, du Service de Santé*. Through this officer all matters which it was necessary to take up with the French were handled.

As the A. E. F. grew and the hospitalization program expanded, it became necessary to detail officers for this work on each of the French military regions, normally twenty into which France is divided. Definite rules were laid down covering the acquisition of hospital sites, the taking over of existing hospitals, the leasing of buildings for hospital purposes, and, in general, for the coordination of the two services Gradually all routine matters affecting the different military regions were handled by the local American liaison officer accredited to the regional French Chief Surgeon's Office. Only such questions as involved definition of policies were referred to the central office.

The early establishment of this intimate cordial liaison with the French undoubtedly contributed to a very considerable extent in the development of our hospitalization program. The French *Service de Santé* under the administration of both M. Godard, and later of M. Maurier, as *Sous Secretaire d'Etat du Service de Santé*, gave every possible assistance in the working out of a very difficult and complicated task. While French organization and methods differ materially from the American, there was never any desire manifested by them to require us to conform to theirs. The most complete harmony prevailed and, as stated above, every possible aid was given us, even to the point of crippling their own service, in supplying hospitals and medical material.

PROFESSIONAL SERVICES

Though not an integral part of this group, the Office of the Director of Professional Services was established at these headquarters primarily through the good offices of the A. C. of S., G-4. The wisdom of effecting this intimate liaison of the Professional Services with this group was fully justified by the results achieved. Calls for the assignment of surgical and other specialist medical personnel to various organizations at the front, particularly evacuation hospitals, were sent direct to this group. By carefully husbanding the limited resources and controlling their distribution, through the Director of Professional Services, it was possible to utilize the services of this high-grade personnel to the maximum advantage of our sick and wounded.

During the height of activities, the Professional Services comprised approximately 4,000 officers, nurses, and enlisted men, specially selected for their professional attainments and formed into teams such as surgical, shock, and gas, and so mobilized as to permit them to be sent fully equipped for the work to be expected of them, on short notice, to any part of the front where their services were needed or an emergency existed. * * * It is desired to insert into this record the fact that these services were organized and efficiently directed by Colonel William L. Keller, Medical Corps.

INTER-DEPARTMENTAL RELATIONSHIP AND COOPERATION
AT G. H. Q., A. E. F.

[This section of the report comments upon the spirit of helpful cooperation manifested in the various staff sections.]

* * * * * *

RELATIONS WITH THE FRENCH

This report would not be complete without reference to the cordial spirit of cooperation shown by the French, and their willingness to assist to the full extent of their resources.

Through the French Mission at these headquarters, repeated requests were made for hospitals, hospital trains, ambulances, etc. This help, without which it would have been impossible for the Medical Department to have satisfactorily discharged its obligations, was always forthcoming.

Later, a medical officer, Medecin Major Petit, of the French Medical Department, was, at the request of the A. C. of S., G-4, attached to this group and rendered particularly efficient service in maintaining the close liaison between the two services.

[The remainder of this part of the report lists personnel on duty in G-4-B, commends the office personnel, and pays tribute to the Medical Department personnel of the A. E. F.]

PART II

SUPPLY

In order to recount the development of strategic supply for the Medical Department of the A. E. F., a detailed sketch of its inception and growth will be given. Generally speaking, from both the developmental and operative viewpoint, this subject may be divided into the two phases of procurement and distribution.

I. PROCUREMENT

Automatic Supply Schemes: The original supply studies made by the General Staff and promulgated in the late summer of 1917 contemplated placing supply procurement for the A. E. F. as much as possible upon an automatic basis and assumed the early establishment in France of a 90-day reserve. The accumulation of this 90-day reserve was of primary importance and had of necessity to be incorporated into any procurement plan. Of the total reserve, 15, 30, and 45 days' supply were directed held in the Advance, Intermediate, and Base Sections, respectively.

The automatic unit was the amount of supplies necessary for 25,000 men for one month, and the method of obtaining the reserve was by shipment to France for all troops embarked (with troops when possible), of a four months' supply in addition to initial equipment. It was anticipated that troops en route to A. E. F. would upon arrival at their final station in France have consumed 30 days' supply. This, therefore, would leave a remaining increment of 90 days, which would accrue to the credit of the department in depot storage in France. Thereafter, for each 25,000 troops in France there would be shipped to the A. E. F. one increment of automatic supply.

Building a Supply Reserve: After a tedious detailed study the automatic supply schedules for the Medical Department were elaborated, approved by the General Staff of the S. O. S. and G. H. Q., and forwarded to Washington for their acceptance. They were accepted by the War Department by cable and put into effect June 1, 1918. Up to this time the accumulation of a 90-day reserve for the Medical Department in France had been purely theoretical and not in any sense an actual fact. For one reason or another, but largely because of tonnage, embarkation and debarkation difficulties, the authorized reserve of Medical Department supplies in France did not arrive in correct proportion to the increased strength of the A. E. F. Between April 1, 1918, and October 1 of that year, huge drafts of troops arrive in France. There was absolutely no relationship between their numbers and the amounts of initial and replacement medical supplies which were laid down in France. Naturally these deficiencies were met from stock in A. E. F. depots, with a corresponding sacrifice in reserve. It is believed that certainly a large part of these difficulties may also have been attributable to a lack, in the early days, of good medical representation upon the docks in the U. S. and in France.

Obviously, if the original studies were correct, it was essential that the reserve of supply arrive in France ahead of troops and that it should include complete initial equipments. It was known to the Supply Division, Chief Surgeon's Office, for months that this was not taking place, and it was therefore necessary to give almost equal consideration, in the automatic supply, to the question of accumulation of a reserve as to the automatic factor. There was included, therefore, in automatic factors a proportionately large item of reserve in an attempt to balance depot levels. This meant practically an inflated automatic. This was carefully considered in the letter of transmittal which accompanied this study when it was sent to the War Department. A policy was outlined in this communication of modifying these schedules every month in connection with the level upon items in depot.

Depot stocks at all times in France were unequal and it was known that the modification of this automatic factor would be extremely necessary until these levels flattened out. This would be largely influenced by the success or failure of the Supply Division in the United States in shipping to France the proper reserve.

In the early days of the procurement problem large quantities of useful medical stores were accumulated upon docks in the United States for early shipment to France. Fortunately for the Medical Department, this materiel being available and other supply services being somewhat less fortunate, considerable space was on hand in bottoms coming to France, with the result that prior to December, 1917, sufficient medical supplies arrived to enable the Chief Surgeon's Office to handle the situation. There developed, however, after this time a starvation period in which the supply situation was at all times critical, and only the most strenuous efforts and extremely good judgement of those charged with distribution saved the day for the Medical Department in France.

Purchase of Supplies in Europe: Throughout the period of July to August, 1917, every effort was being made by the General Staff to organize and establish upon a firm basis a system of A. E. F. purchase. Resources in Europe were never negligible, but for the Medical Department the unfortunate side of the situation was that our people needed materiel for immediate delivery, and although considerable quantities were at times quickly obtained, the majority of orders placed required at least six months for delivery.

This materially complicated all efforts to conserve tonnage by acquiring supplies in Europe. With a line of communication several thousand miles long, a large newly-formed army with a new and unusual problem on its hands, the question of forecasting needs to be met by the markets in Europe was an extremely difficult problem. This involved questions of mobile equipment and innumerable smaller items, many of which were already preempted by the British or French. It very largely amounted to accepting for late delivery any materiel which might be available and necessitated acceptance of supplies which under different circumstances would not have been considered for a moment.

The General Purchasing Board which was established in PARIS and London had associated with it a Representative, in both places, from the Medical Department. The Representative in PARIS in the early days was under the Chief Surgeon's Office, Headquarters, A. E. F., although the Chief Surgeon, Line of Communications, was directly responsible for questions of procurement and distribution, and as regards the question of purchase, this status was a complicating feature and it later became the policy of transmitting orders to the Medical Representative with the General Purchasing Board through the Office of the Chief Surgeon, Line of Communications.

The presence in Europe of Medical Department supply men as observers prior to the entrance of the U. S. into the war would have greatly facilitated matters of purchase and, in fact, questions of procurement and distribution generally.

Tonnage Allotments: For the period prior to December 1, 1917, there are no accurate figures for the amount of medical or Red Cross tonnage which came to France. During the following three months, however, it is known that approximately an average of 1,000 short tons of supplies were received in Europe for the Medical Department.

In the earlier studies on tonnage it was estimated by the authorities in the United States that Medical Department tonnage would represent approximately 1% of total A. E. F. tonnage. It was later definitely known that if shipments continued along any such basis on accumulation of reserve in France would never occur, and that the real needs of the situation could be met by allotting to the Medical Department approximately 1.8% of the total tonnage. Such points emphasized the need of better liaison between the Chief Supply Officer and the Surgeon General's Office. Although one supply officer went from this side for a short stay, a real interchange was never established.

In February, 1918, reserve in depots dropped down to the level of approximately 20 days or less. At the request of the Chief Surgeon's Office, the question was energetically taken up by cable with the United States in an effort to clear the docks of accumulated stores and in the course of the next two months medical tonnage jumped several hundred per cent. At this time a forecast of tonnage requirements was carefully worked out, but unfortunately was based on erroneous assumptions with reference to troop movements. It was later found necessary to materially modify this forecast but the original work served as an excellent basis for this revamping. The inability of all supply divisions to foretell accurately the strength of the A. E. F. as of any future date was always a complicating feature.

On or about April 15, 1918, there was established a system of tonnage allotments to the various supply services. These allotments were largely based upon a statement from the United States of ship space available. Every effort was made by the General Staff to give the Medical Department a fair share of these allotments. For a period of about three months these allotments of tonnage were filled by the authorities at home and even slightly exceeded. For a considerable period of time it was indefinite as to whether or not the Red Cross tonnage was included in that of the Medical Department. This valuable auxiliary service was, however, later given separate tonnage allotments and this hazy situation was cleared up. By an additional system of using lighters at United States ports for filling in the chinks on vessels the Red Cross was able to bring to France large quantities of the most useful type of medical supplies.

After August 1, 1918, tonnage allotments made in the A. E. F. to the Medical Department were greatly in excess of shipments actually received and the level of the depot stocks again began to fall off at a dangerous rate. One of the greatest difficulties was that of maintaining a level which was consistent for all items. This was primarily due to the difficulty of properly modifying the automatic schedules because of the large time element intervening between the shipment and actual receipt of the automatic supplies for any particular month. During the summer of 1918 a change was made in the reserve requirements and the 90-day period was reduced to 45. This was of more theoretical than practical assistance to the Medical Department because even a 45-day reserve had never been attained.

Call upon the United States for exceptional and emergency supplies, although authorized for all services, was seldom found necessary by the Medical Department inasmuch as practically all replacements on medical supplies were susceptible to an automatic arrangement. A certain amount of unusual and exceptional equipment and replacements was, however, obtained upon requisition by cable and otherwise from the United States.

II. DISTRIBUTION

During June, July and August, 1917, large quantities of medical supplies accumulated upon the docks at St-NAZAIRE. Every effort was being made to acquire suitable permanent storage facilities for the Medical Department in the various sections of the A. E. F. As the result of strenuous efforts of individuals the supplies which accumulated at the dock were gotten under temporary shelter and later, as space became available, loaded on cars and shipped to interior points in France.

Establishment of Medical Supply Depots: At an early date a depot was established at COSNE, which later grew into Intermediate Medical Supply Depot No. 3. This depot was always the Medical Department's main full stock distribution point, and from this establishment the entire distribution system was largely elaborated. For a considerable period of time practically all supplies were concentrated at COSNE and likewise distributed therefrom. This depot was situated upon a secondary line of transportation with reference to the A. E. F., L. O. C. and somewhat midway between NEVERS and PARIS. It is now known that the selection of this site as a main receiving and distributing depot from the Medical Department point of view was unfortunate, but at the time of its acceptance the more suitably located points had been preempted, and this location was taken over to meet an absolute emergent need; and even under the circumstances the site was turned over to the American authorities by the French with a string attached and considerable pressure was later brought to bear to have this establishment released again to French control. This release actually occurred after the signing of the Armistice and all supplies were tran-shipped to GIEVRES where the work of detailed issues were taken over by that depot upon the abandonment of Intermediate Medical Supply Depot No. 3 at COSNE.

All classes of medical supplies were concentrated at COSNE, and the storage space rapidly grew to approximately 80,000 sq. ft. In addition thereto, large quantities of stores were concentrated in the open and under canvas at this depot. All depot personnel arriving in France were trained and broken in under the supervision of the officers at this depot, and as rapidly as needs developed trained units were sent out to organize and manage other depots as they were established.

Advance Medical Supply Depot No. 1 at IS-sur-TILLE, and Intermediate Medical Supply Depot No. 2 at GIEVRES were early put into operation. The former, an extremely important unit organized in connection with the regulating station at that point, largely took over the question of distribution to troops and units in the Advance Section. It was not, however, until considerably later that this depot was made a full stock unit and prior thereto its activities were largely confined to the supply of combatant organizations. The problem of supplying the numerous fixed Medical Department organizations in the Advance, Intermediate, and Base Sections continued to be a responsibility of the main depot at COSNE. As the situation developed the depot at GIEVRES was increased in capacity and utilized largely for shipments of carload lots. Small issuing depots were gradually established at the main base ports and gradually larger Base Storage Stations were installed at these places.

Establishment of Army Dumps (Medical): As the PARIS Group was organized, and later the First Army became organized, the establishment of army dumps became essential. In connection with the purchasing business and hospitals in and around PARIS, there had been previously established in PARIS a small medical supply depot, and although this unit was utilized somewhat along the line of an army dump, it was not essentially that type of depot. The first army dump established was at LIEUSAINT, and this was organized and administered for the purpose of supplying combat units in the PARIS Group, and later the First Army. The supply table authorized for an army dump, and which in common parlance later became known as the LIEUSAINT List grew out of the establishment of this army dump. The original basis of this list was the replacements necessary for one combat division for 8 days, and the officer in charge of this distribution point was authorized to maintain in storage as many times this amount as there were combatant divisions in his sector. This practically constituted a stock maximum for his depot. Practically this same system, although with a modified list, was adopted for use in planning the distribution of medical supplies when the offensive operation directed towards the reduction of the St-MIHIEL salient, and later against the ARGONNE-MEUSE sector, were in preparation. Gradually, however, a policy was developed of establishing corps or army dumps for which there was authorized a definite fixed stock maximum without reference to the number of combat units to be supplied, but based more upon the number of such dumps established in relationship to the known number of divisions to be employed in the operation. Such dumps, for instance, were established at TOUL, SOUILLY, VAUBECOURT, FLEURY, and les ISLETTES, and in the order named.

Towards the end of hostilities the problem of distribution from the supply echelons at the base to those in the most forward areas had been worked out with exceeding care and were about to become effective when combat activity ceased. They were no more nor less than an elaboration of the policies under which the units had been previously functioning, but the later plans were better balanced and all echelons much more clearly defined. This was also true as regards the important technique of filling the calls of forward units from the unit next in the rear.

Medical Supply Echelons and Systems of Replenishment: Essentially this scheme of distribution involved the use of six echelons. They were as follows:
    Divisional medical supply unit.
    Army or corps medical supply park.
    Army advance medical supply depots.
    Advance S. O. S. depots.
    Intermediate depots.
    Base storage stations.

It was the policy to establish in each base section, as the need developed, a samll issuing depot to cover the local distribution problem, and in all S. O. S. sections there were established as parts of hospital centers similar units. These hospital center depots requisitioned and issued all medical supplies for their own center.

The divisional medical supply unit normally indicated the need of all divisional organizations upon a consolidated requisition, which after passing through the office of the division surgeon and G-1, was forwarded for filling to a corps or army dump. Many times the division medical supply officer was far removed from the division surgeon and the division staff generally and as a result numerous requisitions had to be sent to the nearest corps dump in a most informal manner and without any vise or approval.

This was recognized as a necessity and such contingencies were provided for by authorizing the dump personnel to honor such emergent calls. It was found in practise that such authorizations increased the confidence of those in the forward areas and that the end result was that of better and closer cooperation with all.

The logical stock for army or corps dumps would include only items of combat equipment and supplies and trench stores, and divisional units would naturally only requisition such articles, but in the early days of the development of the corps echelon it was necessary for these dumps to carry limited replacements for such units as mobile and evacuation hospitals. It was very soon learned, however, that this produced a useless dispersion of equipment difficult to obtain and quickly rendered immobile a unit which of necessity must remain mobile. It therefore became the policy to confine items on the fixed stock maximum of such dumps to those of combat matériel and trench stores alone. Just as soon as this decision was made it necessitated the establishment of a new echelon, inasmuch as large hospitals in the Advance Zone would be required to replenish their stock from an advance supply unit.

It was therefore contemplated to establish immediately (and sites were actually selected) full stock army advance medical supply depots on a basis of one per army. This unit, although carrying a complete stock, carried its items, insofar as quantity was concerned, upon a very limited time basis. The functions, then, of this larger unit would be primarily to fill the calls of the army or corps dumps, and secondarily to fill requisitions from medical units in the Advance Zone. The latter was precluded as far as possible by distribution from the rear through Controlled Stores. The limit of the fixed stock maximum for dumps would have been decided by Army G-4 upon the recommendation of army chief surgeon, and again could be modified only through the same channels. Such a policy precluded the possibility of a dump becoming so overloaded as to become immobile. The method of call by dumps upon the army advance unit would normally be in any informal manner. Thus, depot officers in rear echelons in order to fill the calls from forward dumps had only to know shortages in authorized stock maximums.

Just as it was necessary to establish for army or corps dumps fixed stock maximums, so also was it essential in the case of army advance medical supply depots. These units, although full stock and relatively large depots, have of necessity to be able to move at very short notice. It was therefore necessary to give such stock considerable thought and detailed study, particularly in view of the fact that the matériel within this depot would be turning over at frequent intervals, since fixed upon relatively so low as time basis. It must be remembered in connection with this advance unit that it was necessary for the officer in charge to fill the calls from not only army dumps alone, but also from fixed and mobile sanitary units.

The method of call from units such as base and evacuation hospitals, etc., upon the Army Advance Medical Supply Depot was formal, inasmuch as requisitions were made out by unit supply officers at proper intervals, and with the approval of the commanding officer of the unit were forwarded direct to the depot for filling. This was obviously the simplest manner of handling this situation, but simplicity in a large combat force is not the only consideration, and at the outset our people were acting in conflict with existing orders and regulations which controlled the passage of requisitions through the various G-1's and G-4's, including the General Staff officers in command of regulating stations. The paragraph in general orders, however, with which we were in conflict was later abrogated in favor of certain services whose problems of supply distribution were so peculiar as to demand such action. The confused points in the effort to standardize distribution for all services as they then existed in the supply orders would have been completely cleared up in the rewriting into one order G. O.'s 31 and 44, A. E. F., 1918. The army advance M. S. D. was essentially an army unit and under the direct control of the army commander, through his chief surgeon.

The next unit in rear, although geographically situated within the Zone of Advance and actually within what was to become the Army Service Zone, was an S. O. S. controlled depot. Numerous medical department units of various natures and entirely under S. O. S. control from the administrative viewpoint were geographically located within this area; and it was the intention to write into new orders a definition of policy with reference to these institutions. Advance Medical Supply Depot No. 1 at IS-sur-TILLE had heretofore been an advance section depot, and still of course under S. O. S. control. At about the time of crystallization of the plans for distribution, this supply unit was made an intermediate full stock depot. Its chief function was to fill the calls coming back from the army advance units on the right of the line. It had, however, like other full stock depots, a function of secondary importance, that of supplying replacement to certain of the fixed and mobile units. In addition thereto, the responsibility of furnishing initial equipment and restocking divisional units in divisional training areas was assigned to IS-sur-TILLE. The latter responsibility was in no sense a small one, since divisions arrived in training areas from two sources, i. e., coming out of the line for rest and reequipment, and arriving from the U. S. with practically no equipment or supplies. As combat activity increased the former grew of less importance inasmuch as the divisions leaving the line did not as a rule leave the army area. Their reequipment would then have fallen to the advance army depots. The first great duty, however, of this unit was that of filling the requisitions of the army advance medical supply depots. The technique of this procedure was made absolutely simple, inasmuch as here it was only necessary for the officer in charge of the army unit to submit to the forward S. O. S. unit a semi-monthly stock report. Differences between the report and the known stock maximum formed the basis for filling the call. This method of filling the calls of this unit precluded the possibility of its becoming over-loaded. The officer in charge of the forward S. O. S. depot would be assisted in filling the calls from the forward echelons by Controlled Stores.

The depot at IS-sur-TILLE was normally restocked from COSNE and GIEVRES and later even from base storage stations in the base sections. Considerable quantities of supplies resulting from European purchase were also concentrated at this depot. From this depot regular semi-monthly stock reports to the Chief Surgeon's Office were submitted. A copy of this report was also sent to Officer in Charge Intermediate Medical Supply Depot No. 3 at COSNE. A list of supplies existed for IS-sur-TILLE which were shipped automatically from COSNE. Increases or decreases could be made in the automatic as shorts or overs were indicated upon semi-monthly stock reports. In this way the stock of this depot was kept up. Certain classes of matériel had of necessity to be kept well replenished at IS-sur-TILLE, and during the starvation period this was an extremely difficult task, since it meant to the COSNE depot that practically the entire stock upon numerous items would have to be released to the Advance Section.

For a considerable period of time the depot at GIEVRES remained under the control of COSNE. Its stock reports were combined with those of the latter depot and generally speaking it was considered practically a part of that unit. Later the two were placed under entirely separate administration and GIEVRES was used entirely as a distribution depot for carload lots. Requisitions arriving elsewhere for filling were filled in part upon telegraphic and telephonic authority from GIEVRES when carload lots were involved. This depot was a splendid group of permanent storage buildings, but except during the last few months of hostilities absolutely unsuitable in structure for detailed issues.

Controlled Stores Policy: During the summer of 1918 the policy of Controlled Stores was developed and put into execution. This system centralized in one office distribution control up to the limit of depot requisitions and such other large shipments. Although the primary object of Controlled Stores was to place distribution under a comprehensive scheme in one office, it was also the object to centralize the huge question of accountability. Its establishment in the A. E. F. was in conformity also with accepted policies in vogue in the United States. This system would throw into one office a record of all large receipts and at the same time all large requests. Having such data at hand, distribution was clearly facilitated and with a resulting great conservation of effort.

Equalization of Stock: Upon the first and fifteenth of each month a complete stock report from each S. O. S. Depot was sent by courier to the Chief Surgeon's Office. From these stock reports Controlled Stores compiles a consolidated stock sheet upon essential items for the entire distribution system in the rear echelons. From this sheet is produced an equalization of stock sheet and shortages and excesses are leveled off as they appear in the various depots by shifting through Controlled Stores the stock of essential items in the S. O. S. By the consolidated sheet absolute shortages are clearly indicated and copies of the sheets connected with the equalization of stock are sent to the various section surgeons and depot officers concerned. A policy of strict economy upon items short had of course been previously announced. It was manifestly unnecessary for depots to concern themselves about stock upon essential items except in emergency, since the machinery of Controlled Stores provides for their equitable distribution. All other items, however, were procured by depots through prearranged automatics or by requisition.

III. TRANSPORTATION - AMBULANCES

Procurement: The problem of obtaining motor ambulances in the U. S. must have presented many difficulties if we are to judge by the meagre shipments which have arrived in France.

It is believed that in any future war enough of this type of transportation will be available to cover our needs only if plans for quantity procurement exist before the need arises. During the early days of the A. E. F. the procurement of motor ambulances and motorcycle side-cars for the Medical Department was a responsibility of that organization, and the questions arising in connection therewith were handled by the Transportation Division of the C. S. O. Upon the formation of the Motor Transport Service, however, the procurement of motorcycles was taken over by this service, and ultimately motor ambulances were shipped to France on M. T. C. tonnage upon the basis of estimates submitted by the Medical Department Experience so far gained in the course of the war has made it clear that two types of ambulances were needed: the light Ford for front line service and the heavier G. M. C. for evacuation ambulance companies and for service in the S. O. S. Information to this effect was cabled to the U. S., but not until November, 1918, did any Fords arrive intended direct for the American Army. The question of spare parts and repairs in general was, early in 1918, also taken over by the M. T. C. Prior to this, and later, a hopelessly inadequate quantity of spare parts for ambulances came to France. Estimates covering this situation were submitted and the M. T. C. was at all times kept informed of the number and general distribution of ambulances in the A. E. F. Even up to the present date, however, it has been necessary to dismantle a certain number of incoming new machines in order to keep others on the road.

Method of Shipping Ambulances From U. S.: Ambulances were shipped to France with organizations only until about October, 1917. This was soon found impracticable as the various units were dispatched immediately to training areas or stations in the interior of France, and it took considerable time with the facilities available for unloading boats before their transportation could be forwarded to them; also in transit many machines were badly damaged through faulty loading, being so knocked about that a number were only fit for salvage purposes after being taken off of the ships.

The Medical Department in home territory decided to ship all ambulances in a knocked-down condition to save tonnage space and to have them set up by a skilled body of men after their arrival at the Base Port of St-NAZAIRE. At this time notice was received that ambulances would come into this port only, but the few ambulances which did reach France were unloaded not only at St-NAZAIRE, but also at BREST, Le HAVRE, La PALLICE, BORDEAUX, and later on at MARSEILLES. There was never any way of determining in advance how many ambulances would arrive at any of these places nor when to expect them. It was a common occurrence for the chasses to arrive at one port and the bodies at another, making it necessary from time to time to drive chasses overland to where the bodies were available.

Utilization of Ambulances to Distribute Rations to Troops. The U. S. Army Ambulance service with the French army was operating in France approximately 80 sections of 20 Ford ambulances each, and further maintained a reserve of this transportation in its reserve parks and base camps. During June, July and August, 1917, a large number of Ford ambulances, space for which was available on ships, were transported to France and accumulated near the docks at St-NAZAIRE. Without question, a tremendous excess of these vehicles existed over and above the actual needs of the Medical Department and the U. S. A. A. S. at that particular time. The motor transportation situation in the A. E. F. during these months was extremely acute, and at the request of the transportation people a material number of these ambulances were transferred to divisions and other units and by them converted into light trucks, with the result that the transportation situation of the combat troops in the advance section, with reference particularly to rations, was tided over. The other results, however, was that the reserve upon this item for the Medical Department was practically wiped out.

Shortage of Ambulances: Ambulances are required for the evacuation of the sick and wounded in every section of the theatre of operations. From the beginning to end of combat activities the greatest dispersion of units existed, and upon arrival at destination, detached organizations immediately clamored for ambulance transportation. As a matter of necessity such calls had to be met as far as possible. Incoming divisions required filling up of their missing quotas, and an evacuation service at hospital centers and along the L. O. C., at base ports, etc., had to be established. Before December, 1917, there had already developed an acute shortage of ambulances, and shipments from the U. S., because of procurement and tonnage difficulties, were under our estimated need, and although cable after cable was dispatched setting forth our emergency needs along this line, the shortage continued to accumulate. The vital question of estimating the need was greatly hampered by the absolute lack of tables of organization in S. O. S., corps, and army units. Existing tables indicated transportation for combat and depot divisions alone. As early as possible, however, an estimate of the situation was made which resulted in the Medical Department assuming that from front to rear a minimum of 120 motor ambulances per division in France would be required. The number of vehicles required for the A. E. F. to cover past shortages and future needs was estimated and the results of these estimates were included in cables referred to above. Only during the months of September, October, and November, 1918, was it apparent that the number of motor ambulances which the authorities in the U. S. stated that they would float would have any influence upon reducing our accumulated shortage. Shipments had heretofore not even covered current needs.

DISTRIBUTION

Assembling Ambulances: With the motor ambulance shortage remaining at all times acute, the real problem of distribution was to decide how to supply ten ambulances from a total stock which ranged from zero to about four.

A unit of skilled mechanics known as the U. S. Army Ambulance Assembly Unit, composed of three officers and sixty enlisted men, arrived about November, 1917, and was sent to St-NAZAIRE. It was contemplated that enough ambulances would be assembled and available at this base port for incoming organizations to pick them up upon landing and drive them overland to their interior destination, as traffic conditions would not permit all ambulances being sent by rail to those destinations. As a matter of fact, ambulances never arrived in such quantities for this scheme to be put into operation. It soon became necessary to split up this unit into a number of small detachments to take care of the ambulances arriving at each of the various ports. The efficiency of this unit was greatly impaired as a result of its wide dispersion, and not infrequently it happened that one port would be working steadily day and night while another for months at a time had almost nothing to do. Owing to the uncertainty of arrivals it was never possible to direct nonworking detachments to the port of greatest activity because the moment this was done ambulances would come in at the port they had just left.

For a considerable time after this ambulance assembly unit had arrived, ambulances already set up would come in marked for different divisions or organizations. No attempt was made to supply the divisions with these vehicles as they had either already been furnished with new machines or else the organizations themselves were not yet in France. These set-up vehicles had their marks painted out and were distributed to other organizations in France in accordance with the needs of the service. All spare parts and accessories with which they were frequently found loaded were removed at the base ports and utilized in the equipment of other vehicles.

There were never any ambulances in reserve at any of these ports, as there were orders on hand far in excess of the supply, and vehicles were shipped to organizations overland as fast as they were assembled. Owing to the great lack of chauffeurs available for the Medical Department, divisions and other units were directed to send personnel to the ports to drive the machines assigned to them overland to their stations. It was of frequent occurrence for unskilled personnel to be used for this purpose and this fact, together with the wild driving and untuned machines, resulted in a great many ambulances reaching their organizations in a deplorable condition. Later on it was practicable for the transportation of ambulance companies and field hospitals to be ordered for temporary duty at each of the ports to help in assembling ambulances, upon completion of which this personnel drove them forward to the Training Areas of divisional organizations.

In the S. O. S. base hospitals and hospital centers were directed to send personnel to base ports for ambulances, and after these ambulances had reached the hospitals, individual units located in the S. O. S. were supplied with ambulance service either from the hospital pool, or else ambulances were detached from these hospitals for service to the units located in the contiguous territory.

Ambulance Accountability: All ambulances arriving in France were invoiced to the Medical Supply Depot at COSNE, but no ambulances save a few (shipped through error) ever reached that place, since no facilities were available at COSNE for the assemblage of ambulances. Organizations receiving machines were directed to make weekly reports of their transportation to the Chief Surgeon's Office, which reports were checked against the distribution reported by the base ports and a copy of the location of ambulances was sent to the Medical Supply Depot, COSNE, by the Chief Surgeon's Office. Each organization sent a memorandum receipt for its vehicles directly to Medical Supply Depot No. 3, thus making the latter place the only accountable office for ambulances in France. It is believed that this accountability, if not handled entirely by the Motor Transport Corps, should be centered in the Office of the Chief Surgeon of the American Expeditionary Forces and under the provision of general orders which control the policy of accountability for materiel in general.

Pooling System: The principle of supplying individual units, such as regiments, service battalions, signal companies, etc., with ambulances was found to be expensive, both as regards supplies and upkeep of these vehicles, so that in order to conserve our resources and obtain the greatest use of the limited number of vehicles on hand, definite pools of ambulance transportation were established at all hospital centers, base hospitals, and in each base section. These pools were under the direct control of the Chief Surgeon's Office, which office established a school located in TOURS for the instruction of officers and chauffeurs in the handling of these vehicles, as well as the necessary army paper work. With the exception of the Chief of the Transportation Section of the Chief Surgeon's Office, all officers handling these pools were of the Sanitary Corps. Weekly reports were sent by each pool to the Chief Surgeon's Office showing the number of cars on hand, trips made by each, amount of gasoline, grease, etc., consumed, as well as the nature of service performed by each ambulance in the pool. The records of one pool are checked against those of another, and competent inspectors sent around on tours to see that each pool was giving the maximum of service and that its transport was maintained in the best possible condition.

G-4 Control over Issues: No direct control from the Chief Surgeon's Office was kept over the operation of ambulances assigned to divisions or units serving in the Zone of Advance. Organizations serving in that zone were supplied with transportation in accordance with the tables of organization, but only upon receipt of priority orders issued by G-4, General Staff, G. H. Q. Since there was no Table of Organization covering organizations located in the S. O. S., organizations in that area were supplied from the aforementioned pools in accordance with their needs. As frequently happened, ambulances were detached for the purpose of temporary duty, returning to the parent pool when the unit moved out of the S. O. S. or no longer required the transportation. This allowed a very elastic use of ambulances located in the S. O. S. and owing to the great shortage of ambulances in France, it was frequently necessary, as well as possible, for all of the ambulances in one pool to be sent to units so as to augment the supply for the purpose of unloading hospital trains and similar emergencies, upon the completion of which duty they would return to their regular station.

Demobilization Plans: It is contemplated that with the cessation of hostilities and the return of troops to the United States our divisional sanitary trains and other organizations having ambulance transportation will be directed to leave their ambulances at the pools of large hospital centers such as those at MARS and MESVES, proceeding from thence to their port of embarkation. The ambulances at such concentration points will be carefully inspected by officers and skilled mechanics, and those cars which are fit only for salvage turned in to the large salvage depots of the M. T. C. Ambulances which are serviceable will be driven from here by the personnel of an evacuation ambulance company to BORDEAUX, St-NAZAIRE, or other ports for shipment back to the United States, as it is believed that a large number of them will be required shortly for service in America, now that our sick and wounded are being sent back in increasing numbers. Temporarily, it is desired to have in the advanced region a location such as JOINVILLE to which ambulances from returning divisions can be rapidly inspected and some of them diverted for service and replacement with the Army of Occupation.

IV. HOSPITAL TRAINS

PROCUREMENT AND DISTRIBUTION

Abandonment of Proposed Plan of Using Box Car: In connection with the transport by rail of the sick and wounded from the battlefronts, at one time it was contemplated that a large part of the evacuation for the American army would be accomplished by adapting ordinary box cars to hospital train purposes, by introducing into them fittings for supporting tiers of litters, these fittings to consist of metal posts capable of being screwed into the roofs and floors, so that they would take up little space and could be cleared out readily when not wanted, thus enabling cars which had brought in wounded being easily transformed into their original status and to go back to the front conveying supplies. Some of these fittings actually arrived in France but were never used. The idea seemed sound as the trains would answer a double purpose and the maximum of efficiency would have been secured. It was found, however, that in practice this method would cause unnecessary suffering to the sick and wounded and greatly inconvenience traffic arrangements.

In the earlier days of the war, both the British and French armies adopted this procedure but found it difficult to secure the requisite number of freight cars when required, and a great deal of time was consumed in cleansing and making fit these cars before they could be used for hospital purposes. Also after such use more time was consumed in cleansing them before food supplies and similar articles could again be loaded into them. Both Governments soon abandoned this system and obtained completely equipped hospital trains for the purpose of evacuating wounded.

Purchase of Standard Hospital Trains: The American Government from the start, profiting by the experience of the Allies, promptly placed orders for the Medical Department for hospital trains of the latest and best type to take care of its needs. This was done after receipt of information by the Chief Engineer Officer that the joint memorandum presented by him and the Chief Surgeon to the Chief of Staff on July 21, 1917, relative to the purchase and lease of hospital trains, had been approved.

Owing to the great distance from the United States and the shortage of cargo space, no coaches were imported from the U. S., the trains being obtained from the leading English and French railway companies, the great majority from England where the quality and supply were more satisfactory for our purposes. Soon after the arrival of the American Expeditionary Forces, a conference was held between the Director General of Transportation and the Chief Surgeon, relative to the number of trains that would be required. A tentative estimate was made for 10 hospital trains to be supplied for each 500,000 troops.

French Trains: About August, 1917, the French General Staff was requested to supply 6 hospital trains, and instructions were sent to the Medical Liaison Officer at London to arrange with the British authorities for the obtaining of 5 hospital trains of the same type then being supplied to the British army. The French Government replied that owing to the shortage of rolling stock available, it would be impossible for them to supply more than two of the trains desired. One of these trains was to be supplied by the *Compagnie des Wagon-Lits,* and the other to be composed of coaches obtained from the ORLEANS---PARIS-LYON Mediterranée Railroad, and Etat Railways.

The French officials also informed the Chief Surgeon that it would be impracticable to sell these trains outright to the American Government so that an informal agreement was made for the rental of these two trains at the price of 150 francs a day, together with a rental of about 17 francs a day for the necessary cooking utensils and operating room appliances with which the train would be equipped. All expenses for the transformation of the coaches for hospital trains to be paid by the American Government, as well as the expense of the restoration of these coaches to their original condition, when they were returned after cessation of hostilities.

Under date of December 3, 1917, the Chief Surgeon informed the French authorities Train No. 50 was acceptable and that he was prepared to take possession of it for the A. E. F. Personnel was put aboard and train sent on its maiden trip December 16, 1917. Train No. 51 was accepted for service with the A. E. F. on February 11, 1918.

British Trains: The trains obtained from Great Britain were supplied through the agency of the British Railway Executive Committee which appointed a special subcommittee to make all arrangements relative to design, equipment, transportation, etc., in conjunction with advices transmitted to them through Medical Liaison Officer in London. Under authority of letter dated August 1, 1917, the Chief of Staff, A. E. F. authorized that officer to purchase 2 hospital trains from the British Government; August 12, 1917, 10 additional trains of the same type were authorized; and December 17, 1917, the Commander-in-Chief further authorized the purchase of an additional 3 British trains. Up to December 31, therefore, a total of 15 hospital trains had been ordered from Great Britain and 2 from France.

All the British trains were delivered at the Port of Le HAVRE, where representatives of the Transportation Department were put aboard and the train sent to NEVERS, for final mechanical inspection, after which supplies and personnel were put aboard by the Medical Department and trains immediately put into service.

Trains for Sitters: Under date of July 31, 1918, 23 additional standard hospital trains of the British type were authorized, and arrangements made with the British authorities for their inspection and transportation to France. Under date of November 7, 1918, an order for the purchase of 20 corridor trains, for sitting cases only, to be obtained from the British Government, was transmitted to the General Purchasing Board.

At the time of the signing of the Armistice a total of 19 British and 2 French trains had been delivered, and it was found possible in the interest of economy to cancel 29 additional trains ordered in England; this was done at the earliest possible date and so ended the question of procurement.

Designation of Trains: Hospital trains in France with the A. E. F. were numbered consecutively from 50 up; Trains 50 and 51 being the only ones obtained from the French Government. These two trains were never as satisfactory as those obtained from British sources. The rolling stock, particularly of Train 50, supplied by the *Compagnie des Wagon-Lits*, was of ancient vintage and absolutely impossible to keep warm in the winter months or even in active service for any great period of time at a stretch because of the worn out materials of which it was composed.

Eventual Disposition of Hospital Trains: At a meeting held in PARIS, December 7, 1918, in the office of the Fourth Bureau, *Minister de la Guerre, Francaise*, a representative of the Chief Surgeon's Office, in conformity with authorization of G. H. Q., dated December 3, 1918, offered to return Trains 50 and 51 to the French Government, which offer was accepted. At this meeting the French officials were informed that no bills had as yet been received for the construction or rental of Train 51, and was informed that this was a matter that the French Government would attend to after the conclusion of the terms of peace. Bills for this train would then be submitted to the American Government. The French officials desired both hospital trains sent to PARIS where an official from the Fourth Bureau would inspect them and definitely accept the return of these trains from the A. E. F.

Information has recently been received from the British railway officials that they are willing to buy from the United States the hospital trains furnished the A. E. F. whenever they can be spared.

Schedule for Hospital Trains: In the S. O. S. it was practicable for the Chief Surgeon to obtain *Marche A* schedules for hospital trains, which enabled them to be moved expeditiously in the S. O. S.

In the Zone of the Armies Class C schedules were the best obtained, resulting often in as long as three or four days to obtain a *marche* for hospital trains operating in that region. Under such consitions it was necessary for a large number of trains to be garaged in the Advance Areas, so that they would be readily available when *marches* could be secured, and a great many trains, as high as 40 at one time, were borrowed from the French. The French trains were very uncomfortable for patients to ride in, as well as being of very limited capacity, carrying only from 60 to 80 patients, as compared with 400 lying cases or 650 mixed classes possible on the regular standard sixteen-coach A. E. F. hospital train.

Persistent efforts have been made by the Medical Department and the Transportation Department to secure suitable garaging stations where 5 or more of these trains could be kept when not in active service, especially during the winter months.

At the present time 5 or more of there trains are garaged at PANTIN, near PARIS; MONTOIR, near St-NAZAIRE; and at BASSENS, near BORDEAUX. Only the few trains required for active service, it is believed, will be kept near one of the regulating stations in the Zone of the Advance because of the great danger in winter weather of broken pipes from freezing, as well as the impossibility of keeping the staff and personnel warm on these trains when no engine is attached.

V. LIGHT RAILWAYS

During the St-MIHIEL and ARGONNE offensives some use was made of the narrow gauge (60-centimeter) railway lines, to evacuate casualties. Hospital Trains were formed from the returning cars and appliances that were readily removable were attached to the flat gondolas of this system, so that it was possible with a train composed of an engine and ten cars to transport some 80 lying cases. This method of transportation would have been very saving of ambulances, and it is believed had the war continued for even a few months more a great deal of use would have been made by the Medical Department of the 60-cm. railway for evacuating casualties.

At the time of the signing of the Armistice, some 500 cars were available for purposes of evacuation and it was practicable to manufacture others as fast as need for them developed. Those cars, however, which were used in the St-MIHIEL---ARGONNE-MEUSE operations were built with the center of mass too high for the rough construction of the light railways in the sector, and derailments were so numerous as to cause, in many instances, abandonment of this system.

Practically without exception, the necessities of a smooth-working machine were available to the Medical Department of the A. E. F., in inadequate amounts. The data given in this summary apply entirely to materiel, including supplies, equipment, ambulance, and hospital trains, but from other reports it will be seen that the status of medical personnel was about equivalent to that of materiel, and shortages along this line ranged from 40% in April to about 20% in October, 1918.

It will be seen, therefore, that the Medical Department was called upon to handle its side of a rapidly developing combat problem in the forward areas and the concomitant hospitalization and supply problems in the rear with the most inadequate materiel and personnel. Generally speaking, therefore, our greatest problem was to decide upon priorities of distribution and to determine upon the best possible method of utilization of our limited resources. Situations developing therefrom became at times so acute that it seemed inevitable that the cracking point would be reached before the respite of a winter season came. That such a catastrophe did not occur was due solely to the continuous efforts and driving force of an already much overworked personnel. To develop standards for the future based upon the equipment, supplies and medical department personnel actually available to the Medical Department of the A. E. F. would be a great injustice to the valiant men and women who made a success of the Sanitary Service in the face of the ever-present difficulties which have been so briefly touched upon above.

VI. SUMMARY

Criticisms: Lack of detailed and coordinated supply plans.

Absence of medical department supply representatives as observers in Europe prior to entrance of the U. S. into war.

Shortage of administrative officers in supply divisions in France, thereby causing great delay in completion of tonnage forecasts and automatic replacement schedules for Medical Department, A. E. F.

Lack of tables of organization for units other than the infantry division, thereby precluding accurate estimates upon the need in equipment, supplies, and transportation.

Impossibility of estimating ultimate strength of A. E. F. as of any future date.

Lack of adequate medical department supply representation upon docks at ports of embarkation and debarkation.

Failure to establish proper liaison by exchange of officers between Supply Division of the Chief Surgeon's Office and that of the Surgeon General's.

Lack of proper medical representation with the Administrative and Coordinating Sections of the General Staff prior to March 15, 1918, during which period the larger policies of supply were being developed.

Absence of a definition of policies and a clear division of responsibilities in supply matter between the Office of the Chief Surgeon, G. H. Q., and L. O. C. prior to March 15, 1918.

Lack of coordination of procurement and distribution of certain classes of supplies between the Medical Department and American Red Cross; this consisted largely of a failure to adequately analyze the procurement problem.

Great lack of personnel trained in medical department supply work.

Great shortage of motor transportation for assignment to depots for short haul trucking.

Great lack of coordination between shipment of units of personnel and initial equipment for those units from the U. S.; great quantities of such equipment which should have been in France awaiting its unit either failed to reach the A. E. F. or only did so many months after the personnel for same had arrived. This was the greatest single factor causing the reduction of reserve medical supplies in France.

The selection of site for main receiving and distributing depot at improper point on railway line.

Great dispersion of A. E. F., with lack of corresponding and proper dispersion of supply depots.

Tremendous shortage of light and heavy motor ambulances, which shortage in both vehicles and spare parts continued to accumulate up to the signing of the Armistice.

Impracticability of securing a sufficient number of hospital trains in Europe and because of tonnage situation our inability to augment supply by procurement in U. S. A.

VII. SUGGESTIONS

Basic Principles of Supply: With the cessation of hostilities, the problems of strategic supply ceased to exist. To attempt, therefore, to suggest a plan which might approach what would have been the ideal method of medical supply control within the A. E. F. would be like plotting one of the several solutions of a paper problem. One of the great lessons learned over here, however, was the need of definite and well-coordinated plans. The absence of any scheme of action was a manifest embarrassment to the Medical Department, and it is believed that while the facts are fresh in mind a plan which with modification might fit any overseas expedition, should be suggested. However imperfect such an outline may be, it will form a provisional basis from which something really acceptable may be developed by those who later study the valuable experience and many lessons resulting from the American effort in France.

Without question, a War Plans Division of the General Staff in some form will exist after the war. To speak of deliberately producing war plans sounds strangely like the very Prussianism which for the past many months we have hoped to see eliminated, but the maintenance of a Regular Army along presupposes the existence of plans for its expansion and utilization in time of need. Such plans must be developed during the days of peace. It is to be expected, therefore, that a military policy for the U. S. will be developed as a result of the lessons of this war. The manifest interest of the Medical Department in operation plans must be recognized to the extent of no longer considering that department merely one of the Services of Supply, and it is to be hoped that this change of attitude will be incorporated into any policy which may be developed.

Within the War College and the several sections of the General Staff adequate representation will doubtless be given the Medical Department. Such details will be essential to the development of the Medical Department's share in plans for the future, and such a system will also develop a number of medical officers trained in the duties of General Staff work. With a remodeling of our army educational system there will be available for such details officers who have shown aptitude in such work, from amongst the graduates of the new line and staff schools. Presumably each main section of the General Staff will have a Medical Representative thereon and it is believed that the activities of these officers might well be coordinated through a supervisory group in one of these sections. It has been suggested that this section be the Coordinating Section if such a group is created in the U. S. The organization then of the Medical Department representation with the General Staff would be analogous to that of the A. E. F. One of the chief functions of this supervisory group should be that of developing the Medical Department side of the plans for future operations.

A not inconsiderable amount of detailed work connected with such a study would be with reference to questions of function, personnel, organization, equipment, and transportation for Medical Department units. Before plans for the Sanitary Service of an Expeditionary Force could come into conference, such details would have to be determined at least in provisional form. In general, as regards any expedition, it would furthermore be necessary to know the objective to be attained, climate to be expected, length of front anticipated, lines of communication to be established, nature and number of base ports available, size of the force to be employed, and the length of time of its utilization. Such data being available, a well-balanced sanitary service could be recommended, and out of conference there would come a definite problem for the M. D. The above sequence would follow for each operation planned, and from a series of such studies there would have developed a very large but concrete problem of procurement and organization for our department.

The problems connected with organization are of interest here only secondarily. Our greatest interest is centered in procurement of matériel. Out of the problems of procurement of matériel there will develop one of about equal importance, that of distribution. Before we can proceed further in the matter of procurement and distribution of matériel, consideration must be given to certain other parts of the plan. An Expeditionary Force is usually reinforced progressively and the details of this progression with attached time element must be known. Having this information, it is possible to work out a shipping program and upon the basis of the Priority Schedule to forecast the tonnage requirements.

The ship space allotted the Medical Department should provide for the necessary initial equipment, replacement supplies, reserve stores, and a sufficiency of strictly Medical Department transportation, and the priority established should permit of the necessary shipments of this material coincident with or in advance of the shipment of troops. The amount of supplies and transportation to be held in reserve within the expedition will be largely dependent upon distance from source and such other procurement, storage, and traffic difficulties. This, however, like other general policies, will be announced for the information of all concerned. The question of the shipment of initial equipment is one that is vital to any force. There is no more complicating factor as regards supplies than that of unit of personnel arriving for which there is no initial equipment. Such equipment, like other matériel, has a more or less definite consumption factor and must be stocked in reserve. Supply Depots, therefore, carry items of initial equipment and for these depots to attempt to supply new units arriving from reserve stocks is fatal to that reserve. The equipment, therefore, for each unit should be laid down at the destination of that organization in anticipation of its arrival. To attempt to ship an organization and its equipment upon the same boat has been found to be impracticable and should not, ordinarily, be attempted unless conditions materially change in the future.

During the days of peace, heavy, bulky and expensive items of equipment gradually become part of supply tables. The advisability of producing supply tables solely for peace times and separate and distinct tables for campaign must here be given consideration. In the interest of economy in ship space, a most radical elimination must be practised in an effort to get down to essentially a war basis. The extent of this elimination will have a noticeable influence upon the reserve accumulated and tonnage consumed---provided of course the game is played conscientiously by all services. At the conclusion of hostilities in France in November, 1918, after several processes of elimination, our supply tables for all classes of materiel were far too elaborate, and that deeper cuts were not made was for politico-diplomatic reasons rather than for lack of appreciation of the need. Radical elimination, however, must be practised equally by all services, else we will see very bulky and heavy items that have been eliminated by one service being brought to the Expeditionary Force by another. The question of standardization must be gone into just as thoroughly as that of elimination. It is believed that the importance of this equipment and supply study alone justifies the existence of a permanent board to continuously study and keep up to date just such questions. Such a board will undoubtedly spend much of its time at a field experimental school and must work under the supervision of the Purchase, Storage and Traffic Section of the General Staff.

Upon the final production of a complete list of equipment and supplies detailed data with reference to weight and volume must be compiled in connection therewith. These weight and volume figures must refer to standard shipping packages of the item in question and must indicate clearly the number of such items contained therein. It therefore becomes necessary to include in specifications to manufacturers a requirement that they furnish the necessary tonnage data. When such information has been obtained, it should be compiled in such form as to make it readily possible to go from weight to volume and vice versa for any item upon the supply table when prepared for shipment. Statistics of the exact same nature as those described above must be compiled for the standard types of motor, horse, and rail transportation, to be used by the Medical Department of an Expeditionary Force. Given such information as these statistics on weights and volumes, together with the shipping program of the force, the question of forecasting tonnage requirements becomes relatively a simple matter, provided, of course, there exists for all units, whether Medical Department or otherwise, accepted and approved Tables of Organization indicating personnel and transportation allowed.

We have thus far settled upon the units to be utilized and the matériel that should be sent overseas as their initial equipment. In connection with this, it must be borne in mind that a full initial equipment should include everything necessary to make that unit self-sustaining for a definite period of time, from a Medical Department viewpoint. From this point it would now seem natural to proceed to the immediate plans for procuring and distributing the materiel for the force, but such is not the case without considering another factor of great importance. This is the factor of consumption or the wastage to be anticipated in initial equipment and supplies during service. This factor, together with an estimation of the needs along the lines of exceptional supply, will form the basis for our figures for the replacement of matériel. The former factor, that of consumption, is the real basis for an automatic supply, or for its subsequent modification. We must, therefore, produce complete and theoretically perfect schedules for an automatic replacement of all equipment and supplies and be prepared to make, tentatively at least, a list of exceptional supplies and equipment which may be needed, depending upon certain varying circumstances. Having prepared such lists and the schedules of automatic supply, we are in position to definitely say what materiel must be shipped overseas for any particular expedition and within what time element. We have, therefore, before us a definite procurement problem.

There now exists a Purchase, Storage and Traffic Section of the General Staff in Washington. This section is responsible, with certain exceptions, for questions arising in connection with matériel in home territory. In preparing for the future it is believed that all questions of procurement of matériel will be responsibilities of this section of the General Staff, and the various services will merely indicate the bases of their procurement problems together with the necessary specifications upon items. The question of contracts for equipment and supplies emanating from one central source will have amongst other advantages that of precluding competition between the various War Department Bureaus in the question of procuring supplies. It will further the matter of standardization and elimination and will place squarely up to one section of the General Staff the responsibility of obtaining and holding in storage ready for shipment all necessary matériel for an Expeditionary Force. This means good supply coordination and a thorough investigation of our National military resources, including those of transportation and storage. Such a progressive move is going to call forth larger appropriations for the purpose of producing a reserve in home territory of military stores. This will further necessitate a more careful study of the possibilities of standardization and elimination, since reclamors against such appropriations are almost sure to be heard.

With the advent of hostilities, supply divisions in home territory must be immediately prepared to release from storage large quantities of materiel for shipment overseas. These supplies will be released from the reserve of both perishable and nonperishable stores which will have been accumulated up to the point of equilibrium between consumption and replacement. Consideration must here be given to the fact that within an Expeditionary Force a reserve must also be accumulated. This will materially increase the burden placed upon the Division of Procurement. Supply Divisions must further be prepared to immediately supply trained units of personnel to cover the need for advance supply representatives, purchasing agents, dock representatives, details to the General Staff, and personnel for general distribution purposes. This, therefore, contemplates the accumulation of a reserve of trained supply officers and men. In home territory when an overseas expedition is engaged against the enemy, there exists not only the large procurement problem for forces at home and abroad, but also the problem of home distribution and release of matériel for shipment overseas. Whether control of this distribution is vested in a War Department Bureau or in a section of the General Staff there is certain to be required a carefully worked out scheme of Controlled Stores in order that available resources may be utilized to the best ends.

The development of storage and distribution within an Expeditionary Force depends largely upon the existence or nonexistence of an actual combat problem for troops upon arrival. In other words, the lines of communication may consist solely of the ocean route, or may consist of that and in addition thereto a long railway haul up to enemy territory. With the former, for an indefinite period, combat supplies only must be pushed forward as the fighting troops progress and real bases and land lines of communication, with attendant back area formation, will only be developed slowly. With the latter, the problems of distribution which exist at home will be largely duplicated but will be supplemented by those of actual combat. Distribution plans, therefore, within an Expeditionary Force vary according to circumstances, from the simple supply of combat replacements to a complete and elaborate system of Controlled Stores and other details of supply distribution.

The distribution plans which were developed for the forces in France were the result of many months of trying experience. It is true that in actual practice some of them did not really exist, but had the war gone on the entire scheme would have been in actual use. * * *

The first great need is a well organized supply division in the Chief Surgeon's Office, with single and absolute control. The main sub-divisions of this office will be those of procurement and distribution. Under the former will fall local purchasing and procurement from home territory. The officer in charge of this work must have an exact duplicate of the automatic schedules that are in the hands of procurement and distribution officers at home. To him will fall the task of properly modifying these lists in keeping with depot levels. He must also anticipate the need of exceptional equipment and supply and be prepared for many emergency requests for same. This work will require an assistant trained in cable work. This assistant must have accurate knowledge of every cable sent or received which refers in any way to supply. The question of the initiating of orders to purchase locally is a responsibility of this subdivision. Procurement must develop in cooperation with distribution, a system of storage, depot, and tonnage reports, for upon such reports that office is wholly dependent in the matter of stock levels, storage space available, and the checking of receipts against tonnage allotments. This office must further be in a position to furnish for any period a forecast of the needs of the department in ship space. There should be, therefore, a tonnage and statistical section of the Supply Division, and this work properly falls under procurement. The proper coordination of procurement activities will require the most careful liaison between the Division of Supply and those of Transportation and Hospitalization, for they represent the market to which the goods are distributed. To the Office of the Chief of the Supply Division there should be detailed a representative of the Matériel Section of the American Red Cross and likewise a supply representative from the Medical Department should be on duty with the American Red Cross if useless expenditure of money and needless duplication of effort is to be avoided. Interest in this coordination will be divided between distribution and provurement, and this liaison is, therefore, properly a subsection of the Division of Supply.

The subsection, distribution, will, like procurement, have several subdivisions. Chief amongst these will be that of Controlled Stores. Into Controlled Stores will flow reports of receipts from home territory and all large requests for issue. Further details of the work of this section will be referred to later.

The next most important branch of distribution is that of depot inspection. The sphere of activities of this office must be from the base ports to the divisional supply units. Close touch must be maintained between inspection and depot and supply officers from front to rear. In this way the greatest assistance may be rendered to the Medical Department Chiefs, of all units, combat or otherwise, in questions of supply. At the same time this is the only method by which we may preclude under - or over - stocking in units and in those smaller depots which do not ordinarily make depot reports, and it will be through such inspections that information is obtained by procurement relative to new and exceptional needs of troops. Such a system of inspections will greatly reduce the detail travel which would ordinarily have to be undertaken by those in charge of procurement, and particularly distribution. A considerable part of the time of these latter officers must be spent on the road, but the time thus spent should be very largely devoted to the large questions of policy and to the observation of results obtained.

In connection with the Division of Supply, or probably as a main division of the Chief Surgeon's Office, there must be a division of finance and accounting. The question of property accountability in an Expeditionary Force will be wholly dependent upon the breadth of the interpretation placed upon Field Service or other regulations bearing upon this matter. It is believed that the continuance of real accountability within an overseas expedition was never contemplated and if a sufficiency of trained administrators is available, such accountability would never be needed. A certain degree of responsibility and informal invoicing and receipting between the Supply Divisions at home and abroad, and between depots and units overseas will be required, and it is presumed that money accountability will always be strictly maintained. Such matters as finance, however, are outside of the question here to be considered. A division of finance and accounting will be an important adjunct to a Supply Division and such accountability of property as must exist should be maintained in one office.

Controlled Stores receives requisitions from depots, certain Medical Department units, and from section surgeons, that part of requisitions which cannot be filled from the stores under their control. It is contemplated that distribution of Controlled Stores may extend up to including the Second Echelon of Supply, that of Army Medical Dumps. The execution of the details of equalization of stock falls to the subdivision Controlled Stores in cooperation with the statistical personnel. The Office of the Section Surgeon is one of the points to which certain supply control must be decentralized. These offices pass upon requisitions of units with their territory and direct issues from depots most suitably located within their sections, forwarding calls for such amounts as their depots are unable to supply to Controlled Stores. The control of hospital centers should remain in the Office of the Chief Surgeon, and requisitions from hospital center depots which have been passed upon by center commanders will, therefore, be forwarded to Controlled Stores, which may direct the issue. Issuing depots, up to the Third Echelon (Army Medical Supply Depots) normally forward their calls for replacements to Controlled Stores. The needs of the Second and Third Echelons, which have fixed stock maximums, are automatically met by an informal call or by stock reports to the echelon next in rear. Such calls, however, may be filled either wholly or in part, when sufficient reason exists therefor, by relaying the call to Controlled Stores.

Certain storage space and certain supplies received from home territory are the sole property of Controlled Stores and records of the daily flow in and out of these stores must be kept. Supplies under control will be kept in decreasing amounts from base sections forward. They will normally be held in large base storage stations and in other large non-detail issuing storage depots from which carload lots may be readily shipped. Ultimate disposition of such stores may be from receiving and sorting stations at the docks, or not until such stores have been for some time in an Intermediate Depot, depending upon the need. One of the greatest fields of usefulness of Controlled Stores will be that of laying down initial equipment at destination of units in anticipation of their arrival, thereby relieving a local distribution point of a very appreciable load. The diagram previously referred to shows at the left a line of railway. This is really intended to indicate all distribution and whether by rail or otherwise. The need at depots of independent motor transportation will be great for every echelon of supply. There are many times when rail transport is either hopelessly blocked or not suitable to the need. At least depots and auto-truck pools should be convenient to one another.

Except as heretofore indicated, questions of supply arising within the Army Combat Zone are handled by Group Chief Surgeon or by the Chief Surgeon of the highest combat unit present. The control of army supply units must be left to the authority who has authorized their maximum stock allowances, and, as previously stated, in text above, this is done by Army Chief Surgeons and Army General Staff Sections (G-4).

The forward echelons have been more or less covered under the development of strategic supply, but an additional word in connection therewith and with the diagrammatic sketch may be useful. The divisional unit is an extremely useful addition to our division and must be retained. Medical dumps at Army Parks will ordinarily be needed on a basis of about one per corps. Their sole function should be that of supplying the need of the several divisions actually in front of them. They must also be prepared to assist each other with either supplies or transport in emergencies. Naturally these dumps are not full stock units. The several dumps of an Army are refilled in the manner already outlined from a full stock Army depot. These larger depots, on a basis of one or more per Army, must be pushed as far forward as reasonable safety will permit.

To these last named units will fall the task of supplying the Army and Corps Medical Department units and in emergency also certain S. O. S. units such as forward Base Hospitals. Furthermore, combat units in rest and reserve which may be too far in rear of dumps must forward their requisitions to these depots. The greater bulk of replacements to these larger Army Depots must come automatically from the still larger S. O. S. controlled depots in the rear (Advance-Intermediate Depots). These units are also full stock depots and have functions similar to the Army units. They are, however, in immediate touch with and are controlled by distribution, although a portion of their stock is at the disposition of the Section Surgeon. These Advance-Intermediate Medical Supply Depots are normally stocked through Controlled Stores as a result of the equalization of stock, insofar as essential items are concerned. Upon other items an automatic replacement system from the next echelon in rear may be established if deemed wise or these holes in stock may be filled by call upon Controlled Stores.

All depots and storage stations in rear of the Advance-Intermediate Depots except the small local distribution points are a part of Controlled Stores. One or more large full stock and detail-issuing depots (as shown above) might well be in a position to establish an automatic flow of supplies to the forward units from the Intermediate Section. This echelon will still remain a part of Controlled Stores, however, and may yet further be utilized to cover the local distribution need. Such units would normally receive the results of purchase. The proximity of good rail and road facilities to these depots is of paramount importance and sites for such units must be selected with great care. All other large units in rear are merely duplications of one another, inasmuch as they are for carload lot shipment, are not full stock, do not make detailed issues, and are a part of Controlled Stores. Such stations are enlarged and duplicated as the force grows and as the number of Base Ports is increased.

* * * * * *

Respectfully submitted,

S. H. WADHAMS,
Colonel, General Staff.

Chaumont, France,

December 31, 1918

C-in-C Rept. File: Fldr. 127: Report

Appendix C [Engineer]

4th Section

GENERAL HEADQUARTERS, A. E. F.,

Chaumont, Haute-Marne, April, 1919.

From: Chief of Group

To: A. C. of S., G-4, G. H. Q., A. E. F.

    1. Pursuant to instructions the following report is submitted on the activities of this group:

Our decision to enter the war presented a number of complex problems. Even before his departure from the United States, the C-in-C was brought face to face with questions of engineering and transportation, including consideration of port and railway facilities, shelter for men and animals, provision for hospitals, and for covered and open storage for the vast quantities of supplies which would be needed. This, in turn, entailed investigation as to possible sources of lumber, steel and other materials of construction, as well as the amount and character of equipment with which to accomplish the program.

    2. Questions of this character therefore engaged the attention of the C-in-C's staff from the very outset, and were a material factor in the decision to relieve the Administration and Operations Sections of the General Staff of portions of their duties and to create a 4th Section, to be known as the Coordination Section.

    3. * * * At first it was organized more or less loosely into four groups, or subsections, one of which handled general staff questions of all sorts originating in or relating to the Engineer Department, including the construction program, labor assignments, statistics as to the status of construction and supplies, and relative activities.

    4. Prior to the removal of the main office of the Chief Engineer to Headquarters, S. O. S., at Tours, communications pertaining to the Corps of Engineers were conducted directly between representatives of the Chief Engineer and the various sections of the General Staff. In the preparatory stages of the A. E. F., prior to the beginning of combat operations, it was inevitable that the greater part of these questions relating to construction and transportation should centralize in the Coordination Section. There was, however, an appreciable amount of business connected with the organization, equipment, and training of engineer troops which required presentation and discussion with the other general staff sections.

    5. Upon the publication, therefore, of G. O. 31, G. H. Q., 1918, and on account of the varied nature of the duties pertaining to the Corps of Engineers, the Chief Engineer received authority to organize a branch office at G. H. Q. The duties assigned to this branch office had to do with the control and distribution of engineer supplies, particularly those required by the troops at the front (in cooperation with G-4); with the acquisition and dissemination of military information, not only in enemy territory, but behind our own lines as well (in cooperation with G-2); the organization, equipment, training, and employment of engineer troops (in cooperation with G-1, G-3, and G-5).

    6. To facilitate the transaction of business, this portion of the Chief Engineer's Office was placed in close proximity to the office of G-4, and the officers at all times cooperated with each other in closest harmony.

    7. As our forces increased in number, the volume of business devolving upon G-4 naturally increased in proportion. Its internal organization was therefore changed with a view to decentralizing and more nearly paralleling the field organization of the A. E. F. Under this organization, Group C of G-4 was established and became more closely indentified with the Corps of Engineers than had been possible under the earlier organization.

    8. Its duties involved consideration of a large variety of co-related subjects, including construction, forestry, engineer supply, labor, light railways, and roads.

In addition, in cooperation with G-1, it passed on tonnage questions affecting supplies, particularly those required in direct support of operations against the enemy; it handled questions presented at G. H. Q. relative to the activities of the General Purchasing Board and supervised, for its own use, the collection and presentation of statistics concerning construction facilities, state of supply, and all operations affecting the latter.

9. On May 1, 1918, the Engineer Supply Section of the branch office of the Chief Engineer was incorporated in G-4-C, but, for purposes of record and as a matter of convenience, this activity was maintained as a distinct unit complete with its own personnel and records. By this means, shipments of the tremendous quantities of engineer supplies called for at the front were coordinated with the requirements of other bureaus, and the allotment of available transportation was readily made, while at the same time details were handled by officers who were acknowledged experts in all questions of engineering material and equipment.

10. From March to December 31, 1918, the total tonnage of engineer supplies received from the United States was 1,496,489. Total tonnage received from all sources, 3,255,121. On 11 November, 1918, total covered space occupied by engineer supplies was 764,000 sq. ft; total open space occupied 14,352,000 sq. ft. Nine storage depots were maintained.

Repair shops were operated to care for engineer supplies. Shops made 100 firing platforms for 75-mm. guns, 30 ponton wagons, one hundred 500- gallon water tanks, and completed more than 2,000 orders before the Armistice.

Seven cement mills were operated by engineer troops, producing 55,000 tons or 315,000 barrels of cement during five months operation. Concrete pipe amounting to more than 100 miles was made for A. E. F. use.

* * * * * *

11. The duties of G-4 connected with Engineer construction were of a general nature and concerned the location and magnitude of the various projects, rather than the details of their construction. The latter were administered by the Chief Engineer, A. E. F., through a division of his office in charge of the Director of Construction and Forestry. Officers representing the Director of Construction and Forestry were attached to G-4-C and were, to all practical intents and purposes, members of this Section. Their duties consisted in keeping in close touch with the work of construction and forestry, making frequent inspections and noting progress, compiling data, and advising on questions arising in connection with this work. The officer in immediate charge of forestry matters at G. H. Q. had executive functions also, particularly in connection with the acquisition of standing timber in the French Zone of the Armies. He also was charged with the management of a project for the supply of fuel wood, which was an activity involving close cooperation between the Quartermaster and Engineer Departments. These activities of the Forestry Service might ordinarily have been administered from Headquarters, Advance Section, S. O. S., but were administered from G-4, G. H. Q., as a matter of convenience, largely because of the close cooperation which was required with the French Military Mission of these Headquarters.

12. The most striking achievements of the Division of Construction and Forestry are summarized as follows:

Shelter for troops: A total of 15,039 barracks was erected which represented 285 miles of barracks placed end to end.

Hospitalization: Space for 280,000 beds provided, of which 145,913 represented new construction. New construction was equivalent to 7,700 hospital barracks, 20 x 100 ft., which represented 146 miles in wards.

Ports: Docks for ten vessels were constructed at Bassens. These were 4,100 feet long and were equipped with switching facilities, warehouses, etc. For three months the average daily tonnage discharged at American Bassens was 3,700 tons. Docks at other ports for the use of seagoing ships were completed or partially completed when work was stopped by the Armistice. Eighty-nine berths, totaling 7 miles, were either built or acquired from the French.

Lighterage: Dock 750 feet long at St-Loubes was completed; 84 lighters and 7 derricks barges were constructed.

Railroads: 947 miles of standard gauge railroad (most of it in yards) were completed, approximately the distance between Chicago and New York; 6-mile cut-off at Nevers, requiring a bridge across the Loire River 2,190 feet long, was built.

Storage depot warehouses: Covered storage space constructed 21,972,000 sq. feet or 500 acres, providing space for 90-days' reserve supplies for 2,120,000 men.

Remount depots and veterinary hospitals: Remount space was provided for 39,000 animals and veterinary hospital space for 23,000 animals.

Water supply and sewerage: Much work was done to give pure water to troops. Supply of water for many large cities was chlorinated under engineer control. Four million gallons per day were developed by artesian wells in Bordeaux region. Pipe for sewerage in the Mesves hospital project alone required 28 miles and for water supply the same amount. Large municipal water supply developments were made at Brest and St-Nazaire.

Refrigeration: Refrigeration plant built at Gièvres with daily capacity of 5,200 tons of meat and 375 tons of ice. Three other plants built.

Bakeries: Mechanical bakeries to produce 500,000 pounds of bread every 24 hours were constructed at Is-sur-Tille. Construction of bakeries of 80,000 pounds capacity in 3 other cities was stopped by the Armistice.

Power plants: Electric power was obtained from existing sources and by new construction in the form of central stations and transmission lines.

Oil and gas storage: By construction of tanks at sea coast, storage was provided for 150,000 bbls. Sixty-nine 300-barrel tanks and one hundred-fifty 150-barrel tanks were manufactured for distributing stations. Seventeen complete storage stations including pumps were put in operation.

Forestry: 91 mills were in operation in October. The total production to Dec. 1 was 189,564,000 ft. board measure of lumber; 2,728,000 standard gauge ties; 923,560 narrow gauge ties; 1,739,000 poles and pit props; 892,200 steres of fuel wood; 38,200 pieces of piling. The fuel wood, if corded, would extend 375 miles.

In addition to this fuel wood, the fuel wood project previously mentioned produced sufficient wood to make the total distance 1,325 miles, or approximately 2,120,000 cubic meters.

13. A detailed account of the operations of the Division of Construction and Forestry has been rendered by the Chief Engineer to the C. G., S. O. S., and does not pertain to this report. * * *

14. Questions concerning labor assignments, as presented at G. H. Q., were of the most general nature, and consisted largely in making allotments to the armies of the necessary labor units, arrangements being made in conference with G-3 at G. H. Q. and with the C. G., S. O. S. The details connected with acquisition and assignment of civilian labor were administered by a Labor Bureau, operated for a time under the supervision of the General Purchasing Agent and subsequently under the supervision of the C. G., S. O. S. A detailed report of these activities is not included with this report on the activities of G-4-C, but will be found with the report of the C. G., S. O. S.

15. The construction of light railways and roads, under the immediate supervision of G-4, G. H. Q., was limited to the Advance Section, S. O. S. and to army areas. The Department of Light Railways and Roads was in fact a division of the Office of the Chief Engineer, and was maintained at G. H. Q. until the signing of the Armistice. Details of a general staff nature were discussed directly between the Director of Light Railways and Roads and the officers of G-4-C. The operation of light railways was, necessarily, an army function, and detailed reports in connection therewith will be found in the reports of the C. G.'s of the armies and with that of the Chief Engineer, A. E. F. Similarly, the construction of roads will be covered by the same reports. The following figures are, however, given as indicative of the magnitude of these operations, viz:

On the day the Armistice was signed, the A. E. F. was operating 2,240 kilometers of light railway, of which 1,740 kilometers had been taken from the Germans and the balance had been newly constructed or rebuilt. Up to February 1, 1919, our light railways had handled a total of 860,652 tons of material, of which, 166,202 tons were ammunition. In one week, 10,600 tons of ammunition were handled. In six nights, 23,135 soldiers were carried, and the light railways played a very important part in moving forward to the combat lines and assisting in the evacuation of sick and wounded. The daily net tonnage handled in October, 1918 was 8,100 tons. In one week 10,700 tons of rations were handled. On November 11, 165 locomotives and 1,695 cars were available for use. In five hours on one occasion, 135 men laid 14,200 feet of light railway track, or slightly under 3 miles. Ten shop buildings, 70,000 sq. ft. total area, were erected at Abainville above Gondrecourt. The shop project occupied 125 acres and shop employees had erected 2,300 cars and repaired 140 locomotives.

In the S. O. S. alone, exclusive of the Advance Section, 300 miles of road had been maintained and repaired, and 90 miles of new road had been constructed. The mileage of roads worked over in the Advance Section, including army areas, has never been fully calculated, but subsequent to the Armistice there had been engaged about 34,500 troops of all arms of the service other than engineers, 34,000 civilians and 15,000 prisoners, in an attempt to restore these roads to approximately the same condition that they were in when the American Expeditionary Forces arrived in France.

These forces are exclusive of 43,000 engineer troops engaged in construction, and 18,500 engaged on forestry projects, all under the Director of Construction and Forestry.

16. Questions relative to tonnage requirements, the activities of the General Purchasing Board, and the collection and presentation of statistics were of a general character and do not permit of extended description. The shortage of tonnage necessitated a careful consideration at all times of the requirements of the various supply departments, and an allotment of the tonnage in accordance with their immediate or prospective needs. This in turn necessitated the consideration of probable combat activities and confidential advice to the heads of supply departments as to the probable theater of operations, the consumption of material of various classes, and other data required for their guidance. Eventually the activities in respect of statistics in connections with G-4 were consolidated with those of G-1 and placed in charge of a Statistical Section of the General Staff which was attached to G-1 for general supervision purely as a matter of convenience.

17. At all times G-4-C has been able to work in closest cooperation with other groups of G-4, the officers of which have uniformly been animated by that spirit of cooperation necessary to successful teamwork in any organization. Similarly it has enjoyed relationships with the Officers of the French Military Mission which have been of a most helpful character.

18. [This paragraph lists personnel assignments to the group.] * * *
19. [This paragraph lists certain appendices which are not printed.] * * *

G. A. YOUNGBERG,
Colonel, G. S.,
Deputy A. C. of S., G-4,
Chief of C Group.

C-in-C Rept. File: Fldr. 138: Report

Appendix D [Motor Transport]

4th Section, General Staff   GENERAL HEADQUARTERS, A. E. F.,

Paris, December 23, 1918.

Memorandum for A. C. of S., G-4.

In compliance with your instructions, the following report is submitted on the activities of G-4-D, G. H. Q.

I. GENERAL

1. The agencies which handled the motor transport problem for the A. E. F. changed several times during the war, each change involving a modification of the relations to each other and of the policies to be followed. It is first necessary to consider what these agencies were.

2. At the outbreak of the war, the present functions of the Motor Transport Corps were in general under the Quartermaster General. On the creation of the A. E. F., the Chief Quartermaster, A. E. F., handled the supply of motor transportation as he handled all other Quartermaster supplies, under the supervision of G-4, G. H. Q. The repair of motor transportation also fell to the Chief Quartermaster. The operation of motor transportation by any centralized agency was a question which had never been considered in our service, at least to the extent that any approved policies existed in the matter. It was assumed that operation was merely a question of driving vehicles; that no particular problems existed in this line; and that operation, repair, and the supply of spare parts did not bear so close a relation to each other as to require centralized control.

3. Motor transport supply grew to such an extent in the A. E. F. that it was necessary for the Chief Quartermaster to establish a separate branch of the Quartermaster to handle it. This branch was called the Motor Transport Service and was created by G. O. 70, H. A. E. F., December 8, 1917. By this order the Motor Transport Service was charged with supply of motor vehicles, spare parts, tools and accessories, gasoline and lubricants; handling of repair; technical supervision of motor vehicles. It was specifically not charged with operation.

4. On February 16, 1918, the Service of Utilities was created as a branch of the S. O. S., and among other things was put in charge of motor transport. This had the effect of transferring the Motor Transport Service *en bloc* from the Chief Quartermaster to the Service of Utilities. It also had the effect of making the Motor Transport Service somewhat more independent than formerly; probably because the Service of

Utilities, being a new organization and having control of an extraordinary variety of matters, desired at first to exercise only the most general supervision of its component parts.

5. This arrangement soon proved to be inadequate. The following serious defects developed:

(a) The work of the Motor Transport Service grew to such an extent that it became undesirable to leave it under any other service. A separate service was needed.

(b) Technical supervision as prescribed in G. O. 70 amounted to the control, from a service standpoint, of Motor Transport Service activities in the armies (and elsewhere), such as in the case of other services was performed by their service representatives on various staffs. In addition, it involved the supervision of the handling of delicate machinery, a problem more technical in its character than any other service (except the Air Service) had to meet. It was necessary that, with the creation of a separate service, that service have representatives on the various staffs of the A. E. F. with ability and power to carry out this supervision.

(c) For tactical reasons it was considered unwise to give the Motor Transport Service for the present any operating authority in the armies. But these reasons did not apply in the S. O. S. As motor transport was then (as always) short, and as centralized operation was demonstratably economical, it was desirable to give the Motor Transport Service operating authority in the S. O. S.

(d) Air Service transportation had been wholly excluded from the control of the M. T. S. Motives of economy made this undesirable.

(e) It was desired to combine the supply of gasoline and motor oils with that of other lubricants and place them under the Quartermaster Corps, not the separate Motor Transport Service.

6. While these considerations were coming to the front, the S. O. S. was established. This created an echelon between G-4, G. H. Q., and the services, namely G-4, S. O. S., thereby involving a further readjustment of policies.

7. On May 11, 1918, G. O. 74, H. A. E. F., was published. This order (a) created the Motor Transport Service as a separate service as regards the A. E. F. and (along the lines indicated in par. 3 above) made the following additional changes in G. O. 70 of 1917:

(b) Authorized service representatives of the Motor Transport Service on the principal staffs of the A. E. F.

(c) Gave the Motor Transport Service operating control over ordinary cargo and passenger transportation in the S. O. S. (also over a paper reserve in the armies; which, however, was never created).

(d) Included the Air Service transportation under Motor Transport Service control.

(e) Removed the supply of gasoline and oil from the Motor Transport Service.

It further made certain provisions:

(f) For the control of distribution in France of various types of vehicles; and

(g) For the acquisition of personnel now in France, by the M. T. S.

Both the latter provisions were couched in general terms, and many complications arose in interpreting them.

8. The Motor Transport Service still remained under the Service of Utilities.

9. On July 11, 1918, by G. O. 114, H. A. E. F., the Service of Utilities was abolished; the name of the Motor Transport Service was changed to Motor Transport Corps; and the Motor Transport Corps was made an independent service under the S. O. S.

10. Corresponding changes had been carried out, after delays, in the United States On April 18, 1918, by G. O. 38, W. D., a Motor Transport Service was organized under

the Chief Quartermaster. On August 15, 1918, by G. O. 75, W. D., a Motor Transport Corps was organized as a separate corps. The latter was modeled on the Motor Transport Corps, A. E. F., G. O. 75 being largely a literal copy of G. O. 74, H. A. E. F., 1918.

11. Further reorganizations in the United States have since been made. By one, a portion of the duties allotted by G. O. 75 to the Motor Transport Corps (i. e., purchase, production, inspection and payment) were turned back to the Quartermaster Corps. Still later, the motor transport work was divided between the Motor Transport Corps and the Director, Purchase, Storage and Traffic under the General Staff, eliminating the Quartermaster Corps. The specific orders covering these changes are not at hand.

12. It will thus be seen that the Motor Transport Corps did not crystallize into its final form, in the A. E. F., until four months before the Armistice and more than a year after the A. E. F. was organized. In the United States it came at a still later date.

13. Any readjustment such as the many listed above involves changes in personnel, changes in relations with other departments and bureaus, changes in policies, and a period of weeks or months of inevitable confusion and cross-purposes before the new system is working smoothly. The matter has been gone into in detail, not only to facilitate an understanding of what follows, but to show the great difficulties the Motor Transport Corps has had to meet as a result of these continual reorganizations. It is to be hoped that in the future a fixed policy can be decided on which will enable the Motor Transport Corps in time of peace to build up an organization not requiring great modifications under the pressure of war conditions.

14. There follows a brief description of the activities of the Motor Transport Corps. This is written primarily from the viewpoint of G-4, G. H. Q., which shaped the general policies; but it is unavoidable that the description also covers the functioning and activities of the corps itself. Incorporated therein are criticisms of policies shown by practice to have been incorrect. Where the term Motor Transport Corps is used, it is to be understood to mean either the present corps or whichever of its predecessors handled the work at the time in question.

15. The activities of the Motor Transport Corps supervised by G-4, G. H. Q., are supply, repair, operation, and technical supervision and will be considered in this order.

II. SUPPLY

16. The property handled by the Motor Transport Corps may be divided into three main classes:
   A. Motor vehicles,
   B. Spare parts, tools, and accessories,
   C. Repair plant.
For each class, there are three operations to be considered:
   Determination of needs,
   Acquisitions,
   Distribution.
The three classes of property will be considered in order.

A. MOTOR VEHICLES

17. The basis of estimated needs of motor vehicles was the tables of organization of the Army. These have been shown in some cases to be quantitatively wrong---prescribing too many or too few vehicles. This is an error unavoidable in peacetime determinations and has been largely corrected. A more serious error exists in them,

however, having its roots in the system by which the Tables of Organization were drawn up.

18. There appears to have been no single authority, passing on questions from a purely motor transport viewpoint, which had final decision on the incorporation of motor vehicles into the Tables of Organization, and responsibility for their supply. It was left to the various services---principally the Quartermaster Corps, Chief of Engineers, Ordnance Department, Signal Corps, and Medical Corps. Which service made the decision and acquired the responsibility was apparently decided on two principles: (a) In the case of vehicles for a body of troops belonging to a techncial service, it fell to that service to decide; (b) In case of vehicles whose use is connected, more or less remotely, with the functions of a technical service, it fell to that service to decide. The two principles are not simultaneously applicable to all cases, and the final result appears to have been reached by a series of compromises. As an illustration of the first principle, the Medical Department, by Tables of Organization, supplies the motorcycles of the divisional sanitary train and of various sanitary detachments in the division, though the motorcycles are quite ordinary motorcycles. As an illustration of the second, the Ordnance Department, by Tables of Organization, supplies ammunition trucks, apparently because they are used to haul ordnance property.

19. This arrangement has two bad results, from a production standpoint:

(a) Several departments are competing in the market for an identical product.

(b) Each department seeks to devise vehicles exactly designed to meet special requirements. From this results the presence in our Tables of Organization of a great number of special vehicles. Some of these have never arrived in France, or never arrived in quantity; ordinary vehicles having been substituted for them successfully. Some are really ordinary vehicles disguised under a fancy name---creating vast confusion in offices. A large number of unnecessary, inadaptable, and wasteful. The best-known example of these is the steel-bodied ammunition truck. A four-wheel-drive cruck with cargo body will haul ammunition; also cargo. An ammunition truck will haul ammunition but has no space for any bulky cargo.

20. In determining our future Tables of Organization, the final decision should be with a Motor Transport Corps board, acting under the General Staff, which should adopt certain standard makes, chasses, and bodies. It should consider the needs of all services demanding special vehicles, and ascertain whether one of its standard vehicles ---possible with movable attachments---cannot meet each need. To a considerable extent this has been done in the United States in recent months.

21. The basis of requirements, then, was the Tables of Organization. There seems however to have been difficulty in the United States in interpreting and consolidating these, and the A. E. F. has had to furnish the United States with forecasts of our needs for some months in advance. These forecasts were based on the Tables of Organization, on troop arrivals, on estimates for S. O. S. needs not covered by Tables of Organization, and on estimates of replacements. They were drawn up by the Motor Transport Corps, in consultation with the other services.

22. Based on these estimates the appropriate bureaus in the United States arranged for the construction and delivery of the vehicles.

23. In the early days of the A. E. F., when the difficulties of supply from the United States were still great, a number of vehicles were purchased in European markets. Largely as a result of this, there were at the time of the Armistice about 160 makes of vehicles* in use in the A. E. F., of which 112 (70%) represented only 2 1/4% of the total number.** The relation of a variety of makes to maintenance difficulties is

---

* *Counting cars and trucks, even of the same make, separately.*
***Cars, trucks, and motorcycles only.*

discussed below. It will only be said here that a large portion of our difficulties in maintenance has been due to this cause. Our future policy should limit the variety of makes as much as possible, and the adoption of any make as standard should involve an obligation on the manufacturer to furnish a continuous supply of parts. About the beginning of 1918, G-4, G. H. Q., adopted as a policy that no vehicles should be acquired for the A. E. F. unless satisfactory to the Motor Transport Corps from this maintenance standpoint.

24. Shipments of vehicles to France were arranged as for other property; tonnage allotments were made each month to the various services, which then cabled to the United States what to ship. Up to June, 1918, each service imported on its own tonnage the vehicles for whose supply it was responsible. Thereafter, by direction of G-4, G. H. Q., all motor vehicles came on Motor Transport Corps tonnage. This involved close cooperation of the Motor Transport Corps and other services in the preparation of tonnage cables.

25. It should be noted here that it has been extremely difficult to obtain motor vehicles from the United States. Since the increased shipments of troops began in the early summer of 1918, the shortage of vehicles has grown steadily, both absolutely and (in most cases) relatively. It has never been possible to obtain tonnage allotments in any month sufficient to wipe out this shortage; but very large allotments have been made to the Motor Transport Corps in July, August, September, October, and November. The vehicles called for on these allotments were available in the United States; but in spite of the strongest representations by G-4, G. H. Q., in the first three of these months only about 35% of the vehicles called for were received. The situation has since improved, especially in the November floatings. The cause of this is unknown, but is probably due to the confusion caused by the reorganizations in the United States and to lack of liaison there with the Embarkation Service. * * *

26. Distribution of vehicles was in general governed by the rules of G. O. 73, 1917 (and later G. O. 44, 1918). To develop a smooth distributing system and minimize detail work at G. H. Q., the following policies have been adopted in this matter:

(a) At first, vehicles were distributed by the various services as indicated by Tables of Organization. This meant that often several services would be distributing the same type of vehicle; and as each service supplied only certain arbitrarily specified units, and as some services were much better supplied than others, there was no guarantee that transportation would go where it was most needed. It was obvious that only one service should handle any one type of vehicle. By G. O. 74, 1918, the Motor Transport Corps was given the distribution of all ordinary cargo carrying and passenger carrying vehicles. By a subsequent decision * * * it was specified which service should handle each of the vehicles in Tables of Organization.

(b) As regards the vehicles distributed by the Motor Transport Corps (the only ones under discussion in this section of this report), the chronic shortage in the A. E. F. forced G-4, G. H. Q., in March of 1918, to place these in Class IV, where they have since remained.

(c) The detailed needs of the S. O. S. are known by the Commanding General, S. O. S., particularly as in general no Tables of Organization exist for the S. O. S. Therefore, a fixed percentage of all incoming vehicles were turned over to the Commanding General, S. O. S., for distribution as he saw fit; with these he was required to handle all S. O. S. needs. The percentage adopted was at first 25%; in the spring of 1918 it was reduced to 10% and has since remained there (except for a period in the early fall of 1918, when it was temporarily increased to 30% to repay certain loans of the S. O. S. to the armies). G-4, S. O. S., handled the distribution of this 10%.

(d) With the meaning 90%, G-4, G. H. Q., handled the needs of the combat troops, schools, and miscellaneous.

(e) Issues to any unit were the entire allowance of that unit, or such fraction thereof as was available; and were to the commanding officer of the unit. He had the Tables of Organization to guide him in making distribution within his unit, if he saw fit. If he desired to depart from the Tables of Organization, it was, his right. This policy was applied first to divisions and independent brigades, etc.; when the armies were formed, it was applied to armies. It has created some dissatisfaction; individual units have at times claimed that they have not been given their fair share. Similar claims have been made, in behalf of the combat troops of their services, by the Medical Corps, the Engineers, the Air Service, and (notably) the Signal Corps. Nevertheless it is believed that the policy is correct. If a commanding officer is really too incompetent to distribute the transportation of his command properly, he should be removed. If he is not removed, his prerogatives must not be infringed on. Further, the policy creates a decentralization of work which is essential unless G-4, G. H. Q., is to be swamped with detail work.

(f) Initial issues to units having a Tables of Organization allowance are made without requisition. It was often months before an initial issue would be completed, and continual requisitions as reminders were useless paper work. But this involves a record at G. H. Q. of the actual shortages in units. This may be obtained (1) by keeping track of what the unit has received; (2) by periodical reports of what the unit has. The objection to method (1) is obvious to anyone who knows how fleeting and transitory is army property---especially when self-propelled. The objection to method (2) is that it requires decentralization into the hands of large and responsible units such as armies if it is to work. A suitable record system was not worked up until the First Army was formed. At present, bi-weekly reportes of motor vehicles on hand are received from the armies, listing by divisions and independent units; itemized by cars, motorcycles, bicycles, light delivery trucks, cargo trucks (by capacity tonnage), and machine shop truck units. A card record by units is also kept of issues made, as a check.

(g) Replacements have been treated like initial issues, except that requisition therefor is made from time to time. This was due to the shortage being so great that it was not desired to hypothecate an uncertain quantity of vehicles in advance for replacement purposes. This policy was a mistake. The issue to a unit of a certain number of vehicle involves (unles it is merely for an emergency) an obligation to maintain the unit at that strength, If there are not enough new vehicles coming in to maintain old units and equip new ones, the solution is not to refuse replacements to the old ones, but to reduce their permanent stock, by withdrawal, to a point where it can be maintained. As long as motor vehicles are Class IV, every army or independent unit should have an automatic replacement credit. Such a credit was actually established for the armies, just before the Armistice; but the Armistice caused a change in policy which forced its abandonment.

27. Based on the above policies, the following is the system of distribution. G-4, G. H. Q., receives from the armies their reports of vehicles on hand. It receives from miscellaneous sources, not in the army, emergency requests. It receives daily from the Motor Transport Corps a list of vehicles available for issue. It is informed of the operations contemplated by the C-in-C. Based on this, it decides what issues will be made; informs the units to whom they are to be made; and directs the Director, Motor Transport Corps to make the issues. The Director, Motor Transport Corps, is responsible that they are made.

28. The Motor Transport Corps machinery of distribution is as follows. It receives vehicles at the various ports. At each port it has a reception park, at which vehicles are set up (if crated), cleaned, oiled, assigned a number, and put in running condition. On receipt of issue orders from G-4, G. H. Q., it either delivers the vehicles with its own personnel or notifies the unit to send personnel to take delivery. In general, for

units at the front, the Motor Transport Corps makes delivery as far as its reception park at Dijon, the unit sending there for it; units in the base and intermediate sections send personnel to base ports. These rules are not invariable. The Motor Transport Corps organizes and routes the convoys. For vehicles of special types issued by other services, the Motor Transport Corps puts them in running order and holds them for orders from the Chiefs of the services.

B. SPARE PARTS, TOOLS AND ACCESSORIES

30. It was realy realized that the problem of spare parts supply (which was the crux of the upkeep problem) would be extremely difficult. A single motor truck has about 3,500 kinds of parts, of which about 80% are peculiar to that make and type. For the vehicles in France when the Armistice was signed 90,000 kinds of parts were in stock---Many times the number of individual articles handled by any other service; more than the number handled by all other services combined. (And there were thousands of parts not in stock.) A satisfactory solution of the spare parts difficulty involved the following:

 (a) Information in the hands of manufacturers of the average expenditure of various parts, by a given type of vehicle, in a unit period.
 (b) A steady supply of parts on this basis.
 (c) Extensive depots, with thousands of bins, for housing the parts.
 (d) Skilled personnel to handle them.
 (e) An organized service of distribution.
 (f) Economy in use.

These requirements were met in varying degrees. They will be discussed in order.

31. *Point a:* Tables along these lines were compiled in 1917 by the Quartermaster Corps on the basis of manufacturers' experience in civil life. They have never been corrected for field conditions. They are, therefore, defective and should be so corrected---a very difficult process.

32. *Point b:* The policy was adopted that when a vehicle was shipped to France, there would be shipped in the same month 3 months' supply of parts (as per the tables) and, each month thereafter, 1 month's supply. This would create a 90 days' reserve of parts in France, of which 30 days was to be kept in the Advance Section. Much time and effort was needed to put this into effect. By the latter part of 1918, the system was working quite well, and about a 60-day reserve was maintained of the standard makes. But there were many makes in France---especially those purchased in Europe--- for which parts could never be obtained. This was one of the greatest difficulties faced by the Motor Transport Corps, and it arose from ill-considered purchases of vehicles made without any arrangement for their maintenance in the future. This is an error which we cannot afford to repeat.

* * * * * *

Parts have been manufactured in the A. E. F.; notably to meet the demands for parts which developed unexpected weaknesses---such as the Nash Quad steering knuckles and Ford ambulance front springs.

33. *Point c:* This was an ordinary construction problem. It faced the usual difficulties of shortages in labor and material. Permanent buildings were utilized where possible.

34. *Point d:* Such personnel was very short, like all Motor Transport Corps personnel. This general question is discussed later.

35. *Point e:* The general organization developed was as follows. The parts were shipped from the United States. They were handled as Class III property. They were

sent first to the main depot (Nevers, later Verneuil) which sorted them. Verneuil was a retail depot for the Base and Intermediate Sections and a wholesale depot for the advance depots (Langres, organized very early; St-Ouen, organized with the Paris Group; Sampigny, organized in the Argonne fighting). The armies established, where necessary, dumps or distributing points forward of the advance depot. Requisitions, etc., were handled as for other Class III supplies.

The system of distributing parts by a circulating convoy was first developed, it is believed, by the Air Service, whose units were much scattered and had at first standardized transportation. It was used by the Motor Transport Corps, when the First Army was first organized, for distribution to divisions. Later it was largely abandoned. This system requires considerable transportation and certain special trucks or trailers, but has many advantages, especially for small scattered units. Its possibilities should be given careful consideration in determining future policies.

During the Argonne fighting, the shortage of parts in the First Army was so critical that it was necessary for G-4, G. H. Q., to order shipped to Langres and Sampigny 50% of all parts received at Verneuil. This relieved the shortage considerably; but it is not believed to be a desirable permanent policy. It was made necessary largely because the shortage of personnel, pressure of work, and other difficulties at the advance depots made it impossible for these depots to specify to Verneuil exactly what they wanted.

Some difficulty was encountered by manufacturers packing an assortment of parts in each package. This increased labor of sorting and, if several of a certain part were wanted, made it necessary to go through several boxes in order to get them together. Bulk shipments would obviate this.

It is a difficult technical matter to make out a requisition for parts so that the items can be identified. This again involved technical personnel to make out and review the requisitions.

36. Point f: If the motor vehicles of the A. E. F. had been properly operated and kept in shape, there would have been an immense reduction in the demand for parts. This is a most important factor, often lost sight of, in the spare parts problem. The question of proper operation will be considered below.

37. The supply of tools and accessories was handled along the same lines as that of spare parts.

C. REPAIR PLANT

38. The character and use of repair plant is described below. The supply of this plant was partly by specified calls on the United States for unit plants and partly by an automatic system similar to that for spare parts, the United States shipping monthly a fixed quantity of tools and machinery as replacements for worn out machinery in existing plants on the basis of tables prepared from manufacturers' experience.

III. REPAIR

39. The extent of the motor transport repair problem was not at first appreciated by the Quartermaster Corps, and the Motor Transport Corps suffered from this lack of prevision. Two other services, the Ordnance and Air Service, early made provision to handle the repair of the motor vehicles which they were charged with obtaining and issuing, and which they reasonably assumed they would be charged with repairing. Both these services provided light mobile machine-shop plants for this purpose, so constructed that they would also be able to handle other special repair work of the Service. The Air Service also projected large plants for major repairs of motor vehicles (at Romorantin and Dijon) and a spare parts depot at Romorantin. The Quartermaster Corps

prepared mobile plants also, but not enough. It also early started the temporary plant at Nevers (subsequently succeeded by the permanent plant at Verneuil) and some smaller repair plants at Langres and elsewhere.

40. When G. O. 74 was published, a peculiar situation existed:

(a) The Motor Transport Service became responsible for repairing all motor vehicles.

(b) Its plant was inadequate and took a long time to obtain in the United States; machinery and especially hand tools were at a premium.

(c) The Ordnance and Air Service had previously been responsible for a great deal of the repair now turned over to the Motor Transport Corps. They had a large amount of repair plant in France, and their orders for the future were putting pressure on the factories at home. But they claimed that they could not turn over this plant to the Motor Transport Corps, because it was also designed to handle other types of repair work for which they were still responsible.

41. A compromise was finally worked out and approved by G-4, G. H. Q. The Motor Transport Corps took the responsibility for all major repair and drew up a scheme of personnel and plant for handling it, which was incorporated in the Motor Transport Corps Tables of Organization and approved by G. H. Q.; and took over certain plant from the Air Service. It took the responsibility for, and placed in its Tables of Organization the plant for minor repairs, except that for certain specified vehicles, which the Air Service and Ordnance handled with their mobile plants, which were left with them. The Motor Transport Corps was responsible for the supply of spare parts for these latter.

42. In solving the repair problems, the Motor Transport Corps assumed that there were three degrees of repair, beyond what could be done by a driver with his own tools:

> Minor repair,
> Major repair or overhaul,
> Reconstruction.

Minor repair was in general work that could be done by light plant in one day. Major repair or overhaul was in general work that could be done by more elaborate plant in ten days, involving the replacement of not more then 30% of all parts (by cost). More elaborate repair was reconstruction, which also involved salvage and the manufacture of new parts. These definitions were not rigid, and the different classes of repair graded into one another.

43. The plant provided for minor repair was the service part, In the armies, the service part was mobile. In the S. O. S., equivalent plant and personnel were used. Mobile units were authorized for the S. O. S., but due to the shortage nearly all in the A. E. F. were actually with the Army.

44. The plant provided for major repairs was the overhaul park. * * * This unit was divisible into four independent parts, as regards both personnel and plant.

45. The plant provided for reconstruction was the reconstruction park. Only two were in existence. This unit is not provided by Tables of Organization; in practice, the parks were established with the personnel and plant of several overhaul parks and a large amount of heavy machinery.

46. Vehicles of the armies needing repair were sent to the nearest army service park. If not susceptible of repair here, they were turned over to the S. O. S. and sent to an overhaul park. If not there repairable, they were sent to a reconstruction park.

47. In general, vehicles repaired at a service park were returned after repair to their units; vehicles sent to overhaul or reconstruction parks were dropped from the records of their units (which were furnished a replacement) and after repair were reported by the Motor Transport Corps as available for assignment, as in the case of new vehicles. These rules were not invariable.

48. As regards location of plants, territorially and with respect to units, the following general policies were adopted by G-4, G. H. Q.:

(a) Service parks with armies, 1 per division. Per corps, 1 per division in corps. Per army, 1 per division in army. To army artillery and similar units, numbers proportional (by number of vehicles) to division allowance. These to be located at the discretion of division, corps, and army commanders. * * *

(b) Service parks in S. O. S., at discretion of S. O. S.

(c) Overhaul parks, distributed along the fronts. Average distance from front, 30 miles ± 50%. Located on railroads and main communications. 19 of these are the allowance for an army of 1,300,000 or about 1 per 4,500 vehicles (excluding bicycles). Their distribution depends to some extent on the concentration of vehicles. Typically, however, a park should handle certain makes rather than the vehicles of certain units. With the districting of makes in units, this distinction disappears.

(d) Reconstruction parks, in intermediate section, on main line of communications. One for foreign makes (Romorantin); one for American makes (Verneuil).

49. In practice these policies were approximated only. The supply of mobile service parks and of overhaul parks never reached that required by the above. Districting of makes by unit was very incomplete when the Armistice was signed, and the selection of an overhaul park to do a certain job was usually made territorially.

IV. OPERATION

50. As stated in Part I, the first policy as regards operation of motor transportation was that the Motor Transport Corps should have nothing to do with it. By G. O. 74 this was changed, the Motor Transport Corps being given operating control of Class A transportation, defined as cargo-carrying or passenger-carrying vehicles used for general transportation purposes in the S. O. S., and the motorized portions of such reserve trains as may be held in or in rear of an army, under control of the army commander. No such reserve trains were ever created, and the Motor Transport Corps has operated only the S. O. S. vehicles specified.

51. All such S. O. S. vehicles were assigned by G-4, S. O. S., to the commanders of base and intermediate sections. By these commanders they were assigned to local pools; and in the case of trucks, were usually organized into operating units. Pools and truck units were under the command of Motor Transport Corps officers, and the vehicles were driven by Motor Transport Corps personnel. In the case of passenger-carrying vehicles, the pool received applications for transportation and dispatched the necessary vehicles to accomplish the transportation. In the case of cargo transportation, the usual method was for one or more truck units to be turned over to the officer in charge of a certain work. This officer indicated what was to be hauled, where and when. The Motor Transport Corps officer commanding the units was responsible that the hauling was carried out.

52. The routing and convoying of trucks to units to which they were assigned, was also an operating function.

53. The question of giving the Motor Transport Corps operating control over trucks in the armies has been extensively discussed. It was recommended over a year ago by certain officers of the Motor Transport Service. It was forced into attention by the Allied High Command, acting through the Military Board of Allied Supply, early in August of 1918. Somewhat later the C-in-C pledged the American Army to an adoption of the plan, along the general lines of the French system, and involving also traffic control. Plans were worked out, but had not been put into effect when the Armistice was signed. For this reason, it is not thought desirable here to describe the plans, which were carefully considered and in great detail. * * * It is believed that the question of pooling of trucks, centralized operation, and traffic control, * * * should be most carefully considered in the future.

54. Whatever be the decision with regard to the operating control of the Motor Transport Corps, that corps should have extensive powers to dictate the technical operating policies in the army, i. e., to see that correct and economical methods of driving, caring for vehicles, cleaning and lubricating, making minor repairs, etc., are understood by all personnel in the army---whether or not Motor Transport Corps---concerned therein. This implies that the Motor Transport Corps shall have extensive training functions, both for its own personnel and for that of other branches. Motor vehicles are complicated and delicate machinery; their first cost and cost of upkeep are so great, and the demand for them in modern war so enormous, that nothing should be left undone to ensure a thorough understanding of them by those that handle them.

* * * * * *

V. TECHNICAL SUPERVISION

56. Over all vehicles of Class B (see G. O. 74) the Motor Transport Corps exercised technical supervision as regards their operation and use. This was accomplished---

    (a) By the Motor Transport Officer of the division or other unit to which the vehicles belonged. This was done by a close supervision of the handling of motor vehicles of the command, the Motor Transport officer, as a staff officer of the command, pointing out any errors or abuses which were being committed and if necessary reporting the matter to his commanding officer.

    (b) By the Inspection Branch of the Motor Transport Corps, one of whose duties was to keep in touch with all Motor Transport officers and see that proper doctrines and policies were adopted.

VI. SUMMARY OF CRITICISMS OF PAST POLICIES

[This section repeats in summary the recommendations made in preceeding paragraphs of the report.]

* * * * * *

VII. PERSONNEL

69. The general question of motor transport personnel has not been touched on in the above, not being directly connected with the work of G-4. Mention should however be made of it in this place, because the continual shortage of personnel has been perhaps the most serious drawback from which the Motor Transport Corps has suffered. Of the four new services created during the war, three (the Air Service, Chemical Warfare Service, and Transportation Department) have been well supplied with personnel. In the case of the Motor Transport Corps, no adequate plan for placing it at proper strength was worked out until the Tables or Organization of August 23, 1918. Previous to that time, the Motor Transport Corps, while a branch of the Quartermaster Corps, had merely such personnel as the Quartermaster Corps desired to detail for that duty; and when it was removed from the Quartermaster Corps it took with it merely that personnel.

By the tables of August 23 the total personnel was 44,485. This was made to correspond to an army of 1,300,000. Almost before the tables were approved, and before the Motor Transport Corps personnel actually in France had reached one third of that figure, the strength of the A. E. F. had passed 1,300,000. Steps were at once taken to have the authorized strength of the Motor Transport Corps increased to correspond to the increase in the A. E. F., but up to the time of the Armistice approval of this had not been received. Practically this made no immediate difference, because on the date of the Armistice the total personnel in France was about 25,000, a little more than half the amount authorized, and little more than one third of the proportional amount that should have been authorized for the then strength of the A. E. F.

A particularly serious item of this shortage was that regarding officers of rank and experience belonging to the Regular Army. The Motor Transport Corps had far less than its share of these for the simple reason that it had never had them to begin with and under the pressure of war conditions could not get them. The announced policy of G. H. Q. has at all times been that Regular Army officers should be reserved as far as possible for combat duty and should not be transferred away from such duty for S. O. S. functions. Had this policy been followed out to a logical conclusion it would have involved removing from the other services such of their Regular Army officers as were suitable for combat duty or else effecting a transfer amont the services of Regular officers, in order to equalize the proportion. For quite obvious reasons that was not done. The old and well-established services, such as the Quartermaster Corps, Ordnance, Engineers, etc., had the officers to begin with. The Motor Transport Corps did not have them and could not get them.

In September, a War Department decision was made to the effect that the enlisted personnel of divisional supply trains should be Motor Transport Corps personnel. This had the effect of adding, on paper, an indefinite number of enlisted men to the rolls of the Motor Transport Corps. Practically it was of no value to the Motor Transport Corps during the emergency of the war, as this personnel was engaged in combat duty with divisions and could not be withdrawn therefrom. The practical effect was merely to change the label of these men.

The inherent difficulty in this matter was the same one which lay at the root of most of the difficulties of the Motor Transport Corps, i. e., it was a service created hurriedly under war conditions, the greater part of the work being done under the extremely pressing war conditions of the spring to early autumn of 1918. The remedy has already been stated. In the period of peace which has now commenced for the United States, the Motor Transport Corps must be developed at leisure along definite lines in such a way that it can meet war conditions without any further changes or additions of personnel than are necessary for other branches of the service.

GORDON R. YOUNG,
Lieut. Colonel, Engrs.,
G-4-D, G. H. Q.

C-in-C Rept. File: Fldr. 152: Report

Appendix E [Quartermaster]

4th Section (Quartermaster) GENERAL HEADQUARTERS, A. E. F.,

[Undated]

QUARTERMASTER ASPECT OF STRATEGIC SUPPLY

The functions of the Quartermaster Corps in the American Expeditionary Forces were first defined by G. O. 8, G. H. Q., 1917, which, in eliminating from its responsibilities such traditional quartermaster functions as building construction, rail and water transportation, left the corps free to develop its operations almost purely as a supply service. To supply proper was added the function of salvage, a feature hitherto quite undeveloped in any army, but recognized early in our European operations as a vital element in conserving our none too abundant overseas resources.

There were, of course, other quartermaster responsibilities, such as the pay of the Army and graves registration, which, while important, are not strictly supply functions and therefore will not be touched on in these notes.

Nor is the Motor Transport covered here, because early in the operation of the A. E. F., it was erected into a separate service and has a history of its own, while the Remount Service, though remaining technically under the Chief Quartermaster, has also had a practically independent existence.

The Quartermaster aspect of strategic supply therefore resolved itself in the A. E. F. into a determination of requirements for the supplies with which it was concerned, their procurement from the United States or European sources, the storage needed for their preservation and efficient handling, determination of their distribution along the lines of communication and within combat areas, and, finally, the salvage of what would otherwise have been waste.

This order will govern in the following outline.

I. REQUIREMENTS

The first and one of the most difficult tasks of the Quartermaster Corps was the determination of the quantities of each item which would be required by the A. E. F.

There were three prime factors to be considered: Strength of the force to be supplied; the quantity such strength would require for consumption; and the quantity required for strategic reserves.

The first of these factors---the strength to be supplied---was an unknown quantity, but that difficulty was solved by the method of reducing all requirements to terms of units of 25,000 men, the number of such units to be supplied being determinable in advance in the United States as the progress of training and shipping facilities became known.

There remained for the Quartermaster Corps in France to determine:

1. REQUIREMENTS OF QUANTITIES REQUIRED FOR CONSUMPTION

This problem again resolved itself into requirements for:

(a) *Articles consumed on issue:* These were articles such as subsistence, forage, fuel, and gasoline. Of this, forage was simple enough, given the animal strength and authorized issue. Subsistence was more complex since, in addition to the authorized issue, there was the question of sales commissaries and hospitals to consider. Experience in the United States was first taken, with allowances, as a basis for subsistence requirements, but after the accumulation of data on actual consumption it was found that important differences from previous experience prevailed and requirements were adjusted accordingly.

Fuel consumption theoretically could be and was estimated on authorized issues, but widely varying conditions in billeting areas and at the front, and the different sorts of fuel which had to be used---coal, wood, coke, charcoal---made any close calculation difficult. As for gasoline, the consumption varied with the quantities of motor transport and airplanes in use with the nature of the activities predominating from month to month, whether training, trench warfare, or open combat.

(b) *Articles of equipment requiring replacement after wear:* Here were included clothing, vehicles, harness, wagons and carts, and most all Quartermaster equipment.

The basis for determining the requirements was the amount of the original authorized issue, plus an estimate of the replacement requirements for each item under an average of the conditions confronting the A. E. F. This average of conditions itself presented great difficulties, including as it did seasonal variations, the varied activities of the S. O. S., the training areas, and trench and mobile warfare. The British and French experiences were taken into consideration, due allowance being made for differences in character and use of clothing and equipment, and, as soon as experience permitted, a table of weighted averages of consumption was prepared covering the more important items of clothing and requisitions were adjusted thereto.

(c) *Items for permanent installations:* For this class of items, including salvage machinery, refrigerator plants, and mechanical bakeries, the guide to determining requirements lay in the board outlines of the plan of development of the A. E. F. with its extended lines of communication and the urgent necessity of making the A. E. F. self-sustaining and independent of French resources to the utmost degree.

2. REQUIREMENTS OF QUANTITIES REQUIRED FOR RESERVES

In view of the length of our trans-Atlantic lines of communication, the length of our lines across France, together with the hazards of submarine warfare and mines and the acute state of rail transport in France, it was obvious that, to safeguard lives and operations of the A. E. F., very liberal reserves must be established and maintained in France.

These reserves were early fixed at 90 days, and although shipping and home difficulties of production did not permit of the Quartermaster Corps ever attaining that figure in most items, the 90 days' reserve remained the theoretical goal until the fall of 1918, when the serious tonnage situation and the accelerated troop program forced a reduction to a set standard of 45 days' reserve.

II. PROCUREMENT

The requirements of the A. E. F. having been determined as outlined above, the even more difficult problem of procurement had to be faced. Owing to the shortage of almost all supplies in Europe, the prime dependence of the A. E. F., of necessity, was on the resources of the United States, supplemented for tonnage-saving purposes by whatever could be obtained from England or the Continent.

The methods utilized were as follows:

1. PROCUREMENT OF SUPPLIES FROM THE U. S.

So far as was possible, and to an extent at first thought impossible, calls on the United States were put upon an automatic basis. That is, the requirements for one month of the average group of 25,000 men having been estimated and the probable troop movements being known, the Quartermaster General at Washington could figure by simple arithmetic the quantity of each sort of article required to be shipped during each coming month and so govern his manufacturing and inland shipping problems accordingly. Obviously the method was not perfect, since the equipment requirements of troops vary with the arm of service, as in such items as wagons and rolling kitchens, but while theoretically imperfect the approximation arrived at by taking as a basis the requirements of a complete division served admirably.

The actual application of the policy of automatic supply developed into three sorts of requisitions being sent to the United States:

(a) Exceptional supply. This was the inevitable exception to the general rule of automatic supply.

For material which was not a regular item of troop supply, such as special machinery, special calls had to be made.

Special calls had also to be made from time to time to meet emergency needs for quantities of regular items over and above the product of standing calls. All such requisitions were designated Exceptional Supply and it was understood they were for one shipment only and not be be in any sense a standing call.

Forage and gasoline had always to be carried under the head of Exceptional Supply because although in theory forage could have been shipped on an automatic basis, it was a fact that by reason of the large proportion of animals acquired by requisition or purchase in France and Spain and the partial supply of hay by the French, it was not possible for the home office to figure A. E. F. forage requirements ahead, while as for gasoline the interrelation of the A. E. F. supply with that of the French and the wide variations in consumption from month to month made it necessary to call month by month for the specific quantity required.

(b) *Initial supply:* To equip troops as they arrived with such articles of equipment as were not supplied in the United States and also to create and maintain the established 90 days' reserve for all troops in France, requisitions termed Initial Supply were made on the United States. The quantities shown on these requisitions for initial supply were calculated to cover the initial equipment requirements of arriving troops and also three times their monthly consumption requirements. This held for all sorts of automatic supply except subsistence on which the initial supply was figured at four times the estimated monthly consumption on the theory that the average convoy was one month in transit from dock to dock and arriving troops would therefore land with three months' supply if they were shipped with four. As a matter of fact the troops on transports were provisioned independently and the supplies produced by A. E. F. requisitions not touched, but inasmuch as tonnage was never enough to bring over the full product of the A. E. F. requisitions this theoretical excess of requisition was ignored.

To obtain the amount of supplies to be shipped in a given month as the project of A. E. F. requisitions for initial supply, the Quartermaster General took the number of units of 25,000 men to be shipped in a given month and multiplied the quantity set down for each item by that factor. To illustrate, if 200,000 men were to be shipped in October and escort wagons stood at 100 on the table of Initial supply the requirements for shipment in September were 100 x 8, or 800 escort wagons; this shipment being made in September because it was essential that the initial supply should arrive with or before each shipment of troops, and by reason of the slower crossing freighters, initial supply had to be shipped a month before the troops on whose strength its quantity was based.

(c) Automatic supply: Some confusion has been caused by reason of the fact that while almost all quartermaster supplies came over on an automatic basis, the term Automatic Supply as used in quartermaster requisitions and correspondence has uniformly carried a more restricted significance.

The term Automatic Supply was used in contra-distinction to Initial Supply and Exceptional Supply and represented the quantity of each item estimated as required for consumption by a unit of 25,000 men in one month, consumption being understood to include both actual consumption, such as that of foodstuffs, and consumption by issue in replacement, such as that of clothing, spare parts, etc. The determining factor for quantities to be shipped as Automatic Supply was the number of troops actually in France at the time the supplies arrived. For example, if the strength of the A. E. F. on

November 1 was 1,750,000 men, the multiplier to be used on the automatic supply tables in determining August shipments was 1,750,000 ÷ 25,000, or 70. This on the theory that shipments took an average of 30 days from dock to dock, and, assuming an even flow, August shipments with an average date of August 15 would therefore arrive in France at an average date of September 15. With 15 days allowed for handling and placing supplies in depots, it was necessary that the quantity required for the strength of October 1 should be shipped from the United States in August.

2. PROCUREMENT OF SUPPLIES BY PURCHASE IN EUROPE AND ENGLAND

While the main dependence of the A. E. F. for supplies was necessarily on the United States, it was obviously vital that the resources of Europe be availed of in the largest possible measure in order to save ocean tonnage, since tonnage was the crux of the whole supply problem.

In the beginning, the Quartermaster Corps, like other supply services, did this purchasing independently, but soon its purchasing operations were coordinated with those of the other departments under the control of the General Purchasing Board, of which the Chief Purchasing Officer, Quartermaster Corps, was a member. The purchases of the Quartermaster Corps in Europe reached an enormous total, over $382,000,000 up to December, 1918, and embraced a wide variety of supplies obtained in France, England, Spain, Italy, and Switzerland. To illustrate the variety and volume it may be added that on November 11, 1918, there were over 5,000 separate purchase orders outstanding, with quantities in some cases running into the millions.

In order not to disturb unduly the European market, it was necessary to obtain the consent of the government of the country concerned before any considerable purchase could be consummated, and the whole matter of local purchases was regulated by series of conventions with the Allies embodied in A. E. F., General Orders, of which G. O. 30, 1918, is typical, restricting, as it does to small emergencies, purchases which could be made without reference to and the consent of the French authorities. While necessary for the mutual protection of Allied interests, this procedure added greatly to the difficulties of the situation. Always there was involved the most delicate handling of matters with the various French departments, notably the Ministry of Armament.

The negotiations for coal and its transportation from England, which was throughout the main source of supply for the A. E. F., were equally difficult and delicate, forming so important a chapter of the program of supply that they are covered in a separate memorandum.

The purchases of the Quartermaster Corps fall into four general classes as follows:

(a) *Straight purchases, without replacement of raw material:* While probably most numerous, purchases of this class were exceedingly difficult to negotiate because of the scarcity of raw materials and the natural reluctance of the other Allied governments to permit the A. E. F. to consume their supplies without replacement either of raw material or, where the particular raw material was abundant, the use of the purchasing privilege as a lever to obtain allotments of A. E. F. tonnage for bringing over other materials which were short.

(b) *Purchase, with replacement of material:* Into this category falls a substantial part of the A. E. F. European purchases.

For example, in order to purchase rice flour in France in an emergency, it was necessary to import in A. E. F. bottoms and equivalent quantity of rice. Yeast had to be compensated for the barley and rye. For metal products generally, an equivalent tonnage of bulk metals had to be brought over.

(c) *Purchase, by cession from Allies:* In some instances valuable quantities of much-needed Quartermaster supplies were obtained by direct cession from the military stores of our Allies. Thus the French supplied at one time some 2,000 *fourgon* wagons to help out at a time when the A. E. F. was desperately short of horse transport. In this case, no direct replacement was involved, while in other instances, such as the supply of shoes by the French to cover a serious shortage in the fall of 1917, a later replacement of raw material was required.

(d) *Purchase, involving special production:* In addition to the straight purchases of supplies as above, there was a tremendous amount of actual production work done by and under the immediate supervision of the Quartermaster Corps in France. This production comprised:

(1) Production by the Quartermaster Corps with its own personnel and material in plants, some erected by the Quartermaster Corps, others leased. Examples of this were the Sheet Metal and Hollow Ware Shops at Bourges and the Coffee Roasting and Grinding Plant at Corbeil-Essones with its capacity of 1,300,000 rations per day. Also the immense development of the A. E. F. bakeries, capable on November 30, 1918, of turning out 1,830,000 pounds of bread per day.

(2) Production by French manufacturers using established plants, but with material supplied by the Quartermaster Corps and under Quartermaster Corps supervision. Of this character were a very large production of hard bread, for which flour was supplied, much metal ware manufacturing, and the plants for manufacturing chocolates and candy.

(3) Fuel wood production. This was vitally important and of a still different type, involving the exploitation of French natural resources by the A. E. F. To such dimensions did these operations attain that in the fall of 1918, over 10,000 men were employed solely on fuel wood production.

(4) Vegetable production. Here again there was an exploitation of French resources, and while the Armistice intervened before the Garden Service reached large proportions, the actual accomplishment achieved was considerable and the plans for 1919 extensive.

III. STORAGE

The required quantities of supplies having been estimated and procured, the problem of storage was next in order.

The factors determining the A. E. F. storage plans were, first, the requirements of the base ports for storage reservoirs to facilitate ship unloading; second, the requirements for storage of reserve supplies at convenient points; and, lastly, the requirements of storage for daily shipments direct to troops engaged in combat.

Beyond these regularly organized storage facilities of the Line of Communications, there was local storage of a more informal character---railheads, parks and dumps---providing a quantity of supplies readily available for emergency issue and practically in the hands of the troops.

Also, there were certain items of supply which presented special problems of their own---gasoline, fuel, bread, and the cold-storage of meat---and these will be touched on individually.

But as a whole the storage of the A. E. F. was divided into two groups: That on the Line of Communications (S. O. S.) and that in the combat units,

1. STORAGE ON THE LINE OF COMMUNICATIONS

The Quartermaster general storage and issue depots on the Line of Communications embraced on October 1, 1918, over 7,100,000 sq. ft. of covered storage, all in use, not to speak of over 4,400,000 sq. ft. of open storage space used in conjunction with the warehouses, and this total of over 11,500,000 sq. ft. was made to serve only by the most strenuous efforts in keeping stocks flowing and in stacking in the most economical manner.

(a) *General depots:* The general storage depots of the Quartermaster Corps were planned as of three classes.

(1) *Base depots:* These base depots were located in or immediately adjacent to the ports at which supplies were discharged. They served two distinct purposes: First, as a reservoir into which to pour and store supplies unloaded in excess of the available

railroad facilities for shipment from shipside to the interior; and second, as reserve storage depots. While the storage capacity of such depots as St-Suplice (at Bordeaux) and Montoir (at St-Nazaire) was huge, the storage feature was distinctly secondary from the standpoint of strategic supply.

The docking facilities at the ports being utterly inadequate, in spite of the enormous dock construction accomplished, the problem of first urgency was speed in unloading of ships, to prevent congestion in the ports and accelerate the ships' turnabout. If abundant railway facilities had been available, this could have been accomplished by the constant flow to the interior of cars loaded at shipside. But railroad cars and motive power were always short, aside from the fact that haste in loading and unloading brought cargo out of the holds in a condition which ofttimes necessitated sorting and classification before shipment. The solution was found in the base depot at or near the port, into which went, by shuttle trains, all cargoes for which cars could not immediately be had for the long haul up-country, and where classification could be made and balanced shipments made in regular marches to the intermediate and advance storage depots.

The plan and operation of a base depot of this type is well illustrated by the port of Bordeaux, as developed by the A. E. F.

Beginning in November, 1917, when two ships was the maximum which could be unloaded at one time, docks were built which by November, 1918, were capable of unloading 15 ocean steamships at one time. Three lines of standard gauge railway track ran on the docks along the shipsides, with traveling cranes to swing cargo direct from hold to car and with sheds behind the tracks for classification and overflow. Great railway yards were built and standard gauge tract laid to St-Suplice, some nine miles distant, where an immense storage depot or reservoir took up the slack in the incoming shipments, using constantly from 1,600 to 2,000 railway cars in the shuttle service and making possible an even flow of daily shipments up-country to the maximum of the railway capacity. Where in November, 1917, only 26,056 tons were unloaded, November, 1918, saw 236,563 tons of cargo unloaded at this port, not to speak of 6,933 animals and 2,027 troops.

Naturally, all this construction and operation required a large force, and with over 100,000 troops in this one base section the administration of the section and the coordination of all its activities required a complete staff organization.

(2) *Intermediate depots:* The plan of development of the A. E. F. supply system, premised upon the general scheme of prospective operations on the northeastern frontier of France and in Alsace-Lorraine, involved centrally located storage where the accumulated reserves could be maintained in readiness and where the advance depots could be kept filled to their established levels.

At the beginning such an intermediate depot was established in old French warehouses at Nevers, but this purely temporary establishment was fast outgrown and meanwhile the great storage depot of Gievres was created and was still growing when the Armistice was signed.

Beginning in the summer of 1917 with nothing but a flat expanse of fields and patches of pine woods, the Gievres depot in November, 1918, required an operating force of about 20,000 men, the plans included about 165 miles of railroad track, and the Quartermaster Corps along was using 108 warehouses averaging 50' x 400', or a total of about 2,160,000 sq. ft. of covered storage space, in addition to about 2,000,000 sq. ft. of open storage space.

The average warehouse 50' x 400' could hold about six days' supply of each ration article for a division of 28,000 men. This was probably about a million rations. The number of railway cars loaded and unloaded daily by the Quartermaster Corps alone at Gievres ran sometimes as high as 750 and up to the time of the Armistice the quartermaster section of the Gievres depot had handled over $200,000,000 worth of supplies.

Gièvres was selected as the location for the principal intermediate depot because of its strategic location on the main line of the American used railway communications, about half way between the ports and the Advance Section and was so situated that the main American traffic lines from all the ports, except Marseilles, could ship there without back haul.

Although intended primarily as a reserve storage depot, its central location gave Gièvres a Flexibility which, in addition to its regular shipments to the advance depot, permitted of direct supply to combat troops, first west, then east of Paris in emergency. Thus it functioned in advance depot through the regulating station of Creil for the 1st Division when in line near Montdidier, later for the Paris Group about Château-Thierry through the regulating stations of Le Bourget and Noisy-le-Sec. Afterwards, through St-Dizier, the Gièvres depot supplied direct close on to 800,000 men of the First Army and, finally, Gièvres is sending her daily trains through Liffol-le-Grand to supply the Third Army in the Rhineland.

While during most of this time the haul from Gièvres to the regulating stations, let alone the further haul on to the railheads, was too long to commend itself to the best practice for an advance depot, it served the purpose well at a critical period when military necessity upset premeditated plans as to the sphere of activity of the American Army, and by its ability to supply northwest, north, or east demonstrated the wisdom of the location from the standpoint of strategic supply.

The general plan of the depot embraced both east and westbound receiving and classification yards with parallel ladders of tracks, on one side of which the warehouses were built while the other side was left for open storage.

Each of the supply services had its own section of the depot set apart and the whole project as to construction, warehousing, labor, distribution, and apportionment of the chronically short car supply was coordinated by the commanding officer of the depot as a member of G-4. This commanding officer practically functioned as a regulating officer for the prompt shipment of automatic supplies; priority of shipments and the proper make-up of trains were among his responsibilities. * * *

(3) *Advance depots:* The only permanent advance depot included purely as such in the A. E. F. storage development was that built at Is-sur-Tille.

Like Gièvres, this was a depot for all services, the Quartermaster Corps having finally 17 warehouses at Is-sur-Tille with an aggregate of about 400,000 sq. ft. of covered storage and using about 500,000 sq. ft. of open storage space.

While Is-sur-Tille served its purpose well, supplying up to 700,000 men[*] at one time, from the standpoint of experience its principal interest was to develop the fact that it was a mistake to attempt to unite a storage depot and a regulating station, this, probably under any conditions and certainly without yard facilities and trackage far in excess of those at Is-sur-Tille or likely to be feasible of construction anywhere.

Although, early in the operations the regulating officer was given supreme control over all traffic actually moving in and out of Is-sur-Tille, the anxiety of the supply services to crowd supplies forward congested the yards to the stopping point at the most critical moment, just before the St-Mihiel drive. The situation was only relieved by transferring part of the responsibility for supply of the First Army to Gièvres as an advance depot regulating through St-Dizier. This relief coupled with an extension of the powers of the regulating officer so as to give him absolute control of the organization of shipments to the Is-sur-Tille depots made it possible to clear the yards and resume orderly forwarding of daily shipments. But it is certain that the best results can never be obtained by complicating a regulating station with depots utilizing the same yards. Advance depots should be as close up behind the regulating station as the reasonable safety of large aggregations of stores permits, but must be sufficiently separated from it not to interfere at all with the handling of traffic in the regulating yards and the unconfused handling of the daily divisional trains or *rames.*

---

[*] *The number of men actually supplied through Is-sur-Tille on August 30 was 1,036,785. This included 796,785 through the American station and 240,000 through the French station.*

In operation the Quartermaster advance depot functioned along the lines of an ordinary storage depot except that the bulk of its ration, forage and fuel shipments was automatic, that is, was based not on specific requisitions for particular articles but on strength reports of men and animals submitted weekly or oftener and against which, until changed, the required supplies were shipped daily. In some cases this was done by making up trains for specific divisions; in other cases standard ration cars were loaded to be made up in *rames* by the regulating officer according to the needs of his several railheads. The standard ration car held about 27,000 complete rations, less the meat, bread, and fresh vegetable components.

The internal management and arrangement of the depot was of the usual type.

(b) *Local depots:* In conjunction with the larger functions of the Quartermaster general storage and issue depots as described above, these depots and numerous smaller depots, base hospitals, and other formations maintained less important stocks of ration and Quartermaster supplies and issue to local organizations in the usual manner of post quartermasters in time of peace. Such were the stocks of the post quartermaster at Tours, the quartermaster depots at Valdahon and Issoudun, and perhaps fifty others.

(c) *Gasoline storage:* Storage for gasoline presented a special problem. The French method of distribution to their armies was almost entirely in the form of *bidons*, or cans, of 50 liters capacity, which were filled at bases and shipped forward by rail and truck.

While this *bidon* system presents the advantage of high mobility, it also involves an enormous supply of the containers to cover the long turnabout from base to front lines and return and tends to serious congestion of transportation facilities. Accordingly, it was decided for the A. E. F. to adopt the American methods of tank storage, railway tank cars between storage points and motor tank truck distribution for local consumption---in short, bulk distribution as against package distribution.

Large seaboard tankage was obtained into which arriving tank steamers could pipe their cargoes without delay. Then the Motor Transport Service having determined the routes to the front areas to be used by their convoys from the ports, smaller tankages were installed at suitable points along these routes, these local tankages to be kept filled by flow of railway tank cars from the ports. Railway tank cars were brought from America to the number of nearly 600, as was all the gasoline, and over 500 motor tank trucks.

While installation of tankage was pushed, even to the point of beginning an installation at Chermont-en-Argonne while the site was under almost daily bombardment from the air, it was not possible to keep up thus with the rapid troop movement. The *bidon* supply method, therefore, had to be continued on a large scale.

As a problem of strategic supply in a war of movement, it would appear from A. E. F. experience that the best solution for gasoline is a combination of storage tanks, motor tank trucks, and *bidons*. The portable tanks of 150-barrel capacity set down into the earth and connected in series to give capacity desired, permit of sending solid trains of railway tank cars to advanced railheads and appear to be the solution of the advanced storage problem. Motor tank trucks working forward from this railhead storage can refill *bidons* at the most advanced points.

At the conclusion of active hostilities, the A. E. F. controlled in France a storage capacity for over 11,000,000 gallons of gasoline and had consumed nearly 44,000,000 gallons, the consumption for October alone being over 11,000,000 gallons. No figures are available as to the average consumption of organizations, and if available, would not be of special value---the requirements varying so widely not only with the degree of motorization but with the character of warfare and length of haul from railheads. ***

(d) *Cold Storage:* The French people have never been accustomed in any large degree to the use of frozen meat, and it was therefore natural that their armies, to a considerable extent, should depend for meat supply upon the slaughter of animals by butchers attached to organizations. For the American Army in France, this was not either possible nor desirable, the cattle not existing in France in any quantity surplus to French needs, and American soldiers prefering frozen beef to the inferior product of camp butchery.

But the cold storage facilities of France, outside of a few large cities, were extremely limited, and one of the first large projects started was the cold storage plant, with a capacity of over 10,000,000 pounds, erected as a part of the Gièvres depot.

The U.S.S. *McClellan* anchored in the port of St-Nazaire, had a 1,500-ton cold storage capacity and was used as a receiving ship pending construction of refrigerator plants on shore at the ports. Arrangements were made for such cold storage of all the A. E. F. ports, either by construction entirely by the A. E. F. as with the 4,000-ton plant built at Bassens, or by cooperation with French owners in building or enlarging plants in which space was leased, as at St-Nazaire, Brest, and Le Havre. The main dependence of the A. E. F., however, during the period of active operations was on the Gièvres plant. A large number of American refrigerator railway cars was brought over, and the frozen meat shipped in them from shipside to Gièvres, where it was refrozen if necessary, stored, and shipped in refrigerator cars as required by the troops. Practical butchers detached from butchery companies were stationed at regulating stations and railheads to examine arriving meat, trim, and wash it and, as a result of this system the meat came to the messes in prime condition. There probably has never been an army which has continuously had such excellent beef even at the very front under combat conditions and with the longest line of communications in all history. The percentage of loss has been infinitesimal.

At the time of the Armistice the cold storage capacity of the A. E. F. plants, owned and controlled, was over 26,000,000 pounds and plans had been approved which would have more than doubled these facilities. * * *

(e) *Fuel Storage:* The location of fuel storage was necessarily determined in part by the character of the material. The problem was somewhat different for coal and for wood.

(1) *Coal:* The coal supply of the A. E. F. was all brought from England and was handled throughout in closest cooperation with the French coal supply. Of course, a purely A. E. F. coal dumps were maintained at the ports and in conjunction with the principal intermediate and advance depots, but the arrangement by which the A. E. F. coal importations from England were virtually pooled with the French supply lent a high degree of elasticity to supply throughout France. While for the most part the American armies were furnished with coal from American dumps there was a large aggregate of tonnage provided from French local reserves for scattered units, such supply being charged on the general debit and credit account and obviating the necessity for a multitude of small shipments.

(2) *Wood:* This was a very different problem from the supply-storage standpoint. The fuel wood of the A. E. F. was practically all of A. E. F. production and the prime problem was to locate the cuttings near the main points of comsumption so as to minimize transportation. To a considerable degree this proved feasible, especially in the Advance Section where the training areas with their large aggregations of troops were in the midst of the wooded country of the Haut-Marne and the Vosges. In pursuance of this general policy, wood-cutting units were at times sent to work in advance of railheads and during the Meuse-Argonne operations wood-chopping companies were producing firewood in the Argonne forest actually within range of occasional shells, the men sleeping in dugouts. The result was a substantial saving of rail transportation at a time when railroad cars were expecially short.

It should be noted, however, that, to a very considerable extent, the problem of wood supply automatically solved itself during the Argonne fighting; the quantity of trees felled and splintered by shell fire provided about all the fuel required, and the organizations engaged in the action made almost no calls on the rear for wood.

(3) Charcoal and Coke: These fuels, required for use in trench braziers where no smoke could be permitted and in bakeries, were supplied through the same channels as coal, that is, from depot stocks through the regulating officer, being shipped automatically on strength reports. * * *

(f) *Bakeries:* For that part of the A. E. F. located with any degree of permanence, as in the S. O. S. formations, the question of bread supply was simple. Field bakery companies or units of bakery companies were located at all points of considerable consumption and supplied garrison bread to the neighboring troops.

For the combat troops, much more of a problem was presented. Two alternatives were open: One, supply by attaching field bakeries to organizations; the other, to create large production bakeries at points in the rear and ship bread with the rest of the ration as a daily automatic supply.

The first alternative was backed by the fact that by baking at the front, not only could the men have fresher bread, but no small amount of transportation would be saved, since one carload of flour produces about six carloads of field bread, and the bread for a division, in the shape of 4-lb. field bread, required the use of nearly three French 10-ton freight cars per day.

On the other hand, with divisions shifting positions rapidly, going in and out of the line sometimes after a few days, it was highly desirable to reduce the installations to be moved to the absolute minimum, and that, added to the constant danger of bombing, led the French after four years' experience to rely almost entirely upon large central bakeries back of the regulating stations. The British practice was the same, and since in the early stages of the A. E. F. operations the railway car shortage was not as acute as it later became, the example of the Allies was followed and the policy of shipping bread from a central bakery in the rear adopted.

To that end, the very modern mechanical bakery at Is-sur-Tille was projected and built, with a capacity up to 750,000 lbs. per day, and two other similar mechanical plants had been ordered.

It should be noted however that the principle of shipping bread from the rear in this manner presupposes stabilized warfare and railheads well up to the front, and in a war of rapid movement, the fact that bread requires six times the shipping space of the equivalent flour would probably turn the scale in favor of field bakeries with troops.

On the other hand, if warfare is absolutely stabilized, as with armies of occupation, there would seem to be no question that the field bakery operating locally presents the greater advantages, and in fact preparations are now in the making to send field bakeries to supply the Third Army in the Rhineland, both to give the men fresher bread and garrison bread instead of field bread and also to save bulk in transportation on the long haul to the Rhine.

The conclusion therefore appears to be that while bread supplied from the rear is a simpler proposition and saves trouble at the front, the field bakery with organizations has weighty arguments in its favor and the conditions of the moment must govern the method to be adopted. If supply is to be from the rear, French experience is to the effect that the central bakery should be located behind, but not far behind, the regulating station and a special bread track allocated in the regulating yards on which a solid bread train can be run in from the bakery and cars picked off as required in making up the divisional *rames*.

2. STORAGE IN COMBAT UNITS

(a) Railheads. For subsistence, the railhead stocks constituted the only stockage in the army areas, outside of the authorized reserves actually in the hands of troops. This railhead stockage was under the control of the regulating officer, except in the case of G-4 reserves as explained later, and was of two distinct types.

At the railheads controlled from Is-sur-Tille, the stockage of subsistence was usually equivalent to five or six days' rations and forage for the strength being supplied. Daily ration trains containing more or less balanced shipments were unloaded into warehouses and the issues to organizations made from these warehouses. In short, these warehouses were miniature depots. This system made for continuity of supply, gave a high degree of protection against any rail interruption, and also expedited issues and avoided loss of time by divisional trains in waiting for arrival of the railroad trains. On the other hand, the system was not flexible of calculated to care for large and unexpected movements of troops from one railhead to another. When such movements did occur, large accumulations of supplies were almost always left at the abandoned railheads to be moved later at the expense of much costly transportation.

The railheads controlled through St-Dizier were of quite another type, planned and operated on quite a different theory. Utilizing the French daily *rame* method of sending up each day balanced rations for the required strength, issues were made direct from the railroad cars and only one or two days' stock maintained for emergencies. This method g gave more flexibility, a railhead could be created in a moment at any point where a train could be unloaded. For example, the Verdun railhead being bombarded one day as a ration train came in, it was only necessary to pull back the *rame* a couple of miles to a point where the rails ran alongside the highway and there the balanced issue was made complete. This would have been impossible under the Is-sur-Tille system of railhead depots and it is believed the French *rame* system forms the logical method of supply.

At certain of the St-Dizier railheads in addition to the emergency stock maintained by the regulating officer there were ration stockages set up by G-4 of the Army, known as G-4 reserves, and not to be touched except on orders from G-4.

At some of the Is-sur-Tille railheads, stocks of clothing were also maintained, but there was no clothing at all at the St-Dizier railheads.

In both cases, railhead officer was responsible solely to the regulating officer, reported to him daily his stock on hand, and functioned as his agent and representative. * * *

(b) Army Parks or Depots. To provide a reserve of quartermaster equipment in the Army itself, there was established a stockage known as an army part or depot. The first such park was created at Lieusaint, near Melun, during the operations of the Paris Group about Château-Thierry. This was intended and really served as emergency reserve only, ordinary requirements coming up from depot in the usual way.

When the First Army began its Argonne-Meuse operations and had to depend upon supply from Gievres during a period of most active fighting, with heavy casualties, much gas, and consequent large requirements for renewal of clothing and equipment, the Quartermaster army depot as established at Fleury became in fact a depot of general issue. The methods of requisition and issue there utilized reduced formalities to the minimum, the location was within trucking range of all the First Army organizations, and there can be no question as to the usefulness of the institution under the very difficult railroad conditions prevailing. The stocks accumulated were probably unnecessarily large in some items, but this was in process of correction at the time of the Armistice. It is also true that the ease of drawing tended to extravagance. But the large outstanding fact is that the supplies thus on the ground had a considerable part in keeping the First Army fit for action during the continuous operations of October and November.

The Second Army had also started to stock an army depot at Toul, intended to carry a 15-day stock of clothing, equipage, and miscellaneous quartermaster supplies from which would be filled all the smaller requisitions of the command. The Armistice, however, came along before this depot was fairly under way.

In neither army did the corps or division parks or dumps assume any definite or important form---in most cases not existing at all, in others as rather haphazard affairs.

In the First Army each division was ordered to have with it 500 complete outfits of clothing, including blankets. These were carried in the division gas hospital as a gas reserve under the exclusive control of the division surgeon. The Second Army carried the same gas reserve of clothing at railheads---a less desirable practice.

In conclusion, it may be said that while the combat operations of the American armies, as army organizations, were not of long enough duration to develop any very complete experience in army stockage practice, the army depot or park did thoroughly demonstrate its usefulness. * * *

IV. DISTRIBUTION

The system of requisitions and supplies to troops is completely covered by General Order 44, G. H. Q., 1918, and therefore, need not be repeated here.

V. SALVAGE

The salvage activities of the A. E. F. were divided between the collection of abandoned and unserviceable material, at the front and elsewhere, and the repair and reclamation of this material in workshops set up in the S. O. S., and to a much smaller degree in shops organized in the army area.

Americans, as a rule, are proverbially wasteful. The American soldier is no exception, and the waste of material inevitable in combat is prodigious.

It was the function of the Salvage Service to attempt to reduce this waste to a minimum, and in spite of a handicap of insufficient and often incompetent personnel, the work actually accomplished was very large. For example, the one item of blankets sterilized, washed, repaired, and shipped from the salvage depots from April to October, 1918, reached a total of over 750,000, representing a cash value in America of over $3,000,000 and a large volume of tonnage.

The principal salvage depots where the bulk of the work was done were located at St-Pierre-des-Corps, near Tours, and at Lyon, with smaller shops at other centers. These large plants each employed several hundred enlisted men and several thousand French women and of necessity had to be located in centers of considerable population. Such could not be obtained near the front and, as a consequence, a very long railroad haul was involved, keeping the salvage material out of circulation for a correspondingly long time. In the Second Army an attempt was made to relieve this situation and speed up the reissue of salvaged material by establishing a number of small shops in towns and villages in the back army area, and, if hostilities had not ceased, this excellent plan would doubtless have been more largely developed and helped materially.

One other important fact should be noted here, the inability of the Salvage Service, as a purely S. O. S. formation, to either control or organize salvage in the armies.

If the army happened to have a capable salvage officer, things went well; if the chief salvage officer of the army was less competent or energetic the work lagged. In either case, the chief of the Salvage Service had no authority, was not even consulted in the designation of the army salvage officers, and had no control over the methods pursued. In any future salvage organization, pains should be taken to so organize that the responsibility for salvage throughout the forces should be a single responsibility.
* * *

VI. QUARTERMASTER CONTROL BY G-4, G. H. Q.

The supervising and coordinating functions of G-4, G. H. Q., so far as related to quartermaster activities, were entrusted to a subgroup known as G-4-E.

This group maintained the closest liaison with the Chief Quartermaster, A. E. F., keeping in daily touch with the general situation as to the quartermaster supplies and establishments, in order to act intelligently and promptly as the technical situation changed supply conditions, emergencies developed, and the demands of the several armies required coordination.

To accomplish this, close liaison reports were had daily of the total subsistence on hand in all quartermaster depots, and also from Gièvres and Is-sur-Tille, as advance depots, came daily reports of subsistence stocks in relation to strength each was supplying that day. * * * Daily reports were also received from the regulating officers showing subsistence stocks at all railheads, and the whole food resources of the A. E .F. were thus constantly known.

Daily reports of Quartermaster depot stocks and of stocks in the army depots were required for the principal articles of clothing and equipage, and with complete semi-monthly reports covering all stocks in Quartermaster Depots and all purchases contracted for by the Quartermaster Corps, the quartermaster supply situation was known at all times and any necessary constructive or corrective measures could be promptly taken.

C. W. HALSEY,
Major, General Staff.

C-in-C Rept. File: Fldr. 169: Report

Appendix F [Signal]

4th Section, General Staff   GENERAL HEADQUARTERS, A. E. F.

Chaumont, Haute-Marne, March 15, 1919.

TELEPHONE AND TELEGRAPH SERVICES

GENERAL

It has been the function of the Signal Corps to provide adequate facilities for the transmission of communications the nature and importance of which was such that they could not be transmitted through the mails or courier system. The means used to the greatest extent in providing this liaison system were the telephone and the telegraph. The operations consisted of two phases, one for the requirements in connection with the creation and the administration of the machinery for supplying the combat units, and second for the liaison between the command and the adjacent combat units.

The provision of telephone and telegraph service for the American Expeditionary Forces presented a problem of considerable magnitude on account of the location of the combat units with respect to the ports of entry from which they were supplied. The provision of facilities for the general command and administration up to the combat units was based originally on the use of the French system existing at the inception of the American Expeditionary Forces. General conditions known in the office of the Chief Signal Officer of the Army at Washington relative to the scope and extent of the French system indicated that certain additional lines would have to be constructed by the American Signal Corps. Accordingly, conferences were held in the office of the Chief Signal Officer of the Army in Washington and a hypothetical net was worked out on which the original orders for materials and apparatus were based.

Upon the arrival of the American command in France the immediate problem was to establish adequate means of telephone and telegraph communication between the units located at Paris and Nevers, the former place being decided as the point of command for the American Expeditionary Forces. The Chief Signal Officer, A. E. F., proceeded to establish relations with the French authorities to the end that existing facilities would be used as required, to the extent to which they were available.

It developed in the early conferences that the long duration of the war with its demands on the allied manpower and raw materials and the already heavy traffic on French facilities would preclude the securing from that system of any considerable portion of the facilities required. Accordingly, tentative plans for the basis of ordering material and apparatus were completed to cover a flexible and extensive all-American system. The American system was designed to supplement and reinforce such facilities as could be secured from the French system. Cordial relations were established with the military and civilian telephone and telegraph authorities of France and England and advantageous arrangements were made in which the American Expeditionary Forces were to be provided with means for telephone and telegraph communications of urgent military importance to the extent that the existing French and British systems would permit.

Comparisons between the Continental and the United States standards of telephone and telegraph systems and devices were made and as a result any extension to the existing systems were made on the basis of American standards throughout, employing those items of equipment or apparatus which were standard in American practice and which would involve the least difficulty with respect to manufacture and transportation. Likewise the methods of liaison within the combat units of the French and British armies were minutely studied and standards of equipment and materials were decided which would employ the most efficient means of communication taking into consideration the habits of the American Expeditionary Forces in the use of the telephone and telegraph as a means of liaison. These standards have been revised continually to meet the ever-increasing difficulties and changes in conditions.

BEGINNING OF A TELEPHONE AND TELEGRAPH SYSTEM

The French telephone and telegraph system was used exclusively in the early stages. The first Signal Corps telephone office was opened at Paris on June 15, 1917. From June to August small telephone systems were established at the various base ports in France. The first Signal Corps telegraph line to be put into operation in Europe was leased from the French between Paris and Nevers and was equipped with French instruments remodeled by Signal Corps personnel for the American type of operation. This telegraph line was opened August 9, 1917. The Signal Corps system was expanded until offices for telephone and telegraph service were in operation at the American headquarters at Paris and Cosne, Vierzon, Dijon, Nantes, and Bordeaux. It soon became evident that on account of the limited wire facilities in the French system, the Signal Corps of the United States Army would have to build an extensive system of communication, and accordingly plans were formulated for the construction of a pole and wire line from the first base port, St-Nazaire, to the rear of the zone of combat operations which would eventually be occupied by the United States Army.

It was foreseen at this time that available Signal Corps personnel should be brought to France ahead of the combat units which they would later be assigned. Accordingly requisitions for personnel were placed and the first telegraph battalions arrived in France on August 20, 1917. They were assigned to duty in the construction of the above-mentioned line, the initial portion being between Dijon and Gondrecourt. The arrival of additional Signal Corps personnel and the construction of the necessary facilities over and above those which the Signal Corps were able to obtain from the French system were completed as rapidly as supplies and available personnel would permit.

The first extensive Signal Corps telephone exchange was installed in France and the new General Headquarters of the American Expeditionary Forces at Chaumont. It was put in operation on September 1, 1917, and provided service to the various offices as rapidly as they were occupied.

Combat divisions of the American Army began to arrive in their divisional training areas in France in the latter part of December, 1917. Telephone and telegraph lines were extended to these areas for the purposes of general command and supplies administration. At the same time the nets for training purposes were established within the training areas.

During October, 1917, it became evident that the volume of communication between the War Department at Washington and the American Expeditionary Forces was increasing to such an extent that the existing facilities across the English Channel were rapidly becoming inadequate. Accordingly the Chief Signal Officer, American Expeditionary Forces, visited England in November, 1917, and perfected arrangements for the laying of a four-conductor cable across the Channel and for the necessary telephone and telegraph lines in England. Pending the carrying out of these projects, immediate arrangements were made for one telegraph line from London to Paris, where it connected with the already established Signal Corps system to Chaumont. The Signal Corps service over this system was inaugurated from Chaumont to London by General Pershing, who sent the first official message to the American Ambassador at London. The special American cable was laid across the Channel and connected to the Signal Corps office in Paris and London by the leased land lines on February 25, 1918. Arrangements were also made in November, 1917, with the Western Union Company under which that company reserved part of their system from London to New York for official American Expeditionary Forces communications, thereby giving direct service between General Headquarters, American Expeditionary Forces, and Washington, D. C.

ENLISTED FORCE MESSAGE CABLE SERVICE

Shortly after the arrival of the Chief Signal Officer, American Expeditionary Forces, in France, he took steps to organize a cable service at reduced rates for the interchange of communications between members of the American Expeditionary Forces and their relatives and friends in America. Official announcement of this service was made in a memorandum June 17, 1917, Headquarters, American Expeditionary Forces, signed by Brigadier General (then Colonel) Russel.* On account of cable congestion between London and the United States it was necessary to suspend this service on October 25, 1918.

THE COMPLETED SYSTEM

The completed telephone and telegraph system of the American Expeditionary Forces at the signing of the Armistice consisted of a means of liaison between all units of the American Expeditionary Forces. For purposes of description it may be divided into four parts; namely, (1) net for the general command, administration, and services of supply; (2) net for the command, administration, and supply within the combat zone; (3) special net for the Transportation Service; and (4) net for the United States Navy in France.

(1) *The net for the general command, administration, and Services of Supply:* The meager wire plant available in the French system for the use of the American Expeditionary Forces necessitated the construction of standard American pole and wire lines from General Headquarters at Chaumont to the Headquarters of the Services of Supply at Tours, to the training areas in the vicinity of Chaumont, to the headquarters of the First Army at Souilly, and to the headquarters of the Second Army at Toul. Also, American built lines were necessary to connect the Headquarters of the Services of Supply with the base ports at Brest, St-Nazaire, and Bordeaux, and a second line from Tours to Chaumont by way of Paris. The connections between the Headquarters, Services of Supply, and the Headquarters of Base Sections Nos. 3, 4, 6, and 7 consisted of lines leased from the British and French civil systems.

The lines built by the Signal Corps were so planned and routed as to provide direct connections with the Signal Corps system for a large majority of the American Expeditionary Forces units in France. In order to provide adequate service over the leased lines it was necessary to take over from the French civil authorities the maintenance of these lines. The result of this operation was highly successful, but in spite of the careful attention to these lines it has been impossible to secure the high degree of efficiency from them as has been secured from the American-constructed lines in France.

**Brigadier General Edgar Russel, Chief Signal Officer.*

At all centers of activities in the American Expeditionary Forces, except the very smallest, local telephone installations were made and telegraph offices were opened. For the very small units, connections were made to the long line system where practiable; otherwise connections were made with the French and British civil and military systems.

The plan covering the Signal Corps system in France has continually had as its basis the fundamental principle that whatever facility was put in it should be of such a character as to provide the greatest amount of service commensurate with the expenditure of material and labor and the tonnage required. To this end the lines constructed were so equipped, operated, and maintained as to obtain a maximum efficiency. For example, four single wires between Tours and Chaumont were equipped and operated to provide three telephone circuits and 16 telegraph circuits. These practices permitted the utilization of a minimum of tonnage from the United States, and the result throughout has been a flexible system whereby telephone communications over small copper wires have been made possible throughout the American Expeditionary Forces, a result over similar distances not having even been approximated in the French system. For example, the long line system consists of copper wire approximately 2-1/2 mm. in diameter, whereas the longer lines in the French civil system consist of wire approximately twice this diameter.

The latest developments in the art of printing telegraph terminal apparatus have been utilized in the telegraph system. There were two primary considerations in the adoption of this highly useful instrument; namely, (1) that another type of special personnel could be utilized and to that extent reduce the requirements for Morse telegraph operators, the total requirements for which otherwise would have been such as to interfere seriously with the means of communication in the United States which was so necessary to the prosecution of the war; and (2) it also provided another factor of flexibility in that there were two distinct ways of transmitting telegraphic communications. This type of operation had been installed between Chaumont and London, Chaumont and Tours, Tours and London, Chaumont and Paris, and Tours and Paris. The telegraph operating forces at the points of origin and destination of the larger volume of telegraph traffic were of the highest type and the most expert operating staffs that have ever been collected. Likewise, in the telephone service, women highly trained in switchboard operation were brought from the United States to serve at the larger centers. These women, to a large extent, were able to speak French and this made it possible to secure the maximum efficiency in the combined use of the French and the American systems. Their work has been one of the main factors in the success of the telephone service for the American Expeditionary Forces.

(2) *Net for command, administration, and supply in the combat zone:* The telephone and telegraph net in the combat zone was maintained under the most severe conditions. Due to the customs of the personnel of the American Expeditionary Forces as regards the use of the telephone service for administrative purposes, the net in the different units had to be of considerable extent. They provided connections from the army command at army headquarters to the command and administration centers throughout the armies to the most advanced posts on the fighting front. These nets in many cases were constructed, operated, and maintained under the most trying circumstances. In comparison with the French and the British systems they were the most complete in the Allied forces.

(3) *Special net for the use of the Transportation Service:* Special telephone and telegraph lines were equipped and turned over to the Director General of Transportation, American Expeditionary Forces, for use in connection with the administration and operation of that department in moving A. E. F. personnel and freight over French railroads. These lines extended from the headquarters of the Services of Supply to the principal base ports and up to the railheads in the combat zone. Special Signal Corps personnel was detailed to the operation and maintenance of these lines.

(4) Net for the use of the United States Navy in France: For the use of the United States Navy a special telephone and telegraph net was provided by the Signal Corps, United States Army, between London and the Navy stations along the coast of France. This net was made possible by the use of existing French lines where they could be secured by lease and throughout the other sections by the construction of standard American lines. Local telephone and telegraph systems were installed where required at the larger centers, bases of operation, and observation points extending along the coast of France, from Le Havre on the north to Cap Ferret, south of Bordeaux. This system provided an adequate and a most satisfactory means of communication for the United States Navy, a fact to which the commanding officers of the Navy have attested many times.

TELEPHONE AND TELEGRAPH ACTIVITIES AFTER THE SIGNING OF THE ARMISTICE

The rapid forward movement of the occupying armies presented unusual difficulties with respect to the extension and establishment of wire lines of communications. It was necessary to build extensions across "No Man's Land" at two points and to overhaul and repair enemy military lines ahead of "No Man's Land" and to establish lines for military purposes from the civil nets beyond.

The main axes of communication for the occupying armies are routed from Chaumont through Souilly, Verdun, Etain, Briey, Thionville, Trèves, to Coblenz, and from Chaumont through Neufchâteau, Toul, Briey, Luxembourg, Trèves, to Coblenz.

These main axes were pushed ahead and service established to the advance points ahead of the units for which they were provided. The army network for the occupying forces is made up largely of the military and civil lines found in the occupied area, which have been taken over by the Signal Corps. In addition to providing the command net and local nets for the occupying forces, a general command net to the Inter-Allied Command at Luxembourg was established in the American area, which was extended from this area by the signal services of the allied forces throughout their respective areas. This Inter-Allied command net was completed in the American area prior to its completion in any of the other Allied areas.

Continual supervision is given to the amount of traffic over the system operated by the Signal Corps. The lines which were leased from the French system are being returned to that service as rapidly as the United States military operations will permit.

[The remainder of this part of the report consists of statistical reports showing the cost of an equal volume of commercial service at commercial rates, main lines in occupied areas as of March 1, 1919, Signal Corps pole and wire plant as of October 31, 1918, telephone system as of October 31, 1918, telegraph and telephone traffic by months, and a map of the telephone and telegraph system of the American Expeditionary Forces.]

* * * * * *

SUPPLY SYSTEM

In May, 1917, General Pershing with his staff left the United States for Europe, and upon arrival established his headquarters in Paris, France, and arranged for the arrival of the American Expeditionary Forces, the first of which arrived in July of that year. Conferences were held by the General Staff while en route to France regarding requisitions for supplies from the United States which were placed as soon as they arrived in Paris. These requisitions were estimated to care for an expeditionary force of 30,000 men. This was in accordance with the first studies of the General Staff for an initial force, which was later changed to 500,000, and afterwards to 2,000,000. At the time of the Armistice arrangements were being made to take care of 4,000,000 men.

THE FIRST SIGNAL CORPS GENERAL SUPPLY DEPOT

In August, 1917, the first Signal Corps general supply depot was established at Nevers, Niévre, France, but up to this time no supplies based on the requisition already placed had arrived from the United States. There had also been established in Paris the Office of the Purchasing and Disbursing Officer, Signal Corps, who had contracted for a large amount of signal corps supplies to be purchased in France during September, 1917. In the Office of the Chief Signal Officer, Line of Communications, Paris, the Supplies Division was established which prepared the necessary records and acted on all requisitions for signal corps issues in France. This continued until January, 1918, at which time the Nevers Depot had grown to such large proportions that in order for requisitions to be handled more expeditiously and because of the slowness of the French mails, the Supplies Division of the Office of the Chief Signal Officer, Line of Communications, was moved to the Depot at Nevers and all requisitions for supplies were acted upon at that point.

THE ESTABLISHING OF AN ADVANCE DEPOT

On January 14, 1918, the American Expeditionary Forces were planning for an army of 2,000,000 troops, there being at that time about 200,000 in Europe, which were either in training areas or in the Toul sector. It was decided to establish an advance Signal Corps depot in order that equipment could be delivered to combatant troops with a minimum of delay. This depot was opened at Is-sur-Tille and had the function of keeping all troops in the Advance Zone of the Army supplied with signal material. The stock of this depot was kept up by means of a maximum and minimum list which included all signal corps material necessary for combatant troops and work behind the lines, which was obtained automatically from the Signal Corps general supply Depot at Nevers or from the disbursing officer at Paris.

PROCUREMENT

In the latter months of 1917 each service of the American Expeditionary Forces was making purchases independent of all other services, which caused more or less competition in the markets of Europe. Early in 1918, the purchasing officers of the various staff corps were organized and made members of the General Purchasing Board, with the General Purchasing Agent of the American Expeditionary Forces as president thereof. From that date on, all purchases in France, which were made with the view of reducing tonnage from the United States, were coordinated; the Signal Corps, realizing that it was possible to procure in Europe large amounts of material needed for line construction, and even combat uses, organized a Procurement Section, the duties of which were to place requisitions in the United States for supplies which could not be procured in Europe, these requisitions to be prepared so that shipments of supplies would arrive in proportion to the arrival of troops. These requisitions were so made that they were automatic in every way, and should the proportion of troops be enlarged by the General Staff for any one month, it was only necessary to cable the United States the percentage increase in requisitions. As to wastage and maintenance of signal corps supplies in France, the tonnage of signal corps supplies needed to maintain each member of the Expeditionary Forces, together with a percentage of wastage per man per month was accurately figured. Thus the flow of signal corps supplies (which could not be procured in Europe) from the United States was placed on an automatic basis, similarly to the flow of foodstuffs and other supplies for troops.

On the other hand, a survey of the markets of Europe was made and orders placed for a varied amount of material, the principal items of which were over 200,000 crossarms and 100,000 poles for main telegraph and telephone lines, and 3,000 radio sets of all kinds. It was found that almost all factories in France had been taken over by the French government and that they were working at a maximum of production, the output being used almost exclusively for the French armies. It was necessary for the Signal

Corps in its survey of Europe to find factories which had not been taken over by the French government for its own Army's production and to so develop the resources of these factories in order that additional supplies could be turned out for the American Army.

An instance of this was the manufacture of pole-line hardware at Imphy Steel Mills, near Nevers, which was made possible by the cooperation of the French government. In the latter part of 1917 and early in 1918, the Signal Corps was constructing along its main line of supply in France from St-Nazaire to Neufchâteau a telegraph and telephone line consisting of ten wires of standard construction. A great shortage was being experienced in bolts, lag screws, transposition brackets, and other pole-line hardware, due to the fact that the production in the United States had not yet been speeded up to meet the requirements of the Signal Corps in France, and also due to a shortage in ships' tonnage. The Signal Corps arranged through the French government for the manufacture at these steel mills by turning in iron poles which were melted down and made into such pole-line hardware as was needed to complete this and other urgent telephone and telegraph projects in France.

A representative of the Signal Corps was sent to various cities in southern France, where by working in constant liaison with the French authorities he was able to procure for the Signal Corps a large amount of tools such as pliers, hammers, wrenches, climbers, and other supplies urgently needed by the Signal Corps. Also as a result of this survey of southern France it was possible to place orders for certain supplies which up to that time it was thought impossible to manufacture in France. A survey was also made of the surplus stock of other staff departments of the American Expeditionary Forces and, where possible, by working in conjunction with these departments and by turning over to them slow-moving stock of the Signal Corps, which they needed, we were enabled to procure over 2,000 shovels and 30,000 pounds of friction tape. These items were urgently needed by both combatant troops in the Zone of the Armies and telegraph battalions doing construction work behind the lines.

Due to our efforts in Europe and our automatic requisition placed upon the United States, at the time the Armistice was signed there was an adequate reserve in Signal Corps depots to maintain and equip over 40 fighting divisions, and the situation as regards supplies had been so standardized that there was no further fear of a shortage of any one article needed by the Signal Corps in France.

The signing of the Armistice changed these conditions and required that our efforts towards cancelling requisitions and contracts for material in Europe be inversely proportional to our procurement theretofore. This subject was immediately taken up and requisitions in the United States and purchase orders in Europe cancelled to the extent that was thought expedient, thus causing a saving to the United States, as far as the Signal Corps was concerned, of $73,229,159.71. The Purchasing Division of this Office was later changed from a purchasing agency into a sales department, and arrangements are now under way whereby, when approved, the Signal Corps will be enabled to dispose of its surplus supplies in Europe at an advantageous price, figuring original cost, plus transportation.

INSPECTION

Detachments were supplied by the Division of Research and Inspection, Signal Corps, and stationed at all supply depots and factories in France manufacturing signal corps supplies. These inspectors passed on all material before issues were made, which assured that all equipment conformed to standard before it reached the troops for whom it was intended.

REPAIR SHOPS

Large repair shops were established at the supply depots which repaired all material arriving in a damaged condition. These shops also salvaged all material which was returned after being used in the field.

METHOD OF HANDLING REQUISITIONS

In the early part of 1918 all requisitions for supplies for troops in the Zone of Advance were first approved by G-4, General Staff, of the unit to which they were attached, and forwarded direct to the depot at Is-sur-Tille where issues were made without further reference, the items which could not be supplied from that point being extracted and forwarded to the Signal Corps General Supply Depot No. 1 at Nevers, where, if available, supplies were issued; if not, they were either made in the shop or ordered purchased and delivered by the disbursing officer at Paris. All requisitions other than those for the Zone of Advance were forwarded direct to the Signal Corps Depot at Nevers, and were filled at that point.

REORGANIZATION

In April, 1918, it was decided that all staff corps should be consolidated within the Line of Communications and that General Headquarters at Chaumont should be tactical headquarters only. To do this the Headquarters, Line of Communications was moved to Tours, France, which is on the main line of the 600-mile telephone line from St-Nazaire to Neufchâteau, and the Hq., S. O. S., was established at that point. With this arrangement, an entire reorganization of the whole scheme of supply for the Signal Corps was inaugurated and the Division of Supplies was established at Tours, under the Chief Signal Officer, A. E. F., who approved the issue of all signal corps supplies.

METHODS OF ISSUING SUPPLIES TO COMBATANT TROOPS

All combatant organizations left the United States without their signal unit equipment which was supplied to them after their arrival in France. This was issued to them, as soon as they reached the training area, from the Signal Corps Intermediate Supply Depot. When their preliminary course of training had been completed they were moved to the Zone of the Armies where expendable material and equipment lost in action was replaced from dumps located in the Zone of the Armies. Material not available at these dumps was extracted and forwarded to the advance depot for issue and if not available at that point a requisition was sent to these Headquarters for further action. With the advance depot in such close proximity to the Zone of Operations it was possible for an organization to get the necessary supplies within 24 hours by means of trucks or special trains which were run daily from the advance depot to the various railheads. Before the Armistice was signed there had been established three army parks which served the needs of the First and Second Armies and the Paris Group. Over 45 divisions were supplied with their entire unit signal equipment and over 60,000 miles of wire, 16,000 telephones, and 8,000 switchboards were issued to these organizations.

CHANGE OF LOCATION OF THE SIGNAL CORPS GENERAL SUPPLY DEPOT FROM NEVERS TO GIEVRES

In June, 1918, it was decided to move the Signal Corps General Supply Depot from Nevers to Gièvres due to congestion at that place, the Nevers depot having grown from nothing to a depot embracing 56,000 square feet of covered storage and 218,000 square feet of open storage with no possibility of enlargeing itself. Also there were better transit facilities at Gièvres, and in accordance with a plan of the General Staff to centralize a number of supply depots of the various staff corps at that point the move was made at this time. Signal Corps depots were later established at St-Sulpice, Montoir, and Montier-chaume to care for the immediate areas of the S. O. S. in which they served and to act as storage depot for equipment for the front. Also a photographic depot was established at Paris which supplied the photographic needs of the entire A. E. F. and acted in relation to the armies in the same manner as the advance depot at Is-sur-Tille. A radio depot was opened at Orly Field, near Paris, which issued supplies in accordance with the needs of the Air Service at that point. Before the Armistice was signed there were 7 Signal Corps depots and three Army Signal Corps Parks with a storage space as follows:

	STORAGE SPACE	
	Covered	Open
Signal Corps Advance Depot 1, Is-sur-Tille, Cote D'Or.	70,000 sq. ft.	600,000 sq. ft.
Signal Corps Intermediate Depot 2, Gievres, Loir-et-Cher.	64,750 " "	
Signal Corps Intermediate Depot 3, Montierchaume, Indre.		
Signal Corps Base Depot 4, Montoir, Loire-Inférieure.	25,000 " "	
Signal Corps Base Depot 5, St-Sulpice, Gironde.	52,250 " "	
Signal Corps Photographic Depot 6 Paris, France.	6,200 " "	
Signal Corps Radio Depot 7, Orly Field, Paris.		
Army Park A, Toul, Meurthe-et-Moselle.	7,500 " "	
Army Park B, Lieusaint, Seine-et-Marne.	9,000 " "	12,000 sq. ft.
Army Park C, Parois, Meuse.		
Total Covered Storage Space,	350,000 " "	
Total Open Storage Space,	1,500,000 " "	

PERSONNEL AT THE TIME OF ARMISTICE

On November 11, 1918, the organization of the Supplies Division, including base ports, depots, and disbursing officer, Paris, consisted of 74 officers, 924 soldiers, and 13 civilian clerks.

STATISTICS

Combatant organizations were furnished with sufficient Signal Corps supplies to function properly at all times.

The principal items obtained in Europe were tools, telegraph and telephone equipment, and wire.

Sufficient outside distributing and outpost wire was shipped to France which, if stretched out, would make a circuit of the earth at a latitude of HAVANA, Cuba, 23,090 miles.

Sufficient lead covered cable was shipped to France to reach from DETROIT, Mich., to SAN FRANCISCO, Cal., 2,548 miles.

Material for over 3,000 miles of light line construction was erected in the Zone of the First Army alone.

Enough cross arms were purchased in France for over 40,000 miles of heavy and light line construction and enough poles for 3,000 miles of standard 10-pin construction.

Probable cancellations of Signal Corps orders in Europe amount to over $9,000,000.

The total value of cancellations by the Signal Corps, A. E. F., was over $73,000,000. This includes the value of cancelled orders placed on the Chief Signal Officer of the Army by Chief Signal Officer, A. E. F.

[The remainder of the report consists of a tabular statement of the Purchasing and Disbursing Section, quantities, lists of items of signal equipment obtained in Europe and in the United States, a chart of supply as of November 11, 1918, and an organization chart.]

* * * * * *

[UNSIGNED]

C-in-C Rept. File: Fldr. 170: Report

Appendix G [Liaison]

4th Section, General Staff   GENERAL HEADQUARTERS, A. E. F.,

Chaumont, Haute-Marne, May 25, 1919.

REPORT ON G-4, G. H. Q. REPRESENTATION WITH FRENCH AND INTERALLIED GENERAL HEADQUARTERS

The establishment of a section of G-4 with the corresponding section of the French General Staff, known as the Direction de l'Arriere, took place in the latter part of June, 1918, at the time when the American divisions were first going into the line at the Chateau-Thierry salient. It has been realized for some time that the method of transacting business hitherto employed with the French General Staff, i. e., passing through the French Mission at Chaumont, had many disadvantages and that efficiency demanded the placing of a qualified American Officer, or officers, in the actual French offices with which the business was being done. Colonel (then Major) John R. Kilpatrick, General Staff (then Quartermaster Corps), who had been regulating officer at Mantes for the 1st Division in its Cantigny action and had subsequently organized the regulating station of Le Bourget, was on the request of General (then Colonel) Payot, detailed as G-4 representative with the *Direction de l'Arrière*. He was given on office at Provins at French General Headquarters and subsequently on July 15 Captain (then Lieutenant) Chapin, General Staff (then Cavalry), was added to his office force. On August 23, Col. Kilpatrick was relieved from this duty, eventually to be made Chief Regulating Officer for the A. E. F. and Captain Chapin for some time was the sole representative. During an enforced absence of Captain Chapin on account of illness, Captain O'Donnel Iselin, Field Artillery, represented G-4 for about one month and at the end of November, 1st Lieutenant Thomas H. McKittrick, Jr., Infantry (then 2d Lieutenant), was obtained from G-2, S. O. S., to be assistant to Captain Chapin. Lieutenant McKittrick returned to the United States in April, 1919 and was replaced by Captain William S. Davenport, Sanitary Corps, who is at present on the duty.

On October 15, General Payot was relieved from duty as Assistant Chief of Staff charged with the *Direction de l'Arrière* at the Headquarters of Marshal Petain to become *Directeur General des Communications et des Ravitaillements aux Armeés*, or in other words, head of the 4th Bureau of the staff of Marshal Foch. The G-4 representative followed General Payot, the offices moving to Lamorlaye in the Department of the Oise.

The establishment of the *Directeur General des Communications et des Ravitaillements aux Armeés*, coinciding approximately (i. e., within 14 days) with the signature of the Armistice, establishes definite division in the work carried on by the G-4 representative and therefore permits of the following two period to be covered in this report, namely:

    a. *Direction de l'Arrière*, French General Headquarters, July 1918 to Armistice.

    b. *Direction Générale des Communications et des Ravitaillements aux Armeés*, Allied General Headquarters, the Armistice and after.

- 183 -

Before passing to the chronological outline of the work of the office, a brief outline of the organization of the French staff section with whom we worked will make the later matter of this report clearer.

The *Direction of l'Arrière* corresponds roughly with Section 4 of our General Staff, being that section of the French General Staff which is charged with the direction and coordination of all the Services of the French armies for three purposes: First, to organize the communications of the different armies; secondly, to organize the transportation of every kind within the territorial Zone of the Armies; thirdly, to insure the supply and take care of the evacuations of all kinds from the armies. At the head of this staff section is an *Aide-Major Général* charged with the Direction de l'Arrière, whose functions approximately correspond to the Assistant Chief of Staff, G-4, G. H. Q. He is in direct charge of the eight sections of the *Direction de l'Arrière* proper and the responsible chief of the Services hereinafter referred to, which function side by side with the *Direction de l'Arrière*.

[The report here discusses the organization of the *Direction de l'Arrière* proper and the establishment of the *Direction Générale des Communications et des Ravitaillements aux Armées*.]

* * * * * *

As will be seen from the chronoligical summary of the activities of this office which follows, the character of the work underwent a complete change with the establishment of the *Direction Générale des Communications et des Ravitaillements aux Armées*. While at Provins with French General Headquarters, our activities related to organization, transport, and supply matters between the French and American Armies. Since the move to Lamorlaye was made and General Payot became the Interallied Staff Chief, our activities broadened in scope considerably, and while we had certain requests for supplies and minor transportation problems to be worked out, the vast majority of the questions assumed an interallied aspect and required the adjustment of points of view substantially different from one another. The office began, as well, to take on questions which came within the jurisdiction of the 1st Section of the General Staff, Civil Affairs Section, and to a less extent with Economic Commission in Paris.

A. FRENCH GENERAL HEADQUARTERS, JUNE 1918, TO ARMISTICE

The general character of the work at the time Colonel Kilpatrick was assigned to the duty was chiefly the establishment, in cooperation with the French, of the installations necessary to serve our armies then being organized, together with the methods by which an interchange of commodities of all kinds could be made with the French. At this period, June and early July, 1918, we had but one regulating station, namely that of Is-sur-Tille, in full operation. Through the help of General Payot and his assistants, the combined regulating station of Le Bourget and Noisy-le-Sec was organized to serve our Paris Group and later that of St-Dizier was established for our First and Second Armies.

Along with the establishment of the regulating station went the choosing of sites for, and the installation of, remount depots, veterinary hospitals, hospitals for evacuation of the wounded, and field bakeries.

The remount and veterinary hospital questions were carried on largely by Lt. Col. R. H. Williams, Quartermaster Corps, Chief Remount Office, Advance Section, S. O. S., with Captain de Laperouse of General Payot's staff. Col. Williams made frequent trips to Provins and with the aid of the French staff established remount depots and veterinary hospitals necessary in the area of the Paris Group, the G-4 representative simply facilitating the meetings between the remount officers concerned.

The establishment of a line of hospitals for the evacuation of wounded within a certain radius from the west to the southeast of Paris was a large question with which we were concerned with the *Service de Santé* (Medical Dept.) for some time. This particular question involved obtaining decisions from three different sections: First, the *Direction de l'Arrière* proper as to the general question of emplacements; secondly, the *Service de Santé* (French Medical Dept.) from the point of view of sanitation and suitability of the site for hospitalization; thirdly, with the *Directions des Transports Militaires aux Armées*, from the point of view of railroad connections. The matter had about reached a definite conclusion at the time the divisions were withdrawn from the Paris area and the First Army area set up.

The finding of sites for aviation depots and aerodromes was another question which occupied a large part of the office work. In this, as in the other installation matters, several points of view had to be considered and these were taken up in the following order. First, the advice of the *Direction de l'Arrière* proper was obtained as to the general question of emplacements; secondly, the problem was studied from the point of view of railroading with the *Direction des Transports Militaires aux Armees*. No site could be obtained until the same had been considered in the way indicated and frequent misunderstandings arose with the American Air Service due to the failure of this branch to understand at first the precise method of attacking the problem. We were frequently beset with requests, even demands, from the aviation headquarters in Paris for the immediate granting of a site, which had appeared to an aviator to be desirable from the aviation point of view solely. At one stage of our work several aviation officers came to Provins much incensed because a particular location could not be accorded them but when it was pointed out that the use of this emplacement was simply impossible from a railway point of view, they understood the matter and accepted a substitute site which General Payot and Major Kilpatrick picked out. It was not until November, however, just before the signature of the Armistice, that the whole general question was thrashed out between the Air Service and General Payot's staff and a complete understanding reached. This occurred at a conference in General Moseley's Office at Chaumont. * * *

The obtaining of emergency supplies for the American Army from the French armies, and vice versa, was another distinct type of business with which we had to do. Our calls on the French consisted in ammunition, other ordnance property such as canteens, munition wagons, etc., hay, gasoline, and fresh vegetables. With the establishment of our new regulating stations in the First Army area, we also made considerable calls for telegraph poles. The French called upon us for such commodities as oats and flour. The obtaining of the supplies requested from the French was always a very easy matter, at least from the point of view of their General Headquarters. The officers consulted at once responded to the requests and did everything in their power to assist us in obtaining immediate delivery where possible. It was never necessary to write a formal letter in the first instance, the business generally being transacted orally with confirmatory letters when the thing was done. If satisfaction could not be given within the exact terms of the request, every effort was made to fill the same as closely as possible. For example, on September 3d I received a rush telegram from G-4, G. H. Q., asking for the delivery to the First Army of 50 tank trucks of a certain gallon capacity or carload trucks capable of being equipped with casks to carry approximately the same capacity and thirty-five steel or wood reservoirs of about 5,000-liter capacity. This telegram came in at 10 a. m. and by 11:30 complete orders had gone out to fill the request, specifying what could actually be delivered and the substitute measures to be taken for the material not available. Letters were then exchanged confirming the transaction and the whole matter occupied not 24 hours time. This efficiency was carried out in every other section of the staff for any requests which we made.

Supplies of food and other commodities comprised within the scope of the articles dealt with by our Quartermaster Corps were obtained through the Intendance Section of the *Direction de l'Arrière*. This section, functioning under Commandant Boudot, controlled the disposition of all such supplies for the armies throughout France through a chain of depots of four categories strategically situated with reference to the regulating stations through which the supplies moved forward to the armies in action. * * * The maintaining of the stocks in the depots in question at a given level developed upon the Ministry of War in Paris, but as soon as the commodities were placed in the depots, they passed under the exclusive control of the *Direction de l'Arrière*, and without orders from this staff could not be released for distribution. The same efficiency which characterized the work of the other sections existed in this one and Commandant Boudot and his officers never failed to give absolute satisfaction to all requests addressed to them. This was true even in the most active times throughout the summer of 1918 when we made calls for all sorts of emergency supplies with which this section dealt.

The questions of railway transportation with which we dealt were chiefly in obtaining special train movements, either troop or hospital trains. The main body of movement of large units was carried on by the *Directions des Transports Militaires aux Armées* in consultation with and according to orders received from the 3d Bureau (Operations) of French G. H. Q. and these accordingly were carried on outside the work of our office. Special moves of hospital trains, however, and the routing forward of certain supplies, were attended to by us with the *Directions des Transports Militaires aux Armées* and in this branch we met the same cordial cooperation as we had found in the other sections. At about the end of August a serious block of our supply trains from Gièvres to St-Dizier occurred, and in this particular instance the full weight of the *Directions des Transports Militaires aux Armées*, backed by General Payot and his staff, cleared up very quickly a situation which threatened serious consequences. The first intimation of trouble reached our office officially on August 31 and in General Payot's absence Col. Delalain at once took the matter in charge so that by September 1, or within 24 hours, an extremely dangerous situation had been cleared up.

Another large railway question with which the office had to deal concerned the establishing of 2d line regulation stations to supplement the forward regulating stations of movement. This matter was the subject of a large conference in Paris on Sept. 20, but the Armistice intervened before a great amount of work could be done by either army looking to the establishment of the proposed installations.

During the first phase of the office work indicated above, General Moseley and General Payot consulted each other frequently, both at Provins and at Chaumont, regarding the active matters of ordinary business and further regarding the organization of G-4 in its relation to the S. O. S. which would approximately parallel the French organization of the *Direction de l'Arrierel* General Payot was very anxious that we model our bureaus on his and facilitated in every way a study which was made between his section and General Moseley's. The Armistice alone prevented the reorganization from being put into effect. The conferences held between General Moseley and General Payot inevitably smoothed out many of the complicated questions which were continually carried on between the two Headquarters.

B. DIRECTION GENERAL DES COMMUNICATIONS ET DES RAVITAILLEMENTS AUX ARMEES, ALLIED GENERAL HEADQUARTERS, THE ARMISTICE AND AFTER

At about the end of August a discussion at French General Headquarters began to arise regarding the possible appointment of General Payot as Chief of the 4th Section of Marshal Foch's staff, in which position the French authorities wished him to exercise the general control over all allied supplies and transportation. The proposition of the establishment of this Interallied G-4 had been definitely turned down by both the British and American High Commands on the ground that Marshal Foch's Supreme Command dealt only with matters of military operations. In early October, however, the 4th Section of Marshal Foch's staff, called the *Direction Générale des Communications et des Ravitaillements aux Armées* was established by a Decree of the President of France and in the middle of the month General Payot was installed in his new duties. The first result of this was the immediate necessity of enlarging the American representation and from a single officer and a field clerk we grew to an organization of two officers, a field clerk, a sergeant major, an interpreter, and a stenographer.

The most important matter which was transacted before the signature of the Armistice was the general plan drawn up by General Payot and discussed at an interallied meeting regarding the measure to be taken to rebuild the railway lines in the territory which was, at that time, being evacuated by the retreating German armies. This conference marks the first of many such interallied meetings which were to characterize the work of the G-4 representative from now on. The matters discussed at this particular meeting never came to a definite settlement, however, due to the signature of the Armistice.

On November 14, 1918, the representatives of the 4th Sections of the staff of each of the allied armies were called in conference to study the instructions of Marshal Foch which had been drawn up to give effect to the clauses of the Armistice interesting the staff sections involved. At this conference the various Interallied Military Commissions charged with railway transportation, Rhine navigation, application of various articles of the Armistice, etc., were constituted. * * *

The Armistice, as was expected, at once changed the aspect of many problems with which previously we had had little difficulty. The most important of these was the general question of railway transportation which hitherto had moved relatively smoothly from the point of view of French General Headquarters. From now on, however, the difficulties incident to the advance of the armies over a broken line of communication, coupled with the interjection of French politics into the situation, made General Payot's work, and that of the *Directions des Transports Militaires aux Armées*, most difficult. Early in December matters were at such a state that the transportation representatives were called together in conference at which the situation was explained but not improved in any particular measure.* * * Throughout these difficulties, which terminated in February by the French Ministry returning the railroads to their civilian owners, Colonel [E. M.] Boquet, the *Directions des Transports Militaires aux Armées* and General Payot never ceased their efforts to give the utmost satisfaction possible to the American requests. No one of the Allied armies received from the hands of the *Direction Générale des Communications et des Ravitaillements aux Armees* any treatment radically different from that accorded to any other, either in this particular situation or any other with which this office had to do.

A second important change brought about by the Armistice, and a situation in which many delicate questions had to be treated, was the evacuation by the American Army of its installations on French soil. To adequately deal with this matter the French government organized a separate section of the Ministry called the Ministry of Industrial Restitution and the Ministry of the Liberated Regions. Requests began to come into the *Direction Générale des Communications et des Ravitaillements aux Armées* from these bodies, as well as from the Ministry of War, pressing General Payot to compel the American Army to vacate many installations in which it had made semipermanent establishments. Factories and other industrial buildings, barracks, and similar military establishments needed for the demobilization of the French armies, were continually demanded. General Payot was, however, able to retain for us the installations which we most particularly needed and it was due to his cooperation and activities with the Ministry in Paris that a situation, which at one time forshadowed considerably strained relations, was smoothed out.

By the beginning of December a section for the Administration of the Occupied Territories was created in the staff of the *Direction Générale des Communications et des Ravitaillements aux Armées*, and as this section corresponded with the American Assistant Chief of Staff for Civil Affairs, this office gradually became involved in many of the questions of civil administration. The questions in these matters which were of a routine character such as proposed postal regulations, circulation rules, and the like, were simply forwarded through us to the proper staff section for action. There were, however, certain questions which came up for active discussion in the interallied conferences held at Lamorlaye where marked divergence of views between the French, Belgians, British, and ourselves necessitated the finding of some middle course. The most important of these questions was the method by which requisitions should be settled in the occupied territories and this gave rise to numerous propositions and counterpropositions from G-4, the Asst. C. of S., Civil Affairs, and the *Direction Générale des Communications et des Ravitaillements aux Armées*. Eventually the matter was settled at a conference and the French armies adopted our point of view, due in no small measure to the manner in which General Payot supported General Smith [Brigadier General Harry A. Smith, American Assistant Chief of Staff for Civil Affairs] in our side of the question.

A matter which concerned G-4 and the Asst. C. of S., Civil Affairs, equally was the supply of the civilian population of the left bank of the Rhine with the foodstuffs which were to be furnished by the Supreme Economic Council sitting in Paris. The carrying on of this supply was ordered done by the armies by the Economic Council, and the organization of the Military Commission which has the matter in hand took place in February at General Payot's office. * * * This Commission has functioned by numerous meetings held at given intervals at Lamorlaye and the occupied territories, at which meetings, the G-4 representative has always been present. At the present writing the questions with which this Commission deals are gradually being absorbed by the civilian authorities. With the signing of the peace, in all probability its functions will cease.

The evacuation of France by the enemy, and the occupation of Germany, involved the *Direction Générale des Communications et des Ravitaillements aux Armées* in the establishment of telephonic and telegraphic communications from an interallied point of view and the G-4 representative was called upon by the Chief Signal Officer to attend numerous conferences held for these questions, and, in general, to endeavor to facilitate the relations with the *Direction Générale des Communications et des Ravitaillements aux Armées*. Many difficulties were encountered during the three months which followed the Armistice due to a lack of definite organization within the French armies in relation to the other Allies. Telephone and telegraph systems were interfered with and many of the efforts of the Interallied Staff were rendered negligible until matters were finally straightened out.

Immediately upon the signature of the Armistice the project of supplying the Armies of Occupation by way of the Rhine was brought up by General Moseley to General Payot, and received his hearty approbation. In the latter part of January an informal meeting was held at Lamorlaye, following which, negotiations were opened with the Dutch government and the establishment of the Rhine as a line of communication and supply became a reality. This matter, however, did not become an Interallied affair, as had been the expectation of Payot, for each army carried on its work at the base ports as it desired, making use, however, of the Interallied Rhine Navigation Commission for the movement up the river for its supplies. The only active work which this office had to do in this matter lay in the negotiations which terminated in an Interallied meeting at Rotterdam at the end of January.

One of the most important questions treated at this office during this period was the question of the division of spoils of war recaptured from the enemy during the course of the advance of the Allied Armies. In this matter the American and French point of view differed considerably and frequent propositions and counterpropositions were exchanged until the matter was settled by a conference held in PARIS on April 23, at which the practical measures to be taken were decided upon. Throughout this matter, the American Army maintained its willingness to return to the original owners all property which could be identified as having originally belonged to French and Belgian citizens. On the other hand, we maintained certain legal principles which we believed to be sound, and the difficulty of the situation arose from the fact that the French could not agree with us on these legal points. For more than two months the matter was under discussion, all classes of property being involved, but in the end the parties concerned agreed to disagree on the law and worked out practical principles to give satisfaction to all concerned.

At the present writing the administration of the occupied territories has passed to a Civilian Commission, and in the near future, the supply of the civilian population of Germany will likewise pass. The American Army is quickly withdrawing from all its installations in France and the functions of the *Direction Générale des Communications et des Ravitaillments aux Armeés* are gradually becoming less and less. What has been a most interesting and vital work is, at present, practically terminated and a relation of almost a year with General Payot is ending to the great regret of all those who have come in contact with him.

Respectfully submitted.

May 25, 1919

L. H. PAUL CHAPIN,
Captain, G. S.

C-in-C Rept. File: Fldr. 184: Report

Appendix H [Troop Movement]

4th Stction, General Staff   GENERAL HEADQUARTERS, A. E. F.,

Chaumont, Haute-Marne, March 26, 1919.

Memorandum for: Assistant Chief of Staff, G-4.
in compliance with your memorandum of November 27, 1918, the following report of the activities of G-4-H is submitted.

The magnitude of the plans for the A. E. F., and the rapidity with which it was transported to France resulted in the distribution of its forces over an area extending from the base ports to the battle line in the northeast corner of France. The problem of debarking these troops without congestion of the ports and transporting them without delay from the ports to the various camps, training centers, and depots, necessitated carefully laid plans for locating and employing every unit immediately upon its arrival in France.

This was effected (1) by compiling a Priority Schedule or organization of the A. E. F. divided into 5 phases, identifying with an item number every unit to be organized in America and sent to France, and arranging the units in a general way in the order in which they were to be sent to France. (2) By placing with each section of the General Staff the duty of issuing timely orders to the port commanders (through the Commanding General, Line of Communications, or later Commanding General, S. O. S.) effecting their assignment to commands and travel to first destination.

This duty, together with the maintenance of the Order of Battle was assigned to the Coordination Section, General Staff (or 4th Sec., G. S.) by G. O. No. 8, 1917, and placed by the Chief of Section in a separate subsection. later G-4-H.

To carry out this duty it was necessary for G-4-H to establish means for obtaining the earliest possible advice as to the prospective and actual departures from the U. S. and to identify all units so reported with the role that they were intended to play in the activity of the A. E. F. This was done by the receipt of (1) a weekly cable from the War Department listing all units scheduled for early convoy during the succeeding ten days, identified by means of their priority schedule item number and (2) cables from the Navy Department through the commander of the U. S. Naval Forces Operating in European Waters reporting the departure of every ship carrying military passengers. The later reports were received about seven or eight days after the ships sailed from the U. S.

Upon receipt of these reports and identification of all troops the plan made for their employment by interested staff sections and services were ascertained and coordinated and the orders issued to the C. G., S. O. S. governing their disposition and assignment to a command. In the case of units assigned to the S. O. S. no further orders affecting their movements were issued from these Headquarters, their disposition thereafter being left to the Commanding General, S. O. S. Disposition for all combatant troops was received from the Operations Section (G-3).

It was also the duty of G-4-H to distribute to all interested staff sections and services the information received regarding prospective and actual departures from the U. S., arrivals at the ports, and the assignments made of incoming troops.

In addition to the assignment of new units G. O. No. 8, 1917, placed the duty of maintenance of the Order of Battle with the Coordination Section, G. S.; later it was placed under the First Section, G. S., in the reorganization of the staff by G. O. 31, 1918.

For this purpose, reports were received from base port commanders of all troop movements originating at base ports and from the commanding officers of troops reporting their arrivals at destination. These reports were consolidated by G-4-H and issued to all interested staff sections and services and also used for the compilation of the Battle Order. These reports continued to be received and published by G-4-H after the Order of Battle was placed under G-1 and were used by the latter section as data for that purpose.

The establishment of Troop Movement Bureaus at Chaumont and Tours greatly improved the method of obtaining advice regarding troop movements. The Troop Movement Bureaus arranged for all movements of over 100 men and received reports from the railway transport officers at points of departure and destination of all movements affected.

The placing of the maintenance of the Battle Order under the First Section, G. S., and leaving the assignment of units with the 4th Section, G. S., by G. O. 31, 1918, resulted in an illogical distribution of duties between the two sections. The preparation of the Priority Schedule, the identification and assignment of units arriving in France and the maintenance of the Order of Battle are so closely allied that they should be performed by one staff section.

                    C. Z. CASE,
                  Capt., cav., G-4-H.

C-in-C Rept. File: Fldr. 185: Report

Appendix I [Regulating Stations]

4th Section, G-4-I, General Staff GENERAL HEADQUARTERS, A. E. F.,

[*Undated*].

This Section of G-4, G. H. Q., is headed by the Chief Regulating Officer who supervises and coordinates the work of the various regulating stations and railheads. It is through these latter agencies that G-4 discharges its responsibility in respect to supply and transportation arrangements for combat. Regulating stations are, in effect the control points in the system of supply and through them pass the subsistence, ammunition, equipment, and material destined for the armies. They serve to direct the stream of supplies and regulate the rate of flow to railheads, which are the points at which delivery is made to the supply trains of the larger combat units. In addition to controlling the flow of supplies, the regulating stations are distributing points upon which replacements and organizations are moved for forwarding to their proper organization or positions in the line. The operation of hospital trains in the evacuation of the wounded and disabled to the rear is also an important function of these stations.

A regulating station can well be compared to an hour glass. Just as the sand passing from one chamber to the other is regulated by the narrow neck in such a way that the flow is maintained with absolute regularity, so also are the supplies and troops moving from the great reservoir of the S. O. S. forward into the Zone of the Armies controlled and directed by the regulating station, carrying the simile farther, when the hour glass is reversed the narrow neck again controls the flow of the sand back into the first chamber. So also the regulating station controls the movement rearward of hospital trains, salvaged materiel, troops going into rest areas, and empty supply trains.

It is not the intention to describe here the operations and functions of the regulating stations. * * * A more detailed discussion is contained in the reports of the regulating station at Is-sur-Tille and the regulating station at St-Dizier. Some interesting figures and facts taken from these reports are:

Is-sur-Tille Report. The station was established on November 26, 1917, and was the first regulating station to operate under the supply system outlined in G. O. 73, Dec. 12, 1917, G. H. Q., A. E. F., and as amended in G. O. 44, March 23, 1918, G. H. Q., A. E. F. There was also established at Is-sur-Tille the largest of our advance depots. Statistical records of this regulating station January 1 to November 11, 1918, disclose the following figures:

1. On November 11, 1918, there were stationed at Is-sur-Tille for administration and depot labor, 600 officers and 20,000 men.

2. Total rations issued:

   To men 98,106,097
   To animals 13,907,992

   Maximum daily issue:

   To men 796,285
   To animals 122,779

3. Carloads freight received 118,214
   Carloads forwarded (exclusive of troops) 102,686

4. Is-sur-Tille yards, newly built, American-made standard gauge railroad tracks . . . . 90 miles

5. Open storage space employed: Six million square feet Depot warehouse space: One and one-quarter million square feet under roof.

6. Storage capacity for ten million rations.

7. Operated the largest bakery in the world; daily capacity 800,000 pounds of bread.

8. Evacuated over 70,000 sick and wounded men.

The maximum operation was reached in August, 1918, when from August 2 to August 30 the number of men and animals for the supply of whom this station was responsible jumped from 374,749 to 796,785 men and from 36,130 to 122,779 animals. On August 30, 1918, 1,036,785 men were supplied, this figure, however, included 240,000 French.

During the month of August, in preparation for the St-Mihiel attack, approximately 2,000,000 reserve field rations, 500,000 reserve forage rations, 500,000 gallons of reserve gasoline with proportionate amounts of lubricants and large quantities of engineer, medical, ordnance, and chemical warfare supplies were distributed at parks which were established in close proximity to the front.

St-Dizier Report. This station commenced operation August 28, 1918. The striking feature of this regulating station, as well as the station located at Le Bourget, was that there was no advance depot established to serve it, and as a result the intermediate depot at Gièvres was called upon to act as an advance depot for the supply of the troops regulated through these points. The principal facilities used both at St-Dizier and Le Bourget had been installed by the French as a part of their system of regulating stations and consisted primarily of excellent railroad yards for the reception and make-up of trains from which several railroad lines radiated to the front. To maintain regularity in the flow of supplies and to give the greatest amount of flexibility in the shifting of supplies as divisions changed their location, regular daily marches or schedules over which the supply trains were forwarded were arranged between Gièvres and these stations. At the same time the regulating station developed what is known as the *rame* system, which consisted of blocking out the trains into sections, each section containing the supplies and material for a division. * * *

The largest number of troops and animals supplied from St-Dizier was 718,000 men and 126,700 animals. The daily average was approximately 675,000 men and 115,000 animals. During the St-Mihiel and Argonne-Meuse offensives 476,000 men and 10,712 officers, consisting for the most part of casuals, replacements, and small organizations, were regulated by St-Dizier. 263,000 men and 10,712 officers were actually detrained at this point and new orders given them. A total number of 140 officers and 3,290 enlisted men were on duty at this station on November 11, 1918, but it must be remembered that there were no depots located at this station as at Is-sur-Tille. The number of carloads of freight received and forwarded through the classification yards at this station during these offensives was 47,000; this does not include however large quantities of ammunition, quartermaster supplies, engineering material, rail, ballast, and other railroad construction material which were forwarded in through trains to parks, dumps, and other points where construction was under way. 75,000 tons of engineering material alone were handled. Railroad construction material sufficient to construct an entirely new railroad from Aubreville to Apremont and enormous quantities of road ballast and filler for the repair of the highways and material for the repair of the Verdun---Sedan railroad passed through this station during the first phase of the Argonne-Meuse offensive. The total number of evacuations through St-Dizier between September 5 and December 1, 1918, was 196,018 of which 191,965 were Americans. The number of hospital trains operated from St-Dizier was 529 of which 365 were French and 164 American. * * * At the commencement of the Argonne-Meuse engagement our most advance railheads were along the Four-bis Line (the standard gauge railway line connecting Ste-Menehould with the Verdun line). During the first phase of this engagement a standard gauge railroad was built from Aubreville to Apremont and the railheads for the advance troops at the beginning of the second phase were moved forward to Challerange, Grand Pré, Châtel-Chéhéry, Apremont, Verennes, Charney, Brieulles, and Dun-sur-Meuse.

This report also takes up in brief the development of the French regulating stations and the operation of the American regulating stations at Creil and Le Bourget. The former was established first for the supply of the 26th Division during its final training on the Chemin-des-Dames near Soissons, and later used for the supply of the 1st Division while it was in the line with the French at the time of the Cantigny offensive. The regulating station at Le Bourget regulated for the troops of the Paris Group during the German Aisne offensive and the Château-Thierry---Soissons counteroffensive. The number of troops served through this station was approximately 300,000. The evacuations between June 4 and October 26 were 58,450 and the number of hospital trains operated 297 of which 116 were American trains and 181 French trains.

The most difficult problem which confronted the regulating officer at Le Bourget was the rapidity with which troops were moved from one part of the sector to another. The development of the divisional *rame*, which contained one day's supply of rations, forage, gasoline, and oil and such material as may have been loaded at the depot for the particular division, gave great flexibility in the placing of supplies. Consequently if a division moved from one area to another, or from one part of the sector to another, the *rame* could be readily shifted to the new location of the division. Thus when the 2d Division was rushed from Gisors by motor truck to the vicinity of Chateau-Thierry to reinforce the French durung the Aisne offensive, the *rame* for that division, which had already been forwarded to that point, was stopped en route and returned to the regulating station at Le Bourget where it was reforwarded the same day to Meaux, which was to be the division's new railhead the following morning. This same division, several weeks later, just before the commencement of the Soissons counteroffensive, was again shifted by motor truck from La Ferté-sous-Jouarre to a point south of Soissons to join the 1st Division and the *rame* for this division which had already been made up in the Est railroad yards at Noisy-le-Sec had merely to be shifted over the belt line to Le Bourget and forwarded by the Nord railway system to Crépy-en-Valois, where the division was supplied the following morning. As the counterattack progressed, seven new railheads were established for these divisions in a period of eight days, but the troops were supplied with the same regularity as they had been during the time preceding the attack.

* * * * * *

WILLIAM K. DUPRE, Jr.,
Captain, C. W. S., G-4-I.

For Chief Regulating Officer
Col. J. R. Kilpatrick, G. S.

C-in-C Report File: Folder 96: Report

Machine-Gun and Small Arms Activities

GENERAL HEADQUARTERS, A. E. F.,

OFFICE CHIEF ORDNANCE OFFICER,

Chaumont, Haute-Marne, November 11, 1918.

[Extract]

From: Chief Inspector, Machine Guns and Small Arms, Ord. Dept., G. H. Q., American E. F.

To: Assistant Chief of Staff, G-4 (Through: Col. Casad)

1. To insure an efficient service of supply and maintenance of rifles machine guns and automatic rifles for the American army at war a study was first made by the writer of the British and French services. This study showed that each service contained certain desirable features but that neither the British nor the French methods and facilities would entirely meet our needs.

2. It was evident that our army would be confronted with a much greater problem than either the British or the French as our troops would have several types of machine guns, automatic rifles, rifles and pistols, with the necessary great assortment of accessories, spare parts, etc.

3. Our army was at that time planned on 30 divisions; our corps on 4 combat and 2 replacement and training divisions. American divisions contained 224 machine guns for infantry machine gun companies and machine gun battalions, and 36 for artillery batteries, besides 768 automatic rifles. Our corps, therefore, contained as many machine guns and automatic rifles as the French army of 12 divisions.

4. General Principles of Supply. Rifles: The study of this subject clearly showed but one satisfactory solution and that was that each soldier should come to France with a rifle and that he should carry a rifle forward into battle. The adoption of this solution would also enable the main rifle repair facilities to be located in base shops near the training areas and that only sufficient rifles for maintaining the divisions would have to be repaired at the front.

5. Machine Guns and Automatic Rifles: The supply and maintenance of machine guns and automatic rifles required a different solution from the solution adopted for rifles.

6. The American troops would necessarily be equipped with several types of each of these weapons and this material was difficult to obtain and, further, as the shortage of any one of a number of items would put a whole crew or company out of action, it was evident, that supply and repair centers for automatic arms should be established in each army zone.

7. The automatic rifle was a new and untried weapon and it was reasonable to expect heavy losses of these rifles due to the killing of gun crews or the malfunctioning of the weapons and that both supply and repair facilities must be established in the army zones.

8. By the establishment of automatic arms centers in each army zone, all material of this class salvaged, could be repaired at the front, thereby saving railroad transportation to the rear and again to the front.

9. After several years experience the French army adopted the above solution of automatic arms centers for each army, and these centers met every test of war.

10. Advance Bases for the Mobile Shops and the Establishment of Army Machine Gun and Small Arms Centers: Our divisions at this time were equipped with French Hotchkiss machine guns and Chauchat automatic rifles and with Springfield and Enfield rifles and with three types of pistols. Great difficulty was being encountered in getting spare parts for these various weapons especially the French weapons. It was impracticable for the shops to requisition these supplies on rear depots and wait a week or longer for the receipt or nonreceipt of same. There were over a thousand different kinds of parts and many mistakes were made by the depots in filling requisitions. To operate efficiently it became clear that we should establish advanced bases for the mobile repair shops (machine-gun and small arms sections), in the army zones and these bases should carry machine guns, automatic rifles and spare parts for all small arms.

11. These solutions were approved by the general staff and authority was granted by G. O. No. 43, A. E. F., 1918, to establish advance units of army ordnance parks for machine guns and small arms in each corps area.

12. The first of these units was established at Void (Meuse), at the intersection of the Paris-Nancy, Neufchâteau-Commercy highways. Its success was instantaneous. A table of organization for one of these units was prepared by this office and approved by the General Staff, A. E. F., copy attached. Also attached is a copy of amended table based on the experiences of the First and Second Armies, which is recommended for approval.

13. When first established this unit consisted of a repair center for major repairs as well as a base for the mobile shops. The demands of the service caused additional articles of automatic arm equipment to be added from time to time, and when preparations were being made to launch the St-Mihiel attack it became imperative to carry a complete stock of machine gun and automatic rifle supplies within easy reach of the troops and the unit therefore became, as a result of experience, a rear automatic arms center.

14. French Supplies of Hotchkiss Machine Guns and Chauchat Automatic Rifles: There was great difficulty in obtaining Hotchkiss machine guns and parts and Chauchat rifles and parts from rear depots as the French Ministry of Armament would only replace each month the actual expenditures of the previous month. This resulted in the depots being unable to meet demands. The writer proceeded to French GQG., and made arrangements to fill our requisitions immediately upon receipt of same and to ship this material to our army machine-gun centers.

15. An officer and ten men were stationed at the French regulating station at Noisy-le-Sec to handle this material and convoy it to destination. This arrangement enabled us to receive French supplies in 4 days after a telegram was sent ordering same. Without this arrangement we would have been unable to meet the demands of the Argonne battle.

16. Machine-gun equipment consists of many items a shortage of any one of which will cause a breakdown of the service. These supplies must be within easy reach of the troops.

17. Immediately upon completion of the St-Mihiel attack, the First Army was transferred to the Argonne sector and many new divisions were added to it. Void was the only advanced machine-gun unit and additional arrangements had to be provided at once, for Void had not only to take care of its own sector but the additional burden and responsibilities of the Verdun sector. This office directed the establishment of an advanced echelon from Void for each of the three corps participating in the battle. One echelon was established at Nixeville; one at Brabant-en-Argonne; and one at Les Islettes.

18. The beginning of a second unit similar to Void was started in the French C. A. A. at Vaubecourt, by transferring Major Sabin and 15 mechanics from the temporary army part established at Lieussaint (near Paris), for the Chateau-Thierry offensive and sending equipment and supplies there from Void. This 2d unit was quickly enlarged and later transferred to Parois, where it gradually assumed all the duties and

responsibilities of machine gun and small arms supply and repair for the First Army. A copy of pamphlet on the organization and functioning of an Army Machine Gun and Small Arms Center, including a plan of operations, for the center and advanced echelons is appended.

19. With a Center in each army, the distribution of supplies to the armies became a very simple matter, the supplies being allocated to each army by G-4, G. H. Q.

20. The Control of Issues: In normal periods of position warfare the issues of machine guns, automatic rifles and pertaining equipment were made upon regular requisitions through the division ordnance officer to the army ordnance officer, who in turn sent these requisitions to the army machine gun centers. All shipments from these centers were made by trucks. Divisions usually sent trucks for the supplies but when this was impracticable the center delivered the supplies with its own trucks.

21. In periods of active fighting in position warfare or during offensive operations, advanced echelons or dumps of the army machine gun and small arms centers were established in each corps area, carrying full stocks of machine gun supplies and instructions were issued authorizing company commanders to make direct call on these echelons for whatever was needed. These echelons were a great success.

22. Authority to make direct call was objected to by some supply officers but experience has shown that supply officers were often many miles in the rear and could not easily be found.

23. In case of a general advance the advanced echelon followed the troops, maintaining a close liaison with the center and with divisions.

24. Reports were received from all divisions commanding the work of these centers.

25. AUTOMATIC SUPPLIES: Automatic supplies in connection with machine guns and small arms is intimately connected with maintenance facilities and methods. In the preceding part of this paper it was stated that each soldier came forward armed with a rifle, therefore, the question of supplying rifles to combatant troops in the army zone was almost one of automatic supply. Very few rifles had to be shipped forward for issue as rifles salvaged on the battlefield were reissued after repair by division mobile ordnance shops and army machine-gun centers.

26. The Installation of a System of Automatic Supply of Spare Parts for all Small Arms: Infantry regiments were equipped with spare parts chests for rifles and pistols but there were no spare parts for machine guns in the division excepting the parts in company spare parts kits. There were no spare parts for automatic rifles (Chauchat) in the division. The depots maintained an accountability system and were seriously hampered in filling these requisitions and invoicing the supplies. The troops in turn were greatly delayed in the receipt of spare parts. Regimental and machine gun battalion ordnance personnel had not received any special training and it was impracticable during battle for these men to attempt to repair arms or to receive supplies. Hundreds of requisitions from regiments and machine gun battalions for as many items of spare parts were flooding the depots.

27. Necessity for Machine-Gun Parts in the Division: There were no machine-gun spare parts in the division other than the parts carried by companies. A shortage of a few important machine-gun parts would not only put the gun out of action but also its entire crew. G. O. No. 43 called in all rifle spare part chests, and all pistol parts, requiring all repairs to be made by the mobile shop. It also provided a supply of spare parts for machine guns and automatic rifles in the division by putting these parts in the M. O. R. S. and, therefore, immediately available.

28. An available reserve of machine guns, automatic rifles, rifles and pistols for exchange purposes or for replacement purposes during an emergency were also placed in the mobile ordnance repair shop.

29. All repairs were thus centered in the mobile shops under the immediate supervision of the division machine gun inspector. Organizations sent in damaged weapons to

the shop and were given serviceable weapons in exchange. There was no waiting or delay.

30. The division machine-gun inspector, in the ordnance mobile shop, inspected machine gun companies and kept a check on their spare part kits and made the companies feel that they could obtain parts in the division and that there was no necessity to hoard up parts. Guns which did not function satisfactorily were remedied or exchanged. Hundreds of requisitions for spare parts immediately ceased coming into the depots and spare parts were no longer wasted. Troops commenced getting good service and ceased worrying about small arms generally. In case the division lost a few guns the shop replaced the loss at once.

31. A stockcard system was prepared by this office and distributed to each mobile repair shop. This system included printed forms for the parts of each weapon, on which was recorded the parts salvaged; parts used in repair and parts required. One copy of these forms was sent every fifteen days to the army machine gun and small arms center as a requisition for the automatic replacement of parts used or for parts required. As there are over a thousand parts for the various arms in use it can readily be seen what labor and difficulty would have been caused without some such simple and efficient system in use.

32. Machine Gun and Automatic Rifle Salvage: While salvage proper comes under G-1, the value and importance of this material and the good military reason for avoiding shipping material to the rear and again shipping it to the front, all machine gun and automatic rifle salvage was directed to the army machine-gun centers where it was worked over and again put into service. This material includes many articles besides the weapons, such as carts, harness, ammunition boxes, belts, feed strips, etc.

33. Rifle Salvage: As each soldier came forward carrying a rifle, it was not economical to repair great quantities of rifles at the front and then ship them to the rear. Rifle chests were not available and many rifles which were repaired at the front and shipped to the rear, had to be repaired again.

34. Each divisional mobile shop was authorized to keep on hand for exchange or replacement purposes during normal times 100 rifles, and during battle to have on hand sufficient rifles for the requirements of the division. These additional rifles should be obtained through salvage and repaired.

35. The principal needs for the issue of rifles at the front were to men returned to duty from an evacuation or other forward hospital, and to separate detachments or organizations such as signal or engineer troops. The only other demand of importance was a special case of which two new divisions thrown into the Argonne battle, came out of battle short several hundred rifles less than riflemen. Our experience shows that a stock of about 2,000 rifles in each machine-gun center is ample for all forward issues.

36. During the month of October, 1918, regional replacement depots, were established in forward areas and rifles shipped from base depots forward, to these depots. With the establishment of these forward replacement depots a great many more rifles would necessarily be repaired in the army machine gun and small arms centers.

37. Summary of Accomplishments: The American divisions serving with the American army are equipped with three types of machine guns: Hotchkiss 8-mm, Vickers and Browning caliber.30; three types of automatic rifles: Chauchat 8-mm, Chauchat caliber .30 and Browning; two types of service rifles: Springfield and Enfield; and three types of pistols: Colt automatic, Smith and Wesson, and Colt caliber.45, besides auxiliary weapons such as shot guns. American divisions serving with the British are equipped with British arms and one division with the French (93d) is equipped with French arms.

38. There were many changes of types of automatic arms due to varying conditions of supply and service of divisions and these centers were called upon to effect many of these changes. For instance, the 80th Division arrived in France with American Vickers machine guns. It was ordered to serve with the British and to receive British Vickers machine guns and British Lewis guns. The division was later ordered back to

the American army and was again equipped with American Vickers and American caliber .30 Chauchats. Brownings arrived for the division as it came out of battle and the division was for the fourth time equipped with machine guns and automatic rifles of a different type. In several cases these changes were made when divisions came out of battle, to be thrown in again after a few days rest and refitting. A statement is appended showing these changes of equipment D.

39. Additional burdens were thrown upon these machine gun centers when a division equipped with American arms was attached to one of the armies of our Allies. The 36th Division had just been equipped with Brownings when orders were received attaching to the French Fourth Army. The 37th and 91st Divisions, equipped with American Vickers machine guns were ordered to duty with the French army in Belgium. To care for these 2 divisions a temporary machine gun center was established at Couderkerque - Branch, near Dunkirk.

40. During the St-Mihiel attack and the 1st phase of the battle of the Argonne the machine-gun center at Void was maintaining the equipment of 20 divisions, in numbers of arms as follows:

		TYPES OF ARMS	
Machine guns	4,500		3
Automatic Rifles	15,350		3
Rifles	352,000		2
Small arms	234,500		4
Total	606,350	Shot guns	1
			13

There were actually 1,138 spare parts for these weapons.

41. These machine-gun units had reached such a degree of importance that it became necessary to distinguish them from temporary general supply and other units and the General Staff, G-4 (General Moseley), directed that the establishment at Parois in the First Army area should be designated the First Army Machine Gun and Small Arms Center (M. G. and S. A. C.) and the establishment at Void, in the Second Army area should be designated the Second Army Machine Gun and Small Arms Center.

42. These highly important establishments were thus given a standing worthy of their performance. They have provided every want of the machine gun-service as a whole and every requirement of automatic rifles for the American armies in the greatest battle in our history. They have also repaired the necessary quantities of rifles at the front. The losses of automatic rifles were extremely heavy, often amounting to over 50% after a few days of battle. It was and is at this writing the pride of these establishments that the animals of a machine gun battery may be driven up to the center, and a complete battery of carts, guns, etc., driven away.

43. No other army in the history of the world has ever had so many types of complicated small arms: To send a modern army thus equipped into battle would have been looked upon, before entering this war, as folly. We found a condition which had to be met and overcome and that we have done this successfully reports from divisions attached hereto will bear witness.

44. Recommendations: It is recommended that the army machine gun and small arms center become a permanent unit in the organization of an army and be incorporated in War Department tables of organization for an army and bear a similar relation to the army as does the army artillery park, with the addition of supplying all machine gun and automatic rifle requirements. Rifles and pistols will be repaired at these centers but when general supply depots are established, rifles and pistols and all pertaining equipment will normally be iseued from general supply depots.

45. A table of organization for one of these units was prepared and approved by the general staff, and an amended table based on experiences of the First and Second Army Centers is submitted for approval in the A. E. F., and to be incorporated in War Department tables. This table of organization does not include a single item not found necessary by the combined experiences of these two centers.

46. When first taking the field, the organization is sufficiently mobile to carry necessary material and supplies for immediate use of troops and mobile ordnance repair shops, and when the organization settles down into temporary quarters the cargo trucks become available for hauling supplies from base depots to the center and for delivering supplies to advanced corps echelons or direct to divisions in combat.

* * * * * *

A. E. PHILLIPS,
Col., Ord. Dept.

C-in-C Rept File: Fldr. 93:   Report

Ammunition Supply

GENERAL HEADQUARTERS, A. E. F.,

Chaumont, Haute-Marne.

AMMUNITION SUPPLY

1. The supply of ammunition for the A. E. F. was obtained by the Chief Ordnance and from two sources, i. e., by manufacture at home and by purchase in Europe.

2. As a large number of cannon of French and English manufacture were used by the American E. F., a supply of ammunition for the same was obtained from these two governments under contract, and the ammunition obtained was to suffice until production at home was adequate.

3. After mentioning as above the method of obtaining the supply of ammunition, it is proposed herein to treat the subject of ammunition supply after the same has been delivered to the A. E. F.

AMMUNITION SUPPLY FACILITIES

1. On August 7, 1917, a decision was made by the General Staff that the total supply of ammunition in France would be a 90-day reserve, computing one day's reserve to be the average expediture of a particular cannon over a long period of time.

2. This reserve was to be stored as follows: 45 days in the Base Section, 30 days in the Intermediate Section and 15 days in the Advance Section. It was therefore necessary to provide adequate storage facilities in the three sections enumerated above, at first on the basis of an army strength of 30 divisions and later in August 1918 amended so as to provide sufficient storage space for ammunition for 80 combat divisions in France by July 1919, the building program to be so arranged as to progressively meet the needs as the troops in France increased.

3. It was decided at a later date in June 1918, that the reserves of ammunition in France would consist of the 90 days, heretofore mentioned, in the depots of the

S. O. S., plus that ammunition required with the guns and in the depots of the divisions, corps, and armies, in the Army Zone, which in most cases approximated 30 days of average fire, making the total reserves in France from the guns back approximately 120 days of average fire.

4. The quantity of reserves to be maintained in France was again amended in October 1918 to consist of a 45 days average fire supply in the depots of the S. O. S. and 30 days average fire supply in the Army Zone, making a total of 75 days average fire reserve in France from the guns back. This latter decision was taken as the result of a conference between representatives of the General Staff, the Chief of Ordnance Officer, A. E. F. and Mr. Stettinius, representing the War Department, and the reduction was necessary for two reasons, first to reduce the requirements of powder to conform to the production capacity, and secondly to reduce the ocean tonnage required for transporting ammunition from the States to France. The quantity of reserves of ammunition to be maintained in France in every case affected the storage and handling facilities required.

5. The original plan of providing space for ammunition reserves required for 30 divisions was to be carried out and upon completion of this building program, it was planned to build such additional storage facilities as would be required, based upon conditions existing at the time of the completion of the original building program. The requirements of covered storage space for a 90 days reserve of average fire for 30 divisions was as follows:

Base Section	1,844,167	sq. ft.
Intermediate Section	1,229,444	sq. ft.
Advance Section	614,722	sq. ft.

On November 11, 1918, the following storage space for ammunition had been provided:

Base Section:	540,000	sq. ft. - St-Loubes
	30,000	sq. ft. - Usine Brulée (near Nantes)
	11,200	sq. ft. - Miramas (Marseille)
	90,000	sq. ft. - Montoir (St-Nazaire)
	671,200	sq. ft. - TOTAL
Inter. Section:	400,000	sq. ft. - Foecy (or Mehun)
	465,000	sq. ft. - Issoudun
	865,000	sq. ft. - TOTAL
Adv. Section:	295,000	sq. ft. - Villers-le-Sec

6. While the storage space available on November 11 did not meet the proposed theoretical requirements, it was sufficient to adequately meet all needs, as ammunition from the States had not arrived in quantities anticipated and we were drawing a great portion of our artillery ammunition from French Depots. As a matter of fact we had approximately 550,000 sq. ft. of unoccupied storage space on November 11 which was to be utilized in the near future by the receipt of large shipments of artillery ammunition from the States.

AMMUNITION STORAGE FACILITIES

The following ammunition storage depots were built or proposed within the Zone of the S. O. S.:

BASE SECTION:

St-Loubes depot, near the city of Bordeaux. This depot consisted of 36 wooden storehouses, each 50 ft. by 300 ft., giving a total of 540,000 sq. ft. of covered storage space, or a holding capacity of about 60,000 tons of ammunition. Ammunition for this depot was unloaded at the docks at Bassens, ammunition was promptly loaded into depot at St-Loubes. When unloaded at Bassens, ammunition was promptly loaded into lighters or cars and hauled to St-Loubes, where it was sorted on sorting platforms and then stored in designated sheds. There were 14 sorting platforms at the triage at St-Loubes, each 18 ft. by 300 ft. long.

Montoir depot, near port of St-Nazaire, consisted of six wooden buildings, each 50 ft. by 300 ft., giving a total of 90,000 sq. ft. of covered storage space. This depot was a temporary one, as a permanent depot was to be built at Donges, which depot was to provide storage space for ammunition received at the port of St-Nazaire. The Donges depot was to consist of 27 buildings each 50 ft.by 300 ft., giving a total of 405,000 sq. ft. of covered storage space, or a holding capacity of about 45,000 tons of ammunition. Ammunition would have been handled by rail from the docks at St-Nazaire to the depot of Donges. Considerable grading and track work had been done on this depot but no buildings erected and construction was discontinued on November 11.

Usine Brulée depot, near port of Nantes, consisted of three wooden buildings, each 50 ft. by 200 ft., giving a total of 30,000 sq. ft. of covered storage space. This depot was located three miles from Nantes and was used for a sorting depot and not as a storage depot. It was utilized for handling ammunition unloaded at the port of Nantes and after ammunition was sorted there, it was shipped to storage depots in the Intermediate Section. It was not contemplated to build a large storage depot for ammunition at or near the port of Nantes, as it was thought the quantity of ammunition arriving at that port from the States would not justify the erection of a large storage depot.

Miramas depot, located 35 miles from the port of Marseille, consisted of one building 130 ft. by 280 ft. and was used as a sorting station for ammunition arriving at the port of Marseille. The ammunition after sorting was shipped to the interior depots. All ammunition received at the ports of [Le] Harve, Brest, La Pallice and Rochefort, was forwarded by rail to depots in the interior and was not sorted at the base ports.

The large storage depot built at St-Loubes to serve the port of Bordeaux and the one proposed at Donges to serve the port of St-Nazaire, were designated to serve ports where it was contemplated the greatest portion of ammunition received from the States would arrive. This, by reason of docking conditions at these two ports and their location with respect to the two great mainlines of railway communication. It was thought unnecessary to build large storage depots at other ports for the reason that the ammunition received at those ports would not justify such construction.

INTERMEDIATE SECTION:

Foecy depot, near Mehun, Department of the Cher, consisted of eight wooden buildings, each 50 ft. by .1,000 ft., giving a total capacity of 400,000 sq. ft. of covered storage space and a holding capacity of about 45,000 tons of ammunition and to be used for small arms and artillery ammunition.

Issoudun depot consisted of 31 wooden buildings, each 50 ft. by 300 ft., giving a total capacity of 465,000 sq. ft. of covered storage space or a holding capacity of about 52,000 tons of ammunition, and to be used for small arms and artillery ammunition.

La Chapelle depot was designed for storing trench and aerial bombs and grenades. This depot was to have a capacity of 120,000 sq. ft. of covered storage space or about 13,000 tons. Considerable grading and track work had been done on this depot prior to November 11, 1918, when work was suspended. However no building had been erected.

The depot site at Foecy was selected to provide storage space on the main line railway from the port of St-Nazaire and the depot site at Issoudun was to provide a storage depot on the main line railway from the port of Bordeaux. Both of these were selected after consideration of the traffic conditions, both as concerned shipments coming from the rear and expedition of shipments to the front or to the depots in the

Advance Section. The bomb depot site at La Chapelle was also selected for the above reasons and a separate depot was to be constructed for bombs to remove the possibility of explosion by storing bombs and grenades in a depot where large stocks of artillery ammunition were stored.

The location of these intermediate ammunition depots were also selected with a view to their serving American troops operating on the western front to the north and west of Chalons as Advance Depots. They later proved well located in this respect while serving American Troops operating in the vicinity of Chateau-Thierry.

ADVANCE SECTION:

Villers-le-Sec depot consisted of sufficient wooden buildings to provide 295,000 sq. ft. of covered storage space and construction had begun prior to November 11 on an extension of about 120,000 sq. ft. of covered storage space, giving a total capacity of 415,000 sq. ft. of covered storage space. In addition to the above platforms were constructed at this depot providing about 100,000 sq. ft. of storage space for small arms ammunition. This depot was so designated as to provide storage facilities for all types of ammunition used by the American Armies.

Chamoy-St-Phal: The site for this depot was selected about November 1, and plans were being prepared when the Armistice was signed on November 11, at which time instructions were given to suspend action on plans on construction of this depot.

Both of the depots in the Advance Section were selected on the following basis:
(a) Traffic conditions with respect to receiving shipments from the rear.
(b) Traffic conditions with respect to serving Army Depots at the front.

METHOD OF SUPPLY

1. Under General Order No. 44, A. E. F., dated March 23, 1918, the method of distribution and supply of ammunition was laid down.
2. This provided that ammunition for organizations in training in the Zone of the Service of Supplies would be procured through the Chief Ordnance Officer, A. E. F. and that this ammunition would be supplied based on allowances made for training by the General Staff.
3. All ammunition issued to the Armies at the front was supplied through the agency of G-4, G. H. Q. In order to expedite supply, certain amounts of ammunition in depots, called credits, were placed at the disposition of the Armies by the G-4, G. H. Q., and against these credits the Armies ordered shipments made to the Army Depots in the Zone of the Army without further authority from G-4, G. H. Q. Credits were usually based on a certain period of time and covered theoretical requirements of the Army during that period of time, based on the guns emoloyed and the degree of activity of the front on which the Army was operating. All ammunition desired in excess of credits was secured through G-4, G. H. Q., who coordinated the requirements of the Armies and distributed the ammunition based on the relative needs of the various armies, and on the necessity for accumulating reserves for future contemplated operatins.

SUPPLY OF AMMUNITION THROUGH FRENCH DEPOTS

1. Due to the very active operations of the American Army after August 1, 1918, and due to the fact that a large amount of artillery was employed under the direction of the American Armies, a great quantity of artillery ammunition for this cannon was obtained from the French Depots, because sufficient quantities of certain types of artillery ammunition had not been received from the U. S. to care for our needs. In

view of the above, it is felt that there should be incorporated in this paper a review of the method of obtaining the above ammunition from the French depots since it concerns the supply of ammunition and particularly since it covers a period of time during the most active operations of the American Expeditionary Forces.

2. About July 24, at a meeting of the Military Board of Allied Supply, it was determined that in view of the fact of contemplated important operations of the American armies, of an offensive character, and in view of the fact that sufficient American artillery ammunition was not available for these operations, the ammunition stocks of the French and American armies could be pooled for all cannon common to both armies and that French and American depots would serve indiscriminately the French and American armies; that requisitions for ammunition upon French depots would be made by the French *Direction de l'Arrière* at the request of the 4th Section, American G. H. Q., and requisitions upon American depots would be made by the 4th Section of the American G. H. Q. upon the request of the French *Direction de l'Arrière*. The above pooling agreement to have no reference whatsoever to any former definite contracts for ammunition that had been placed by the American Government with the French Government; but it was felt the pooling of ammunition was necessary for the accomplishment of the common cause.

3. About August 15, 1918, prior to the commencement of the St-MIHIEL offensive and during the period of preparation for that operation, the French G. Q. G., 4th Bureau, and the 4th Section G. S., American G. H. Q., each attached to the 4th Section of the American First Army a liaison officer who was authorized to control the issues of ammunition to the American army from both French and American depots. This arrangement obviated the necessity of having the army apply to the American G. H. Q. for artillery ammunition which must necessarily come from French depots. Under this arrangement, application was direct to the French G. Q. G. for ammunition and the needs of the American army were met through this method of supply, therefore the supply was greatly expedited.

4. Upon the formation of the American Second Army, the liaison officers, representing the 4th Bureau, French G. Q. G. and the 4th Section American G. H. Q., acted on the supply of ammunition from French depots for both of the American Armies. This arrangement continued in effect until the signing of the Armistice and while it was felt that the quantities of American ammunition of all types would have been sufficient in a few months to take care of the needs of the American Armies, the arrangement of pooling ammunition had proven so satisfactory that no doubt the same would have continued in effect. Of course insofar as possible, the French Depots would have supplied French Armies and the American Depots would have supplied American Armies, but in case of need, each of the Allied had the right to use the ammunition of the other, based upon their relative needs.

SUMMARY OF ACCOMPLISHMENTS

1. The results attained in the supply of ammunition have shown that the system of supply in principle is correct, for the supply did not fail at any time during the operations of the A. E. F. It has been demonstrated that to assure the supply of ammunition, the issues of same should be controlled by a central authority such as that exercised by G-4, G. H. Q., in liaison with G-3 of G. H. Q.

RECOMMENDATIONS

While the original plan was to maintain reserves of ammunition, distributed in the S. O. S. as follows:

        3/6 - Base Section
        2/6 - Intermediate Section
        1/6 - Advance Section

it was demonstrated later that after sufficient storage facilities had been created at the base ports to provide storage in order to relieve dock conjestion and to assure what might be termed as iron reserve, if by accident ammunition in the advance depots should be lost, that no distinction should be made between quantity stored in the various Zones of Supply, but that all ammunition, not stored at base ports, should be placed in advance Depots, so located as to provide rapid shipments to Army Depots.

* * * * *

TRANSPORTATION CORPS

C-in-C Rept. File: Fldr. 320: Report

Transportation Corps

HEADQUARTERS, SERVICES OF SUPPLY, A. E. F.,

Chaumont, Haute-Marne.

PART I

FOREWORD

[Extract]

When the United States entered the war it became apparent that transportation would play a larger part in the history of American arms than it had ever played before. Army officials were not ready with a transportation organization but they had already recognized the fundamental fact that transportation in France for the American Army should be handled by transportation men. For three years England had been meeting and solving transportation problems that confronted her expeditionary forces and what was known of British achievements led the general staff to propose a commission to study military transportation in France and in England. The Secretary of War selected a commission of five, four of whom were transportation men of note in civil life and the other a regular army officer who was an engineer of marked ability. These officers were Major William Barclay Parsons, who had a record of great achievement, particularly in the construction of subway systems in New York City; Major W. J. Wilgus, formerly Vice-President of the New York Central Railroad, and of nation-wide reputation as a railroad builder; Captain A. B. Barber, Corps of Engineers, United States Army; Mr. W. A. Garrett of the Remington Arms Company, transportation expert; and Mr. F. de St. Phalle, motive power and rolling stock expert and an official of the Baldwin Locomotive Works. With two clerical assistants this commission sailed from New York on May 14, 1917, and arrived at Liverpool on May 23. After the official and formal reception was over the members of this commission divided the work and began an exhaustive study of military transportation in Great Britain and particularly the organization of the British transportation department. On May 28 the commission went to France and two days were taken up in formal receptions. In their discussions with the French officials the members of the commission kept constantly to the fore two questions. What did the French railroads need? What was the most important immediate work for America to do? The answer was prompt. Many miles of rail; hundreds of locomotives; 800 work-shop operators; 5,000 trained railroad men; and 20,000 laborers merely to start with. What the subsequent necessities would be only time, prolonged negotiations, and careful consideration would show. This starter was a large order in itself, but this order was filled and things done subsequently made the first accomplishments pale into insignificance.

During a two days' trip Minister Claveille explained at length the characteristics of the ports through which he expected the American army would pass. He named St-Nazaire, Cherbourg, Nantes, La Pallice, French Bassens, and a proposed new port at Bassens, the construction of which was thought should be undertaken by the Americans.

General Pershing and his party arrived in France on June 13, 1917, and on June 17 the commission made its formal report to him.

While the commission was in England and France procuring advance detailed information necessary properly to handle transportation problems, Mr. S. M. Felton, President of the Chicago and Great Western Railway, one of the best known and ablest transportation men in America, and an advisor to the Chief of Engineers of the Army, who eventually became Director General of Military Railways, took up the Army's transportation problem which he handled in the United States during the war with the energy and thoroughness expected of him. Engineers of ability were drawn into the service, and the commission reported from time to time by cable. The reports were gone over carefully and steps were taken to procure a great deal of the equipment which, it was already apparent, was absolutely essential.

Colonel Harry Taylor, afterwards Brigadier General, was detailed by the Commander-in-Chief as Chief Engineer Officer, A. E. F., and immediately upon his assignment he began for the Transportation Department. In the large staff which General Pershing brought over with him there was only one railroad man, Captain L. A. Jenny. Soon after the arrival of the Commander-in-Chief and his staff, the two civilian members of the Railroad Commission found it necessary to return to the United States, Major Parsons joined his regiment, the 11th Engineers (railway), and Captain Barber went to general staff duty. This left Major Wilgus the only member of the commission to continue with the Chief Engineer Officer, and he devoted all of his time to transportation.

As the expeditionary forces at that time had not sufficient personnel, either technical or clerical, there was nothing with which to inaugurate a transportation branch of the Engineer Department and Major Wilgus was obliged to assume his duties with the sole help of one officer until the middle of August, 1917, when a force of draftsmen, stenographers, and clerks arrived. His first task was to prepare a bill of material for an army of undetermined size for one year in advance. This involved pure assumption, guided, however, by observation gained during the trip of the commission to France and to the several ports. This bill, afterwards known as Requisition No. 6, included all kinds of track and other railroad material, motive power and rolling stock, trains, and port equipment. The requisition was completed July 2 and cabled to the United States July 14, 1917. Thereafter it was used as a basis for ordering A. E. F. transportation material in the United States.

In ordering this amount of track material, motive power and rolling stock it was necessary to outline a general policy of military railroad operations in France. The situation, it was concluded, was such as to warrant the operation by the American army of its own locomotives and cars manned by an American personnel, for transporting its supplies from the seaboard to the front over the French lines somewhat in accordance with methods known in the United States as trackage rights. The adoption of this policy meant that, while the Americans would have control of the personnel of their trains, all movements over French railroads would be governed by the rules of the French.

It became necessary to order sufficient locomotives and cars from the United States to handle what, it was estimated, would be the army's requirements, and to arrange for the forwarding of railroad personnel in sufficient volume to meet the needs. Again, the adoption of this policy made it necessary to arrange for sufficient personnel to supervise American railway troops, but always with the idea that the American supervisory forces would, of course, be subordinate to those of the French railways.

It was concluded that the handling of American traffic thus, to a large extent under its own control, was an absolute necessity as otherwise the success of American arms might fail should the supply of personnel and equipment by the French fall short of American needs at a critical moment. It was recognized that this procedure and the additional burden on the French railroads would require on the part of America the construction of new yards, water supply, engine terminals and other facilities to go with the assumption of responsibilities of this kind; also the construction of many other facilities such as multiple-track, cut-offs, and regulating stations, all with the view of removing any special restrictions that might hamper the maximum train movements. Along with the need of this method for securing the maximum capacity of existing French railways was the requirement of large storage depots with their yards and engine house facilities and the need of ample material for advancing the road into the enemy's territory when the time came that the enemy would be forced towards Berlin.

The Commander-in-Chief at the very beginning of the study of the transportation problem laid down one idea, which became the basis of all transportation operations. The idea was that always there should be ninety days' supplies for the expeditionary forces. Of this amount, supplies for forty-five days were to be held at base storage, thirty days at intermediate storage and fifteen days at advance storage at the regulating stations.

In formulating this policy certain lines of communication were adopted, viz: from Bordeaux, on the Gironde River, and from St-Nazaire to Nantes on the Loire River, via existing double track lines to a junction near Bourges, thence easterly and northerly by way of Nevers and Dijon to Is-sur-Tille, from which point several lines radiated towards the sector extending from Epinal to Nancy. Over this line it was expected that American supplies could be transported to the extent of 25,000 tons a day. When the tonnage exceeded these figures, the second line of communication was to diverge from the above mentioned route near Bourges, thence by way of Cosne to Laroche, Nuits-sur-Ravieres and Chatillon and Neufchateau, from which tentacles extended to the sector. Over this second line of communication it was expected an additional 15,000 tons a day could be handled. When the total requirements of the army exceeded 40,000 tons a day, a third line of communication was to come into play extending from a point on the Loire River at Tours northerly through Orleans and Troyes to Neufchateau and beyond. This line was to handle an additional 10,000 tons a day. When the daily requirements to the army exceeded a total of 50,000 tons, a fourth line of communication was to be added and other lines as needed. The result was, plans were made so that when the Armistice was signed preparations were well under way to take care of 4,000,000 men by June 1919 on a basis of 50 lbs. per man per day, making the total daily requirements of the army at that time 100,000 tons.

In carrying out a comprehensive plan of this kind, one of the first questions arising was the character of the rolling stock to be used on the French railroads. It was concluded that the locomotives, if practicable, should accord with the American practice and should be of a capacity that, as nearly as possible, would be limited only by the bridges and clearances of the French railroads. It was decided also that the cars should be of American type, with a capacity, as nearly as possible, consistent with the same limitations as for locomotives and equipped with air brakes but with French couplers and buffers instead of American devices. The outcome of these decisions on equipment was that the Transportation Department was furnished with consolidation locomotives with a tractive effort of 36,000 pounds, and cars of 30 tons (60,000 pounds) capacity, with the usual permissible over-load of ten per cent. Hence the policy adopted in the early days of the Transportation Department, then a function of the Chief Engineer, A. E. F., committed the American Expeditionary Forces to running its own trains, made up of American locomotives and cars and manned by American personnel, under trackage rights over French railroads from the sea to the front, a distance of about six hundred miles, by several routes.

In addition to defining the general policy in the way American supplies and troops should be transported in France, it was necessary to reach a conclusion as to improving the management of all ports and the manner in which the new ports should be created so as to meet the needs of the American army. Early in June, 1917, American and French officers visited the French ports. The outcome of this visit was a recommendation for improvement at some places and for new ports; one at what has since become known as American Bassens, near Bordeaux, with ten new berths. Another was at La Martiniere to the front line railroad. Plans were made for these locations, bills of material prepared and piling timbers and iron were cabled for from the United States. It had been found that these were unobtainable in Europe. During the month of August, 1917, construction of the ten new berths at American Bassens was approved. During this time, St-Nazaire was being used as the principal American port. Also, orders were placed in the United States for sixty Gantry cranes.

In conformity with the decision of General Pershing that there should always be ninety days' supplies on hand, it was recommended that ample space for open and closed storage should be provided first at Bassens and St-Nazaire,. It was also suggested that there should be intermediate storage depots on the southern, or Bordeaux route, at Chateauroux, and at Gievres on the northern route. Then too, it was deemed advisable that there should be ordnance depots at Issoudun, on the southern line, and an ordnance depot at Mehun, on the northern line.

* * * * * *

By General Order No. 20, August 12, 1917, the Commander-in-Chief established the Line of Communications, with Brigadier General R. M. Blatchford in command. The work of transportation belonged naturally to this service and Major Wilgus, Assistant Director of Railways, was transferred from the personnel of the Chief Engineer Officer, A. E. F., and made a member of the staff of the Commanding General, Line of Communications as Director of Railways.

In the early part of August the Commander-in-Chief approved an outline of organization submitted by the director. By this plan the Transportation Department was to control the operation, maintenance and construction of such railways as might be turned over to the American forces by the French authorities, and the supervision of all movements of American troops and supplies over lines operated by the French authorities. It was to include all railways, both permanent and temporary, constructed or controlled by our forces involved in the supply or transportation of the army, exclusive of light railways in the Zone of the Armies. The plan favored by the Director of Railways was one modeled after one by the British army. It was built on departmental control, whereby the several branches of the service were to be under heads who were experts in their particular lines. An alternative plan after the French scheme was also submitted. It was commonly known as the divisional system, under which the various branches of transportation in each territory are grouped and headed by one officer. The director pointed out some advantages of adopting an organization after the British system with modifications to suit American needs. It would follow methods already familiar to the French in their dealings with the British. It would lend itself more readily to centralizing responsibility for a given service, as, for instance, the movement of trains through from the point of trans-shipment at tidewater to destination, including terminal switching, main line movement over French railways, and distribution by way of lines under military control in the army zones. The situation in this respect was widely different from that of the French, who were not hampered by having a large portion of their operations by lines over which they did not exercise full control. Then, too, the departmental plan would permit the selection of officers suited to their several specialties. Moreover, it would avoid the need of seeking men of more than ordinary capacity whose experience and temperament must fit them for supervising branches of the service with which they had not had detailed experience. In addition to all this, the first plan would leave each department head unembarrassed by the necessity of dissipating his time in supervising matters other than the one of dominant importance under his charge.

On July 29, 1917, the Commander-in-Chief cabled to the Secretary of War that a thorough study of the transportation history of the Allies had convinced him that the operation of railroads must be under a man with large experience in managing commercial railroads at home. He asked that the ablest American railroad man available should be sent to him after the most careful selection. He added:

> After the most disastrous result with inexperienced military men, the British selected the ablest man they could find to have charge of transportation. The question here is mostly one of operation and managing in intimate relation with the French, who retain the general control which is necessary to handle commercial transportation. The question of railroad transportation, of course, involves equipment and maintenance and new construction at the front as the army advances.

Adopting the recommendation of the Commander-in-Chief, the Secretary of War sent over Mr. W. W. Atterbury, Vice President in Charge of Operation of the Pennsylvania Railroad. Mr. Atterbury brought a letter from the Secretary of War to the Commander-in-Chief. He had been told that, as Director General of Transportation, he would act directly under the orders of the supreme authority, that authority from the United States being the General Commanding the Expeditionary Forces. Mr. Atterbury arrived on August 31, 1917. In the meantime, the Commander-in-Chief, not having heard from the Secretary of War on the subject, had named Major Wilgus, afterwards Colonel, Director of Military Railways, and Major Wilgus had started to work. When Mr. Atterbury arrived he found transportation plans under way under the direction of Major Wilgus and, approving what had been done, signified his readiness to withdraw and return to the United States. But it was decided that he should remain and take charge, and he was formally appointed Director General of Transportation on September 14, 1917, without commission. He accepted a commission as brigadier general in the national army October 8, 1917.

The Director General's first task after his appointment was to find out what was to be done, how to do it, and what help was needed. To this end he went over the plans of his predecessors and made an inspection of the railroads of France and the ports the American army was to use. On his return to Paris he took up the question of organization.

At no time had the transportation officers of the American army contemplated any transportation novelty or engineering curio. Mr. Atterbury's decision to adopt the principle of construction and operation and maintenance so long used successfully in America, coincided with the plans already made. Therefore, he approved the proposition, mapping out a railroad organization very much like the commercial railroad organization in the United States. At this time it was intended that the Transportation Department should include operation and construction of the standard gauge lines of communication as well as the narrow gauge line in the advance section and all highways, the light railways and railroads being a separate subdivision. The army was to use the French railways. Therefore, there were adjustments to be made. In France material had been scarce and labor plentiful; hence material expensive and labor cheap. In America material had been comparatively plentiful and labor scarce; hence material had been comparatively cheap and labor expensive. Naturally, America had developed labor saving devices that speeded up machinery. In Europe interest had been low and the need of speeding up to such an extent as had been done in America had not been felt in France. During the period of preparation and while Mr. Atterbury was laying his plans, this scarcity of material recurred. Three years of aggressive warfare had tried the resources of France and in the summer of 1917, the enemy's submarine operations had made inroads on the available resources. So to a land with different customs, with a different language, came the American army transportation men to apply the methods of operation and construction that had made American transportation the best in the world.

This was the state of affairs when the appointment of Mr. Atterbury as Director General of Transportation was made on September 14 by General Order No. 37, G. H. Q., 1917, whereby the Transportation Department was established as one of the technical services of general headquarters. By this order Major Wilgus was detailed Deputy Director General, Brigadier General W. C. Langfitt, as Manager of Light Railways and Brigadier General C. H. McKinstry as Manager of Roads.

In addition to the three subdepartments, this order provided that there should be a deputy director with each American army to be the personal representative of the director general; a general manager; a business manager, and an engineer of construction. The general manager was made responsible for the operation and maintenance of all broad gauge lines, including equipment and terminals. He was to be assisted by general superintendents; a general superintendent of motive power; a superintendent of maintenance of way; superintendent of transportation, and superintendent of telegraph and telephones. The business manager was charged with the responsibility of all purchases, accounts, statistics, disbursements, supplies and all stores except those on line, in which case they were under a division superintendent. The business manager's assistants were a purchasing agent, chief accountant, a chief of bureau of claims, a statistician and a treasurer.

The construction of all new broad gauge lines, terminals, docks, shops, sheds and other structures, was given over to the Engineer of Construction, and the Manager of Roads was held responsible for the highways within the zone occupied by the American forces. The Manager of Light Railways was to look after the construction, operations and maintenance of all light railways for the use of American forces. Later on, March 12, 1918, all construction work was turned over to the Department of Construction and Forestry and directed by the Chief Engineer, A. E. F. The Director General of Transportation procured the services of Mr. J. A. McCrea, General Manager of Long Island Railroad, as General Manager of the Transportation Department. As Business Manager he secured Mr. C. M. Bunting, Comptroller of the Pennsylvania Railroad; as Engineer of Construction Mr. H. C. Booz, Assistant Chief Engineer of the same line. All three of these gentlemen were commissioned colonels. Because of his knowledge of men who had made their mark with the railroads in the United States, and because of the work he wanted them to do in France, the Director General sent a cable to the United States naming the men wanted, and the Director General of Military Railways there, Mr. S. M. Felton, made an effort to secure them.

Construction and repair of standard gauge railroads was transferred from the Engineers to the Transportation Department by G. O. No. 56, Hq., S. O. S., November 19, 1918. A few days after the signing of the Armistice, the Commander-in-Chief made it a part of the duty of the Transportation Department to carry out the agreements of the American Expeditionary Forces with the Allies in reference to the operation, exploitation and repair of railroads which had been assigned to Americans. It was in carrying out this policy through the order above quoted, that the Director General was given charge of construction again. To give it the necessary facilities for the additional duties, the order transferred the 11th, 12th, 14th, 15th, 16th, 21st and 22d Regiments of Engineers (Railway) from the Engineer Department to the Transportation Department. By the same order the Engineer Department was directed to furnish the Transportation Department with material, supplies, tools, and labor necessary for the performance of the work in hand. The most of the work done under this order was in the zone of the advance, and with the personnel, tools and material given it, the Transportation Department was enabled promptly to carry out the wishes of the Commander-in-Chief.

The Army Transport Service was transferred from the Quartermaster Corps to the Transportation Department by General Order No. 78, G. H. Q., December 18, 1917. The need for this change had been apparent for some time. It had appeared soon after the Transportation Department began its work. Under the arrangement prior to this, the unloading of ships and loading of cars was controlled by one department and the hauling of freight (from) to the ports by another. As long as this handling of freight was thus dually controlled, differences were bound to arise, which could not help but lessen efficiency, and these delays were always annoying and might become dangerous. The single control gained by the transfer resulted in the elimination of this handicap, and in the more expeditious handling of supplies and a saving of organization. With the broad features of organization decided upon, the Transportation Corps began work under the departmental system. By March 1, 1919, it had 1,523 officers and 52,101 men and in addition 154 officers and 9,793 enlisted men were attached making a total of 1,677 officers and 61,894 men under the supervision of the D. G. T.* * *

* * * * * *

PART II

PROCESS OF ORGANIZATION

Soon after General Atterbury became Director General of Transportation he mapped out the broad lines of his organization, as already indicated, on the principles applying to commercial railroad organization in America. Although this gave him a machine with which to work, it was recognized that at best this plan of organization could not be more than a basis. For the first time in history a commercial railroad organization was superimposed upon a military organization and the two did not and could not fit into each other. It was obviously necessary to modify both.

The difficulty to be adjusted was three-fold. In the first place, American railway officials were called upon to operate over systems of railroads whose facilities were not then adequate to sustain the burden equal to the French needs plus the needs of the American army. Moreover, they had been developed and were operated by methods widely different from the railways in the United States.

Again, there was nobody connected with the American railroads who had been trained before the war for military railway service. What little business the railroads had had with the army had always been that of common carrier and shipper. Even in the Mexican Campaign this relation prevailed, and it is not stating any new fact to say that no new ideas of transportation had been gained by either from that expedition.

In the third place, there were no officers in the regular army before the war who had any working knowledge of railway operation or of any but the broadest and most obvious phases of transportation problems. This was not to be wondered at because the army had had no occasion to study transportation technically nor had there ever been any likelihood that it ever would have to.

The result of these conditions was that the technical transportation officers, newly commissioned, and the trained military men talked different languages and each had to learn that of the other before any real progress could be made in the process of organizing to the point of maximum efficiency. It was difficult for military men to understand why railway organization and operation could not be made to fit firmly established military theories and it was equally difficult for the railway men to understand why the strictly military officers should insist upon this thing and that thing, which the army regarded as military fundamentals, when they were so much at variance with transportation fundamentals. This, in brief, is a statement of the obstacles in the way of adequate Transportation Corps organization. How were they overcome? The military men, recognizing their lack of knowledge of transportation proposed dual control. In other words, they proposed that the heads of the various transportation organizations should be military men who should have technical advisers. The transportation men pointed out that dual control was as far from the desired efficiency from a military standpoint as it was from a transportation standpoint. The steps taken to settle this contention and ultimately to place the transportation men in control, giving them efficient military advisers, were the several stages of organization which made the Transportation Corps efficient and made possible the delivery of supplies to the troops promptly and in sufficient volume.

The Transportation Department was authorized by General Order No. 8, G. H. Q., July 5, 1917. This order made the Department one of the technical services of general headquarters, reporting through the Chief Engineer Officer. In theory all construction work was to be carried on by the Transportation Department but a footnote to the assignment of duties placed construction under the Commanding General of the Lines of Communication. The reason for this was that not enough construction troops assigned to the Transportation Department had yet arrived in France to do the work necessary and the Engineers continued to do it. At this time Major Wilgus, and Engineer Officer, was in charge of transportation matters. By General Order No. 20, G. H. Q., August 13, 1917, the Line of Communications was organized and it included the Service of Military Railroads with Major Wilgus on the staff of the Commanding General as Director of Military Railroads. This order set forth that the service was to include operation, maintenance and construction of such railways as might be turned over to the American army by the French authorities and it was to have the supervision of all movement of troops and supplies. The order stated further that the Service of Military Railways was to include all railways, permanent or temporary, constructed or controlled by American forces exclusive of light railways in the zone of the armies.

Soon after this Mr. Atterbury arrived from the United States and General Order No. 37, G. H. Q., Sept. 14, 1917, which appointed him Director General of Transportation also made the Transportation Department once more one of the technical services of general headquarters. The organization plan published in the same order was the authority for including in the staff of the Director General the department heads already indicated. The order also directed that, until such time as the number of construction troops in France warranted a division of engineer troops and labor of the Line of Communications, all construction work should continue to be done under the Commanding General of the Line of Communications.

The Commander-in-Chief made a further study of the problem and he decided that rail transportation should be organized as a separate department of Army Field Headquarters and coordinate with existing administrative staff and supply departments, since it occupied in this war a function apart from the Quartermaster Corps and the Engineer Corps. A cable to this effect was sent by him September 21, 1917, recommending that an organization be established to be known as the Railway Transportation Corps, its officers to be temporary officers of the national army and not qualified for purely military duty, a distinction which should be clearly observed. This recommendation was approved by the War Department October 26, 1917 but no provision was made for the transfer of men or units to the corps. The Army Transport Service was transferred to the department in December, 1917.

On January 23, 1918 general headquarters asked for suggestions for the revision of General Order No. 8, 1917. The Director General of Transportation and his staff made exhaustive study and then submitted a number of recommendations. Among these were:

(a) That authority be given to enlist men in the R. T. C. and organize all soldiers now or hereafter to be employed in this department other than regularly organized units.

(b) That the name of the Railway Transportation Corps be changed to Transportation Corps, services other than railway now being included.

(c) That the Transportation Department and Lines of Communication, at least as far as the purely business functions were concerned, be consolidated into one department with a single responsible head.

(d) That the work of the General Staff be decentralized by committing to competent managers an increasingly large share of the business and administrative routine.

(e) That the Director General of Transportation be given the usual disciplinary authority and an opportunity for adequate housing, police and sanitation of his own troops, such as possessed by a division or department commander.

One of the results of these recommendations was that the Commander-in-Chief convened a board of three general staff officers and one transportation officer to consider: first, what changes, if any, should be made in the organization of the whole supply service to relieve the Commander-in-Chief of the immediate direction thereof and place the entire responsibility upon some competent authority; second, what changes, if any, should be made as a result of the findings on the first proposition. This board met February 8, 1918. After a week of study and investigation it recommended the establishment of a service of the rear. This service was to consolidate procurement, transportation and supply as branches of equal standing and responsibility. The Commander-in-Chief approved the findings of this board but circumstances intervened which caused him to change his mind and no order was ever issued to this effect.

On February 16, 1918, General Order No. 31, G. H. Q., was issued creating the Service of the Rear. Under the Service of the Rear, and coordinate with the other departments was created a Service of Utilities. The Transportation Department was made a branch of the Service of Utilities and the control was placed under a new head, a military rather than a railway man, thus giving the Director General of Transportation only secondary control. The Commanding General, Service of the Rear, interpreted this order to make the Transportation Department subordinate to rather than coordinate with the other branches of the Service of Utilities. On March 19, 1918, the Commander-in-Chief in a telegram corrected this impression.

The board continued its proceedings upon instruction of the Commander-in-Chief and recommended a simpler form of administration, clearer definition of duties and a direct line of responsibility for results. It was pointed out by the board that this could be accomplished first, by localizing purely local agencies and placing upon local authorities the responsibility within their respective spheres, but preserving central authority for all matters of general policy and the control of general operations, particularly as to transportation; second, by having the Director General of Transportation under the direction of the Commanding General, Services of the Rear, retain control of the personnel of the Transportation Department and determine the location and scope of their employment. It was added that the responsibility for the efficient operation of Transportation Department should be placed directly upon the Director General of Transportation without the intervention of section commanders. No further action was taken at this time, however, save to amend General Order No. 31 by changing the name Service of the Rear to Services of Supply.

Under the Service of Utilities the idea of a strictly military man in control, with a technical assistant, as urged by the purely military officers, reached its highest development. But, as the technical railroad men had contended, this principle was found unworkable so far as transportation was concerned, and on July 11, 1918, General Order No. 114, G. H. Q., was issued, which abolished the Service of Utilities and made the Director General of Transportation responsible directly to the Commanding General, Services of Supply. This placed the entire control of the Transportation Corps with the

Director General of Transportation, as he had suggested in his memorandum to the General Staff on July 23.

The Internal Organization: But thus far the organization of the Transportation Corps has been considered in relation with other branches of service and with the Commander-in-Chief. While this was being developed, the internal development of the corps was taking place step by step. Until April 1918 the interior economy had to be governed most largely by the exigencies of the arrival of troops. The first outline of a definite and continuing plan of organization for a Railway Transportation Corps was made in April. Several attempts had been made before definitely to organize and provide personnel, but each of these attempts had been made on a basis of existing conditions and very limited expectations. The status of the corps was so indefinite that it was impossible to look far enough into the future and make plans for the ultimate detailed organization. The bulk of the personnel was to be made up from Engineer and Quartermaster units. It is true there did exist a Railway Transportation Corps composed of a limited number of officers and enlisted clerical and technical personnel, but this was intended to serve merely as a headquarters organization. It was created in February, and by the first of April the limits of its elasticity were already reached. During February and March tonnage rating and traffic density charts were made as the result of studies of the needs of the army, and with these charts as a basis, an estimate prepared of the personnel required to handle supplies for the A. E. F. in keeping with the constant increase. This estimate was made by a railroad man and was solely a railroad man's estimate of operating needs, and was in no sense a military plan of organization. The military officers of the Transportation Corps made a study of it and converted it into a military table for a Transportation Corps. The assignment of rank to technical duties were made partly on a basis of rank necessary for certain duties, and partly on accepted ratios in grades for the army in general. No attempt was made radically to depart from custom or take the stand that various railway positions could not be governed by accepted standards for the line. After this information was consolidated, it was put in the form of a telegram, which was submitted in the rough draft to the Chief of Utilities, under whom the Director General of Transportation was then operating. The Chief of Utilities hestitated to approve it because he believed the estimate was far too large.

The last day of May the Director General of Transportation forwarded a letter developing a proposed staff and line organization. While approved as a tentative form of organization, exception was taken by the Chief of Utilities to the scope of the duties given some of the officers; i. e., the General Superintendents of lines, Division Superintendents, etc., he thought should not be permitted to exercise military as well as technical command, because, in his opinion, all their time and attention should be taken up with operating duties. A further objection was made to the statement of duties of the Engineer of Construction, insofar as the table made him responsible for the execution of all plans prepared for design and construction in the Transportation Department. The organization was approved by General Headquarters, but the Chief of Utilities assigned the actual work of construction to the Department of Construction and Forestry.

Meantime studies were being made of the railway personnel situation and the difficulties encountered under existing organization. No unit under the jurisdiction of the Director General of Transportation in April, except the 19th Engineers, had ever been given a fair opportunity to organize under its own tables. The units were composed mostly of men who had been hurriedly thrown together either in France or in the United States, and were, therefore, more or less poorly disciplined and poorly equipped. Commissioned personnel was lacking and had to be picked up from any possible available source. Naturally some of the men thus obtained were unsatisfactory for their duties. The necessity of operation without proper personnel had caused many improvised measures to be taken which had badly confused the situation. One of the results of the study was the conclusion that an infantry regimental table would meet the needs of the transportation service better than the former engineer regimental or engineer battalion organization, because the engineer organization was too small to provide the personnel necessary to operate an entire grand division of railroad. The infantry organization was unsatisfactory also, but it was the lesser of two evils.

It was believed that an infantry regiment would be large enough to provide the personnel to operate a grand division, and that it could be operated under a General Superintendent, who would also be the military commander of the regiment. The actual military administration, however, was to be delegated to his Lieutenant Colonel, who would be a purely military officer.

As the months went up, however, many defects in this plan of organization cropped out. Finally after prolonged negotiation and much argument to bring the General Staff to an understanding of the real needs of the department, and then after the General Staff had convinced the War Department, in turn, a fluid organization was reached under which the Transportation Corps did operate as long as it remained in France. This organization was based upon a personnel of six thousand officers, with ranks according to certain stated proportions, and two hundred thousand enlisted men in the various grades. After the approval by the War Department by cable on October 3, 1918, the plan was made effective by General Order No. 52, Hq., S. O. S., which was issued under instructions from the Commander-in-Chief on November 12, 1918. This order was broad in its scope and left to the Director General of Transportation freedom to work out the details as the needs of his organization demanded. The Transportation Corps had been working on these details pending the publication of the proper orders, and as soon as General Order No. 52, Hq., S. O. S., was published, General Order No. 35, Hq., Transportation Corps, was promulgated, also on November 12, 1918 (the day after the signing of the Armistice), carrying out the details authorized by the War Department and defining the organization in detail.* * *

The principal features of this order, copy of which is attached, was to divide the headquarters organization and to set forth the territorial boundaries of each Grand Division.* * * Subsequent to the promulgation of General Order No. 35, Hq., Trans. Corps, the work of organization went along in its due course smoothly and efficiently.

While all this was going on, however, it is not to be understood that the officers of the transportation service had been sitting idly by and waiting for somebody to map out their duties before they went to work. During all these months the hundreds of thousands of tons of supplies were being brought across the Atlantic, landed at the ports, and shipped to the front. Thousands of cars and hundreds of locomotives were being erected, and American trains operated by American railroad men were rushing across France with the dispatch and efficiency expected of American railroad men. Port and railroad facilities were being planned by the Engineers, and were constructed and turned over for operation. All these things were done by the Transportation Corps with its make-shift organization because it was realized by the Director General of Transportation and his staff that the object of the transportation service was to transport supplies, and other things were details. How these things were done will be told in the places of this report which deal with the various divisions of the service.

PART III

DEPARTMENT OF BUSINESS MANAGER

When the Director General of Transportation decided upon a Business Manager on the general lines of a railroad organization in America, he decided that purchases, disbursements, accounts, statistics and claims should be entrusted to him. Carroll M. Bunting, then Comptroller of the Pennsylvania Railroad, was requested to be the Business Manager, and I. A. Miller, the Chief Accountant of the Operating Department of that road, to be his assistant. For the position of Chief Statistician, Disbursing Officer and Claim Agent, J. R. Black, Jr., Special Agent for the Accounting Department of the Pennsylvania Railroad, E. H. Reynolds, President, Peoples' Trust and Savings Bank, Chicago, and C. A. Walter, Special Agent for the Accounting Department of the Pennsylvania Railroad, were selected. This personnel arrived in Paris October 9, 1917, and reported immediately to General Atterbury.

At first some difficulty was experienced in obtaining definite records of material ordered or already purchased for transportation purposes because the Transportation Corps had not jurisdiction over all the activities affected by it. Later when it got control of the ports and other branches of transportation, this difficulty was obviated. It was found that no authority had been granted for the Transportation Department to conduct its own purchases or make its own disbursements. All materials ordered from the United States by requisition or cable for use of the department were handled through the Corps of Engineers and paid for through Engineer appropriations and were consigned to the Chief Engineer, A. E. F.

After securing such records and other data as could be obtained regarding orders placed in the United States for transportation purposes, the General Purchasing Agent was consulted as to the advisability of the service establishing its own organization in the A. E. F. Because the French government had promulgated regulations covering the purchase of material, equipment and supplies in France, and that the consent of the various French commissions was necessary before a purchase could be consummated, and also because the Transportation Department had no disbursing fund from which to make payment for its purchases, and the Engineer Corps already had a purchasing organization working under the General Purchasing Agent and the General Purchasing Board, it was decided not to establish an independent purchasing organization, but use the Engineer purchasing office.

The wisdom of having all A. E. F. purchases made by the General Purchasing Board was fully demonstrated. So far as the Transportation Service has been concerned, orders were filled with greater despatch and better terms were secured, and it is believed that the quality has been higher than would have been even remotely possible had there been indiscriminate purchasing by each service. The General Purchasing Board has served the needs of the Transportation Service in a manner which has been highly gratifying to the officials of the service, and which must be gratifying to the board itself.

This conclusion was reached with the understanding that the department of the Business Manager would receive the requisitions from the Transportation Corps organizations, would coordinate them, and then place them with the Engineer purchasing officer. At the same time, on account of the scarcity of ship tonnage and the necessity for conserving such tonnage so as to import from America the minimum quantity, extra efforts were made to secure as much of the supplies as possible from European sources. The Engineer purchasing officer was already organized to undertake this work, and, therefore, it was decided that the disbursing organization would not be needed by the Business Manager of the Transportation Corps.

The original plan for organizing the Transportation service also contemplated the construction of warehouses and storage depots for the receipt and distribution of transportation material. But when these materials began to arrive from the United States shortly after the organization of the Business Manager's Department, it was necessary to make some immediate arrangement. Therefore, the Corps of Engineers was again asked to handle this. This developed a serious situation later on. The Corps of Engineers had ordered for its purposes much material of a character similar to that ordered for the Transportation service and difficulty was ultimately encountered by the Transportation Department in getting possession of its own materials, because these common articles found their way into the Engineer depots and their identity became lost. To remedy this condition, arrangements were made with the Engineers to issue from their depots on transportation requisitions such material as was needed that was found in the Engineer stores. While this resulted in some delay in securing transportation material, there is no doubt it reduced to a minimum the stock of American material in France, and often put the Transportation Department more quickly in possession of some of the material it actually needed.

In the meantime information had been collected in regard to contracts and leases made for the operation of the Transportation Department, and about December 1, 1917, the Director General undertook the operation of the base ports, including the discharge and handling of transports. This necessitated the compilation daily of statistics in order that the authorities concerned could have accurate knowledge of port operations. When additional personnel was assigned to the Business Manager's department, it was organized into three sections, as follows:

1. A STATISTICAL AND ACCOUNTING SECTION: To have jurisdiction over the compilation of statistics regarding operations under the jurisdiction of the Director General of Transportation, as well as the handling of any accounts in connection with these operations.

2. A REQUISITION AND MATERIAL SECTION: To handle all demands for transportation supplies, keep record of the receipt and distribution of supplies, keep record of the receipt and distribution of supplies ordered for the Department in the United States, as well as a record of stock on hand and other details in connection with supplies.

3. A CONTRACT, CLAIMS AND ADJUSTMENT SECTION: To supervise the preparation of contracts, keep record thereof, and handle all matters in connection with any claims arising through the requisitioning of land, damage to property, etc., and to establish a record of the service rendered by the Transportation Department to the French railroads, or materials furnished or services rendered by the French to the American Transportation Department.

Statistics and Accounting: The Statistical Bureau was established November 1, 1917, and the work performed by it from that date until January 1, 1918, was principally of an investigating character of the ports of St-Nazaire, Nantes, and Bordeaux, in determining the kind of records that would have to be kept, and in devising blank forms necessary for this purpose. At the outset the bureau worked with a view of getting the maximum amount and highest grade of work out of its officers and enlisted men. To this end some weeks of extra hours were observed in educating both officers and men in the kind of accounting deemed best for the corps. This was entirely in addition to the work necessary to keep up with current business. The officer in charge of the bureau held classes of instruction to explain to the men the importance and purpose of the statistical data compiled and the necessity for exercising extreme care to avoid errors, which, if not detected, would affect the usefulness of the statistics as a reliable measure for judging results and directing future operations. These classes were not only beneficial so far as the results were concerned, but they had distinct additional advantages to the men for subsequent civil life, and also served the much desired purpose of arousing enthusiasm and interest of the men in their duties.

The Statistical Bureau never stopped work. The force, whether at headquarters or in the field, was divided into two shifts, one worked from 8 a. m. until 6 p. m., and the other from 6 p. m. until 8 a. m. In the headquarters day force there were six officers and nine enlisted men; in the night force, one officer and twenty-four enlisted men; on detached service, eight officers and seven enlisted men.

On account of the necessity for accuracy and the tedious nature of the work performed, it would have been desirable to have had three instead of two shifts at headquarters, but the shortage of available personnel made this impossible. The personnel on detached service worked at ports to supervise and assist the port organizations in the preparation of daily, weekly and monthly reports.

All operations were reported on a daily basis, which, from January 1, 1918, to May 1, 1918, ended at 6 a. m., the reports from the base ports being submitted as soon after this hour as possible by telegraph. When the headquarters were removed to Tours, on March 24, 1918, increased facilities, both telephonic and telegraphic, were provided, and arrangements were made on and after May 1 to have all records close as of midnight and transmitted to headquarters before 5 a. m. by telephone, but when delays occurred in making connections, the information was telegraphed. With these increased facilities, an effort was always made to have the reports of operations for the preceding day in the hands of the proper Transportation Corps officials by 9 a. m.

For the purpose of relieving the organizations at the ports of the responsibility of accounting and giving them greater freedom to work out problems of efficient operation and to insure accuracy and reliability in the reports submitted to the Statistical Bureau, it was found necessary to have representatives at the ports, reporting to and receiving instructions directly from the Statistical Bureau. The duties of these representatives involved the supervision of the manner in which the basic data was compiled to insure its correctness before being submitted. It was necessary, also, that these men should have a comprehensive knowledge of the details of all reports and be thoroughly experienced in the work of the bureau. Consequently, the men were recruited from the office personnel and officers were detailed for one or two months work with the headquarters force before being assigned outside.

There were brought from the United States such mechanical devices as were considered necessary for the Statistical Bureau. These included machines for additions, divisions and multiplications for determining average and percentages; nonlisting machines for verification and easy multiplications and additions; listing adding machines of various kinds and duplicating devices. These machines were found indispensable, as, in view of the shortage of clerical labor, the daily work of the bureau could not have been accomplished. The duplicating machines were particularly valuable in view of the fact that it was extremely difficult to obtain printed blank forms and special ruled paper, with other stationery and office supplies. These articles purchased, as the months went by, justified themselves owing to the scarcity and high price of this class of material in France.

One of the best known, most important, and most comprehensive statements prepared by the Statistical Bureau was the Daily Summary of Boat, Dock, Car, and Barge Operation, commonly known as Form 66. This report showed the essential information contained in the daily reports received from the various departments, eastbound boat operations, westbound boat operations, and status of erection of locomotives and cars. Forty copies of this form were issued daily for the use of the Commanding General, S. O. S., various sections of the General Staff, the Director General of Transportation, the Deputy Directors, Director of Army Transport Service, Port Superintendents, Business Manager, General Manager, Engineer of Construction, Transportation Department representatives at Naval Headquarters, and the Transportation Corps Historical Officer.

A monthly report of vessel movements at base ports was compiled, showing separately the trans-Atlantic, crosschannel and interport service, the names of vessels, date delivered to the A. T. S., cargo on board on arrival, cargo unloaded prior to and during current month, average discharge per boat per day, cargo unloaded from date of arrival to close of current month, cargo remaining on board at close of month, record of diversions to other ports, cargo of ballast, troops and passengers loaded for outward movement, and date released by Army Transport Service. Copies of this report were furnished to the General Staff sections, S. O. S., the Director General of Transportation, the Director of the Army Transport Service, each Port Superintendent, and the Historical Officer. The information contained in this report was of particular value to the Port Superintendents because it showed in detail the operations of various vessels and was available as a basis for compiling statements relating to arrivals, departures, and performances while in port.

There was also compiled a supplementary monthly report showing the classes of tonnage unloaded at each port by commodities and service, the total tonnage unloaded, the percentage of each commodity to the total tonnage, and an analysis of the total classified tonnage for trans-Atlantic, crosschannel, and interport service.

Early in April 1918 the Statistical Bureau began the preparation of statements of boat detention. These statements showed the number of boats released and the total days and average days detention per boat. Weekly statements were also compiled from March 1, 1918, showing similar information, which was changed to ten-day statements beginning July 1, 1918.

It was necessary that the Statistical Bureau be equipped to furnish at short notice statistical data relating to the detailed operations of the various branches of the Transportation Service, and statements were compiled, showing such information as the following:

(a) Tonnage handled on each dock at all ports.

(b) Performance and efficiency of gantry cranes as compared with other unloading equipment.

(c) Analysis of car situation at particular base ports or for certain classification yards in the interior of France.

(d) Special reports upon the time and cause of port congestion.

(e) Analysis of the cause of detentions of boats in ports and the days elapsing for turn-around movements in trans-Atlantic, cross-channel, or interport services.

(f) Many other special statements relating to operations of the Transportation Service.

The Statistical Bureau prepared cables for the Chief of Staff and for embarkation as follows:

(a) A weekly cable of transport operations in which was included cargo from the United States discharged at all ports; estimated tonnage evacuated from the ports; probably departure of vessels during the following week; unusual delays; amount of cargo and ballast of vessels sailing from France; repairs needed upon arrival at American ports. On May 1, 1918, an additional paragraph was inserted covering unusual delays to vessels in French ports. On July 23, 1918, further information was incorporated covering activities for previous periods of trans-Atlantic tonnage discharged by vessels, and the total cross-channel tonnage.

(b) A monthly cable showing probable departure of cargo vessels from French ports for loading in the United States during the following month, together with the total amount of tonnage that such vessels would probably carry on the eastward return voyage.

(c) Beginning August 3, 1918, a tri-weekly cable was begun. It was submitted each Tuesday, Thursday, and Saturday, and contained the names and dates of vessels arriving from the United States; the names of vessels with cargo sailing for the United States, or with Ballast and personnel, the latter being classified as to officers, men and civilians; and a statement as to the health of the personnel. This cable was continued on a three-day basis until the signing of the Armistice, since when it has been submitted daily.

(d) Beginning October 12, 1918, there was sent a weekly cable showing the status by ports as of Saturday night; the number of ship days lost awaiting berths; and the number of idle berths for the previous week covering berths permanently assigned to the A. E. F. This cable was discontinued November 16, 1918.

A study of the increasing amount of tonnage unloaded at the ports and the rate of increase in the tonnage evacuated, showed an insufficient car supply, which in April, 1918, was controlled largely by the French. Disproportionate accumulation of tonnage at the docks was evident. It was, therefore, necessary to have statistical data which would reflect the exact situation regarding the receipt and dispatch of loaded and empty cars at all points under American jurisdiction. Therefore, forms were devised and put into use on May 1, 1918, which would show this information in detail. These statements were based upon reports from the American Railway Transportation Officers, commonly known as R. T. O.'s. Because of the need for obtaining special data from the R. T. O.'s special arrangements were made whereby officers from the Statistical Bureau delivered lectures at the R. T. O. School at Angers from June 1, 1918, until the close of the school after the signing of the Armistice.

In connection with Form 66 above referred to, a statement of the daily car situation was made. This showed the cars ordered, cars erected during the day, cars under erection, cars on hand at the shops but erection not started, total at shops, total at ports, total in France, and total on sea. There was also included in the daily statement classes of equipment received already erected, such as petrol tanks from England, railway wagons for fighting tanks from England, and twenty-ton gondola cars from Spain. Similar information was submitted daily on the status of the erection of locomotives.

To summarize, the Statistical Bureau reported daily, weekly, and monthly on every activity of the Transportation Service, and because of its machinery, was enabled to make certain that every report was accurate.

Requisitions and Distributions: The arrangements of the Transportation service with the Engineer Supply Officer for the purchase and filling of requisitions have already been shown. When units in the field became more familiar with conditions existing in France, requisitions began to come in for authority to purchase from local French firms where material was available, and it was decided by the Business Manager that emergency purchases which could be made in accordance with regulations, should be authorized, but that all such purchases should be made only upon authority issued by him. This condition was decided upon in order that all records of materials could be kept by the proper department. An arrangement was made with the Engineer Supply Officer whereby payments of all emergency purchases would be made upon proper certification by the Business Manager. This had its effect in the organization of the Bureau for Requisitions and Distributions, because it necessitated an additional subdepartment, of which there were three in all. The first one was for procuring transportation material in the United States and the preparation of all cablegrams and information in connection therewith. The second was for requisitions and purchases in France. The third was for a record of all materials requested from the United States, the purchase of same, and their distribution upon arrival in France.

When the Service of the Rear was established, the department of Construction and Forestry, and the department of Light Railways and roads were organized under the Chief Engineer, thus leaving the Director General of Transportation in charge solely of the standard gauge railroads and the Army Transport Service. The department therefore handled only such materials as were for transportation use.

Therefore, plans were made for a central material depot for the Transportation Corps, which was to be located at Nevers, with a corps supply officer in charge. When the Armistice was signed and all additional construction was cancelled, the plans for a large depot were somewhat modified, but Nevers was still maintained as a storage depot for transportation material, and since its establishment, distribution of material has been handled from it.

Upon the cessation of hostilities, considerable reduction in requirements became apparent. Immediate efforts were made to cancel in England and France all contracts which the Engineer and other services had entered into at the request of the Transportation Corps, and a considerable number of cancellations were made in the United States for material on order there.

Contracts, Accounts and Settlements: Although it had been intended, at its inception, for this bureau to handle claims against the Transportation service, the institution of the Rents, Requisitions, and Claims Service of the American E. F. relieved it of this work, and it devoted its activities entirely to contracts, accounts and settlements. All formally executed agreements, contracts, and leases involving the activities of the Transportation service have been made under the supervision of this bureau, which has been charged with the assembling of data relating thereto, and with their preparation and execution. The bureau has also acted as a liaison between the various branches of the transportation service and the Board of Contracts and Adjustments of the A. E. F., while the latter board has furnished advice as to the legality and form of all contracts. On account of the difficulty experienced because of the late start of this department and the lack of personnel, it was found hard to bring the work up to the maximum of efficiency and to place all kinds of contracts at the very beginning of each operation. A great many arrangements had been entered into by representatives of the transportation service covered only by letters of proposal and acceptance. However, efforts were made subsequently to consummate formal agreements wherever possible, and as nearly as possible, the representatives of the Transportation Corps conform to the requirements of army regulations in respect to the procurement of services, etc.

To this end representatives of the bureau investigated conditions under which every enterprise involving the procurement of services was entered into covered only by letters of proposal and acceptance, and as nearly as possible has corrected any apparent omissions. By January 1, 1919, a complete file of all contracts, agreements, leases, and letters of proposal and acceptance had been made.

It was necessary to keep a record of all cars owned by the United States or those loaned to the American E. F. by or through any of the Allied Governments, and at the same time show the disposition of these cars. Without interruption, this work progressed until a complete record was available showing to whom all equipment charged against the transportation service is assigned, and when any of the equipment had been turned over to any of the Allied Governments or the French railroads, proper record of such transactions was made. In addition, it was necessary to keep an accurate record of the disposition of all locomotives owned by the United States, as well as those loaned to the A. E. F. or rented from the French or Belgian Governments, and those loaned by the Belgian Government and subrented to the P. L. M. and Etat railroads. This department has procured receipts covering all locomotives turned over to others than members of the A. E. F. and also reports showing the condition of locomotives when put into service, giving a list of tools thereon, together with a list of any tools or parts missing upon arrival in France.

It was found necessary to make an investigation at the various base ports of payments being made on account of the expenses of the various ships in the Army Transport Service, to find whether such payments were properly chargeable against the United States or ship owners, with the result that an arrangement concluded to have all payments on ship accounts reported to the proper authorities in the United States or the American authorities in England, so that proper charges will be borne by the vessel owners when final settlement is made. Also, investigations had to be made and accounts kept with various American firms employed by the Transportation Corps for the erection of port equipment.

With a view to final settlement at the end of the war, a record was kept of all authorizations by G-4, General Staff, S. O. S., and by the French services for the installation of transportation facilities and the information thus procured is being assembled so that at the final accounting a determination may be made as to the justness of the charges rendered by the United States or to the United States.

Owing to the uncertainty of the basis of settlement upon which reimbursements were to be made to the A. E. F. for services performed for the French, or vice versa, no account was kept in this bureau of services so rendered, instructions having been issued to the various branches of the Transportation Corps performing these services to keep the accounts in question. But since the signing of the Armistice, this information has been gathered and is now being arranged for a final accounting. To do this, it has been necessary to obtain data in regard to the maintenance of French tracks by the American forces, the use of American personnel on French trains and in French shops, the use of American personnel in A. E. F. shops repairing French-owned or loaned equipment, French material brought in on American transports and handled and rehandled by the American forces, American personnel assisting in unloading French vessels, space on docks for storing French material, and detachments loaned to the French, or other miscellaneous services that may have been rendered.

As one of the conditions of the use of French docks by American forces, the A. E. F. was to pay to the several Chambers of Commerce at the base ports, rental in the shape of dock dues. After considerable negotiation, in which efforts to obtain a schedule of these rates were unsuccessful, the whole matter was referred to the Finance Officer of the A. E. F. who is making a settlement with the French Government.

In addition to the locomotives brought over from America and erected in France, it was necessary for the A. E. F. to procure a number from the Belgian Government; the settlements to be on a basis of the net amount due either Belgium or the United States after consideration had been given to the value of the machinery turned over to Belgium to be used in her shops, the cost of the machinery to be applied against the rental due Belgium for the use of her locomotives. The net difference is to be charged either to the United States or the Belgian Government. A complete record of these transactions has been kept by this bureau, and is in such shape that proper statements can be made on call.

PART IV

DEPARTMENT OF ENGINEER OF CONSTRUCTION

Under the organization created by G. O. No. 8, G. H. Q. 1917 series, the Director General of Transportation was charged, inter alia, with the responsibility for". . . the construction of all railroads and canals under American control." The Director General of Transportation, by G. O. No. 1, Hq. D. G. T., November 6, 1917, created the department of the Engineer of Construction with Colonel H. C. Booz at its head.

Under the reorganization pursuant to G. O. 31, G. H. Q., February 16, 1918, whereby the Service of Supply was created, within which was a Service of Utilities, the actual construction of facilities was put under the Department of Construction and Forestry and the duties of the Engineer of Construction were limited to inception and design of all transportation facilities including ports and railroads, negotiations with the French authorities for the approval of such facilities as would affect the existing French Railroads or ports and procuring land for these facilities through the proper French authorities.

By G. O. No. 23, T. S., July 14, 1918, Lt. Colonel (later Colonel) H. M. Waite relieved Colonel Booz, who was recalled to the United States and, in turn, Colonel Waite was relieved by Major (later Lt. Colonel) H. W. Hudson, in accordance with G. O. 34 T. S., dated November 1, 1918. By G. O. 46 T. C., dated December 24, 1918, Major E. W. Clark succeeded Lt. Colonel Hudson.

On November 6, 1917, the Department of the Engineer of Construction had a personnel of 13 officers and 8 civilian draftsmen. At the signing of the Armistice, November 11, 1918, it had 43 officers, 76 enlisted men and 12 civilian draftsmen.

As from time to time, the organization of the services in the rear of the army was changed to meet new conditions and to profit by experience, so the organization of the Department of the Engineer of Construction varied. The organization is best typified by its status at the cessation of hostilities. * * * The subdepartments at that time were those of executive officer, port facilities, water supply, railroad facilities, designing and structural engineer. In addition, there were engineers assigned to specific districts in those parts of France where construction was being done, and survey parties who gathered the data necessary for the development of designs.

Scope of Its Activities: Although the department was not formed officially until November 1917, considerable work had already been done in studying the general scheme and in preparing standard designs.

In May, 1917, members of the American General Staff, in conference with the French Government, obtained permission to utilize certain existing French berths. The first of these was at St-Nazaire and subsequently, as necessity arose, additional berths were assigned at Nantes, French Bassens, Pauillac and La Pallice. The Railroad Commission, of which Major W. J. Wilgus was a member, early came to the conclusion that the question of port facilities was the keynote of the success of the A. E. F. in France, and that additional facilities, far in excess of those assigned by the French, must be found. Accordingly, when Major Wilgus was assigned to duty under the Chief Engineer Officer, A. E. F., immediately he bent his efforts to the design of new ports and to the preparation of a bill for the transportation material and equipment needed.

The congestion of the Channel Ports, due to their use by the British army, and the submarine menace in the Mediterranean Sea, narrowed the search for additional port facilities to the Atlantic ports south of the Channel and made it necessary to find sites for the construction of new ports. Furthermore, the French Government in designing the American railroad lines of communication, had offered certain French railroads terminating at St-Nazaire, La Pallice, and Bordeaux, where existing French berths were designated as available for the use of the A. E. F.

After much study, sites for the new ports were selected (a) on the south side of the Loire River at La Martiniere for a 10 berth port and (b) for another 10 berths at Bassens adjoining the French wharf of the same name on the Gironde River just north of Bordeaux.

The Commander-in-Chief directed that storage facilities should be provided on the 90-day basis. To provide for this storage, sites were selected, all American storage depots designed, and a general system planned with Base Storage Depots located at Montoir to operate in conjunction with the port of St-Nazaire and at St-Sulpice---Izon to operate with the ports of French and American Bassens, Intermediate Storage Depots at Gievres and Montierchaume and Advanced Storage Depots to be used also as Regulating Stations at Is-sur-Tille and Liffol-le-Grand. Sites for Ammunition Storage Depots at the ports were selected at St-Loubes on the Dordogne River and at Donges on the Loire River and for Intermediate Ordnance Depots at Mehun and Issoudun.

Later as the demands of the increased tonnage grew, depots for port storage were designed to be located at St-Luce for the port of Nantes, at Aigrefeuille for the ports of La Pallice and Rochefort, later at Miramas for the port of Marseille, and at Pleyber Christ for the port of Brest. In addition to these there had been selected and designed at the time of the cessation of hostilities other storage depots in advance of the Intermediate Section at Troyes, Tavaux and Rugles, although nothing ever came of them.

The ramifications of modern warfare made a broad field to be covered in the design of transportation facilities. They included storage depots, engine terminals, car shops, hospitals, camps for the various arms, ammunition storage, wharves, piers, railroad classification yards, repair shops, remount depots, Air Service Depots, Forestry operations, passing sidings, increased station facilities, etc. Also the adaptation of existing French port and railroad facilities to meet the needs of the American army's supply system and the additions to these facilities in order that the existing ports and railroads could bear the added burden imposed upon them by the American tonnage made the problem extremely complex. It required much investigation, study and negotiation. Each service had to be consulted, the French ideas adjusted and the plans designed so as to get maximum results for operation with the minimum effort of construction as the Department of Construction and Forestry had a large task confronting it. Naturally the confliction of ideas originating from so many sources, French as well as American, added to the difficulties. The matter of obtaining official French approval produced delays, but gradually these difficulties were ironed out, and with ideas coordinated by experience and the delays reduced, the machinery began to move much more smoothly. Plans were made and approved covering installations which totalled 316 different transportation items, and work had been completed, was under way, or was projected, by which the anticipated army of 4,000,000 men could have been fully served by transportation. This program was greatly modified after November 11, 1918, to the point of incorporating only essential features.

Filed with the report of the Chief Engineer Officer, in connection with the activities of the Department of Construction and Forestry, are ground plans of the following projects which are typical of the designing done by the Engineer of Construction in carrying out the A. E. F. program:

1. Bassens
2. Montoir - Base Storage Depot
3. St-Sulpice - Base Storage Depot
4. Gievres - Intermediate Storage Depot
5. Montierchaume - Intermediate Storage Depot
6. Liffol-le-Grand - Regulating Station
7. Is-sur-Tille - Regulating Station
8. St,-Loubes - Ammunition Depot
9. Romorantin - Air Depot
10. Saumur - Engine Terminal

In order to obtain a clear idea of the activities attending the aception of designs, it is necessary to give the method by which not only the American authorization but also the French approval was secured. It is to be noted that the larger railroad lines in France radiate from Paris as a hub and that the lines of communication assigned for the use of the American army crossed these main arteries of traffic practically at right angles. In all, five of the six main lines of French Railroads were utilized. Connections, multiple tracking, passing sidings, engine terminals, cut-offs and additional water facilities were necessary in the congested districts and affected the following French Railroads with whom negotiations had to be started in order to obtain the concurrence of the officials for the various projects desired: The Paris-Orleans, the Paris, Lyon Mediterranee, the Est, the Midi, and the Etat.

Each of the projects, after having been designed and authorized by the proper authorities of the American army, was submitted to the French Government, which in turn forwarded them to the French Railroad affected for approval. Because of wide difference in operating methods and railroad traditions, the early plans were seldom accepted as designed and counterpropositions were frequently offered. To cut red tape and to avoid delays, it was decided finally to submit the design directly to the railroad affected, and after meeting with the road's approval, to submit the design to the French Government and the American Army Staff.

Furthermore, on account of difficulties of ocean transportation, lack of personnel, and because connections had to be made with existing lines, it was frequently necessary to call upon the French Railroads to furnish both labor and material. The bills for such services and material were rendered by the local French Railroad Officials through the main office of the railroad, to the French Government thence to the Director General of Transportation. These bills had to be checked and certified by the Engineer of Construction.

The French Railroads were under the War Ministry, which, acting through the Ministry of Public Works, of which M. Claveille was the head, gave the official approval for installations. The Minister was assisted in this work, at first by a bureau designated as the Fourth Bureau, and later by a board called Franco-American Special Services.

All plans authorized were sent to the French officials through the Deputy Director General of Transportation at Paris, thence to the French Railroads, Marine Service or Government Department affected for action. This approval carried with it the acquisition of the necessary land and contained the stipulations under which the work was to be undertaken, setting forth the manner in which, the labor and materials were to be supplied and the cost met. Another feature included in this approval, insisted upon by the Director General of Transportation, was the clause that "in event any or all of the facilities being retained by the French Government. Railroad or Service, credit should be given to the American army for the work performed and the materials furnished."

Besides transportation plans originating through the Engineer of Construction, projects were sometimes initiated by the French Railroads or Marine Service, in which case they were sent through the French Bureau to the Director General of Transportation for acceptance.

At first negotiations were tedious and cumbersome. Later, owing to the establishment of semi-monthly conferences at Paris at which the various representatives of the French Railroads and Services and the representatives of the operating and construction departments of the Director General of Transportation were present, matters were adjusted more expeditiously and satisfactorily.

The proper American authority for authorizing the various projects differed under the various plans of organization. At first the Director General of Transportation, acting under the Commander-in-Chief, arranged directly for such installations. Later, under the organization of the Services of Supply, the Chief of Utilities became the proper authority. Finally, after July 11, 1918, the proper authorization came from C. G., S. O. S., G-4.

Planning Port Facilities

PORTS: The ports at which berths were contemplated for the use of the American army were divided into five groups as follows:

(1) Channel Group: Le Havre, Honfleur, Rouen, Cherbourg, St-Malo, Granville.

(2) Brest Group: Brest, Lorient, St-Brieuc.

(3) Loire River Group: St-Nazaire, Montoir, Donges, Usine Brulee, Nantes, Les Sables d'Olonne, La Pallice, Rochefort, Tonnay-Charente, Marans.

(4) Gironde River Group: Bordeaux, Pauillac, Blaye, St-Loubes, American Bassens, French Bassens, St-Pardon, Bayonne, Talmont.

(5) Mediterranean Group: Marseille, Toulon.

At some of these ports existing French facilities were not changed. At others French facilities were adjusted to the use of the American traffic by eliminating turntables, by installing lead tracks. crossovers and connections which would permit direct shifting and utilization of American equipment. At other ports entirely new installations were designed and constructed.

Le HAVRE: At Le Havre, a deep draft port, two berths were assigned to the A. E. F. at the Bassin Bellot. The only work needed was to adjust tracks to make them available for American cars. At the docks on the Tancarville Canal warehouses were designed, construction authorized, and work had begun when the Armistice was signed. At the existing wharf at the Quai de Maree plans were made to provide additional tracks and warehouses. The project, however, was cancelled.

ROUEN: Designs were made for the construction of a two berth vessel wharf at Cleres Cailly and for a wharf and ammunition storage layout at Grand Couronne. While the construction at the first was authorized, neither of these projects were ever started.

BREST: The port of Brest was a deep water port, but the facilities originally assigned to the American army were suitable only for handling troops, troop baggage and package freight, by means of lighters. At Pier No. 3 a ramp was levelled, a deck built and stiff leg derricks installed. A two berth wharf, know as Jette-de-l'Est, was completed in November 1918, and equipped with cargo masts. A three berth wharf was designed for Digue-du-Sud to be connected with the mainland by a double track trestle. The construction was begun in October 1918, but was stopped after the signing of the Armistice. Additional facilities had also been contemplated and a general scheme of improvement near the Château-du-Brest.

ST-NAZAIRE: It soon became apparent that the capacity of this port could be increased by the addition and rearrangement of tracks and crossovers but that no additional wharves were needed, except an extension to make Berth No. 9 a lighterage wharf. These plans did not mature. Part of the extension and rearrangement of tracks was done in 1917, including the laying of a third track to provide an additional outlet from the docks. It was also planned to install twelve gantry cranes at two of the berths and the proper track rearrangement was designed. This work was cancelled on account of the cessation of hostilities.

MONTOIR: The site originally selected for a port on the Loire River was changed from La Martiniere to Montoir because of the railroad construction necessary to connect La Martiniere with the main line and because of the development of the Montoir storage yard. After considerable investigation and controversy with the American Officials and the French, designs were made for the construction of an 8 berth pier to provide for deep draft vessels, the pier to be 3,280 feet long and equipped with cranes and warehouses or sheds. A double track trestle approach was also designed.

This work was under way, but after the Armistice the design was modified so that only 1,275 feet of the pier, to accommodate 3 vessels, was completed.

DONGES: Donges was chosen as as site for an ammunition port. This project located on the Loire River, was isolated from other operations as required by French Regulations for ammunition storage. The designs called for a two-berth vessel pier, but it was enlarged later, on account of the anticipated increased shipments of ammunition from the United States, to provide four berths. At the time of the cessation of hostilities this work had just been started and the project was cancelled.

USINE BRULEE: At this point, just west of Nantes on the Loire River, the French had under construction a reinforced concrete structure providing for two berths. These were completed by the French in July 1918, and turned over to the A. E. F. It was found that, in order properly to operate the cranes located on platforms off shore, it was necessary to fill in the open space between the crane platforms and the bulkhead, and to do some construction to bring the railroad tracks within reach of the cranes. This work, the construction of warehouses adjacent to the tracks, and the additional track facilities were completed.

A three berth wharf was also under construction by the French, but was not completed when the Armistice was signed.

NANTES: The construction of the wharves already begun on the Island of Ste-Ann, at the Quai-de-Pirmil and the Quai-d'Antilles, was continued by the French and some of the berths completed and turned over to the American army by the fall of 1918. Adjacent to these berths and to the Etat Railroad Yard on the Island, considerable increase and alteration of existing tracks was designed and several warehouses planned. Much of this work had been completed before new operations were stopped.

Les SABLES D'OLONNE - TONNAY CHARENTE: These two minor ports were used by the A. E. F. mostly for unloading coal. Only minor track changes and coal storage facilities were undertaken. This work was practically complete on November 11.

La PALLICE: At this point, existing French wharves were slightly changed to accommodate American traffic and facilities handling cars. It has been the intention to erect eight electric gantry cranes and provide necessary additional track facilities, but the Armistice intervened.

ROCHEFORT: Four existing French berths were assigned to the A. E. F. at Rochefort. Construction of an additional 2-berth pier and the installation of make-up yards to serve it and the existing berths was authorized, but the work was never begun.

PAUILLAC: Two berths at this port were assigned to the A. E. F., but were used almost exclusively by the navy. Additional tracks were laid and minor track changes were made but no extensive construction work was necessary although a plan had been prepared for additional facilities in event the war continued.

St-LOUBES: At this location on the Dordogne River a lighterage wharf 750 feet long, equipped with standard gauge locomotive cranes, was built for unloading ammunition. Next to the wharf was the ammunition storage. The project was completed and in operation before the fighting ended.

AMERICAN BASSENS: As early as July 1917, it was decided to build an American port in the vicinity of Bordeaux on the Gironde River. Piles, sawed timber, steel I-beams and the necessary hardware were ordered from the United States. Simultaneously a contract was made with the Phoenix Construction Company of New York City whereby equipment and tools were to be sent from the United States and the work of building the docks undertaken.

The earliest complete plan prepared by the Transportation Service for this work is dated September 24, 1917, but the original scheme for the design had been evolved at a much earlier date. The plan called for the construction of a wharf 4,100 feet long, deemed sufficient for berthing 10 vessels. On the wharf, four railroad tracks were planned, the three nearest the string piece spanned by over-head electric gantry cranes, thirty of which were to be 5-ton capacity and ten of 10-ton capacity. Warehouses were laid out in the rear of the wharves providing 215,000 sq. ft. of storage space, and behind these two railroad tracks so depressed as to bring the car floors on a level with those of the warehouses. Beyond these depressed tracks, additional warehouses were designed. The whole area around the warehouses was to be paved with concrete. Adjacent to the wharf, receiving and departure yards were laid out providing for circular movement of cars to and from the docks.

From the outset, difficulties were experienced in obtaining material from the United States, both as to quantity and quality. Work on the wharf proper was actually begun on November 17, 1917, and while the quality of the material, especially the piling, was poor, the material was used because the port was needed at the earliest possible date and the prospect for obtaining timber of better quality was remote.

As late as December 26, 1917, none of the steel I-Beams required to sustain the anticipated load properly had reached Bassens. On account of the great need for completing the wharf, a committee was appointed to make a survey of the entire situation to determine the advisability of continuing construction along the lines of the original design. The report of this committee, which was later approved, eliminated the use of the gantry cranes because their additional weight required the use of the gantry cranes because their additional weight required the use of the steel I-beams and timber of superior quality than that on hand. A modified ship gear had been designed with which to equip the wharf, but the delivery and quality of material improved and the construction of two of the berths was carried out as originally planned. They were completed for the reception of the heavy gantry cranes in March, 1918.

The increased tonnage program demonstrated the need for unloading ships rapidly, and the splendid performance of the gantry cranes on these two berths demonstrated their efficiency. So on August 18, 1918, the C. G., S. O. S., authorized the strengthening of the remaining eight berths and the erection of the additional thirty-two cranes to equip the wharf as originally planned. This work was begun on September 4, 1918, and the last of the gantries was put in service on January 25, 1919.

FRENCH BASSENS: A wharf at this point had been constructed by the French and six berths were used by the A. E. F. from October 1917. The French completed the construction of four additional berths in October 1918. Warehouses, providing 100,000 sq. ft. of storage space, and the additional track work to develop the full efficiency of the docks and allow for a circular movement of cars were designed. The whole work, however, was not completed until February 1919. The outlet for trains from French Bassens is through the yard provided for American Bassens adjoining.

BASSENS AND St-PARDON: Lighterage wharves, each 600 feet long, were designed for the above locations but when the fighting ceased only that at St-Pardon had been started.

TALMONT: The location of a new port at Talmont was the subject of much controversy. The site was opposed by the Transportation Service and by the French. Eventually, however, a 10-berth wharf was designed by the Section Engineer of the Department of Construction and Forestry and authorized together with a 16-mile railroad connection. A port storage yard was designed in the Officer of the Engineer of Construction. The work was begun in August 1918, but cancelled by the cessation of hostilities.

TOULON: At this port, the French Naval Base for the Mediterranean, two piers were assigned to the use of the American army, and designs were made providing tracks, warehouses and unloading devices so that these piers could be used to handle ammuniton. The tracks were completed but the remaining work was not.

MARSEILLE: When the accelerated troop movement, which necessitated increased tonnage, reached such a point that additional port facilities were necessary, the work of navy in the Mediterranean made it possible to use Marseille. This deep water port is the largest in France and it was proposed to provide facilities here for handling 10,000 tons a day. Plans were made for track changes to provide switching and facilitate handling American equipment on the docks in the Bassin de la Gare Maritime and on Mole G. The latter was to be completed by the French. Additional tracks to hold the loaded and empty cars in the vicinity of the docks were projected. It was intended to install sixteen American gantry cranes and warehouses on Mole G. The construction was under way when the cessation of hostilities brought the American participation in this work to a close.

In addition to the ports mentioned, studies had been made for the improvement of berth and track facilities at other French ports mentioned in the several groups, but nothing further was done after the signing of the Armistice. In all, the A. E. F. used 28 different ports and had 89 berths definitely assigned to it. It was intended to provide facilities at the ports so that by June 1919, 101,000 tons per day could be handled.

Railroad Facilities: On the Lines of Communication designated for use of the American army the American tonnage was imposed in addition to the burden of French civilian and military traffic. A complete study of these facilities was required and showed that to carry this increased burden successfully, many of the tight places would have to be relieved and present facilities enlarged as well as new projects installed. This included increasing existing and, in a number of cases, constructing new engine terminals and water supply facilities, multiple tracking, new connections and crossovers, the lengthening of sidings, cut-offs and the installation of new large reception, classification, departure and storage yards and branches to serve plants constructed by the various services of the American army.

In addition to the three Lines of Communication already mentioned, the opening of the port of Marseille made it necessary for the American army to utilize the lines of the Paris, Lyon Mediterranee Railroad up the Rhone Valley from Marseille and connecting with the first lines of communication at Chagny. Also, as more ports became available for the American army, other lines came into use, notably the main line of the Etat Railroad from Brest to Le Mans and thence by the Paris-Orleans Railroad from Le Mans to Tours, where connection was made with the first line of communication, and also of the small line from Bayonne to Bordeaux.

It has been estimated that the total railroad mileage utilized by the American army exceeded 5,000 miles.

Storage Depots: On account of the storage system as directed by the Commander-in-Chief, to which allusion has already been made, sites were selected and plans made for general storage depots.

These depots were designed to include receiving, classification and departure yard facilities, with engine, storage, water and special facilities, such as bakeries and refrigerating plants. After considerable study, the so-called Herring Bone system for the layout of the warehouses and tracks to serve the same was adopted. This allowed for great facility and ease in operation, since by having tracks on each side of the warehouses, with the intervening space to be utilized for open storage, materials could be loaded and unloaded to and from the warehouse at the same time and the short groups of houses permitted a larger number of cars to be placed where needed without interference with another group. It also was adapted readily for further expansion and was regarded as the most economic use of materials. The ratio between open and covered storage was as two to one and while the yards varied slightly according to their location and use, this general design was followed.

PORT STORAGE YARDS

MONTOIR: As a result of investigation made in September 1917, the site of Montoir was chosen as being the best available for the location of a storage depot to serve the port of St-Nazaire and also the pier which it was proposed to build at Montoir. In September 1917, a plan was prepared for an initial small yard. This plan was followed by one providing for a much larger development. It provided an ultimate of 236 miles of track with 1,025 turnouts, 180 warehouses having an area of 4,125,000 sq. ft. and, approximately, 10,000,000 sq. ft. of open storage space. The work was started in October 1917, and continued until the signing of the Armistice, at which time there had been installed 125 miles of track with 400 turnouts, and storage aggregating 2,066,000 sq. ft. in area and approximately 7,000,000 sq. ft. of open storage space. The complete layout is about 2 1/2 miles long by one mile wide, and covers and area of 1,200 acres.

St-SULPICE: This site was selected in 1917 and is about nine miles eastward from the port of Bassens which it serves. Plans were prepared for providing an ultimate of 147 miles of track, 623 turnouts, 144 warehouses having a total area of 2,263,000 sq. ft. and open storage space amounting to 6,860,000 sq. ft. Construction was started in November 1917. In November 1918, when further new construction work was cancelled, there had been completed 91 miles of track with 305 turnouts, covered storage space amounting to 2,341,000 sq. ft. and open storage area totalling 3,000,000 sq. ft. The complete layout is about 3/5 of a mile wide and 2 1/2 miles long, covering approximately 850 acres.

AIGREFEUILLE: This site, at the junction of the main line from La Pallice and Rochefort, was recommended for a port storage depot by a board of officers in May 1918. The plan provided for an initial installation of 23 miles of track with 102 turnouts and 9 storehouses giving a total of 204,000 sq. feet and 429,000 sq. ft. of open storage. The complete layout covers an area of 310 acres. Only a small portion of this work was complete when it was cancelled by the cessation of hostilities.

MIRAMAS: This site was selected in May 1918, for a storage depot to serve the port of Marseille. It is located adjacent to the existing French yard at the junction of the two double track lines of the Paris-Lyon Mediterranee Railroad, 33 miles northwest of Marseille. Pending the completion of that part of the Miramas layout which was to be immediately installed, arrangements were made with the French for the use of storehouses at the French depot located at this point. The plans provided for an ultimate of 108 miles of track with 474 turnouts and 120 warehouses giving a total of 2,496,000 sq. ft. and 10,000,000 sq. ft. of open storage space. The layout covered an area of approximately 1,020 acres. The engine facilities were to be taken care of by the French engine facilities under construction. Only a small percentage of the work had been completed when the project was cancelled.

PLEYBER CHRIST: This site, 32 miles from Brest, was selected after considerable reconnaissance on account of the difficulties of the terrain in this section of Brittany. It was to be a storage depot for the port of Brest and the plans prepared in October 1918 provided for 42 miles of trackage with 244 turnouts and 36 warehouses giving a total of 816,000 sq. ft. and an open storage space amounting to 2,000,000 sq. ft. The layout covered an area of 360 acres. No work was started when the war ended.

Ste-LUCE: This location was selected as a port storage for the port of Nantes and the plans included an ultimate construction of 23 miles of track with covered storage amounting to 267,000 sq. ft. and open storage of 956,000 sq. ft. At the time of the cancellation of further work approximately 15 miles of track had been completed, with 125,000 sq. ft. of covered and 556,000 sq. ft. of open storage.

INTERMEDIATE STORAGE DEPOTS

GIEVRES: This is the largest of the A. E. F. depots and is located on the main line of the Paris-Orleans Railroad between St-Nazaire and Saincaize, being 208 miles from the former point. The site was selected in August 1917 and the layout ultimately provided for 264 miles of track with 1,152 turnouts and 195 warehouse aggregating 4,410,000 sq. ft. with 10,387,000 sq. ft. of open storage. The project covers an area of approximately 2,600 acres. At the time of the signing of the Armistice, 132 miles of track with 3,552,000 sq. ft. of covered and 6,000,000 sq. ft. of open storage had been completed.

MONTIERCHAUME: This site located near Chateauroux and approximately 227 miles from Bassens, was selected in August 1917. The plans called for an ultimate track installation of 225 miles with 1,000 turnouts, 180 warehouses totaling 4,079,000 sq. ft. and 10,000,000 sq. ft. of open storage space. Construction was started in March 1918 and at the time of the cessation of hostilities there had been completed 49 miles of track, 305 turnouts, covered storage amounting to 1,123,000 sq. ft. and about 5,000,000 sq. ft. of open storage space. The yard as planned covered about 1,040 acres.

ADVANCE STORAGE DEPOTS AND REGULATION STATIONS

IS-sur-TILLE: This location was adopted in August 1917. The French prepared the plans originally for the yard layout. These plans were revised to meet the needs of the American operation. The yard is located at the Junction of the Paris, Lyon Mediterranee and the Est Railroads and is approximately 436 miles from St-Nazaire. The layout involved 95 miles of track with 60 buildings providing 1,847,000 sq. ft. of covered storage and 5,110,000 sq. ft. of open storage. Construction was started in the latter part of 1917 and by November 11, 1918, 95 miles of track with 1,355,000 sq. ft. of covered and 4,186,000 sq. ft. of open storage had been completed. The layout covers 840 acres.

LIFFOL-le-GRAND: This site was agreed upon for a regulating station about the same time that Is-sur-Tille was selected. It is located on the same line of communication, 467 miles from St-Nazaire. The plans provided an installation of 72 miles of track with 318 turnouts and warehouses giving 408,000 sq. ft. of covered storage and open storage space amounting to 1,444,000 sq. ft. Construction was started April 1918. When the work was cancelled there had been completed 42 miles of track with 180 turnouts. All the warehouses as planned amounting to 408,000 sq. ft. and 584,000 sq. ft. of open storage space had been served by tracks. The area of the project is 580 acres.

As has been stated, studies and plans had been made for storage depots at Rugles, Troyes, and Tavaux, but these subjects had not gone beyond the plan stage at the cessation of hostilities.

Engine Terminals: A careful study made of the existing French engine facilities showed that, to handle the American traffic in addition to the French, it would be necessary not only to increase the capacity and to speed up the existing plants, but also to build entirely new ones. Accordingly, engine terminals were designed and afterwards constructed at Saumur, Cercy-la-Tour and at Perigueux and also at the storage depots at Montoir, Gievres, Is-sur-Tille, St-Sulpice, Montierchaume, and Liffol-le-Grand, as well as at the storage yard at Aigrefeuille and St-Luce and the proposed storage depots at Pleyber Christ, Rugles, Troyes and Tavaux. Work was started on engine terminals on the secondary line of communications at St-Germain-du-Puy, Etais, and Poincon. All of these, however, were cancelled before much work was done. Smaller installations were also provided for the ordnance and ammunition storage yards at Mehun, Issoudun, and Jonchery. At all of these plants, provisions were made for inspection, ash and repair pits, storage, coal and water facilities, the necessary standing tracks, a loop or wye for turning locomotives, and also for machine shops for the making of minor repairs. The layouts were made so that cross movements could be avoided and the engines turned and made available for the next run as expeditiously as possible. Had hostilities continued it would have been necessary to augment the existing French facilities on the lines from Brest to Tours and from Marseille to Chagny and also to construct new terminals on the third line of communication between Tours and Bricon. The cessation of hostilities made these unnecessary although investigations had been made and plans were being prepared.

Main Line Improvements: Certain improvements along the existing main lines were required as has been set forth, the most notable of these are as follows:

NEVERS CUT-OFF: The purpose of this construction was to enable the American traffic to avoid the congested station and yards at Nevers. The cut-off was proposed by Major Wilgus in September 1917 and although the French objected, as they were in favor of the construction of a new yard and a double track through the congested district, the American plans were finally approved and construction started. The work involved 162,000 cu. yds. of excavation and 428,000 cu. yds. of fill, a bridge and trestle approach 1,400 feet long over the Loire River and a canal crossing. Also a single track bridge to take the east bound track over the existing main line of the Paris-Lyon Mediterranee. The project is a double track railroad 5.5 miles in length and made a saving of 8.6 miles for train operation. It has been in service since October 19, 1918.

FOR-TRACKING PONTVERT TO BOURGES: The lines of communication from Bordeaux and St-Nazaire converge at Pontvert while the second line of communication branches to the north a short distance east of Bourges at St-Germain-du-Puy. It can therefore be seen that the existing two tracks form the neck of a bottle and would become congested when the traffic from both the ports of Bordeaux and St-Nazaire would have reached considerable magnitude. In order to avoid this congestion, it was decided to put two extra tracks on the section from Pontvert to Bourges, it not being necessary to go beyond Bourges as 4 tracks already existed between that point and St-Germain-du-puy. This work was completed about the time of the signing of the Armistice.

PERIGUEUX WYE: In order to avoid the necessity of a switchback into the town of Perigueux, a wye connection, 0.4 miles long, was constructed. Although a small project in itself, it is an important item in time saving and in relieving congestion of traffic.

DOUBLE TRACK THROUGH NANTES: The main line of communication from St-Nazaire and Montoir passed on a single track through the city of Nantes. This was not sufficient to provide for the additional traffic which the American army proposed to handle. After much difficulty and much negotiation, permission was finally obtained from the authorities of the city of Nantes to permit a second track to be laid through the city. This track was three miles long and the work was completed and in operations in May 1918. handle. After much difficulty and much negotiation, permission was finally obtained from the authorities of the city of Nantes to permit a second track to be laid through the city. This track was three miles long and the work was completed and in operations in May 1918.

FOURTH TRACK BASSENS TO St-SULPICE: In order to take care of the shuttle traffic between bassens and its storage depot at St-Sulpice, plans were made to add two additional tracks to the existing double track line of the Paris Orleans Railroad between these points. Only one of these tracks was actually constructed as the traffic never reached the point where it was necessary to have the fourth track installed. The work on the third track has been completed.

Miscellaneous Projects: In addition to these projects, the details of which have been set forth, plans were made and construction done on many other projects to serve the needs of the American army. Particularly, difficulties were encountered in the selection of sites and in making the layout for ammunition storage depots, as the French regulations on such depots were very strict, and, also varied from time to time. Designs for ammunition depots were made for port storage at St-Loubes and Donges, for intermediate storage at Mehun, La Chapelle---St-Ursin and at Issoudun; for advance storage at Jonchery, also called Villiers-le-Sec. Plans had been made but not yet authorized for ammunition storage depots near Miramas, near Troyers and near Tavaux.

Numerous plans, designs for which were usually initiated by the Department of Construction and Forestry, were gone over and forwarded to the French for approval for the installation of forestry projects. Plans were also made for the serving of salvage depots, remount stations, hospitals, air artillery, infantry and concentration camps, car erecting facilities and for facilities to serve Motor Transport, the Ordnance and Inland Waterways and Quartermaster Departments at numerous points.

Special Studies: With a view to anticipate the needs of the transportation, a special department was charged with the study of the entire French railroad system and its adaptability to the increased needs of the American army. These included the preparation of tonnage charts, the study of possible routings, capacities of lines, determination of engine runs and the proposed location of yards, regulating and other facilities. Also of the routings and possibilities of the French canal system and of the lines to be used and facilities required for the possible advance of the American army to the Rhine.

Water: This department was charged with the design of all facilities supplying the lines of communication with the necessary water for locomotives and troop trains. Hence was included the provision not only for water at the various engine terminals, but also for the roadside water stations.

Under the original organization, studies were made including both available sources of water supply to the point of distribution and also the distribution system itself. However, when the actual construction was turned over to the Department of Construction and Forestry, the work of the Engineer of Construction was, theoretically, limited to the design and distribution system. The department of Construction and Forestry was charged not only with the construction but also with the requisition of all supplies and investigation of all sources of water supply which could be used by camps, hospitals and other facilities as well as for transportation. In practice, however, detailed studies were made of water supply by the officers of this department and at the time of the signing of the Armistice, the number of studies had reached 268, of which 105 plans had been completed. The question of roadside water stations was a particularly difficult one because the French plants were in general supplied by only a four inch main which caused a great delay to locomotives in taking water. It was planned to have many of the French water stations reinforced and to utilize 10-inch standing pipes and thereby greatly facilitate the movement of trains. Owing to the fact that the work of installation of these roadside water stations was progressing very slowly and that materials were not sent promptly and in sufficient quantities from the United States, the water facilities of the American army for transportation purposes, were fast reaching a critical stage. Had hostilities continued, extensive and expeditious work would have been necessary in order to prevent congestion and to meet the transportation requirements.

PART V

DEPARTMENT OF THE GENERAL MANAGER

Among the responsibilities placed on the Director General by General Order No. 8, G. H. Q., July 5, 1917, were the operation and maintenance of all railways under American control, the operation of terminals, and the control and maintenance of all rolling stock and motive power. This part of his responsibility the Director General placed in the hands of a General Manager, whose department was authorized by General Order No. 1, Headquarters Trans. Dept., November 6, 1917. In this order he appointed Colonel J. A. McCrea, General Manager. On the General Manager's staff were appointed Lieut. Colonels N. L. Howard, H. H. Adams, Nettleton Neff, and H. H. Maxfield; Majors E. B. Cushing, V. R. C. King, and R. A. Crammes; Captains C. E. Carson, F. E. Kennedy, H. N. Williams, and F. P. Paten, and First Lieutenants J. A. Appleton, F. C. Bryant, G. T. Sheehan, H. L. Kyle, G. A. Kendrick, F. A. Parker, J. D. Farrington, and E. A. Craft.

By General Order No. 29, Hq. Trans. Service, September 26, 1918, Colonel McCrea was relieved to become Deputy Director General of Transportation in the Zone of the Advance. By the same order Colonel F. Mears was made General Manager for S. O. S. and Lieut. Colonel H. H. Adams for the Zone of Advance. This order also appointed Colonel George T. Slade, Deputy Director General, S. O. S. Colonel Mears reported to Colonel Slade and Lieut. Colonel Adams to Colonel McCrea. Colonel Slade left for the United States February 6, 1919, and left Colonel Mears reporting directly to the Director General of Transportation.

Immediately upon his appointment as General Manager, and the announcement of his staff, Colonel McCrea began active direction of railroad operations for the Transportation Department. By the time the department had authorized, the lines of logical communication, as indicated already in this report, had been fixed* * * The first line having been decided upon, it was necessary to map out this territory into railroad divisions with a view to future operation.

Lieut. Colonels Neff and Maxfield were accordingly sent out by the General Manager, and reported on the condition of the railroads and the territorial divisions in February,

1918. They found the roadway and track in fair physical condition in spite of the heavy traffic and lack of maintenance during the previous three and one-half years; a serious lack of motive power, and an even more serious car shortage. The big French terminals at St-Pierre-des-Corps, Bierzon, and Nevers were already handling traffic which taxed their facilities and it was apparent that, when the American army started its own railroad operations, other terminals than those already established by the French would be necessary.

The 1st Division made was as between the northern and southern lines. The northern lines included the main line from St-Nazaire to Is-sur-Tille and any lines which might later be operated to the north of this. The southern lines included the territory between Bassens or Bordeaux and the junction of the main east and west line at Bourges.

It was decided that the divisional system in use on most American railroads would be employed in spite of the fact that the French use a highly developed departmental system. Accordingly, in March 1918, a General Superintendent was appointed for the northern lines and one for the southern lines.

American railroad operation in France divides itself into three phases:

First: The American army was in the position of a large commercial shipper over the French railroads; during this phase all troops and all freight for the American army were handled on the French railroads, French equipment and French personnel alone being used.

Second: The American army operated its own terminals and by its engines, cars, and crews, gave substantial aid to the French.

Third: Upon which we were about to enter at the time of the signing of the Armistice; that in which the American army would have taken over a section of the French railroads and operated it with American personnel and under the American system.

From March 1918, when the first General Superintendents were appointed, until June is the period of the first phase. The French railroads handled all freight and troops with their own personnel and equipment. Practically the only American agency in active touch with the railroads being the R. T. O.'s, who were stationed at the more important passenger and freight stations to look after American interests.

The American traffic handled by the French amounted to about 6,000 tons a day during the first half of April, 1918, but this figure was expected to reach 20,000 tons a day by August, 1918. In order to meet this situation it was necessary for the American army to supply its own cars, enough locomotives to handle its own traffic, and to supply the French with locomotives and crews to meet their own increasingly grave lack of motive power and personnel. It was estimated that, to take care of the needs of an army of 500,000 men, 900 locomotives and 18,175 cars would be necessary, the total supply of freight cars in France being only 362,000.

When the headquarters of the Transportation Department was moved from Paris to Tours, steps were taken to put the organization on a more workable basis. Owing to the lack of personnel but little could be accomplished during the first few months as no operating troops had arrived from the United States. A considerable number of casual officers were, however, arriving from week to week, and these were assigned at headquarters to help plan for the future operations; or, were sent out with titles of Division Superintendents and Master Mechanics assigned to what was to be the territories previously agreed upon as those which constitute the future operating divisions.

Very early it was necessary to establish an effective liaison with the French railroads. A regulating commission, at the head of which was commandant Andriot, of the French General Staff, was placed at Tours, and this commission was given power to act as an intermediary between the American railroad administration and the 4th Bureau of the French General Staff at Paris, which was in charge of transportation. All requests of the American army upon the French railroads for transportation were to be made through the Regulating Commission, and all requests of the French railroads upon the American service were to be made through the same channel.

Under the General Manager, in addition to the General Superintendents, was appointed a General Superintendent of Motive Power, Colonel H. H. Maxfield, and a General Superintendent of Transportation, Lieut. Colonel V. R. C. King. The General Superintendent of Motive Power was to be in charge of the erection and maintenance of all locomotives and cars and the General Superintendent of Transportation, of all transportation matters, keeping in close touch with the other departments of the army, in order to anticipate and meet their needs. Under the General Superintendents were Division Superintendents, each in charge of a specified territory, and each of whom had upon his staff a master mechanic for the upkeep of locomotives and equipment, and trainmasters to look after the actual details of operation.

This organization was established only in the territory behind the regulating stations. The transportation in the Advance Section was largely under the control of the regulating officers appointed by G. H. Q., although Colonel H. H. Adams was assigned as Assistant General Manager, Zone of the Advance, and attached to the Assistant Chief of Staff, G-4, at G. H. Q., to look after the transportation problems in that territory and act in liaison with the General Staff.

Under the General Superintendent of Transportation was a Superintendent of Freight Transportation and a Superintendent of Passenger Transportation. The Superintendent of Freight Transportation controlled a Car Record Office and a Car Order Office. The Car Order Office was to assemble requests for empty cars and assist in getting this equipment for the forwarding services, according to priority of shipment established by G-4 of the General Staff. To the Car Record Office the movement of all cars both loaded and empty was reported, special emphasis being given to the movement of American cars. But records also were kept of the movement of all French cars carrying American freight. Reports were telegraphed each night to the Car Record Office from every station where a representative of the Transportation Department was, giving the numbers, initials, contents, destination, and point of origin of every car carrying American freight that had passed through, arrived at, or departed from the station during the day. Thus a complete check was kept on the movement of a car from the beginning of its journey to the end. The bureau had charge also of tracing lost cars, and rendered great assistance to the forwarding services.

The Superintendent of Passenger Transportation acted in a supervisory capacity over the transportation of all A. E. F. personnel. Under him was organized a Troop Movement bureau, which arranged with the French for all schedules of troop movement. Although the bureau was in existance from January 1918, no official recognition was given it until General Order No. 105, G. H. Q., July 1, 1918. Previously troop movement from the ports was arranged directly with the French by the Base Commanders on instruction from the General Staff. But after the appearance of General Order No. 105, all troop movement was arranged by this bureau. Two bureaus were established: One at the Headquarters, S. O. S., and the other at G. H. Q., the first, making arrangement for movement within the S. O. S., and the second for any movement taking place in the Zone of Advance. A third bureau was established in January 1919, in Paris, to arrange for the movement of men on leave. The operation of the bureau will be described later.

Another activity under the Superintendent of Passenger Transportation was the Lost Baggage Bureau, which was established to trace and locate officers baggage and that of other American E. F. personnel lost in transit.

The General Superintendent of Transportation kept in touch with the Regulating Commission through an American officer stationed in the office of Commandant Andriot.

The General Manager's Staff also included as Assistant General Manager, whose duty it was to take care of some of the operating details, a personnel officers and an officer in charge of the instruction of R. T. O.'s, under whose supervision came the R. T. O. School at Angers, and to whom the Chief R. T. O.'s on the staff of the General Superintendents referred for decisions. All correspondence from the R. T. O.'s passed through the Division Superintendents and the General Superintendents to the General Manager and were referred by him to the R. T. O. Instructor, who, however, only issued instructions over the General Manager's name, thus keeping intact the Divisional System.

An Engineer of Maintenance of Way was appointed in November 1918, but due to the signing of the Armistice and the consequent reduction in operation, this position was considered unnecessary and abolished on December 1, 1918.

In June a second Regulating Commission was established at Perigueux, but after three months of operation it was decided that transportation matters could be better handled through one office, and the Perigueux Commission was discontinued.

Contract of Operating Methods: Before describing the actual work of the Transportation Department in France it is necessary to take up some of the chief differences between American and French railroad operation. The chief difference was that of centralized control, in the case of the Americans, and local control, in the case of the French.

Before it could be hoped to operate trains on a satisfactory basis it was seen that a new system of communication would have to be established over our lines, as the French system of telegraph and telephone, running only from station to station, could not meet the needs of the American Service. A sector telephone system was, therefore, installed from St-Nazaire to Is-sur-Tille, from Bourges to St-Florentin and Liffol-le-Grand, and from Bordeaux to Bourges and Vierzon. The line was cut at each division terminal so that the operation of trains over any given division was under the control of a Chief Dispatcher at that point. In addition to the selector telephones, telegraphic communication was also put in on all lines over which American trains were operated. This service proved entirely satisfactory; and, in fact, better communication was afforded on the lines operated by the Transportation Service in France than on many good railroads in the United States.

On September 27, 1918, Colonel McCrea, General Manager, was appointed Deputy Director General, Transportation, in the Zone of the Advance, Colonel Mears was appointed General Manager. From this time on the Transportation Service in the Zone of the advance was organized along the same lines as in the S. O. S. Colonel H. H. Adams, previously the representative of the Transportation Service on G-4, G. H. Q. Staff, was appointed General Manager, and the lines in the Zone of the Advance divided into three Grand Divisions with the same operating organization as existed in the S. O. S.

In the S. O. S. there were six Grand Divisions known as the A, B, C, D, E and F lines until November 12, 1918, when the whole Transportation Department was reorganized by General Order No. 42, Hq. S. O. S.

The French Chef de Gare has absolute control over the movement of all trains through his station, and no train is permitted to depart without his consent. The trains are run on a series of schedules or marches, beginning at one minute after midnight. The marches of trains in the direction of Paris are even numbered, and those in the opposite direction are odd numbered, and are spaced twenty minutes apart. Each train is given the number of its march, to which is prefixed the key number of the district over which the train travels. For instance, the key number of the district between Vierzon and Tours is 62,000; thus a train departing from Vierzon to Tours at 12:01 a. m. would be numbered 62,001, and a train departing from Tours to Vierzon at the same hour would be numbered 62,002. The corresponding trains departing twenty minutes later would be 62,003 and 62,004, respectively, etc., throughout the entire twenty-four hours. On a double track railroad, therefore, seventy-two trains per day in each direction is the limit of the traffic that can be handled. As a matter of actual practice this limit is never reached on account of road delays, terminal congestions, etc.

On the French railroads all runs for train and engine crews are turnaround runs, the crew starting from its home terminal and returning to the home terminal at the end of the day. The system of putting crews on rest at an outlying point, common in American railroad practice, is entirely unknown in France. The trains are blocked from station to station. All signals are under manual control, and, with the exception of certain distant signals, no permissive signals exist.

The French rolling stock is very light and air-brake equipment on freight cars was almost unknown before the advent of American constructed cars. The average French car has a capacity of about ten tons. The American cars used in France had a capacity of thirty tons.

The French motive power is of good design and construction, and well adapted to the needs of the country under ordinary conditions, being, as a rule, lighter than the power generally used on our freight trains, due to the fact that higher speed is maintained and lighter trains are hauled than in the United States. On account of the fact that the ordinary freight car has no air-brakes, and that a great many of them are not even equipped with hand brakes, it was necessary to place a certain number of brake cars in each freight train, the number varying on the several roads according to the grades and the length of train handled. On the P. O. Railway each train must contain at least three brake cars, one at the head end, one at the rear, and one in the middle, whereas, on the Etat Railway seven brake cars is the minimum number.

Owing to the fact that the traffic was very well balanced, no central system of car distribution had been evolved. The Chefs de Gare generally had enough empty cars at their stations to take care of local needs. If not enough cars were available, a request was made on the nearest division terminal for the necessary number. The same was true in regard to motive power, and no definite system seemed to be in vogue for the balancing of motive power along the lines.

The records kept at stations of freight cars appeared to the average American railroad man as primitive. The cars were recorded in a book in the order of their arrival and not under the car number, as usual in the United States. As a rule, even the small stations are equipped with loading platforms and freight houses; the construction generally being of stone, very solid and excellently adapted to the needs of the traffic.

Freight Movement: It was the operations of the storage plants that the Transportation Service entered the second phase of its activities. In addition to the terminals at these storage plants, two other important terminals were constructed, one at Saumur, where a junction was effected between the Etat Railway from La Rochelle and the P. O. line from St-Nazaire, and another at Marcy, midway between Bourges and Dijon.

In May and June five battalions of railway men were assembled in France, the troops being picked at the classification camps at St-Aignan and Blois from the line regiments. These men were former railroad employees in the United States. They were assembled at such points along the line as Saumur, St-Pierre-des-Corps and Gievres, and for a period of thirty days were instructed by representatives of the French railroads. Miniature signals were made and classes held at the camps in order to familiarize the men with signal operation, and a résumé of the rules of the Etat, P. L. M., P. O., and Est Railways was translated from the French and assembled in standard book form. The book contained the essential rules for French railroad operations showing the signal aspects in colors. It was thought that men thoroughly familiar with this information would be able to qualify and run trains on the French roads. As soon as the instruction was finished the men were turned over to the French and used as much as possible to handle American locomotives, which had begun to arrive and were being used by the French to haul American freight.

The increasing number of troops which began to arrive in France in March had put a tremendous burden on the French railways, because the amount of freight unloaded at the ports reached 25,000 tons daily at the end of May. Therefore, a request was made by Marshal Foch that railway troops from the United States be given priority, and it was asked that 25,400 railroad men be sent over in June and July. Although this program was not fully realized, about 15,000 operating men arrived in France before the end of July and immediately steps were taken to instruct these men and put them into service. They were stationed at Nantes, Saumur, Gievres, Marcy, and Is-sur-Tille, and, on the line from Bordeaux, at Bassens, Perigueux and Montierchaume. Meanwhile, engine houses were being erected as fast as possible and the water supply was being looked into with a view to future operation. However, because of the need of thirty days' instruction for the men it was not until September that the first trains, operated entirely by Americans, began to run from the coast to the regulating stations.

It was agreed that Americans should operate their own trains as much as possible, solid American trains to be made up at the ports and run through to the American terminals. So far as possible no American trains were handled in French terminals as these were already congested and could not take care of additional traffic. Freight runs were, therefore, made on the main line from Montoir to Saumur, from Saumur to Gievres, from Gievres to Marcy and from Marcy to Is-sur-Tille, instead of using the French terminals at Angers, St-Pierre-des-Corps, Vierson, Nevers, and Dijon. Although this kept French terminals from being further congested, some difficulty arose on account of the fact that the runs of the French pilots, one of whom was on every American train as conductor, did not coincide with the regular French train runs. The lack of through communication from American terminals to French terminals further complicated this and it frequently was difficult to arrange for marches for American trains after they were made up in American yards.

It was believed that American trains could be run more safely and more economically if operated with air brakes, but this was forbidden by French operating practice. Accordingly, in June a conference was held between representatives of the P. O. and P. L. M. Railways and some members of the 4th Bureau and members of the American Transportation Corps in Paris. It was agreed that a test train should be run from Montoir to Is-sur-Tille. Americans hoped to prove the feasibility of the use of the air brake. The test was conducted on June 17, 1918. The train was made up of 37 loaded American cars, box, flat, low and high side gondolas, with one empty box car, fitted with seats, at the rear of the train for the observers. Air brakes were used throughout and the French operating officials were convinced that the plan was entirely feasible. Another test train was run from Vierzon to Is-sur-Tille, on June 24, made up of both American cars and French cars, the American cars only being fitted with air brakes. This test was successful also, and as a result of the performance of these two trains the Minister of Public Works issued an order, on July 4, 1918, authorizing the operation of American trains with air brakes over any part of the lines of communication. It was stipulated that the trains so operated should consist either entirely of American equipment or of not more than one-third of French equipment. Where the train contained French cars, the French cars were to be placed behind the American cars.

Another point involving much discussion was that of tonnage ratings. The French claimed that our tonnage ratings were much too high and that we would not be able to do what we planned. A thorough survey of the lines was made and account taken of the curvature and gradients. It was found that the French, in computing their tonnage ratings, used a greater margin of safety than was common in American operation, and that in the main their ratings more nearly approximated the facts than our own. Trains were limited to a length of not more than 500 meters, including the locomotive. But this limitation was not so much due to the type of power used by the American army as to the length of the passing sidings on the French railroads.

A feature of freight operation peculiar to the Americans was the convoy system. This system was largely after the system used by the British army on the railroads in the north of France. It involved sending an armed guard, or convoy, with every important shipment. Until the signing of the Armistice each shipping service provided its own convoys, and in addition, the Transportation Service tried to supply guards for American trains for important shipments. As long as this practice was in effect the convoy system was not a success. The authority of the convoyer was somewhat obscure, and the fact that the same train might be convoyed by several forwarding services, as well as the train crew and the guards provided by the Transportations Services, led to the evasion of responsibility on the part of all concerned and to no real protection for the freight. It was recommended, in January 1919, that the entire system of convoying freight be turned over to the Provost Marshal General to be carried out by the Military Police, because of the respect for which their authority was held both by Americans and the French. This recommendation, however, was disapproved and the Transportation Service was instructed to provide its own convoys. Twelve transportation companies are now being organized at the classification camp at St-Aignan. Those of these men who convoy trains will be put into the same camps with train crews and called at the same time as the crews. They will be armed and will have authority to arrest or fire upon any persons breaking into or otherwise molesting government freight. The runs made by the guards will be the same as those made by train crews. Thus the men will have their full period of rest between hours of duty, and it will be possible for them to stay awake at all times during the journey and keep close watch on their trains. Two men are thought to be sufficient to guard each train. In addition to the train guards, the Transportation police will also guard supplies on the docks at the base ports.

Below is shown the average daily freight train density during November and December 1918. The points given are the division terminal stations. It can be seen from the table* * * that the traffic increases at Saumur, where the line from La Rochelle joins the line from St-Nazaire to Is-sur-Tille. However, the line from Gievres to Cosne takes over a large part of the business which it was intended originally to handle through Is-sur-Tille, but which was discontinued upon the completion of the regulating station and terminal at Liffol-le-Grand.

From	To	Eastbound Trains	Westbound Trains
Montoir	– Saumur	12	7
LaRochelle	– Saumur	7	5
Saumur	– Gievres	15	15
Gievres	– Marcy	7	5
Marcy	– Is-sur-Tille	14	11
Gievres	– Cosne	9	6
Brest	– Rennes	4	4
Rennes	– St-Pierre-des-Corps	4	4
Bassens	– Perigueux	7	4
Perigueux	– Montierchaume	5	4
Montierchaume	– March	4	4
Cosne	– St-Florentin	8	5
Montargis	– Sens	2	3
St-Florentin	– Chattillon	3	2

Troop Movement: Until some time after the signing of the Armistice the actual operation of troop trains was conducted almost entirely by the French, although not infrequently some American equipment and some American crews were used in the operation of these trains. However, the trains were operated as between French terminals and not as between American terminals as in the case of freight.

Upon being notified by the Commanding Officer of a district that orders had been received for the movement of a certain number of troops, the R. T. O. telephoned the request to the Troop Movement Bureau, giving the number of men and the points of origin and the destination. The Troop Movement Bureau gave this information to the Regulating Commission and requested that transportation be supplied. The Regulating Commission got the schedule from the French railways and it was passed back through the same channels to the Commanding Officer of the district.

In the case of casuals or small detachments, the schedule supplied by the French was usually one of the regular passenger trains. In the case of a large movement of troops, however, involving a whole train or more, a special schedule was given and equipment sent to the point of entrainment. The R. T. O. supervised the entrainment of the men and their baggage, and from that point to the point of detrainment, the French were responsible.

Certain exceptions to this rule are, however, notable. In February 1918, a special train for the use of the American army was established between the Headquarters, S. O. S., at Tours, and G. H. Q., at Chaumont. This train was provided with first, second, and third-class coaches, one of the first-class coaches being a couchette, and another a wagonlit. A dining car was added to this equipment in August so that officers could have meals at a reasonable price and not be compelled to carry their food with them.

In October it became apparent that it would be necessary to establish a regular train running from the S. O. S. to the Zone of Advance daily to pick up small detachments of replacements and casual troops going from one area to another. Accordingly, on October 8, 1918, a daily train, known as the rocade train, was started from Tours to Is-sur-Tille, picking up on the way small detachments that could not be handled by the regular passenger trains because of the congestion, but which were not large en enough to justify a special train movement. This train was later run through to Toul, Headquarters of the Second Army. After the signing of the Armistice and the occupation of the territory on the Rhine a daily train connecting with the rocade train was run from Toul to Coblez to take up detachments of replacements to the Third Army.

The cessation of hostilities made possible the release of a certain amount of freight equipment and steps were taken to establish a better regulated and more comfortable service for troops from the concentradion areas to the ports. Ten trains of American box cars were fitted up with latrine facilities in each car. These trains were of fixed consist and designed for use between Le Mans and Brest and St-Aignan and St-Nazaire.

Another improvement was the establishment of a kitchen car service on the troop trains. When the troops were moving from the ports towards the fronts, they were fed en route with travel rations carried in the car. The results were far from satisfactory, particularly so during the cold weather, when the journey frequently took three or four days. During this time the men had only cold rations, which, although abundant, were not sufficient to keep them in as good physical and mental condition as would have been the case if they had been able to have hot meals. Coffee stops, however, had been provided along the lines of communication at that time. With the establishment of the regular service from the concentration areas at St-Aignan and Le Mans to the ports, a kitchen car service was installed. Each train of fixed consist had attached a flat car or a box car upon which were two rolling kitchens and a water tank. Another car was fitted up as storage for rations and sleeping quarters for the mess crew. The cars were stocked at terminals and when the train was made ready to take on troops a hot meal was cooked. The men were fed at the first convenient stop, when the food was carried back in G. I. cans to the cars and distributed under the supervision of the non-commissioned officer in charge of the car. The results of this service were immediately apparent and were gratifying. Similar sets of kitchen equipment were attached to the rocade trains from Tours to Toul.

In December 1918 and January 1919 attention had to be given to the transportation of a large number of men on leave. A meeting was held on December 23 in Paris at which were present representative of the Transportation Service, the French railroads, and the 4th Bureau. All the leave traffic had been handled by commerical French passenger trains, except in case of large movement. It was now believed that, owing to the fact that sixteen leave areas had been opened and the attitude had become much more liberal in regard to leaves, active steps were necessary to place this traffic on a more substantial basis. The French were requested to furnish our men with the same facilities as the French soldiers on leave, and were further asked to give our leave trains the same accelerated schedules as those given to the French leave trains. To both of these demands they agreed promptly. A service was arranged from Is-sur-Tille to Menton, on the Riviera. This was to take care of a thousand men daily in each direction. The service was put into operation on January 23, 1919.

On February 10 an express train, on a fast schedule, was started from Paris to Menton, via Dijon and Lyon. This train was more particularly for the benefit of officers and nurses going to the Riviera on leave. The Paris-Menton train consisted of first-class accommodations for 300 and third-class accommodations for 240. Dining car service was supplied. Both the trains from Is-sur-Tille and from Paris to Menton were operated entirely by the French. But as in the case of the Tours-Chaumont train, they could be used only by Americans. In return for the establishment of this service the American army agreed to restrict all American travel to and from these points to these trains, and to forbid officers or men to use the French commercial trains. This was done to avoid disputes constantly arising between the Americans and French civilians and French officers because of arbitrary occupation of reserved seats, etc., which had become, at certain points, cause of much friction.

One of the most serious problems in the transportation of troops is the prevention of personal injury. The accident rate of troops travelling over our lines of communication had been high. These accidents were for the most part clearly due to the carelessness of the men and the lack of discipline. During the warm weather the temptation was great for soldiers to get out of cars where they were crowded and to ride between or on top of the cars, or with their legs and heads hanging out the doors. The clearance between cars and bridges and tunnels in French railways is considerably less than clearances in the United States. In many instances it is only six inches. An active campaign was started by the Transportation Service, posters and warning notices being supplied by the R. T. O.'s to be distributed among the troops at points of entrainment. Although these measures unquestionably helped the situation, they were never thoroughly effective because the commanding officers, in the majority of cases, did not attempt to enforce restrictions laid down by the Transportation Service.

For the transportation of wounded, the Transportation Service has sixteen hospital trains completely equipped with ward cars both for officers and men.

R. T. O. SERVICE: A distinctive feature of the railway organization in France was the establishment of the R. T. O. Service. This system was patterned after the one in use in the British army where railway transport officers were placed at the more important freight and passenger stations to keep track of freight shipments and to aid the members of the army passing through.

The difference in language makes it very difficult for officers and soldiers to get proper information regarding train schedules and the handling of baggage and freight. The R. T. O.'s were installed with the view to assisting them and consequently taking off the hands of the French the burden of dealing with a great number of passengers unfamiliar with the language and customs. For this purpose a number of officers were secured in the United States who had had railroad experience, and, whenever possible, some knowledge of the French language. Upon arrival in France they were sent to the school which had been established at Angers, where they were instructed in French railroad methods and the way shipments of troops and freight were made. About 220 of these officers were stationed in France in the more important stations and terminals. In addition to making all arrangements for troop movement and supervising all detrainment and entrainment of men and material as mentioned above, the R. T. O.'s rendered important service in furnishing information and handling baggage. They were also required to keep permanent record of all shipments arriving at and leaving their stations, and were the only authorized intermediaries between the French railroads and the army services. The R. T. O.'s were not confined to the main line of communication, but were stationed all over France at leave areas, or important junctions, and several were stationed in England and Italy.

Erection and Maintenance of Equipment: The General Superintendent of Motive Power was charged with the erection and maintenance of all motive power and rolling stock belonging to the American army in France. The original estimate of requirements for locomotives and cars for an army of 500,000 men in France was 980 locomotives and 19,500 freight cars. To save shipping, locomotives and cars were sent over either partially erected or knocked-down. It was necessary, therefore, to establish shops at, or near, the ports for the erection of this equipment.

The locomotive erection shop was built at St-Nazaire, and a shop for erection of freight cars was established at La Rochelle. The erection of locomotives began in November 1917 and the erection of freight cars in March 1918. Although the number of locomotives erected to April 30, 1918, was only 212, it had reached 1,202 by December 31, 1918.* * * In October the number of locomotives on order anticipated the needs of an army of 4,000,000 men by June 1919. The 98,000 freight cars on order at the same time was to meet the needs of this new army. After the signing of the Armistice, however, orders were cut down, and the only locomotives and cars which continued to arrive in France were those which were already under construction in the factories in the United States.* * *

For the repair of cars and engines, the Motive Power Department took over the P. L. M. shops at Nevers, which had been in the course of construction at the time of the outbreak of the war. These shops were finished and taken over by the 19th Engineers.

The Mechanical Units were stationed in French railway shops at various points throughout France, where they were employed in the repair of French cars and locomotives, a total of 53,438 cars being repaired by our men up to December 31, 1918.* * *

There were many French cars in bad order, in the small stations all over the country, which could not be repaired owing to the scarcity of labor. The Motive Power Department proposed that it be given authority to purchase the needed spare parts in France, to make the necessary repairs and to bill the French government in order to get these cars back into service again. This was authorized by Minister Claveille.

At the time of the signing of the Armistice a second plant at La Rochelle for the erection of freight cars was being built. With the two plants in operation in addition to certain facilities offered by the British at their plant at Audruicq, it was estimated that the total out-put after December would be 4,700 cars a month. The cessation of hostilities, however, caused a suspension of this work.

During the first few months all engines erected in France by the Americans were turned over to the French railroads through the Etat Railway. After the Transportation Service began to operate its own trains between its own terminals, all surplus power not needed for our own immediate use was turned over for the use of the French according to an agreement made in Paris in July. In cases where the engines were not permanently assigned to French service, but a surplus existed in our own terminals, the practice was to send surplus engines from Gievres, for instance, to Vierzon light, upon the call of the French at which place the French agreed to have trains made up and waiting.

On December 1, the P. O. Railway had 136 American engines, the P. L. M. 139, the Etat 85, the 6Bis line 40, and also 606 engines were employed entirely in American service. Of these, 459 were in road service, 74 in switching, 24 en route, 41 in the shop, and 80 in reserve. In addition, the Transportation Service procured 176 Belgian engines, of which 104 were used in switching service. The others were in the shop nearly all the time. The distribution of locomotives was handled by the General Superintendent of Transportation. * * *

Coal Supply: It was intended at first to handle coal for the Transportation Service separately from that of the other services. All the coal was brought from England and for the most part landed at the smaller ports on the west coast and on the channel. Then it was forwarded in solid trainloads to such points as Gievres and Nevers, where the coal was stocked in piles. The original intention was to have a pile of 100,000 tons at Nevers and two other piles of similar capacity at Gievres. This supply was only to be used as a reserve. At other points, chiefly at the division terminals, smaller piles were kept, usually from 7,000 to 15,000 tons in a pile. It was finally seen, however, that the coal situation could not be handled separately for the Transportation Department, and the piles at Nevers and Gievres were turned over to the Depot Quartermasters at those points and the coal requisitioned as needed.

Maintenance of Way: The maintenance of way performed in the Transportation Service was largely limited to the maintenance of tracks in American terminals and furnishing, sometimes, a few men to assist the French. The most important maintenance work was that done on the Etat Railway between Le Mans and Rannes, and between Tours and Le Mans.

When the Armistice was signed it was contemplated double tracking the line from Tours to Le Mans, the work to be performed by the American army and billed against the French railroads. Had the war continued, the work of maintenance would unquestionably have assumed a very important character. Although the condition of track on the French roads was good in the spring of 1918, the tremendous traffic and the heavier cars and locomotives of the American army had worked a marked change for the worse by fall. It was believed that during the rainy season serious consequances would result unless a large force was employed to restore it to normal. The French were able only to supply about two to three men for track work where ten had been used before the war. Furthermore, the French wartime labor was of a much lower grade than that of peace time. However, on December 1 the position of Engineer of Maintenance of Way was abolished, and all projects for further construction and maintenance indefinitely suspended.

At the close of the war recommendations had already been made to the French with a view to the taking over of a considerable section of the railways forming the main lines of our communications with a view to operating them entirely with American personnel and according to the American practice. It is believed that had this been done the train density on these lines could have been greatly increased if the terminals had been enlarged sufficiently to handle the increasing traffic as was planned.

PART VI

ARMY TRANSPORT SERVICE

Preliminary Report of A. T. S. Operations: Prior to the entry of the United States into the war the Army Transport Service was operated as a department of the Quartermaster Corps through the Water Transportation Branch of the Office of the Quartermaster General in Washington. Shortly thereafter radical changes were made in the organization in the United States. All matters pertaining to procuring and allocating tonnage and managing vessels, including operation of docks, wharves and terminals, were placed under a civilian organization, the Shipping Control Committee, formed in the early part of 1918 and given the powers of the War Department and of the Shipping Board relative to vessel procurement, allocation and operation. The members of the Committee were Mr. P. A. S. Franklin, Chairman, Mr. H. H. Raymond, and Sir Connop Guthrie, with Captain Cletus Keating, Q. M. R. C. as Secretary. While no definite limit was placed upon the authority and jurisdiction of the Shipping Control Committee relative to vessel operation, their efforts were confined mainly to the procurement and allocation of tonnage and the loading of vessels in home ports. They did not attempt to exercise jurisdiction over the operations of the Transport Service in Europe, contenting themselves with the appointment of Major Alfred Huger, Q. M. C. as permanent representative of the Shipping Control Committee with G-1, General Staff, S. O. S., following an inspection of facilities and methods in Europe by Mr. H. H. Raymond, a member of the Committee. The European representation of the Committee was of great value to the Army Transport Service authorities in France in obtaining the allocation of the necessary tonnage for the European Transport Service of the A. E. F. and in securing prompt action from the Committee in regard to the proper loading of vessels to suit the facilities of ports to which destined.

Organization of the Service in Europe: The Army Transport Service of the A. E. F. was at first operated under the Quartermaster Corps with Captain H. B. Moore, Q. M. R. C., an officer who had accompanied the Commander-in-Chief to Europe, in direct charge of the work as Director of Docks. On December 18, 1917, under the provisions of G. O. No. 78, G. H. Q., Series of 1917, the A. T. S. was transferred from the Chief Quartermaster, Line of Communications, to the Transportation Corps, Service of Utilities, Captain H. B. Moore being appointed Director, Army Transport Service. On January 1, 1918, Colonel R. E. Wood, Infantry, was appointed Director, A. T. S. with Major Moore as his assistant. When on April 6, 1918, Colonel Wood was relieved from duty with the A. T. S. for return to the United States to act as Quartermaster General, Major Moore was appointed Acting Director, A. T. S., and appointed Director, A. T. S., on May 6, 1918, serving as such until December 5, 1918, when he was relieved by Brigadier General Frank R. McCoy, who, upon his appointment as Deputy Director General of Transportation, was on January 2, 1919, relieved by Brigadier General S. A. Cheney. On May 24, 1918, the Army Transport Service was reorganized and a standard organization prescribed for all ports with corresponding divisions in the Office of the Director, thus enabling the necessary control and supervisions of port operations and a comprehensive development of the terminal organizations. Due to long continued lack of personnel it was not possible to complete the organization for several months, but prior to the signing of the Armistice the organization had been practically completed and stood as follows:

Headquarters Organization Army Transport Service

Director - A. T. S.	Brig. General S. A. Cheney, U. S. A.
Deputy Director	Lieut. Colonel E. B. Cushing, T. C.
Executive Officer	Lieut. Colonel O. D. Miller, T. C.
General Inspector	Major D. W. MacCormack, T. C.
Supervisor of Operations, and Chief, Troop and Cargo Division	Lieut. Colonel J. A. Coates, Q. M. C.
Supervisor Terminal Facilities	Lieut. Colonel R. W. Stovel, T. C.
Chief, Inland Water Transport	Lieut. Colonel L. E. Lyon, T. C.
Chief Marine Engineer	Major George C. Cook, T. C.
Property Officer	Captain Frank Staples, T. C.

Port Organization: The organization at base ports comprised:
(a) General Superintendent, with an Assistant General Superintendent, in charge of each group of ports.
(b) Superintendent in direct charge of each port having an A. T. S. organization.
(c) Camp Commander reporting to the General Superintendent but in direct charge of stevedore troops and of all purely military affairs.
(d) Executive Officer in charge of Administrative Division comprising correspondence, records, statistice, finance and personnel.
(e) Supervisor of Operations in charge of all matters pertaining to marine operation and with supervision over the work of the Marine Superintendents, Superintending Engineers, and Port Stewards.
(f) Superintendent, Troop and Cargo Division, in charge of all matters pertaining to handling of troops from ship to dock and of cargo from ships hold to delivery to Transportation Service in departure yard.
(g) Supervisor of Terminal Facilities in charge of the procurement, inspection and maintenance of all terminal facilities, including dock, wharf and warehouse structures, yards and terminals and of all electrical and mechanical equipment and installations.
(h) Property Officer charged with the procurement, custody and issue of all supplies including stevedore gear.

Personnel: Starting with a few officers, and 491 civilian stevedores, known as the Transport Workers Battalion, the personnel of the Army Transport Service was gradually increased until at the time of the Armistice it consisted of approximately 800 officers, 22,000 enlisted men, 2,509 civilians and 901 German prisoners, a total of 26,210. There was, however, an acute shortage of both commissioned and enlisted personnel during the entire period of active operations.

Port Facilities: The first step taken towards the provision of Port Facilities for the American Expeditionary Forces was in May 1917 when a commission headed by Colonel Maurier of the 4th Bureau of the General Staff of the French army and comprising among its members Captain Asher C. Baker, U. S. N., retired, and Major, now Colonel, J. A. Loga U. S. A. made a survey of the ports available for the use of the A. E. F.

St-Nazaire was recommended by this commission as the first port to be used for the following reasons:
(a) This port was served by two double track railroads and was directly on our lin of communication.
(b) There was a large remount station perfectly equipped where over 300,000 horses had been landed.
(c) There was sandy soil and good facilities; also good water for camps.
(d) There was a maximum depth of water over the sills of 29 feet and 29 feet over the bar.
(e) The outer harbor, on account of outlying shoals, was well protected from submarine attack.
(f) This port had the best crane facilities of any available for the use of the A. E. F. including two heavy lift cranes with a capacity of 150 tons or over.

Bordeaux was the second choice because:
(a) It was not used by the French, was free, and offered possibilities of further development.
(b) The connection from the main line was over an easy grade and simple.
(c) St-Sulpice offered a splendid location for our warehouses.
(d) The Railroad thru Periguex offered a not very much used line connecting directly with our main line of communication.

(e) The depth of water was 26 feet, but the soft mud made it perfectly safe for vessels to ground without strain or danger.

(f) There were existing lighterage and towage facilities at Bordeaux.

The utilization of the port of Brest was not looked upon with favor as:

(a) It had no commercial facilities.

(b) There was no berth available where vessels drawing 27 feet could come alongside the dock, consequently everything had to be handled by lighter.

(c) The commercial port as well as the arsenal was absolutely congested with munitions for Russia and Roumania.

(d) The railroad haul was over heavy grades and was 200 miles longer than St-Nazaire and in order to reach our line of communication it was necessary to run over a single track line from Le Mans to Tours.

(e) The possiblity of expansion seemed out of the question on account of mountainous country and the necessity of handling immense amounts of material to make a storage yard.

(f) There was no level ground within any reasonable distance for establishing a storage yard or warehouses. Despite its many disadvantages the use of this port later became necessary as it was the only one available to the A. E. F. which could accommodate the deep draft interned German liners which were converted into troop transports.

Port Facilities Assigned to or Developed by the A. E. F.: Early in July 1917 berths as follows were assigned to the A. E. F. with the provision that as they were made use of the A. E. F. should construct new berths at Bassens, La Martiniere and l'Usine Brulee:

St-Nazaire - 5 berths. 4 in the basin of St-Nazaire and one on the Quai-de-Maree
Nantes - 4 berths along the Quai-des-Antilles
Bassens - 7 berths ready or about to be finished
Pauillac - 2 berths
La Pallice - 2 berths and in addition the berth with the 40-ton crane when necessary.

From time to time as was necessitated by the rapid growth of the A. E. F. additional berths were secured and new ports opened up until at the time of the signature of the Armistice the port facilities assigned to or constructed by the A. E. F. were as follows:

French Berths:	Permanently assigned	71
	Usually available	14
Berths constructed by A. E. F.		12
	Total	97
Lighterage wharves constructed by A. E. F.		2

A. E. F. terminal Projects: The French port terminals being entirely inadequate to meet the rapidly growing needs of the A. E. F. an extensive construction program was laid out, approved, and well under way, but in the main abandoned upon the signature of the Armistice. A brief statement of approved projects with present status appears below under each port.

Ports operated by the Army Transport Service: For administrative purposes the ports operated or to be operated by the Army transport Service were divided into groups, as follows:

CHANNEL GROUP: Havre, Rouen, Caen, Cherbourg, and Honfleur.
UPPER COAST GROUP: Brest, St-Malo, Lorient, and Granville.
LOWER LOIRE GROUP: St-Nazaire, Montoir, and Donges.
UPPER LOIRE GROUP: Nantes, and subsidiary small ports in vicinity.
CHARENTE GROUP: La Pallice, La Rochelle, Rochefort, Tonnay-Charente, and Marans.
GIRONDE RIVER GROUP: Bassens, Bordeaux, Sursol, Blaye, Furt, Pauillac, St-Loubes, St-Pardon, and Talmont.

MEDITERRANEAN GROUP: Marseille, Toulon, and Cette.

OPERATED INDEPENDENTLY: Bayonne (on Bay of Biscay 125 miles south of Bordeaux) (Eventually to have been operated with the Gironde Group).

Les-Sables-d'Olonne (midway between La Rochelle and St-Nazaire).

BRITISH PORTS: London, Southampton and Liverpool in England
Glasgow in Scotland
Barry, Cardiff and Swansea in Wales
Belfast in Ireland.

CHANNEL GROUP

Le HAVRE: Opened August 2, 1917, with Capt. Claude D. Liebman, Q. M. U. S. R. in charge, who was on August 21, 1917, relieved by Major J. L. Gilbreth, Q. M. C. On February 20, 1918, Captain John A. McDonald, Q. M., U. S. R., was appointed Superintendent, Army Transport Service. This port was used mainly for troops, but in addition handled a large amount of coal and general cargo, the bulk of which was shipped by barge to Paris and thence by rail to destination. Prior to March 1918 this port was used solely for troops arriving in English vessels and for A. E. F. cargo carried as commercial tonnage. Six berths were permanently assigned to the A. T. S. two trans-Atlantic in March 1918, and two cross-channel in June 1918, all well equipped with cranes and warehouses. Two more cross-channel berths were assigned in September 1918 with the understanding that the A. E. F. would provide tracks and warehouses, which work was started but abandoned after the Armistice. Cargo however was unloaded at these two berths by using some American locomotive cranes which the French had purchased and mounted on concrete pontoons. The French had planned some very large dock improvements for deep draft vessels in the outer harbor and completed three berths in the early fall of 1918. These were assigned to the A. E. F. which under took to install tracks, warehouses and crane equipment. Plans had been completed and approved for this work, but it had not been started at the time of the Armistice and was abandoned.

ROUEN: The first transport was handled at this port on May 25, 1917, but a permanent organization was not effected until on March 3, 1918, Lieut. A. E. Manning, Q. M. C. was sent to open up the port as Acting Superintendent. On September 21, 1918, Captain, now Major, E. H. Arne, Transportation Corps was appointed Superintendent. The cargo handled was principally coal from England, lumber from Sweeden and general cargo for interior movement by barge. The A. T. S. had no specifically assigned berths at this port, but could always unload from four to five cross-channel vessels with existing facilities. plans had been completed and approved for the A. E. F. to construct and equip a two-berth wharf for cross-channel general cargo vessels and also another two-berth wharf not far from Rouen, at a location known as Grand Couronne, for the purpose of handling trans-Atlantic vessels carrying ammunition. This last involved the creation of an ammunition storage area which had not received French approval at the time of the Armistice, when both projects were abandoned.

CAEN: No A. T. S. organization was stationed at this port. A considerable quantity of engineering material from England was landed here from commercial vessels, A.T.S. matters being handled by the General Superintendent at Le Havre.

CHERBOURG: Opened June 23, 1918, with Captain E. J. Dillon, T. C., in charge. This port was used almost exclusively for the debarkation of troops from England, its use being necessitated by the great increase in the embarkation program during the summer and fall of 1918. No berths were ever specifically assigned to the A. E. F. at this port, but berths and crane facilities were available for the discharge of from 2 to 3 cross-channel vessels at all times. There were certain other French berths not used to capacity by either the French, British, or ourselves and consideration was given to the possibility of their further use by the A. E. F. but the difficulties in the way of improving the rail transportation serving this port were such that nothing was done although it was contemplated that as our tonnage increased we would utimately have to unload considerable coal at Cherbourg. This port was closed December 15, 1918.

HONFLEUR: This port was used to a limited extent principally during the months of August and September 1918 for the discharge of Engineer, Chemical Warfare, Ordnance, and Q. M. cargo from chartered Swedish vessels, Lieutenant Leonard R. Weitzel, T. C. being in charge under the direction of the General Superintendent, A. T. S., at Le Havre.

UPPER COAST GROUP

BREST: Opened November 12, 1917, with Captain F. W. Green, R. T. C. in charge, who was relieved on July 1, 1918, by Lieut. Colonel C. A. Stern, T. C., and he in turn on February 20, 1919, by Lieut. Colonel John O'Neill, T. C. Brest was the principal port for the direct movement of troops from the United States to France. In November 1917 the A. T. S. was assigned a lighterage wharf 760 feet long and for the first six months of its operation all troops and troop cargo were unloaded by lighter. In May 1918 a moderate draft vessel berth known as Pier No. 5 was obtained, followed in September 1918 by the assignment of a similar berth. In the spring of 1918 the A. E. F. had prepared extensive plans for the improvement of this port including the proposed construction of several deep draft vessel berths. The first construction undertaken by the A. E. F. was a two-berth wharf know as Jetty del'Est which being well along at the time of the Armistice was carried to completion during December 1918. Plans had been prepared and approved covering the construction by the A. E. F. of a three-berth wharf known as the Digue-du-Sud and the provision of warehouses, tracks and crane equipment for the two assigned berths. Work on the Digue-du-Sud was about to commence but both projects were cancelled on the signature of the Armistice. Apart, therefore, from the Jetty-de-l'Est the A. E. F. construction at this port was not extensive, consisting only of improving the original lighterage pier with shed and derrick equipment and more recently adding shelter and rest facilities for embarkation purposes.

St-MALO: This is a coal port opened February 24, 1918. The first boats put in here were handled by officers sent out from Brest and no permanent organization was formed until on October 11, 1918, Lieut. E. C. Foudriac, T. C., was sent here as Acting Superintendent. Coal with a small quantity of engineering material from England was practically the only cargo handled. No berths were assigned to the A. T. S. until late in the summer of 1918 when two, partially equipped, were assigned and arrangements made by the A. E. F. to complete the crane equipment and to make minor track changes. Work had not been started at the time of the Armistice and the plans were abondoned.

LORIENT: This port was opened about the first of August 1918, but no A. T. S. organization was maintained here, the port being handled by officers sent down from Brest as necessary. While a few A. E. F. vessels with special cross-channel cargo were unloaded at this port with existing facilities, the tonnage was small. The French, however, had under construction a one-berth wharf in the outer harbor know as the Quai-de-Kergoise for which they had ordered the necessary crane equipment in the United States. It was anticipated that this berth would be completed in the spring of 1919, at which time it was to be assigned solely to the use of the A. E. F.

GRANVILLE: This port was opened on August 23, 1918. No permanent organization was effected, vessels putting in there being handled by officers sent out from Brest as necessary. The A. T. S. was permanently assigned one berth which was used for handling cross-channel coal vessels with French crane equipment. It was planned that the A. E. F. complete the crane equipment but the project was abandoned on the signature of the Armistice.

LOWER LOIRE GROUP

ST-NAZAIRE: Opened on June 26, 1917, with Colonel S. D. Rockenbach, Q. M. C., in charge and Captain H. B. Moore, Q. M. R. C., as Director of Docks. In August 1917 Colonel Rockenbach, in addition to his duties as Base Quartermaster, assumed the title of Superintendent, Army Transport Service. Later changes in port superintendents were as follows:

Colonel R. E. Wood, Inf.	October 1, 1917
Lieut. Colonel N. L. Howard, Engrs.	December 1, 1917
Major Charles H. Mann, Q. M. R. C.	February 20, 1918
Major F. W. Green, T. C.	July 1, 1918
Lieut. Colonel W. S. Olsen, T. C.	February 20, 1919

This port, in addition to handling a considerable number of troops was, on account of the number of berths immediately available for the use of the A. T. S. and of the existing cranes including several heavy lift cranes, for many months the principal port of the Army Transport Service in France and the port at which the bulk of the heavy lifts such as locomotives and guns were handled. Five berths were nominally assigned to the A. T. S. in July 1917 although they have been considered and reported as four due to one of the two-berth wharves being able to accommodate but one trans-Atlantic vessel. Six additional berths were assigned in January 1918, two in March 1918 and two in August, making a total of 14 berths all told. These berths were turned over with such crane equipment and warehouses as existed at the time but in order to use American cars many track changes were necessary, in some cases requiring that tracks be cut existing masonry warehouses. A few timber warehouses were added, as well as certain derrick and locomotive cranes, but although this port was the first occupied by the A. T. S., only absolutely necessary improvements and additions to equipment were possible until the larger items of new construction were well in hand. However prior to the Armistice, plans had been made for extensive improvements, including the construction of a lighterage wharf on a sloping quai in the basin; installing 12 heavy electric gantry cranes, together with suitable platforms, on the four berth continuous quai along the north side of the larger basin; and supplementing the mechanical equipment to give each of the assigned berths at least four crane devices. All of this work however was cancelled subsequent to the Armistice.

MONTOIR: The earliest plans for A. E. F. dock construction contemplated a five-berth port in the Loire River at La Martiniere not far from Nantes and in July 1917 material for this construction was ordered from the United States. However, later consideration proved this project to be unsatisfactory on account of lack of necessary depth of water, and following further studies it was decided to build the new port at Montor adjacent to St-NAZAIRE and directly opposite the large Montoir storage yard. Owing to the lack of construction materials and the difficulty of getting this project satisfactorily located due to the peculiar nature of the river bottom at this point there was considerable delay in getting the work started. Work was well along on the construction of an eight-vessel pier to be equipped with thirty-two five-ton one-track gantry steam cranes at the time of the Armistice, following which it was decided to complete only enough of the pier for three vessels. This work was practically completed except for crane equipment. In the late summer of 1918 plans were also made to provide a 400 foot lighterage wharf adjacent to the large vessel pier but this project was cancelled.

DONGES: In order to safely and economically handle the movement of ammunition and explosive material it was necessary to provide for certain wharf construction suitably located with regard to ammunition storage. It was proposed to locate one such wharf with a capacity of two vessels at Donges on the north bank of the Loire River a few miles upstream from Montoir and St-Nazaire. Work was well started at the time of the Armistice and plans were under consideration for its increase to a four-berth wharf when the work was abandoned.

UPPER LOIRE GROUP

NANTES: Opened October 20, 1917, with Mr. C. B. Backmin, a civilian employee, in charge. Further changes in superintendents were:

Captain Gabe Filluel	October 24, 1917
Captain E. P. Morrison, Engrs.	January 20, 1918
Major W. D. Wells, T. C.	May 6, 1918

Nantes with its various subsidiary ports stretching for 14 miles along the banks of the Loire was used for the discharge of light draft cross-channel vessels and occasionally for deeper draft vessels which had been lightened at St-Nazaire. The principal cargo handled was coal, general merchandise, munitions and heavy artillery. Although four berths at the Quai-des-Antilles were the first officially assigned to the A. T. S. at this port, the first berths actually turned over were one at the Quai-de-la-Fosse which is the older section of the harbor and two at the newer and well equipped Quai-des-Antilles. These were followed by one additional berth at the latter quai and two at the Bras-de-Pirmil, the construction of which the French are now completing. The French also built and turned over to the A. E. F. a two-berth wharf at Usine Brulee, a few miles below Nantes, the A. E. F. providing the track and warehouse equipment completing same about midsummer 1918, since which time these two berths have been used principally for ammunition pending the completion of the A. E. F. project at Donges. This made a total of eight permanently assigned berths in the Nantes territory although additional berths mainly for colliers were usually available. While the A. E. F. was constructing the warehouses and tracks for the two berths at Usine Brulee, the French were pushing to completion a third berth at this point for which it was also intended that the A. E. F. should provide tracks and warehouses. It was planned that the A. E. F. should remodel this dock, since as originally built it had not proved satisfactory due to the cranes being located too far from the vessels on the one hand and from the loading tracks on the other. The A. E. F. also undertook to provide tracks and warehouses for the four assigned berths on the Quai-de-Pirmil completing the work on two, the construction of the other two not yet being finished by the French.

CHARENTE GROUP

LA PALLICE AND La ROCHELLE: Opened October 31, 1917, with Lieut. Colonel T. B. Hacker, Q. M. C., in charge. Later changes in port superintendents were as follows:

Major E. B. Cushing, R. T. C.	December 6, 1917
Major George T. Newbury, R. T. C.	May 23, 1918
Captain George A. Heyburn, T. C.	November 23, 1918

La Pallice and La Rochelle may be properly considered as one port. The old port is located at La Rochelle and the new port at La Pallice. Practically all the A. T. S. operations were conducted at La Pallice, but a few light draft vessels were handled at La Rochelle. Owing to the location of the car erection shops at La Rochelle these were the principal ports for the handling of car parts. The principal cargo handled was care parts, locomotives, lumber, rails, horses, forage, oil and general cargo, with deck loads of auto trucks and tractors from England. Two berths at La Pallice assigned in July 1917 were first used in October of that year, a third being assigned shortly thereafter. In the summer of 1918 an arrangement was made whereby the A. E. F. moved two large electric cranes from the south to the north side of the basin, being then assigned the four berths comprising the south side and the control of the tracks serving this side of the port. In October a fifth berth was assigned. Use was also made, from time to time, of an oil berth in the outer port and the French, about the time of the Armistice, completed the construction and equipment of a second oil berth in the outer harbor intended for A. E. F. use. The five berths in the basin were used for general cargo, principally car parts, and were equipped with certain cranes. Plans had however been made to completely equip two of these berths with heavy duty electric gantry cranes and to reenforce the crane equipment on the other berths. Certain track changes were planned to facilitate the use of American cars, some of these being completed and the balance with the entire crane program abandoned following the Armistice. No berths were assigned to the A. T. S. in the basin at La Rochelle although certain coal vessels were unloaded here and the French had promised the assignment of at least one coal berth when it became necessary. No changes in tracks or crane equipment were contemplated.

ROCHEFORT: Opened February 16, 1918, with 1st Lieutenant, now Major, E. A. Craft, T. C., in charge. The pringipal cargo handled was coal, with a small amount of general cargo. The A. T. S. was first assigned three berths in this port and a fourth added in midsummer 1918. One of these had no crane equipment, two had but three cranes between them while the fourth was well equipped with American pier cranes and constituted an excellent berth for unloading coal. Other berths were also available from time to time including a second well equipped coal berth which enabled the satisfactory handling of a large amount of coal at this port. It was planned to complete the crane equipment for the assigned berths and to construct a two-berth timber pier in the basin. Prior to the Armistice it was decided to proceed with the additional two berths but to make it a floating pier rather than a pile and timber structure. A material rearrangement of the tracks serving the basin and the two proposed berths was also contemplated and had just been started when the entire program was abandoned following the Armistice.

TONNAY-CHARENTE: Opened June 20, 1918, and operated as a coal port by the Rochefort organization, no separate A. T. S. organization being established. Berths were available for the handling of from two to three cross-channel coal vessels at all times, but no berths were specifically assigned although it was expected that ultimately the A. T. S. would be given the entire use of one or two of the existing berths. No A. E. F. construction was planned at this port.

MARANS: Opened early in August 1917 and operated as a coal port under the immediate jurisdiction of La Pallice, no local A. T. S. organization being maintained. Facilities were available for the discharge of a least one vessel at a time but no specific dock space was assigned to the A. T. S. nor were any plans made for A. E. F. construction at this port.

GIRONDE RIVER GROUP

BASSENS: Opened October 26, 1917, with Captain E. V. Rhodes, Q. M. C., in charge. Changes in port superintendents were as follows;

Major H. B. Moore, Q. M. C.	January 28, 1918
Major E. V. Rhodes, Q. M. C.	March 22, 1918
Major C. A. Stern, T. C.	March 27, 1918
Major J. H. Elliott, T. C.	June 26, 1918
Lieut. Colonel John Quinn, T. C.	December 27, 1918

This port has been used for the handling of both troops and cargo, the principal cargo handled being horses, coal, construction, material, explosives, subsistence, and general cargo. Following consideration of the port problem by A. E. F. and French authorities in June and July 1917 it was planned that about 40% of the A. E. F. cargo would be brought into the Gironde and handled principally at the new port of Bassens about six miles below Bordeaux on the north shore of the river. There the French had already completed several berths of a ten-berth wharf and were willing to assign some of these to the A. T. S. as the tonnage required. The first was turned over in October and the first A. E. F. cargo boat unloaded at this wharf in November 1917. Three more were assigned in November and one in December 1917 and one in January and four in July 1918, thus giving the A. T. S. control of the ten French built berths in connection with which the A. E. F. constructed certain warehouses and made some necessary track changes. These berths were equipped with twenty-nine raised pier cranes to which the A. E. F. planned to add twelve more so that each berth would have at least four. The American cranes were not yet delivered. In addition to the ten-berth wharf at French Bassens, the A. E. F. in July 1917 planned to create just downstream from the French location a ten-berth American port complete with tracks, warehouses and cargo handling equipment. Orders for the necessary material were cabled to the United States in July 1917 and Washington made a contract with the Phoenix Construction Company to send a force of civilians to France to construct this work. These civilians arrived shortly after but the materials did not come until later and before work was started the project came under the supervision of the 18th Engineers (Railway) who were mainly responsible for its completion under the authority of the Director of Construction and Forestry. After a trying wait of several months for material, work was started in November 1917 and this wharf was first used for A. E. F. cargo in April 1918 following which the ten berths were rapidly completed and put in service. This piece of dock construction with its many large warehouses and railway trackage is the only all American dock project concluded prior to the Armistice and it stands as the evidence of what the A. E. F. would have been able to accomplish along the lines of a port construction program had the war continued. Unfortunately however, this otherwise excellent performance is somewhat marred by the history of its crane equipment. When this dock project was first planned in July 1917 it was planned to equip it with forty heavy duty electric gantry cranes, each crane spanning three railroad tracks, there being four crances to each vessel, three of the cranes per berth having a five-ton capacity and the fourth having a ten-ton capacity. The cranes were ordered in July 1917 and were ready for shipment from the United States the first of January 1918. However, in the meantime differences had arisen as to whether or not these crane devices were those best adopted to handling cargo and the discussions continued until, at the end of 1917, when certain long piling expected from the States failed to arrive, the matter of crane equipment was reconsidered by a board which rendered a decision based primarily on the lack of adequate piling, that only two berths out of the ten would be constructed of sufficient strength to carry the gantry cranes and that the other eight berths would be finished up with lighter construction which prohibited the use of the gantry cranes. The two berths on which the gantry cranes were to be installed were those last completed and the eight cranes on these two berths were not completed and put in service until June 18, 1918. In the meantime and while excellent crane equipment was lying at the docks in the United States for the remaining eight berths, its shipment to France was prohibited and six or seven timber gantry frames carrying fixed derricks which were to be used in the same manner as ship's tackle were erected on the remaining eight berths. One of these was tried out and while giving good service for a certain class of goods, did not prove itself to be flexible enough to meet the varying conditions and the rest of the devices were not completed. Also in midsummer while the original cranes were still lying at the port of embarkation in the United States other gantry devices with derricks were ordered from the States, although none were ever received. During the entire first half of the year 1918 those responsible for the original design of the dock and its equipment endeavoured to persuade the authorities of the wisdom of reverting to the original plans and finally in August 1918 after over six months had been wasted a reconsideration was had and it was decided to reinforce the eight berths to carry the necessary load and erect all forty gantry cranes as originally planned. Subsequently this work was carried along rapidly although the last of the forty cranes was not put in service until January 1919. In addition to the creation of this ten-berth American wharf the A. E. F. planned to construct 600 feet of lighterage wharf as well as a vessel repair shop. The former was cancelled by the Armistice, while the latter was continued.

BORDEAUX: No berths were assigned to the A. T. S. in the port of Bordeaus itself, although a few cross-channel vessels were handled there and a considerable number of troops debarked from vessels of the French Trans-Atlantic Company.

SURSOL: (Bordeaux) This is a privately owned French dock a lettle upstream from Bassens consisting of seven berths including two well equipped coal unloading berths. Some coal and general cargo was unloaded herefrom Army Transports by French contract labor, but no space was definitely assigned to the A. E. F. although an effort was made to secure the permanent assignment of at least one coal and one other berth.

BLAYE: This is a two-berth coal port used for unloading coal destined for Italy. Arrangements attempted for the rerouting of this coal and thus making this port available for the use of the A. T. S. were never concluded and consequently no A. E. F. cargo was handled.

FURT: An existing small port on the north bank of the Gironde used for unloading oil. No facilities were assigned specifically to the A. T. S. although some oil was unloaded here during 1918 and it was contemplated using this port for oil up to an average of 400 tons daily.

St-LOUBES: This location, a few miles upstream from the mouth of the Dordogne River and near the St-Sulpice storage yard, was selected as one of the sites for an A. E. F. ammunition wharf and storage yard. As trans-Atlantic vessels could not berth at this point, it was decided to construct achorages, or dolphins, at the mouth of the Dordogne River and load the ammunition on lighters which would in turn be unloaded at St-Loubes. The 750 foot lighterage wharf with sorting sheds and storage yard was practically finished in October 1918. It was planned to equip this wharf with ten 15-ton locomotive cranes which were on order but pending their delivery three lighter cranes were used. The use of this terminal had just well commenced at the time of the Armistice, since when it has been used for reloading ammunition for the United States, as well as for handling some general cargo.

St-PARDON: The A. E. F. planned to construct a 600 foot lighterage wharf, equipped with derrick, at St-Pardon, a little upstream from St-Loubes, on the Dordogne River, and practically at the eastern end of the St-Supice storage yard. This terminal was planned to increase the general unloading facilities in the Gironde district. Cargo would have been lightered to St-Pardon, from vessels anchored at the mouth of the Dordogne River, in the same manner as ammunition for St-Loubes.

PAUILLAC: Two out of the six berths at this port were assigned to the A. T. S. and used by them jointly with the Navy during most of the year of 1918, the Navy having priority on their use. They were equipped with small hydraulic cranes which were not very effective, but the dock construction was so light that no plans were made for the improvement of these facilities. Arrangements are now being made for the use of Pauillac as a port of embarkation.

TALMONT: During the discussion prior to the actual beginning of construction at Montoir: that is, during the fall of 1917 and the spring of 1918, consideration was given to the alternate possibility of constructing a ten-vessel port at Talmont at the mouth of the Gironde on the right bank. Owing to the relatively greater amount of work that would have to be done at Talmont not only in the way of dock construction but particularly in rail connections and rail storage yards, and also owing to the more exposed position of the harbor, the decisions were always in favor of the Montoir project. When, however, in the summer of 1918, it became evident that we would not only have to use every available port, but in addition build a large number of new berths to handle the anticipated tonnage, it was decided to proceed with Talmont as well as with Montoir and extensive plans were made and approved for the creation of a ten-vessel port, somewhat similar to American Bassens. A large amount of construction material had been ordered from the United States and assembled in France and a construction track run to the site and work well started when, following the Armistice, the whole project was abandoned.

MEDITERRANEAN GROUP

MARSEILLE: Opened June 1, 1918, with Major, now Lieut. Colonel E. B. Cushing, T. C., in charge. Changes in superintendents were:

Major W. B. Ryan, Engrs.	October 10, 1918
Major, now Lieut. Colonel, W. J. Reiss, T. C.	January 3, 1919

This was a general cargo port handling mainly subsistence clothing, forage, motor vehicles, aircraft, machinery, railroad steel, oil, gasoline and a few locomotives. Six existing berths were assigned to the A. T. S., all well equipped with warehouses and two having excellent hydraulic cranes, although in bad repair. The other four had rather poor hydraulic cranes which it was planned to replace, although this was never done. In September 1918 two berths without warehouses, tracks, or crane equipment were assigned and in October 1918 another berth with warehouses, but poor crane equipment, making a total of nine, all of which were returned to the French during February 1919 following the closing of Marseille as a cargo port. In addition to the two berths without tracks mentioned above three more berths were to have been assigned at the same pier, known as Mole G, and plans had been approved for the construction of large warehouses thereon and for its equipment with tracks and sixteen high power electric gantry cranes which would have made it one of the best piers in France. This work which had just been started was abandoned after the Armistice. It was also planned to put modern crane devices on six other berths which had been or were to have been assigned. The tracks serving the assigned berths were not such as to permit the use of American cars, consequently plans were made for practically an entire rearrangement of the water front tracks serving the A. E. F. piers. This work was well under way at the time of the Armistice following which it was in the main abandoned.

TOULON: The French Ministry of Marine placed three deep-water berths in the naval base at the disposal of the A. T. S. which it was intended to use in the handling of ammunition. The A. E. F. was to make certain track changes and provide crane equipment consisting of twelve standard gauge 10-ton locomotive cranes and eight 5-ton, one-track gantry cranes all of which had been ordered. None of the berths were in condition to operate by November 11, 1918, when the project was abandoned.

CETTE: The use of this port for A. E. F. traffic was investigated and it was at one time anticipated that at least three of the berths then occupied by the British could be obtained. It was purposed to equip them with one-track gantry 5-ton steam cranes which were ordered. These arrangements were not concluded prior to the Armistice and the A. E. F. never made use of this port.

OPERATED INDEPENDENTLY

BAYONNE: Opened March 26, 1918, with Major E. V. Rhodes, Q. M. C., in charge. Major Rhodes was relieved as Superintendent by Major C. G. West, Q. M. C., July 8, 1918. Principal cargo handled was coal, one shipload of railroad ties from Portugal and deck loads of tractors and wagons from England. While no berths were specifically assigned to the A. T. S. at this port, facilities were available for handling up to four or five cross-channel boats at well equipped existing berths. On account of the long railway haul to the A. E. F. lines of communication and the limitations of the Midi Railway, the existing facilities at this port could not be used to capacity, and consequently no effort was made to improve them as this would have involved as a first step taking over and operating the Midi Railway from Bayonne to Bordeaux.

Les SABLES D'OLONNE: Opened August 20, 1918, with Major J. Campbell, Engrs., in charge. The principal cargo handled was coal and coke with a small amount of general cargo. Three berths suitable for light draft cross-channel vessels were assigned to the A. T. S. in August 1918 on the understanding that certain track changes around the pier would be made. There were three small locomotive cranes at the port to which the French added two more in September. In addition to the track changes it was proposed to add several locomotive cranes and two inclined boom coal unloading devices which would have given the A. T. S. three good coal berths. The work was abandoned following the Armistice before any of the crane equipment had arrived or the track changes were well started.

British Ports: Operations in Great Britain were started shortly after the United States entered the war under the direction of Lieut. Colonel H. F. Ruthers, Q. M. C., of the Embassy Staff. Captain R. C. Stone, Q. M. C., was assigned to duty as the first Superintendent, A. T. S., January 30, 1918. On September 27, 1918, Colonel M. C. Kennedy, R. T. C., was designated as General Superintendent, A. T. S., in addition to his duties as Deputy Director General of Transportation, Captain Stone being assigned to duty as Assistant General Superintendent. On December 14, 1918, Colonel Kennedy was relieved by Colonel Houston as General Superintendent, A. T. S. All matters pertaining to the debarkation and embarkation of troops were handled by Captain, now Major, W. S. Franklin, T. C., who on January 9, 1918, was assigned to duty in London serving as Assistant to the Deputy Director General of Transportation and Liaison Officer with the British War Office.

The ports at which operations were conducted in Great Britain were:
London: Loading general cargo for France.
Barry, Swansea, and Cardiff: Coal and general cargo for France
Belfast: Loading potatoes for France
Liverpool and Glasgow: Debarkation of troops from the United States
Southhampton: Debarkation of troops from the United States and embarkation for France.

Troops Debarked and Tonnage and Animals Unloaded: The following table summarizes the troops debarked and tonnage and animals unloaded at all ports during the period June 1917 to February 1919 inclusive:

		TROOPS	TONNAGE	ANIMALS
June	1917	12,162	24,524	
July	"	3,562	23,780	2,899
August	"	14,502	28,355	
September	"	22,359	33,853	110
October	"	37,771	98,585	
November	"	29,521	124,641	
December	"	37,522	113,825	3,774
January	1918	47,763	162,016	3,694
February	"	33,455	192,239	6,559
March	"	62,348	288,038	8,547
April	"	84,948	397,969	2,232
May	"	162,885	487,197	
June	"	221,288	607,274	
July	"	301,526	641,959	
August	"	242,207	715,258	
September	"	311,969	767,648	1,839
October	"	217,614	919,488	2,582
November	"	112,626	920,972	20,881
December	"	6,574	910,059	11,801
January	1919	936	740,562	
February	"	474	442,089	
Total		1,964,012	8,640,331	64,918

* * * * * *

Tonnage loaded for westward movement: The tonnage loaded for westward movement since the Armistice is as follows:

November 11 to 30,	1918	12,106	
December	"	84,904	
January	1919	91,169	
February	"	60,878	
Total		249,057	Tons

Floating Equipment: Throughout practically the entire period of operations in France the A. T. S. has been seriously handicapped by the lack of floating equipment such as tugs, lighters, and barges, troop-tenders and floating derricks.

TUGS: Two tugs were ordered in June 1917 and five more in September 1917. The first tugs to arrive from the United States did not reach Franch until May 1918. By the end of 1918 a total of nineteen American tugs had arrived which, with three allocated by the British and two chartered from the French, made a maximum of twenty-four tugs operated by the A. T. S. at the ports. The tugs used on the inland waterways were furnished almost entirely by firms operating under French Military authorities although thirteen tugs were loaned to the Inland Waterways Division by the British I. W. T.

LIGHTERS AND BARGES: It was early evident that a large number of lighters and barges would be needed for port operations but with the exception of twenty obtained from the French, at Brest, and a few chartered from private owners at other ports, the A. E. F. had to rely on its own resources. Twenty 500-ton wooden lighters were ordered in September 1917 and arrangements effected in Washington to have the Stewart Construction Company build them in France, using lumber sent from the United States. The first was completed and put into service the end of March 1918 and the last of the lot, which had been increased to twenty-five, in July. In the meantime arrangements had been made for the construction of additional lighters of 300-ton capacity from French timber. Between September 1918 and the cessation of work following the Armistice, a total of forty-nine such lighters were built and put into operation. In October 1917 Washington purchased seven 1,500-ton steel barges. The first two sent across were lost in making the trip the other five arriving between September and November 1918. In the latter half of 1918 the British Admiralty allocated some eighty barges to the use of the A. T. S., half of which were used on the inland waterways and half at the ports. The following tabulation indicates the number of barges in the service of the Inland Waterways Division at the time of the Armistice and source from which obtained:

Chartered from owners	178
Bad order barges purchased under authority of French Government and repaired or under repair	48
Allocated by British Admiralty	56
Loaned by British I. W. T.	12
Total	294

TROOP TENDERS: Two tenders for unloading troops at Brest were ordered in November 1917 and although Washington promptly commandeered two such vessels they did not reach France until May 1918. At the time of the Armistice there were seven tenders in service at Brest, four having come from the United States, one allocated by the British and the other two borrowed from the navy.

FLOATING DERRICKS: The early receipt of heavy locomotive parts from the United States and the lack of floating derricks in the French harbors necessitated the ordering of three floating derricks in 1917, subsequent orders increasing the total to eighteen. Owing to the hulls of the first two being lost in crossing the Atlantic it was not until September 1918 that the first floating derrick was put in operation at St-Nazaire followed the same month by the second. Two others have been put into service since the Armistice, making a total of four floating derricks of from 75 to 100-ton capacity now in operation and one complete floating derrick received but not put in operation.

Vessel Repairs: Under the direction of Major G. C. Cook, T. C., Chief Marine Engineer, a total of 584 vessel repair jobs were handled by the Marine Engineering Division in France, 84 being exclusively by A. T. S. forces and 500 by contract under A. T. S. supervision. The repairs contracted for totaled 1,500,000 francs, or an average of 3,000 francs for each job. Two vessel repair shops had been constructed, one at St-Nazaire, which was practically in full operation, and one at Bassens in operation though not entirely completed.

Inland Water Transport: The French railroads having been severely taxed to handle their traffic prior to the commencement of A. E. F. operations in France, consideration was early given to the utilization of the inland waterways as a means of diverting part of the A. E. F. traffic from the railroads. Preliminary surveys of the inland waterways were made in October 1917 by 1st Lieut. G. C. Graeter, E. O. R. C., under the direction of Brig. General W. C. Langfitt, N. A., and by Lieut. R. L. James, acting for the Advisory Purchasing Board. These preliminary reports indicating that considerable relief might be obtained thru the use of the rivers and canals, Captain, now Lieut. Colonel, L. E. Lyon, T. C., was detailed by the Director General of Transportation to make a further study of the situation and upon approval of his report was placed in charge of what was later known as the Inland Waterways division, Army Transport Service. Barge operations were started in February 1918, the principal movement being on the Seine between the ports of Le Havre and Rouen and Paris with a small movement from Paris to interior points. Up to the end of January 1919 there had been handled by this division over the inland waterways of France a total of 381,673 tons.

European Service Division: The organization of this division was necessitated, first, to provide for the transportation of coal purchased in Great Britain and, second, for the transportation of miscellaneous supplies for the A. E. F. purchased in Great Britain and European countries in order to reduce to the minimum the strain upon the trans-Atlantic service. In September 1917 an order was placed for vessels of the lake type built as coal carriers of approximately 3,000 tons capacity drawing from 18 to 20 feet of water. None of these arrived in France until June 1918 but in the meantime 51,000 tons of American shipping was secured by taking vessels from the trans-Atlantic trade. Two large grain vessels, the Wm. O'Brien, 8,000 tons and the Ockenfels, 7,500 tons, dead weight actually in European ports were requisitioned by the Army Transport Service and turned over to the British Admiralty in exchange for the movement of 15,000 tons of coal per month from the United Kingdom to French bay ports. British commercial vessels sailing short of their marks were also used for the transportation of general cargo from ports of the United Kingdom, approximately 4,000 tons per month being carried in this manner. A total of 44 Swedish vessels were also employed in this service under the Baltic and White Sea Time Charter - 1912 - Form A. With the arrival of the first lake boats about June 15, 1918, the tonnage of the European Service Division increased rapidly, the growth of the fleet being indicated in the following table:

MONTH		TONNAGE ASSIGNED TO EUROPEAN SERVICE	CARGO CARRIED
June	1918	207,720	152,257
July	"	213,210	171,100
August	"	290,000	190,000
September	"	*	214,500
October	"	305,000	283,255
November	"	*	281,956
December	"	*	285,494
January	1919	*	227,813
February	"	*	159,736

* Totals not available.

The principal cargo handled by the European Service was coal from Wales, Engineer, Ordnance, Chemical Warfare, and Quartermaster supplies from England, potatoes from Ireland; railroad ties and steel from Portugal; and onions and dried fruit from Spain. Major H. B. Moore, Q. M. U. S. R., was designated as the first head of this service under the provisions of G. O. No. 7, October 26, 1917. Upon the reorganization of the Army Transport Service on May 24, 1918, Major, then Captain, Edouard de Wardener, T. C., who had been in general charge of this operation under Major Moore, was designated as Chief of the European Service Division, with 1st Lieutenant Arthur Barber, T. C., as his assistant. These officers remained in charge of this important branch of the service until their release subsequent to the Armistice.

Embarkation Service: In anticipation of the signature of the Armistice, plans were prepared for the return movement of the American Expeditionary Forces, and on November 11, 1918, a tentative program was submitted to the General Staff recommending the use of the ports of St-Nazaire, Bordeaux, and Brest, with preference in the order given; Brest to be used only for deep draft vessels and such others as could not be taken care of elsewhere due to congestion at the other ports. The Embarkation Branch, Troop and Cargo Division, Office of Director, in charge of Major W. S. Franklin, T. C., handled for the Army Transport Service all matters pertaining to the embarkation of troops in liaison with G-1, General Staff, S. O. S. The return passenger movement up to the end of February 1919 is shown in the following table. The heading troops comprises all military or militarized personnel of the A. E. F. including officers, enlisted men, field clerks, nurses, etc. Under civilians are grouped civil employees of the United States Government, Red Cross, Y. M. C. A., K. C. and other auxiliary personnel and such military or civil representatives of Allied governments as were carried on American vessels.

	TROOPS	CIVILIANS
Prior to Armistice (approximately)	15,000	
November 11-30, 1918	12,155	1,210
December 1918	73,270	777
January 1919	114,831	388
February 1919	177,331	1,737
Total	392,587	4,112

Handling of Food Administration Ships: Early in December 1918 arrangements were made at the request of Mr. Herbert Hoover for the handling by the Army Transport Service of ships consigned to the United States Food Administration. An investigation was made of the ports in the Adriatic by Major H. H. Haines, and of Rotterdam and Antwerp by Lieut. Colonel E. B. Cushing, T. C., and Commander J. C. Fremont, U. S. N. An army personnel under Colonel E. S. Walton, Q. M. C., as General Superintendent, with Major H. H. Haines, T. C., as assistant, was furnished to handle the Food Administration ships at Constantinople, Salonica and ports in the Adriatic. The Food Administration organization soon being able to handle these ships, arrangements were made for the relief of the A. T. S. personnel.

Supply and Evacuation of the Third Army: With the establishment of the Army of Occupation in Germany consideration was given to the utilization of the Rhine as a means of relieving the strain upon the French railroads, particularly in what had been the Zone of the Armies. A survey of the ports of Antwerp in Belgium and Rotterdam in Holland was made by Lieut. Colonel E. B. Cushing, T. C., Deputy Director, A. T. S. and Commander J. C. Fremont, U. S. N. Their report favored the establishment of Rotterdam as the American Base. This project being approved, arrangements were made to forward an A. T. S. personnel to that port on February 27, 1919, with Lieut. Colonel E. B. Cushing, T. C., in charge of all matters pertaining to the Transportation Corps and Lieut. Colonel J. A. MacDonald as General Superintendent, A. T. S. Consideration was also given to the use of this port for the evacuation of units of the Third Army.

Return of Ports to French: Following the conclusion of the Armistice, immediate steps were taken to reduce the number of ports operated by the Army Transport Service and to release as many berths as possible at ports where operations must continue. During the latter part of January and February the ports of Marseille and Le Havre were closed, other than for the handling of troops, Rouen at the same time being closed entirely. There still remained at each of these three ports a certain amount of cargo to be disposed of and the routine of winding up the ports completed. No more ships were sent to the small coal ports and upon the discharge of the vessels then at or en route to Rochefort, La Rochelle, Marans, Tonnay-Charente and Les-Sables-d'Olone, they likewise were closed. St-Malo continued in operation as a coal port for two or three months longer. The program was to center operations, so far as was practicable, at Bordeaux and St-Nazaire for troops and cargo, Brest, Marseille, and Le Havre for troops only, and La Pallice for cargo until the embarkation authorities in the United States could arrange to ship solid carges of locomotives and car parts destined for the French. Until such time as no A. E. F. cargo came on these vessels, the A. T. S. organization was maintained at this port.

SOS Hist. Dup.: File 9-I: Study

Transportation Facilities Required

En Route, s. s. *ESPAGNE, December 28, 1917.*

(1) This study primarily has been made with a view to ascertaining the possibility of placing 900,000 men in France by July 1, 1918. However, it has been found that, even though it may be possible to furnish the required exceedingly large increase in tonnage for so doing, other conditions obtained that make impossible the transporting of such a large volume of troops and materials over the French railroads from the seaboard to the front. It seems to be clear that, with a reasonably large increase in ocean tonnage, say from the existing 780,000 to 1,500,000 tons, the necessary materials and men for improving the situation in France may be transported so that, within the next four to six months, the way will have been paved for the desired increase rate of troop movement, in this matter guaranteeing the presence in France by next fall, say November 1, of the desired force of 900,000 men, provided that a further increase in ocean tonnage to 2,500,000 tons may be brought about by next July, followed by a still further increase to 3,100,000 tons by November 1. The reasoning that has led up to this conclusion is set forth in the following analyses:

UNDERLYING CONDITIONS

(2) General Nature of Problem: In the preparation of this study it is assumed that four corps, of six divisions each, are desired to be placed on the western front in France by July 1, 1918, together with an additional 33 1/3% for the service of the rear, a total force of 900,000 men, of which 190,000 are assumed now to be in France. Therefore, the problem to be met embraces the movement, within a period of six months, of 710,000 men with their animal and mechanical transport and supplies, from various points in the United States to the seaboard, an average distance of say 1,200 miles; thence across the Atlantic Ocean, a distance of say 3,200 miles, and thence from various ports in England and France, by rail and water, to the battle line, a further distance of say 600 miles and upwards, the aggregate distance being in excess of 5,000 miles.

(3) Troops, Including Animal and Mechanical Transport: To attain the figure of 900,000 men on July 1, it will be necessary to ship troops at the average rate of 118,000 men per month.

It has been estimated that, of this monthly number, 30,000 may be brought via England, thereby utilizing to the utmost the cabin space of British cargo vessels plying between the United States and England. As the French state that they cannot handle more than 5,000 men per week, or say 20,000 per month, via Le Havre, it would be necessary to move the remaining 10,000 per month through some other French port, as for instance Cherbourg or Brest. The British have stated that the increasing need of their cross-Channel boats for on leave men will make it impossible for them to furnish cross-Channel transportation for our troops, but the opinion is held by members of the United

States Army Board recently appointed for investigating that subject, that this objection can be overcome. It should be noted that, if such a large number of troops is moved from a port in England, say Southampton, to Le Havre, Cherbourg, and Brest, additional convoy as well as carrier service will be required. It is proposed that the troops moved via England will bring with them their light baggage only, their animal and mechanical transport to be moved direct from the United States to France.

It will be seen that, on this theory, an average of 30,000 men per month would be moved via England, leaving 88,000 men per month to be sent direct to France in United States bottoms.

An average of one animal, with its paraphernalia per 5 to 7 men, is assumed for the animal transport, or say 180,000 animals, in which number is included belated shipments for the portion of the army now in France. Necessary provision also is required for motor trucks.

(4) Supplies: For the various services of the army supplies are required for: (1) maintenance or upkeep (2) for reserves, and (3) for initial construction. The first is taken at 50 pounds per man per day, this being predicated on the actual results obtained by the British, about 30 pounds per man per day, plus an additional 20 pounds per man per day to cover coal and construction material necessitated by our longer lines of communication. 30% of the maintenance tonnage is assumed to originate in Great Britain, this consisting largely of coal. The second is taken at a 90-day reserve for the portion of the supplies coming from the United States, on the basis of 30 pounds per man per day, plus a 30-day reserve for the part originating in Great Britain on the basis of 15 pounds per man per day, all to be gradually accumulated during the six months' period. The third applies to the large initial tonnage that is pressing for movement to meet the demands of the various services of the army for construction purposes. The Transportation Department alone has demands that exceed 600,000 tons. For the purpose of this estimate it has been assumed that, in the aggregate the other services of the army have an equal tonnage, making the total for all services say 1,200,000 tons. It should be understood that no exact information is available as to the initial tonnages ordered by the army services other than the Transportation Department, and that, therefore, this estimate of their needs is a pure assumption predicated on fragmentary information that points to its general correctness. The movement of the initial tonnage has been distributed thus:

January	250,000 long tons.
February	250,000 " "
March	200,000 " "
April	200,000 " "
May	200,000 " "
June	100,000 " "
Total	1,200,000 " "

These tonnages are assumed to originate, 70% in the United States and 30% in Europe.

On these bases the average daily movement of supplies, in long tons, will be approximately as follows:

Month	From U. S.	From Europe	Total
Jan. 1	17,330	2,270	19,600
Feb. 1	19,180	3,060	22,240
Mch. 1	19,020	3,860	22,880
Apr. 1	20,870	4,650	25,520
May 1	22,720	5,440	28,160
June 1	21,570	6,230	27,800
July 1	23,420	7,030	30,450

From this it will be seen that the average monthly movement in long tons will range from 590,000 in January to about 900,000 in June, and that the total to be moved in the six-month period will approximate 4,500,000 tons.

(5) Summary: Thus, to raise the strength of the American Expeditionary Forces in France to 900,000 men by July 1, there will be required the shipment within six months of at least 710,000 men, 180,000 animals with proper proportion of mechanical transport, and some four and a half million tons of supplies, over a distance of approximately 5,000 miles, in which operation is involved trans-shipments at the two seaboards, passage across an ocean infested with the enemy's submarines, and movement over railroads which are already congested in the United States and France.

TRANSPORTATION IN THE UNITED STATES

(6) Railroads: The undersigned, having been in France since last spring, is out of touch with the railroad situation at home, but he understands that matters are unsatisfactory owing to congestion at the seaboard and elsewhere. The opinion is hazarded that this may be remedied to a large extent by eliminating the handling of nonessentials such as parlor cars, a large proportion of the sleeping car service, and freight that is used for construction that does not serve a war purpose. Also, if not already done, it would seem that good will come from the pooling of terminals under single-headed management, especially at the ports, coupled with the construction of connecting lines where necessary to facilitate interchange between the various railroads so that the facilities of all may be used to the best advantage. The adoption of this general plan should also make available suitable areas, contiguous to the railroads and removed from the congested waterfront, for the storage of supplies awaiting embarkation.

(7) Ports: Judging from the manner in which cargoes have been received at the French ports, it is evident that much difficulty is being experienced in the United States (a) in the convenient selection of suitable materials for obtaining the full capacity of the ships (b) in the orderly selection of materials with a view to the discharge of the ship with the least delay, and (c) in the giving of proper attention to the forwarding of materials in the order of their priority and in self-contained lots that will permit of their prompt utilization. It would seem that these difficulties will be largely minimized if a closer relationship is established between those charged with the responsiblity of loading the vessels in the United States and those in France responsible for the discharge of the vessels and the transportation of troops and materials to the front. Hence, coordination is recommended, if possible, through a single official who will have jurisdiction over operations on both sides of the ocean and thereby bring about the best use of the facilities through a knowledge of of what is to be moved in the way of men and material, loading of vessels in such manner as to admit of their prompt release in France, the establishing of uniform rules and regulations for the preparation and rendering of reports of various kinds, and the dispatching of ships to the ports best suited for their reception through the giving of

advance notices of dates of sailing and character of cargo. It should be added that every effort should be made to utilize the stock of steel billets for the French at American ports, said now to amount to some 80,000 or 90,000 tons, in the obtaining of full ship loadings, this being particularly desired because of the obligation that the United States has undertaken to move these billets in exchange for manufactured products which have been furnished to us in France.

OCEAN TRANSPORTATION

(8) Army Transport Service: In arriving at the shipping required to move troops and their animal and mechanical transport, it is assumed that 7 gross register tons will be required per man, in which is included his pro rata share of animal and mechanical transport in the case of troops that are moved direct from the United States to France, and 2 gross register tons per man for the movement from the United States to France for the animal and mechanical transport of the portion of the troops that is to be moved, together with light baggage, via England. The 7 gross register tons are made up of 4 1/2 tons for the troops proper, 1 1/2 tons for the animal transport, and 1/2 ton for mechanical transport, these figures agreeing quite closely with similar estimates that have been prepared by the British. The time required for a round trip between the United States and France is taken at an average of 50 days for both troop and animal vessels, and 56 days for cargo vessels. For the cargo movement between England and France 21 days are assumed for the round trip. 25% of the results obtained through the use of these factors has been added as a proper allowance for contingencies, embracing casualties, accidents, repairs, storms, etc. 5% of the troop ship tonnage has been assumed to be available for supplies. An arbitrary amount of 22,000 tons has been added for the cross-Channel service between Southampton and La Havre, Cherbourg, and Brest.

The required gross register ship tonnage ascertained through the use of these data, the tonnage understood to be available at the present time, and the estimated additional needs are as follows:

Date	Required	Available	Estimated Additional Needs
Jan. 1	2,580,000	780,000	1,800,000
Feb. 1	2,730,000	780,000	1,950,000
Mch. 1	2,770,000	780,000	1,990,000
Apr. 1	2,920,000	780,000	2,140,000
May 1	3,070,000	780,000	2,290,000
June 1	3,010,000	780,000	2,230,000
July 1	3,160,000	780,000	2,380,000

A detailed comparison of the estimated requirements in gross register tons, the available shipping and the shortage, as of January 1 and July 1, follows:

	ESTIMATED REQUIREMENTS		AVAILABLE	SHORTAGE
January 1:				
Troop and Animal and Mech. Transports		1,430,000	518,000	912,000
Cargo Vessels---				
Maintenance	170,000			
Reserves	450,000		262,000	888,000
Initial Const.	530,000	1,150,000		
		2,580,000	780,000	1,800,000

	ESTIMATED REQUIREMENTS		AVAILABLE	SHORTAGE
July 1:				
Troop and Animal and Mech. Transports		1,430,000	518,000	912,000
Cargo Vessels---				
Maintenance	1,070,000			
Reserves	450,000			
Initial Const.	210,000	1,730,000	262,000	1,468,000
		3,160,000	780,000	2,380,000

(9) French Requirements: The French claim that we are under obligations to furnish them with bottoms for the prompt movement of steel billets, and also locomotives, cars, track material, etc., which they say we have not only promised to do for them, but which they state are necessary for the French railroads of the troops and supplies of the American army pending the arrival in France of our own materials of the same nature. The figures given above are based on a 70% load factor, which is assumed to be sufficiently liberal to allow for space which may be used for these heavy articles.

(10) Summary: As this question of shipping has such a vital bearing upon our success in this war, being, after all the crux of the situation, it seems absolutely necessary that all vessels, subject to such action on our part be immediately commandeered for war purpose, and only such part thereof as may be essential for indirect war purpose be used otherwise than in the transportation of troops and supplies for our Expeditionary Forces in France. Otherwise stated, because of what is at stake, it would seem beyond question that all commercial considerations for the present should be abandoned, and that every effort should be bent to the use of all available shipping for but one object, the winning of the war.

If the result of the analyses that follow should show that, even should it be found to be possible to supply the full amount of shipping required to place 900,000 men in France by July 1, other limitations exist that would prevent the full utilization of such shipping, then a revision of these needs will be necessary for the harmonizing of the shipping that can be used to the best advantage in the light of the other conditions that may limit the placing of such a large force in France within the next six months.

TRANSPORTATION IN FRANCE

(11) General: This phase of the problem includes: (a) the discharge of vessels in the French ports and the classification of supplies for their various destinations; (b) the forwarding, over the existing standard guage French railroads, of troops and supplies from the ports to points in the Intermediate and Advance Sections; (c) the continued movement of troops and supplies from regulating stations in the advance section over standard guage railroads exclusively under the control of the American army to the railheads; and (d) the distribution of troops and supplies from the railheads via 60-centimeter gauge light railways and roads, to the front.

Stated differently, the transportation problem in French involves the movement of troops and supplies from the seacoast to the trenches, a distance of some 600 miles, in which operations are involved the discharging of vessels, terminal and main line handling over standard gauge railroads, continuation of such movement over light railways to the battle line, and the construction and care of highways that are used in connection with the operations of the American army.

(12) Ports: The American army has now at its disposition the following French berths:

Name of Port	Numbers of Berths	Permissible Maximum Draft
St-Nazaire	10	28'
Nantes	7	19' to 24' (av. 22)
Usine Brulée	2	22'
La Pallice	4 (inc. oil berth)	26' to 28'
Pauillac	2	27'
Blaye	1	-
St-Loubes	1	-
Furt	1	-
Bassens	4	25'
Total	32	

We now have under construction at Bassens a new 10-berths port of which it is estimated that 5 berths will be ready for use by Arpil 1, and the entire 10 by May 1, provided material reaches us in time from the United States.

Actual experience at the northern French ports used by the British, points to an average discharge capacity of 600 long tons per day per 400' berth, which figure has been adopted in the berths at Bassens after their assumed date of readiness, April 1. In the case of the British use of French port, the low average of 600 tons per berth per day is brought about by a number of undesirable conditions such as lack of unified control and the discharge of a large portion of the freight in 12 to 14-hour single shifts per day. With the perfection of our port management under a single control, and with ample facilities so as to permit the working of two or three shifts per twenty-four hours, it would seem possible to better the British results. However, in the case of our use of the French berths, no improved results have been assumed, but at the new American berths at Bassens it is assumed that the output can be gradually increased so that, when the 10 berths go into use on the assumed date of May 1, 700 tons per berth per day will be handled, on June 1, 900 tons, and on July 1, 1,400 tons.

On these bases the following number of berths will be required, it being understood that the tonnage originating in Great Britain, consisting largely of coal, will be handled at berths not included in this calculation.

Date	French Berths	American Berths (Bassens)	Total
Jan. 1	30	0	30
Feb. 1	33	0	33
Mch. 1	33	0	33
Apr. 1	31	5	36
May 1	27	10	37
June 1	22	10	32
July 1	17	10	27

It will, therefore, be seen that the number of French berths now at our dispositions, together with those that are under construction by American forces, should be about equal to the demands for placing 900,000 men in France by July 1. To do this, however, will require the kindly consideration by the French of our needs so as to enable us to continue to use their facilities, which they are very anxious shall be returned to them at the earliest possible date; it will also require the best of management on our part, the prompt receipt of construction materials, such as for instance, I-beams on order, and ample stevedore forces and supervisory personnel promptly to release ships and keep troops and material flowing continuously through the ports without congestion.

The above-mentioned required number of berths does not include those that are to be used for the handling of troops at Brest, Cherbourg, and Le Havre where it is believed that sufficient facilities may be found for that purpose.

To get the most use out of the ports thus placed at our disposal every means should be taken to get the full usage of the shallower ports, as for instance at Nantes, Bassens, and Bordeaux. The loading and dispatching of vessels should have this in mind, so that those of the shallower drafts may be sent to these ports, and not to the others, which should be reserved for the deeper drafts.

Plans are now being prepared for a new port at Montoir, adjoining St-Nazaire, where it is proposed to construct two piers with 8 berths at the start, later to be increased to four piers with 16 berths, the permissible vessel draft being 30'. This work, however, cannot be completed within the period under consideration.

While this study indicates that there are at the present time sufficient French berths to enable us to handle the flow of troops and supplies for starting the building up of a force of 900,000 men in France by July 1 next, it should be borne in mind that to do this we require at once sufficient stevedores to handle the material. Based on an average output of 4 tons per man per day and making due allowance for ineffectives, some 6,000 stevedores are required on January 1 and 10,000 by July 1. There are now in France say 2,000 stevedores, so that there is an existing shortage of some 4,000 men for serving the above estimated shipping requirements. Therefore, even though the required shipping were available, there is not now on hand a sufficient force of stevedores.

(13) French railways: It is the present intention to use two principal lines of communication for the A. E. F., one originating at the ports in the Loire River Basin, viz, St-Nazaire, Montoir, and Nantes, and running thence easterly to Pont Vert, near Bourges, where a connection is made with the other route, which originates at the ports in the Gironde River Basin, namely Bordeaux (Bassens) and Pauillac. From Pont Vert to Bourges both lines follow the same route, at the latter point splitting, the southerly one passing through Nevers (Saincaize) and Dijon to Is-sur-Tille, and thence to Neufchâteau; and the other passing to the north through Cosne and Châtillon to the same terminus, Neufchâteau. The port of La Pallice, on the Atlantic coast, is served by the French railroad that connects with the above-mentioned northerly proposed line of communication at Saumur. The use of the tracks of four railway systems are involved in this plan, the Etat Ry., Paris-Orleans Ry., Paris---Orleans---Mediterranee Ry., and the Est Ry.

The main line mileage involved both routes roughly may be taken at 1,000 miles. It is planned by the French that up to a movement 25,000 tons per day traffic will move by the southerly route through Nevers, Dijon and Is-sur-Tille, and that the tonnage in excess of that figure will be diverted to the northerly route via Cosne and Châtillon.

It is the intention that ultimately the troops and supplies for the American army will be moved over the above-described French railroads in American 30-ton cars, hauled by American locomotives and manned by American crews, all in a manner quite similar to the practice in the United States under which the trains of one railroad are permitted to operate over the rails of another in accordance with what are termed trackage rights. To carry out this plan a supervisory personnel is being organized, consisting of managers, general and division superintendents, maintenance officials, and station agents and operators, all to work in parallel with similar French railway officials, who will, of course, continue to administer their own properties and direct the train movements, as is usual under similar conditions in the United States. In addition to the supervisory forces and the train and engine crews, the American army is expected to furnish a proper quota of maintenance forces to care for its own locomotives and rolling stock and also to aid in the maintenance of track.

(14) Train Service: Based: (a) on the handling of 900 troops per 50-car train, (b) on a proportion of one animal to 5 men and 400 animals per train, (c) on one-quarter as many trains for mechanical transport as for the animals, (d) on 650 long tons per freight train, (e) on one-half of the reserves and initial construction material being stored or used in the vicinity of the ports so as to require no main line train service, and (f) on an addition of 25% to the number of trains thus ascertained, for fluctuation in movement and for supplies obtained locally, the maximum required number of trains per day in each direction is estimated to be as follows:

Jan. 1	32
Feb. 1	38
Mch. 1	40
Apr. 1	45
May 1	50
June 1	52
July 1	58

With the lengthening of sidetracks and other operating improvements it is probable that, with our comparatively heavy type of consolidation locomotives, more useful tons per train can be handled than has been estimated, but for this purpose it has seemed best to use a conservative figure. It may be added that the small tonnage per French train is to be ascribed to the heavy maximum gradients, usually 1% and comparatively high freight train speeds, usually 18 miles per hour.

Our proposed Lines of Communications west of Pont Vert apparently will not be overburdened with the above-mentioned number of trains, which, of course, will be halved for each route. From St-Nazaire to Pont Vert the existing maximum daily number of trains in each direction is 33, with an ultimate daily capacity of say 60, the difference between the two, 27, being about equal to our requirements of from 16 to 29 trains each way daily.

From Bassens to the points of junction at Pont Vert there is apparently a similar meeting of our requirements, except from Bassens to Courtas where the available margin between the existing maximum movement of 42 and the available maximum of 60, say 18 trains, is comparable with our requirements of from 16 to 29. However, improvements in the block system in that territory and careful operation would seem to offer promise of taking care of this situation without the necessity of building additional tracks.

East of Bourges the existing traffic is comparatively light, and no trouble is anticipated in handling our above-mentioned needs.

Therefore, it appears that, from a main line standpoint, our estimated number of trains may be moved over the proposed Lines of Communication with, however, the performance of certain new work outlined below; but until much of this new work is completed it will not be possible to handle the estimated train service.

(15) Proposed Improvements: For the facilitating of main line movements work is either under way or projected, as follows:

At Nantes, the double-tracking of the single-track link through that city, and the building of a connection between the Etat and P. O. railways.

Between Bassens and St-Sulpice, the construction of a third, and possibly a fourth, track to obviate the use of the main line for the handling of supplies passing from the port to the storage depot at St-Sulpice.

At Perigueux, on the southerly route, a cut-off for obviating a reversal in the direction of trains.

At Nevers, a cut-off involving a crossing of the Loire River for obviating main line movements through Nevers.

Between Pont Vert and Bourges, two additional tracks, making four in all, made necessary by the centering in that territory of the increased traffic from both the northerly and the southerly routes.

Additional tracks to avoid interference with yard operations at Montchanin.

At Dijon, a cut-off for obviating grade crossings of traffic.

Various side track extensions.

In addition to improvements required for facilitating main line movements, there are projected or under way the new 10-berth group of piers at Montoir.

Also construction is under way or projected for large storage depots with their attendant yards and other facilities, at St-Sulpice and St-Loubes near Bassens, Montoir near St-Nazaire, St-Luce near Nantes, Gièvres, Châteauroux, Mehun, Issoudun, Is-sur-Tille, Villiers-le-Sec, and Liffol-le-Grand.

Motive power and rolling stock facilities are projected or under way at Bassens, St-Sulpice, Montoir, La Rochelle, Clamecy, Saumur, Perigueux, Gièvres, Châteauroux, Nevers (general repair shops), Gercy-la-Tour, Is-sur-Tille and Liffol-le-Grand.

Construction is about to be started on a large regulating station at Liffol-le-Grand, and it is prabable that a second large facility of this kind will be determined upon at another location similarly situated in relation to the front.

In addition to the construction work outlined above, there will, of course, be required the building of standard and 60-centimeter gauge railroads, with attendant facilities of various kinds, in the zone of the armies, this applying not only to the territory occupied at the present time but also that which later is expected to be won from the enemy.

It will be seen that, before it will be possible to transport and supply the flow of troops required to build up a force of 900,000 men in France by July 1, a considerable portion of these improvements must first be completed so that the Line of Communications effectively may handle the required number of trains. Hence a large proportion of available shipping will be needed for the transporting of construction troops and materials in advance of a further increase of combatant forces.

The conclusion to be drawn from these figures is that there is not now in France sufficient motive power to handle the combined needs of the British and French, and the building up of an American army to the strength of 900,000 men by July 1 next. The best that can be done is to hasten the arrival of American repair forces to aid the French in the rehabilitating of their power, at the same time that every effort is made to equal or exceed the above-mentioned rate of 100 new ones to give the aid that they have repeatedly asked of us in the bringing over of locomotives ordered by French railways and now awaiting shipment in the United States

(17) [16?] Cars: Based on an average load per loaded car of 18 long tons, and an average daily movement per car of 100 miles, together with 25% added for sanitary, immobile and on leave trains and contingencies, the car requirements are estimated as follows:

Jan. 1	11,300
Feb. 1	13,200
Mch. 1	14,400
Apr. 1	16,300
May 1	18,400
June 1	20,000
July 1	21,900

These figures include not only freight cars for the movement of supplies, but also passenger and baggage cars for the movement of troops, etc. Rather than attempt to manufacture passenger and baggage cars of European type in the United States, it would seem best to furnish our full quota in freight cars, in exchange for a portion of which there will be turned over to us by the French our proper share of passenger and baggage equipment.

As above stated, for the required flow of troops necessary to build up the desired force of 900,000 men by July 1, there will be needed on January 1   11,300 cars.

Although we now have on order in the United States two lots of cars, the first of 9,000 and the second of 10,000 the total that has so far arrived is   0   "

                                                                     Shortage   11,300 "

Although the French originally gave us to understand that our car requirements would be met by the French railroads, it has since developed that they will be unable to do so because of the unexpected demand of the Italian campaign, and also, they claim because of an excess of bad order cars over what was normal before the war to the extent of 11,196 cars of the French type, or the equivalent of 5,598 of the American 30-ton type; also it is stated that the excess bad order passenger cars aggregate 922.

(16) [17?] Locomotives: Following is a statement of the number of locomotives required based on 80 miles per locomotive per day (including locomotives out of service), for troop, transport and supply services, and 50 miles per switching locomotive per day, and adding 25% for sanitary and on leave trains and contingencies:

          Jan. 1   558
          Feb. 1   670
          Mch. 1   747
          Apr. 1   856
          May 1   966
          June 1   1044
          July 1   1156

These take into acount the moving of all of our troops and their animal and mechanical transport, supplies, sanitary trains and soldiers on leave, with our own power. Originally it was not intended that we should be called upon to do otherwise than handle our own supplies, and the fact that the French formerly stated that, if we furnished for general use in France 300 locomotives by October 15, our needs would be taken care of by the French railroads without further demands on us in this regard. However, the French now strongly intimate that we will have to supply enough locomotives to take care of our needs, and that so far we have failed to do this in that we have furnished them but 10% of the 300 that were to have been delivered by October 15 last.

As shown above, for the movement required to build up 900,000 men in France by July 1, there will be required on January 1   558 locomotives.

Including locomotives so far delivered to the French and those that are awaiting erection or are still on shipboard in France, there will have been supplied from the United States by January 1 say   100   "

Therefore, we are now short of the loccmotives required to handle the estimated volume of traffic   458   "

Before we can start to bring troops to France at the required rate it will be necessary first to bring over, or otherwise cause to be provided, this shortage in motive power.

There are now said to be in France 483 bad order locomotives in excess of what was normal before the war. The French state that, if we will furnish 2,400 skilled workmen and 1,600 laborers, a total of 4,000 men, these excess bad order locomotives can be repaired within from four to six months; and that these, together with the 300 that they state we have promised them, will go far towards meeting our needs. On this basis at the end of six months, assuming that we can erect in France at the rate of 109 new locomotives monthly, we would have say 700 locomotives, plus the 483 required French locomotives or a total of 1,183, in contrast with the 1,156 which are estimated to be required for the serving of an army of 900,000 men.

W. J. WILGUS,
Colonel, R. T. C., N. A.

G-1, GHQ, AEF: 009.1 DGT: Memorandum

Study of Tonnage Requirements

1st Section, General Staff GENERAL HEADQUARTERS, A. E. F.,

Chaumont, Haute-Marne, May 21, 1918.

Memorandum for: A. C. of S. , G-1

    1. A note, dated March 31, 1918, from the C-in-C. As understood, this referred to a report dated March 7, 1918, from Colonel Wilgus (errand to U. S.) and to a memo which I prepared dated March 25, 1918, on daily tonnage required for 2,000,000 men. This number to be in France at end of 18 months, or by September 1, 1919.

    2. Perhaps the changes (increased troop movement, etc.) made later than either the report or memo in question, make a statement now on the differences in tonnage figures noted by the C-in-C unimportant. However, any reliable data on requirements, A. E. F., in France, as at this time, based on latest information, must be important.

    3. Major Ryan conferred with Colonel Wilgus at Tours April 8/9, 1918. It may be stated briefly that the study of Colonel Wilgus' tonnage, etc., included with his report of March 7, 1918, was made in December 1917:

    (a) At that time he assumed that there were 190,000 men in France, and that there would be in France 900,000 men by July 1, 1918.

    (b) He assumed there would in France by July 1, 1918   180,000 animals.

    (c) He assumed that transportation, initial constructions and installation, supplies and tons of materials all of which should be France by July 1, 1918, would amount to   600,000 short tons.

    (d) Also that initial construction and installation materials for all other services to be in France by July 1, 1918, would amount to   600,000 short tons,

    (e) Finally, he took, as a basis for supplies per man per day, as below:

    1. Maintenance or upkeep per man per day, 70% from the U. S., and 30% from England   50 lbs.

    2. Reserves per man per day, for 90 days, to come from the U. S.   30 lbs.

Reserves per man per day, for 90 days (coal, etc.), to come from England   15 lbs.

    4. Major Ryan, in preparing his memo dated March 25, 1918, after providing for movement from the U. S. of construction and initial installation materials, at rate of 100,000 tons per month, April 1918 to March 1919, inclusive, 12 months (the same aggre-

gate tonnage of this material as assumed by Colonel Wilgus for movement during only 6 months, January to June inclusive, 1918), took an arbitrary basis, in pounds per man per day, based on 300,000 men in France April 1, and arrival of 100,000 men per month to September 1919 (total 2,000,000), per man per day   4. lbs.

5. Necessarily on these bases, quite different, the total tonnage per month, or per day was quite different. The actual movement of troops or supplies to France up to date has not conformed, even nearly, to that contemplated by Colonel Wilgus last December.

6. The foregoing, Paragraphs 3, 4 and 5, simply an explanation of differences between two forecasts. The following is submitted, considering the troop movement to France as now arranged, or understood, and the tonnage to be unloaded at French ports; April to December, 1918, based on cablegram 1048 of April 6, 1918. This cablegram states that the War Department has given positive assurances that 5,680,000 tons of supplies will be unloaded at A. E. F., French ports April to December inclusive, 1918. This based upon an average turnaround of cargo, or supply, ships of 60 days. It is assumed the War Department must have calculated that this tonnage of supplies April to December 1918, inclusive, will be, and must be, sufficient to cover all maintenance, reserve, and other supplies. Ordnance munitions, etc., also construction and initial installation materials, based on the number of troops A. E. F., in France, and to arrive France during during this year to December, inclusive. It is suggested that an inquiry should be cabled to the War Department, as to the division or allotment of tonnage between the several army services, and also for construction and initial installation materials, taken as a basis, by the War Department, in connection with this aggregate total tonnage of supplies to be unloaded at French ports, April to December, 1918, stated per this cablegram 1048, of April 6, 1918, as 5,580,000 tons. Such cable also to make inquiry as to the relation, according to the War Department's calculations, between this tonnage of supplies, etc., and the number of troops which, under arrangements as made, or to be made, will be with A. E. F. in France during 1918.

7. A statement shown to Colonel Logan in London (April 1918), at the offices of the Allied Maritime transport Council, American Section (Mr. Stevens, Mr. Morrow, Mr. Shearman, etc.), gave the tonnage to be forwarded from the U. S. as follows:

	Long Tons	Short Tons	Daily unloading required Short Tons
April	407,000	455,840	15,200
May	463,000	518,560	16,725
June	488,000	546,560	18,220
July	653,000	731,360	23,600
August	747,000	836,640	27,000
September	710,000	795,200	26,500
October	727,000	814,240	26,266
November	743,000	832,160	27,740
December	748,000	837,760	27,025
	5,686,000	6,368,320	

In addition, not included in foregoing figures, there is coal from England, which will be required, delivered at French ports for A. E. F. at rate of 5,000 tons per day, and other supplies from England, which may aggregate from 1,000 to 1,500 tons per day, the latter loaded on decks of coal ships, and delivered at Le HAVRE. (The general supplies purchased in England mentioned as delivered, Le HAVRE, are shipped on British ships - not A. E. F. colliers.)

(a) Coal from Welsh ports, delivered to A. E. F. at French ports, amounted to about 40,000 tons in January 1918
" 40,000 " " February "
" 30,000 " " March "
" 60,000 " " April "
" 24,000 " up to May 17, 1918

(b) Not including coal and oil from tank ships, the unloading at all A. E. F. French ports (including Le HAVRE) daily average was:

For March 1918   8,355 short tons
For April 1918   11,285 short tons

On basis of unloading May 1 to date, the May daily average, excluding coal, may reach   13,000

(c) It will be seen that the average unloading at French ports, during April, and to date in May, is lower than the average called for on basis of the War Department's advices covering the tonnage which must be unloaded from April to December, inclusive, 1918.

8. The total tonnage (ship space) cabled from the U. S. in March 1918 for April allotment, was 261,350 short tons.

The report receiving in May, stating the tonnage of supplies actually forwarded from U. S. ports during April 1918, shows:

Quartermaster supplies	171,473
Ordnance supplies	72,626
Engineer and Transportation Supplies	103,417
All other services	26,168
Total tonnage shipped	373,684

(a) Included in the Ordnance tonnage - 72,626 - stated as shipped from U. S. in April, was French replacement steel, tons, 2,000 lbs., 33,900

(b) The tonnage allotted from the total ship space cabled from the U. S. in March for April allotment was for:

Quartermaster supplies	127,000
Ordnance supplies	23,000
Engineer and transportation supplies	74,285
For all other services	37,065
Total	261,350

9. The total tonnage (ship space) cabled from the U. S. in April 1918 for May allotment, was   325,000

(a) The tonnage allotted from this total ship space advised from the U. S. for May 1918 allotment, was for,

Quartermaster supplies	130,875
Ordnance supplies	46,406
Engineer and transportation supplies	90,905
For all other services	56,814
Total	325,000

10. The total tonnage (ship space) cabled from the U. S. in May 1918 for June allotment was   350,000

(a) The tonnage allotted from this total ship tonnage space advised from the U. S. for June 1918 allotment was for

Quartermaster supplies	127,118
Ordnance supplies	42,700
Engineer and transportation supplies	99,215
For all other services	80,967
Total	350,000

11. These allotment figures for April, May and June, should be noted, in connection with the tonnage which the War Department advised, by cablegram 1048 of April 6, 1918 (also the information received from the London Office of the U. S. Shipping Board), must be unloaded at French ports. (Par. 6 of this memo.)

	Unloading required Short Tons	Cabled from U. S. for Allotment - Short Tons	Actually shipped, Short Tons
April	455,840	261,350	373,684
May	518,560	325,000	---
June	546,560	350,000	---

If loading at U. S. ports and unloading at French ports must go forward, at rate as advised by the War Department, such supply movement presumably based upon requirements of A. E. F. (troops) to be in France from month to month as now agreed, it is clear that supplies largely in excess, not only of tonnage allotments made to and including June, based on cable advices from the U. S., but also in excess of the supplies actually shipped in April, must come forward to meet the requirements of A. E. F. in France. The shortage in tonnage actually shipped in April, 373,684 tons, as compared with 455,840 tons, which the War Department figures, stated must be unloaded at French ports in April, must be made up in months following. Again if we find that during May there will have been actually loaded at U. S. ports considerably less than 518,560 tons, the War Department's scheduled unloading tonnage for that month, the shortage will have to be made up in months following, and so on, with any shortage loaded at U. S. ports during any month, for unloading at French ports, as compared with the War Department's scheduled unloading, the shortages cumulative, if the War Department based its unloading figures on the requirements of A. E. F. (troops, etc.) in France, and figured these requirements correctly.

12. What are the absolutely essential requirements of A. E. F. in France represented in pounds per day per man? Based on all information obtainable, and saying nothing for the moment of transportation (including coal) and initial construction and installation materials, the essentials should not be stated in pounds per man per day, at less than 30 lbs. Included in this 30 lbs. per man per day, there is allowed for ordnance, ammunition, air service and motor transport not to exceed 6 lbs.

13. Troop arrivals A. E. F. as advised, at this date, are as follows:

		A. E. F. number of men
May 1, 1918, total A. E. F.	432,000 men	
Arriving during May	200,000 "	
Average for the month of May		532,000
June 1, 1918, total A. E. F.	632,000 men	
Arriving during June	220,000 "	
Average for the month of June		742,000
July 1, 1918, total A. E. F.	852,000 men	
Arriving during July	220,000 "	
Average for the month of July		962,000

14. As we are now in the month of May, take the essential supplies on basis of 30 lbs. per man per day, for May, June, and July, 1918, on basis of A. E. F. (troops) for those months as stated, and we have tons, 2,000 lbs. per day, required in France.

	Number of men	Tons, 2,000 lbs. per day	Tons, 2,000 lbs. for the month
May	532,000	7,980	247,380
June	742,000	11,130	333,900
July	962,000	14,430	447,330

15. Comparing the tonnage to be unloaded at French ports, as stated by the War Department (Par. No. 6 of this memo) with the tonnage of essentials required by A. E. F. on basis of 30 lbs. per man per day, we have:

	War Dept. daily unloading required	Essentials daily 30 lbs. per man per day	Balance, daily for transportation and initial construction materials
May	16,725	7,980	8,745
June	18,220	11,130	7,090
July	23,600	14,430	9,170

16. The daily tonnage apparently available after providing for absolute essentials, during the months of May, June, and July, based on the War Department's advices, covering the tonnage which must be unloaded at French ports, (and of course loaded at U. S. ports), is from 7,000 to 9,000 tons per day, or from 200,000 to 300,000 tons per month. This is the maximum tonnage per month which can be allowed for all transportation and construction or initial installation materials, together with ordnance (including steel for French replacements) ammunitions, air service and motor transport, in excess of 6 lbs. per man per day, even if the War Department's schedule of unloading is maintained.

(It is not believed it will be maintained.) Based on British experience in this war, ammunition, regarded as supplies of first urgency, or priority, may alone equal 6 lbs. per man per day. In such case all other ordnance, air service, motor transport, transportation and initial construction materials of all services must be limited to a tonnage of from 200,000 to 300,000 tons per month, figuring upon loading at U. S. ports, and unloading at French ports, maintained on basis of the War Department's tonnage schedule April to December 1918. If the loading at U. S. ports and unloading at French ports continues to fall below the tonnage schedule of the War Department, the tonnage space for all supplies and materials not included in the basis of 30 lbs. per man per day, must be correspondingly reduced.

17. It is believed that the tonnage must fall below the War Department schedule, if for no other reason, than that the War Department figured upon an average turnaround for cargo ships of 60 days. The average turnaround, up to date, is considerably longer than 60 days. Moreover, the tonnage tons of 2,000 lbs. reported actually shipped in April, 373,684 short tons, is under the War Department's basis for that month, which was 455,840 short tons, by 82,156. Again, the cabled report, just received of supplies loaded at U. S. ports during the first 10 days of May states a total of 129,410 short tons. On this basis the loading at U. S. ports during May will not exceed 500,000. The War Department's schedule for unloading for May is: 518,560 short tons, and for June, 546,560 short tons.
(See par. 7 of this memo.)

18. The essential supplies on basis of 30 lbs. per day for the average number of men A. E. F. during May, 532,000 (see par. 15 of this memo) which calls for 7,980 short

tons per day, and 247,380 tons for the month of May, would be well covered by 500,000 short tons, with an excess of 252,620 short tons for transportation and construction or initial installation supplies and materials and all other supplies not included in the 30 lbs. per man per day. But, the rate of unloading for May, nf maintained at rate of 13,000 tons per day (not including coal), or 400,000 tons, would provide only about 150,000 tons of supplies and materials in excess of the 247,380 tons, which are represented as essential supplies for the average number of A. E. F. troops during May, 532,000 men, at 30 lbs. per man per day. (We are also figuring on providing for 90,000 horses.)

19. Included in supplies and materials for June shipment are the following, which do not represent any part of the essential supplies taken to provide 30 lbs. per man per day, although these supplies (which follow), are, under existing conditions essential, next to food, forage, etc. For example, we must provide for transportation:

Transportation	Tons 2,000 lbs.	
107 Standard Locomotives	11,556	
200 Refrigerator Cars	5,200	
1,200 Box Cars	21,600	
150 Tank Cars	2,750	
380 Flat Cars	5,085	
400 Gondola Cars	6,600	
Transportation Construction	4,204	
Total		57,035
Motor Transport	9,613	
Standard Gauge Rail and Fastenings	15,247	
Light Rys. and Roads Construction and Equipment	5,773	
Forestry	2,108	
Water Supply	2,266	
Replacement Steel, French (Ordnance)	12,753	
Total		104,795

There are other supplies and materials to come forward from the U. S. in June which could easily raise the tonnage shown above from 104,795 tons to 150,000. These supplies and materials are needed, but they are not included in the essentials taken to make up the basis of 30 lbs. per day, which must be delivered in France in June.

20. The 30 lbs. per man per day for the average number of troops to be in France during June (742,000 men), represents 11,130 short tons per day, or 333,900 for that month. (Par. 15, this memo.) 150,000 tons additional, supplies and materials, stated in foregoing paragraph 19, represents (tons of 2,000 lbs.) an additional 5,000 tons per day, or 16,130 tons per day (not including coal), and a total for the month of June 1918 of 483,900.

(a) Will we be able to unload at A. E. F. French ports in June an average of 16,130 tons per day (exclusive of coal? The average unloading during this present month, May, to date, is 13,000 tons.

(b) Still it must be borne in mind that even at this rate of unloading for June 16,130 tons per day (if we do it), or 483,900 tons for the month, falls below the War Department schedule, 546,560 tons, by 62,660 tons.

21. The position for July will be as follows: Average number of men A. E. F. in France, 962,000. Essentials on basis of 30 lbs. per man per day, represents 14,430 short tons per day. (Par. 15, this memo.) 150,000 tons additional supplies and mat-

erials, as stated Par. 19, this memo, represents an additional 4,839 tons per day, or 19,269 short tons per day (not including coal), and a total for the month of 579,339.

(a) Will we be able to unload at A. E. F. French ports in July, an average of 19,269 short tons per day, exclusive of coal? Again, even at this rate of unloading for July (if we do it) we fall behind the War Department's scheduled tonnage for that month, 731,360 short tons, by a shortage of 134,021 tons.

22. Conslusions, Recommendations.

(a) Proposed cablegram to Chief Staff, Washington.

With reference to your cablegram 1048. It is assumed that the aggregate tonnage to be unloaded April to December inclusive, as stated, was arrived at based on troop movements to this side as now arranged, and essential requirements of all services here. Request information by cable stating the figures used, if possible, for each month April to December, representing tonnage of each service, aggregating the tonnage stated, in short weight tons. These figures desired for purpose comparison with ours.

(b) It will not be safe to allot tonnage space from the U. S. for supplies and materials for transportation, locomotives, cars, rails, motor transport, construction, and replacement steel or other material, in excess of 150,000 tons per month.

(c) Of these supplies and materials, and others, which are not included in the essentials (aggregating 30 lbs. per man per day, based on the average number of men A. E. F. in France, or to be in France). Transportation material and equipment, and construction materials for transportation, including motor transport (trucks) are most needed, and should be given priority of shipment to France, after the essentials making up the 30 lbs. per man per day.

(d) The minimum average unloading which must be maintained at French ports, exclusive of coal, is as follows:

		Tons of 2,000 lbs.
May	Daily	13,000
June	"	16,000
July	"	19,000

This is to provide for essential supplies based on the number of A. E. F. (troops and animals in or to be in France, as now arranged), at 30 lbs. per man per day, and in addition for 150,000 tons per month of transportation materials and equipment, motor transport, and construction materials.

(e) While movement of supplies, equipment and materials, as herein indicated, with minimum average daily unloading at French ports, during May, June and July 1918, 13,000 short tons, 16,000 and 19,000 respectively, will not meet the unloading schedule of the War Department (Par. 7 of this memo), it is believed that absolutely essential requirements (based on 30 lbs. per man per day), also transportation, construction and initial installation requirements to the extent of 150,000 short tons per month, not included in the 30 lbs. per man per day, will be met.

(f) It should be borne in mind, that the coal needed for locomotives, is an essential requirement for the transportation necessary to serve A. E. F. This coal will amount to 5,000 tons daily, not included in any tonnage figures before mentioned in this memo. The cross channel ship transport, required for this coal, must be assigned to that service as soon as possible. The existing A. E. F. coal reserve is inadequate, moreover, it is in possession of French authorities, which might, under certain conditions, be an unsatisfactory position for A. E. F. coal urgently required for A. E. F. transportation service.

W. B. RYAN,
Major, Engineers, N. A.

C-in-C Report File: Fldr. 149: Report

Inspection of Motor Transportation

GENERAL HEADQUARTERS, A. E. F.,

OFFICE OF INSPECTOR GENERAL,

Chaumont, Haute-Marne, April 28, 1919.

FROM: Colonel C. C. Carson, I. G.

TO: The Inspector General, G. H. Q., American E. F.

    1. This investigation and inspection was made during the period March 1 - April 28, 1919, by Colonel C. C. Carson, I. G., assisted by Colonel J. J. Grace, I. G., Lieut. Colonel C. O. Schudt, I. G., and by four captains, technical inspectors, viz: Captain N. E. Tourtellotts, C. A. C., Captain F. E. Stockwell, C. A. C., Captain L. E. Brown, C. A. C., and Captain E. L. Bull, Tank Corps, in compliance with instructions from the Commander-in-Chief February 16, 1919, directing certain information concerning the Motor Transport Corps to be secured, and that an inspection of motor transportation be made.

    2. The motor transportation in the hands of the three Armies was inspected, the Motor Transport Corps establishments in the army areas were visited, visits were made to the principal overhaul and reconstruction parks, and a study was made of documents and correspondence on file at the Headquarters of the Motor Transport Corps at TOURS.

    3. The following facts were ascertained:

    (a) HISTORY: The history of the Motor Transport Corps as such dated from the issuance of General Order No. 70, G. H. Q., A. E. F., December 8, 1917. Before this time the activities connected with the purchase, operation and maintenance of motor vehicles were carried on by the Quartermaster Corps as a part of its general duties. In April, 1917, there was some motor transportation on hand which had been procured for use in the Mexican Punitive Expedition, and was then in use at certain posts in the United States. Four truck companies were organized and these, with one motor park company, for repair work, left the United States on June 12, 1917, arriving at St-Nazaire on June 27, 1917. These four truck companies were the nucleus around which the present Motor Transport Corps was formed, the various steps to its present organization being as follows: December 8, 1917, General Order No. 70, G. H. Q., A. E. F., created a Motor Transport Service of the Quartermaster Corps, with the following functions:

    a. Technical supervision of all motor driven vehicles in the A. E. F.

    b. Reception, organization and assignment of motor vehicles.

    c. Organization and operation of spare parts depots and the supply of gasoline, lubricants and miscellaneous supplies.

    d. Operation and maintenance of repair shops and garages.

    e. Maintenance of reserve vehicles for replacements.

    February 16, 1918, General Order No. 31, G. H. Q., A. E. F., created a Service of Utilities and place thereunder the Motor Transport Service. May 11, 1918, General Order No. 74, G. H. Q., A. E. F., amplified to a certain extent the duties of the Motor Transport Service and in addition provided that all motor vehicles by whatsoever corps or service originally procured were to be brought under the supervision of the Motor Transport Service, the only exception being tractors of a type designed primarily for traction purposes and tanks. This order also provided for the detail of an officer from the Motor Transport Service to each army, corps, division, the army artillery, and to each base section of the S. O. S. as Motor Transport Officer of the command, and further provided that all questions arising in future with reference to the design or construction of motor vehicles would be decided by consultations between the staff corps or service concerned and the Motor Transport Service.

July 11, 1918, General Order No. 114, G. H. Q., A. E. F., abolished the Service of Utilities, changed the title of the Motor Transport Service to Motor Transport Corps and placed it under the Commanding General, S. O. S.

No fundamental changes in the Motor Transport Corps have taken place since, any apparent changes in organization being only a change in methods to comply with the provisions of General Order No. 74, G. H. Q., A. E. F., May 11, 1918.

(b) ORGANIZATION: The organization of the Motor Transport Corps as it exists in the A. E. F. at present really had its inception in the appointment by the Chief Quartermaster, A. E. F., of one of his staff, as officer in charge of motor transportation under the Quartermaster Corps. This appointment was made on August 16, 1917. The only organizations on duty in the A. E. F. at that time were the Motor Truck Group, First American Expeditionary Force, and one motor park company, the motor park company being organized for repair work. Some additional vehicles had been purchased in Europe to meet urgent local demands by the Depot Quartermaster in Paris and by the Signal and Engineer Corps, these units being responsible for the upkeep of their own vehicles. At the same time plans were being considered in the United States to organize units for the repair of motor transportation, to purchase machine and hand tools, and to design standard shops and equipment.

The first public official recognition of a service solely engaged in motor transportation problems was given by the issuance of General Order No. 70, G. H. Q., A. E. F., December 8, 1917, which created a Motor Transport Service of the Quartermaster Corps. This order, however, in great part recorded and made official the activities of the Motor Transport Service which had been conducted for some months on almost the identical lines of the order. In other words the Quartermaster Corps had within its organization the suborganization known as the Motor Transport Service and this organization was then carrying out the provisions of the order to the limit of available personnel. All personnel was furnished by the Quartermaster Corps but provision was made for a representative from each corps or service having motor transportation to be attached to the office of the Chief, Motor Transport Service, as his assistants.

A Service of Utilities was created by General Order No. 31, G. H. Q., A. E. F., February 16, 1919, and this order placed the Motor Transport Service under the Chief of Utilities. However, the duties of the Chief of Utilities in connection with the Motor Transport Service consisted principally in coordinating it and certain other services. The personnel which had been a part of the Motor Transport Service of the Quartermaster Corps, became the personnel of the Motor Transport Service with the exception of the personnel in charge of the supply of gasoline and lubricants who remained with the Quartermaster Corps. Much freedom was given the Motor Transport Service by the Chief of Utilities, but no provision had been made for the supply of additional personnel to provide for the great expansion taking place at this time.

With the constant expansion of the American Expeditionary Forces and the new problems arising therefrom, a policy was finally arrived at which was the result of many conferences among heads of departments, etc., and the Chief, Motor Transport Service and his assistants. General Order No. 74, G. H. Q., A. E. F., May 11, 1918, was issued after many of its provisions were accomplished facts. This order acquainted the A. E. F. as a whole with the duties of the Motor Transport Service and permitted the preparation of tables of organization with a view to providing adequate personnel. It also provided that in addition to the personnel of the old Motor Transport Service of the Quartermaster Corps which was to remain with the Motor Transport Service, all personnel then under training in the operation of motor vehicles and pertaining to other branches of the service was to be attached to the Motor Transport Service.

By General Order No. 114, G. H. Q., A. E. F., July 11, 1918, the title of the Motor Transport Service was changed to the Motor Transport Corps and it was created a separate corps under the Commanding General, Services of Supply.

The Tables of Organization now in force in the Motor Transport Corps was approved by the War Department August 15, 1918.

The Motor Transport Corps as now organized consists of a Director, Motor Transport Corps (brigadier general), a Deputy Director, Motor Transport Corps (colonel), and an Executive Officer, Motor Transport Corps, (lieutenant colonel), as the Headquarters Staff, Motor Transport Corps. The Headquarters offices is sub-divided into an Executive Division, a Supply Division, a Repair Division, an Operations Division, and Inspection Division, a Plane and Projects Division, and a Training Division, each division being in charge of an officer with the necessary assistants. Base and intermediate sections are administered by a Section Motor Transport Officer. Each section is further divided into districts and each district is provided with a District Motor Transport Officer who acts as an assistant to the Section Motor Transport Officer. In the zone of operations, each Army is provided with a Motor Transport Officer known as the Chief Motor Transport Officer, who has charge of all Motor Transport Corps activities in the Army, and who is assisted in his work by Corps and Division Motor Transport Officers. The Tables of Organization provided for the various officers named, together with a sufficient number of assistants.

(c) PERSONNEL: a. General Statement: When the original project for the A. E. F., provided for an army of 1,300,000 men, was drawn up in August 1917, the Motor Transport Service in the office of the Chief Quartermaster, A. E. F., estimated that about 40,000 men would be needed for the Motor Transport Service of this force. This was cut to 10,000 by the General Staff, A. E. F. During the winter of 1917-1918 it became apparent that this number would be inadequate, and repeated requests were made by the Chief, Motor Transport Service, for permission to submit a new project. These requests were verbal, and were made by the Director, Motor Transport Service, at staff conferences at Chaumont. When the Motor Transport Service moved from Chaumont to Tours in March, 1918, it was plainly seen by all concerned that an increase in personnel was necessary. Permission was therefore granted in April to submit a new project. This project, completed in the early part of May, provided for the operation of a large portion of the motor transportation belonging to combat units, and called for a total of about 100,000 men. This was forwarded to G. H Q., and on June 24 a cable was sent to the United States requesting the formation of a Motor Transport Corps. This Corps was not to be charged with the operation of vehicles in combat organizations and was to have a strength of 44,485 men. On August 15, this project was approved in Washington. The personnel of 10,000 allotted to Motor Transportation, was given a place on the original priority of shipments schedule, but after March 21, 1918, because of the great need for combat troops, the percentage of motor transport men among the personnel arriving in France showed a steady decrease. Beginning in August, 1918, a system of monthly priority requests was adopted in the A. E. F. and the Motor Transport Corps was allotted such numbers of men as was thought proper by the General Staff. This was invariably a fraction of the number requested by the Motor Transport Corps, due to the priority which was as a matter of necessity given to combat troops. However, of the Motor Transport Corps personnel requested by the A. E. F., less than 50 percent were sent by the United States. This was due to influenza, to late dates of drafts, and to a failure on the part of the Motor Transport Corps in the States to obtain, before late in the fall of

1918, permission to induct specially qualified men into the service for Motor Transport Corps work. A study of the cable and letter correspondence between the S. O. S. and Washington shows that the Motor Transport Corps of the A. E. F. continually made requests for special units and for specially qualified personnel which for some reason were never complied with.

The A. E. F. and Washington had authorized a strength of 44,485 Motor Transport Corps troops for an Army of 1,300,000. On this basis, there should have been an M. T. C. personnel of 52,000 in the A. E. F. at the time of the Armistice. The actual number was about 26,000.

    b. Commissioned Personnel: The Motor Transport Service, being a new service created during the war, was unable to secure officers of rank and experience, belonging to the Regular Army. The policy of G. H. Q. was that Regular Army officers should be reserved so far as possible for duty with combat units. At the time of the Armistice the officers of the Motor Transport Corps, A. E. F., numbered about 1,100, of whom 14 were Regular Army officers. This commissioned personnel consisted of officers of the Quartermaster Corps, Engineers, Artillery, and Infantry who were serving with service parks motorized trains, etc., at the time of the organization of the Motor Transport Corps in September, 1918, and of officers commissioned from time to time in the Motor Transport Corps. Officers selected for duty with motor organizations were supposed to be those having had experience with automobiles. In many cases they were men who had been advertising men, salesmen, and manufacturers where officers who had had actual experience in operation were needed.

    c. Enlisted Personnel: Motor transport companies were slow in arriving from the States and there was always a shortage of trained drivers and mechanics. Personnel arriving from the States was usually insufficiently trained, and much damage to motor transportation may be attributed to this fact. It appears that recruits were classified as automobile drivers on their own statements, and it was found necessary to test drivers before entrusting them with valuable vehicles. As an illustration the following is cited: The commander of a large organization newly arrived from the States was directed to turn out one hundred of his best truck drivers for test. Thirty were found to be qualified drivers. Seventy admitted that they had had more or less experience in driving Fords, and had stated upon entering the service that they were chauffeurs, in order to secure agreeable work. A large percentage of the men who came over for repair work were men who had worked in automobile factories. American factory methods make specialists of men, but do not turn out all-around mechanics. This point was emphasized by the Motor Transport Corps, A. E. F., in its communications to the United States, and every effort was made by them to secure men of the proper type.

    d. Training in the United States: Training of personnel for the Motor Transport Corps commenced at Camp Johnson, July 10, 1918. This school had a capacity of 2,500 men. Enlisted men sent to the A. E. F. were given a course of from one to three weeks. The Motor Transport Corps in the United States planned to establish three additional shcools, to commence about October 1, 1918. In addition another school, with a capacity for 10,000 students was planned for the training of the specially qualified men who were to be inducted into the service for the Motor Transport Corps in the fall of 1918.

    e. Training in France: The first acquisition of trained personnel for Motor Transport Service, aside from the truck companies brought over with the first convoy, came when the American transport with the French Army was, in part, taken over. This was a volunteer organization of Americans who had joined the French for ambulance and other transport work. About three hundred of these entered the American service, and, of these, some eighty-five were commissioned in the Motor Transport Corps, between November 1917, and November 1918. The supply train of the 26th Division, one-half of the supply train of the 41st and part of the 42d Divisional train received valuable training with the volunteer organization mentioned above.

The 1st Depot Division of St-Aignan conducted a school, with instructors who had been trained with the French, and a number of drivers for the combat divisions received this training.

A motor transport school was established at Decize (Nievre) and the first class entered July 5, 1918. The first class for officers and officer candidates for field service entered August 26 and the first for training for park service entered November 4, 1918. At the time of the Armistice, 125 officers and 2,045 enlisted men had completed courses at the school. The school was visited by the inspector and two of the assistants and was found to be a model institution.

(d) EQUIPMENT: A. Sources: At the beginning of the war the Ordnance Department, Air Service, Medical Corps, the Engineer Corps, Signal Corps, and the Quartermaster Corps, all went into the market for motor transportation. These departments worked on this problem independently and often found themselves in competition for the same product. Their field was the markets of the United States, France, England, and Italy. Before December, 1917, each of these departments in the A. E. F. purchased in Europe whatever necessary material they could find, but after that date this power was vested in the newly created Motor Transport Service of the Quartermaster Corps. This was done more as a measure of economy than as one to standardize the class of transportation procured. This, however, did not prevent all of these departments from continuing to design and procure their own vehicles in the United States.

While to a certain extent the idea of coordination had been considered, yet at the signing of the Armistice it had been but poorly realized. The question of upkeep which is the vital point of motor transportation had been considered but slightly. For instance the Medical Department contracted for large numbers of ambulances, but no spare parts. Other departments designed and floated what are know as special vehicles, that is what is considered special to their service. The Ordnance, the Air Service, and the Quartermaster Corps brought over mobile repair shops.

One by one each of the above departments turned over to the Motor Transport Corps what they had thus accumulated in the way of motor transportation in the A. E. F. The Air Service was the last to do so, and the entire transfer is only now being completed.

At the time of transfer the greater part of the property was in use. A physical transfer was impossible. The condition of the property can only be surmised, but from the fact that some of it had been in service more than a year, and that it had seen very hard service, the condition must have been poor. Another consideration complicating this question was that a number of vehicles, particularly the foreign makes, were by no means wew when purchased. In addition to the five principal supply departments all procuring vehicles independently, there was a considerable accumulation of vehicles that finally came into the Motor Transport Service pool from a variety of sources, principally donations to Hospitals and other organizations, vehicles purchased from company funds and brought over on baggage allowances, and converted vehicles. Vehicles of welfare organizations the Y. M. C. A., the Red Cross, and other welfare organizations all contributed to the introduction of a variety of types of transportation in the A. E. F., which, while it did not come into the Motor Transport Corps pool, yet was assembled and maintained by that corps.

b. Types: The above system not only led to a multiplicity of makes and types of machines, but also was responsible for the accumulation of a large number of useless and salvaged vehicles. On December 14, 1918, the records show that there was on hand in the A. E. F. the following number of different types of the vehicles mentioned:

Vehicles	Number of different types	
	American Make	Foreign Make
Motor cars	31	50
Light delivery	11	13
1 1/2 to 2-ton trucks	19	18
3 to 4 ton trucks	21	21
5-ton trucks	10	7
Motorcycles	5	11
Ambulances	10	7
Tractors	6	6
Caterpillars	6	0
Trailers	37	0
Machine Shop and Repair trucks	13	4
Kitchen trailers	2	2
Omnibuses	3	3
Reconnaissance	3	0
Laboratories	14	11
Tank trucks	8	2
Totals	157	155

The list above comprises every conceivable form of motor transportation. They were not all obtained in quantity, and many of the above types contained but one vehicle. Some of these were for experimental purposes and therefore did not have any special bearing on the operation of the Motor Transport Corps. The types of vehicles which perhaps caused the greatest difficlties to all concerned were the special vehicles. Unfortunately, some of these, such as the Nash Quad, were obtained in larger quantities and in the early stages of the war, so that this particular vehicle was in the hands of many of the organizations.

Many of the above vehicles were but slightly related, and few of the parts of one type interchangeable with those of another type. Even some of the so-called standard commercial vehicles which are listed above had modifications intended to better fit them for military uses.

c. Shipment: Shipments of vehicles and equipment to France were arranged, as for other property, on a tonnage allotment. Until June, 1918, each department imported on its own tonnage, thereafter it came over on the Motor Transport Corps tonnage. This was covered by monthly cables, specifying in detail the amount of each class of property desired floated. The question of spare parts was covered definitely by what was called the automatic supply. These cables were sent about two weeks in advance of the month for which they were operative. In addition to this, a system of weekly letters to and from the States was established April 19, 1918, and officers were sent back and forth between the States and France with particular directions as to shipment. With all this, however, liaison with the States poor. There is a vast discrepancy between the allowance of tonnage and the amount actually docked on this side. The records show that throughout the months of July, August, September, and October, 1918, but 25 per cent of the alloted tonnage was used, notwithstanding the fact that letters from the States written at that time stated that there was abundant Motor Transport Corps material on the wharves of the United States.

It appears also from these letters that during this time the material suffered considerable damage in transit, due principally to faulty crating and careless handling. At first vehicles were brought over uncrated as deck cargo, and naturally did not arrive in good condition. After repeated remonstrances, this was corrected. Another unfortunate error which occurred almost up to the last was sending over used vehicles, some of them showing many thousand miles of travel. In the beginning, the vehicles were brought down to the docks of the United States under their own power and loaded without being crated, and when they arrived in France they had to be completely overhauled. There was a difference of opinion between the Embarkation Service in American and the Motor Transport Corps on the question of crating the vehicles for shipment, but after constant pressure by the Motor Transport Corps the crating and boxing of vehicles was permitted. Thereafter the material arrived in better condition.

    4. Priority: The monthly cables gave priority of shipment based on the allotment of tonnage by G-4, G. H. Q. The indications are that at times priority meant nothing as shown by the following extract:

> Weekly Letter No. 5, June 26, 1918. (From the U. S.) The ports at present are congested with huge quantities of material so that any system of priorities is practically inoperative. For instance analysis of shipment made in May shows that a large quantity of material not covered at all on the priority schedule was floated, the reason being that it was in the ports and in the way, and had to be moved either abroad or back into the country, in order to make it possible to operate the ports. It is believed that the steps in progress now in connection with motor equipment depots will rapidly clean up the ports so far as M. T. S. material is concerned, and make it possible to operate shipments on strict priority schedule,. At present it is not possible to do this.

In all these priority cables, spare parts, which throughout the war was the most vital point, was given its proper proprtional weight. The percentage of spare parts received to that for which tonnage was available was the same as for other motor transport material, about 25 per cent, but it appears that such non-essentials as radiators, hard tires, bumpers, skid chains, and wheels predominated. From July 1, 1918, to November 30, 1918, 20,000 tons of spare parts were floated, of which 10,000 or fifty per cent were tires and tubes which were never used.

    e. Handling at Base Ports: It was found that the ships manifests could not be depended upon, so representatives of the Motor Transport Corps were detailed to watch all cargoes from the sides of the ships and keep the headquarters Motor Transport Corps informed of arrivals, whereupon the necessary instruction were issued for its disposition. At each of the base ports was established a Motor Reception Park where motor vehicles were uncrated, assembled and made ready for issue to the departments, including the Navy. This work was done by mechanics skilled in this line of work and was fairly well done, except at times when the material came in too rapidly to be handled, and at the signing of the Armistice there was quite a large accumulation of vehicles to be assembled. The park at St-Nazaire, which was the largest one of these, turned out in the month of November, 1918, 2,321 trucks and 436 passenger cars.

    f. Convoy System: Prior to June, 1918, some vehicles were forwarded from base ports by rail, but thereafter, due to the shortage of rolling stock in France all vehicles were driven in convoy formation overland. Sometimes these vehicles were convoyed by personnel sent from the organizations for which they were destined, but the greater part of them were convoyed by the Motor Transport Corps to distributed point. Each convoy operated on specified routes under carefully formulated regulations, and under charge of a pilot, who was usually an officer. Each night the pilot reported by telegraph to the Operation Department his whereabouts and the condition of his convoy. Records and charts showing the location of each convoy at all times were kept and preserved. An examination of these records over several months indicates that this method operated satisfactorily, and with a small percentage of vehicles not arriving promptly at their destination.

    (e) OPERATION: a. In the S. O. S. Early in the war it was decided that 75 per cent of the motor transportation arriving would be assigned to schools, training centers, and combat troops, the remaining 25 per cent to remain in the S. O. S. All assignments were made by the Director, Motor Transport Service. About May 1, 1918, due to the fact that full knowkedge of the relative needs of schools, training centers, and combat troops was lacking in the Motor Transport Service, these assignments were taken over by G-4, G. H. Q., A. E. F. The 25 per cent which remained under the control of the Commanding General, S. O. S., was assigned specifically to units and organizations by the Director, Motor Transport Service, until the issuance of General Order No. 36, Headquarters, S. O. S., August 7, 1918, which provided for the assignment of motor transportation to section commanders. In June, due to the necessities of the service, the proportion to remain in the S. O. S., was changed from 25 per cent to 10 per cent, and in addition to this reduction, orders were issued by G. H. Q., A. E. F., under date of August 19, 1918, to the effect that 2,300 vehicles types would be delivered by the S. O. S. to Dijon within seven days. In order to repay the loan of the 2,300 vehicles mentioned the proportion to remain in the S. O. S. was changed to 30 per cent for a time in the autum of 1918.

The great demand for motor transportation in the S. O. S. caused the establishment of a pool at Tours as an experiment. This proved so successful that pools were established at many other points in the S. O. S. Upon the issuance of General Order No. 36, Headquarters, S. O. S., a letter of instructions was sent to all section commanders outlining the pool system and directing the division of the section into districts with a pool in each district. Roughly the pool system provided for the control of all motor transportation in the district by the District Motor Transport Officer acting under the District Commander. A number of vehicles, the daily use of which was assured, were assigned to units or organizations, the remainder being kept as a district reserve to meet extraordinary demands. The District Motor Transport Officer was reponsible for the supply of all spare parts, gasoline, lubricants, etc., for the upkeep and operation of motor transportation and was also in charge of repair work, being provided in many instances with a repair shop. This system was further modified by the establishment of Motor Transportation Centers which in some cases were established within the districts with a view to reducing the empty hauls, and the final organization developed was that a transportation center under the local commanding officer who provided, under the pool system, for the needs of all S. O. S. troops in the vicinity.

b. In the Armies: In the early part of the war, motor transportation was being landed in France by several staff corps and services and issued direct to units therof. Later, with the scheme of combining all the motor transportation arriving from the States, issues were made direct to divisions and separate brigades, and, when the First Army was organized, direct to the Army. Unit commanders were then enabled to distribute their transportation as they saw fit. It was never possible to issue to any organization its table of organization allowance of transportation, hence unit commanders distributed the transportation in accordance with the problems to be solved rather than with reference to tables or organization. The pool system, with some modifications, was in use in all combat organizations. As to the actual administration of the use of vehicles, the divisions differed, though all transportation was in accordance with orders under the Assistant Chief of Staff, G-1. In some divisions the Supply Train Commander despatched cargo vehicles, in others this duty fell either to the Division Motor Transport Officer, or to an officer specially detailed to this duty in the office of G-1. As to passenger vehicles, these were generally in a Headquarters garage under an officer of the Headquarters Troop, and the vehicles were either dispatched by the officer in charge of the garage or by some officer specially detailed for this duty in the office of G-1. Transportation assigned to an organization and replacements thereof were usually procured by personnel from the organization in question from the Organization Parks at Dijon and Langres; however, on occasion deliveries of motor vehicles were made direct to organizations at the front by the Motor Transport Corps.

The combat organizations were on numerous instances given material aid in executing changes of position and in transportation of supplies from regulating stations to the front by means of provisional organization of truck trains from the S. O. S.

(f) TRAFFIC CONTROL: Traffic control was never developed, either in the S. O. S., or the zone of operations. The French Army, under stress of necessity, established traffic control points whenever necessary, the result being that French motor transportation during the latter part of the war was never used except when a military necessity arose. The amount of American travel by automobile reached such proportions that General Orders No. 1, Headquarters, S. O. S., was issued March 13, 1918, with a view to its control, and the Provost Marshals and Military Police were directed to establish traffic control posts to enforce its provisions. The control posts were established at certain points but were taken off as a rule between 8:00 p. m. and mid-night, and, so far as can be determined, reports made to commanding officers were not properly followed up in order that disciplinary action could be taken in cases of unauthorized use of automobiles. They were continually used for trips which could have been performed as well by rail transportation. A general order is now in preparation by G. H. Q., A. E. F., with a view to reducing necessary travel by automobile, the substance of which was telegraphed to the Third Army under date of March 30, 1919. An inspection of the motor transportation of the Third Army made between the 7th and 17th of April, showed that but two organizations, the 3d and 98th Divisions, had established traffic control posts as required by the order in question.

(g) MAINTENANCE: There were three classes of repair parks: Service Parks, which took care of minor repairs; Overhaul Parks, that cared for major repairs, and Reconstruction Parks, that reconstructed, or rebuilt, badly worn or damaged vehicles.

Service Parks were classed as mobile when serving with troops, and semi-mobile or immobile when located in sections where the operation of vehicles was more or less permanent. The size and equipment of these units are based upon the number of vehicles allotted to the park for repair. A Service Park Unit consisted of one officer and 35 men, and included specialist personnel for the different operations connected with ordinary repair work. For Service Parks, a suitable number of these units were assigned, depending upon the number of vehicles to be maintained. One hundred of these Service Park Units were organized, sixty-four being with the First, Second, and Third Armies, and the remainder at various S. O. S. stations. The majority of these units were inspected in the course of this investigation and they were found in general to be efficient and well managed organizations.

Eight Overhaul Parks were established, charged with the periodical general overhaul of all motor vehicles, and with such emergency work as was beyond the capacity of service parks. The majority were in the Advance Section. They had a capacity of from 100 to 200 trucks at a time, with other vehicles in proportion. Six of these parks were inspected. They were found to be well equipped, well managed, and functioning efficiently.

M. T. C. Reconstruction Park No. 772 commenced operating at Verneuil in July, 1918. The site was a poor one, but was the only one available, and was adopted because of certain railway transportation and strategic considerations. It was forseen that the drainage problem would be a difficult one, but an inspection and study of the plant shows that little intelligent attention was given to this. In the operation of the Park, too many service jobs were undertaken and this caused the plant to develop into an unwieldy service overhaul and reconstruction park combined. This also prevented the adoption of approved efficient shop methods. The failure of spare parts to arrive in France made it necessary to do a certain amount of manufacturing. With its splendid shop equipment Verneuil was able to manufacture quantities of spare parts on several occasions, and to be of great assistance to the Motor Transport Corps. Certain manufacturing was also done for the Engineers, Signal Corps, and for the Ordnance Department. This giving of so much attention to manufacturing diverted the plant from the use for which it had been intended---the reconstruction of damaged vehicles. At the inspection of this plant it was noted that there was practically no inspection system.

Reconstruction Park 713-A commenced operating at Romorantin January 1, 1919. It was charged with the reconstruction of vehicles of foreign makes. The site was an ideal one, and the buildings and much of the machinery were taken over from the Air Service who had operated their shops at this place during hostilities an inspection and study of this plant shows that it is economically and efficiently operated. Only a small percentage of service jobs are undertaken and there is no unnecessary manufacturing.

(h) SPARE PARTS: There has been much complaint throughout the A. E. F. concerning the dearth of essential spare parts. The original plan provided that Washington should ship six months supply with each 100 vehicles of a type, and that therafter an authomatic supply was to be established. Experience showed that to obtain any article or articles from the States by definite requisition required about 6 months.

It must be understood that spare parts are not an articles of commerce. Each manufacturer plans for a sufficient number of parts for his product plus the number of spares that his experience shows will be needed for his trade. Orders for large quantities such as are needed in war time must be placed in advance and provision made for their manufacture.

The automatic list was supposed to go into effect July 1, 1918, and each month cables were sent to Washington specifying the exact number and kind of vehicles to be floated, and also the amount and kind of spare parts and accessories. Numerous cables and letters and the continued efforts of three officers travelling between France and the States failed to produce results, and the spare parts never arrived in adequate quantities. The Motor Transport Corps, A. E. F., repeatedly requested Washington to float spare parts in advance of, or with, shipments of any particular type of vehicles, but this was never done. Many shipments that should have arrived during the months of hostilities have now arrived in France, and it is believed that the principal reason for their non-arrival when needed was the congested condition of American ports, as stated elsewhere in this report. The spare parts that did arrive were well and promptly distributed, and quantities of parts for distribution were manufactured at Bordeaux and Paris as well as at the Reconstruction Park at Verneuil. There was also a great shortage of tools. Many vehicles arrived from the States without tools or accessories or with incomplete sets. All repair personnel arriving before September 30, 1918, came without the necessary hand tools, etc., that would have permitted them to be of immediate service. It was necessary to make purchases in France, England, and Spain in an effort to make up these shortages.

In this connection, it must be stated that motor transportation in the A. E. F. was subjected to use which was quite without precedent in American experience. The stress of war service was expected to cause demands for spare part, but it was not anticipated that valuable government property would be neglected or misused to such a great extent as has been the case. Drivers were, as a rule, half-trained, reckless, and poorly disciplined. Vehicles were overloaded, were driven at excessive speeds over hard roads, and were necessarily left exposed to the elements when not in use. Little attention was given to keeping vehicles lubricated, adjusted and clean. This caused rapid deterioration, and a consequent demand for spare parts and replacements. Officers, in general, did not show a proper appreciation of their duties and responsibilities in connection with the upkeep and use of motor transport.

(i) SALVAVE: During Operations: General Order No. 74, 1917, G. H. Q., discontinued property accountability, but specifically retained responsibility. The Salvage Service was created January 16, 1918, and various orders were published contemplating the reception from all departments of such salvage material as could not be used in these departments. Following this, responsibility became a fiction, rather than a fact.

General Order No. 58, G. H. Q., April 18, 1918, prescribed that motor vehicles should be sent for salvage to the temporary Reconstruction Park at Nevers. This was not generally observed. The general understanding by officers as to the meaning of salvage was the stripping of vehicles of their component parts and applying of these parts to the same uses on other vehicles. Other than as stated above there are no published orders on this subject but it was understood by the officers of the Motor Transport Corps that this power was vested in the Reconstruction Parks alone.

The approved practice of salvaging was as follows: When vehicles could not be repaired in the Service Parks, authority would be granted by G-4 to ship them either to the Overhaul Parks or the Reconstruction Parks, as the necessity demanded. This was only done, however, after an inspection of the vehicles by a representative of the Motor Transport Corps. The receipt given to the responsible officer for this material served as a means for procuring replacement as well as for clearing responsibility. Inasmuch as during operations there was seldom any transportation available for replacement, and as responsibility had become a fiction, organizations were loath to turn in their transportation for salvage but preferred to keep it, though unserviceable, for replacing parts of other vehicles.

No inspections were made to enforce the rules of salvage, and as a result, there accumulated at railheads large numbers of disabled vehicles, usually known as salvage dumps. These dumps were unguarded and anyone was at liberty to search them for spare parts. There is evidence that in many cases the desired spare parts were broke off vehicles by violence. When combat units left sectors they abandoned their dumps, and new units came in and carried on in a similar manner.

Salvage in the S. O. S.: The approved practice of salvage as above described was attempted in the S. O. S. but its principles were frequently departed from. The overhaul parks did not ship for salvage to any great extent, but handled their own salvage. This was not a bad plan at the overhaul parks where there were suitable facilities for such work, but some of the small service parks also attempted this operation, which was neither economical nor practicable, for them, with their limited facilities.

Salvage since the Armistice in the Armies: After the signing of the Armistice, the work of salvaging government property was commenced. Inspections of motor transportation were made under the direction of the Motor Transport Corps of the Armies. Attention was given to many details which the pressure of more important events had caused to be overlooked. The approved method of salvage as described above was in general put into operation. There was no rail transportation available, so that such material could not be sent overland was collected in dumps.

These dumps in the first Army were abandoned for some time until a corps of Air Service mechanics under Motor Transport Corps officers took charge, about January 25, 1919. After this the material was evacuated to the reconstruction parks as rapidly as possible. The report of the officer in charge of the reclamation of the dumps at Dun-sur-Meuse, Grandpré, Dombasle, Baleycourt, Souilly, and La Frana-Fermen, shows that considerable property, consisting of about 1,400 vehicles and a large supply of spare parts had been left unguarded for many days and that much damage had resulted from this and other neglects.

Salvage in the S. O. S.: After the signing of the Armistice there was no material change in the method of salvaging in the S. O. S., except that the release of pressure of other work permitted more time to be devoted to the care and recovery of property. Vehicles of American make intended for salvage, which could not be handled elsewhere, were sent to Verneuil, and those of foreign make, to Romorantin. This resulted in the accumulation at these places of the majority of the disabled vehicles in the A. E. F. These vehicles upon arriving at Verneuil were piled by means of a steam crane, sometimes four vehicles high, in disorder and in a hopeless tangle. In this case valuable government property has been grossly neglected and unnecessarily subjected to further damage. At Romorantin this condition does not prevail, but on the contrary the vehicles are carefully unloaded and parked, and suffer no material damage after arrival.

(j) PRESENT CARE OF TRANSPORTATION: The motor transportation of the First, Second, and Third Armies was inspected and also that pertaining to many S. O. S. units. In making this inspection, it was necessary to establish a standard in order that just criticisms could be made. This was assumed as somewhat above the conditions that it was believed would be found in general, and criticisms were based on this standard. This standard, is, however, too low. The standard as to cleanliness and care should be that of American Naval craft, field guns, coast defense guns and fire control apparatus and this standard has nowhere been approached in our service.

In January, 1919, the Motor Transport Corps formed a corps of Inspectors and took up the work of improving conditions in the S. O. S. commanding officers of the various Army units have, since the Armistice, generally shown a commendable interest in their motor transportation, and conditions are improving.

4. CONCLUSIONS: The instructions of the Commander-in-Chief of February 16, 1919, may be interpreted as requiring answers to the following three questions:

(a) What care is now being taken of Motor Transportation?

Seven officers have been engaged for a period of two months in inspecting vehicles, repair establishments, garages, etc. A formal report has been made in the case of each place or organization inspected, and these reports have been followed up, in order to correct deficiencies. The inspectors have endeavored to give advice when possible, and to make constructive criticisms. There was much neglect and carelessness during hostilities, but conditions show constant improvement and motor transportation is now being generally well cared for. However, a proper standard has not yet been attained in the A. E. F.

(b) Was the organization of the Motor Transport Corps well planned and executed?

All available documents were studied and many officers were interviewed in the search for information on this subject. The organization was entrusted to officers well qualified for the work, and whose experience had fitted them for the task. It was well worked out, and is substantially that proposed to the Staff by the Motor Transport Service of the Quartermaster Corps in August, 1917.

(c) How has the Motor Transport Corps functioned?

The Motor Transport Corps was a new service, reaching its final status four months before the Armistice. But few experienced officers could be spared for this service. It suffered continuously from shortage of personnel, and was always short of material. Considering its many difficulties, it is believed that the Motor Transport Corps functioned remarkably well.

5. RECOMMENDATIONS: Because of the demobilization, it is not considered that recommendations are desired or could be acted upon if made. It is, however, recommended that a study be made of the Motor Transport Services of the French and British Armies, with a view to collecting data to be made use of in a Motor Transport Corps, which will doubtless be an important branch of the new United States Army.

C. C. CARSON.

ASSISTANT CHIEF OF STAFF, G - 5, GHQ, AEF

C-in-C Rept. File: Fldr. 215: Report

Final Report of Assistant Chief of Staff, G-5

5th Section, General Staff   GENERAL HEADQUARTERS, A. E. F.,

Chaumont, Haute-Marne, June 30, 1919.

FROM: A. C. of S. G-5

TO: Chief of Staff

[Extract]

1. In compliance with your instructions, I submit the following report of the operations of G-5.

[The report continues with a list of the general headings used in the report and a partial list of appendices.]

* * * * * *

ORGANIZATION

3. The General Staff of the American Expeditionary Forces was at first, in accordance with our Field Service Regulations, organized into three sections, Administration, Intelligence and Operations. Training and military education were to be handled by a subcommittee of Operations.

4. In August, 1917, Operations and Training were separated. G. O. 8, July 5, 1917, assigned duties to the Training Section as follows:

Supervision of centers of instruction and staff schools. Preparation of courses of training.

Coordination of school training and that imparted to troops.

Preparation of training manuals and simmlar literature.

Methods of tactical inspections.

Training bulletins.

Sits with Operations Section in matters affecting organization and equipment.

Inspection of schools and methods of instruction.

5. G. O. 31, February 16, 1918, reorganized the General Staff into five sections. Training became the fifth (G-5). Duties were assigned as follows:

General directions and enunciation of the doctrine of instruction and training throughout the command.

Supervision of centers of instruction and staff schools. Preparation of courses of training.

Coordination of school training and that imparted to troops.

Preparation of training manuals, with incorporation of changes suggested by actual experience.

Translation of training manuals and similar literature.

Methods of tactical inspections.

Training bulletins.

Sits with Third Section, General Staff, in matters affecting organization and equipment.

Inspection of schools and methods of instruction.

Inspection to insure efficiency and thoroughness in training throughout the command.

SCHOOLS

6. Both the training committee of G-3, and G-5, after the separation, made careful studies of the whole training problem for the forces in France; and in reaching their solutions received the ready and very valuable assistance and cooperation of the French and British Staffs.

7. Training divides itself naturally into two parts, the training of officers and the training of men; in other words, the training of individual instructors and the training of organizations. It is by no means sufficient simply to appoint officers and tell them to train their men. Before one can instruct others he must have some knowledge of the subject he is to teach.

8. Therefore, in improvising an army or in a great expansion of an existing army, the first difficulty is in making a corps of officers who can serve as instructors for their men. Having competent instructors, the training of the soldiers and of the organization is a relatively simple process. Not only are line officers difficult to improvise but staff officers and staffs are much more so. After our arrival in France, both our Allies emphasized the need of staffs and the relatively long time required to train and educate their members. Both the French and the British urged prompt steps toward a beginning.

9. Some of our young officers received more or less training in the camps at home, but all nevertheless required further schooling and orientation as to new weapons and formations after arrival in France.

10. In attacking this problem, the American staff, as stated before, had the interested assistance of the French and the British. Both were glad to tell us of their experiences, of their difficulties, and of the manner in which they had met these. Both services had found it expedient to establish and maintain continuously through all operations a great system of schools wherein they trained replacements in officers and men. This was the case in both services, notwithstanding the fact that the French had a relatively strong framework of officers and noncommissioned officers, while the British, whose situation was more nearly like our own, had only their small regular establishment to build upon.

11. We frequently hear it said that the best school for war is war. No idea could, however, be more fallacious. One has only to visualize the conditions at the front to appreciate how limited is the view of any man and how little opportunity he had to understand what is actually occurring and why. This is particularly so in the underground warfare we found when we came to France. If one cannot understand the how and the why of what is happening on the battlefield, he cannot there learn to make successful war. Service in battle hardens officers and men, an important part of training, but it does not school them.

12. The training of officers was affected by the general replacement scheme. From the reported losses of our Allies, it early became certain that we should need in France at least 50% of our first-line strength in replacements, ready at short notice to fill the regiments depleted in action. For various reasons, a six-division corps was adopted. Each corps was to have four combat divisions and two replacement divisions. One of these replacement divisions was to be established in some convenient training area behind the general position of the combat divisions. Its function was to hold and train replacements in officers and men all the way from the division commander to the private soldier. It was then, upon demand, to forward officers and men of all grades to the

first line divisions. The sixth division of the corps, forming the second of the two replacement divisions, was to be called the depot division and to be stationed near the ports. It was to receive drafts from the United States and give them little more than individual training, including target practice. From the depot division men would be sent to the replacement division for the completion of their training. It was found impracticable to carry this replacement scheme into full effect. But it enters into training matters because upon it was necessarily and conveniently hung the entire school system for the Expeditionary Forces.

13. The divisions at the front, i. e., the four combat divisions of each corps, should remain mobile; that is, they should have no more excess baggage in the way of schools or installations back of the line than was absolutely essential, and their location could be expected to shift more or less continually. To maintain schools at maximum efficiency, their equipment and installation should be stationary. Moreover, up to a certain point, the larger the institution, the more economical it is in overhead and in instructor personnel. On the other hand, the resulting institution must not be too unwieldy to administer. The replacement division was expected to remain continually in one area. If the corps schools were located nearby, it could conveniently furnish troops for labor and demonstration. It was decided, consequently, that the area of the replacement division should, in principle, accommodate a group of schools for the corps.

14. Based upon a study of the French and British systems, including in that study visits to their fronts and their best schools, the memorandum and project quoted below was submitted, and approved on August 30:

Headquarters American Expeditionary Forces

Office of the Chief of Staff

Training Section

Paris, August 27, 1917.

MEMORANDUM FOR THE CHIEF OF STAFF.

SUBJECT: School for American Expeditionary Forces.

1. A study of the French and British systems of the training of troops in France indicates that the following school project will best meet the needs of the American Army:

(a) In each division a system of troop training under the direct supervision of the division commander involving such incidental school instruction as may be desirable in the training of the division and for the purpose of producing instructors in corps schools.

(b) A center of instruction for each corps for the purpose of training replacements of all grades and commanders of all units. This naturally places the center of instruction at the location selected for the first replacement division of each corps and contemplates that each group of corps schools shall instruct commanders of proper grades for four combat divisions, assuming that the organization of corps recommended at these headquarters will be approved in full. Until the system is in complete operation, it will also be necessary to train at corps schools a number of officers who will ultimately become instructors in Army Schools.

(c) A center of instruction for the entire Army in France, to be known as the

Army Schools. This group should include a General Staff College and such other schools as may be necessary to train instructors for all corps schools The Army Schools should be under the direct control of these headquarters in order that the doctrine which should actuate the entire system of instruction and control our ideas of combat may be transmitted from the General Staff through these schools to all units of the army.

As these schools will train a great number of men comparatively unfamiliar with actual operations, the group should be placed in close contact with large bodies of troops. The necessity for economy of administration and uniformity of instruction requires that the schools be grouped together so far as practicable. They should, moreover, be on or near the main lines of communication, close to the zone of the army, but far enough away from the front to be comparatively safe from hostile aircraft. They should be so located as to insure permanency, but not in such locality as to influence future actions in regard to the front to be occupied. All of these conditions may be satisfied if the second replacement division of the first corps, which would ordinarily be placed near one of the bases on the west coast of France, were moved forward instead into a suitable divisional cantonment in the area bounded by Orleans---Montargis---Troyes---Chaumont---Langres---Gray---Dijon---Châlons---Nevers---Bourges---Issoudun---Blois. The various army schools should be so grouped with respect to the division as to permit the members of any or all of the schools to attend any or all of the demonstrations conducted by troops without in any way detaching troops for this purpose from divisions at the front or in any way impairing efficiency of troop training in the replacement division itself.

2. It will be impossible to put this system into complete operation until the entire first corps has reached France. Under the present schedule of troop arrivals, this will occur about November 15 next. In the meantime, it is necessary to meet the needs of army training as they arise and to utilize existing facilities to the best possible advantage. Thus the schools at Saumur and other points may be used for the training of the 2,200 reserve officers to reach France not later than September 15. Mailly may be used for our heavy artillery school; Arnouville-les-Gonesse may be used for the training of our antiaircraft guns; but these widely scattered schools should be regarded as expedients only and every effort should be made to bring all of our institutions for army training into close proximity, if possible, into the area above referred to, where the second replacement division of the first corps should be located as already outlined.

It may be necessary to depart from this plan in some cases but departures from the plan should be accepted only if compelled to by circumstances beyond our control.

3. Should it be found impracticable to concentrate the Army Schools and the second replacement division in the area named, then it is thought that both the division and the schools should be placed near one of the bases on the west coast of France. Should this be found impracticable, which is highly improbable, then it will be necessary to locate the schools at a number of widely separated points. In order that the best possible solution may be secured, it is thought necessary to designate at once the prospective commandants of these schools, acquaint them with the situation and direct them to make necessary study of the corresponding British and French schools and submit recommendations in regard to the organization, equipment, personnel and curriculum best suited to our neecs. While this work is in progress, the Operations and Training Sections, working in cooperation and with the French General Staff, should locate the exact area best suited for this work and take the necessary steps to place the schools and the division in the area selected.

4. It is therefore recommended:

(a) That the following officers be designated as prospective commandants of schools as indicated:

* * * * * *

(b) That the French government be advised of the decision of these headquarters to place the second replacement division and the schools named in the area referred to and that the Training Section, in cooperation with the Operations Section, be authorized to take the necessary steps to accomplish the results desired.

5. A skeleton outline of the entire school project drawn up originally by Lieut. Colonel Fox Conner and Major Drum, as modified by the Training Section, is hereto attached.

* * * * * *

PAUL B. MALONE,
Lieut. Col., Infantry, DOL,
Chief of Training Section.

HEADQUARTERS, A. E. F.
August 30, 1917

Approved by direction:

J. G. HARBORD
Chief of Staff.

SCHOOL PROJECT FOR AMERICAN EXPEDITIONARY FORCES

Per Combat Division	No schools – Troop training.	
Per Army Corps	**ARMY CORPS CENTER OF INSTRUCTION** (Located at 1st Replacement Division of each Army Corps and under supervision of Div. Commdr.)	

OBJECT	(A) TRAINING	(B) ARMY CORPS SCHOOLS
1. Training replacements. 2. Training various commanders of all units, etc.	1. Drafts of all arms received from Base Replacement Division. 2. Training of men to be non-commissioned officers of all arms.	1. The Corps Infantry School. Section A – Plat. and Sec. Comdrs. " B – Rifle Co. Comdrs. " C – M. G. Plat. and Co. Comdrs. " D – Trench Mortar; (3"-Stokes); and 37-mm. " E – Lines of Information.

ARMY CORPS CENTER OF INSTRUCTION (Cont'd)

OBJECT   (A) TRAINING   (B) ARMY CORPS SCHOOLS

    2. The Corps Artillery School.
       Section A – Lieuts. and Btry.
                 Comdrs. (3"–& 6"–How.)
          "   B – Instrument Sergts.
                 and Range Finders.
          "   C – Lines of Information
                 (radio, telephone
                 and signal).
          "   D – Artillery Information,
                 Firing Charts, Sound
                 Ranging, Flash Ranging.

    3. The Corps Engineer School.
       Section A – Co. and Plat. Comdrs.
          "   B – Sappers School
          "   C – Pioneers school
                 (Engrs., Inf., Cav.,
                 and F. A.)

    4. The Corps Cavalry School.
       Section A – Mounted Service School.
      NOTE: Captains and Lieutenants
            attend Inf. and Engr. Schools.

    5. The Corps Gas School.
       (For all arms of the service).

    6. The Corps Signal School.
       Section A – Co. and Plat. Comdrs.
          "   B – Special N. C. O.'s.

    7. The Corps Sanitary School.
       Ambulance and Field Hosp. Co.
       Officers.

    8. The Corps Aeronautical School.
       Section A – Combat Aviation School.
          "   B – Combat Balloon School.

    9. The Corps Field Officers School.
       All Lieutenant-Colonels and Majors
       (includes school course and visits to
       all schools).

Army Schools

ARMY SCHOOLS
(Located at 2d Replacement Division of I Army Corps and under supervision of Gen. Hq.)

OBJECT

1. Training instructors for Corps schools.

2. Training special officers.

    1. The General Staff College, A.E.F.
       Special officers selected for General Staff work.

    2. The Army Line Schools, A.E.F.
       Section A - Inf. Lts.   ) Trained to in-
       "   B - Art. "   ) clude co. and btry.
       "   C - Engr. "   ) comdrs. duties.
       "   D - Signal"   )
       "   E - Capts., Majors, and Lt. Cols. of all arms.
       "   F - Line of Information. (Liaison of all arms).
       "   G - Sanitary Service.

    3. The Army Candidates School, A.E.F.
       Training soldiers to be officers.
       (If necessary, to be divided into sections
       for each arm).

    4. The Army Antiaircraft School, A.E.F.
       Section A - Artillery
       "   B - Machine Guns.

    5. The Army Artillery School, A.E.F.
       Section A - Heavy Artillery
       "   B - Trench Artillery
       "   C - R. R. Artillery

    6. The Army Signal School, A.E.F.
       Section A - Telegraph
       "   B - Telephone
       "   C - Radio
       "   D - Visual Methods
       "   E - System Operation.
       "   F - Carrier Pigeons.

    7. The Army Aeronautical Schools, A.E.F.
       Section A - Aviation School
       "   B - Balloon School
       "   C - Inf. and Art. Observers, organization
                and training

    8. The Army Sanitary School, A.E.F.
       Complete outline to be announced later.

9. The Army Engineer School, A.E.F.
   Section A – Sappers School
   "   B – Pioneer School for Engrs., Inf., Cav., and F.A.
   "   C – Bridging.
   "   D – Mining.
   "   E – Searchlights
   "   F – Ranging.
   "   G – Topography.
   "   H – Camouflage.

10. The Army Inf. Specialists Center, A.E.F.
    Section A – Automatic Weapon.
    "   B – Musketry, Bayonet and Sniping
    "   C – Grenade, Trench Mortar, 3"–Stokes and 37-mm.

11. The Army Center of Information, A.E.F.
    Conferences and demonstrations for all generals
    and colonels of all arms.

12. The Army Tank School, A.E.F.

13. The Army Gas School, A.E.F.

Army Corps Base Training Center

BASE TRAINING CENTERS
(Located at 2d Replacement Division of each army corps and under supervision of division commander).

OBJECT	(A) TRAINING	(B) BASE TRAINING SCHOOLS
1. Training new drafts.	Training new drafts individually of all arms and services.	Section A – Cooks and Bakers. " B – Clerks " C – Mechanics " D – Saddlers, Horseshoers and Stable Sergeants. " E – Drivers and Packers. " F – Chauffeurs. " G – Telephone Operators. " H – Telegraph and Radio Operators.
2. Special classes of soldiers.		

Hq., Amexforce, Paris, August 30, 1917.

   Approved by direction:

                                J. G. HARBORD
                                Chief of Staff.

15. The broad outlines of this scheme were carried into effect. As was however to be expected, some modifications in details were required, or were found expedient, to meet later developments. In this report it will be sufficient to touch briefly on the schools and their purposes.

16. Army Schools: Unless there was some coordinating influence, the several corps schools provided for above would probably begin to diverge soon in the direction of their tactical thought and tactical training. This necessity for coordination was to be met by the establishment of a group of army schools, one of whose great functions was to be the training of instructors for the sorps schools. The mission of the corps schools was to train officers and selected noncommissioned officers as rapidly as possible so that they might return to their organizations and, in turn, train their soldiers. Upon completion of each course officers were graded in accordance with the work they had done, the best being rated as instructors for corps schools. In principle, these were to be sent to the army schools and there be given intensive additional training. They were then to return to troops and be given front line service until they were recalled for duty as instructors at some one of the schools.

17. Those were the governing principles. But men graded as of instructor caliber were necessarily of very fine quality. All of our staffs were being constantly expanded and new ones created so that the demand for good men was enormous. Our instructors, too, when they went to front line duty suffered an undue proportion of casualties. With it all, the scheme of systematic progress through corps and army schools, duty at the front, and return to schools as instructors, had many setbacks. But little by little as the war progressed we were able to approximate more and more closely the original scheme.

18. In addition to these broad functions of the corps and army schools, the army schools contained in the original scheme an army general staff college for the training of staff officers and candidates' schools for the training and selection of soldiers to be promoted to the grade of officer. By these two schools it was proposed to meet the needs of the Forces in the two directions in which the greatest difficulties were anticipated; by one producing a steady flow of officers up into the lower grades, and the other a steady flow of officers into our constantly increasing staffs. Langres, after reconnaissance of many suggested locations, was selected for the group of army schools. General McAndrew was the first Commandant.

19. General Staff College: The Staff College opened for its first class on November 28, 1917. Brigadier General A. W. Bjornstad was its first Director. He was assisted by four French and four British officers who had had wide experience in staff duty in their respective services. The College graduated four classes with a total of 537 officers. Classes were continually increased in size to meet the constantly increasing demands for graduates. The one intended to begin January 1 of this year was to contain 500 members. All courses were three months in length. As rapidly as our own officers became available and competent, the foreign officers were relieved and our own substituted. At the closing of the College, January 1, 1919, all were American but one Englishman and one Frenchman. The first classes were largely composed of regular officers who had had tactical training. But the number of such was very limited. The Line School, also at Langres, accordingly came to serve as a feeder for the Staff College, receiving officers of shorter previous military training for a three months' purely tactical course. The Line School had four sessions and graduated 488 officers.

20. Candidates' Schools: From the figures furnished us by the French and the British, it was plain from the beginning that our officer casualties were going to be very great. To meet this there would be the officers to come from the United States with replacement troops. Then, on request from this side, the War Department early sent to France a total of about 6,000 surplus officers, captains and lieutenants, graduates

of the training camps at home. Some of these were sent through British schools, some through our own corps schools, some through the Line School at Langres, and some through two special schools established under General Bullard, largely with French instructors, at la Valbonne and Valreas. At the same time candidates' classes at Langres, Saumur and Mailly were started. Their product was expected fully to meet the periodical losses based upon the figures of our Allies. But our wastage in officers was enormous from the beginning and beyond all of our anticipations. The S. O. S. absorbed great numbers, so did all staffs, many became sick; when active operations began, the casualties among platoon and company commanders were exceedingly heavy. The 6,000 surplus from the United States, several thousands promoted from the ranks of the divisions as the result of schoolings and examinations in the United States, and the product of our candidates' schools were all absorbed and disappeared. Early last fall (1918), we were facing a serious shortage in officers, only efficiently to be met by a tremendous expansion of all candidates' schools. The schools for infantry candidates were gradually being transferred to la Valbonne, near Lyon, where by January 1 we should have had 22,000 candidates constantly under instruction and would have been graduating between 5,000 and 6,000 every month. At the same time, it was expected that the artillery candidates' school at Saumur would be graduating about 800 each month, the engineer at Langres about 400, and the signal at Langres about 200. Actually we graduated altogether from candidates' schools in France 6,895 infantrymen, 2,384 artillerymen, 1,332 engineers and 365 signalmen, or a total of all arms of 10,976. Courses were ordinarily three months long, although to meet imperative demands for officers several courses had to be considerably shortened.

21. The candidates' schools were based upon the idea that men who displayed qualities of leadership with troops should be selected by their organization commanders as officer material, and that these candidates should be sent to schools where they would receive three months' intensive training under uniform methods, and be carefully tested to weed out those who by deficient education or for other reason showed themselves unsuited to commissioned rank. The schools received much criticism from those who believe that the only necessary instruction is received at the front or with units; but all nations properly accept and use the school idea as the most rapid, uniform, and in every way economical means for the education of the officer.

22. All of our many schools were important but the two described above were unquestionably the most important.

23. Corps Schools: The corps schools were carried through in general as outlined in the original scheme. Courses were at first of five weeks' duration; they were early shortened to four weeks. No cavalry school was established because we had no first line cavalry. Classes at the Sanitary School were found too small to warrant separate schools for each corps so all were shortly consolidated at Langres. The artillery schools were also early discontinued because of lack of material and a duplication of work which was being satisfactorily performed at artillery organization and training centers and at Saumur. The aeronautical schools were after a time consolidated at the II Corps schools, and the field officers classes were consolidated at Langres.

24. Corps schools were organized by these headquarters. The I Corps schools were for a time supervised by the headquarters of that corps, but when the German menace became serious last year, it was realized that headquarters of corps were going to be too much on the move to have direct charge of their schools. The I Corps schools then reverted to the control of G-5, and the others were never released to the control of their corps. Only three corps schools were organized as it was found that this number could handle the personnel for all of the divisions that ever came to France.

25. The corps schools graduated 13,916 officers and 21,330 noncommissioned officers, a total of 35,246.

26. Other Schools: Saumur. The old French cavalry school at Saumur was taken over for our field artillery school in 1917. Its first classes were reserve officers of the 6,000 from the United States. While classes for battery officers continued to be held, the main function of the school soon became the training of all artillery candidates.

27. Heavy Artillery School was for the training of officers assigned to railway and tractor artillery, and of artillery soldiers in the work of artillery specialists. The school held its first courses at Mailly later moving to Angers. Eight regular courses were completed. The school graduated 1,071 officers and soldiers.

28. A very successful field artillery school covering much the same courses as those intended for the corps schools was established at Valdahon about the time of the Armistice and continued in operation for several months. Especial stress was laid upon close support of the infantry, to facilitate work with which a fine battalion of infantry was assigned to the school.

29. An artillery center of information, established at Langres and afterwards moved to Treves, held four courses in artillery studies for general and field officers. It graduated 110 officers, among whom were 15 general officers of artillery and 13 of infantry.

30. In addition to the above, and as contemplated in the original scheme, schools were established in the depot division at St-Aignan for cooks and bakers, clerks, mechanics, saddlers, horseshoers, stable sergeants, drivers, packers, chauffeurs, and telephone, telegraph and radio operators.

31. In all schools every effort was made to secure a constant rotation between duty as instructors and duty with troops at the front. It was considered absolutely essential that our instructors should be thoroughly conversant with affairs and conditions at the front and that they should have the prestige which goes with successful duty thereat. The courses in all of our schools were entirely too short for efficiency, but, under the circumstances, they constituted a reasonable compromise between the demand for haste in all of our preparations and what was desirable.

TROOP TRAINING

32. Programs: The 1st Division reached St-Nazaire towards the end of June, 1917. That division, composed almost entirely of recruits, had its first training in France in the Gondrecourt area, alongside and in reality under control of a French division. The differences in language, temperament, and methods caused little progress to be made. With the organization of a training section at these headquarters, in August, 1917, it was decided to write a detailed program for the 1st Division and supervise its execution. It was also decided that the training of all divisions as they arrived in France should be in conformity with the programs written and supervised by these headquarters. These should be based upon progress of the divisions before arrival in France, and the anticipated time before they would have to go into the line. Unless a program was prepared in this manner and adherence thereto rather rigidly compelled, it was found that entirely too great diversity in ideas prevailed among division commanders as to methods, and that uniformity and rapidity in the production of a satisfactory efficiency in training could not be expected. Moreover, members of the Training Section had been in France from the beginning, had visited the best of the French and British Schools and were familiar with their methods of training. The Training Section was therefore better prepared to draft a program which would work than was a division headquarters just over from the United States. The 1st and 2d Divisions, and all succeeding ones, were trained in accordance with this plan.

33. French officers, as advisors and critics, were attached during the first period of training; and until the military situation of 1918 rendered this impracticable,

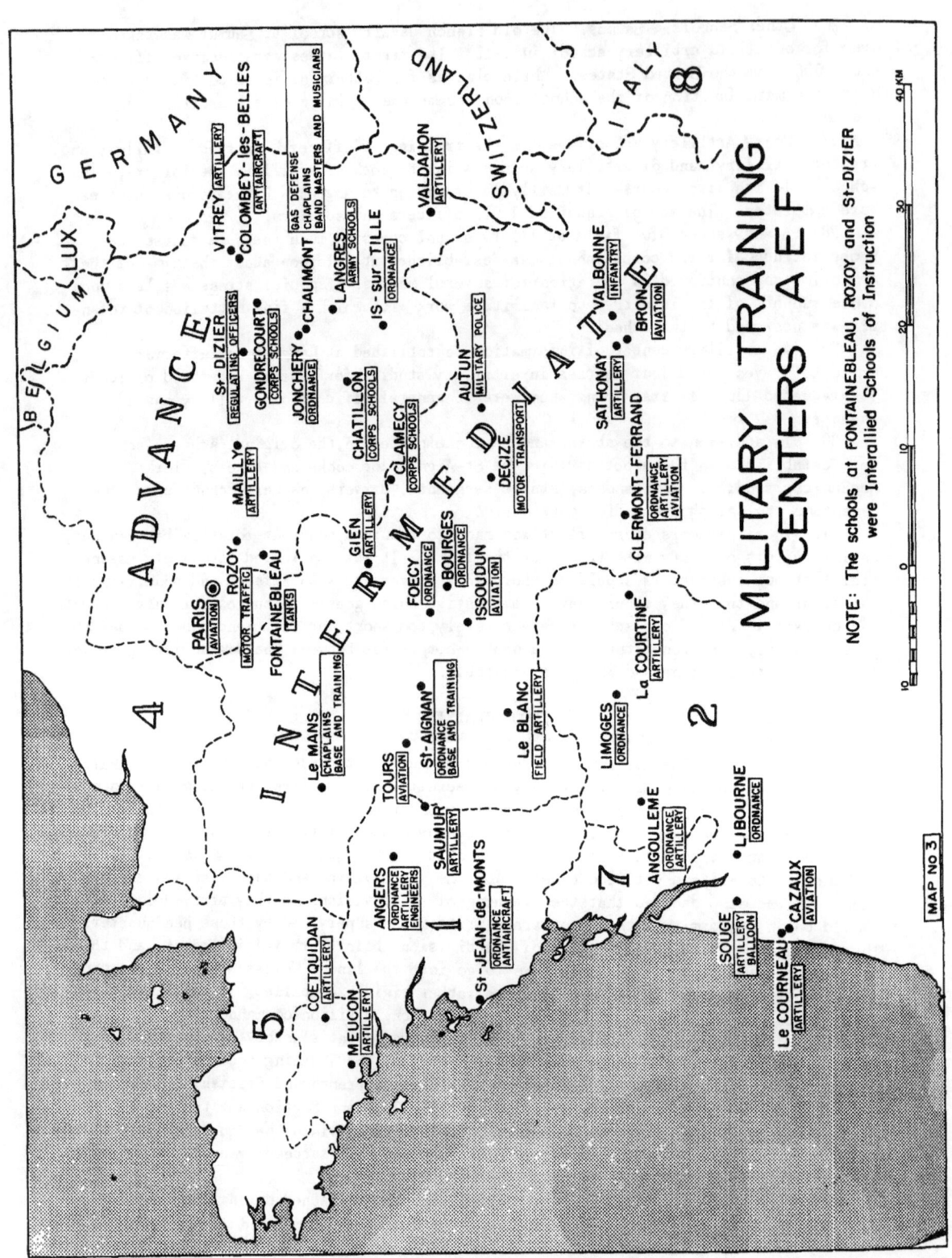

two French battalions were attached to each American division for demonstration purposes.

34. In the fall of 1917, it seemed that divisions could be allotted a training period of about three months after arrival in France. Early programs were accordingly for that period. Short as was the period covered by these programs, it was soon found that circumstances invariably prevented their being carried out as drawn. Early in 1918, consequently, the Section began to prepare simply a short four weeks' program for the first phase of the training, leaving the programs for later phases to depend upon what the enemy situation afterwards permitted.

35. The basic idea of three months' training was, however, retained. The attempt was always made to get four or more weeks of preliminary training for small units, to fit the troops to go in by battalion with French units for a second period of three or four weeks in a quiet defensive sector where there would still, however, be enough happening to harden and accustom them to all sorts of fire and make veterans of the individuals. Starting with the early programs for 1918, during the first training period, terrain exercises in communication and connection were weekly given the regimental, brigade, and division commanders and their staffs to accustom them to functioning together under assumed conditions, which were made to resemble as closely as possible the incidents likely to be met when against the enemy. During the second period our higher commanders and staffs would be working with the corresponding French headquarters as observers and students. The third and final period then would come with the withdrawal of the division to a training area behind the line where another four weeks of training, chiefly for the higher units in the attack, was to take place. This constituted the very modest scheme adopted for the training of our divisions in France. But even this it was not always found practicable to give them. During the emergency of last May, June, and July several divisions, usually selected from those which seem to have made the greatest progress in the United States, had to be put into quiet sectors with considerably less than the preliminary four weeks of training, and in only a few cases did any division get a full four weeks in the last period. The time actually obtained for this last period usually ran from six days to two or three weeks.

36. Field Artillery Camps: While highly desirable to train our complete divisions at one place in order to accustom the arms to work together, it was found impracticable to put the artillery through its first phase with the remainder of the division. To secure suitable firing grounds, to take advantage of existing French installations, and to facilitate equipping with French materiel, the artillery brigades upon arrival were sent to camps in the interior of France. There they received their first phase training, usually of about six weeks, under their proper officers but assisted by a corps of competent instructors. The brigade then joined its division in the line during the second phase, unless as frequently happened, the enemy situation compelled brigades to be used with infantry of other divisions.

37. These camps afforded the only practical solution of the problem of equipping and training rapidly a considerable number of artillery brigades. During the summer of 1918, as many as sixteen brigades were under training at one time at various points in France.

38. Work was confined almost wholly to technical training. The size and location of the camps were necessarily based on the terrain available for firing. The French authorities were generous in their allotment of terrain for this purpose, but the sites available were isolated with respect to the general sphere of American activity.

39. The system of a standardized camp organization with a selected staff of instructors at each camp insured rapid progress along predetermined lines. Supervision of the brigades under training was relatively simply, as the instructors made frequent reports. The issue and upkeep of equipment was facilitated. Supply and administrative facilities were permanent and occupied very little of the time of brigades under

training. Firing facilities were well organized, and ready for instant use by incoming units.

40. The tendency of the system was, however, to relieve the brigade commander and his officers from the task and responsibility of instructing their men. The fact that the instructors were placed at the disposition of the brigade commander could not alter the fact that officers of the brigade actually and of necessity attended classes conducted by the instructors. It was obviously impossible for the officers to be the real instructors of their men in subjects in which they themselves were being schooled. But the successive instruction first of the officers and then of the organizations by these officers was not practicable under the conditions. The system, though faulty in principle, actually gave very gratifying results.

41. The system separated the artillery from its division and from supervision by the division commander. Contact with the infantry was, for the time being, lost. In fact, in several divisions, the division, less the artillery, and the artillery each saw considerable fighting, but were never together prior to the Armistice. This condition was partly due however to the fact that the infantry of a division was sometimes relieved from the line while the artillery supporting it at the time was left in place.

42. Another incident of the intensive instruction in artillery subjects of both officers and men was a tendency to neglect discipline and kindred phases, as well as mounted instruction and field service. These matters were susceptible of correction, however, by supervision and suitable instructions.

43. Heavy Artillery: The establishment of organization and training centers for heavy artillery was authorized on March 12, 1918. The first four numbered centers were devoted to the units of the heavy tractor guns and howitzers, two to each type. Organization and Training Center No. 5 was devoted to the training of truck and tractor drivers; ammunition trains, etc. Organization and Training Center No. 6 was for the Railway Artillery Reserve.

44. In addition to the organized American centers of instruction and training, full use was made of existing French and British plants. Officers were sent to British motor transport schools at St-Omer; to French Railway School for Artillery for instruction in standard and 60-cm. railway methods; to the French Trench Artillery Center of Instruction at Bar-sur-Seine; and to the front for short periods of observation.

45. Coordination with United States: From time to time, cables were forwarded the War Department, suggesting methods and doctrine, reporting deficiencies in arriving divisions and recommending measures for correction.

46. To economize in time of training after arrival in France, the War Department was requested in the fall of 1917 to send ahead of each division a staff officer familiar with training in the United States to report with previous schedules to G-5 at these headquarters. The training program for the first phase in France was framed to supplement and complete what had been done in the United States.

47. Arrangements were also made with the War Department by which each division should cause approximately one-third of its officers and noncommissioned officers to precede it to France long enough to go through one of the corps schools before the arrival of the division. These officers were then able to meet their division and give it the last thing in the development of methods and tactics on this side.

48. Divisions with British: With the coming of the great German offensive in March of last year the transportation of our troops was speeded up to the limit of available shipping. The tactical situation made it expedient to send the divisions arriving in British bottoms to train with the British. Ten divisions (less their artillery) which reached France in May and June were placed in the British Sector and were so trained. Programs for their training were written by these headquarters (G-5) after consultation with the training section at the British G.H.Q. Programs and methods of training were much the same as in French areas, except that assistants for

these divisions were British officers and men instead of French. Periods were divided into three phases: A preliminary one of four to six weeks in a training area re-equipping and training higher units; followed by a tour in the line by battalion in in British units, and finally a short period for smartening up and training higher units. But here as elsewhere the German interfered and compelled the shortening of the last period in most cases and the first period for half of the divisions.

49. Difficulties: With American divisions scattered from Switzerland to the Channel, G-5 spent a busy summer in 1918. To illustrate its difficulties, a memorandum for the Chief of Staff, dated July 4, 1918, is quoted below:

GENERAL HEADQUARTERS

AMERICAN EXPEDITIONARY FORCES

France, July 4, 1918.

MEMORANDUM FOR THE CHIEF OF STAFF.

SUBJECT: Training.

1. Secret memoranda of the French G. H. Q., dated May 1 and June 19, make it clear to the French commanders to whom these are addressed that they must control the instruction of American regiments training with French divisions and impregnate the American units with French methods and doctrine. That such was the understanding of the French officers has long before this been evident.

2. In view of these memoranda, I desire to point out the present unsatisfactory situation so far as training is concerned. American units are scattered from the North Sea to Switzerland. Proper inspection and coordination of their training from these headquarters is, therefore, extraordinarily difficult. Some are tactically under the French and some under the British. Many are closely affiliated with decimated French and British divisions.

3. The offensive spirit of the French and British armies has largely disappeared as a result of their severe losses. Close association with beaten forces lowers the morale of the best troops. Our young officers and men are prone to take the tone and tactics of those with whom they are associated, and whatever they are now learning what is false or unsuited for us will be hard to eradicate later.

4. In many respects, the tactics and technique of our Allies are not suited to American characteristics or the American mission in this war. The French do not like the rifle, do not know how to use it, and their infantry is consequently too entirely dependent upon a powerful artillery support. Their infantry lacks aggressiveness and discipline. The British infantry lacks initiative and resource. The junior officers of both allied services, with whom our junior officers are most closely associated, are not professional soldiers, know little of the general characteristics of war, and their experience is almost entirely limited to the special phases of war in the trenches. And judging from the memorandum of May 1 (page 9, Operations in Open Country), even the high command has ceased to think of a great decisive offensive. Notwithstanding all of the efforts made to prevent such, the many French and British instructors scattered among our divisions have spread French or British doctrine, or a combination of both, through our Service.

5. Neither the French nor the British believe in our ability to train men or in the value of the methods adopted by us. Both forget that in dealing with our

officers and men they are dealing with men of different characteristics from those of their own people, and that methods which produce excellent results with the French or British officer or soldier may not be the best for the American. Distrusting our methods as they do, both French and British find many means of blocking our wishes and instructions. What we build up, they to a certain extent pull down. There is consequently much friction, much lost motion, and much valuable time wasted.

6. The tutelage of the French and British has hindered the development of responsibility and self-reliance upon the part of our officers of all grades. All of our commanders from the division down have constantly at their elbows an Englishman or a Frenchman who, when any difficulty arises, immediately offers a solution. A great fraction of our officers have consequently permitted themselves to lean very largely upon their tutors with a resultant serious loss in initiative and the sense of responsibility. The assistance of our Allies has become not an asset but a serious handicap in the training of our troops.

7. Berlin cannot be taken by the French or the British armies or by both of them. It can only be taken by a thoroughly trained, entirely homogeneous American army, in which the sense of initiative and self-reliance upon the part of all officers and men has been developed to the very highest degree. An American army can not be made by Frenchmen or Englishmen.

8. It is appreciated that many other factors besides training must guide in the disposition of American units. But it is desired plainly to point out that the present dispersion of American divisions among foreign organizations and under foreign commands renders supervision, inspection and training after American standards almost impossible. The training of a homogeneous American army, by which alone is a decisive victory possible, can best be attained by concentrating all of our troops on an American sector, including a suitable training zone behind the front, in which all control is vested in American authority, with no French or British instructors at schools or with divisions, and with all missions confined to the duty of liaison.

9. I strongly recommend that the earliest practicable opportunity be taken to secure our emancipation from Allied supervision.

H. B. FISKE,
Colonel, General Staff,
A. C. of S., G-5.

50. The time came when we had a front of our own, and when the correctness of American doctrine and methods received somewhat general recognition.

51. Doctrine: The fundamental doctrine always insisted upon can probably best be indicated by a few quotations from the statement of principles introducing all training programs, and extracts from certain cablegrams to the United States:

THE GENERAL PRINCIPLES GOVERNING THE TRAINING OF UNITS OF THE

AMERICAN EXPEDITIONARY FORCES

1. The general principles governing the training of troops of the American Expeditionary Forces will be announced from these Headquarters. Strict compliance with these principles will be exacted and nothing contrary thereto will be taught. Among these principles are the following:

(a) The methods to be employed must remain or become distinctly our own.
(b) All instructions must contemplate the assumption of a vigorous offensive.

This purpose will be emphasized in every phase of training until it becomes a settled habit of thought.

(c) The general principles governing combat remain unchanged in their essence. This was has developed special features which involve special phases of training, but the fundamental ideas enunciated in our Drill Regulations, Small Arms Firing Manual, Field Service Regulations and other service manuals remain the guide for both officers and soldiers and constitute the standard by which their efficiency is to be measured, except as modified in detail by instructions from these headquarters.

(d) The rifle and the bayonet are the principal weapons of the Infantry soldier. He will be trained to a high degree of skill as a marksman both on the target range and in field firing. An aggressive spirit must be developed until the soldier feels himself, as a bayonet fighter, invincible in battle.

(e) All officers and soldiers should realize that at no time in our history has discipline been so important; therefore, discipline of the highest order must be exacted at all times. The standards for the American army will be those of West Point. The rigid attention, upright bearing, attention to detail, uncomplaining obedience to instructions required of the cadet will be required of every officer and soldier of our armies in France. Failure to attain such discipline will be treated as lack of capacity on the part of a commander to create in the subordinate that intensity of purpose and willing acceptance of hardships which are necessary to success in battle.

[Cable P-85-S to AGWAR.] *August 8, 1917.*

* * * * * *

Paragraph 3. Study here shows value and desirability of retaining our existing small arms target practice course. In view of great difficulty in securing ranges in France due to density of the population and cultivation recommend as far as practicable the complete course be given in United States before troops embark. Special emphasis should be placed on rapid fire. *PERSHING.*

[Cable P-178-S to AGWAR.] *September 24, 1917.*

Paragraph 1. Referring paragraph 3 my number 85, longer experience conditions in France confirms my opinion highly important infantry soldier should be excellent shot. Thorough instruction and range practice as prescribed our small arms firing manual very necessary. Allies now fully realize their deficiency in rifle training. Difficult secure areas for target ranges in France even now when crops off ground. Much greater difficulty soon when plowing begins. After ground secured in France considerable time required for troops to construct ranges and improvise target material. In theatre active operations this time should be available for intensive training, new weapons and formations. Therefore strongly renew my previous recommendation that all troops be given complete course rifle practice as prescribed our Firing Manual before leaving United States. Specialties of trench warfare instruction at home should not be allowed to interfere with rifle practice nor with intensive preliminary training in our schools of soldier, company and battalion. *PERSHING.*

* * * * * *

October 20, 1917.

Paragraph 16. . . . Recommend that instruction of divisions in United States be conducted with a view to developing the soldier physically and in knowledge of sanitation, inculcating high standards of discipline, producing superior marksmanship both on the range and in field firing exercises in large bodies. Close adherence is urged to the central idea that the essential principles of war have not changed; that the rifle and the bayonet remain the supreme weapons of the infantry soldier and that the ultimate success of the Army depends upon their proper use in open warfare. To this end it is recommended that intensive training in all the phases of open warfare be accepted as the principal mission of divisions before embarkation, trench warfare and the use of the special arms being taught in connection with the assumption of the offensive from an intrenched position. If divisions arrive trained to these standards the completion of their training in the methods of trench warfare may be accepted as the mission of the training section at these headquarters. . . . *PERSHING.*

[Cable P-952-S to AGWAR.]

Paragraph 1. . . . Subparagraph A. With reference to paragraph 16 my 228, paragraph 4 my 348, and paragraph 1 my 408, again strongly urge absolute necessity of making open warfare prime mission training in United States and that training in United States for trench warfare and for specialties for use in trench warfare be kept distinctly in subordinate place.

Subparagraph B. Training for trench warfare relatively short process best completed in France in atmosphere of front and with instructors who are familiar latest developments. While trench warfare somewhat complicated so far as work of staffs is concerned, it makes relatively small demands upon initiative and resource of subordinate commanders and troops. Incidents trench warfare, both in attack and defense, largely foreseen and provided for, so trench warfare assumes character carefully rehearsed routine.

Subparagraph C. Open warfare on other hand demands initiative, resource, and decision upon part of all commanders from highest to lowest, and requires that all organizations be made into highly developed flexible teams capable rapid manoeuvering to meet swift changes in situation.

Subparagraph D. Construction efficient divisions for trench warfare therefore relatively short process. On other hand sufficient training to make handy divisions for open warfare matter considerable time. Areas lacking in France for extensive manoeuvering and time will not be available after arrival in France. Moreover greater part special weapons for trench warfare issued troops after arrival France.

Subparagraph E. During this war successful operations across trenches have again and again been nullified because training in open warfare had not been sufficient to give officers and men resource and initiative required for exploitation success.

Subparagraph F. Great battle now raging makes certain that too much trench warfare militates against successful conduct great operations. Morale troops long accustomed duty in trenches lowered thereby. When driven into open men have feeling nakedness and helplessness. Current great battle also emphasizes extraordinary value highly trained riflemen and machine gunners.

* * * * * *

PERSHING.

52. A constant demand for the offensive and for training in open warfare will be noted. There never was any question in the mind of these headquarters that the German lines could be broken by American troops. With this idea of the offensive as the only possible role to fit the American characteristics and mission in the war went also the idea of an aggressive self-reliant infantry as the basis of all organization. That idea will be found running through the Notes on Recent Operations prepared by this Section after each offensive of 1918, Memorandum for Corps and Division Commanders dated August 5, 1918, and Combat Instructions dated September 5, 1918. Only with troops imbued with this offensive spirit could decisive results be obtained, and the United States did not enter this war for anything less than a decision.

53. It will be noted also that a great deal has been said about the rifle and its value. Some Americans think the rifle is obsolete. But the facts are American rifles, and American rifles almost alone, saved Paris and prevented a decisive German victory, and American rifles when used in later attacks proved their superiority over other weapons on the field.

54. Inspections: All schools were as a rule directly under this Section. Visits and inspections were of constant occurrence. Tactical inspections of troops likewise were the function of this Section and were constantly and systematically made. In theory, what the Section tried to do was not to disturb any one in his work but to join the troops and simply observe. Deficiencies were corrected as far as possible by suggestion and instruction, only when absolutely necessary to correct some considerable failure were orders issued. The policy, therefore, was not simply to issue paper programs of training, but to follow such up and make certain that there was a reasonable degree of compliance.

55. Observation of Operations: It was plain that the Section would be utterly unable to train troops unless it had a clear understanding of conditions at the front. For this reason during the quiet periods visits to our trenches were frequent from the beginning. And after American troops began to attack, this Section habitually had at least one member with each first line division. These having no responsibility or duty other than to observe, were in an extraordinarily fine position for cool judgment as to what was happening and why. After each phase of our operations, defects were commented upon in Notes on Recent Operations, of which four were promptly published.

AFTER THE ARMISTICE

56. Problem: With the Armistice a new and serious problem was presented. Everybody, of course, wanted to go home immediately. For almost all concerned that, however, was a physical impossibility. Many changes were necessary in the personnel of commands and staffs, and, in replacing heavy casualties, organizations had to assimilate many thousands of new men. The enemy situation was not clear. For possible use against the enemy, for the national prestige, and to give the words of the Government of the United States an adequate material backing in the peace conferences, it was essential that in the most rapid possible manner these replacements in higher commands, staffs, officers, and men should be trained and our three armies converted into highly efficient teams. A great deal of work of a military kind must therefore be done just at a time when most men wanted to forget all about soldiering and think only of going home. Moreover winter was coming on with its prospect of nearly continuous bad weather.

57. Rather strenuous programs for the first months were ordered and their execution compelled by suitable inspections. As fast as divisions rounded into form and the enemy situation rendered their use less likely, the programs and instructions from these headquarters made less and less demands upon the troops and more attention was given to the amusement, athletic, and educational features.

58. Target Practice: With all of the divisions in training an excellent opportunity was afforded at this time to carry through a systematic course of instruction in the rifle and the pistol. The Macnab system was used. Col. Macnab joined the section to supervise the work. He first trained his instructors on the great ranges at Le Mans (totalling 775 rifle targets) and then sent them at the rate of one or more to a regiment to transmit their knowledge to the troops. Interest was general, scores were very high. A great mass of men who not only know how to shoot but, more important, how to teach others to shoot are consequently being turned back to civil life, where their presence will for many years be of incalculable benefit towards national defense.

59. Musketry: In natural sequence after target practice comes combat firing under conditions as nearly similar to battle as they can be made. Target practice teaches individuals to fire at known distances. The instruction in musketry teaches individuals how to group their fire at the will of their leader so as to get the greatest benefit from their team play. A thorough course in musketry was carried through in all divisions in accordance with bulletins written in this Section by Col. Fulmer.

60. Competitions: Beginning the 5th of May, a highly successful rifle, pistol, automatic rifle, machine gun, and platoon musketry competition was conducted at the Nemours range near Le Mans. The extensive ranges were in splendid shape, not only for known distance individual firing but with elaborate installations for the musketry and machine gun problems. Great interest was manifested. 1,179 officers and men competed in the rifle, 783 in the pistol, 41 in the automatic rifle, 11 platoons in the musketry, and 5 platoons in the machine gun competition. An International Competition between our own team and the teams of our Allies began on June 23. Teams and individuals participated from the United States, France, Canada, Italy, Roumania, Belgium, Portugal, and Greece. The American team won first place in the Rifle and the Pistol team matches, and Americans held the first eighteen places in the individual rifle match and the first eight places in the individual pistol match. Both in this competition and in the Inter-Allied games in Paris every effort has been made to convince all participants that the Americans were holding fair play and equal opportunity to all as far more important than winning events. It is believed that effort was successful.

61. Education: Early in 1918, the Y. M. C. A. suggested the advisability of preparing some sort of educational scheme for the necessarily long period of repatriation and demobilization which would come at the end of the war. Before the Armistice the beginning of divisional schools had been ordered, and the draft of a more comprehensive order was ready for publication as soon as the Armistice was accomplished. A rather extensive system of education was put into effect on January 1, with constant extension later in character and number of schools and in number of students. In brief, the schools comprised post schools, with primary and grammar courses, divisional educational centers where high school subjects and vocational training were given, a great group of more advanced vocational schools at the shops centering at Decize, the American University at Beaune with college courses, and an agricultural annex at Allerey nearby, university courses at a number of French and British universities, and an American art school at Paris. Exclusive of short lecture courses, roughly 200,000 men were students in these various schools. Of them, 2,000 were at British Universities; 6,000 at French; 350 at the Paris art center; 4,800 in the Decize vocational group; 6,000 at Beaune, and 3,000 at Allerey. The remainder attended the post and divisional schools, some of the latter of which themselves attained the proportions of high educational centers.

62. Athletics: Nothing appeals to the American and retains his interest like all forms of athletics. Nothing, therefore, could be done that would so help our average man to tide over the long wait to go home as well as a great scheme of athletic contests for him to participate in or to observe. Great benefit of course also accrues to the physique of all concerned.

63. To get the utmost possible value from athletics every effort has been made to secure the maximum number of players in all events. These were held a series of eliminations in all contests; boxing, wrestling, football, baseball, basketball, track events, the pentathlon, tennis, golf, polo, etc., etc., which culminated finally for the Army in the great championship games in Paris in June. These were followed by Inter-Allied games at the invitation of the Commander-in-Chief which, in number of participants and quality of entry, probably surpass any of the past Olympic contests.

MISCELLANEOUS

64. Publications: The Section is charged with the publication of training manuals and translations. The translating department was always a busy one. In the beginning, since American troops seemed most likely to serve in the French front, the basic manuals for our training were adaptations of translations from the French. This policy was believed best until our infantry had attacked sufficiently to permit rewriting our Infantry Drill Regulations in the light of our own experiences. French translations were modified for publication to conform to American methods and temperament and the fundamental idea of an offensive, self-reliant infantry whose chief weapon was the rifle. In 1918, the Infantry Drill Regulations were revised by this Section. The first part dealing with the offensive was published in December, 1918. The second part containing the defensive, ceremonies, etc., was published in June, 1919. Studies have also been prepared on military policy for the United States, on organization, on military education. Staff manuals, small arms firing regulations, pamphlets on musketry, and the separate manuals for the special weapons have been prepared and published.

65. Composition Section: The Section as at first organized contained two officers in a subsection for infantry matters, two for artillery, three (including a French officer) for translating and distributing manuals and pamphlets, one for engineer matters, and a section adjutant.

66. As the work of the Section expanded additional officers were assigned to the various subsections mentioned above and to take charge of the work of the several special arms and services.

67. [This paragraph lists the organization of the G-5 in the fall of 1918 and in the spring of 1919 showing the titles of the various subdivisions and the rank and numbers of the officers therein.]

* * * * * *

CONCLUSION

68. This sketch of the activities of G-5, though necessarily brief, would be incomplete without a tribute to the splendid quality of the officer and soldier material composing our Forces. Without the keen intelligence, the physical endurance, the willingness, and enthusiasm displayed in the training area as well as on the battlefield, the successful results so quickly obtained would have been impossible.

69. This view finds striking support in the estimate of American troops by a keenly observant and experienced enemy. A German general staff officer of high rank has stated that the attack of the American troops west of the Meuse (Meuse-Argonne), delivered with an impetuosity which the German Staff had not believed possible after so short a period of training, had gained the decision for the Allies and brought about the ruin of the German Army.

70. Unquestionably our infantry was strongly impregnated with the offensive spirit which constitutes the great essential towards successful war. Before the Armistice, many of the veteran divisions had acquired not only this spirit but most of the other

elements of a fine discipline. All were tending toward such. But for the maintenance of a proper perspective, it must be remembered that to the end most of our divisions were lacking in skill. Given plenty of time for preparation, they were capable of powerful blows; but their blows were delivered with an awkwardness and lack of resource that made them unduly costly and rendered it impracticable to reap the full fruits of victory. In a highly trained division, commanders of all grades operate with a definite plan of maneuver calculated to concentrate the efforts of their units upon the spot where the enemy is weakest, where therefore the most damage will be done at the lowest cost; skulking is practically eliminated; the infantry is so skillful in the use of fire and natural cover to further its advance that ground is gained with a minimum of casualties; the battalion with all of its accompanying weapons works smoothly as a team in which all parts mutually assist all others; the artillery through long practice gives the infantry close and continuous support; and unforeseen situations are met by prompt, energetic and reasonable action. This describes no impossible standard, simply the one which must be attained unless success in war is only to be gained at extravagant cost. Towards this standard our divisions were gradually working, but few had actually attained it. The truth must be recognized that this war has not reversed all the lessons of the past by proving that tacticians can be made in a few months training or service at the front; or that handy, flexible, resourceful divisions can be made by a few maneuvers or by a few months' association of their elements. To conclude that such has been proven would be to go far indeed from the truth and would be fatal to the adoption of a logical military policy for the future of our country.

71. List of appendices follows. Only the original of this report is forwarded. A duplicate with all appendices is filed in the records of G-5.

H. B. FISKE,
Brigadier General, General Staff,
Assistant Chief of Staff G-5.

C-in-C Rept. File: Fldr. 246: Report

Divisional Training

[Extract]

POLICY AND DOCTRINE

1. The general outlines of the policy adopted by the American Expeditionary Forces were contained in a report on training which was approved and forwarded to the War Department on July 11, 1917, the following being pertinent extracts from that report.

AMERICAN EXPEDITIONARY FORCES,

Paris, July 11, 1917.

From: The Commander-in-Chief

To: The Adjutant General of the Army,
          Washington, D. C.

Subject: Training

    1. Enclosed herewith is a memorandum on training, discussed and agreed to at a conference between officers of these headquarters and the officers of the mission headed by Colonel Chauncey B. Baker.

    2. The question of training is necessarily covered in outline only but it is essential that we adopt the broad principles of this work at once and it is therefore recommended that the principles contained in the accompanying memorandum be adopted without delay.

    3. Paragraphs 1 and 6 of the memorandum are of special importance.

JOHN J. PERSHING,
Major General, U. S. A.

TRAINING

The subject of training troops in France and in the United States prior to departure for France received consideration and approval as indicated:

    1. PLACE OF INSTRUCTION: The question of which troops should be instructed in France and which in the United States cannot be definitely settled until the War Department establishes a roster of troops which will show the approximate dates of departure for France.

    It is evident that the first troops to arrive must receive their training in France. However, it is also clear that a great many troops will not reach France for nearly a year. The training of these later troops should not be delayed until their arrival in France. Much can be accomplished in the United States if efficient instructions and advisors are available.

    It is therefore recommended that an approximate roster of departures be established and the place with the extent of training to be given thereat be arranged accordingly.

* * * * * *

    3. FRENCH AND BRITISH ADVISORS: The committee is of the opinion that in physical training, close order drills and disciplinary instruction, and musketry, the systems in vogue in the army of the United States are entirely adequate. It is believed that in musketry the use of panoramic landscape sketches in target designation should be put into more general use. Commanders in charge of instruction should not be limited in their expenditure of ammunition. In one exercise given at Chalons in the presence of 4 American officers, 40,000 rounds of small arms ammunition were used. Attention is invited to the use that may be made of short ranges, under 100 yards, for much of the musketry instruction to be given.

    In physical training, especially by the French, it has been generally observed that much use is made of obstacle courses over which the men are advanced at all gaits, loaded with various combinations of equipment for long distances, over all sorts of such obstacles as would be encountered on the battlefield.

    The committee recommends the drafting of regulations to provide for the utilization elsewhere of those men who in the course of their physical training demonstrate their unfitness for active military service.

The committee desires to call attention to the vital importance of establishing in the United States at the earliest possible time, schools for the instruction of specialists in all the special branches of instruction necessary for the infantryman. Since we have practically no qualified instructors, these schools must at first be for the training of instructors who in turn must train others in schools within the organizations, until a fair amount of the training has been disseminated among the troops. To establish these first schools in the United States with the least practicable delay, the board recommends the utilization of French and British officers and noncommissioned officers as advisors to our own officers, who will be the commandants and instructors in these schools. It is recommended as a minimum that one officer and one noncommissioned officer in each special subject be sent to each of our 16 divisional training areas.

* * * * * *

4. ARTILLERY TRAINING: The question of artillery training was discussed in its outline, the following points being considered:

(a) At Home: Schools should be established for the training of instructors in the various special lines of work such as, light artillery; heavy artillery; aerial observation; signal service; trench mortars; antiaviation work; etc., etc. As soon as instructors have thus been trained they should be utilized as such with the troops. A central coordinating and school inspection service was also suggested.

(b) In France: It was stated that artillery organizations arriving in France in the near future would necessarily be lacking in instruction in the material which they are to receive and in the various special lines of artillery work developed during the present war. To meet this condition it was stated that the following general plan had been developed but that the plan had not yet been worked out in all its details and submitted in complete form to the Commander-in-Chief, American Expeditionary Forces, for his approval. As the successive brigades of field artillery arrive they will be sent to Valdahon where they will receive their new material and their horses and where they will take up their preliminary training. This training will include the familiarizing of officers and men with their new material, the conduct of fire utilizing forwarded observers and aerial observers, and in all the various special lines of work. It is intended that all specialists shall be trained in sufficient numbers to permit the transfer from each brigade to the next succeeding brigade a sufficient number of officers and men to be of real assistance in the instruction of the succeeding brigade. To aid in the instruction of the first few brigades the French have already placed or made arrangements to place at our disposal a considerable number of specialists in all lines. Balloons and aeroplanes will also be placed at our disposal at Valdahon for the preliminary instruction of officers as aerial observers. The further instruction of aerial observers will be carried out in our own aviation centers to be established in France. After a short period at Valdahon 2 officers will be selected from each brigade and sent to the French front for training as artillery information officers. The general plan involves sending battalions for short tours at the front before sending the brigade to join its division for divisional training. Although it is intended to leave the brigades at Valdahon under the control of the division commander it will be necessary, on account of the fact that one brigade must replace another at Valdahon, for the Headquarters, American Expeditionary Forces, to exercise a certain coordinating influence.

It was also suggested that it was believed to be advisable to establish in France a central school for the training of officers promising to become battery commanders. It was stated that the French authorities had made a tentative offer of the facilities at Saumur for this purpose but that the question had not yet been thoroughly studied.

5. TRAINING OF STAFF OFFICERS: One of the features of this war is the great development of staff duty of various kinds, particularly in the operations and intelligence sections. With us a greater demand will be made upon the staff on account of the fact that we have to organize, train and equip armies before operations can begin. It is believed that the success of our operations depends to a great extent upon solving this problem and that the solution lies in sending to France without delay as many officers as practicable for staff training.

The French authorities have offered to open their staff schools and to permit our staff officers to serve on French staffs for training purposes. They believe that three months training of this nature will be sufficient for an officer who has already had some military experience.

It is therefore recommended that the officers selected for duty in the operations and intelligence sections of divisions and army corps be sent to France to receive staff training three months in advance of their units.

6. EXTRA RESERVE OFFICERS: It is recommended that after a limited number of officers have been trained and have had the experience of serving in the line in France, they be sent to the United States to assist in instructing troops.

A large number of extra officers will be needed as instructors for the schools to be established in France and to assist in the training of new units as they arrive in France. In addition, a number of extra officers will be needed to perform the duties of assistants in the corps and army staff operations and intelligence sections.

It is believed that the best method of meeting the conditions mentioned above is to select and send to France without delay extra reserve officers. It is estimated that the following officers will be needed for this purpose per division:

```
Operations Section . . . . .10) Includes officers for
Intelligence Section . . . .14) corps and army staffs.
Infantry . . . . . . . . . .96
Artillery. . . . . . . . . .40
Cavalry. . . . . . . . . . . 1
Engineers. . . . . . . . . .15
Signal . . . . . . . . . . .10
Medical. . . . . . . . . . .15
Quartermaster. . . . . . . . 5
Ordnance . . . . . . . . . . 2
         Total         208
```

The above number of officers should be sent for the division now in France as soon as the reserve officers' training camps have terminated.

2. As stated the first divisions to arrive necessarily had to receive their training in France. The time that would be required to prepare these divisions for combat could not be determined accurately in advance, as they were largely composed of recruits; also a number of the organizations and a considerable number of officers belonging to those divisions would have to be used in preparing the way and building up the organization necessary to handle the large number of troops that would arrive later.

3. The plan of training for divisions which had completed the basic elementary training in the United States contemplated a period of three months training. One month of this was to be for acclimatization and instruction in small units from battalion down; the second month to be spent by battalion with French units in a quiet defensive section where there would be enough activity however to continue the process

of hardening the officers and men and accustom them to all sorts of fire; the third month to be spent in a training area and to be devoted to correction of deficiencies noted in the second month and to training the higher units, including the complete division, especially in open warfare.

4. The fundamental doctrine approved by General Headquarters, A. E. F., was contained in a statement of general principles included in the training program issued for the 1st Division early in October 1917 and continued in the programs furnished all divisions that followed. [See Rept. A. C. of S., G-5, preceding.]

* * * * * *

5. These principles enunciated so early in the history of the American Expeditionary Forces have remained unchanged and have received a thorough test in the rapid march of events and the part played by American troops therein between May 28 and November 11, 1918. That the doctrine of training and combat approved by General Headquarters of the American Expeditionary Forces was thoroughly sound has been demonstrated by the work of American troops at CANTIGNY, in the operations around CHATEAU-THIERRY, at St-Mihiel, in the MEUSE-ARGONNE, on the St-QUENTIN Canal and the operations on the SCHELDT River in Belgium.

6. In view of the comparative density of the population in France and the fact that every piece of ground capable of being cultivated was necessary to produce supplies for the French people and for their army, it was important that the instruction of our men in individual rifle practice and the training of officers and men in musketry should be given as far as possible in the United States. Recommendations emphasizing the necessity for this training were cabled to the Adjutant General of the Army on August 8, 1917, and September 24, 1917. [See Rept. A. C. of S., G-5, preceding.]

* * * * * *

7. The statements * * * regarding the fundamental importance of the proper training of the infantry arm in rifle practice and musketry were reiterated from time to time in subsequent cables regarding training both of divisions and replacement troops, and the value of the proper training in the use of the rifle has been demonstrated in all the operations in which American troops participated.

8. Until we had developed our system of schools and were able to produce instructors in sufficient number and with the necessary experience in use of new weapons and methods, French and British officers of experience would be able to render valuable assistance to us both in France and in training in the United States. Both governments were exceedingly anxious to render us every assistance possible in this regard. As a result of our observations it was evident that each army excelled the other in the handling of certain weapons or in certain technical work so that advantage could be taken of the best in both by using officers and noncommissioned officers of both armies. Accordingly recommendations were made that French and British officers and noncommissioned officers be sent to the United States as advisors on training, as follows:

(a) For the central training committee in the War Department one officer for each arm of the service.

(b) For each division one officer and one noncommissioned officer for each of the following subjects:

From British Army: Machine guns, trench mortars, bayonet fencing, gas defense, sniping.

From French Army: Automatic rifle, bombing and rifle grenade, liaison, pioneer work.

(c) For artillery and other arms, the number to depend on number of schools established for training instructors.

9. The scheme of training adopted for divisions in France contemplated training during the second phase in quiet sectors of the line, with the assistance of French units until such time as it might be practicable to train with experienced units of our own forces.

10. The French War Department placed a number of officers and noncommissioned officers at our disposal as each division arrived, who were used in an advisory capacity within each division and for purposes of liaison with the French military authorities during the periods of training in the line and during operations. Similar assistance was rendered by Marshal Haig to the divisions trained in the British area and we are deeply indebted to those officers of both armies and to their superiors for the opportunities given to us to profit by their veteran experience.

11. The officers of both armies who were assigned to our divisions worked earnestly to aid us in every possible way and, while we have undoubtedly derived a large amount of benefit from their assistance which was made absolutely necessary by our unpreparedness, yet the net results were not of unmixed benefit. Fundamental differences in basic methods and ideas and differences in national characteristics mingled to make the task of the foreign advisor a difficult one; methods that produced desired results in French and British units were not always those best suited for Americans. The proper assimilation of the information received and its application to our own organization without diverging from our own doctrine was no easy problem especially for our large number of new officers. In a large number of organizations commanders of all grades depended too much on these foreign instructors thereby retarding the development of instructors of our own and with resultant loss of initiative and responsibility.

12. Coordination of training in the United States and France. In order that there might not be any waste of time or effort, to secure proper coordination of training and to insure that the training proposed to be given in France would be a proper supplement to that given in the United States, it was advisable to establish close relations between the training section at these headquarters and the personnel in charge of training in the War Department.

13. The proposals to effect this were contained in the report on training forwarded to the War Department on July 11, 1917, from which the following is quoted:

2. TRAINING COORDINATION: In order to secure coordination and uniformity in training and equipment of all troops, it seems advisable to establish close relations and connections between the troops in France and those being trained in the United States. Experience in the theatre of war will gradually develop new conditions and methods, and these will frequently change as the war continues. Then again, it is realized that many theories and principles have been and will be published which later experiences show to be erroneous. These errors can only be definitely disclosed by the troops associated with actual fighting and hardly by the forces being trained in the United States.

In view of the foregoing it is recommended that a central training and equipment committee, consisting of officers of all arms, be established at the War Department, for the purpose of recommending the policies and regulations for the training and equipment of the troops in the United States. This committee should be authorized to maintain close relations with the headquarters of the American Expeditionary Forces in order to secure accounts and up to date information, etc.

14. Subsequently a series of cablegrams marked training was initiated in the first of which there was submitted for War Department approval a statement as to the mission of the training staff in Washington and the training section in France. This division was based on the fact that training areas in the United States were comparatively open,

maneuver grounds extensive and the facilities for open warfare training excellent. Special trench weapons would not be available for the home divisions for sometime and the intricate trench systems which characterize the training areas in France would not exist in the United States. For these reasons, it was felt that training in open warfare was the natural mission of troops in the United States, the completion of their training in trench warfare the natural mission of the troops in France. Provision was also made to have a staff officer familiar with status of training of each division precede it to France and report at these headquarters with copies of training schedules so that a proper training program could be prepared based on progress of the division in the United States and be ready for prompt issue to division on its arrival. This cable and the War Department cable approving in general the recommendations made were as follows:

    No. 228-S
    October 19

    AGWAR Washington

        Paragraph 16. For Chief of Staff Training Reference paragraph 3 my 92 August 10, paragraph 4 my 147 September 8 and paragraph 10 your 266 first corps schools were established yesterday. Army General Staff College organized and ready to receive the 100 officers referred to in paragraph 9 your 195 September 19 for course of approximately four months. Officers of French and British General Staffs assistants at Staff College. Gas training an essential feature of instruction for trench warfare. Organization of army gas school in connection with training and experimental work of regiment of gas engineers deemed important and necessary. This school will be center of training for gas projection and in conjunction with army aeronautical school will conduct important experimental work in dropping gas from aeroplanes. The school will furnish valuable data to gas experts in the United States, will coordinate gas training here and unless specifically ordered to the contrary the army gas school will be established. Training of 1st, 2d, and 26th Divisions in progress under programs prepared by the training section. Work started in revision of portions of infantry drill, field service and field artillery drill regulations to meet special conditions of warfare. Results will be forwarded. Recommend that instruction of divisions in United States be conducted with a view to developing the soldier physically and in knowledge of sanitation, inclucating high standards of discipline, producing superior marksmanship both on the range and in field firing exercises in large bodies. Close adherence is urged to the central idea that the essential principles of war have not changed, that the rifle and the bayonet remain the supreme weapons of the infantry soldier and that the ultimate success of the army depends upon their proper use in open warfare. To this end it is recommended that intensive training in all the phases of open warfare be accepted as the principal mission of divisions before embarkation, trench warfare and the use of the special arms being taught in connection with the assumption of the offensive from an intrenched position. If divisions arrive trained to these standards the completion of their training in the methods of trench warfare may be accepted as the mission of the training section at these headquarters. In order that there may be continuity of work the advance agents of each division should report at these headquarters with copy of program of training and statement of results accomplished. This is the first of a series of cablegrams headed training which will be sent in order to coordinate the work here with that in the United States. Written report follows.

                                                               PERSHING.

No. 352-R
November 2, 1917

PERSHING
AMEXFORCES

* * * * * *

Paragraph 6. Your recommendations as to instructions of divisions here are approved and being carried out with the exception that it is believed advisable to impart some specialty training for the purpose of sustaining interest of troops. See pamphlet infantry training Adjutant General's Office Document 656. All instruction in specialty will be carefully supervised along the lines indicated by French and English advisors.

* * * * * *

15. As a further means of coordination and to enable each division to take up its training on arrival in France with the assistance of instructors belonging to the division who had had the advantage of instruction in the most recent methods and developments, recommendation was made to the War Department that a number of officers and enlisted men be sent a sufficient length of time in advance to enable them to complete a course of instruction in one of our schools by the time the division arrived. The War Department approved this recommendation and an advance school detachment consisting of 314 officers and enlisted men of all arms preceded each division to France. Cables covering this recommendation and others referring to the coordination of training in the United States and France follow:

No. 298-S   *France, November 20, 1917.*

AGWAR Washington

Paragraph 3. For the Chief of Staff. Training Cablegram No. 3.

Subparagraph C. The fundamental principles governing conduct of fire for field artillery remain essentially unchanged. Officers properly trained in conduct of fire our own arm quickly acquire proficiency in use French material. Field Artillery officers arriving in France are frequently ignorant volume 3 field artillery regulations. Recommend all be thoroughly trained in conduct of fire and that all be required to know volume 3 thoroughly as part of training in United States. Report from field artillery training camps forwarded today by mail.

* * * * * *

PERSHING.

Headquarters, A. E. F.
No. 348-S   *France, December 8, 1917.*

December 7

AGWAR
Washington.   Via Anglo

* * * * * *

Paragraph 4. For Chief of Staff. Training cable number 4.

Subparagraph A. Referring paragraph 6 your cablegram 352, War Dept. document 656 had been received and examined. In my opinion this pamphlet is not in harmony with recommendations contained in paragraph 16 my cablegram 228 in regard to the training of divisions in United States. The first paragraph of War Department document announces that in all the military training of a division, under existing conditions, training for trench warfare is of paramount importance. The program of training contained in this document is prepared accordingly and subordinates all instruction to training for trench warfare. My views in regard to the training of divisions were expressed in documents furnished visiting Major Generals and forwarded you Nov. 13, and in letter furnished General Scott on his departure for the United States. I invite attention to paragraph 16 my cablegram 228 and repeat my recommendations contained therein that intensive training in all the phases of open warfare be accepted as the principal mission of divisions before embarkation, trench warfare and the use of special arms being taught in connection with the assumption of the offensive from an entrenched position. It is urged that future programs of training for divisions in the United States be prepared accordingly.

PERSHING.

No. 338-S *Headquarters, A. E. F.,*
France, December 17, 1917.

ADJUTANT GENERAL, WASHINGTON

* * * * * *

Paragraph 2, For Chief of Staff. Training Cablegram Number 5. The I Corps schools are now prepared to train approximately 1000 officers and men in all branches of service. Arrangements under way for organizing the II Corps schools which will train approximately the same number. Heretofore officers and noncommissioned officers have been detached from each division upon arrival in France to receive instruction in corps schools and their places have been left vacant during training at schools or have been taken by officers of other divisions resulting in extensive changes in officer and noncommissioned officer personnel. It is highly desirable that this change in personnel be avoided and that training be expedited asmuch as possible. To secure this result about one-third of the officers and noncommissioned officers of each division should be sent to France in advance of their organizations by sufficient interval of time to permit them to complete course in corps schools and join their own divisions upon arrival and begin at once training of troops in latest development trench warfare. This personnel should be in France at least five days before date of beginning of course. Not practicable to permit students join after course begins. Each course lasts five weeks. Sessions corps schools commence on January 7, February 4, February 18, March 18, April 1, April 29. Should send from infantry regiment: To attend schools company platoon and section commandrs, from rifle companies four captains, 12 1st lieutenants, 8 2d lieutenants, and 12 sergeants; to attend trench mortar and 37-mm. school, from headquarters company 1 lieutenant and 4 sergeants; to attend signal school from headquarters company 1 lieutenant and two sergeants; to attend field officers school, 2 field officers from regiment. From machine-gun organizations, one-third the officers in each grade and one sergeant from each platoon. From each brigade divisional artillery, 59 officers as follows: Four field officers to attend field officers school, 10 officers for instruction wireless or telephone, 10 as aerial observers, 15 orienteurs, 20 instruction in firing; soldiers as follows: 30 instruction in material, 20, in wireless, 20 in telephone, 20 in observation and liaison. From sanitary train, one-third officers all grades. From engineer regiment 1 field officer to take field officers course, 3 captains and 2 lieutenants to take engineer company commanders course, 4 lieutenants and 6 sergeants for each pioneer and sappers courses. From field singal battalion, 3 junior officers and also the division signal officer. In connection with detail of signal corps officers your attention is invited to series of cablegrams on this subject of which paragraph 4 B our 340 is the last and still remains unanswered. Total number sent from United States to attend as students any one session corps school not exceed 600 officers and soldiers.

* * * * * *

PERSHING.

16. The necessity for proper supervision of training to be certain that it is being carried on along efficient lines, following sound doctrine and producing desired results was shown by the lack of proper instruction exhibited by troops that arrived here during the latter part of 1917, and the first months of 1918. To correct these deficiencies, in order that we might be able to count on organizations reaching France trained in the basic elementary principles of open warfare, individual target practice and musketry and that officers in command of all units would actually be required to take active part in the instruction, cables were forwarded to the War Department on December 22, 1917, and April 18, 1918, giving conditions as found and making recommendations:

No. 408-S
December 22
Headquarters, A. E. F.

ADJUTANT GENERAL, WASHINGTON   Via ANGLO

1. For Chief of Staff. Reference training of troops in states, deficiencies noted here indicate first great laxity on part of division and brigade commanders in requiring officers to learn their duties or to perform them efficiently; second almost total failure to give any instructions in principles of minor tactics and their practical application to war conditions. Officers from colonels down and including some general officers are found ignorant of the handling of units in open warfare including principles of reconnaissance, outposts, advance guards, solution of practical problems and formation of attack; third no training whatever has been given in musketey efficiency as distinguished from individual target practice on the range. Many officers of high rank are hopelessly ignorant of what this training consists of. Pershing.
  A. Division and brigade commanders must be brought to realize that their duties include something beside routine administration and they must be required to conduct the training of their units in the above particulars. All the higher officers must be held directly and personally responsible for the instruction of their commands and should be compelled by study and application to become competent to conduct and supervise personally the instruction of their officers in theoretical and practical work and should conduct exercises themselves until subordinates are competent to do it. It is not enough for division commanders merely to issue orders on these subjects but they must themselves be required to teach

them in every detail. Necessary supervision by inspectors or by officers of the War Department in charge of training should be ordered to prevent ignorant and incompetent officers in high places from retaining command. Pershing.

      B. Suggest that the importance of work in practical application of tactics and thorough training in musketry for all units be taken by General Morrison and that these subjects be presented to our troops in great detail by his office, also that all officers of whatever rank, including those in the regular army, be held up to a high standard of accomplishment. Many of our high regular officers do not know how to instruct men practically and they should either be compelled to learn or be removed. Pershing.

      C. I would recommend General Blatchford as assistant to General Morrison as Blatchford's experience in musketry should be invaluable. Too much importance cannot be placed upon this sort of training as exemplified in our school of musketry at Fort Sill, the elements of which should be thoroughly pounded into our infantry. Pershing.

PERSHING.

No. 952-S   *France, April 18, 1918.*

AWAR WASHINGTON

      1. For the Chief of Staff. Conditions found among troops recently arriving in France indicate insufficient attention being paid in United States to training in open warfare and relatively too much time being devoted to trench warfare. Pershing.
[See Rept. of A. C. of S. G-5, preceding for Subpar. A - F, incl., this cable]

* * * * * *

      When driven into open men have feeling nakedness and helplessness. Current great battle also emphasizes extraordinary value highly trained riflemen and machine gunners. Pershing.

      G. Recommend therefore following outline for training in United States; thorough instruction in marksmanship to include known distance firing for all men to 600 yards and in battle practice after methods school musketry. Production excellent close order drill to further high discipline. Thorough instruction both officers and men in open warfare. Small units should be thoroughly grounded in patrolling, in all forms of security, and in attack and defense of minor warfare. Problems for such should customarily be prepared by next higher commander. Pershing.

      H. In training field artillery following considered most important: Perfection of mounted instruction over difficult ground and at increased gaits, care of horses, accurate laying by frequent verification and computation, observation of fire with most stress on fundamentals and some advance and lateral observation, manipulation of sheaf, rapid preparation and conduct of fire without maps, rapid reconnaissance and occupation of positions under tactical situation, changes of position by echelon, ammunition resupply, telephone. Map laying and refinements of position warfare best taught in France and should be subordinated at home to points emphasized.   Pershing.

I. During training of small units commanders of divisions brigades and regiments should be engaged in a series of terrain exercises involving use brigades and divisions in open warfare. Director for such exercises should be carefully chosen for his competency and should freely criticize. Advisable frequently to conduct these terrain exercises with framework system of liaison or communication, including infantry and artillery aeroplanes, signal battalion, liaison groups of brigades and regiments. By painstaking use these means considerable progress will be made towards development of brigade and division teams before troops are trained to point where large manoeuvers are of value. Finally complete divisions should be worked out in a series of carefully thought out manoeuvers to accustom all parts and all arms to function together.   Pershing.

J. By means these exercises and manoeuvers determination should be obtained as to ability commanders exercise their functions. Prompt elimination of unfits should follow.   Pershing.

K. Suggest further for education higher commanders establish at suitable geographical points centers of instruction to which should be sent division and brigade commanders infantry and artillery for instruction after methods of Leavenworth, laying stress upon terrain exercises in command and communication or liaison similar those outlined in preceding paragraphs. By demonstration and practice these centers of instruction should familiarize artillery and infantry with best means for production highly developed teamwork these arms required in modern battle.   Pershing.

L. Recommend that production staffs be considered function staff college in France. Plant now in operation here working along best lines with assistance excellent instructors Allied services. Not wise establish another plant in United States since almost certain teachings two institutions would soon diverge.   Pershing.

M. Suggest further that matter of increasing responsibility and training sergeants be considered. Sergeants need habit command, schooling, and prestige to be able at once replace officer when down. Suggest among means schools be established for servants and sergeants be messed separately in organizations and their intercourse with other soldiers be minimized.   Pershing.

N. Major Requin of French Mission en route United States has memorandum which in general agrees my idea peoper coordination training between United States and France. Broadly France complete training for trench warfare and educate staffs; United States train for open warfare and production tactical commanders reducing training trench warfare to distinctly secondary place and attempting nothing in trench warfare beyond battalion in defense.   Pershing.

PERSHING.

17. Divisions were arriving in France which had received large consignments of recruits shortly before departure from their camps for ports of embarkation as late as the middle of April 1918. It was found also that large numbers of men had been taken from time to time from divisions scheduled for early overseas service for use in staff departments on account of special qualifications and for other causes. No doubt these conditions were unavoidable but it resulted in divisions composed of men of various degrees of training and necessarily hampered the development of the divisions into properly balanced fighting units. With the great increase in troop movements in May and

June these conditions were continued and measures were taken to segregate recently drafted men of insufficient training so they might be given special training and brought up to standard before being sent into line. Cables from and to the War Department on this subject with cable of July 18, 1918, submitting recommendations regarding training of new divisions to be organized follow:

No. 990-S
April 24, 1918

AGWAR WASHINGTON

    1. Have learned from division commanders and staff officers recently arrived from the United States that large numbers of recruits have been assigned to divisions designated for service in Europe. The same lack of training is found in replacements as already reported in previous cables. In view of the urgency of the situation here there is no time to drill raw recruits in France in elementary work. To send them into the trenches or into battle without requisite training would mean useless and unwarranted loss of life. Therefore urgently recommend that no men be sent over who have not had at least four months intensive training and who have not also had full and thorough instruction in target practice and that a limited number of divisions be broken up to accomplish this if necessary. Attention invited to original project which contemplated organization of 7th Division for training recruits.
    2. Reference target practice have been informed that none of our troops have had practice above 300 yards. Consider this very grave oversight that should be corrected as soon as possible. Target practice should embrace instruction in skirmish firing and practical application of the principles of fire direction, control and discipline with especial emphasis upon instruction of younger officers in musketry as applied to tactical problems in open warfare. Request advice as to action taken upon above recommendation and also information regarding what instruction has been carried out in divisions to come over within the next three months.
    3. Regard it most imperative that there be no delay in calling out a new draft and the entire summer season devoted to instruction and training so that new troops may be thoroughly and systematically trained without disturbing organizations when formed. Believe German offensive will be stopped but Allied aggressive must be undertaken as early as possible thereafter and American forces must be in position to throw in their full weight. Recommend that a call be issued at once for at least one million and a half men. Having in mind large replacements of losses that are sure to occur, and the delays of organization equipment and training of new drafts this is the smallest number that should be considered.

* * * * * *

PERSHING.

No. 1259-R
Dated May 7, 1918

PERSHING
AMEXFORCES

    1. With reference to paragraph 1 your 990, troops sent you have been best available. Divisions became depleted during the winter on account large number

being taken for staff corps and other unavoidable causes, and lack of equipment for replacements. Conditions will begin to improve early in July so that eventually only those divisions with at least six months training will be sent. Questions of breaking up divisions for trained men has been fully considered, as was the one of organizing 7th Division, and it was decided that depot brigades and replacement camps are better solution. Breaking up divisions now would not help situation.

   A. With reference to paragraph 2 your 990, your information that target practice for troops has not been had above 300 yards incorrect. Course provides instruction to include 600 yards as well as combat firing and practical application of principle of fire control and discipline. School of Musketry established Camp Perry, Ohio, for instruction of officers and noncommissioned officers as instructors in divisions.

   B. With reference to paragraph 3 your 990, 643, 198 white and 73, 326 colored men, total 716,524 have been drafted since January 1, including May draft. Draft will be continued monthly to maximum capacity. Impracticable to draft million and half at one time. Draft already called will fill and divisions now organized and all other troops for second and third phases. Question of organizing new divisions under consideration. We now have troops of all classes under training in replacement camps.

                    McCAIN.

No. 1543-R
June 16, 1918

PERSHING
AMEXFORCES

   By reason of the increased number of troops shipped every month, the length of time portions of them have had in training camps at home has correspondingly diminished. At the last minute the final combing out of each division always leaves a number of vacancies which have to be filled by transfer of men from other divisions and the instruction which a division has is not homogeneous but there are in each division a number of men, sometimes numbering several thousand, who have less instruction than the rest. These facts are undoubtedly known to you but the department desires you to obtain from each division commander when he reports a report as to the number of men who have now been in service four months, three months, and two months, and that you adjust the training of the men who have had the least training accordingly before using them on the battlefield. It is assumed by the War Department that you do this anyway, but the Secretary of War desires this to be established as a policy. March.

No. 1337-S
June 19, 1918   McCAIN.

Adjutant General, Washington

For the Chief of Staff and Secretary of War

   1. Reference your 1543. The reasons for sending men with insufficient struction is fully appreciated in view of the large increase in number of troops sent over during past three months and the inequalities in training are fully

considered here. The plan of separating recently drafted men from divisions and giving them special training for a longer period than the others before being put in the line had already been adopted. It will however reduce the fighting strength considerably of several divisions soon to be ordered into the line.

2. This situation emphasizes the importance of establishing the rule at home of keeping divisions intact, both as to officers and enlisted men, from the time they are organized until they are sent to France. The plan of using divisions through which to pass large numbers of men for instruction is very detrimental to thorough training of the divisions. It need not be pointed out that it takes much time to consolidate a division into homogeneous fighting unit and build up its esprit. Almost without exceptions, division commanders complain of the methods that have been followed. I recommend that in future the training of replacements and of special troops of all kinds be kept distinct from that of divisions.

3. Our inspection of divisions recently arrived shows that the training is uneven and varies much in different divisions. It appears superficial in many cases and generally lacks spirit and aggressiveness. In most of these divisions little attention has been given to training in open warfare, and in this regard younger officers are especially deficient. The training appears to have been carried on in a perfunctory way and without efficient supervision. The general impression is that division officers have leaned too heavily on French instructors whose ideas are not ordinarily in accordance with our own. General March will recall French opposition to our ideas of training especially as to musketry and open warfare, but the soundness of our methods is now accepted by the French who themselves have published similar orders on instruction of troops.

4. I recommend the maintenance of an efficient training staff at army headquarters, made up of thoroughly competent officers qualified to direct and supervise the training of our units according to approved principles and experience of our own army. It seems advisable at this time to suggest the adoltion of some plan of exchange between here and Washington of officers especially fitted to supervise the training of troops.

PERSHING.

No. 1597-R
June 25, 1918

PERSHING
AMEXFORCE

* * * * * *

1. The policy recommended in paragraph 2 your 1337 has already been adopted and is nos in operation. It was necessary to wait for certain camps to be vacated before it could be put into full operation. Of the June replacement draft the infantry and field artillery were drawn from divisions not on schedule for early shipment. That is the last draft that will be made on divisions. March.

* * * * * *

McCAIN.

No. 1482-S
July 18

AGWAR WASHINGTON

* * * * * *

1. For Chief of Staff. Developments war situation render utmost importance new divisions referred to in your 1630 be uniformly trained throughout, if possible before departure from United States. Important also before arrival each division that I should be able accurately to estimate extent training undergone.

 A. To secure desired results I am having prepared for submission to your four months program for all units of new division, embodying therein my ideas absolute essentials for warfare this theatre operations. Will forward this program by courier at early date. If meets your approval, recommend it be published for guidance new divisions.

 B. For attainment uniform standard essential program be followed by all without substantial modification.

 C. Officers all grades usually pay little attention programs unless execution same closely supervised. To secure compliance therefore recommend constant general staff inspection of all training. Believe members general staff should visit small units each division when beginning period of training to insure program understood and properly initiated; should visit again in middle of period and observe progress work; should finally inspect during last two weeks to determine whether adequate results obtained.

 D. On these visits general staff should give all possible assistance by suggestion and explanation.

 E. Recommend final inspection of divisions by general staff be made basis prompt relief manifest incompetents all grades and that such relief take place before departure division for France.

 F. General staff inspectors should be empowered issue orders for immediate correction all deficiencies.

 G. Suggest highly desirable training branch general staff be composed best qualified troop leaders our army. In view supreme importance training these new divisions, properly qualified officers should be made available for duty training branch from practically all sources.

 H. To increase prestige training branch and facilitate prompt transmission their business recommend this committee be made separate section general staff, be located in War Department, and report direct to Chief of Staff.

 J. Recommend further that all new divisions scheduled for sailing after January 1 be stationed in southern portions United States in order to enable their training continue without interruption throughout winter.

 K. If several arms are dispersed for early training, I strongly recommend each division be completely assembled during last two months its program in order produce necessary teamwork of combined arms.

PERSHING.

Information contained in cable of August 8, 1918, stated that plans were being formulated to carry out above recommendations.

18. In September, 1917, the War Department directed the commanding generals of all national guard divisions and their chiefs of staff to proceed to France for a tour of observation of approximately one month. A similar tour was also ordered for commanding

generals and chiefs of staff of national army divisions on completion of the tour of observation of national guard division commanders.

19. These officers spent twelve days with a British front line division and twelve days with a French front line division observing all kinds of actual front line work, including operations of division staff; visited schools and training centers of both armies; and saw the systems of supply in use by our Allies. On completion of their tours of the front these officers were ordered to General Headquarters of the A. E. F. where they were made familiar with the work that was being done by the various sections of the general staff and by the chiefs of staff departments, visited divisional areas occupied by our troops, and saw the billeting arrangements and training schools in operation. They were informed as to the object sought in the training in France, and furnished copies of training programs prepared for first three divisions, copies of our complete school project and cables regarding training which had been sent to the War Department.

20. This visit of these officers was useful as a means of establishing the coordination in training which was so much desired. In a memorandum furnished them signed by the Chief of Staff, A. E. F., the salient features of the school project and scheme of training in the A. E. F. were pointed out and their attention directed especially to the general principles governing training of the American Expeditionary Forces as published in the training program prepared for the 1st Division and already noted in this report. The memorandum continued:

> The tendency noticed in discussions among officers to depart from this sound doctrine should be constantly checked. The disposition to regard the introduction of a variety of new weapons to meet the special conditions of trench warfare as evidence of a complete departure from all our former principles of combat should be constantly opposed, and the attention of all officers should be fixed upon the ultimate object of all trench operations, namely, warfare in the open conducted in all essential elements according to the principles found in our standard manuals. The doctrine taught by the general staffs of all the great armies in this war confirms this opinion which was maturely considered by the Commander-in-Chief before its promulgation, and will be adhered by him in directing the training of troops in France.

21. Early in May 1918, the War Department directed that a certain number of signal corps and coast artillery corps officers who had had instruction and training in France be returned to the United States each month to assist in instruction there, these officers to be replaced by an equal number sent from the United States. Artillery officers were to be divided among those who had instruction in heavy artillery, anti-aircraft artillery, trench artillery.

22. In July 1918, this provision was extended to officers and noncommissioned officers of infantry, including machine-gun units; field artillery and engineer regiments to provide instructors of our own for organizations of new divisions about to be formed in the United States. These were to be selected from those who had had training in France, experience in the face of the enemy and had been proved efficient. A similar plan was later put in effect for officers for following duties in new divisions: Quartermaster corps, general staff duty, divisional machine gun officers, intelligence officers and battalion scout officers.

PROGRAMS

23. Very early in the history of the A. E. F. it was decided that the training of all divisions as they arrived in France should be in conformity with programs written and supervised by these headquarters. Members of the training section charged with the

preparation of these programs had visited the best French and British schools and centers of training and were familiar with the methods in use in those armies. They would have the advantage of observation of results obtained in training of the various divisions and would be in a better position to draft a consistent program conforming to our doctrine than a division headquarters recently arrived from the states. Moreover this plan ensured uniformity in methods and rapidity in the production of satisfactory efficiency that would not be practicable if the preparation of basic training programs were left to division commanders, with the probable great diversity of ideas that could be expected.

24. Accordingly a program was prepared for the training of the 1st Division and issued to that division on October 6, 1917. Programs were after that prepared for each division either prior to or immediately after its arrival in France, all programs being based on the progress the division had made in the United States. Separate programs were prepared for divisions trained in British areas and also for our colored infantry regiments which trained and served with the French army.

25. These programs were based on 36 hours instruction per week with a minimum working day of six hours, Sundays and holidays excepted. They contained the general principles governing the training of our forces which have been quoted, a brief outline of the function of our schools, general rules covering march and discipline, directions concerning personal appearance and military courtesy and an outline of the general plan of training followed by a list of publications to govern in training and the detailed schedule.

26. As already noted our plans called for three months training divided into three phases:
    (a) Training of small units.
    (b) Training of small units in sector.
    (c) Training of larger units and correcting deficiencies developed during tour in trenches.

27. During the first phase terrain exercises in command and communication were prescribed for regimental, brigade and division commanders covering various problems in attack and defense, both in open and trench warfare. In these exercises all means of communication were required to participate. By this means the development of the staff and command into well organized teams proceeded at the same time as the training of the smaller units was taking place. During the second period our higher commanders and staffs worked with the corresponding French or British headquarters as observers and students.

28. The early training programs prepared for divisions covered the entire three months period of instruction. It was soon found however that these programs providing for three months in the future had little chance of being completed as drawn due to various exigencies created by changes in the military situation. Consequently, early in 1918 a change was made and the programs issued divisions on their arrival provided for a four weeks period and covered only the first phase of training, leaving programs for later phases to depend upon what the enemy situation permitted but retaining the basic idea of three months training which was to be given whenever practicable.

29. For the terrain exercises prescribed, corps headquarters was required to prepare and conduct the division problems, division headquarters those for brigades, etc. During the third course at the army staff college problems were prepared by the students of the staff class under supervision of the instructors and furnished to some of the divisions in training. This gave the members of the class excellent training for their subsequent work but this practice was discontinued when location of divisions began to change rapidly to conform to military situation.

30. The training of divisions which had returned to back areas after a tour in the line was regulated by memorandum for corps and division commanders dated August 5, 1918.

After two or three days for rest and cleaning up, regular training was resumed five hours per day five days per week. Terrain exercises for larger units, maneuvers for all units from platoon to division inclusive, and daily target practice for infantry including practice at the longer ranges of 500 and 600 yards were prescribed, corps commanders being charged with direct supervision of training of their divisions.

AREAS

31. Naturally the location of the training areas for our divisions and other units had to be based on the location of our ports, our line of communications, and the sector of the line in which the American army would eventually operate.

32. Very soon after the arrival of the Commander-in-Chief and his staff in France, a board of officers visited several areas which had been selected by the French in the general vicinity of Gondrecourt and Neufchateau as training areas for divisions and the camp at Valdahon which had been offered for the preliminary training of our field artillery brigades.

33. Eventually there were located nineteen divisional training areas, six miscellaneous training areas and one heavy artillery training area in the area included in the pentagon Bar-le-Duc---Nancy---Vesoul---Semur---Auxerre. This location was near enough to the front to bring the units in training in the atmosphere of the front and facilitate the sending of units to front line for the second phase of training without too great a loss of time. The areas were also close to the main arteries of supply from our base ports, and General Headquarters of the A. E. F. was approximately in the center of the area.

34. While it was most desirable to train our complete divisions in one place in order to secure the absolutely necessary cooperation in action, it was found impracticable to train artillery brigades with the balance of the division as very few of these areas offered any opportunities for artillery firing and permitted training of other units at the same time. In order to secure suitable firing grounds, take advantage of existing French installations and facilitate equipping with French material, artillery brigades were sent to organization and training centers for the first phase of their training. These centers were situated for the most part near the west coast.

35. In order to obtain sufficient billeting space so as to avoid an enormous construction project it was necessary to distribute the organizations of a division mostly by battalions over a large area; divisional areas averaged something over 500 square kilometers or approximately equal to an area 20 miles long by 10 miles wide. This made the assembly of units for training of regiments, brigades and divisions a matter which involved a great deal of time and bivoucking on the part of the troops.

36. The areas available for training in the proximity of the billets were usually very meagre and restricted to camps sets aside by special provision of law where trenches might be dug and firing take place in certain specified directions. Ground for open warfare training was difficult to obtain while crops were on the ground but usually any farm land could be used so long as growing crops were avoided. It was likewise difficult to secure target ranges especially for the longer ranges on account of the density of the population. This condition was accentuated when plowing began and during the time crops were on the ground, in view of the urgent necessity for conserving all food. Material necessary to improvise the necessary targets was likewise difficult to obtain.

37. It was for these reasons that the War Department was urgently requested from the beginning to make open warfare the main function of training in the states and to make instruction in rifle practice and musketry, especially at the longer ranges, a matter of prime importance there.

38. In December 1917, several more divisional areas were selected in the interior of France and in close proximity to our lines of communication for use in case of congestion in the regular divisional areas. These were to be used for a comparatively short time but occasion for their use never arose.

39. The number of divisions increased so rapidly during the summer of 1918 that it was necessary, in order to simplify questions of supply and equipment, to select several additional areas conveniently located with regard to our base ports where divisions could have first phase of their training.

40. Divisions arriving during September and October 1918, were assigned to these and equipped therein. The same difficulties regarding adequate target ranges and maneuvering ground were met here as in the training areas in the advance section.

* * * * * *

JAMES B. GOWEN,
Colonel, Gen. Staff, G-5.

C-in-C Rept. File: Fldr. 264: Report

American Expeditionary Forces Publications

[June 30, 1919].

It was planned that the A. E. F. Base Printing Plant would print the training publications that were required. However, this plant had so much other work to do that it was able to print only a very small fraction of the work that was required by this section. The printing plant of The Adjutant General, A. E. F., printed practically all of the small pamphlets that were gotten out by this section. Great credit is due the officer in charge of the printing plant of The Adjutant General, A. E. F., for the assistance he has given G-5, G. H. Q., in getting out promptly important training instructions to troops. Practically all books have been printed by the publishing houses of France.

The following named publications were translated from the French text, changed in some cases to agree with our organization, and published to our army:

A. E. F. NO.	TITLE	NO. ISSUED
2	Liaison for troops of all arms	63,048
5	Provisional drill regulations for field artillery — 75-mm. gun	23,451
6	Manual of the chief of platoon of infantry	29,065
14	Drill regulations for the 155 how.	9,065
69	Firing tables for the 155 how.	15,980
80	Aerial observation for artillery	18,771
90	Mine warfare	4,727
160	Offensive conduct of small units	86,494
160-A	Supplement to offensive conduct of small units	35,311
170	Handbook of the 155-mm. Filloux gun material, with inst. for its care	250
194	Manual of wire entanglements, Ad. No. 1 to engineer field manual	21,630
230	Manual of the 37-mm. gun	18,640

231	Regulations for M. G. companies equipped with Hotchkiss machine guns, Model 1914	14,418
265	Instructions on the defensive action of large units	22,130
266	Manual of the automatic rifle – Chauchat	34,974
514	Organization of the ground	15,226
704	Provisional instructions and complementary lecture on the organization and use of the corrector for the antiaircraft firing of infantry machine guns	19,795
723	Gonimetre Boussole de Batterie	16,756
760	Firing tables – 75-mm. gun	1,112
813	Lecture on the supply of ammunition	4,975
953	Drill regulations for the 155 GPF	3,243
990	Artillery firing	26,335
1020-1	Firing tables for the 155 Fillous gun	3,021
1095	Study and utilization of aerial photos (text)	1,018
1353	Silhouette de Avions	1,508
1356	Volume I, School of the Battery Commander, 75-mm. gun and 155 how.	2,818
1445	Military testament – Colonel de Maud'Huy	4,980

The following named publications were obtained from the British and issued to our army:

40	Notes on the identification of aeroplanes	720
48	Gas poisoning in warfare, with notes on its treatment	5,925
67	Vocabulary of German mil. terms	4,541
132	Notes on the construction of deep gallery shelters	10,281
147	Questions a platoon commander should ask himself on taking over a trench, and at frequent intervals afterward	88,797
166	Scouting and patrolling	2,105
171	Bayonet training manual	27,119
187	The employment of machine guns – Part II	11,527
216	The employment of M. G. Part I	12,610
245	Engr. work during operations	4,810
253	Def. measures against gas	85,346
1344	I have captured a Boche machine gun; What shall I do with it?	10,410
1351	Notes on German heavy and light machine guns	4,179

The following named publications were furnished by the War Department and issued to troops:

7	Machine gun training	9,379
84	Manual for the artillery orientation officer	9,373
267	Manual of the automatic pistol	33,182
550	Light TM DR	30,806
725	Musketry	5,139
807	Organization and construction of battery emplacements	4,945
811	Landscape sketching	4,328
1040	Manual of equipment for machine gun companies, equipped with Hotchkiss machine guns	20,599
1060	Machine gun drill regulations, (provisional)	4,773
1070	Provisional M. G. firing manual	7,118
1073	Description on the Coleman hold and trigger squeeze device	120
1337	Handbook of the Browning machine rifle	4,673

The following named publications were prepared by or under the supervision of G-5, G H. Q., and issued to our troops:

19	Notes on artillery camouflage	8,493
516	Manual for trench art., Part I	3,695
517	Manual for trench art., Part II	3,708
518	Manual for trench art., Part III	3,650
519	Manual for trench art., Part IV	3,809
520	Manual for trench art., Part V	3,725
1060-A	Supplement to M. G. D. R.	2,607
1060-B	Supplement to M. G. D. R.	9,217
1060-C	Supplement to M. G. D. R.	2,526
1078	Practical Supplement to the school of the btry. commander (Vol. III)	4,267
1090	Remarks concerning deficiencies in the training of our units as brought out in some of the recent offensive operations	124
1097	Report of American officer on recent fighting	4,822
1301	Instructions concerning maps	4,896
1308	Trench orders for American forces in France	7,393
1312	Instructions for the defensive action of small units; Infantry, platoon to regiment	64,056
1316	Training bulletin for F. A. brigades	223
1320	Supplement to M. G. D. R. and provisional firing manual	19,613
1322	Notes on recent operations I	14,690
1325	Training memorandum for corps and division commanders	3,669
1328	The artillery informations service	1,820
1332	Handbook for brigade and division commanders	2,564
1336	Map problem: Sanitary service of an inf. div. intrenched for defense	3,303
1341	Corrections for firing tables for 75-mm. guns with American ammunition	3,861
1345	Duties of divisional engineers in mobile warfare	532
1346	Notes on Recent Operations 2	5,215
1348	Combat Instructions	54,968
1349	Duties and relations of engineers	3,886
1352	Map problem - Sanitary service	750
1354	Duties of field food and nutrition officers Volume II, technical supplement to the school of the btry. commander	4,268
1361	Lectures and conferences, army gen. staff college, Part I	248
1362	Lectures and conferences, army gen. staff, college, Part II	250
1363	Lectures and conferences, army gen. staff college	248
1364	Dugouts Don'ts -- Plates	143
1365	Notebook for general staff officers	8,654
1375	Camouflage	1,965
1376	Notes on recent operations 3	19,453
1378	Provisional infantry drill reg.	79,588
1384	Baseball throw for hand grenades	200
1397	Heavy art. school notes, Part X	686

1398	Heavy art. school notes, Part VI	687
1399	Heavy art. school notes, Part IV	685
1401	The school of the btry. commander: Vol l. I (In prep.)	
1402	Vol. II	2,467
1402-A	Vol. II A	2,184
1402-B	Vol. II B	1,655
1403	Vol. III	2,494
1404	Vol. IV (In prep.)	
1405	Vol. V	1,896
1410	Heavy art. school notes, Part II	136
1411	Heavy art. school notes, Appendix Part III	269
1417	Notes on recent operations 4	27,269
1418	Individual instruction in rifle practice	81,104
1419	Heavy Artillery school notes, Part VII (Appendix)	145
1422	Heavy artillery school notes, Part VII	89
1425	Provisional staff manual	878
1428	Heavy Artillery school notes, Part V	46
1431	Heavy Artillery signal manual: In prep.	
1432	Tanks - Organization and tactics	2,810
1433	Defense against gas	4,944
1435	Notes for lectures on preliminary instruction in rifle firing	5,946
1454	Dismounting Browning rifle-plates	12,050
1455	Assembling Browning rifle - plates	12,050
1458	Individual instruction in revolver and pistol practice	16,557
1460	Musketry Bulletin 1-16 A	8,750
1475	Gas manual - Parts I, II, III, IV and V (In preparation)	
1476	Musketry Bubletin 18A, 19A and 22A	8,759
51	Memorandum governing divisional training	234
251	Program of training for the 1st Division	452
255	Revised program of training for the 2d Div.	417
256	Program of training for the 26th Div.	181
544	Program of training for the field bn., signal corps, 26th Division	34
546	Program of training for the sanitary units of the 26th Division	74
700	Program of training in gas defense for divisional antigas school	65
749	Program of instruction for the field signal battalion	28
750	Program of training for the 42d Division	57
759	Program of training for the sanitary units of the 42d Division	42
782	Program of training (First Phase) for the 32d Division	65
818	Revised program of training for the 26th Div.	267
1008	Program of training (First Phase) for Amer. Divs. with the British	529
1010	Program of training (First Phase) for divisions, III Corps	122

1057	Program of training (First Phase) for U. S. Infantry Regiments attached to French divisions	247
1071	Training program for the 2d Division in concentration area	1
1080	Program of training (First Phase) for 83d Div.	161
1081	Program of training (First Phase) for 89th Div.	166
1084	Program of training (First Phase) for 92d Div.	177
1086	Program of training (First Phase) for 37th Div.	165
1087	Program of training (First Phase) for 29th Div.	161
1088	Program of training (First Phase) for 90th Div.	141
1307	Program of training (First Phase) for 6th Div.	242
1309	Program of training (First Phase) for 91st Div.	178
1310	Program of training (First Phase) for 79th Div.	156
1329	Program of training (First Phase) for 36th Div.	201
1340	Program of training (First Phase) for 81st Div.	127
1347	Program of training (First Phase) for 7th Div.	149
1348	Program of training (First Phase) for 88th Div.	143
1358	Program of training (First Phase) for 84th Div.	151
1359	Program of training (First Phase) for 86th Div.	145
1371	Program of training for depot divisions	175
1382	Program of training (First Phase) for 38th Div.	149
1426	Program of training for divisions in training in the U. S.	28
1429	Extract from program of training for divisions	495

SCHOOLS

C-in-C Rept. File: Fldr. 218: Report

Army General Staff College

Langres, Haute-Marne, June 12, 1919.

[Extract]

The arrival of the first divisions of the American Expeditionary Forces in France brought the Americans into contact with certain conditions and requirements which had never before been experienced or anticipated. Necessity, therefore, required that changes be made in the organization of the American army to adapt it to its new environment.

It was soon apparent that the old staff organization was not adapted to meet the many and varied new demands imposed by these new conditions. As a result, the authorities of the A. E. F. decided upon a reorganization of the division and higher staffs and the present staff organization of units of the American Expeditionary Forces was adopted and at once ordered into effect.

The new staff organization required a great increase in highly trained officer personnel for each unit then in the A. E. F. and the ever increasing number of new units made the demands for such personnel far exceed the available supply. The number of officers in the American army trained for staff duty, prior to America's entry into the the war, was indeed small and there were many phases of the modern warfare staff requirements with which even they were not familiar.

Obviously to have the staff organization properly function, it was necessary to have trained staff officers and in order to meet the demands which then did and would continue to far exceed the available supply, it was decided to establish a short and intensive course in staff training for selected officers.

With this end in view, Lieutenant Colonel (now Brigadier General) A. W. Bjornstad was directed to proceed to the town of Langres, Haute-Marne and establish the Army General Staff College, under the supervision of the commandant of army schools, who was in turn subordinate to the G-5 (training) Section, General Staff, G. H. Q.

Colonel H. B. Fiske (now Brigadier General), Assistant Chief of Staff, G-5, G. H. Q., Brigadier General (now Major General) J. W. MacAndrew, then commandant of army schools, and Colonel A. W. Bjornstad, formulated the general outline and scheme of instruction for a three months course and arranged for representative missions of French and British staff officers to assist in the instruction. All details of the course, the method of instruction and administration of the college were left to General Bjornstad, who was appointed Director of the Army General Staff College.

Accordingly, a large number of student officers reported to the director and the first course, Army General Staff College, opened at Carteret-Trecourt Barracks, Langres, Haute Marne, November 28, 1917.

* * * * * *

No American instructors were detailed. The director selected Major Offner Hope, a member of the student body, to act as his assistant. Major Hope was later detailed as an instructor.

* * * * * *

The scheme of the first course was based upon a succession of map problems. Of these problems, twenty in all, each of the first nineteen represented some necessary phase of staff work. The proper solution required a certain knowledge of staff principles involved, as well as the technique necessary to communicate this knowledge to subordinates in the form of orders.

Students were given the entire day each Wednesday and Saturday for the solution of the problem. Two days preceding the problem, lectures were given by the French and British instructors on subjects which had a bearing on the following problem. There were three lecture periods, viz: 8:30 a. m., 9:40 a. m. and 10:50 a. m., the afternoons being left to the students for study. On the day preceding the problem, at 8:30 a. m. another similar conference or lecture was given. At 9:40 a. m., the last problem was again discussed by groups and at 10:50 a. m. an American officer gave a conference called the X Conference in which he coordinated into terms of the American organization, the various points which had been previously touched upon by the lecturers of the Allied forces.

At the close of the problem day, the student was required to hand in his solution to a group leader, who in turn gave him the solution of a fellow student, upon which criticisms and comments were to be made in writing, the student mdanwhile being furnished with a school solution made up by the entire faculty. The students' solution with the comments thereon were returned to the group leader, who in turn reviewed both the solution and the comments and awarded the proper marks to the student concerned. On the next succee ding day, the group leaders held conferences for their groups and again discussed the problems, and the errors and ommissions noted in the solutions which he had reviewed.

In this manner, for each problem the student received five preliminary lectures, solved the problem himself, received the school solution, obtained another officer's ideas by commenting upon another student's solution and a final review and discussion in group conference, had obtained most every angle of the subject of the problem.

* * * * * *

The end of the fourth course marked the close of the Army General Staff College in the American E. F. During its thirteen months of existence 770 officers were enrolled as students of whom 537 were graduated and recommended for duty as staff officers.

* * * * * *

C-in-C Rept. File: Fldr. 219: Report

Army School of the Line

November 17, 1918.

From: Director, Army School of the Line

To: Commandant, Army Schools

[Extract]

1. The following report as to the operation of this school is submitted.
The army schools were authorized under G. O. No. 46, Par. 3, Subpar. 1, A. E. F. dated October 10, 1917, * * *

* * * * * *

The Army School of the Line was organized pursuant to the following letter:

AMERICAN EXPEDITIONARY FORCES,

January 2, 1918.

From: The Adjutant General

To: Commandant, Army Schools

Subject: The Army Line School

1. The Army Line School will be started so as to begin operations during the present month.
2. The student personnel for the first session will be drawn from the army signal, sanitary, and engineer schools. In addition, there may be some officers available from the 41st Division. Students of the special schools above mentioned

will, in principle, take such portions of the course as apply to their particular arm or service.

3. The personnel to be employed in connection with direction and instruction of the student personnel is as yet limited. Colonel Kirby Walker, N. A., and Lieutenant Colonel Willey Howell, J. A., N. A., have been detailed for such duty. In addition, Major Denig and Captain Metcalfe, Marine Corps, and Captain Grandgent, 101st Infantry, will probably report to you later for the same duty.

4. The details of the course will be planned so as to give tactical instruction to all students in such manner as will bring about the study and application of the use of all arms and services in combination, to include the regiment.

5. The scope of subjects should include: Organization, orders, reconnaissance, security, marches and convoys, combat in open and position warfare, sanitary service and liaison.

6. The length of course will not exceed three months, and the first course will be so arranged as will meet the particular conditions which surround it.

7. A program covering the first course will be submitted without delay to these headquarters for approval.

By command of General Pershing:

F. R. KENNEY,
Adjutant General.

Colonel Kirby Walker, Cavalry, reported January 6, 1918 and assumed duty as director per S. O. No. 200, Par. 6, G. H. Q., A. E. F., series 1917.

* * * * * *

The first course was scheduled to cover the period from February 4 to April 30, 1918.

The instruction was planned on the broad ground that the first two months would be devoted exclusively to instruction in open warfare and the last month to trench warfare. The school was greatly hampered by a lack of experienced instructors and proper facilities for conducting a school of the kind but in spite of this fact Colonel Walker planned an excellent course and deserves great credit for building the schedule on the foundation that if officers were properly taught the proper principles as laid down in our field service and drill regulations, that the details as changed by trench warfare would be quickly picked up.

The course covered the following: Organization, 2 conferences, map reading 4 conferences and 3 problems. Solution of tactical problems 1 conference orders 1 conference, information 3 conferences, 3 problems and 1 tactical ride, war game 7, communication. 1 demonstration, security 6 conferences, 4 problems and 1 tactical ride, aerial photography 4 lectures, artillery 4 conferences and 1 problem, marches and convoys 4 conferences 3 problems and 1 tactical ride; camps 4 conferences 3 problems and 1 tactical ride; sanitation 6 lectures and 2 problems; field engineering 2 conferences and 2 problems; field fortifications 4 conferences 4 problems and 1 tactical ride; combat 11 conferences 14 problems and 8 tactical rides.

* * * * * *

The first class comprised 52 officers and was composed to a large extent of captains of the reserve corps who had just arrived from the United States.

The second course was of shorter duration. It began May 31 and ended July 6, 1918.
The course was based on the same principles as the first course but billeting, demonstrations at the infantry specialist, automatic weapons, and signal schools were added and the number of conferences and problems in order subjects shortened to meet the reduced time.

* * * * * *

The third course was practically of two months, duration beginning August 1 and ending September 25, 1918. During this course the same broad principles applied but instead of having the first part of the course devoted to open warfare and the latter part to trench warfare the instruction was given in both so that the schedule as a whole was better balanced and it is believed improved in many ways.
Demonstrations at the trench mortar, engineer and tank schools were added to the course.

* * * * * *

Upon completion of the course the 100 graduates who had stood highest in the class were detailed to attend the next class at the Army General Staff College.
The fourth course was increased to practically a 3 months course beginning on October 7 and scheduled to conclude on January 4, 1919.
On account of the increased time allowed and the previous experience in conducting the schools this is the best course the school has had.
The instruction in the different subjects is followed as far as possible by demonstrations at the different schools and a large number of terrain exercises has been introduced in the course.
In addition a course in the preparation of problems has been added so that the company, battalion and regimental commanders will have a better idea of training their officers and men upon returning to their organizations.
The course comprises instruction by means of: 1. Lectures, 2. Conferences, 3. Demonstrations, 4. Problems and Terrain Exercises.
Lectures are given on the following subjects: Artillery, aerial observation, camouflage, engineer duties of infantry, food nutrition, gas, intelligence, liaison, map reading and march graphics, tactical use of machine gun and automatic weapons. Moving of a division by rail and by truck. Tanks etc.,
Conferences are given in the field service regulations, infantry drill regulations, offensive conduct of small units and combat instructions together with numerous other books and pamphlets, a part of which is herewith enclosed. These conferences include both open and trench warfare.

* * * * * *

The class comprises 208 officers:
Thus making a total of 497 officers who have taken the regular courses.
During the first week of July 1918 the director was directed to prepare a special two weeks course for field officers.
Under these instructions six courses have been held as follows:

```
1st course, July 16-July 29, 1918, attended by 113 field officers
2d  course, Aug. 14-Aug. 27, 1918       "    "  121   "      "
3d  course, Sept. 1-Sept. 14, 1918      "    "   55   "      "
4th course, Oct. 7-Oct. 19, 1918        "    "   53   "      "
5th course, Oct. 24-Nov. 6, 1918        "    "   39   "      "
6th course, Nov. 15-Nov. 29, 1918       "    "   95   "      "
     Total 476 field officers
```

The purpose of these courses has been to give the field officers the recent developments in tactics, the proper coordinating of the use of the different auxiliary weapons attached to infantry and proper use of accompanying artillery and tanks.

* * * * * *

A center of information was established at this school as per following letter:

AMERICAN EXPEDITIONARY FORCES,

T. S. G. S.,

January 15, 1918.

From: The Adjutant General
To: Commandant, Army Schools
Subject: Course at Center of Information, Army Schools

    1. The following extract from memorandum approved by the Chief of Staff, January 14, 1918 is furnished you for your information and guidance:

        It is desired to begin on the 21st inst. the course for infantry colonels and brigade commanders of the 41st and 42d Divisions. It is proposed to have this course consist of subjects which are attached hereto, and will extend over a period of nine days: 21st to 30th inst. inclusive.

    2. Orders have been issued for the attendance of the personnel mentioned in this extract.

    3. Request has been made on the motor transportation division to furnish you four closed automobiles for the use of this class from January 20 to 30.

                  By command of General Pershing:

                          F. P. KENNEY,
                         Adjutant General.

* * * * * *

    2. The aim of the school has been to teach officers the proper principles in combat, both offensive and defensive. The coordination of the different arms and weapons and the issuing of proper orders.

    The aim has been by means of problems to teach them to form correct estimates of the situations thus enabling them to arrive at a proper decision and to issue intelligent orders to carry out the decision.

    It has been impressed on all students that though they may never solve the particular problem in action operations that they solve at the school yet if they form the habit of thinking along the lines as taught that the chances are they will at least form a reasonable decision and if proper orders are issued to carry it out that they will meet with success.

4. The policy of the school has been to consider that the function of the school was to turn out better company, battalion and regimental commanders, and that no matter how much or how little knowledge the man had on his arrival he could be benefited byy the instruction here. With this in mind the school has not been conducted to find out how much or how little a man may know but to impart to him the maximum amount of instruction possible in the time allowed.

J. K. MILLER,
Colonel, Infantry,
Director.

C-in-C Rept. File: Fldr. 220: Report

Army Candidates School

Langres, Haute-Marne, February 15, 1919.

From: The Director

To: The Commandant, Army Schools, American E. F., Langres, France

[Extract]

ORGANIZATION: The Army Candidates School, American E. F., was established at LANGRES, HAUTE-MARNE, France, under the provisions of Section III, General Orders No. 46, G. H. Q., American E. F., France dated October 10, 1917. A director was appointed by General Orders No. 5, Headquarters, Army Schools, American E. F., dated November 20, 1917, and the organization of the school was begun the following day.

* * * * * *

Offices and barracks at Caserne Turenne in the Citadelle of LANGRES were assigned the school on November 24, 1917.

Under instructions contained in letter from the Adjutant General, American E. F., France, dated November 24, 1917, the first course of the school was to begin December 1, 1917, and was to accommodate 600 infantry, 36 engineer and 12 signal corps candidates selected from the 1st, 2d, 26th and 42d Divisions. The first candidates reported on November 30, 1917, and the total number ordered had arrived by December 20, 1917. Instructors began to arrive on December 4, and by December 18 a total of 17 officers had reported for duty.

In addition to candidates undergoing the regular course of instruction, 72 enlisted men designated for a competitive examination for appointment to the United States Military Academy were sent to the school in December 1917, to receive instruction in the subjects of the entrace examination for the Military Academy. Two lieutenants, recent graduates of the Military Academy, were sent to the school as special instructors for this class. These enlisted men were returned to their organizations on March 28, 1918.

The usual difficulties and delays were encountered in obtaining supplies for instruction, and labor for administration. By December 20, 1917, sufficient material had been received to permit the course of instruction to be organized and systematically followed.

GROWTH: The number of infantry candidates was increased to 950 for the course beginning April 1, 1918, and to 2259 for the course beginning August 1, 1918, additional barracks at Caserne Turenne being assigned. On September 15, 1918, Fort de la Bonnelle and the barracks adjacent thereto were assigned to the school and an additional battalion of 1125 candidates organized. On September 25, 1918, Forts de Cognelot and de France were assigned to the school, and a sufficient number of additional barracks erected so that each could accommodate a battalion of 1100 men for the course to begin October 6, 1918. The greatest number of candidates at the school at one time was 4828 on October 26, 1918.

INSTRUCTORS: Instructors for the school were detailed from the divisions by orders from G. H. Q. The captains, in most cases, had never received any tactical instruction and many had apparently received little serious military instruction of any character. At the end of the first course of the school a number of the smartest and most enthusiastic graduates were selected for duty as instructors, and this practice was continued in succeeding courses. These graduate instructors proved to be the best, and were of the greatest assistance in securing uniformity of instruction and in maintaining the discipline and esprit of the school. The sudden expansion of the school in September and October 1918, rendered it necessary to obtain a large number of new instructors, many of whom were but poorly qualified for the duty. This undoubtedly resulted in a lowering of the standard of instruction during the short courses then required. Unfit instructors were relieved as soon as competent officers could be found to take their places.

With remarkably few exceptions, all officers detailed as instructors performed their duties conscientiously and zealously, and made every effort to perfect themselves as instructors.

A total of 183 officers were on duty at the school at various times.

INSTRUCTION: The 1st, 2d, 6th and 7th courses were of approximately 3 months duration. The 3d course was shortened to 8 weeks, and the 4th and 5th courses to 6 weeks on orders from G. H. Q.

A large number of the candidates reporting had received very inadequate instruction, about 30% had never fired any course with the rifle or pistol, and a small percentage from the staff corps and departments had never received any infantry instruction at all. Much time, therefore, had to be spent in rudimentary work. During the short courses, the time devoted to first principles had to be reduced at the expense of smartness and precision.

Candidates were organized into platoons, companies and battalions. The platoon was the unit of instruction, and varied in strength from 55 to 70 men, depending upon the number reporting for the course.

The instruction was progressive, and the subjects included the technical construction and operation of the platoon weapons, the tactical use of those weapons, and finally the tactical handling of them combined in the platoon. The tactical use of the regimental weapons, and their construction and operation, so far as facilities would permit, was also taught. The tactical organization of the ground both on the trench polygon and on varied terrain was a valuable part of the tactical instruction.

After the first course, all tactical instruction was directed by Major Louis Grandgent, Infantry, a keen student of tactics and an exceptionally able instructor. In collaboration with Captain E. Allain, French Infantry, Major Grandgent developed a progressive course in tactics which formed the basis of all instruction. Leadership was developed and correct tactical principles taught mainly in practical terrain exercises. To stimulate initiative and mental activity candidates were required to solve the tactical problems for themselves, errors being pointed out and discussed by instructors. Every effort was made to keep abreast of the latest developments at the front through intelligence summaries and training pamphlets issued by G-5, G. H. Q. The value of the rifle as the prime weapon of the infantry was emphasized in all training; all candidates were given a course in range firing and in such combat firing as facilities would permit.

In addition to platoon leadership the courses of instruction included the use of the compass, map reading and hasty sketching, field fortification and the use of obstacles, relief and occupation of trenches, means of communication, organization and administration, etc.

SPIRIT AND DISCIPLINE: The material sent to the first four courses of the school was of the highest quality; the personnel of the fifth and sixth courses was noticeably lower in quality, and the men sent to the seventh course averaged below the standard both mentally and physically. This may have indicated that the officer material in the divisions was becoming rapidly exhausted, but is quite as likely to have been due to carelessness and indifference on the part of the commanding officers making selections.

The highest state of discipline was maintained at all times, an effort being made to attain the standard of the corps of cadets at the United States Military Academy. The splendid spirit and discipline of the candidates is indicated by the fact that even after the signing of the Armistice, and after it was known that commissions would not be given graduates, there was only a slight diminution of interest and a slight increase in number of infractions of discipline. It was necessary to try by court martial only 75 of the 9686 candidates who attended the school.

The spirit of the school was aggressively American, and it is doubted if a more democratic institution ever existed. A candidate's success depended entirely upon his demonstrated fitness, judged by impartial and unprejudiced officers. The location of the school in France operated successfully against the use of any sort of influence.

CANDIDATES SCHOOL, LA VALBONNE, AIN: Under instructions from the commandant, army schools, the director and supply officer of the school in September 1918, reconnoitered and reported on Camp La Valbonne, Ain, with a view to its use as a candidates school. On September 20, 1918, the supply officer of the school, Captain W. E. Haskell, Infantry, was sent to Camp La Valbonne to take over that camp from the French authorities and prepare it for the reception of 7100 candidates who were to arrive on October 17, 1918.

On October 16, 1918, the director and adjutant of the school were sent to Camp La Valbonne to organize the new school and administer it until a permanent commandant was detailed by G. H. Q. Owing to its distance from American supply centers, great difficulties were encountered in preparing and organizing Camp La Valbonne in the limited time allowed. Some 5,000 candidates arrived before rations, bedding and clothing, and medical supplies were received from the American supply departments. Transportation facilities were inadequate, and only the energy and ingenuity of Captain Haskell and his assistants and the cooperation of the French military authorities prevented serious hardship and suffering.

The course of instruction at Camp La Valbonne began October 21, 1918.

By October 25, 1918, ordnance supplies for instruction, rations and field ranges had arrived and the difficulties in the way of supply were rapidly being improved.

On October 26, the school, organized into six battalions, was turned over to Colonel C. W. Exton, Infantry, who reported for duty as commandant; the name of the school was changed to infantry candidates school and its connection with the army schools severed.

* * * * *

RECAPITULATION

(Infantry)

```
Candidates commissioned . . . . . . . . . . . . . . . . . 3242 (65 Marines included)
     "     recommended as eligible for commissions . . . 2354 (22 Marines included)
     "     relieved . . . . . . . . . . . . . . . . . . . 4077 (49    "        "    )
     "     died . . . . . . . . . . . . . . . . . . . . .   13
                                                           9686
```

S. L. PIKE,
Lieutenant Colonel, Infantry.

C-in-C Rept. File: Fldr. 221: Report

Center of Artillery Studies

Treves, July 12, 1919.

From: The Director, Army Center of Artillery Studies, A. E. F.

To: The Chief of Field Artillery, War Department, Wash., D. C.

[Extract]

    1. In accordance with instructions contained in Par. 2 of a letter from the Adjutant General, G. H. Q., A. E. F., to the Commanding General, Third Army, dated June 15, 1919, the following final report covering the entire operations of this center is forwarded to your office, together with all records pertaining to the center:

    2. The development of the war impressed upon the French army the necessity for meeting the following needs: First, the training of higher artillery commanders and their staffs in the preparation of artillery plans and orders; second, the necessity of acquainting higher commanders of other arms, especially the infantry, with the various methods, powers, and limitations of artillery, and of giving to higher artillery commanders a better understanding of what the infantry might require from them. In order to meet these two needs the French army established a center of artillery studies, where high ranking infantry and artillery officers, removed from the care of duties with troops, should have an opportunity for study together and for an exchange of views on subjects of interest to both. This center was first established at CHALONS in 1916, but was later removed to VITRY le FRANCOIS. It was in operation continuously throughout the war since that time, with the exception of a short interruption in the Spring of 1918, and it is still in operation. The results obtained there have been successful.

Each class is composed of from thirty to forty officers of the rank of generals or field officers of infantry and artillery and a number of aviation officers. During the war the course afforded an opportunity to assemble a number of officers from the front for a short period of study and conference. It afforded an opportunity for an exchange of personal experiences as to the most recent modifications in military operations at the front, and served to develop a better liaison between the officers of the different arms. The French attached great importance to this institution which is one of the most advanced schools in their system of military training.

As early as February of 1918, G. H. Q. of the American forces foresaw the need for establishing a similar center for our army in France, but various difficulties stood in the way of its early creation. It was not, however, until the end of June 1918 that further steps could be taken in the matter, but at that time there was formed at the headquarters of the First Army Artillery at Bar-sur-Aube a class of officers who pursued a short course similar in nature to the one proposed in this center should it be organized. This class was formed under the direction of Major General E. F. McGlachlin, chief of the First Army Artillery. The officers of his staff formed the class and were instructed by Colonel Louis D'Astorg of the French artillery. About the middle of July the Chief of the First Army Artillery addressed a letter to the Commander-in-Chief of the A. E. F. recommending the establishment of the center of artillery studies. * * * As the result of it Colonel M. E. Locke, Field Artillery, was detailed by orders from G. H. Q. to report to the commandant, army schools at Langres for the purpose of organizing and conducting this center of instruction. He so reported on August 16, 1918 and was assigned to duty as director of the center by Paragraph 8, S. O. No. 225, headquarters, army schools dated August 17, 1918.

It was the purpose to have the center begin the first course of instruction on September 16, 1918. By that time all arrangements had been perfected, the center organized and equipped, the course of instruction prepared and a series of lectures provided. Owing to the fact that operations assumed a large scale at the time scheduled for the opening of the center (September 16, 1918) it was found impossible to secure the attendance of a class of the desired personnel. The need for officers at the front of the rank and attainments constituting such a class was too great to admit of their detail for this course at the time. The signing of the Armistice, however, released a large number of officers from the front and the class of twenty-one officers was therefore ordered to report at Langres for the first course which began on December 9, 1918. Since that time the courses have succeeded one another until four regular courses have been completed. A special course in artillery operations for a class of fifty field officers of artillery sent over from the United States has also been pursued, (June 16/28, 1919). There have been graduated in the four regular courses: 31 generals; 28 colonels; 34 lieutenant colonels; 15 majors and 2 lieutenants - a total of 110 officers. In the special course 49 officers have received certificates of proficiency. * * *

The first course was completed on December 28, 1918 and upon its conclusion it was found necessary to remove this center from Langres as the result of the breaking up of the army schools there. The first course had been so successful as to lead G. H. Q. to decide to continue the center after the breaking up of the army schools. Various prospective locations were considered and the new location was finally selected at Treves, Germany, where the center would be near the bulk of our troops as the time went on. The second course began there on February 18, 1919, and the center has remained there up to this date.

The object of this center as defined by G. H. Q. is: (a) The training of higher artillery commanders and their staffs in the preparation of artillery plans and orders; (b) To inform commanders other than artillery as to the powers, methods, and limitations of artillery. To accomplish this object there has been pursued a course of instruction which involves the preparation of plans and orders similar to those ordi-

narily prepared by the chiefs of artillery of armies, corps, and divisions. Study along such broad lines as is demanded in such a course of instruction was not supplied as far as known in any other American school in France. Briefly, the course includes:
(a) The selection of a number of problems involving the use of infantry and artillery suitable in size to the rank of the student body; (b) Review of the solutions of one committee by the members of another committee; (c) Conferences held at the conclusion of each problem's solution whereat a critique is conducted by instructors of the center's staff and at its conclusion divergent opinions are thrown open for general discussion; (d) A course of reading and lectures on selected subjects thought applicable to such an institution; (e) Demonstrations of artillery fire and exercises of other troops performed by units in the vicinity of the center; (f) At the conclusion of each course a staff ride of from ten to fourteen days over various areas of the recent front. Areas are selected which illustrate the various phases of operations, open warfare, semi-open warfare, and trench warfare with its limited objectives. The areas visited are made the subject of previous study beforehand and the classes are conducted over the ground either by high ranking officers who have personally directed the actual operations there, or by officers of the center's staff who are thoroughly familiar with the ground as the result of frequent visits to it and from study of the operations. These staff rides have been a most valuable feature of the course. They have enabled every officer who took them, to carry away a most intimate understanding of the operations occuring in the areas visited. In after years they will constitute a body of officers especially well adapted to teaching in our own schools at home the military history of the western front.

The course of study in the regular course lasted three weeks; that in the special course 12 days. * * *

The lectures which have been given throughout the courses have been of a very high order. It has been possible to secure as a lecturer on every subject an officer who has distinguished himself in France in that particular subject upon which he lectures. The very best brains of the A. E. F. have been available in this way for the students of this center. Most of these lectures have been mimeographed and distributed through a mailing list to officers of the A. E. F. desiring them. Copies of same have also been supplied to the office of the chief of artillery and to G-5, G. H. Q., A. E. F., where they will undoubtedly be preserved as most of them are military literature of great value * * * The officers selected for duty as instructors on the center's staff have all been most competent and have discharged their duties most efficiently. They have all had extended service at the front and the doctrine which has been taught by them can in no way be regarded as purely academic.

The center has striven to develop the ability of high ranking officers to organize their work so that effective plans for the employment of the artillery may be quickly drawn; to determine the capacity of high ranking officers for the command of large artillery units; to give to officers of other arms attending this center a knowledge of the powers and limitations of artillery, and finally as a result of study together and the exchange of views, to build up between high ranking officers a better understanding of each others needs and how these needs can best be met by each others branch of the service.

As the course proceeded the class was enlarged to include in addition to the infantry and artillery officers, officers of the air service, machine guns, and engineers, so that representatives of all combatant arms of a division were found in the classes. The classes were divided into two or more committees. Each committee made one solution of each problem in the course. The personnel of each committee functioned as a staff; usually the senior infantry general officer acted as the high command, assisted by an infantry field officer and was chief of committee. He laid down the work in the problem required of an army or corps commander. Another infantry general assisted by an infantry field officer did the work of the particular division concerned in the problem. An artillery general with a number of artillery officers acted as chief of corps artillery and handled the corps artillery work of the problem. Another artillery general assisted by artillery officers prepared the plan of employment for the artillery of the infantry division concerned in each problem. The plans for the air service, machine guns, and engineers in each problem were gotten out by one officer of each of those arms assigned to each committee. The effort was made in the committee to have officers of one arm work with officers of another arm in their particular parts of the problem, so as to get a better understanding of how a branch of the service other than their own proceeded in its work. For each problem, each committee therefore turned in one solution which was the product of the work of all its members who had functioned in its solution more or less as staffs would have done in actual operations. Each committee then turned its solution over to another committee for comparison and comment. These comments of another committee were reduced to writing and with the solutions of each committee were made the basis of a general critique by the school staff on all the solutions submitted. At the conclusion of these critiques the solutions of the problems were thrown open for general discussion. Much value resulted from this way of handling the work. The analyzation, comparison, and comments upon three different solutions made by different bodies of men was very interesting and instructive. The character of the officers who formed the student body of these classes, has been such as to make the quality of the work done, very high. The officers of the classes have lived and messed together, have worked together in committee rooms and have had an opportunity for constant and detailed exchange of views in the solution of military problems. The result has been the building up of a liaison between the officers of the various arms attending this center which it is most desirable to attain. It has been the universal expression of opinion of all officers of all arms who have attended the course here that the work has served to give them a better understanding of the other arms of the service, their needs, their powers, their limitations, and their aspirations. They have almost without exception been officers of high rank and professional qualifications; most of them generals, colonels, or lieut. colonels, and a very large proportion of them have demonstrated their professional ability in action during the war. The association of such men together for a short time on any duty is an education in itself.

3. It is not known what policy has been adopted as to the reestablishment of the center in the United States. The establishment of some institution akin to it seems to be very desirable for purposes of study during peace time. The course might be lengthened, say to six weeks or two months. The officers detailed for the course should be of high rank and professional attainments and past records in keeping with the dignity and importance of such an institution. As was the case in Europe it is believed the class should be limited to general officers and to selected field officers of field and coast artillery, with a certain representation of other combatant arms of a division, such as the infantry, aviation, engineers, and machine guns. In such an institution, essentially artillery in its nature, the proportion of officers of other arms would naturally be considerably less than that of artillery officers. The course should be regarded as something in the nature of post-graduate work and should consist of a course of lectures, a series of appropriate tactical problems, visits to various industrial plants, arsenals, etc., and demonstrations by troops especially artillery firing.

4. In order that it may be readily accessible both for lectures and for shortness of travel in visiting various industrial centers, proving grounds, arsenals, etc., and for reasonable accessibility to artillery firing grounds the center should be centrally located. If the artillery camp in North Carolina (Camp Bragg) is continued it would meet the needs as far as artillery fire is concerned. Under such conditions the center might well be located at or near Washington, D. C. It should be placed where there would be close liaison between it and the War Department and the new General Staff

College at Washington, D. C. Its staff should consist of the ablest officers obtainable. The director should be a general officer, preferably one of distinguished service with the artillery in the A. E. F. and as far as possible all members of the center's staff should have had battle experience. The importance of directing such an institution demands that it be directed by an officer of high rank and achievements. We have many such who have served in France as corps, division and artillery brigade commanders.

* * * * * *

M. E. LOCKE,
Colonel, Field Artillery,
Director.

C-in-C Rept. File: Fldr. 222: Report

Infantry Specialists School

Langres, Haute-Marne, November 11, 1918.

[Extract]

August 27, 1917: School project for American Expeditionary Forces, calling for the creation of Army Infantry Specialists School submitted to Chief of Staff, American E. F. by Lieut. Colonel Paul R. Malone, chief of training section.

October 10, 1917: G. O. 46, G. H. Q., orders establishment of Army Infantry Specialists School at Langres not later than November 15, 1917.

October 25, 1917: Lieut. Colonel Robert J. Maxey, ordered from I Corps School at Gondrecourt to Langres to establish Army Infantry Specialists School.

December 17, 1917: First courses opened * * *

January 30, 1918: Pressing need of trained officers with troops obliged school to assume responsibility of training men for commands in line as well as training instructors for junior schools. Second series of courses begin this date.

March 5, 1918: Minor tactics branch organized. Began working out new extended order combat formations later adopted by the American army.

April 11, 1918: Army Automatic Weapons School at Fort de Peigney, center of instruction in machine guns and automatic rifles, incorporated with Army Infantry Specialists School.

July 31, 1918: Following a period of expansion school changed station to Fort de Plesnoy to procure larger quarters and improved facilities. Automatic rifle section joins school from Fort de Peigney.

August 19, 1918: Courses open at Fort de Plesnoy, with numerous additions and amplifications to schedules.

September 10, 1918: Half-day tactical program for entire school introduced. Student battalion organized.

October 31, 1918: Company B, Provisional Training Battalion, assigned to school.

Figures giving the number of courses given in each branch up to December 21, 1918, with strength and number of officers and noncommissioned officers recommended to be instructors, up to November 11, 1918, are supplied * * *

Branch	No. of Courses	Officers Attending	Recommended Instructor	N. C. O.'s Attending	Recommended Instructor
(x) Minor Tactics	8	466	35	265	None
Musketry and Bayonet	8	351	48	281	9
(y) Machine Gun	6	259	31	280	None
Automatic Rifle	20	553	96	400	29
Observation and Sniping	9	333	35	284	None
One Pound Cannon	18	381	30	296	15
Grenades	18	605	77	484	33
Stokes Mortar	17	329	50	354	16
	104	3277 2644	402 102	2644	102
Grand Totals Students		5921	504 Instructors		

(x) Organized March 5, 1918. (y) From April 11 to July 31, 1918.
This table does not include special demonstrations for general officers of army center of information, general and field officers of Army General Staff College and field and line officers of army school of line. There were ten such demonstrations attended by approximately 1,000 officers.

* * * * * *

2. General Policy of School: The general policy of the Army Infantry Specialists School was originally defined as follows, in a memorandum to the Chief of Staff, American E. F., bearing the date of Paris, August 27, 1918.

The army schools - A center of instruction for the entire army. This group shall include a general staff college and such other schools (The Army Infantry Specialists School being mentioned by name in another part of the memorandum) as may be necessary to train instructors for all corps schools. The army schools should be under the direct control of these (general) headquarters in order that the doctrine which should actuate the entire system of instruction and control of our ideas of combat may be transmitted from the general staff through these schools to all units of the army.

From this statement of policy all subsequent processes of these schools proceed.

The first series of courses conducted by these schools (Dec. 17, 1917-January 15, 1918) adhered solely to the purpose defined above, i. e. to train instructors for the corps schools. December and early January witnessed the first overseas contingents from the second officers training camps in the United States, ordered to France as replacements for the early divisions. The I and II Corps Schools were unable to handle all of the new arrivals, so the surplus was turned over to the army schools. Thus, at the beginning of the second series of courses (January 30-March 2, 1918) the Army Infantry Specialists School was diverted from the aim for which they had been created, namely, to supply instructors to the junior schools. It could not, however, relinquish its original responsibility for the selection and training of instructors for the other schools, so, under the stress of necessity, it assumed the dual task of training such instructors and at the same time fitting officers, and later on, noncommissioned officers, for commands in the line.

This state of affairs, at the time regarded as the issue of a temporary necessity, became permanent. The American Expeditionary Forces grew by such swift strides that corps schools could not be created or enlarged rapidly enough to meet the demands made upon them. So, throughout its existence the Army Infantry Specialists Schools continued to perform this two-fold function.

At the conclusion of the series of courses completed December 23, 1918, the Army Infantry Specialists Schools had given 102 separate courses to 3277 officers and 2644 noncommissioned officers. Up to November 11 when hostilities ceased 504 officers and noncommissioned officers had qualified to be instructors for either the army or corps schools. These figures do not include special demonstrations for general staff and field officers to the number of about 1000.

This addition to the mission of these schools necessitated an amplification of their policy, which is covered in G. O. 35, G. H. Q., dated March 5, 1918. This order recites "instructions to govern corps schools", but since the Army Infantry Specialists School had taken over the work of the latter the order is applicable equally to the Army Specialists School.

While courses were arranged primarily with a view to prompt training in methods proper for stationery warfare, it was made clear to all concerned that this was a special form of warfare, and the highest excellence in this form would be of little avail if officers and troops have not the knowledge and training required for the maneuvering in the open fields that we recognized would follow successful operations across the trenches. The school strove to keep the various forms of warfare in their proper place and proportion, and make clear to the students what methods, formations and tactics were suitable for, and should be applied to each kind of warfare. The thorough inculcation of correct tactical doctrine for the platoon, company, battery and battalion has been made the first consideration at these schools.

Tactical teachings were fitted to the natural initiative of our officers and men, and were calculated to develop this characteristic to the fullest extent.

The training given provided for the imparting to the students a thorough knowledge in the specialist branch to which assigned, an outline of the use, capabilities and limitations of the other specialty branches and, by combined exercises, the use tactically of all of the infantry arms. Frequent requests were made by divisions for instructors in the various specialties, for instruction in the divisional areas. These were always granted, and the extent of such instruction was limited only by the number of officers available for such duty.

Constant effort has been made to improve, revise and extend the scope of the several courses as experience dictated. A spirit of individual initiative in the direction of research and experiment was encouraged. Every effort was put forth to stimulate the development of new ideas for the betterment of methods and matériel. This policy resulted in the invention and development by instructors of numerous devices, many of which have served to promote the effectiveness of the infantry specialties.

Instruction looking toward the return to open warfare was introduced in December, 1917. It was developed as the turn of events warranted during the summer of 1918. In September instruction in the different specialties was restricted to one-half day and one-half of each day was devoted to special instruction designed to insure more intelligent and capable cooperation between the various infantry arms, to drill in open warfare combat formations and to field and combat problems.

Particular emphasis was placed on the use of the rifle. It was shown how the individual could be quickly trained and how the fire of rifles and automatic rifles could be combined with movement to insure the taking of hostile machine-gun positions with the minimum of loss, the details of which will be more fully discussed under the heading of musketry and bayonet.

Throughout its existence it is believed that the character of instruction given at the school was kept thoroughly up to date, with reference to the nature of operations at the front. To accomplish this it became the policy of the school to select the additional instructors required by the growth of the institution, from among former students who had been recommended to be instructors and who had returned temporarily to their combat divisions. Instructors detailed from their organizations before American troops had participated to any great extent in the fighting, were ordered from time to time to tours of duty with combat divisions in the line. In this manner there was built up an instructor personnel of experienced line officers, who understood the practical application in action of the tactical theories elucidated at this school.

    a. Musketry and Bayonet
    b. Automatic Rifle
    c. Grenades
    d. Observation and Sniping
    e. One Pound Cannon
    f. Stokes Mortar
    g. Minor Tactics
    h. Gas

a. MUSKETRY AND BAYONET: Musketry training at these schools falls readily into three phases, which may be considered in their order:

1. Preliminary rifle training. It was found that with virtually all classes, previous training in the use of the rifle had not extended beyond the most elemental considerations. It therefore became necessary to begin with the fundamental elements. A system similar to the one outlined by Colonel McNab, Infantry, has been used and most excellent results obtained. The shortcomings of each student were carefully noted and corrected. No great change from old methods was attempted, merely a different application in which each man learned thoroughly a subject before advancing to another. The essence of this phase of the training may be summed up in:

    a. Sighting and aiming drills until proficient
    b. Positions, until proficient
    c. Trigger squeeze, until proficient
    d. Rapid Fire Drills, until proficient

2. Collective Training. Limited range facilities prevented any extended musketry problems and as a substitute landscape targets were introduced and used throughout the course. A landscape target, presenting in miniature a section of terrain, proved as effecacious, if not better, for certain musketry training than would the actual ground itself. The use of such targets enables the presentation of principles and more clearly accentuates errors in the different phases of firing than any other method. By clearly shown errors the maximum of information can be imparted. Training in sight training, vocabulary, target designation and recognition, fire training principles of tactics and fire action was pursued with the best results on the landscape range.

3. Fire and Movement. For the practical application of the rules learned and principles gained from the exercises there followed a series of field and combat problems. These were designed to illustrate the various methods by which the combination of fire and movement may be utilized to cope with a military situation. These problems

varied, one from the other, and it is believed the very essence of musketry centralized in these exercises. Constant and daily practice was given in range estimation, hasty estimation of situations calling for logical deductions and disposition of forces, all to the end that the platoon or company commander would realize the full effects of the fire of his weapons.

Bayonet training, which formed a part of this course, was found to be very beneficial. If it is assumed that this training does no more than to impart confidence to an infantryman, it has served its purpose. As a training to harden muscles to make the man physically fit and alert, it fits in well with any system of musketry training.

Synopsis of Instruction
 a. Preliminary Rifle Training

* * * * * *

 b. Musketry

* * * * * *

 c. Bayonet

* * * * * *

AUTOMATIC RIFLE: American troops have been armed with four types of automatic rifles   the Chauchat, French Model of 1915, and United States Model of 1917, the Lewis gun and the Browning. At all times they have been opposed by the German Light Maxim. Consequently automatic rifle instruction has embraced all of these weapons as well as instruction in the use of the Colt Automatic Pistol and the Smith and Wesson Revolver, which the gunner carries for his personal protection.

The first and fundamental aim in instruction in the automatic rifle section is to impart to the student an expert and thorough knowledge of the mechanical characteristics of the rifle, with particular stress upon the reduction of stoppages. Without this thorough knowledge of the powers and limitations of the rifle no automatic rifle commander can achieve success. Tactics amount simply to the application of this knowledge to the conditions of warfare.

Tactical considerations are taken up in this sequence:
1. Use of the Automatic Rifle in Defence.
   a. Position Warfare.
   b. Open Warfare.
2. Use of the Automatic Rifle in Offense.
   a. Position Warfare.
   b. Open Warfare

In defence, either in trenches or out, the automatic rifle occupies forward positions, and acts by means of its fire alone. In an attack delivered from one organized position against another it acts by combination of fire and movement which are nearly the same in all cases. Rules supplant the need for individual initiative to some extent in trench warfare. In an attack or advance in the open the automatic operates by a union of fire and movement, generally more movement than fire, in contradistinction to trench warfare where fire takes precedence over movement. No new principles of automatic rifle tactics are disclosed in open warfare; that form of combat demands merely the quick and intuitive application of the old principles which stand out more clearly in trench actions.

With the Browning the unquestioned superiority of single shot over automatic fire is emphasized most forcefully. By actual demonstration every student is shown that the

Browning, fired semi-automatically at the rate of one aimed shot a second, produced the most effective class of small arms infantry fire ever achieved with a platoon weapon.

Synopsis of Course

I. Training of the Individual:

* * * * * *

II. Training of the Team:

* * * * * *

III. Training of the Squad:

* * * * * *

IV. Theory of Automatic Rifle Practice:

* * * * * *

V. Pistol Course:

* * * * * *

GRENADES: In this course the student is taught that the grenade is a weapon used by the infantry soldier as a supplement to his primary weapons, the rifle and bayonet.

That the function of the grenade is to reach the enemy underground or behind cover, and force him into the open where he will provide a target for the rifle, automatic rifle and machine gun. That the rifle grenade extends the radius of action of the hand grenade. That combined with covering fire and natural cover several grenadiers can advance and bring effective fire upon hostile machine-gun positions.

Tactical problems in connection with the other arms are given to illustrate the use of this instrument of warfare.

Synopsis of Course:
Theoretical

* * * * * *

Practical

* * * * * *

OBSERVATION AND SNIPING: The aim of the observation and sniping course is to train officers in the duties of regimental intelligence officer and of battalion scout officer, and to train noncommissioned officers to the work of N. C. O.'s in the above capacities.

In the opinion of the officers associated with this course the battalion scout group should be an independent organization. Recommendations to this effect have been made.

In July 1918 the regimental and battalion intelligence officers of the 32d Division received instruction from this branch. After testing the tenets of this instruction in line, G 2 of the division expressed the opinion that the intelligence work of that division was surpassed by none in the army.

The intelligence personnel of the 19th Division was given a special course of instruction in its divisional area. G-2 of that division stated, after months of service in the line, that so long as officers who had received this training were available for intelligence work, the service was highly satisfactory.

Synopsis of Course.
I. Lecture:

* * * * * *

II. Individual Instruction:

* * * * * *

III. Training of regimental intelligence section.

IV. Training of Battalion Scout Group.

ONE POUND CANNON: The course of instruction in this branch lays particular emphasis on the fact that the one pound cannon is a link between the artillery and the infantry, and that it must accompany the infantry in all the circumstances of battle. Every use to which the piece is put is predicated on the assumption that it keeps pace with the infantry.

Practical ways and means for keeping the gun with the infantry, for maintaining liaison between the gun commander and the regimental and battalion P. C.'s, and for keeping an adequate ammunition supply with the guns accompany every phase of the instruction.

This instruction covers advance and defense tactics in both position and open warfare. In position warfare the function of the one pound cannon is largely the delivery of harassing fire. In the advance its main mission is to offset machine-gun fire and to destroy machine guns by direct hits, a fact made possible by the accuracy of the piece.

Synopsis of Course.
I. Lectures for Study and Incorporation into Note Books.

* * * * * *

II. Field Work putting into practical application information contained in lectures.

* * * * * *

STOKES MORTAR: Like the one pound cannon, the Stokes mortar is always an accompanying weapon of the infantry. The roles of the Stokes and one pound cannon, however, are separate and distinct, and it has been one of the principle aims of these courses to train each branch to its proper task.

The one-pounder has a flat trajectory, great accuracy, and a comparatively small killing radius. The Stokes has a high trajectory, only fair accuracy, but a large killing radius. It can cover effectively features of terrain which are defiladed to the fire of the one-pounder to artillery or small arms.

It has been the aim of this course to train the Stokes personnel to accompany the infantry under all circumstances and to recognize and fire upon the proper Stokes targets, and to cooperate with the other regimental arms.

Synopsis of Course.
Theoretical.

* * * * * *

Practical Work.

* * * * * *

MINOR TACTICS: The minor tactics course was designed to cover, as the name implies, minor tactics. The principles underlying the use of all the weapons of the infantry platoon together with the supporting arms were first emphasized by demonstrations and conferences followed by problems designed to illustrate clearly these principles.

One-half day was devoted by the entire school to tactical training, covered by the attached schedule.

The minor tactics section proper took part in these exercises as students, platoon, company and battalion commanders and more extended work in the following subjects:

Organization
Military Sketching
Use of Maps and Compass
  Map Problems
Information
  Aeroplane Maps
  Intelligence, Liaison
Security
  Problems
March Discipline
Combat
  Use of small arms
  Use of tanks
  Camouflage
  Tactical Exercises

C-in-C Rept. File: Fldr. 223: Report

MILITARY HISTORY OF ARMY MACHINE GUN SCHOOL

[Extract]

1. On December 5, 1917, Colonel John H. Parker, U. S. Infantry, officially took over FORT de PEIGNEY from the French authorities and established the army automatic weapons school. This school consisted of two sections, viz.
  (a) The machine gun section.
  (b) The automatic rifle section.

On April 11, 1918, the name of the school was changed to: Army infantry specialist school, Section A, automatic weapons. On August 1, 1918, the name was changed to: Army machine gun school and the automatic rifle section was transferred to the infantry specialist school.

* * * * * *

The classes were as follows:
1. Hotchkiss, December 17, 1917 to January 20, 1918.
   Officers 29
2. Hotchkiss, January 28, 1918 to February 28, 1918.
   Officers 45
3. Special Hotchkiss, January 28, 1918 to February 11, 1918.
   N. C. O.'s 17
4. Special Hotchkiss, March 4, 1918 to March 13, 1918.
   Officers 8
   N. C. O.'s 14
5. Special Hotchkiss, March 8, 1918 to March 15, 1918
   Officers 1
   N. C. O.'s 36

6. Hotchkiss, March 13 to April 7, 1918 and May 11, 1918 to May 18, 1918.
   Officers 15
   N. C. O.'s 36
7. Hotchkiss, March 13, 1918 to March 17, 1918 and April 27, 1918
   to May 18, 1918.
   N. C. O.'s.44
8. Special Hotchkiss, April 11, 1918 to April 15, 1918.
   Officers 52
9. Special Hotchkiss, April 15, 1918 to April 22, 1918.
   Officers 14
10. Hotchkiss, April 15, 1918 to May 18, 1918
    Officers 56
11. Special Course, April 1, 1918 to April 18, 1918.
    Officers 1
    N. C. O.'s 5
12. Vickers, May 27, 1918 to June 22, 1918
    Officers 74
    N. C. O.'s 126
13. Vickers, July 3, 1918 to July 27, 1918.
    Officers 67
    N. C..O's 69
14. Vickers and Hotchkiss, August 21, 1918 to September 14, 1918.
    Vickers
      Officers 52
      N. C. O.'s 44
    Hotchkiss
      Officers 50
      N. C. O.'s 42
15. Hotchkiss, October 1, 1918 to October 26, 1918.
    Officers 75
    N. C. O.'s 53

2. The work in each course included the mechanical operation of various types of machine guns; practice and instruction in known distance machine gun firing; calculations for and practice in various methods of indirect machine-gun fire; a certain amount of machine gun tactics; pistol and grenade practice.

3. The original aim of the school was to provide instructors for corps machine gun schools and other places where specially qualified instructors were required. However, this plan was never carried out owing to the constant arrivals in France of machine gun officers whom it was necessary to train prior to their joining their organizations. For that reason the students in each course prior to the present one have been limited to company officers and noncommissioned officers. These to be utilized as instructors in their respective organizations. There are no records available of any particular instances in which such training as has been given at these schools did or did not save lives or assist in securing successes. It is a matter of general information that such has been the case in many instances but the only authentic accounts could be given by participants in those particular actions.

4. The general policy of the school as recently outlined is: (a) to fit company officers and noncommissioned officers for duty as instructors in their respective organizations in the use of the Browning Machine Gun Equipment. (b) To fit the machine gun field officers to properly supervise the work of their respective battalions in training and in combat. This requires a certain amount of mechanical instruction in the new

equipment together with such tactical instruction as the four weeks course and the facilities of the school permit.

5. Such data as are available are furnished concerning the automatic rifle section during the time it was a part of this school.

F. S. BOWEN,
Col., Inf.

C-in-C Rept. File: Fldr. 224: Report

Army Engineer School

December 12, 1918.

[Extract]

GENERAL OUTLINE: Under the provisions of subparagraph c, paragraph 1, Section III, General Orders No. 46, G. H. Q., American E. F., October 10, 1917, the army engineer school was established, and on October 31, 1917, with Colonel G. R. Lukesh, Engineers, as Commandant, the school was opened at Langres, Haute Marne, France. The months of November and December were spent in preparation and organization, and early in January, courses were opened for students in the following sections of the school:

Bridging
Camouflage
Flash and Sound Ranging
Mining
Pioneering
Topographic and
Searchlight

After a reorganization of the army candidates school, the engineer section was created as part of the army engineer school, January 22, 1918.

On March 1, 1918, the school was moved from Langres to Fort Saint Menge, ten kilometers north of that city. At that time the searchlight section was severed from the school and taken over by the antiaircraft and trench mortar school. The topographic section remained in Langres, operating at the Turenne Barracks. * * *

* * * * * *

On June 25, a school was opened for engineer officers and was called the student officers training camp, ending August 7.

In the latter part of July the topographic section was taken over by the army intelligence school, and in its place was created the artillery orientation section, operating at the Lunette, Turenne Barracks, Langres.

The towns of Bannes, Charmes, Chaney, Charmoilles, Changey, Champigny, Dampierre, Humes, Jorquenay, Lannes and Rolampont were assigned to the army engineer school for the purpose of billeting and training troops.

To perform and assist in the practical and demonstrational work in connection with the school, as well as to undergo training, various engineer organizations and detachments have been assigned to the school from time to time. * * *

* * * * * *

The total strength of the school, although subject to fluctuations, has averaged for the past two months 3,000 officers and men, including staff, students and organizations on duty with the school.

This school gives the full courses of five weeks [of general military engineer instruction for student officers and N. C. O.'s from] the IV, V, VI and VII Corps and a one week course in bridging for students of the I, II and III Corps Schools. In addition, students are sent here for special courses from all branches of the service. Brief demonstrations are given from time to time to students of other army schools. In the five weeks' course the time is about equally divided in the four regular sections of the school: Bridge, camouflage, mining and pioneer.

A brief outline of each section of the school follows:

ARTILLERY ORIENTATION SECTION: In April, 1918, an orienting course for artillery officers was planned, but owing to the impossibility at that time of getting officers relieved from duty at the front, to undergo instruction, there was developed instead, a course in topography and mapping under the supervision of the topographic section. This served to fill the needs of several of the army schools as well as the 29th Engineers (flash and sound ranging).

On August 12, the artillery orientation section began its actual course of instruction * * * The personnel consisted of two officers and two enlisted men, all of whom were from the 29th Engineers. A three weeks' course was given for sixteen officers and ten enlisted men from artillery organizations from various divisions at the front. This was the only course given to artillerymen, due to the same difficulty of relieving men at the front to attend the school.

Due to the highly specialized nature of the work comparatively few students underwent training in this section, those who did so coming from the 29th Engineers. Subjects were covered that were found necessary in certain phases of flash and sound ranging. No regular courses have been followed, schedules being arranged to meet requirements.
* * * The last course in this section ended November 22.

BRIDGE SECTION: The bridge section opened approximately December 15, 1917, with the establishment of the army engineer school. * * * The bridge section was located at Carteret Trecourt Barracks, Langres, remaining there until March, when it moved with the rest of the engineer school to Fort Saint Menge, where its headquarters and heavy bridging site were located. The ponton and light bridging work was carried on at the Reservoir des Charmes, near Bannes, which is about eight kilometers distant from Fort Saint Menge. Due to difficulties in transportation and administration on account of this wide separation of the section, the entire personnel and material were moved on September 9 to the reservoir. The present personnel consists of ten officers and twenty four enlisted men. * * *

* * * * * *

Three regular courses in bridging are followed: The normal course (eighteen days), special course for engineer candidates, and the short course (six days), the last named being the most frequent. Instruction is given in practically all types of ponton, light, and heavy bridging, both as to theory and practice.

The bridge section is the only school of its kind in the American army. It instructs all of the engineer students from the various corps schools, all of the engineer candidates for commission, and all of the corps and army bridging units, as well as giving numerous demonstrations to the army school of the line, army general staff college, trench mortar school and others.

This is the largest section of the school, and approximately 4500 students (officers and men) will have completed a regular course of instruction in bridging by January 31, 1919.

The primary aim of the bridge section is to train in the fundamentals of military bridge construction, the selection of the proper type of crossing to be used under various conditions, both tactical and topographical, and the simplest and quickest way of preparing such a crossing for use.

CAMOUFLAGE SECTION: The camouflage section began its formulation of plans in November 1917, * * *

The courses of instruction, at the beginning, consisted of lectures only, as there was no demonstration field or camouflage material available. In January 1918, a demonstration field was secured at Fort Saint Menge, but owing to adverse weather conditions and lack of material, it was not possible to begin actual work there until March 1. At that time the personnel was composed of two officers and five enlisted men. At present there are four officers and twelve enlisted men on duty with the section.

The section has been in close touch, at all times, with the operations at the front, its instructors making frequent trips for the purpose of gathering material and data for instruction. It has been observed at the front that officers and enlisted men who passed through the camouflage section have applied the principles taught there with great thoroughness and success and have spread their knowledge with good results.

Special instruction was given to artillerymen, both officers and enlisted men. It was planned to regularly instruct each week a class consisting of about ten officers and fifty enlisted men from different artillery organizations, but upon the completion of the fourth class, cessation of hostilities rendered it no longer necessary. Regular courses were originally planned but found impracticable and as a result special courses were given, according to the convenience of the class, for artillery infantry, engineer and camouflage officers and men, varying in length from a day to a month.

In general the subject covered consisted of the study of airplane photographs, the theory and practice of camouflage, its relation to the infantry and other branches of the service, and the camouflaging of excavations, dugouts, ammunition dumps, light railways, batteries, machine-gun positions, trenches, observation posts, camps, huts, and tents. Instruction has been given in camouflage to approximately 3000 students since the organization of this section.

The camouflage section has endeavored to give, through its students:

(a) An understanding and a working knowledge of the practical cmouflage that is erected at the front by the Camouflage Section, American E. F., and

(b) Correct information regarding the military channels through which the services of the camouflage section may be secured at the front.

In its instruction, the camouflage section has had to overcome an almost complete misunderstanding of the subject on the part of students newly arrived from America. Throughout the course, the instructors give the logical, practical reason for everything that is done in camouflage as practiced by the camouflage section. Students are shown photographs of the interior of actual camouflaged battery positions at the front, American, and sometimes, German aerophotographs of these positions, and captured German secret maps of the sector on which the well camouflaged batteries are not marked. In all the instruction, special stress is laid on an understanding of airplane photography, and of how manufactured camouflage materials give to the camera in the airplane the general proportion of shadow and of reflecting surface that the camera finds in a terrain. For artillery officers, reconnaissance is an important part of the course. Students are sent out to select for their batteries, positions in which they could not only fulfill an intended tactical mission, but which could also be successfully and simply camouflaged.

ENGINEER SECTION, ARMY CANDIDATES SCHOOL: On December 1, the army candidates school was organized, and was composed of representatives of all infantry, engineer and cavalry regiments in France. On December 22, 1917 the engineer section, of the army candidates school was officially opened with a class of thirty-six students, who took a three weeks' course of lectures, in pioneering, mining and bridging, and on January 22, 1918, it became a section of the army engineer school. On that date, there was an interchanging of students of divisional and railway troops, to the infantry and engineer courses, leaving twenty seven students in the engineer section.

* * * * * *

On March 9, the candidates were ordered to Fort Saint Menge for practical engineering work, the time being divided between pioneering, bridging and mining. Eighteen of the students of the first class were commissioned as 2d Lieutenants and were sent to the front on April 1 on an observation trip, three of them being retained in this section as instructors.

The second class opened April 1 with ninety-six candidates, an increase of 300 per cent over the first class. Fifty-nine successfully graduated from this class and were commissioned at the completion of the course, June 30. They also had a two weeks' course in the infantry section, army candidates school, after completing the engineer work. Six of these officers were retained in this section as instructors.

The third class opened August 1, with 406 candidates, 324 of whom successfully completed the course and were commissioned October 1. On October 7, 800 candidates were received, and 400 additional ones on November 7. It was intended to keep 1200 candidates regularly, graduating 400 per month, and receiving 400, but due to the cessation of hostilities the class of November 7 was the last to enter. 100 successful candidates were graduated on November 20, and 300 on November 30. The candidates who graduated after November 11 were not commissioned, but given a certificate showing that they successfully completed the course, and this certificate will be given to the remaining successful students.

The aim of the school is to give the students the military and engineering training that will best fit them for duties as engineer officers in the army. All classes of candidates receive instruction in mining, bridging, pioneering and camouflage, from the different sections of the army engineer school. The classes in these subjects are given in the mornings, while the afternoons are taken up with drills, recitations and lectures. Recitations cover the manual of courts martial, infantry drill regulations and field service and sanitary regulations. Lectures by experienced officers take up in a brief way the subjects of mechanics, hydraulics, bridging, topography and landscape sketching, and more thoroughly, company administration and rules of land warfare. Practical work includes the erection of wire entanglements and other obstacles, the use of explosives, the construction revetment and drainage of trenches, some of the simpler phases of mining, the location and erection of camouflage, bridging, and topography and landscape sketching.

The strictest discipline is maintained and this result is accomplished in part by a regular and systematic program of close and extended order drills which not only instil a spirit of discipline but also assist in giving to the candidate a more military bearing and carriage and inspire in him a greater confidence in himself and in his ability to command others. Additional instruction is given in combat formations and in the handling of special weapons.

FLASH AND SOUND RANGING SECTION: The flash and sound ranging section began operations January 5, 1918 * * * The personnel on December 1 consisted of five officers and twenty-four enlisted men.

The primary purpose of this section is to train officers and men of companies from the 29th Engineers specializing in ranging. It is therefore set apart from the army engineer school to a great extent, and although under the jurisdiction of the school its operation is largely under the control of the 29th Engineers. In addition certain courses have been given to the candidates and special lectures and demonstrations have been given at the school and outside.

The operation of the school can be divided roughly into two periods: January 5, 1918-July 20, 1918, and July 20, 1918 to date. During the first period of five and a half months, only Company B, 29th Engineers was trained. This was due to the difficulty of obtaining replacements and the close connection between the school and that organization. During that time no definite schedule could be carried out so the men were available for school duties only at odd times.

During the second period definite schedules of instruction were carried out according to prearranged plans. This has resulted in a much better training for the men in a much shorter interval of time. The present flash course is of four weeks duration, that of the sound, three weeks. During this period, two weeks mobile work, one week flash and one week sound, has been carried out with each class, giving the men a chance in the field to put to actual use, the principles learned at the school, after which the errors made could be corrected and a better line upon the ability of each man obtained.

A record card of each man is kept, giving his qualifications, past experience, record at the school with suggestions how the man should be used at the front. These cards are sent to the front with each individual so that he may be put just where he belongs.

Sound and flash ranging are technical services used for the first time in this war, four years ago being unknown. The chief objects of these services are the location of enemy artillery and the regulating of friendly artillery fire upon enemy targets. In addition, the flash ranging service does a considerable amount of intelligence work such as recording enemy troop movements and new work (dugout construction, new trenches and wire entanglements).

The primary object of this section has been to teach both officers and enlisted men all the theoretical side, and as much of the practical side as is possible away from the front, so that they could quickly take their places in sections at the front and carry on this special work.

Of these two services sound ranging is highly technical, while flash ranging is more of a technical nature than one might assume from a knowledge of the theory alone.

All flash and sound rangers in addition to being soldiers are obliged to learn a work absolutely new which requires a considerable knowledge of mathematics, electricity, drafting, topography, etc., and as not all the students possess the education requisite to a full understanding of the principles involved, it has been necessary to teach elementary electricity, instrument repair, survey methods, map reading and a certain amount of mathematics before flash and sound ranging in detail could be approached.

MINING SECTION: The mining section began its courses of instruction January 5, 1918. * * * At the time of the opening, the personnel of this section consisted of two officers and three enlisted men, and at present there are six officers and nine enlisted men.

* * * * * *

The work of the mining section is both theoretical and practical, the time being about equally divided between lectures and actual construction. The preparation of designs and papers for the board on military engineering, has been an important part of the work, much of which has been published in the engineer field notes. This section has kept in close connection with the operations at the front, instruction being based entirely upon present and future conditions. Instructors and detachments have been sent to the front from time to time for the purpose of gaining practical experience under actual conditions.

Two regular courses are given: The long course (eighteen days) and the short course (nine days). In addition, special courses varying in length are arranged to meet requirements. In general the following subjects are covered: Cave shelters, cut and cover shelters, concrete structures, mine warfare, the use of listening apparatus, mine rescue and demolitions.

Approximately 3100 officers and enlisted men (students) will have completed a regular course in this section by January 31, 1919, in addition to detachments from organizations assigned to the school to assist in the practical work. Numerous lectures and demonstrations have been given to other army schools here and instructors sent out to these schools on other occasions for this purpose.

When the American E. F. started fighting in France, it was soon found that there was a total lack of knowledge regarding safe, shell-proof shelters for the men, and very little was known about mining operations of any kind. This also applied to military demolitions and the handling of explosives. The aim of the mining section has been to overcome these deficiencies, not only among the engineers but also in the other branches of the service which would have to use this knowledge to work efficiently.

Courses have been laid out to fit the particular needs of each branch of the service. Engineers are given lectures and practical work covering all kinds of mining and demolition while other organizations have only taken up the special kinds of construction needed for their work. Officers are given more of the theoretical side while enlisted men spend most of their time in actual underground work.

PIONEER SECTION: The first course of instruction in the pioneer section commenced January 5, 1918 * * * The present personnel consists of five officers and eight enlisted men.

The work of the pioneer section involves a broader scope than that of the other sections, consisting of everything in the way of military engineering not included in the others, particular emphasis being laid upon field fortifications, mapping, entanglements and road construction. A battle sector has been constructed on the drill grounds which includes various types of machine gun and automatic rifle emplacements, trenches (showing two samples of all types of revetment) and an extensive system of barbed wire entanglements.

Two regular courses are given: The long course (eighteen days) and the short course (nine days).

Approximately 2800 officers and enlisted men (students) will have completed a regular course in this section by January 1, 1919. In addition frequent lectures and demonstrations have been given to various classes from outside schools.

In general, the aim of this section is to give the students a logical view of the work which devolves on divisional engineers in active service (excluding mining and bridging), beginning with the simplest basic principles of field fortification, and continuing through the more technical subjects.

STUDENT OFFICERS TRAINING CAMP: The student officers training camp was opened in the latter part of June * * * having a student body of 240 engineer officers sent from various organizations in the American E. F. The course lasted six weeks.

The object of the camp was to fit officers for duty with new combat regiments. To attain this primary object the camp was organized and instruction given with a view to provide the students with a first hand impression of the life of an enlisted man; to teach them how to train new recruits; and to impress them thoroughly with the fundamental principles of discipline. A secondary object was to determine what students were fitted to perform the duties of a higher grade of rank; what students were unfit for service with troops; and what students were unfit for further service in the army.

TOPOGRAPHIC SECTION: Regular courses in the topographic section commenced January

22, 1918 * * * Its function was primarily to give special instruction in the interpretation and restitution of aerial photographs and map reading.

No regular courses were followed and schedules were arranged to meet requirements, considerable instruction being given outside of the school and to other sections within the school. The personnel of the school was also subject to frequent changes.

* * * * * *

NOTE: No data are available on the searchlight section, due to the fact that all records went with that section when it was taken over by the antiaircraft and trench mortar school.

AIMS OF THE SCHOOL: It has been the aim of the army engineer school to give technical instruction to the divisional engineer troops in France in matters with which they are expected and required to be familiar during active operations and to this end the very best personnel available has been gathered together, consisting of both officers and men who have been specialists in their particular phases of work in both civil life and the military service. As a policy the tour of duty at the school has been limited to six months, and always, when possible, has this policy been followed, as it is possible only by a continual, but slow, shifting to prevent the institution from falling into ruts that do not keep abreast of the new developments of the war. The officers have been required to make trips to the front in order to gain first hand knowledge of actual conditions and to discuss with unit commanders difficulties that the latter have encountered with a view to conducting experiments at the school intended to overcome these difficulties. In this sense the school has been a laboratory, some of the output of which has been incorporated in one of the official publications of the American E. F., the engineer field notes.

The principal function of the school has been however, to teach standard engineering practices and in this it has had the assistance not only of experienced officers of our own army but also of the French. Successful results have been manifested in bridging units sent to the front, in artillery officers who have become familiar with the principles of shelter for artillery material and personnel and of camouflage, in flash and sound rangers, who have operated with the artillery, and in engineers who, lacking previous training, have returned to their organizations far better equipped professionally to perform their various duties.

It is believed that the school has been well worth while and has more than justified the expense in material, personnel and effort devoted to it and, while no specific instances can be recounted in which lives have been saved or operations made successful as a result of instruction received here, it can only be assumed that such results have obtained because the very nature of operations waged at the front has necessitated the application of principles on which instruction has been based.

E. K. NEWCOMER,
Lieut. Colonel, C. of E.,
Asst. Commandant.

C-in-C Rept. File: Fldr. 225: Report

Army Sanitary School

Langres, Haute-Marne, November 11, 1918.

CHAPTER I

[Extract]

* * * * * *

As a part of the I Corps Center of Instruction at Gondrecourt, a sanitary school was established * * * Despite the fact that but seven students appeared to take the course, the extensive plans for the first session of that school were carried out per the program up to the point at which the students were to proceed to Base Hospital No. 18 for a two weeks course of lectures and clinics beginning November 5. A few days prior to this date * * * the two-weeks course planned at Base Hospital No. 18 was annulled by the Chief Surgeon, A. E. F., owing to an epidemic of scarlet fever.

Pursuant to G. O. No. 46, H. A. E. F., 1917, Colonel Ashford reported for duty as commandant of the army sanitary school, November 1, 1917. * * * The original plan to employ this school for the training of instructors for corps schools was never extensively carried out. From time to time a few graduates were recommended for appointments of that nature, but the major functions of the school have been (1) to train a few selected officers from each division who would return to their organization and instruct their colleagues and (2) to collect information concerning the work of the medical department in war and distribute this information in mimeographed pamphlets throughout the A. E. F. During the first, second, and third sessions students were drawn from organizations already on active duty in France; all subsequent classes were formed of divisional advance school detachments of ten officers each, whose organizations arrived in France about the time that these advance representatives were completing their course at the school.

Since a division is composed of about 28,000 men it will be seen that if 280,000 divisional troops landed in France per month, the sanitary school would have 100 students per month. As a matter of fact the first class numbered 19 and the largest class which attended the school numbered 99. The courses varied from one month to six weeks and were divided into two parts; a course of lectures and demonstrations at the school and a visit to some sector of the British, French, or American front.

* * * Lectures and demonstrations went on from 8:30 to 12 and from 1:30 p. m. to 5. * * *

The courses in medicine and surgery were conducted by special lecturers, members of the staff of consulting specialists for the A. E. F. * * *

Simultaneously with the school for medical officers, there was established a section for officers of the dental corps. Here the dentist from civil life learned what was expected of him in the army. In a two weeks' course he was instructed in drill and army regulations, first aid, the treatment of hemorrhage and shock, general and personal sanitation, the organization of the medical department with a bird's-eye view of its activities at the front and in the rear, and the principles of plastic surgery. In short he learned how to take care of himself in the field, how to function as a part of the big machine in which he had become one of the wheels, and how to be of assistance in carrying on the duties of any branch of the medical department at the front, where it would be impossible for him to perform operative dentistry. * * *

* * * * * *

OUTLINE OF COURSES:

1. Medico-Military Administration

* * * * * *

2. Military Hygiene

* * * * * *

3. Sanitary Tactics

* * * * * *

4. Military Surgery

* * * * * *

5. Military Medicine

* * * * * *

CHAPTER II

The Work of the School: * * * There are at least four outstanding factors in this new conception of the duties of a medical officer which makes him an active participant in the winning of battles:

(1) The prevention of disease by sanitary arty. and by preventive medicine.

(2) The rapid collection and transporting to the rear of the wounded and gassed, with intelligent first-aid, such as the transportation of fractures in extension, the preventive treatment of shock, the immediate relief of the gassed, and the direct removal in the most comfortable and expeditious manner of all casualties to hospitals adequately provided to fulfill the requirements of modern military medicine and surgery.

(3) The prevention of infection of wounds by the surgical removal of the contaminated dead and dying tissue upon which organisms have heretofore been able to thrive.

(4) The rapid return to duty through convalescent camps of men who have heretofore spent months in the zone of the interior, many never returning to the lines and being lost to the army. Great numbers of those who are so disabled that they can never return to the front lines, can nevertheless be salvaged for duty in the services of supply, releasing able bodied soldiers for the more arduous tasks.

This may be summed up more concisely as (1) the preservation of health, and (2) the salvage of men.

* * * * * *

At the beginning of its career the army sanitary school found itself confronted with the problem of teaching the tactics of medical department units in a kind of warfare with which the American army had had no previous experience trench warfare. Its instructors therefore went to the British and French, where they found two different methods being followed. The British were pushing their hospitals as far forward as possible, where they ran great risk of having them bombed. The French were placing theirs farther to the rear and running the risk of serious infection setting in before the patient reached a hospital equipped for thorough operative intervention. The advantages and disadvantages of both were carefully studied and explained to the students who afterwards visited the front and saw for themselves examples of the points brought out in lectures and map problems.

When the Germans left their trenches and started their drive in March 1918, open warfare was established. The school then studied the problem of the sanitary service of the British and French during retreat and simultaneously saw the sanitary service of the American army adapting itself to trench warfare in quiet sectors. Here the casualties were few and the chief problems were the teaching of Americans to make clean and healthful homes in damp dugouts, the combating of lice and skin diseases, and the organization of effective gas defense measures.

From July 18, 1918, to the cessation of hostilities, the period of the Allied advance, attention has been focussed upon the problem of getting wounded back through road blocks due to destruction of the roads in the country over which advance was being made, and the problem of moving hospitals forward fast enough to keep sufficiently close to the front, so that the haul by ambulance would not be too long. A wealth of first-hand material was accumulated at the school on these questions by trips to the front by classes and members of the faculty and by inviting officers to come to the school immediately after a severe action and narrate their experiences. The map problems given at the school from this time were based on actual battles, even copies of the original orders being at hand. After the student had worked out his solution of a problem the instructor would tell what actually occurred.

* * * * * *

CHAPTER III

The Aims of the School

* * * * * *

To state the proposition in less general terms, it was the aim of the sanitary school to provide a step in the process of turning civilian doctors into medical officers. * * *

* * * * * *

CHAPTER IV

The Policies of the School:

1. The activities of the school have been conducted in accordance with the following policies:

    (a) To comprise in each course a maximum of practical experience, demonstration, and problems, and a minimum of didactic teaching.

    (b) To base all instruction upon a faithful and accurate presentation of the facts, offering practical solutions rather than ideal theories.

    (c) To collect at the school a mass of information on every phase of the work of the medical department as an integral part of the forces in France to win the war.

    (d) To distribute this information as widely and as promptly as possible to medical officers, as well as to sections of the general staff in France and in the United States.

    (e) To keep in touch with the previous training received by students in the United States so as to eliminate duplication.

    (f) To give every student a conception of the functions of all the parts of the medical department machine with the guiding principle of the greatest good for the greatest number.

(g) To create and preserve a military atmosphere in which the cultivation of qualities of the soldier becomes a habit.

* * * * *

C-in-C Rept. File: Fldr. 226: Report

Dental Section, Army Sanitary School

December 10, 1918.

Chapter I

The Instructors

[Extract]

The first session of the dental section of the army sanitary school was held from December 10 to 17, 1917, with twelve student officers. * * *

* * * * *

This history covers the activities of the dental section during the first year of its existence. There have been sixteen sessions and 320 officers of the dental corps have received diplomas. The policy of the school and a consideration of its successes is taken up in another portion of this article.

* * * * *

Chapter II

The Development of the School Policy

* * * * *

The demand for organized instruction was met in the 1st Division and a course instituted by the division surgeon, * * * This instruction anticipated the demand which was later felt for training in first aid bandaging and first aid dressing, and with the exception of the lectures on oral surgery was quite similar to the course which was given during the first session of this school, from Dec. 10 to 17, 1917.

* * * * *

2. DIVISION DENTAL SCHOOL (AND FOR SEPARATE BRIGADES): A course of instruction conducted by the division dental surgeon under the direction of the division surgeon.
    (a) Army regulations (pertaining to officers in particular).
    (b) Manual of the medical department (dental instruction and administration.
    (c) Manual of court martial and military law (administration of military discipline and justice, charges, specifications, trials, etc.).
    (d) Customs of the service.
    (e) Paper work (correspondence, records, reports and returns).

3. CORRESPONDENCE COURSE OF INSTRUCTION FOR DENTAL OFFICERS STATIONED AT BASE HOSPITALS, ENGINEER REGIMENTS AND OTHER ISOLATED COMMANDS: To cover preceding subjects of instruction and conducted from the army sanitary school in accordance with plans followed in the usual correspondence course for medical officers of the army.

4. A POST-GRADUATE SCHOOL OF INSTRUCTION: To be established at the American Red Cross Hospital No. 1, Neuilly, under the direction of the commanding officer. Said course to embrace lectures on hospital administration, admissions, evacuation, records, diet, internal economy, etc.; * * *

NOTE: The course of instruction at the division schools may be handled in six to eight sessions, held two afternoons per week for the period. The duration of the term for instruction at the army sanitary school (dental section), is contemplated as one week. The period of instruction at the post-graduate school may be covered in two weeks intensive study. This may be extended in certain particular cases where deemed desireable for the best interests of the service.

Prior to the completion of the organization of the I Army Corps, although coincident with the plans for corps training, a program was instituted for a school for dental officers a part of the I Corps Army Sanitary School. However, the sanitary school was later moved as a part of the army schools, at Langres, and this course was never given, although the program of instruction was incorporated in the courses which were given during the first two months of the school at this station.

It was the original intention to institute courses of instruction for dental officers not only at the army sanitary school, but throughout the various army corps, as well as in the divisions. In some divisional organizations, good results have been gained, but, as a rule, the difficulties of transportation and the conditions in general have been such as to make continuous training for dental officers impracticable. The plans for corps schools for dental officers was instituted and a program for a course at the headquarters of the I Army Corps was laid out, but, there is no record here that any school was ever established in corps organizations in France for dental officers.

Tentative plans were made in November 1917 to supplement the theoretical instruction in oral surgical prosthesis by a post-graduate course at American Military Red Cross Hospital No. 1, at Neuilly, but this had been subordinated to the larger demands for training impractical field service. The advanced work in oral surgery has been always considered as of less importance than the solution of the problems incident to field service.

It will be recalled that it was not until February 1918, that American troops occupied the front lines to any extent. Prior to this time, the majority of all instruction for dental officers was experimental and speculative, for no one knew and no one could prophesy what combat conditions would be for dental officers. There could be no parallel drawn from the experiences of our Allies, for in no army is the allowance of dental personnel so complete as in our own. Nothing could be foretold of the difficulties which would arise in the transportation of the portable outfits, soon proven to be helplessly bulky. No one could foresee that the dental officer would be called upon for every duty except dental work, in fact, when one recalls such functions as battalion or regimental surgeon, sanitary inspector, censor officer, mess officer, burial officer, and many others, it is apparent that the problem of adequate instruction was a serious one.

After American troops finished their preliminary training and began to occupy different sectors on the western front, it was found that training dental officers in routine subjects of military administration was not sufficient. * * *

This was the problem which confronted the director of the dental section as soon as the facts were known. Two courses were open. In the first place, the elimination of the larger part of the portable dental outfit, in favor of a small, easily transportable equipment, by means of which the dental officer could render the emergency service demanded of him while in combat. Secondly, and by no means less important, it became the obligation of the dental section of the army sanitary school, and the duty of division dental surgeons, to see that dental officers on duty with combat troops were trained in the proper performance of the duties required of them should they replace or function with the medical officers.

To this end, the courses at this school were modified to teach less in detail the more professional and theoretical subjects and to lay more emphasis upon first aid bandaging and splinting, map reading, orientation, field sketching, sanitation, hygiene, and evacuation of the wounded. * * * In brief, the school has gradually developed into a field service institution, and has laid its great emphasis upon the preparation of dental officers for combat service. * * *

The difficulties caused by the too bulky portable outfit were adjusted from the chief surgeon's office * * * and this equipment was reduced, to make a modified portable outfit, and the emergency kit. This latter was carried on the person of the dental officer and his enlisted dental assistant, and made it possible to take care of emergency cases, even though the dental officer was being employed in medical capacities. In other words, dental service could be rendered with this equipment, without regard to transportation difficulties, and even under combat conditions.

While certain subjects and phases of oral surgical prosthesis have been part of the school curriculum, the dental section of the army sanitary school has never been primarily a school for oral surgery. Nevertheless, efforts have been made to bring the best methods in plastic and prosthetic restorations before the student officers. Records are on file as part of the official literature of the school of the work of the French Medical Department in the Maxillo-facial Hospitals of Paris, Lyon and Vichy, as well as of the work of American specialists throughout France. * * *

Chapter III

The Making of a Dental Officer

* * * * * *

The dental section of the army sanitary school in the attainment of its ideals was confronted with four problems, which were intimately associated with the making of a dental officer. The first was to make the dentists from civilian life realize that they were soldiers, and that as soldiers, they had certain duties and obligations. The second was to modify their ideas of professional work, so that the men would be kept effective. The third, was the instruction in the various methods of dental administration, so that the new dental officer would be able to cooperate with his administrative chiefs in an efficient manner. Fourth and last, was the special training for the special man, in oral surgery and in operative procedures.

* * * * * *

Chapter IV

The Period of Organization

* * * * * *

The problem during the first two months of this school was one mostly of working out the question as to whether it should instruct its students in the broader foundation for efficient field service, or, if it should devote its time to the training in the details of dental and medical administration, essential always, but later determined to be subordinate in time of war, to the more pressing needs of field service training.

* * * * * *

The second session, which commenced January 2, 1918, further developed the idea of medical training for dental officers, in that a lecture on general anesthesia was added. However, the lack of clinical facilities prevented the complete success of this branch of the work until the occupation of Camp Hospital 24 by an American hospital formation, when practical demonstrations were made possible.

* * * * * *

Chapter V

The Training in Military Discipline

* * * * * *

The fourth session, held from February 2 to 17, 1918, was marked by some radical changes in the program of instruction. A consideration of the important provisions of army regulations was taken up more in detail. * * *

* * * * * *

Up to the commencement of the fourth session, six lectures of one hour each had been given each day. With the initiation of the training in drill the lecture hours were reduced to five, the hour for drill instruction occupying the sixth period.

It will be noted that, during this period from the fourth to the seventh sessions, the attempt was made to combine field service and practical instructions for combat conditions with the more detailed training in military administration and discipline. This plan was successful, but only for the reason that the problem of the training of dental officers to function properly in times of battle was not sufficiently understood to enable the school to give a comprehensive course concerning it. Furthermore, it was expected that many of the dental officers who seemed especially fitted, would be employed in the special work of oral surgery. This theory was later proven to be a mistaken one, for the demand for men who could do routine dentistry was so great that this special work was assigned to other fields, and the dental officer, not only in combat divisions, but throughout France, was employed for the most part, when he did dental work at all, in the practice of the routine methods of his profession.

* * * * * *

Chapter VI

The Beginning of Clinical Demonstrations

The school had been in operation until May before it was possible to secure any clinical material for instruction purposes. One of the disadvantages of a training institution located in such a town and locality as Langres was that clinical material was not easily available, and, what little there was, could only be drawn with great difficulty from the few French hospital formations located in the vicinity. But with the occupation of Camp Hospital 24 by an American unit, the opportunity arose for the use of clinical demonstrations for the student officers.

* * * * * *

During the first week in June the faculty of the dental section spent several days in studying the work of the French Maxillo-facial surgeons at Hospital 45 at Vichy. It was here that the idea of the cast splint for cases of jaw fracture was being worked out efficiently, and much information towards the improvement of the maxillo-facial work in our own service was gained.

This trip to Vichy formed the basis for a series of lectures which was later given before the dental and medical classes. * * *

* * * * * *

Chapter VII

Medical Instruction for the Dental Corps

Reference to the programs which outline the policy of the dental section previous to July 1918, will reveal the fact that the development towards a practical field service course had taken place, but that this development had been slow. With the seventh session, clinical instruction had been made possible. Soon after this, it had been possible to glean accurate information from the dental officers in divisions concerning just what their difficulties were, together with some suggestions as to the most efficient methods of solution.

In brief, the problem of dental service under combat conditions was two-fold: The dental equipment was too bulky to be transported; and dental work under these conditions of excitement and stress did not seem to be possible. Consequently the dental officer was employed in almost any capacity, and knowing more about medical duties than anything else, he naturally supplemented the work of his medical officer, and, in times of emergency functioned alone in that capacity.

With a view for amplifying the training which was already being given the student officers of the dental section, the commandant of the army sanitary school made the following recommendations in a letter:

June 26, 1918.

From: The Commandant, Army Sanitary School

To: The Chief Surgeon, S. O. S., American E. F.
        (Through Commandant, Army Schools)

Subject: Medical Instruction of Dental Corps

1. It is being constantly reported to the commandant of the army sanitary school that dental officers are being employed to do the work of medical officers not only in the back areas but in those at the front, such as battalion aid stations.

2. In order to meet the demands for knowledge of duties they would be required to perform in first aid and in emergency the commandant of the army sanitary school has provided instructors for the dental section of this school to give them an an elementary knowledge of such first aid work and of the relative positions of medical units on the battlefield and their functions as they might be called upon to perform in emergency.

3. As will be seen from the appended program now being followed, the following is the distribution of the time allotted to the class of the dental section:

		Hours
(a)	Dental hygiene, dental diseases and injuries affecting the practice of stomatology.	15
(b)	Anesthesia, local and general.	5
(c)	General instruction in gas protection and treatment of the gassed.	9
(d)	Purely military subjects.	4
(e)	Drills and setting up exercises.	13
(f)	Purely Medical Subjects.	12
(g)	Administration, general knowledge of regulations, including property accountability and regulations of the medical department.	17
	TOTAL.	75

4. As this gives only 20% of the time to the purely professional side of the dental corps and provides no opportunity, save one hour, for clinics and demonstrations on professional subjects, it is recommended that the previous recommendation some months back, to the effect that some practical demonstrations be given these officers, should be provided in the future by a tour of instruction for the purposes of practical demonstrations to the Franco-American Dental Center now being formed at Vichy, the division of the time of the class being as follows: One week of didactic instruction in the school area and one week of practical demonstrations at Vichy.

5. That division surgeons be instructed to provide for their dental surgeons all necessary instruction in the paper work of the army, drill and first aid, in order to thus reduce to a minimum this elementary instruction at a center like this which should devote its time to the teaching of those things which cannot be learned in a division. Inasmuch as much instruction in first aid, bandaging, etc., should be limited to that knowledge which should be possessed by all branches of the medical corps, it is believed that the proper person to be made responsible for such instruction should be the division surgeon and not a school devoted to the higher branches of professional work. Such instruction can be given, as it has been given for the last six months, but always at the expense of things which cannot be obtained in a division and by duplication of the work of our own faculty, inasmuch as the lectures given our medical officers are too technical to be used by the dental surgeons who, by the way, have but one-third of the time given our medical officers for instruction at this school.

6. The recommendation herein made does not intend to exclude intervention of medical officers at this school in those special and necessary presentations of phases of first aid work which they can best give; in fact the commandant of this school desires to have at least three or four periods at his disposal for the presentation of such medical subjects; but the intention of this letter is to try to have defined the principles underlying dental instruction at this center and have time which is today taken for elementary training in military and medical subjects provided for by division surgeons under the general head of training, instruction which can never bear fruit unless such training is continued over a period far in excess of the time which it is possible to allot to these subjects at this center,

and the dental school here will be enabled to divert its energies to more important subjects and to instruction which could not be given in the division.

> BAILEY K. ASHFORD,
> Colonel, Medical Corps, U. S. A.,
> Commandant.

The results of this recommendation were later made evident in the publication of the policy of the training section of the general staff, concerning the dental section, in the following letter:

July 20, 1918.

MEMORANDUM FOR: COMMANDANT, ARMY SCHOOLS, A. E. F.

SUBJECT: Program of instruction Dental Section, Army Sanitary School

    1. Examination of the program of instruction of the dental section of the army sanitary school and correspondence relating thereto, leads to the following conclusion:

    2. The purpose of this school is to give dental surgeons attached to combat divisions or the S. O. S. instruction in preparation for field service in the A. E. F., which will supplement that given in the training camps in the United States and with troops in France.

    3. General first aid instruction is required for all sanitary troops in divisions in France, and is given in training camps in the United States.

    Instruction in military law, customs of the service, army regulations, and general instruction in military correspondence and reports and returns is given in divisions and training camps in the United States.

    4. In view of the fact that the course for dental surgeons is short and instruction in the subject is available elsewhere it is desired that, instruction in first aid, except as it relates to oral or dental wounds or accidents, military law, customs of the service, military correspondence, army regulations, and reports and returns (except as changed by the A. E. F.) be discontinued in the dental section of the army sanitary school, and the time secured used for instruction in other subjects relating to field duties of dental surgeons.

* * * * * *

    5. There is no immediate probability of a special course centre of oral surgery near the site of the army sanitary school, and until such a centre is established, visits of instruction for student officers of the dental section are deemed impracticable.

> H. B. FISKE,
> Brigadier General, General Staff,
> A. C. of S., G-5.

* * * * * *

Chapter VIII

The Field Service School

It had been the aim of the director of the dental section for several months to present a course of instruction to the dental officers which would embody both the principles of dental service in the field, and the consideration of the multifold auxiliary medical duties which become a part of the life of the dental officer during combat. For numerous reasons, this plan had not been practical up to October 1918. But with the initiation of the plans for the program of the fifteenth session of the dental section of this school, a plan was considered jointly with the director of the army sanitary school, which contemplated the holding of fourteen joint lectures of dental and medical officers, embodying practically all the essential points of medical duties and sanitary tactics * * *

* * * In the first place, in order to give the dental officer some conception of the organization of the machine of which he is a part, one lecture on the organization of the entire American Expeditionary Forces was presented, and also a lecture on the organization of the medical department. This gave the dental officer an idea of the workings of the different sections of the general staff, of the functionings of the services of supply, and of the coordination of the medical department plans with those of the line organizations in a combat division.

Furthermore, in addition to theoretical instruction in sanitary tactics, one afternoon was devoted to practical terrain exercises, in charge of an officer, who was a graduate of the General Staff College, and who had studied the divisional problem from every side.

The previous fourteen sessions had contained as part of the course the preparation of a notebook, which held the different lectures in the form in which they were given. This notebook had been corrected, and was later returned to the student officer, but not until this book had been carefully studied, and the gradings given by the faculty entered upon the student's record, and made part of the official report which was made concerning him.

* * * * * *

Since the beginning of the fifteenth session the effort has been made to carry out the instruction along the lines of practical field service, with a view to helping the man with the division, who needs aid the most, and making the base hospital problem subsidiary to the larger question.

* * * * * *

Chapter IX

The School Curriculum

* * * The purpose of this chapter is to give a summary of the courses which have been offered for instruction, together with a more detailed consideration of the purposes of these subjects than has heretofore been practicable to present.

A review of the work of the past year has resulted in the following classification of the subject matter in the courses of instruction:

I. Military discipline

* * * * * *

II. Military administration

* * * * * *

III. Professional

* * * * * *

IV. General field service problems

* * * * * *

C-in-C Rept. File: Fldr. 227: Report

Army Intelligence School

Langres, Haute-Marne, November 30, 1918.
[Extract]

Our first small, but independent, military operations at Bois de Belleau and the village of Vaux, slightly northwest of Chateau-Thierry, had just been brought to a successful conclusion, when the Intelligence Section of the General Staff at General Headquarters of the American Expeditionary Forces decided to establish an Army Intelligence School in Langres (Haute-Marne).

FOUNDING OF ARMY INTELLIGENCE SCHOOL

Thus after a week's deliberation on the school schedule, and on the choice of instructors, the Army Intelligence School began to function on July 25, 1918. The director and adjutant of the new school, which existed on paper only, arrived about four days before the date set for its opening, in Langres. The complete installation of all the necessary school paraphernalia and dormitory requirements was a monumental task to accomplish within such a short period of time, but it was achieved by the efficient support of the Commandant of Army Schools, General Smith, and the able cooperation of the Quartermaster Department. * * * The first course, from July 25 to September 4, 1918. * * * The second course covered the period from September 30, to November 9, 1918. * * * The third course opened on November 18, 1918, with an eight weeks' schedule, whereas the two previous courses only covered a period of six weeks each. * * *

The total number of students attending these courses was as follows: First course, 41; second course, 56; third course, 41.

OBJECT OF SCHOOL

The main object of the Army Intelligence School when first created, was to turn out officers who were properly trained in divisional and regimental intelligence, and for the interrogation of German prisoners and the exploitation of captured German documents. The first course was, therefore, divided into two main sections -- one being the Regimental and Divisional Intelligence Section, the other the Interrogation of Prisoners and Exploitation of Documents.

The second and third courses were enlarged by the addition of a Branch Intelligence Section, which required a division into three sections.

The five main subjects taught at this school were the German Army Organization and Battle Order, the Interrogation of Prisoners and Exploitation of Documents, Divisional, Regimental and Branch Intelligence, and Interpretation of Airplane Photographs. In addition to these there were numerous other lectures to supplement these five main subjects.

It is of interest to record here what field of study was covered by these five main subjects.

ORGANIZATION OF THE GERMAN ARMY

A knowledge of the organization of the German Army was the basis for all the work in this school and therefore a considerable part of the schedule was devoted to a detailed study of this subject. Not only was the organization of the High Command and units of the army considered, but the subjects of the history of the German Army prior to 1914, the relation of the sovereign states of Germany to Prussia, the existing corps districts and their character, the service liabilities of the German citizen and also the recruiting and training system in force in peace time and war was studied in detail as well.

The German Battle Order lectures and practical work gave the officers a complete conception of the German Army organization and its relation to our intelligence service.

ENEMY ORDER OF BATTLE

The object of this course was to give the officers attending this school a complete conception of the routine of our Battle Order Work at General Headquarters, the value of its application to our own operations and the source of information upon which Battle Order Work and its application depended.

With this object in view the course was divided into a series of subordinate subjects, together with extensive practical work. Battle order can be broadly summed up in the following elements of study: I. Enemy Disposition; II. Character of Fighting Value of Enemy Units; III. Enemy Intentions; IV. Geography of and its Relation to Enemy Tactics and Intentions.

The first of these subjects was covered in a series of lectures on the theory and importance of a knowledge of enemy battle order and was amplified and applied by problems in battle order tracing the development of German concentrations and operations prior to the offensive of March 21. In this practical work the students used the situation of March 1 as a basis and by means of daily problems, founded on the actual reports received at General Headquarters during the period under consideration, developed the disposition of German units in line and reserve up to March 21. A battle order map was maintained showing the daily changes and situation. The use of this map served the subordinate though important function as well of familiarizing the students with the geography of France.

The subject of character and fighting value of enemy units was covered by lectures on Divisional Histories as prepared at General Headquarters, the sources of information used in preparing these histories, together with practical work in the actual writing of divisional histories, based on data obtained from General Headquarter's files.

The subject of Enemy Intentions and the geography as related to Enemy Tactics and Intentions were covered by lectures, covering the tactical and economic value of the field of operations.

INTERROGATION OF PRISONERS

For the interrogation of prisoners and exploitation of documents those students were selected to make a special study of the principles and methods involved, who possessed a good knowledge of the German language. They were not only required to be able to converse fluently, but also to easily read the German script and translate accurately and into good military English.

Lectures on the interrogation of prisoners were given by an instructor who had just returned from the front, and had more experience at that time than any other American officer in the interrogation of prisoners. This experience, gained in the field, was based on theoretical instruction received in the British Intelligence School, followed by a trip to the British and American front. The presence of the two French instructors who were specialists in this branch of the service, therefore, enabled the instructors to combine the best features of the methods employed by the French, English and Americans. The theoretical work of the course was practically applied by having 25 prisoners sent every week to the school, fresh from and active battle front. As soon as the prisoners arrived, the instructors ascertained in what sector of the battle front they were taken prisoners, and the necessary maps were obtained to permit an extensive and thorough interrogation of the prisoners. Demonstrations were also given as to the proper method of quickly handling very large numbers of prisoners, by using some 800 prisoners in a nearby prison camp. These practical tests were invaluable as they accustomed the students to become acquainted with many types of prisoners and entirely removed that feeling of embarrassment and awkwardness which is felt by all interrogators the first time they are obliged to put prisoners through a crossexamination.

EXPLOITATION OF DOCUMENTS

The lectures on the exploitation of documents were supplemented by many hours of practical work in the actual exploitation of German army, corps and divisional orders, letters and post cards from military and civilian sources, notebooks, diaries, soldbücher, and so on, thousands of which were sent to this school by an arrangement with the Intelligence Section of our First Army.

IDENTIFICATION OF ENEMY UNITS

Through the cooperation of our troops in the field, the school also obtained a large number of shoulder straps, cockades, and other parts of the German uniform which were of great service in supplementing the lectures on these subjects.

REGIMENTAL AND DIVISIONAL INTELLIGENCE

The section devoted to the training of divisional and regimental intelligence officers by a series of lectures and practical problems trained intelligence officers for these units. The series of lectures covered the organization and functions of the regimental and divisional intelligence services, observation posts, patrolling, intelligence summaries, and lectures on the outline of information to be secured concerning the enemy.

The practical work simulated as closely as possible the problems confronting divisional and regimental intelligence officers in the field. Practice was given in the location and operation of observation posts. Information secured in observation post practice became the basis of battalion intelligence reports. These reports were then coordinated, and regimental, and subsequently divisional intelligence summaries were written. Thorough training was given in map work and the intelligence officers had problems involving the drawing of enemy activity, shelled area, enemy circulation, artillery objective, liaison, and battle order maps. Problems included drawing up training schedules of their intelligence sections, writing of patrol orders and patrol reports, identification of German shells and fuses, and the writing of operation orders. The practical work was completed by a continuous problem for which the students were organized into a Divisional Intelligence Service with a G-2, Brigade Artillery Intelligence Officer, Brigade and Regimental Intelligence Officers. Field telephone and runners connected these various offices, and conditions were made as similar as possible to actual practice in the field

AIRPLANE PHOTOGRAPHY

The Airplane Photography Section gave a course in map reading and interpretation and restitution of airplane photographs.

The course in map reading included instructions on projections grid, symbols, scales and contours. Practical work was given on contour construction and profiles, map visibility, map construction and field work on reading maps.

The course in Aerial Photographs included a detailed study of British and French books on the subject and instruction and practical work on the interpretation and restitution of photographs, and field studies with photographs.

The purpose of giving instruction in map reading was to insure an officer's ability to read a map correctly, and to emphasize the value of the use of maps in warfare. The purpose for giving instruction in reading aerial photographs was to impart to officers the right conception of the information revealed and confirmed by photographic reconnaissances as to impress them with the value which this source of information is worth to the Intelligence Section.

The Topographic Section was organized January 21, 1918, as a section of the Army Engineer Schools, with classes for a three weeks' course for Intelligence Officers and one week course for Regimental and Battalion Scout Officers.

Instruction was carried on continuously until July 27 when personnel and material were transferred to the newly organized Army Intelligence School.

Instruction was given from January 22 to July 27 to 22 Intelligence Officers; 24 Regimental and Battalion Scout Officers; 23 Branch Intelligence Officers; 20 Tank School Officers, and 13 Engineer Officers (29th Engineers).

Instruction in restitution of photographs was given to enlisted men as follows:

    44   29th Engineers
     9   117th Engineers
    13 - Air Service
    24 - Miscellaneous Units

Field instruction on map work was given to students of the Engineer Schools.

In addition, 13 lectures on the study of Aerial Photographs were given at Corps Schools.

BRANCH INTELLIGENCE

The function of the Branch Intelligence Section was to simulate the Branch Intelligence Officer (hereinafter referred to as P. I. O.), his duties and environment, insofar as local conditions permitted, thus bringing home to prospective B. I. O.'s the actual problems which were theirs in the field.

This goal was attained by the following methods:

    I. General Lectures:

        1. Branch Intelligence
        2. Aviation Intelligence
        3. German Air Service

    II. Detailed Class Room Work:

        1. Methods of Instruction:

           a. The students fill in a map of a chosen area, coloring the woods in green; lakes, canals and rivers in blue; main roads in yellow; and coordinates plainly marked on map.

           b. Skeleton maps; memory skeleton maps.
           c. Jigsaw map puzzle contests.

       d. Name the towns by means of unmarked photographs.
       e. Question sheets.
       f. Map study with photos.
2. General Discussions:
       a. Relations within and without squadron or group of squadrons.
       b. Photo interpretation.
       c. Office personnel organization.
       d. Air intelligence regulations.
       e. Definitions.
       f. Identifications of airplanes.
       g. A day's work.
       h. Dump, airdrome, town and display books.
       i. Variety
       j. Questioning observers and pilots.
       k. Equipment.
       l. Coordinates.
       m. Map study.
3. Observer's Room:
       a. Contents.
       b. Purpose.
4. Forms
       a. Summary of Intelligence.
       b. Observers' reports.
       c. Photo information sheet.
       d. Railroad activity and rolling stock in yards.
       e. Request for photographs.
       f. Report of photographic missions.
       g. Mailing list.
       h. Check list.
5. Flights and reports.
6. Photo assemblages, mosaics, identifications.
7. General review.

* * * * * *

NEED OF ARMY INTELLIGENCE SCHOOL

There is no need to set forth any extensive arguments to establish a justification for the Army Intelligence School, for the absolute absence of any knowledge of Fighting Intelligence in itself created a crying need for properly trained intelligence officers. After the conclusion of the first course, the graduates of the School did such excellent work in the field that our field units immediately began to make demands for more trained officers. Other officers who had an opportunity to observe the systematic and efficient methods used by the trained intelligence officers, put in applications for attendance at the School, and these applications greatly surpassed in number the number of students who could be handled at one time. Upon the formation of new corps headquarters, direct requests were made in several cases for graduates of this School.

DISPOSITION OF STUDENTS

Briefly stated, the lectures and the practical work at the Army Intelligence School resulted in a highly trained staff officer who was able to fill any position, either at regimental, divisional, corps, army or general headquarters. The work of the students was closely observed, and when they were graduated they were recommended for such work which in the opinion of the instructors they were most fitted for, and for which they displayed peculiar aptitude.

USEFULNESS OF SCHOOL ON PRESENT LINES ENDED

As long as hostilities had not ceased the Army Intelligence School should have continued to exist, but with the vanquishing of the enemy there is no further need for this School based on its present lectures and practical work. This is evident as all the lectures and practical work are based on the German military organization and, in view of the political and military changes, much of the knowledge previously required has now become history. It must also not be overlooked that a course in which the lectures and practical work are based on the military organization of one country alone is bound to be narrow and onesided.

CREATION OF A NEW ARMY INTELLIGENCE SCHOOL IN THE U. S.

An Army Intelligence School, however, should under all circumstances be maintained to prevent any such deplorable state of unpreparedness to occur again in our military history as we have experienced. This new school should not confine itself in its subjects to one country, but on the contrary, should encircle the globe. For obvious reasons France is not the proper place for such a school. It should be established as a section of the General Staff of the War College at Washington, D. C., for in its future work, the practical end of it will require, a close liaison with, in fact, may even be a part of our diplomatic and consular service.

C-in-C Rept. File: Fldr. 228: Report

Army Gas School

Langres, Haute-Marne [November 11, 1918].

[Extract]

Authorized by G. O. 46, G. H. Q., A. E. F., Oct. 10, 1917, for establishment at Langres not later than Nov. 15, 1917.

* * * * * *

II. General Plan of Courses of the Army Gas School: The original plan of the army gas school was to give both defensive and offensive gas training; up until January 12 however, owing to the lack of supplies and facilities the only work done by the school consisted of training troops in defensive measures and the giving of short courses to students of other army schools.

The first extended offensive-defensive course was given during the two weeks Jan. 12-26, 1918. No lecture room was available and, as a result, lectures were given in various improvised lecture rooms. No gas chamber was ready nor had a demonstration field been secured, therefore the course had to be theoretical rather than practical. By the time the second course began, a demonstration field had been obtained on the Polygone de Jorquenay near Fort de St-Menge and the theoretical was supplemented by the firing of 4 inch Stokes mortar and emplacing of gas cylinders.

Courses of this type continued intermittently until the middle of April when a new policy was adopted. The courses of instruction in offensive gas warfare were discontinued entirely and three types of courses in defensive measures against gas were substituted. These were of one, two and six day duration respectively.

The six day course was designed for training gas officers and gas N. C. O.'s and consisted of 12-15 hours theoretical instruction and about 20 hours practical instruction. Students were familiarized with the methods of offensive gas warfare, taught in detail defense against gas and, in general, made gas specialists who could supervise and give gas defense training to their own units. As success in gas defense is directly in proportion to the discipline, a high standard of discipline was maintained at all times.

The one and two day courses were given to students of the various other army schools and where possible, to the officers of organizations temporarily in the vicinity of Langres.

The two day course was desirable for all officers because it was sufficiently extensive to give them a good knowledge of gas warfare and defense and to develop and appreciation of the future possibilities of gas and the problems of defense presented thereby. This course was given to all students of the army candidates' school.

Students who were unable to take the two days' course, were given a one day course which attempted to develop a receptive attitude towards gas defense as well as to teach protection. Less attention naturally could be paid to details and therefore the schedules were especially designed to fit the needs of the particular classes. Specimen schedules of the three different types are attached to this history.

In addition, many thousands of officers and men were given several hours drill including passage through a gas chamber. The training was not only given in Langres but to organizations at outlying points within a radius of 50-75 miles.

* * * * * *

The following table shows the number of students attending these various courses:

MONTH	2 WEEKS COURSE		SIX DAY COURSE		TWO DAY COURSE		ONE DAY COURSE		TWO HOUR COURSE	
	Off	Men	Off	Men	Off	Men	Off	Men	Off	Men
Dec.					31					
Jan.	5	4			27	500			50	58
Feb.	19	2					100	25	288	169
Mar.	19	2		33			655	179	235	4129
Apr.			49	96		1038	17	300	9	650
May			50	198			160	59	64	1592
June			63	223	109	420	40		86	1400
July			49	436	130		102	84	69	1600
Aug.			111	850	89	15	247	864		
Sept.			74	785	57	2000	205	120	112	7600
Oct.			76	930	73	1337	18	134	334	12420
Nov.				966		3347	138	72		1300
TOTALS	43	8	473	4577	516	8657	1682	1837	1247	30918

III. Geographical Locations: For a time the school continued to function in Langres, devoting one day of each six-day course to practical operations at the demonstration field. However, with continued growth, the school became cramped for lecture space and drill grounds and therefore a plant was constructed on the demonstration field. The plant finally consisted of six Adrian Barracks and three Swiss huts with a capacity of 250 N. C. O.'s and 30 officers weekly.

Inasmuch as the school was forced to move before this construction was even well under way, the instruction for a time was much handicapped and it was only by much hard work and many long hours on the part of the staff that any results were obtained. For the first class June 11 to 17, the mess hall was at the same time officers' billet and lecture hall while the kitchen served as an office.

As the school grew, difficulties of transportation multiplied and therefore a new location was sought and found in Rolampont, about 11 kms. north of Langres. Here a school with a capacity of 500 N. C. O. students weekly, was constructed and on October 6, the school was moved from the Polygon. Every effort was made towards constructing an ideal camp from the standpoint of sanitation and comfort.

Much credit is due to Lieut. H. W. Brown, Asst. Director, who was in charge of the construction and Capt. H. C. Von Dahn, Medical Officer, for the success which was attained in the construction of this camp.

IV. Principles of Training: The secret of success in gas defense is training and discipline. The policy of the school has therefore been to maintain a high standard of discipline and to give an intensive training in gas defense with the aim of developing an *esprit de gaz* which would spread a good gas discipline throughout the army.

The advantage of good gas training can best be illustrated by the following instances of two different units.

Recently one division that is known to have a high standard of gas discipline was bombarded with 6000 gas shell, Yellow Cross, phosgene and Blue Cross being used, and only six slight casualties resulted.

In one attack against a regiment where 140 gas shell were used, with approximately 250 men exposed, there were 90 inexcusable casualties, and five excusable casualties. Later, after a change of training systems, the following good results were obtained in the same regiment.

```
6 attacks of approx.  400 gas shell    no casualties.
1 attack    "     "   300   "    "     5         "
1 attack    "     "  1999 Yellow Cross Shell  19 casualties although
                     750 men were exposed. The men occupied a
                     heavily wooded area.
```

It was only through the untiring efforts of the staff, who labored week in and week out without hope of reward in spite of discouraging episodes and with an absolute lack of excitement or thrill in the labor, that the school was enabled to turn out the work that it has. It is interesting to note that since April 11, the six-day course has run continuously every week without a vacation.

C-in-C Rept File: Fldr. 229: Report

Army Tank School

Langres, Haute-Marne, November 22, 1918.

From: Colonel G. S. Patton, Jr., Tank Corps

To: Commandant, Army Schools, American E. F.

[Extract]

1. The history of the army tank school, American E. F. commenced when the Chief of Staff of the American E. F., Lieut. Colonel J. G. Harbord, G. S., U. S. A. by direction of the Commander-in-Chief of the American E. F., General John J. Pershing, U. S. A. wrote to Captain George S. Patton, Jr. Cavalry, U. S. A. at PARIS, France, on the date of November 29, 1917 as follows:

    1. By direction of the Commander-in-Chief, you are detailed to duty with the tank service.

    2. It is desired that you undertake the organization of the light tank service.

    3. This letter will serve as your credentials with the renault works, to which it is desired you go on December 3, pursuant to instructions already given you.

J. G. HARBORD,
Chief of Staff.

Prior to the ussuance of this letter pursuant to verbal instructions from the acting chief of the tank service, Lieut. Colonel LeRoy Eltinge, G. S., U. S. A. and from the Chief of the Training Section, Headquarters, Amer. E. F. and by authority of Par. 37, S. O. 153, Hq. A. E. F., November 10, 1917, Captain Patton visited the French Tank Center at CHAMPLIEU in the forest of COMPIEGNE from Nov. 18, 1917 to December 1, 1917, both dates inclusive and the Renault Construction Works, Dec. 3, 1917.

* * * * * *

On December 12, 1918 a report was submitted covering the following features of tank service.
    A. Mechanical
        1. Description
        2. Specifications
        3. Mathematical formula
        4. Changes
    B. Organization
        1. Personnel and Material
        2. Maintenance
    C. Tactical
        1. History
        2. Lessons from fights
        3. Theory of use
    D. Instruction and Drill

2. Captain Patton reported at Headquarters, Army Schools, American E. F. at Langres, Haute-Marne, France, December 18, 1917 accompanied by Lieut. Braine.

3. The interval of time between Dec. 18, 1917, and the arrival of the first officers was spent in going thoroughly into the possibilities of the surrounding country for use as a tank school and the planning of courses of instruction for the first increment of officers.

* * * * * *

The course at Turenne Barracks gave thorough instruction on the 37-mm. gun.

The course at Fort de Peigney gave thorough instruction on the Hotchkiss machine gun and the automatic pistol, 45 caliber and a working knowledge of the German Maxim and the French Chauchat.

These special courses at the two schools above mentioned were completed on January 29, 1918 and all officers of the tank school acquitted themselves very creditably.

* * * * * *

Thereafter all the officers attended classes in a body and underwent the following instructions:

Special map making and reading course at the army school of the line which lasted ten days.

Lectures on the use of camouflage
Lectures on gas defense
Lectures on aeroplane photos

An Atlas Truck which had been considerably damaged was obtained and the engine and transmission were dismantled.

Practical demonstrations were given by Lieuts. Braine, Baldwin and Winters in the construction and operation of the gas engine.

* * * * * *

Due to lack of the equipment which was deemed necessary for training of tank troops the interval between Feb. 17, 1918 and March 1 was spent in the following program:

Signalling
Nomenclature and use of pistol
Infantry drill
Lectures on discipline
Inspections

On March 1, 1918, two Hotchkiss machine guns and one 37-mm. cannon were procured from the army schools and the instruction went forward with some degree of efficiency.

* * * * * *

On March 23, 1918, there was received from the French Government 10 Renault tanks, two-man crew, without ordnance.

Shortly prior to this, sufficient lumber was procured to commence building at the training center the necessary buildings for the school.

With the arrival of the tanks training commenced in earnest and the following courses were given to all the tank corps personnel.

All officers in addition received thorough reconnaissance training and attended lectures in the evening.

Gunnery

* * * * * *

Gas Engineers

* * * * * *

Repair Work

* * * * * *

Map making and reading
Visibility of targets
Patrols
Tank Driving

* * * * * *

General Policy of the School: The general policy of the school from its conception was a thorough training of the tank personnel, officers and men, in the highest ideals of discipline, neatness, devotion to duty and *esprit de corps*. These results were produced by vigorous attention to close order drill, by the enforcement of great personal neatness on the part of officers and men and by lectures pointing out to the men the necessity for the ends sought. Since tank soldiers always act in a more or less isolated way the necessity for very hard discipline and devotion to duty among them is perhaps more important than in the case of any other troops. In addition to the above training of the individual the general training was carried out always with the understanding that tanks exist solely for the purpose of helping the advance of the infantry and that for this reason the tanks must conform to the infantry formation and not vice versa. Instructions in carrying out the end sought in this respect were obtained through manoeuvres with any infantry obtainable and when no infantry could be found then by having tank corps soldiers represent infantry. Each manoeuver was followed by a critique showing in what the tanks had done well or ill. It is believed that the results obtained in their battles shows the soundness of the policy adopted at this school. It is further believed that much better liaison with infantry could have been obtained had the infantry who were detailed to take part with the tanks in an attack been given a similar state of preparatory manoeuvers with tanks.

G. S. PATTON, Jr.;
Colonel, Tank Corps,
Commanding 304th Brigade (1st Brigade) T. C.

C-in-C Rept. File: Fldr. 230: Report

Army Signal Schools

Langres, Haute-Marne, January 31, 1919.

[Extract]

I. Early in the history of the American Expeditionary Forces, it was realized that among the important methods of training, especially for officers, a system of schools of instruction must be included; consequently under the supervision of the 5th (Training) Section of the General Staff, the Army Schools Center was organized and located at Langres, Haute-Marne, France.

* * * * * *

* * * It was therefore recognized that in the scheme of military education signal schools should be organized where the functions of signal troops would be taught utilizing the services, not only of the few of our own officers who had been able to familiarize themselves with conditions by serving with British or French, but also utilizing the services of especially well informed British and French instructors, who were cheerfully supplied us by our Allies.

To meet these requirements, the army signal schools were organized * * * The first course of instruction commenced December 1, 1917, with a class of radio intelligence specialists.

On January 7, 1918, and before the completion of the first course, another class was started, composed of officers and enlisted men from the mobile units and also a class of enlisted men, candidates for commission in the signal corps. These two classes were given the same course of instruction though succeeding classes were separated, due to normal expansion of the school, into separate and distinct courses.

* * * * * *

III. SCHOOL FOR PERSONNEL OF MOBILE UNITS: From the beginning referred to above until the time of the closing of the schools, January 31, 1919, there have been conducted courses for seven (7) succeeding classes of officers and men from the personnel of the mobile units. The students from the earlier classes being selected mostly from field signal battalions, but in the later classes also from telegraph battalions, infantry regiments and in some cases from artillery regiments. * * *

The object of the school for the personnel of mobile units was to familiarize students thoroughly with all signal equipment used in functioning technical means of communication for the mobile troops; to instruct them in the case, adjustment and manipulation of all the apparatus, much of which then in use in the American E. F., was either French or British material, and with which our officers and men were not familiar; and to instruct in the possibilities, limitations and tactical uses of the different means of communication. Since it would be manifestly impossible to organize schools of sufficient capacity to accommodate all our signal troops, it was the aim of this school to so frame the courses of instruction that the graduates would be suitable to impart the knowledge they had received to others on their return to their respective units.

It was naturally impossible to give a thorough course of instruction in the time available, but an attempt was made to review the elements of electricity upon which the operation of signal apparatus is based, and then to make a special study of each of the particular instruments in use. This was accomplished by means of lectures and laboratory demonstrations, followed by practical problems illustrating the tactical uses of the instruments in maintaining communications.

IV. RADIO SECTION OPERATORS' SCHOOL: The radio section operators' school, or as the earlier classes were called, the Radio Intelligence Specialists School, had for its object the training of radio section operators and German speaking listening-in-operators to supply the personnel necessary to operate the listening-in-stations and goniometric stations which our British and French Allies had found were essential in the conduct of their intelligence service. Two classes of students were sent for instruction in this school: First, telegraph operators to be trained as radio operators, and, second, German speakers without any knowledge of the continental Morse Code. The course was designed to give sufficient instruction in radio telegraphy to enable both classes of operators to operate radio sets. The first class at the rate of twenty-five words a minute and the second class, the German speakers, at the rate of fifteen words per minute. The earlier classes in this school were not in all cases permitted to complete the course as the demand for personnel for the radio section was so great and as soon as a man acquired a proper speed as an operator and could operate a listening-in set under normal conditions, he was sent for duty at the work for which there was a demand for his services although he may not have been sufficiently familiar with the instrument to repair or adjust his instruments under unfavorable conditions. During the latter courses, however, we were able to keep the students long enough to give them a fair working knowledge of the instruments.

Six classes have been given instruction in this school. * * *

V. CANDIDATES' SCHOOL: The object of the candidates' school as its name signifies, was to train selected enlisted men who had been recommended by their commanders, and to select from among them and to recommend those for commission whom we considered suitable for signal corps officers. In the first class, the same course of instruction was given as was given to the officers in the school for personnel of mobile units. In the second class a six weeks course of instruction similar to the officers' course, though separate from it, was given, and, in addition, a course in administration, discipline and military matters was given at the army engineer candidates' school. Up to the time of the completion of the second course of the candidates' school, the small number of students had given this school a minor place, the size and needs of the other schools having taken precedence.

At this time, however, it was realized that, in the curriculum of the schools, the candidates' school must eventually become the leading feature, due to the urgent need of signal officers. The increased capacity at the corps schools for the personnel of mobile units permitted us to decrease the size of these classes in the army signal schools. To prepare for this change, a course of instruction for the candidates' school was mapped out including not only the technical work covering practically the same ground as is covered in the officers' school, but which in addition would include sufficient work along other lines to give the candidates some practical knowledge of the use of infantry, for whom, as signal officers, they would be required to furnish means of communication; it also covered such subjects as administration, field service regulations, discipline and other matters with which every officer, in whatever branch of the service, should be familiar. It was considered essential also to include such exercises as would tend to develop energy, initiative and ability to command men.

* * * * * *

The following general course of instruction was planned.
BUZZER PRACTICE
ELECTRICITY:

* * * * * *

RADIO:

* * * * * *

WIRE:

* * * * * *

OTHER MEANS OF COMMUNICATION:

* * * * * *

TACTICS:

* * * * * *

MILITARY SUBJECTS:

* * * * * *

VI. The result of operations during the summer and fall of 1918, and the call from the United States for experienced signal officers to be returned for training the additional units being mobilized there, created a greatly increased and immediate demand for signal corps officers, which had to be supplied from the American Expeditionary Forces, so that the courses of instruction for the third and fourth classes had to be curtailed. This was done by increasing the hours of work and by eliminating some of the nontechnical work which had been mapped out. Also, early in October the chief signal officer informed me that twelve hundred signal corps officers must be supplied through the medium of the army signal schools from enlisted candidates by July 1, 1919. The laboratory facilities at the army signal schools or the possibility of their extension were not considered sufficient to accomplish this and retain at the same time the other courses, but this was arranged by the training section inasmuch as the army radio section was by this time prepared to take up the work of training its own replacements, and the increased facilities of the corps schools could take care of the personnel of the mobile units. It was, therefore, planned to have three distinct candidates' classes at the same time; one class entering each month and one class graduating each month. However, the signing of the Armistice obviated the necessity of continuing this plan and the class starting November 4 was the only class to complete a three months' course and was the last class at the school. After the signing of the Armistice it became evident that there would be no need for their services as officers, the course, as originally mapped out, has considerably changed. It was realized that there would be a lack of interest and a tendency to slight such subjects as administration, field service regulations, and similar Allied subjects; therefore, additional work along technical lines, although not absolutely essential for the instruction of signal officer, was substituted.

* * * * * *

VII. SPECIAL COURSES: There were from time to time special classes sent here not included in the above three schools, but in each case only one course was conducted for each of the special classes: a special radio course for a class of thirteen officers of the air service, and a class of enlisted men from the engineers which was reported as the engineer radio specialists' course. Also, two courses which at the time were reported as artillery radio specialists' course, and, artillery telephone specialists' course. These two latter classes, however, took the same course and are included in the third class of the school for personnel for mobile units.

VIII. METEOROLOGICAL SCHOOL: There was organized and started on March 24, 1918, under the administration of the director of the army signal schools, a meteoroligical school conducted by Major Blair and Major Gale of the signal corps. The courses of the school were entirely separate and distinct from the other activities of the army signal schools and its connection with these schools was a purely administrative one, and no records were kept of the activities or extent of work covered by this school.

The meteorological school moved to Colombey-les-Belles on August 4, 1918.

IX. PIGEON SERVICE: The headquarters of the pigeon service, located at Fort de la Bonnelle, was placed for a time to a certain extent under the administration of the army signal schools, merely insofar as it was controlled by the commandant of the army schools though all its activities came directly under the administration of G. H. Q., American E. F., without reference to the intermediate authority. Therefore, no records were kept at the army signal schools.

X. GENERAL POLICY OF THE ARMY SIGNAL SCHOOLS:

1. The general policy of the army signal schools have been to impart the maximum of of instruction to the maximum number of students in the minimum of time. The instruction to be both theoretical and practical and only enough of the theoretical to enable the graduates to disseminate the knowledge they had gained at the schools.

2. To train the greatest number of students possible in the least time, to perform the function of radio operators in the army radio sections.

3. To select, train and recommend for commission from the enlisted personnel of the signal units, the number of men required as officers for replacements in the signal corps of the American Expeditionary Forces.

4. By lectures and demonstrations to disseminate among the other schools in the area as much general information as possible of the operations of the signal corps.

5. To maintain the schools on as elastic a basis as possible so as to be able to modify the courses to meet the rapidly changing conditions and so as to be able to accommodate any classes for instruction along any of the lines of work with which the signal corps occupies itself, at any time the need might appear for so doing.

XI. RECAPITULATION: The following tables show the number of students in each of the different courses at the school.

* * * * * *

```
        Total number of officers . . . . . . . . . . . . 239
        Total number of candidates . . . . . . . . . . . 515
        Total number of enlisted men . . . . . . . . L . . 718
                            Grand Total. . . .1472
```

C-in-C Rept. File: Fldr. 231: Report

Army Antiaircraft School

Langres, Haute-Marne, November 11, 1918.

[Extract]

At the time the United States entered the war there was no antiaircraft development by the United States * * *

It was decided that an American school for antiaircraft would be necessary and arrangements were made to have such a school conducted by English-speaking French officers * * * A class of twenty five officers reported for this purpose at the French school at Arnouville-les-Gonesse, September 26, 1917.

* * * * * *

The school was given official recognition in Par. 1, Section III, G. O. 46, G. H. Q., dated October 10, 1917, which established the antiaircraft and trench mortar schools * * * There was no connection between the antiaircraft and the trench mortar schools * * *

Upon completion of the first course of study, the student officers and Captain Anderson proceeded to the French front for two weeks experience with batteries.

It was decided that the army antiaircraft and trench mortar schools should be a part of the army schools at Langres. The antiaircraft school included both the antiaircraft artillery and antiaircraft school machine guns. On November 1, 1917, while the student officers were still at the front, Major Hopkins moved the headquarters of the antiaircraft artillery school to Langres.

* * * * * *

Searchlight instruction had been carried on * * * at Fort Mont Valerian and at Langres. Close liaison was maintained with the antiaircraft school, it being recognized that searchlights would be used only for antiaircraft service, but the order definitely making the searchlight school a part of the army antiaircraft school * * * was issued June 10, 1918 (Par. 22, S. O. 161, G. H. Q.).

* * * * * *

A history of the various sections of the army antiaircraft school will be given more in detail.

ARTILLERY SECTION: It was decided to adopt the French methods for antiaircraft artillery and the first course at Arnouville-les-Gonesse was a duplicate of the French course given at the school, but taught by English-speaking French officers, assisted by American instructors.

The first antiaircraft troops, Battery A, 1st Antiaircraft Battalion and the 1st Antiaircraft Battery, arrived at Langres, November 12, 1917. About December 1, 1917, the remainder of the 1st Antiaircraft Battalion and the 2d, 3d, and 4th Antiaircraft Batteries arrived at Langres. The officers who had completed the first course were assigned to these batteries as instructors. About the middle of December two French auto-cannon were loaned to us and were used for the training of these batteries. These two guns were entirely inadequate and after the failure of repeated attempts to obtain more guns, it was decided to move the center of instruction to the French school at Arnouville, where our troops could have the use of the same guns used by the French and also the guns in nearby forts that were part of the Paris defenses. Fort de Stains, near Arnouville, was placed at our disposal. The 1st Antiaircraft Battery was sent to Chaumont to drill at the French guns there, headquarters and supply company and Battery A of the 1st Battalion remaining at Langres to drill with the two auto-cannon. The remaining batteries proceeded to Fort de Stains January 23, 1918. The officers assigned to all the antiaircraft batteries were relieved from active duty with the batteries and assigned to duty at the officers' school, which was reestablished in the Chateau d'Arnouville. Officers who had completed the first course were in charge of the drill of the batteries.

Thirty-one additional officers were detailed from the C. A. C. replacements and were also designated to take the course at the school. * * *

* * * * * *

Arrangements were made with the French to have our American batteries assigned to French batteries for experience at the front and they proceeded for this purpose on April 15, 1918. The 1st Antiaircraft Battery, however, was assigned to the antiaircraft defense of Is-sur-Tille and went there directly.

Arrangements were made with the British to have groups of five American officers take the course at their school at Steenwerck. Twenty officers were given this instruction, the last five leaving the Steenwerck school at the time of the German advance.

The 1st to 7th Antiaircraft Battalions, inclusive, and the 1st to 20th Antiaircraft Batteries inclusive, have received instruction at the school, a total of nearly 5,000 troops and 240 officers.

* * * Officers arriving with the new troops are detached from the troops in order to take the course at the school. The troops themselves are placed in training under officers who have already completed the school course. Two officers are assigned to each battery for this purpose, if possible, but the lack of officers had rendered this impossible in some cases. The course of instruction for troops is six weeks and for officers five weeks, with one week at the front. The course at the officers' school includes practical instruction in the care and use of all antiaircraft materiel and theoretical instruction in the angle of approach and tachymetric methods of fire. In addition, many Allied miscellaneous subjects are studied, such as:

Identification of Targets
Sound Apparatus and Firing by Sound
Selection of Positions
Camouflage
Tactical Use of Artillery with Searchlights
Liaison with Air Service
Gas Instruction
Fixed Antiaircraft Defenses
Visits to Aviation Fields, Gun Emplacements, Listening Stations, and
Proving Grounds

The instruction for troops includes:

Care and Use of all Antiaircraft Apparatus
Gas Instruction
Identification of Targets
Close Order Drill
Physical Exercises
Military Courtesy
First Aid
Signalling

There is also given special instruction for noncommissioned officers.

In addition to Fort de Stains the school is now occupying Forts Montmorency and Mont Lignon, the flying field at Le Bourget and billets in the villages of Sourcelles, Garges, and Villiers le Bel.

MACHINE GUN SECTION: The machine gun section was organized December 2, 1917 * * *

Prior to the arrival of the 1st Antiaircraft Machine Gun Battalion, the staff of the school consisted of the director, senior instructor, four commissioned instructors, chief clerk and a detachment of 16 enlisted men. The work consisted in thorough drilling of the instructors and the enlisted men in order to prepare them for their duties. The machine guns were mounted for antiaircraft defense of Langres and were manned by this detachment.

The 1st Antiaircraft Machine Gun Battalion arrived on May 19, 1918, and the school was moved from Galland Barracks to Perrancey. On May 12, 1918, the aerial firing range, known as the Courcelles-en-Montagne Antiaircraft Firing Ground was assigned to the school. The range is about 25 kilometers in area and because of the two ravines at each end makes an excellent range for this purpose. The ground firing is conducted in the ravines with the targets placed against the side hills. Aerial firing at a simulated moving aeroplane target is very ingeniously arranged by having the guns mounted in ravines and a target mounted on a motorcycle which moves at full speed along a path on top of the steep banks of the ravine. The rider is protected from fire by stonewalls, and the machine gunner sees only the rapidly moving target. The range complete has been built by the troops undergoing instruction.

The machine gun section gives a course of about six weeks and instructs officers and men in the practical work required of an antiaircraft machine gun battalion, as well as in the theory of antiaircraft gunnery. Assigned officers remain with their organizations during the training.

Very strict discipline is enforced in all organizations coming to this section and in addition to keeping up the close order drill, physical exercises, practice marches, instruction is given in the following subjects:

Nomenclature and handling of various types of machine guns
Care, preservation, cleaning, and repairing of machine guns and accessories
Machine-gun drill of all kinds
Stripping and assembling of various machine guns
Use of antiavion mounts and sights
Range firing
Barrage fire
Night firing
Target designation
Use of automatic pistol
Use of range finders and field glasses
Estimation of range

Map reading
Construction of machine-gun emplacements
Camouflage
Visual signalling

Night firing in cooperation with the searchlight section is conducted every Thursday night.

The following organizations have either finished course of instruction or are taking course at present: The 1st, 2d, 3d, 4th, and 5th Antiaircraft Machine Gun Battalions and the 141st Machine Gun Battalion. Special courses have also been conducted for officers and men of the coast artillery corps and field artillery. About 125 officers and 350 enlisted men have taken these courses.

At present there are about 3200 troops at the machine gun section and attending school. The following villages are being used for billeting purposes: Noidant-le-Rocheux, Beauchemin, Perrogney, Montaubon, and Vieux-Maulin. Montaubon, the headquarters of the machine gun section, is about 8 kilometers from Langres.

* * * * * *

SEARCHLIGHT SECTION: Before the searchlight section, army antiaircraft school, was established on June 29, 1918, there had been a detachment of searchlight engineers at Langres for over six months, working under the army engineer school. Additional searchlight troops were being trained at Fort Mont Valerian, which at that time was a searchlight base for the French. Others were assigned direct to the British army to receive their training with British lights at the front.

At the present time this section is located at Champigny * * *

The course is six weeks in length and among the subjects taught are:

Nomenclature, operation, mainipulation, assembling, and care of various types of searchlights
Searchlight crew drill
Searchlight position selection
Night drills
Camouflage
Paraboloid and other methods of sound locating
Signalling, use of field glasses, and telescopes
Theory of electricity and gas engines as pertaining to searchlight equipment
Practical work on telephones; storage batteries, generators, and gas engines
Cleaning, repairing, care and use of automatic rifle
Panoramic sketching
Erection of shelters, etc.

There is an advanced searchlight base and training center at Colombey-les-Belles, where troops who have completed the preliminary training can be sent, pending the receipt of materiel for use at the front.

Up to the present time 34 platoons (45 officers and 1,530 enlisted men) of the 56th Regiment of Engineers have received instruction at the searchlight section.

Because of the separation of the searchlight and artillery sections it has been impossible to obtain in drills the close cooperation necessary between the searchlights and artillery. Cooperation between the searchlights and machine guns has been obtained by transporting a searchlight to the machine-gun firing ground one night a week. It will be noticed that the three different sections are separated and the machine gun section and artillery section are spread out too much for the most efficient administration.

It has been the plan, approved in principle by G. H. Q., to consolidate the three sections into one training area as soon as practicable.

At the present time there have been approximately 578 officers and 12,000 enlisted personnel, who have either completed or are now at the various sections of the army antiaircraft school. The total commissioned personnel of the army antiaircraft school is 71 officers. This number includes the administrative staffs, the instructors and officers assigned to replacement organizations which have been lately organized.

C-in-C Rept. File: Fldr. 232: Report

Army Trench Mortar School

Vitrey, Haute-Saone, September 10, 1918.

[Extract]

The Army Trench Mortar School is a section of the army antiaircraft and trench mortar schools, originally organized by virtue of G. O. 46, H. A. E. F., 1917, and placed under the command of Brigadier General J. A. Shipton, National Army.

The school was first formed at Bourges, France, on October 10, 1917, Colonel F. K. Fergusson, C. A. C., Director. On November 22, 1917, the trench mortar school was moved to Fort de la Bonnelle at center of instruction.

Instruction is given to both officers and enlisted men and in the past, divisional and corps artillery batteries have taken the courses.

Both practical and theoretical instruction is given. Courses in army regulations, customs of the service, manual of guard duty, small arms and military correspondence and paper work, as well as the technical courses in trench mortar work and modern warfare are included. The technical courses provide instruction in gas protection, camouflage, cover and topography as well.

Both theoretical and practical instruction including manning mortars, placing them in correct firing position, firing and correction of fire is given in all English, French, and German types of mortars, all positions in a battery being filled by student personnel.

Trench mortar regulations for the United States army have been compiled and various information pertaining to trench mortars disseminated. Latest information is incorporated in existing regulations by the issue of bulletins from time to time.

In the musuem all forms of trench mortars in the armies of the Allies and the enemy are collected and the courses include instruction for firing captured ordnance in combat.

* * * * * *

The Trench Artillery Center: The trench artillery center was established by authority of Section V, General Orders No. 152. American Expeditionary Forces, September 10, 1918. Its object was to provide for the organization and training of trench artillery units, officers and soldier specialists, and for the development and test of trench artillery matériel. It was regularly established on September 8, 1918. It was organized with a view of equipping and training for front line service five thousand trench artillery troops every four to six weeks.

The Center Area: The trench artillery center was located in the Department of Haute-Saone with headquarters in Vitrey. It comprised the following villages.

	Rated Capacity			Maximum men occupied by at one time
	Officers:	Men	Horses	
Vitrey, including barracks	183	2474	325	2345
Chauvirey-le-Vieil	17	390	28	254
Chauvirey-le-Chatel	33	650	43	649
Montigny	38	890	219	859
Ouge	40	800	64	673
Preigney	29	400	100	303
Pisseloup	29	540	105	284
St-Marcel	25	661	222	580
Betoncourt	31	316	216	156
Norroy le Jussey	10	100	0	0
Bougey	18	200	0	0
La Ferte	43	697	127	0
Villes.	16	1000	70	0
Total	512	9118	1518	6103

The capacities of the villages were rated for occupation in the summer time and actual experience showed that in autumn on account of the crops being stored and the bad repair of the buildings, the towns would accommodate about 85% of their rated capacity.

The Trench Artillery School: Instruction in trench artillery in the American Expeditionary Forces was initiated by detailing 48 coast artillery officers to take a course in the trench artillery school of the French army at Bourges, beginning October 9, 1917, and 12 coast artillery officers to take instruction at the trench mortar school of the Second Army, British Expeditionary Forces at Saint Omer during the same time. On December 1, 1917, these 60 officers under Captain F. E. Williford, C. A. C., established the Army Trench Artillery School at Fort de la Bonnelle, Langres. Upon the establishment of the Trench Artillery Center at Vitrey, September 8, 1918, the Trench Artillery School was moved to that place and made a part of the center activities. Since its establishment the school has graduated 367 officers, and supervised and standardized the instruction of all trench artillery troops. The courses have included instruction in general artillery, the use of trench artillery of all calibers, gas defense, hand bombing, machine-gun instruction, bayonet combat, camouflage, and hippology.

In addition to its regular instruction, the school has written and revised the manuals for trench artillery, received designs for and experimented with new matériel and encouraged the development of this arm. It gave seven demonstrations of the use and development of trench artillery, which were witnessed by several hundred officers. From August 1, 1918 to December 1, 1918 the officers and troops under instruction fired 12,000 grenades, 920 rounds of dummy ammunition and 4,127 rounds of service ammunition. The service ammunition fired totals over 190,000 pounds of metal and 98,000 pounds of high explosive all of which was shot without any injuries to personnel or matériel. In addition, German minenwerfer were fired during the courses and demonstration. The firing of the minenwerfer resulted in one burst in the bore which caused two deaths and injuries to two men.

Ranges: A feature which contributed greatly to the value of the center was the extensive artillery range approximately 5.8 kilometers x 2 kilometers. The varied terrain represented therein permitted extensive maneuvers of all kinds with the firing of service ammunition under conditions closely approximating actual field service. Rifle and pistol ranges were provided for small arms and machine-gun training. Grenade ranges were provided for the training of hand bombers.

C-in-C Rept. File: Fldr. 235: Report

Infantry Candidate School

La Valbonne, Ain, February 3, 1919.

From: Capt. Benjamin Brooks, G-4, Infantry Candidates School

To: The Adjutant General, G. H. Q., American E. F.

[Extract]

1. Pursuant to your letter of December 2, 1918, No. 3603-233-N, the following brief history of the infantry candidates school, is written:

* * * * * *

3. On October 1, 1917, under the supervision of French officers, an American infantry officers' school was established in the part of the camp known as ECOLE-de-TIR. The foreign legion and colonial troops occupied the rest of the camp. The course ended December 15, 1917. 1st Lieut. H. E. Bronson, Infantry, was stationed at the camp, on the close of school, to take charge of American property but was not ordered to look after French property.

* * * * * *

5. Authority for the establishment of a candidates school at La VALBONNE, is given in a letter from General Hallier, Assistant Chief, General Staff of the French army, dated September 15, 1918. This letter was indorsed and referred from G-5, G. H. Q., to Brig. General Harry A. Smith, Commandant Army Schools. The second indorsement was given by General Smith, who referred the proposition to Captain W. E. Haskell, Jr.

6. The formation of the camp should be divided into three parts:
    (a) Initial work done by Captain W. E. Haskell
    (b) The organizing of the school under Lt. Col. S. L. Pike
    (c) The post as commanded by Colonel C. W. Exton

7. On September 6, 1918, Captain Haskell arrived in La VALBONNE under orders to have the camp ready for a garrison of 7,900 men by October 15, 1918, and with authority from General Harry Smith, Commandant of Army Schools, to make all necessary purchases locally or otherwise.

Seven candidates battalions consisting of 1,000 men each were contemplated.

Upon the arrival on September 27, 1918, of Company B, 601st Engineers, consisting of 162 men, and 261 men who comprised the nucleous of a labor battalion, together with one captain and 48 men, Q. M. C., the camp was thoroughly policed, disinfected, and bunks built to accommodate approximately 7,000 candidates.

On October 14, ninety-five 2d Lieutenants detailed as instructors arrived per S. O. 279, par. 7, headquarters, army schools, and from then on officers arrived daily from combat division, detailed as instructors.

From the 2d Lieutenants detailed from headquarters, army schools, Captain Haskell selected two men from each battalion to act as adjutants and supply officers of the seven battalions. Lieut. Reid A. Page, Quartermaster Corps, was detailed as camp adjutant.

The remainder of the officers were assigned to the different battalions as instructors.

8. On October 17, Lieut. Colonel S. L. Pike, Director, and Captain W. P. Hair, Adjutant of Army Candidates School, Langres, arrived under verbal orders of Brig. General H. A. Smith, to complete the organization of the school.

At this time there were only twelve candidates at the school. From then on various contingents arrived. The battalion received their full quotas on the following dates:

1st Battalion . . . . Oct. 18
2d Battalion . . . . Oct. 18
3d Battalion. . . . . Oct. 18 and 19
4th Battalion . . . . Oct. 19 and 20
5th Battalion . . . . Oct. 23
6th Battalion . . . . Never received full quota.
last candidates were received November 14, 1918

9. Owing to the casualties in the divisions of the prospective candidates, the desired quotas never arrived. As the other battalion was not filled as late as November 14, the plan of having a seventh battalion was abandoned.

* * * * * *

11. The 160 men of the 601st Engineers who reported September 27, 1918, left pursuant to telegraphic instructions from G. H. Q. on November 18, 1918; but 261 men who accompanied them remained and the construction under Major Brown's direction was continued by a detachment of the 113th Engineers who reported November 9 and 10, 8 officers and 239 men. The necessary ground was cleared and work commenced, but on November 16, telegraphic orders were received stopping all new construction. Thenceforth the engineers were employed in salvaging lumber, repairing roads in camp, flooring one building with concrete to be used as shops, installing a drainage system for the motor transport park etc.

* * * * * *

15. General Order No. 1, Headquarters, Infantry Candidates School, dated November 12, 1918, states that the organization of this school will be as follows:
    1. Commandant * * *
    2. Assistant Commandant * * * supervises.
        (a) Adjutant's Office
        (b) Personnel Office
        (c) Post Office
        (d) Billeting
        (e) Administration Service Battalion
        (f) Administration other attached troops
        (g) Military Police
        (h) Strength Reports and Graphics

    (i) Hospitalization
    (j) Pay of Enlisted Men
    (k) Care of Service Records and preparation of discharge certificates
    (l) Travel Orders
    (m) Y. M. C. A., Red Cross, etc.
    (n) Reception of Candidates
    (o) Assignment of Candidates to Companies
    (p) Equipment of Candidates
    (q) Arrangements for departure of Candidates and Graduates
    (r) Equipment of Graduates
    (s) Discipline
    (t) Journal of School Activities and Developments

3. Assistant Commandant * * * supervises.
    (a) Q. M. Corps
    (b) Ordnance Department
    (c) Signal Corps
    (d) Engineer Depot
    (e) Police Officer
    (f) Mess Officer
    (g) Motor Transport
    (h) Animal Transport
    (i) Salvage Service
    (j) Construction and Maintenance
    (k) Fire Protection
    (l) Laundries
    (m) Electric Lighting
    (n) Water Supply

4. Assistant Commandant * * * supervises.
    (a) Instruction
    (b) Examination
    (c) Elimination of Candidates
    (d) Graduation
    (e) Discipline

16. Actual instruction began October 21, 1918 with a total of 5835 candidates and occupied 464 hours * * *

* * * * * *

17. It unfortunately developed, however, that the candidates received were not all well chosen. Some were sent positively against their will, having no desire to receive officers commissions. A larger number had never received the necessary elementary education on which to base their studies for a commission. They had never been noncommissioned officers and in some cases were foreigners with but a years residence in the United States and only a night school knowledge of English. Another considerable number, though perhaps having the initial qualifications, lost interest after the signing of the Armistice, or for other reasons, failed to qualify. It was for the above reasons that on:

    November 19, 1918 - - - - - - - - - - 1502 men
    December 6, 1918 - - - - - - - - - - 1642 men
    December 9, 1918 - - - - - - - - - -   82 men
    December 20, 1918 - - - - - - - - - - 754 men
                    Total   3980 men

were transferred from the school to the 2d Depot Division Le Mans, Sarthe.

* * * * * *

19. Instruction ceased January 17, 1919 * * *
20. Twelve hundred and ninety-nine candidates were graduates. * * *

* * * * * *

> BENJAMIN BROOKS,
> Captain, Engineers,
> G-4.

C-in-C Rept. File: Fldr. 236: Report

I Corps School

Gondrecourt, Meuse, November 11, 1918.

[Extract]

Creation of the School: In compliance with Par. 2, G. O. 45, 1917, G. H. Q., A. E. F., the 1st Division School, located on the outskirts of Gondrecourt, Meuse, became the I Corps Schools, the first session of which began October 15, 1917, with about ten Adrian barracks for school buildings, the remainder of the necessary shelter consisting of tents.

Mission: The I Corps Schools form a part of the school project of the American expeditionary Forces, which project has had for its primary object the propagation of the military principles, including the doctrine of combat, announced by the Commander-in-Chief. The mission of the I Corps Schools, like that of the other corps schools, is to train the student personnel for duty as unit commanders in the organizations from which drawn, and there is no doubt but what the schools have filled their mission well. While it may be true that regimental commanders, and company commanders, especially those at the front, may, owing to the scarcity of officers and noncommissioned officers, or to other exigencies of the service, grumble at times about sending officers and noncommissioned officers to the various schools, it is a well-known fact that regimental and company commanders are always glad to have in their organizations officers and noncommissioned officers who have graduated from the schools. It is also the concensus of opinion of those who have gone through the schools that their military efficiency has been materially increased therby.

Organization: When the I Corps Schools were organized, they included the following schools:

- (I) Infantry Schools
- (II) Artillery Schools
- (III) Engineer School
- (IV) Signal School
- (V) Antigas School
- (VI) Sanitary School
- (VII) Aeronautical School
- (VIII) Field Officers School

(I) INFANTRY SCHOOL: The Infantry School was divided into (a) The Tactical School, (b) The Infantry Weapons School, and (c) The Machine Gun School, organized as follows, the subjects indicated being taught in each school:

(a) Tactical School: (Captains and lieutenants of rifle companies only)
Section A: (Lieutenants) Principal subjects: Tactics; map reading; duties of platoon

commanders; liaison. Subordinate subjects: Uses and characteristics of all infantry weapons; observation; intelligence; pioneer work; care of troops. Section B: (Captains) Principal subjects: Tactics; map reading; duties of company commanders; liaison. Subordinate subjects; Care of troops; uses and characteristics of all infantry weapons; intelligence; pioneer work.

      (b) Infantry Weapons School: (Officers and noncommissioned officers of rifle companies.)

         (1) Grenade and Automatic Rifle Section: (noncommissioned Officers.) Automatic rifle; automatic pistol; hand grenades; rifle grenades.

         (2) Musketry and Bayonet Section: (Noncommissioned Officers.) Course in musketry, bayonet fighting, physical training, boxing, patrolling, a little sniping, and intelligence work.

         (3) Sniping, Observation and Intelligence Section: Noncommissioned officers course: (For battalion scout N. C. O.'s, sniping N. C. O.'s, and observation N. C. O.'s) Scouting, patrolling, sniping, observation, intelligence, musketry, bayonet, and grenades.

         Battalion Scout Officers Course: (For lieutenants detailed as battalion scout officers.) Scouting, patrolling, sniping, observation, intelligence, musketry, bayonet, grenades, automatic rifle and pistol.

         (4) Trench Guns Section: Stokes Mortar Course: (For officers and noncommissioned officers of Stokes mortar platoons of Hq. Cos.) Three weeks' work with the Stokes mortar and one week's work with the 37-mm. in the technical and tactical uses of these weapons.

         One-pounder Gun Course: (For officers and noncommissioned officers of one-pounder gun platoons of Hq. Cos.) Three weeks' work with the one-pounder gun (37-mm.) and one week's work with the Stokes mortar, in the technical and tactical uses of these weapons.

      (c) Machine Gun School: (Officers and noncommissioned officers of machine-gun organizations.)

         Noncommissioned Officers Course: Technical handling of machine guns.

         Officers Basic Course: Technical and tactical handling of machine guns.

         Officers Advance Course: Only for officers who have already graduated from the machine-gun course in corps or army schools or who have had practical machine-gun work giving an equivalent amount of instruction.

   (II) ARTILLERY SCHOOL: This school covered instruction in the technical and tactical uses of the 75-mm. and the 155-mm. guns, particular attention being given to the solution of fire problems; also, liaison with infantry and aeroplanes.

   (III) ENGINEER SCHOOL:

      Section A: (For officers of engineer organizations and hq. cos. of infantry, cavalry, and artillery.) Instruction given in pioneer, sapper, and bayonet work, and in minor tactics, musketry, grenades, gas and automatic weapons.

      Section B: (For N. C. O.'s of engineer organizations and hq. cos. of infantry, cavalry, and artillery.) Instruction in wiring, revetment, trenches, mining, dugouts, camouflage, roads, light railroads, explosives, bayonet, musketry, grenades, gas, automatic weapons, and duties of N. C. O.'s in handling working parties.

   (IV) SIGNAL SCHOOL:

      Section A: (For officers and N. C. O.'s of the signal corps.) Line of information for liaison between different units of a division, including instruction in telephones, radio, visual signalling, pigeons, fireworks, aeroplane liaison, storage batteries, gas.

      Section B: (For officers and N. C. O.'s of infantry signal platoons.) Lines of information for liaison within an infantry regiment and to supporting units, including instruction in same subjects as above, except storage batteries.

Section C: (For officers and N. C. O.'s of artillery signal units.) Lines of information for liaison and fire control within the artillery brigades and other units of a division, including instruction in same subjects as Section A, except storage batteries and pigeons.

(V) ANTIGAS SCHOOL:

Section A: (For all student officers and N. C. O.'s of the I Corps Schools.) For each class a one day course in the general principles of antigas measures and in the personal use of protective appliances.

Section B: (For N. C. O.'s) A six day course to qualify N. C. O.'s for the duties of company and battery gas N. C. O.'s.

(VI) SANITARY SCHOOL: Included a course in hygiene, sanitation, management of hospitals, evacuation of patients from the front, and field surgery.

(VII) AERONAUTICAL SCHOOL: The course in this school covered the following subjects, practical and theoretical; photography, reconnaissance, firing, reglage, panel work, and observation.

(VIII) FIELD OFFICERS SCHOOL: The course in this school included tactical walks and the solution of tactical problems.

Discontinuance of certain schools: With the growth of the American E. F., the facilities and accommodations at Gondrecourt proved inadequate, and for this and other reasons, the following schools were discontinued as indicated:

Artillery School	In June 1918
Signal School	In November 1918
Sanitary School	In March 1918
Aeronautical School	In May 1918
Field Officers School	In March 1918

Detail of Students: Although it was planned originally that each corps should have its own schools, and the I Corps Schools were at first under the jurisdiction of the I Corps, on August 6, 1918, the I Corps Schools were placed directly under the jurisdiction of G-5, G. H. Q., the students, consisting of officers and noncommissioned officers, have been detailed from the various divisions, irrespective of corps.

Detail of directors and instructors: The directors of the various schools and the instructors were detailed from graduates of the schools, and, as far as practicable, from graduates who had seen service at the front.

Duration of session: Each session lasted four weeks, with one week's intermission between sessions.

* * * * * *

The last session: The session of November 25-December 21, 1918 was the last session of the I Corps Schools, which, following the Armistice, was discontinued December 21, 1918.

Number of graduates: During the fourteen months of their existence the I Corps Schools graduated 12,535 students.

GONDRECOURT, THE CRADLE OF A. E. F. TRAINING AND INSTRUCTION: When the history of the American E. F. is written, Gondrecourt (Meuse) will have an important place in it, for this little village was the center of the first training done in France by the American Expeditionary Forces. It may be called the cradle of training and instruction of the American Expeditionary Forces in France.

C-in-C Rept. File: Fldr. 237: Report

II Corps Schools

[*April 21, 1919*].

  Acting under verbal instructions of General H. B. Fiske, G. H. Q., Lt..Col. H. L. Cooper, Infantry, did not assume active command of the schools until August 15, 1918. The time intervening between his arrival and taking over the command of the schools was spent in observing the courses of instruction and all forms of work connected with the schools. His observation led to the belief that the schools were not performing their full function because the work of all the schools was not being coordinated. Each school was acting as a separate unit, engrossed in its own particular line with no attempt being made to instruct students in the coordination of all the weapons with which the army is equipped and which were available at the schools for this purpose. By this is meant, for instance, that there was no tactical instruction worthy of the name. Up to this time, apparently, efforts had been made to have students specialize in the course for which they were sent here, but the course failed of its purpose when it neglected to instruct them in the coordination of their specialty with that of the rest of the schools. All attempts apparently made were limited to instruction for trench warfare, but this date, September 1, approximately, the conditions of warfare had changed, and it was considered desirable to build up the offensive spirit and the warfare of movement.

  Another defect noticed was that the commandant of the schools had not organized any board of directors to coordinate work and to consider questions regarding training which are continually arising at such an institution as this. This, in a measure, prevented the instructors from making suggestions with reference to the betterment of the general school work, which was considered rather detrimental. The instructors of the different schools were first made to understand that their share in the responsibility for the instruction in their particular school extended to the correct instruction of the entire student body. This ultimately worked out in a most satisfactory manner, the instructors getting together informally and frequently to help each other in determining the proper use of their particular subject of instruction. After consultation with the directors of the different schools it was decided to make representations to the training section, requesting authority to limit the technical instruction in all the schools to 50% of the time, while the tactical instruction should be pressed to the utmost limit. About this time, Col. McAndrews and Col. Short visited the schools and in talking over the change which it was proposed to recommend, they advised us that a letter would be received directing such instruction. Upon the receipt of this letter, it was noted that offensive tactics were to be insisted on. Inasmuch as all the instructors at the schools had been teaching nothing but trench warfare systems, it was found necessary to organize classes for the instructors themselves. Major J. A. McDermott was placed in charge of the instruction of the instructors and assistant instructors and their schools were required to conform to the instruction therein given. The entire student body was organized into groups, platoons, companies and a battalion the demonstration companies being used to fill in such parts of the battalion as it was not considered necessary to have students execute, namely; the support companies in an attack when the support companies were simply to follow and not to be used tactically. It was found by experience that the first class with which this was tried, very few of the officers had had any instruction in regard to the tactical use and coordination of their arms. Platoon commanders apparently had no conception of the fire power of their platoon. Musketry work, while not entirely unknown to them, was most unsatisfactory. Upon a visit made to the school by General Paul B. Malone, he severely commented to the student body on their lack of ability to command. This was not peculiar to that particular class, as it was found in other classes composing the school. It is believed that this lack of leadership on the part of the unior officers was caused by their lack of knowledge of any of the tactical principles as set forth in our different drill regulations and other manuals. It was noticed that the officers knew their close order drill veryywell, but did not insist on its execution with snap and precision. After the signing of the Armistice it became particularly noticeable that officers would fail to enforce their orders, or as a matter of fact, any discipline among the men under their command. Inquiry has since been made among officers commanding regiments and combat divisions with regard to the method of selecting officers to attend corps schools. I was advised by Col. A. F. Prescott that the officers sent to the corps schools were ordinarily not the officers whom the regimental commanders considered best in their organizations. In a division with which he was connected, he stated there was a tacit agreement among regimental commanders not to send their best men to the schools for the reason that if they came to the schools and made a good record, they would probably be lost to the regiment by being detailed as instructors at the school. A second, and the main reason, that regimental commanders would not send good officers to the schools was because of the danger to themselves of being relieved from command for some error made by the less efficient officers. There is reason to believe that this attitude extended throughout the entire army, with the result that the class of officers on the average who were sent to the corps schooks did not represent the best elements of our service.

Immediately following the signing of the Armistice, there was such a decided let up in all desire to learn and resentment to all discipline, that the task of the instructors at the schools became doubly hard. The court martial record of the school, unfortunately, is large, but there appeared to be no way in which to bring to these officers the realization of their responsibility, except through the medium of a general court martial. On August 12, 1918, instructions were received that the schools would be enlarged to accommodate approximately two thousand five hundred students. This necessitated a complete reorganization of the schools and redistribution of the work, and a closer coordination of problems and other work to prevent different classes from interfering with each other on the target range.

During September, we had in addition to the above, additional work imposed on the schools by the attendance of the division school details from the following divisions: 7th, 81st, and 85th. The officers and noncommissioned officers composing these details were keen to learn, but had apparently had no instructions beyond bayonet work, some throwing of grenades and close order drill. As these details arrived between courses they were given the additional time between the meeting of the regular classes in intensified work to being them up to the standard which it was hoped to make the entire class reach. It is understood that officers were sent from combat division of the A. E. F. to the divisions being organized at home, as instructors. If this is the case, then there should be no excuse for the condition in which these division school details arrived at these schools, unless the instructors sent home were below par.

Conditions having changed on the front, a series of problems were devised which represented most of the conditions which would be met at the front; attack on a strong point, bridge crossing and occupation of a defensive line in open warfare, and problems of like nature. Each one of these problems were taken direct from the infantry drill regulations, using the particular paragraph of the regulations as a sort of a text on which the whole problem was built. All other paragraphs in the drill regulations bearing on, or relating in any way to the text paragraph was then brought to the attention of the students. Mimeograph sheets showing all of these being issued to each student, and the study period in the evening devoted to a study or a conference in which students were urged to ask questions of the instructors. It was found that the interest taken was very much intensified, and furthermore, many students stated that they had never realized what the tactical principles given in the drill regulations had meant. In addition to the above, a careful study was made of the summaries of information which the schools received daily, and many valuable lessons on German methods which were given in those summaries of information were transmitted to the students in order that they might be informed as to what the Germans would probably do under any particular circumstances. The whole effort of the schools was to instill in the student body the idea that offensive movements in warfare of movement or open warfare could only reach their full success when the officers who were conducting it had full knowledge of the tactical formations best to adopt to meet a given condition, and a greater appreciation of the fire power of an infantry unit. The present organization prescribed by infantry drill regulations seem to meet all conditions, admirably, and it was not difficult to instill into the student the idea that an infantry company or platoon of itself had sufficient power to overcome nearly all obstacles if the proper formations were used.

With reference to the coordination of arms, every effort was made to eliminate the distrust which the majority of the students seemed to have of the auxiliary arms. Many students said that it was not worth while to attempt to use Stokes mortars or the 37-mm. guns, as they were of no use any way on the front. Others complained that every thing would be perfectly quiet on the front until these arms appeared, when the infantry were subjected to retaliatory fire because of their presence. After several demonstrations in which the proper method of approach was shown and a demonstration as to the effectiveness of these particular weapons, it is believed that most of the students left the schools with a very different idea than that which they had entertained upon arrival here. This was particularly noticeable in the use of the accompanying gun of artillery. In this connection, however, it is necessary to say that after the relief of the two school batteries, no battery was found of the division which furnished the battery for this work, which was capable of doing the work. It is to be feared that because of the lack of knowledge on the part of the artillery officers commanding the guns that not a great amount of respect was formed for the guns in this particular method of employment. It is recommended earnestly that in any future school that a battery shall be attached to the demonstration battalion so that there will be no false notions instilled in the students by the fact that the guns are unable to function because of lack of knowledge of how the work should be done.

It is considered necessary that in training company or platoon leaders in infantry that the auxiliary arms should be fully capable and invariably present in all tactical schemes.

It was further noted that of the thousands of students who attended this school, most of whom came direct from combat divisions, that the work of the infantry airplane was an unknown quantity then. We were jokingly informed that the panels issued to infantry units made good dish towels and that that was the principal use to which they were put. I did not believe this was possible until I talked with many aviators returning from the line in which they stated that it was almost impossible to get our infantry to locate their position by displaying of the panels. I was tempted at first to believe that this was caused by fear of observation by the enemy, but after a time I became convinced that it was due to the ignorance on the part of our officers and men as to the function of the infantry plane. Many officers have been met commanding battalions and regiments who condemn the air service because of their own ignorance. It is recommended that if any schools such as these be organized in the United States that there should be directly connected with it not less than one air squadron.

From the time of the organization of the schools until October 1918, there had been a British Mission composed of seven officers and eight non-commissioned officers and a French Mission with thirteen officers and five noncommissioned officers The officers of both these missions rendered most valuable service in the first courses of instruction which concerned trench warfare. It was found, however, that they were not entirely in sympathy with our efforts to instruct the students in offensive action in open warfare. While there was no outward criticism of it, they did not enthuse much in this matter. Inasmuch as we believed that the point had been reached when trench warfare would become only an incident between attacks, their service became more or less nominal at the schools. They were finally relieved in October 1918. I believe that the officers sent here in both the French and British Missions were of the finest type of officers. Their services, for such work as they had been trained in, trench warfare, was invaluable and there is no doubt in my mind that they rendered possible the training of large numbers of men which otherwise would have been exceedingly difficult to handle.

The field officers' school which was established by verbal authority of G-5, G. H. Q., January 9, 1919, brought to the school in the first class, seventy-seven officers. This first course was in the nature of an experiment and did not appear to be entirely satisfactory. The officers composing the class were an excellent body of men, worked with enthusiasm and did absorb quite a lot of information which had heretofore been to them simply a theory. The work was limited almost exclusively to practical work such as they would encounter in the performance of their usual duties. It was found, however, that one of the mistakes made in preparing the schedule for their instruction was that the school authorities assumed a complete knowledge of their part of certain subjects, as for instance, map reading, order writing, sending messages, etc., so that during the first class no particular stress was placed on these important subjects. The results obtained in that class were very discouraging. It was found that the vast majority of field officers could not read a map, could rarely make a sketch, could not write a clear, concise message, and had small conception of the general tactical principles employed in offensive movements. As the first class showed such regrettable lack of knowledge on these subjects, the second class was arranged to include a large amount of map work. The results were not at all gratifying. It is recommended that for schools organized in the future, instruction in map work be insisted on in a practical way, as for instance; in reading coordinates; there were only five officers out of fifty seven who could read them accurately and correctly. In the majority of cases it took officers of this class thirty five minutes to find a reading of fourteen coordinates. Each were plainly marked on their maps. Again, in a practical exercise when the class was divided into patrols, and each patrol directed to go to a certain coordinate point on the map and report upon their return what they found at that particular coordinate, only one patrol succeeded in reaching the coordinating point to which they had been directed and in bringing back to the class room a flag which indicated their arrival at the designated point. Unless field officers can themselves use maps with greater facility, it is impossible to see how they can instruct their subordinates.

The schools were closed officially on April 21, 1919. It is believed that the school system inaugurated in the A. E. F. was of immense value to the whole army. It is further believed that its value could be greatly enhanced by a little more preparation and study during peacetimes. It is not believed that a school of this nature can take the place in any manner of the officers' school such as was maintained at Fort Leavenworth, but it is believed that a school of this nature would pay for itself in obtaining a uniform instruction and uniform methods throughout the service. Too often in the past have regimental commanders been allowed to set aside well known principles and evolve others of their own of questionable value. It is believed that schools of the nature of the corps schools should be organized in the United States, and that all officers be required to attend them.

H. L. COOPER,
Colonel, Infantry.

II CORPS SCHOOLS, A. E. F.,
May 10, 1919.

[Extract]

The II Corps Schools were established by Paragraph 1, Section 1, G. O. 14, G. H. Q., American E. F., dated January 23, 1918. The schools were opened February 4, 1918.

* * * * * *

C-in-C Rept. File: Fldr. 238: Report

III Corps Schools

Clamecy, Nievre, April 9, 1919.

[Extract]

The history of the III Corps Schools starts in the month of July 1918. * * *

* * * * * *

PURPOSE: Early in the history of the American Expeditionary Force, the system of schools was planned and was subsequently carried out with certain minor changes. The army schools at Langres were intended to train instructors for the various corps schools which were to be formed as the demand for them became necessary. In October 1917, the I Corps Schools at Gondrecourt were formed, followed by the II Corps Schools at Chatillon-sur-Seine in January 1918, and the III Corps Schools at Clamecy in August 1918.

These schools were originally planned to take officers and N. C. O.'s from a certain corps for a month's training and then return them to their organizations, to serve as instructors therein. They were to function under the command of the corps commander and all the branches of the service were to be represented, * * *

SELECTION OF SITE: The III Corps Schools, having the same function and purposes as the I Corps and II Corps Schools, and being under the same control were organized in August 1918, along the lines that had proved successful in the other schools. Before establishing the school it was necessary to choose a suitable location. This problem, in itself, presented many difficulties. Some of the points that had to be considered were:

(a) A suitable range.
(b) A town with sufficient billets for the instructor personnel.
(c) Locations for barracks conveniently placed as regards water supply, drainage, roads, electric lights, etc.
(d) Conference and study halls.
(e) Easy rail connections to supply depots, location of units from which students are to be drawn.
(f) Desirability of avoiding a divisional area.
(g) Proximity to river, canal, or lake suitable for ponton drill.

In choosing Clamecy, Nievre, for the site of the III Corps Schools, the selection was well made. * * *

* * * * * *

FORMATION: The III Corps Schools came into being July 22, 1918, with the arrival of headquarters, * * * They did not find easy sailing. The spirit of the French inhabitants was distinctly hostile.

No soldiers had ever been quartered in the town before and they did not care to have them. It was necessary to threaten requisition to obtain billets, to rent houses for officers and conference rooms. It was necessary to requisition land for the range. Everything was handled carefully and when the first troops, the 3d Battalion of the 331st Infantry arrived, August 1, the formal arrangements with the French had been settled and it was possible to start building up the school. * * *

* * * * * *

ORGANIZATION: The organization of such a school as the III Corps Schools, in which there were to be many organizations taking part on a rather restricted maneuver ground, where the schedules must necessarily be overlapped and be fitted into the schedule of the other schools, and where it was impossible for each school to have its own buildings and own personnel, sufficient for its needs, required much thought and attention. A study of the methods employed at these schools might be of value in starting a similar school, for due to the change of commandants, two distinct methods were employed and thoroughly tested.

Under the first regime, from the end of August 1918 to the end of November 1918, every effort was made to separate the administrative work of the school, such as caring for the incoming and outgoing students, housing and feeding the students, police and inspection of quarters, etc., from the instruction work. * * *

Under the second regime from the end of the school, March 27, 1919, the tendency was to give more authority and to hold the directors of the schools strictly responsible for their own schools. * * *

* * * * * *

As originally planned, the III Corps Schools were to comprise an Infantry Weapons School, a Tactical School, and Engineer School, a Gas School, and a Signal School. An Aviation School was also contemplated but was never started. On the first course which started on September 2, 1918, the first four of the above-named schools received students. The Signal School received no students until the second course, after which it was discontinued in order to concentrate all the Signal Schools of the A. E. F. at Chatillon-sur-Seine.

The work of the various schools was closely coordinated from the very beginning, it being believed that one of the functions of the corps schools was to install a more perfect understanding and closer liaison between the different branches of the service. Thus all the students of the Tactical, Infantry Weapons, and the Engineer School had instruction in gas; the engineers were given short courses in tactics, grenades, musketry and bayonet, automatic rifles, and machine guns; the musketry and bayonet, grenades, and automatic rifles sections of the Infantry Weapons School, and the Tactical School students were given short courses in pioneer engineer work, and the work of the Tactical School and Infantry Weapon School were very closely coordinated, approximately half of the time of the infantry weapons students being devoted to tactical instruction. In the maneuvers given at the end of each course, the engineers, all the infantry arms, the air service, and signal troops were combined to show the student the relation between the different branches of the service, and let him know what was expected of his arm and what he might expect from the other services. In this way the student went away from the school more or less of a specialist in one arm or one service, but having a clear understanding of the tactical handling of all the arms in attacks and retirements of bodies of troops up to and including the battalion. This, then, in general was the purpose of the schools, to give the student a complete technical knowledge of one weapon, to install in his mind proper tactical ideas and give him a basis on which he could build up for himself correct solutions of any tactical problem that might confront him under actual battle conditions in the line. * * *

GROWTH OF THE SCHOOL: Five courses were given at the III Corps Schools. * * *

* * * * * *

TACTICAL SCHOOL: When first organized, that part of the III Corps Schools which was to concern itself with instruction in the work of the infantry was divided into two main branches, the Infantry Weapons School and the Tactical School, the former teaching the technical of the various special weapons and the latter concerning itself with the subjects of tactics as a whole rather than the use of any particular arm.

The Tactical School with Major H. T. Creswell, Inf., as Director was organized August 20, 1918. * * *

INFANTRY WEAPONS SCHOOL: On August 21, 1918, Major Robert G. Calder, Inf., reported for duty as Director of the Infantry Weapons School. It was the duty of this school to give instruction in the mechanism and tactical employment of the special infantry arms. With this point in view it sought to give each man a thorough technical training in his particular specialty. The mechanism of the pieces was thoroughly covered with the intention of preparing the students to become instructors in their organizations. Throughout the Infantry Weapons School particular attention was paid to the development of the student into a proficient instructor. It was not sufficient for him merely to know the mechanism of his piece and its correct tactical employment in battle. He had to be able to instruct others in these things.

* * * * * *

COURSES: The courses in machine guns, observation and sniping, musketry and bayonet were four weeks in length, while the one-pound cannon and trench mortar sections alternated their students, i. e., each course was completed in two weeks and the student personnel of each was shifted to the other section in the middle of the school term. The same was true of the Automatic Rifle and Grenade courses. The scheme was found to be especially advantageous in the cases of the two headquarters company specialties, the 37-mm. gun and trench mortars, not only because by applications the main essentials in the use of the weapons may be gained in two weeks study but also from the fact that in actual practice the personnel of both the 37-mm. and the Stokes mortar platoons are required to have at least a working knowledge of the two arms.

In the Machine Gun, One-Pound Cannon and Trench Mortar Sections, instruction in the specialty was given both morning and afternoon while in the Musketry and Bayonet, Grenade, Automatic Rifle and Observation and Sniping Sections every afternoon was devoted to instruction in tactics. * * *

* * * * * *

MACHINE GUN SECTION

The machine gun section of the Infantry Weapons School was formed under the direction of Captain Leven C. Allen, Infantry, as Senior Instructor. * * * The range at the III Corps Schools was well adapted to machine-gun work. From the firing point the ground, dotted with bushes, gradually fell away for two or three hundred yards and then ascended to a height of some sixty yards above the firing point, at a range of approximately 1200 yards. Beyond this it fell again, the slope almost corresponding to the trajectory of a bullet at that range. Advantage was taken of this fact by the placing of targets on the forward and rear slopes of the hill for the purpose of observing the effect of direct and indirect fire. An abri, connected by telephone to the firing point was constructed from which zone fire at ranges up to 2500 m. could be observed.

The instruction in the machine gun section included the stripping and assembling of the piece, the mechanism, nomenclature, stoppages of the first second and third positions and means of remedying them. During the first course instruction was given in Vickers and Hotchkiss machine guns. Throughout the other courses the instruction was limited to the Browning machine gun. It took up the elementary machine-gun drills in close and extended order, our rough and broken ground, firing on the thousand inch range using ordinary and landscape targets, firing on the long range at fixed targets at known and unknown ranges, and indirect fire including the calculation and employment of indirect firing data.

* * * * * *

The first course of the machine gun section started at the same time as the other schools. * * *

* * * * * *

AUTOMATIC RIFLE SECTION

1st Lieutenant Postell F. Witsell organized the Automatic Rifle Section of the Infantry Weapons School in August 1918. The range was in the process of constuction when Lieutenant Witsell arrived to take charge of the section. This work was rapidly pushed to completion so that the first class at the school had an opportunity to use it throughout the whole of the course. Handicapped by the lack of sufficient instructors Lieutenant Witsell succeeded in getting the work so organized that proper instruction was given. From the first class of students many good officers and noncommissioned officers were held over for instructors. With these the sections could be divided up into smaller section not over seven or eight working at any table in the study of the mechanism of the guns.

The first course was devoted entirely to the American and British Lewis guns and the American and French Chauchat rifles, with additional work on the automatic pistol.

The second course took up the Browning automatic rifle and dropped the work in the other types of weapon. Instruction in the automatic pistol was abandoned after the third course. The instruction in automatic arms has been balanced between mechanical and theoretical instruction in classrooms, and range and field work. Actual practice in stripping and assembling the weapons had been interspersed with lectures on tactical employment and discussions on the care of the guns, their characteristics, strengths and weaknesses, with a view to avoiding monotony. It has been the experience of this section that interest in the Browning rifle particularly is invariably keen. Range firing, aside from instructing the students in the proper handling of the gun, has been conducted with the purpose of demonstrating the superiority of aimed fire over the great volume of fire which the automatic rifle is capable of delivering. Instruction in the Browning rifle particularly has been devoted to emphasizing the greater destructive power of semi-automatic or single shot fire. For this purpose both maneuvers and known range firing have been conducted to illustrate the difference in fire effect, under identical conditions, of the different classes of fire. In addition to bullseye targets, silhouette targets and bobbing targets have been used for problem firing. During the last course, work in target designation, fire orders and fire discipline and control was added to the instruction given; for this purpose ten landscape targets were added to the range equipment, and every student practiced in controlling the fire of several guns on various targets in the course of a problem. The work of the section in firing has been severely handicapped by poor ammunition, which, giving rise to jams, caused the gun to appear less effective than they are under actual field conditions with good ammunition.

After the second course all instruction pertaining to trench warfare methods was abandoned, and tactical work was devoted to open fighting methods.* * *

* * * * * *

From the opening of the first course of instruction in automatic arms at the III Corps Schools more than eighteen hundred students have been enrolled in the Automatic Rifle Section. * * *

* * * * * *

MUSKETRY AND BAYONET SECTION

The Musketry and Bayonet Section of the Infantry Weapons School was formed by Captain (then 1st Lieutenant) Sherrard Ewing. Captain Ewing had been an instructor in musketry and bayonet work at the II Corps Schools and had no difficulty in getting his section organized and ready to receive the first class of students. The time allowed for this preparation was extremely short but with the cooperation of all the departments of the school material for the range was obtained, targets made, dummies in various positions, bayonet rings, firing points and butts were all constructed, equipment for the students was obtained, the work of the instructors outlined and the course of instruction prepared by the time that the students arrived. As with the other section the work of the first course was handicapped by the lack of sufficient instructor personnel, and sufficient details to carry out the work planned.

The course at the Musketry and Bayonet Section was one month in length but a great deal of this time was devoted to other subjects, thus cutting the time for instruction in the specialty very low. Every afternoon was spent at the Tactical School, one full day was devoted to instruction in gas, three half days and one evening were spent at the engineer field on engineer subjects and night wiring parties and the last two or three days were devoted to the combined maneuvers. It was therefore seen that the instruction must be concentrated and boiled down; every moment of the day must be employed if the subject was to be given to the students in the proper fashion.

The instruction was to consist of lectures and conferences followed by practical work on the range. All instructors were proficient in every subject included in the musketry course, * * * Especial emphasis was laid in the musketry and bayonet course on the importance of the students at these schools becoming proficient instructors while at the school. For this purpose each student was given opportunity to carry on the drill or exercise, the instructor being present and making suggestions as to how he should improve the work. At the end of each period the instructor would take the class himself and show the class how the drill should be carried on to give the maximum of benefit to the individuals making up the section.

* * * * * *

The following number of students were instructed by the Musketry and Bayonet Section:

COURSE	DATE	NUMBER
1st	Sept. 2 – Sept. 29	177
2d	Oct. 5 – Nov. 2	157
3d	Nov. 25 – Dec. 21	203
4th	Jan. 8 – Feb. 5	445
5th	Feb. 17 – March 15	343
	Total ------	1325

* * * * * *

OBSERVATION AND SNIPING SECTION

The Observation and Sniping Section was formed for the purpose of training officers and enlisted men sent to these schools as students to be proficient instructors for the intelligence personnel of their respective organizations. Certain officers from each organization were taken and during their stay at the III Corps Schools devoted their attention to this work. The classes were purposely kept small because of the fact that much of the instruction of this section had to be of an individual nature to be of any benefit. For convenience the course was divided into four parts, the short range, the long range, maps, and patrolling. The instructors were assigned to a division of the work for which they were best adapted and then devoted their attention, thought and time to the exploiting of their part of the course.

* * * The object of the course was alwasy to train officers and N. C. O's in such a way that they could back to their organizations and train the intelligence personnel in observation and sniping. * * * Instruction was also given for the purpose of developing the man into an expert sniper and observer. * * *

* * * * * *

* * * The following number of students were enrolled in the Observation and Sniping Section:

COURSE	DATE	NUMBER
1st	Sept. – Sept. 29	128
2d	Oct. 5 – Nov. 2	143
3d	Nov. 25 – Dec. 21	197
4th	Jan. 8 – Feb. 4	89
5th	Feb. 17 – Mar. 15	64

GRENADE SECTION

The grenade course as given at the III Corps Schools consisted of two weeks work. The students from this course were sent then to the Automatic Rifle Section while in return students from the Automatic Rifle Section came to the grenade section to finish the course of one month at the school. This system of instruction was highly satisfactory for it gave the student an opportunity to judge the merits of the two arms and to understand the method of their employment in assisting one another.

* * * the course planned * * * included instruction in the construction and method of use of the French, British, American, Italian and German grenades; the mechanics and tactics of the Grenatenwerfer; the tactical employment of hand and rifle grenades and the composition and use of the explosives contained in the grenades. Detonators and their action, precautions in the handling and shipment of explosives were also included in the subjects taught. In the field, practice was given in the throwing positions and the throwing of dummy and live hand grenades. With the rifle grenades the instruction comprised the firing positions, and firing for accuracy, for barrage effect and practice in the destruction of a strong point.

Instruction in this section was given in the form of lectures and conferences followed by practical work in the field. * * *

* * * * * *

A total of 1587 students took the course of the grenade section during its existence.

* * * * * *

37 MILLIMETER GUN SECTION

The 37-Millimeter Gun or One-pound Cannon Section was organized in September 1918, by 1st Lieut. Harry L. Grant, Infantry. The course at that time was a one month's course. However, as all the students of this section took tactics every afternoon, and one complete day was spent in instruction in gas and about three days at the end of the course were spent in the combined maneuvers, the time for instruction in the one-pound cannon itself was very limited.

The section was handicapped at the beginning by the lack of sufficient number of instructors and by the lack of materiel. A rangehouse was obtained and the materiel stored there. The range itself was admirably adapted for the purposes of the one-pound cannon. From the firing point, the ground sloped gradually downward for about 300 yards and then ascended to a height about 60 yards higher than the firing point at a range of 1500 yards. Piles of rock in various parts of the range were put up to serve as targets. These were renewed from time to time.

It was the purpose and intention of the instructors to work up enthusiasm among the students for the one-pound cannon. Undoubtedly, this weapon attracts more favorable attention then almost any other weapon adopted from the French army. Its great accuracy, mobility, its rapidity of fire and destructive effect suit it for the purpose of destroying strong points, machine-gun nests and also as a defense against tanks. This enthusiasm was maintained throughout the five courses * * *

* * * * * *

The following number of students were handled by this section:

COURSE	DATE	OFFICERS	N. C. O.'s
1st	September 2 to September 29	26	27
2d	October 5 to November 2	19	46
3d	November 25 to December 21	8	73
4th	January 8 to February 4	23	139
5th	February 17 to March 15	31	116

TRENCH MORTAR SECTION

The Trench Mortar Section of the III Corps Schools was organized in September 1918, * * * It was necessary to send trucks to the II Corps Schools to borrow equipment to start the first course. By the middle of the first course, the ordnance began to arrive and thereafter there was no shortage of ammunition and supplies for this section.

Instruction in the Trench Mortar Section took the form of lectures and conferences followed by practical work in the field. * * *

* * * * * *

The following number of students were handled by this section:

COURSE	DATE	OFFICERS	N. C. O.'s
1st	September 2 to September 29	36	88
2d	October 5 to November 2	47	52
3d	November 25 to December 21	11	145
4th	January 8 to February 4	22	138
5th	February 17 to March 15	14	113

INFANTRY SCHOOL

In January 1919, certain readjustments were brought about whereby the Infantry Weapons School and the Tactical School were consolidated under one name and organization, called the Infantry School. In general, the methods of instruction of the specialty sections were left unchanged, except that the courses in Observation and Sniping, Automatic Rifles, Grenades and Musketry and Bayonet were so rearranged as to include all instruction in these specialties during the morning, the afternoons being devoted to tactics, in which all students of the school except those enrolled in machine guns, one-pound cannon and Stokes mortar took part. Under the new regime the Tactical Section became an integral part of the Infantry School; the instructional personnel was enlarged to meet new requirements, and the course of instruction was somewhat widened. * * * aeroplanes were also used in connection with the combined maneuvers, held during the last week of each course, in which the auxiliary weapons participated.

An innovation which also came into being with the establishing of the Infantry School was the Topographical Section, which with suitable personnel and equipment was made responsible for the supplying of maps and all mimeographed matter pertaining to the school. The two officers in charge of this section also supervised the instruction in map and compass work.

The total commissioned and noncommissioned personnel comprising the instructional staff of the Infantry School was in the neighborhood of one hundred and ninety. * * * Since the founding of the III Corps Schools, a grand total of 7675 students received instruction in the Infantry School or in its predecessor, the Infantry Weapons School.

ENGINEER SCHOOL

The staff ordered by G. H. Q. to Clamecy to open the Engineer Department of the III Corps Schools, arrived August 19, 1918, and found little or nothing upon which to build. It was necessary to choose quarters for the school and make out long requisitions for material necessary to carry out the demonstration work. A field for the engineering drills had to be started also.

Four officers reported to the Director, Major Edwin C. Kelton, all of whom had just come from the front after having passed through the Army Engineer School at Langres. * * * All four officers were from the reserve corps as it was then known, * * *

With a pick and a shovel and a coil of barbed wire borrowed from the Engineer School at Chatillon, the first course of the Engineer School at Clamecy opened on September 2, 1918. The first few days were nightmares in the minds of the instructors, but at the end of the first week a few of the requisitions began to arrive and soon thereafter the two departments of the school took real form.

The Mining Department started building frames for dugout entrances on the side of a steep hill, thereby displaying the necessary features of timbering, etc., just as the sections would go together beneath the ground. The pioneers started specimen stretches of wire entanglement standard type trench profiles, trench traces, types of revetment, etc., and the engineer field quickly became a scene of activity. The students were drilled at this field for 12 half-days throughout the course, amounting to about one-half their time.

* * * * * *

The school officially closed March 27, 1919, although the instruction at the school stopped March 15. During the five sessions, the original four instructors had remained until almost the last but additional officers had been added, so that the close of the school found a staff of 11 officers and 12 noncommissioned assistants. * * *

Association closely with the Engineer School, and under the director, was an elaborate drafting room, carrying on work for other departments of the III Corps Schools, such as blue printing, mapping and a hundred other things. The inception of the department really came with the demand for a map of the field of exercise, which map was completed weeks previous to the official one made by special engineers from Langres. A zincograph and hectograph outfit were added to the drafting room and lessened some of the labor.

One of the biggest questions arising during the five sessions was the proper balancing of technical and practical work, adapting some course just as the abilities of the students warranted. * * *

The following student classes were handled by this school:

COURSE	OFFICERS	N. C. O.'s	TOTAL
1st	52	79	131
2d	41	58	99
3d	34	59	93
4th	67	124	191
5th	39	74	113
TOTALS	233	394	627

This student personnel was made up of men from nearly every National Guard and National Army Division sent over from the states. Only one regular division sent any students.

* * * * * *

GAS SCHOOL

The Gas School differed from the other schools of the III Corps Schools in that its course was only one week in length. This fact put extra work upon director and instructors of the Gas School because of the necessity of receiving and discharging a class of students each week. It was impossible to become fully acquainted with all the students. In addition to the regular students of the Gas School, a one-day course was given to practically all of the students who came to the other branches of the III Corps Schools. This required the handling of approximately 400 students at one time. The school was formed in September 1918, * * *

In the beginning, the primary purpose of the III Corps Gas School was to instruct students sufficiently in German gas warfare methods to enable them upon returning to their organizations to impart information in those organizations, being better able to protect themselves against gas. The approved drills for training troops, and antigas fillings were taught. Without endeavoring to make the work very technical with regard to the chemistry and physics of the German gases, effort was made to teach the psychological and physical effects and to some extent to acquaint the students with the names, odors and actions of most of the more commonly used gases. For this purpose, samples of the gases were demonstrated on the field and their actions noted.

After the Armistice when data which had previously been secret and confidential was permitted to be used in the class room, the time given to gas defense was greatly decreased, active drills with respirators were practically abandoned, and much more time given to gas offense. * * *

* * * * * *

The following shows the number of students given instruction by the Gas School from September 1918, to March 15, 1919. These students were given a six-days' course. In addition, approximately 7,000 students were given a one-day course in gas.

* * * * * *

1945   Total no. of students (six-day course)

SIGNAL SCHOOL

The III Corps Signal School was not opened at the same time as the other of the III Corps Schools, and was in existence for one course only; 34 officers and 135 noncommissioned officers attended.

The instruction was made as practical as possible, difficulty was experienced because of the fact that the students were very unequal in education and training. This practically necessitated the organization of three or four classes, the students of each were graded according to their abilities. To do this in a course of one month's duration was practically an impossibility. * * *

* * * * * *

MEDICAL DEPARTMENT

The Medical Department of the III Corps Schools began with the arrival of the 331st Infantry and the establishment of their infirmary in the French Gendarmerie * * * about August 3, 1918. On August 25, 1918, this organization left * * *

On September 1, 1918, the 318th Field Signal Battalion arrived here with Capt. Clarence E. Dunbar, M. C., as medical officer. Being senior officer, he became surgeon of this station. During his incumbency a French house was obtained to be used as infirmary for officers and soldiers resident in town and a Swiss hut was erected near the men's barracks for a field infirmary. A few available cots were placed in the rooms for cases requiring a few days' treatment while all other seriously ill were sent to Mesves Hospital Center in trucks or whatever transportation was available, there being no ambulances here. The pharmacy and dressing room were in a basement room. During the month of September an epidemic of mumps broke out and soon the infirmary was overcrowded. The 318th Field Signal Battalion left this station about October 5, 1918. During September, the strength of the command was 2,716 and it was cared for by three medical officers. * * *

* * * * * *

On account of the location of the troops it was necessary to operate five infirmaries, one in town, one at the officers' barracks, one at the men's barracks, one at the Demonstration Battalion barracks and one at the Aero Squadron barracks. During January the sick call was very heavy reaching 300 in one day.

Three prophylaxis stations were operated, one at old hospital No. 1, one at the Demonstration Battalion and one at the Aero Squadron. * * *

* * * * * *

The problem of sanitation of this camp has not been an easy one but by the cordial cooperation of the Engineer Department great improvements have been made. All the barracks of the men were located in low, water-soaked fields of impervious clay. For many weeks the barracks had wet floors, it rained constantly, stoves were difficult to obtain and wood was scarce. It was therefore often necessary to wear shoes soaked the day before and the sick rate was high although the men were so well cared for early that the hospital rate was not above normal despite the fact that all officers and men were marked either "Duty" or "Hospital." The barracks area was drained by the engineers and sidewalks laid in front of the barracks All double bunks and those close together were separated by shelter halves so that respiratory diseases were much less easily communicated.

Wastes from kitchens and latrines were removed by the French and used for hog feed and fertilizer.

During November the delousing station was enlarged to 5 Serbian barrels and then a steam sterilizer was obtained which could sterilize the clothes of 100 men every 40 minutes. This was placed in the bath house and is in operation constantly. A test was made by the bacteriologist and it was found that spores were killed by the process, thus demonstrating its absolute efficiency.

Several analyses of the drinking water showed it all to be unsafe for drinking without chlorination or boiling and Lyster bags and other containers have been placed at all necessary and many other convenient places.

The food supply of the camp has always been ample but early in the school the required amount of fresh beef was not furnished the men. The number of hind quarters was also less than the proper proportion but after real efforts, this trouble was overcome. All kitchens have been put in sanitary conditions, * * *

* * * * * *

In addition to the work of these schools, the medical department has had supervision over the medical work of outlying detachments such as the 18th Engineers at Etais, Signal Battalion at Entrain and other detachments within a radius of twenty-five kilometers. * * *

* * * * * *

SUPPLY DEPARTMENTS

Separate from the schools but equally important, are the Supply Departments at such schools as these. Without sufficient ordnance, quartermaster and engineer supplies nothing can be done. In the matter of supplies, the III Corps Schools were fairly fortunate, although the schools were organized at a time when the big drives which concluded the war were in preparation. Still at no time were the schools without supplies. * * *

* * * * * *

SERVICE TROOPS

In the matter of Service Troops, the III Corps Schools have not been extremely fortunate. On August 1, the 3d Battalion of the 331st Infantry, an excellent organization, reported at these schools for duty. It was due to their labors that the school was able to start on September 2. However, on September 21, 1918, this battalion was relieved by Provisional Replacement Unit, made up of raw recruits and men detached from the 49th Infantry. Great difficulty was experienced in training and handling this unit.

* * * * * *

C-in-C Rept File: Fldr. 240: Report

Gas Defense School

Hanlon Field, Chaumont, Haute-Marne, November 23, 1918.

[Extract]

(A) Purpose of the School

The A. E. F. Gas Defense School was authorized by paragraph 2, G. O. 79, G. H. Q., A. E. F., May 27, 1918:

> An A. E. F. Gas Defense School is established at the experimental field of the Gas Corps. It will be under the commandant of the experimental field as far as concerns supply, discipline, quarters for officers and men, and administration of grounds, buildings, and equipment. A director and instructors will be appointed by G. H. Q. upon the advice of the Chief of the Gas Corps. The director will report to G. H. Q. through the Chief of the Gas Corps, on all matters pertaining to personnel and instruction. The commandant of the experimental field will render all practicable assistance to the director of the Gas Defense School. At the A. E. F. Gas Defense School will be maintained a course of instruction in gas warfare, adequate for the training in gas defense of gas officers and gas non-commissioned officers. In order to bring this course to the highest possible efficiency, the director of the school will co-operate to the fullest extent with officers engaged in offensive gas instruction, as well as with those engaged in technical investigations at the experimental field. The director shall keep full records of all persons attending the school, and will submit copies of these records to the commanding officer concerned to the Chief of Gas Corps and to G. H. Q.

Arrangements were made to train all gas noncommissioned officers at the army and corps gas schools. The A. E. F. Gas Defense School was used to train officers for gas duties.

* * * * * *

(C) Location and Capacity of School.

The A. E. F. Gas Defense School was located at Hanlon Field (C. W. S. Experimental Field), 2 kilometres east of Chaumont. When established, accommodations were provided for approximately 70 student officers. Later, the facilities were increased so that about 200 students could be instructed during one course.

(D) Length of Course and Number of Classes Graduated.

The course for battalion or prospective battalion and regimental gas officers (who were not members of the C. W. S.) provided for six days of instruction. A total of 22 classes were graduated from the school.

* * * * * *

(F) When School Began Operations and When Closed.

The first class reported for instruction on June 9, 1918, and the last course started on November 18, 1918.

(G) Brief Outline of Course.

The first courses were very disjointed, due to the haste with which the organization was gotten together. A number of lectures were given, but the scope of each lecture was not clearly defined so that there was a great deal of overlapping, and the sequence of lectures was not such as to maintain or illustrate a definite trend of thought. Furthermore, the practical periods did not directly illustrate the subject matter of the lectures. The final course developed gas warfare in a logical sequence, and specimens illustrating the subjects dealt with in the various lectures were arranged on the walls of the lecture room following exactly the order of subjects in the system of instruction. The same trend of thought ran through the lectures, the practical periods, and the museum specimens. * * *

(H) Number of Officers and Soldiers Graduated.

This school has trained approximately 2,300 officers. Over 75% of these graduated sufficiently well to become battalion gas officers and of the 75%, 25% graduated sufficiently well to become regimental gas officers; or even assistant divisional gas officers, if tranferred to the Chemical Warfare Service.

(I) Special Courses Conducted.

C. W. S. officers who were to assume gas duties were sent to the A. E. F. Gas Defense School for training. In order to equip these officers with expert gas knowledge, it was necessary to add special work for the C. W. S. officers to make the course more complete and scientific. This special work dealt largely with the offensive use of gas.

(J) Visits of Students and Instructors to the Front Line.

Members of the C. W. S. on completing the work were attached to divisions at the front for observation and training under the directions of the division officer. At the end of two or three weeks they were given definite assignments with units. Battalion and regimental gas officers were returned to their units.

The instructors made frequent trips to the front in order to become familiar with the developments in chemical warfare, and to collect enemy gas warfare appliances.

* * * * * *

Approved:

J. H. HILDEBRAND,
Lt. Col. C. W. S.
Commandant

C-in-C Rept. File: Fldr. 243:   Report

Bandmasters and Musicians School

Chaumont, Haute-Marne.

[Extract]

In July, 1918, it being learned that Mr. Walter Damrosch (a prominent musician of New York), was in France, General Pershing, called him to Chaumont, for consultation. From this consultation the A. E. F. Bandmasters and Musicians School came into being.

Mr. Damrosch, having volunteered his help, was requested to arrange for the examination of the bandleaders on duty with the respective bands then in France, to determine their fitness for the position held and their eligibility for commission as such in the newly authorized grades.

During the months of July, August and September, 1918, under authority contained in S. O. 204, G. H. Q., A. E. F., France, July 23, 1918, a board * * * attached to G-5, G. H. Q., A. E. F., France, as consultants, called before them for examination two hundred and two bandleaders. Of this number only twenty six were found proficient. * * *

With the result of these examinations before him General Pershing saw the great need for the immediate establishment of the proposed school and announced its establishment of the proposed school and announced its establishment in Bulletin 84, G. H. Q., A. E. F., France, October, 28, 1918. * * *

With the school established the next question was its housing and officers for its. administration. * * *

The school opened for its first course on November 1, 1918. * * * As quarters the As quarters the school was placed in an old mill situated in Bruxeilles, a suburb of Chaumont. This building, with very little alteration, has been found ideal for the purpose. * * *

* * * * * *

With the establishment of the school was convened a Permanent Board for Examination on Candidates. * * * *

Upon reporting for duty each candidate was required to take preliminary examination in harmony, instrumentation and conducting, and all enlisted men reporting were required to take physical examination in addition.

Based upon the result of these examinations each candidate was classified and special attention paid to his requirements in that subject of which he showed the least knowledge - his needs in other subjects however, were not overlooked.

No effort was made at any time to conduct a final examination. The standing and efficiency of each candidate was determined by careful check of his advance, each week, and his final showing as compared with his standing upon admittance to the school determined his eligibility for commission.

Not all of those who reported for examination were permitted to remain at the school. Some were found wholly inefficient, and, due to the very limited time to be devoted to instruction it was found wisest to report these men as found inefficient to higher authority for action. These candidates were returned to their organizations. * * *

All examinations were conducted by the permanent board.

Three separate courses for bandleaders each of eight weeks durations, were carried through.

All students in these three courses were successfully graduated and were recommended for commission as 2 lieutenants, bandleaders, U. S. Army.

* * * * * *

In addition to the course for bandleaders two courses of instruction in French Horn, Bassoon and Oboe were carried through. These courses were each of twelve weeks duration. This part of the school instruction was not as successful as was desired.

The students sent to the school by regimental bandleaders were, with few exceptions, not adapted to the purpose and to this can be laid the small number of successful graduates. * * *

For the purpose of instruction the following instruments were obtained:

    77 French Horns,
    19 Bassoons,
    46 Oboes.

All of these instruments were of French manufacture. Considerable trouble was experienced in obtaining bassoons and oboes due to the very small number available and the lack of labor in their manufacture. It cannot be said that the instruments of these two classes were of high quality. Due to improper seasoning of the wood of which they were made, there was considerable need of repairs both of bassoons, and oboes, and, it being necessary that the repairs be made in Paris, the school at times was without a sufficient number of these instruments.

The French Horn provided was of high grade and study of this instrument was carried through with very little difficulty. * *

* * * * * *

Through the courtesy of the Directors of the French Conservatoire of music two of the graduates - 2d Lieutenants Walter Charmbury and Charles Haubile - were enabled to enter the conservatoire for a further study of music.

CHARLES J. ELLACOTT,
Captain, Infantry, U. S. A.,
Commandant

C-in-C Rept. File: Fldr. 244: Report

Chemical Warfare Service Training

[Extract]

1. Base Ports.

Originally, replacement and special troops, debarking without knowledge of the defensive methods of gas warfare, were sent directly to forward areas for both equipment and training. Unavoidable congestion and confusion rendered this plan unsatisfactory. Troops were then routed from the ports through intermediate points, and trains were sidetracked while the men were equipped and fitted with masks. This scheme was also defective from many points of view.

The great increase in the number of troops bound for forward areas, as the Allied offensive developed, brought from G-4 a request that equipment and training stations be established at important base ports. In compliance with these instructions, equipment and training stations were established at Brest and St-Nazaire.

The work at Brest may be considered as typical of this kind of instruction. At that port arrangements were made to equip and train about 250 men per hour. This necessitated personnel, facilities, and methods that would ensure thoroughness with a minimum of delay and confusion. Under the command of a first lieutenant the training detachment consisted of two sergeants and four corporals as trained instructors and three privates as fitters and helpers.

The troops in single file entered a warehouse containing a stock of 20,000 masks. After fitting and inspection, masks were removed and the men entered a large lecture hall, where everything possible was done to inspire interest and to impress on the men the vital points of defensive measures. When from 75 to 100 men had been fitted, they were placed in a gas chamber for 5 or 10 minutes.

By this procedure, over, 2,000 troops were handled in a single day. During the period from September 25, 1918, to November 16, 1918, 18,328 men were equipped and trained at Brest. Similar work was carried on at St-Nazaire, and was projected in all of the other important base ports of the A. E. F.

2. Depot Division.

At the depot divisions, organization was effected to give three distinct classes of training, namely: for automatic replacements from the States destined for line units; for infantry labor units, etc., that had arrived with little or no gas training, and which were to go forward as units; and, finally, for casuals who after release from hospitals were being returned to their organizations.

By the depot division scheme, a minimum of 18 hours was allotted for gas training for the automatic replacement troops. This time was evenly distributed through the regular three-weeks' course given to such troops and was devoted to lectures, mask drills, games, and range work, during which masks were worn. Minor mimic gas operations with smoke candles and lachrymatory grenades provided realistic settings.

Complete units, such as pioneer infantry, battalions and regiments, engineer service units, and the like, were trained at the depot and held for three days, during which time they received fifteen hours of gas training. Every effort was made to make the training practical. Work was performed and games were played with respirators adjusted. Members of medical units applied bandages, and carried stretchers through woods and over rough ground while wearing respirators.

The number of men released from hospitals and returned to their units via the depot division varied from a very few to 2,000 per day. After examination and classification, these men were re-equipped. A roster of Class A men was made up and the detachment was marched to the gas chamber. With the exception of short talks on the subjects of mustard gas, sag paste, etc., it was not possible to give these men a course of instruction. The Class A men, however, had had previous gas training.

Manifestly, the success of the C. W. S. organization in a depot division depended upon its elasticity and upon its ability to meeting fluctuating conditions. As the arrival of large replacements could not be foretold at division headquarters, large stores of gas material had to be maintained at all times.

During a ten-month period, the 1st Depot Division handled 330,000 men. Similar work was accomplished at the five other divisions of this nature.

3. Artillery Training Camps.

The largest and most typical of the artillery training camps was located at Souge. There, from small beginnings, a week's course for officers and N. C. O's., with a second week for N. C. O's., was developed. After lectures and drills, which included practical work, a thorough examination was given. All who failed to pass with a grade of 70 or above had to take the course a second time. At the termination of the course, the class was taken to Base Hospital No. 6 where the effects of gas were studied from actual gas casulties. This furnished a great stimulus to general gas training.

When it became evident that gas officers and N. C. O's were not receiving the necessary support from their immediate commanders, a comprehensive brigade lecture course was instituted during the third week of camp training. Results were so successful that the brigade course was moved up to the second week.

To ensure strict gas discipline, all units were subjected to at least three surprise gas attacks under the following conditions:

At night, while the troops were sleeping at their positions, -- to test protection given by sentries, and to correct such carelessness as leaving respirators out of reach, etc.;

While firing was in progress on the range -- to correct errors in laying the piece and in transmitting data;

And finally, during night marches, -- to overcome confusion.

Interest was maintained by furnishing regimental and battalion gas officers and N. C. O's. with live literature on defensive methods.

It was found that there was comparatively little to be gained by instructing the individual officer. Interest created within the unit gave the best results. The conclusion is that all gas instruction should be given simultaneously with the artillery training.

Lectures were given and literature distributed on the use of gas shell by artillery. The Chief Gas Officer and his commissioned assistants held themselves in readiness at all times for conference on this most important problem, and gave technical advice to the artillery men on the problems involved in the use of gas shell by artillery.

As the capacity of the Souge Camp increased from one brigade to five (with auxiliary troops), more than 50,000 men were given instruction at one time. The total of officers and men equipped and trained, including fifteen different artillery brigades, exceeded 150,000. Similar training was given in the other artillery training camps.

4. Miscellaneous Stations.

In the fall of 1918, large numbers of corps and army troops arrived who had had but little gas training in the States. Logically, these men might have been sent to depot divisions; but as such a course would have overburdened the transportation system, they were ordered to billeting areas for a short period of training.

A gas equipment and fitting station was maintained at Is-sur-Tille, where, occasionally, as many as 2,000 men were handled in one day. Later, similar stations were established at St-Dizier and Dunkirk. Such men as might get past all other training and equipment centers without acquiring masks, and at least a small amount of gas instruction, received their training in gas defense at these regulating stations.

* * * * * *

6. Army and Corps Schools.

The largest of the gas schools was the Army School for noncommissioned officers situated at LANGRES (later at ROLAMPONT). The director, a captain, was assisted by eight lieutenants. Six-day, two-day, one-day, and one-hour courses were given for various branches of the service. During the month of November, 1918, 919 men took the six-day course, 3,347 men the two-day course, and 2,312 men the one-day course.

The first corps gas school at GONDRECOURT, which was the first to be established in France, may be taken as representative of the three corps gas schools (gas schools were operated in the II Corps under authority granted by G. O. No. 14, G. H. Q., A. E. F., dated January 23, 1918, and in the III Corps). This was organized shortly after G. O. No. 45, G. H. Q., A. E. F., dated October 8, 1917, combined the first division schools to form the first corps schools. As finally organized, the operating personnel of the school comprised one captain as director, two first lieutenants as instructors, seven sergeants as assistant instructors, and five additional enlisted men for office work. The buildings included an old chateau occupied as headquarters, a large lecture hall, six Adrian barracks, and seven Swiss huts for headquarters. The trench system, complete with all types of dugouts, was large enough to accommodate 300 students. Originally, a three-day course in defensive measures against gas was given. Early in 1918 it became necessary to complete gas training within two days, and, somewhat later, the course for regular students of the first corps schools was reduced to six hours.

Later, however, to meet the requirements of Section 5, Par. 1, G. O. 79, G. H. Q., A. E. F., dated May 27, 1918, which authorized the appointment of a gas N. C. O. for every battalion and separate unit and two gas N. C. O's for each company, it was necessary to provide a special six-day course for noncommissioned officers. This six-day course was attended by approximately 2,400 N. C. O's. The total number of students for all courses in the first corps school was about 8,000, of which 40 per cent were officers who were trained during the earlier months of the school's existence.

7. Defense in the Field.

A chief gas officer and assistants were assigned to every army and army corps, and a division gas officer and assistants to every division. With the publication of G. O. No. 79, G. H. Q. A. E. F., May 27, 1918, the position of these officers in the field was satisfactorily defined. The duties of field gas officers as summarized by that order included:

  The instruction of all gas officers and N. C. O's. within their units;

  The supervision of gas defense training and drill;

  The collection and transmittal to laboratories and proving grounds of all new enemy material;

  The inspection of gas defense measures adopted throughout other units;

And finally, the furnishing of advice on matters relative to gas warfare to the commanders or staffs of the units to which they were assigned.

The scope of this advisory function was broadened by G. O. No. 107, G. H. Q., A. E. F., dated July 2, 1918, which provided that: "Gas officers acting as advisors will be consulted and advantage taken of their technical knowledge and advice in the preparation of all plans involving the extensive use of gas, whether by artillery or other-wise." This included, in addition to artillery and the weapons used by the special gas troops, the use of hand and rifle grenades containing gas, smoke, and incendiary fillings, and the use of smoke producers.

Gas officers in the field collected and transmitted to the proper authorities intelligence relating to enemy gas warfare methods, material, and attacks. These officers prepared schemes for the use of gas, smoke, and incendiary materials by their units or by special gas troops and, on the other hand, they investigated and reported upon all hostile gas attacks and casualties resulting therefrom.

C-in-C Rept. File: Fldr. 245A: Report

Air Service Training

[Extract]

1. Upon the formation of the Training Section, General Staff, one officer was placed in charge of the air service training. Air service training naturally divides

itself into two phases; the training of individuals and the training as a unit. Our aviation was so far behind the other Allied nations that it was found necessary to have a large system of schools in France for the instruction of the individual. The control of this large system of schools, from the viewpoint of personnel, material, courses taught, and methods followed, was of such magnitude that it could not be handled except by a large staff of trained officers. Accordingly the Chief of Air Service, A. E. F., was designated as Director, Army Air Service Schools. He in turn designated an air service officer as Chief, Training Section, Air Service.

2. While the system of air service schools was being built up preliminary efforts were made to start the training of aerial observers for the use of our first squadrons to go to the front with our first divisions. Officers from the 1st Division and from the 1st Artillery Brigade were trained as aerial observers by the French aero squadron on duty at La Valdahon. About twenty coast artillery officers, sent from the states for training as aerial observers, were first sent to the signal school of the I Corps Schools and upon forming of the I Corps Aeronautical School they were given the course of observation at that point. Upon completion of observers' course at La Valdahon the graduates were sent for about a week to French squadrons at the front and were then sent to the I Corps Aeronautical School for further training. Subsequently all classes from La Valdahon and other preliminary observers schools were sent through either the I or the II Corps Aeronautical School (which was formed later) for advance training. due to the lack of a suitable artillery range the I Corps Aeronautical School was discontinued and all observers afterwards sent through the II Corps Aeronautical School.

3. It was planned to carry out the training of our air service units by placing them on airdromes with French units of the same kind as follows:

Observation squadrons at Amanty; pursuit squadrons at Villeneuve; day bombardment squadrons, Viloeneuve; night bombardment squadrons, Cernom; balloon companies, Vadenay.

4. This plan was carried out with regard to the first four observation squadrons, the first two pursuit squadrons, and the first four balloon companies. As soon, however, as American units had had some experience over the lines this policy was changed so that new units coming to the front were placed alongside older American units.

5. The system of air service schools was built up under the chief, training section, air service, and soon began to turn out more pilots and observers than our units at the front could absorb. In order to give them training, arrangements were made with the French whereby these men could be sent to French squadrons, receive advanced intruction at the squadrons and actually carry on work over the lines and be released as we needed them.

6. Arrangements were also made for training airservice personnel in England and officers graduating from the schools in England were sent to the front with English squadrons, where they served for a period of three months and were then released for duty with American units. Two American pursuit squadrons were trained, equipped and sent to the British front by the R. A. F., but were later transferred to the American sector.

7. Upon the development of the training section, air service, the work of the training section, General Staff, with regard to the training of air service personnel became one of determining matters of policy, of supervision and inspection of the work carried out and of liaison in regard to training with other arms.

8. It later developed that there was need of better liaison between the ground and air and accordingly there were established at the corps airdromes a corps liaison school, each course lasting about six days and about 250 men from designated divisions attending each course. All squadron and balloon companies at the front carried out instruction for the officers and enlisted men of their respective units. Endeavor was made by the above means and by participation in maneuvers to increase the efficiency of

liaison between air and ground troops. These courses were conducted by the different corps and armies to which these squadrons and balloon companies were assigned.

9. Air service units were stationed at all the artillery schools and these units were placed directly under the commanders of those schools and were primarily school detachments for the instruction of the artillery. However, at each of these points some instruction of individuals were carried on. Air service units were placed at practically all schools of every branch in order to promote the knowledge of air service among the other arms and all detachments so placed were directly under the school commanders. Arrangements were just being completed for placing air service units and a staff of competent officers in the areas near the base ports in order that divisions arriving in France might have the benefit of air service during their training after arrival. The signing of the Armistice, however, made it unnecessary to carry this into effect.

10. During the Armistice the work of the liaison schools and the participation of airplanes and balloons in maneuvers was carried out to the fullest extent possible. This work was directly under the corps or armies to which the air service was assigned. During active warfare liaison between the front and the schools was carried out at all times, officers from the front spending periods at the schools and officers from the schools serving with units at the front. This resulted in the latest developments of aerial warfare reaching schools after a minimum of time. * * *

C-in-C Rept. File: Fldr. 248: Report

Military Education in the American Expeditionary Forces

[Extract]

1. Special Schools and Students sent to British and French Schools: The British and French authorities soon after our arrival offered to give instruction to a number of our officers at their schools and centers of instruction. Pending the organization and development of our own schools, advantage was taken of this offer and a large number of officers were sent to the schools of our Allies. This assistance was particularly valuable during the formative period of our own school system and the plan was continued until the end of March 1918 when it was practically discontinued except for officers of our divisions that were training in British areas.

2. Approximately 2,000 reserve officers, graduates of the first Officers Training Camps in the United States, arrived in France in September 1917. These officers were distributed among French and British schools, our own artillery schools at Mailly and Saumur, our 1st Division Signal School at Gondrecourt and two temporary schools for the instruction of infantry officers organized by Major General (now Lt. Gen.) R. L. Bullard at La Valbonne and Val Reas. Those officers who were sent to British army and corps schools spent three or four days at the end of their course with British front line units to see practical application in line of what they had been taught.

3. 175 of these officers were given instruction at Val Reas and 525 at La Valbonne. These schools were organized as a temporary measure and took advantage of French plants. American officers were in charge but instruction was given by British and French instructors. The course was for five weeks and only one course was given as our own corps schools had in the meantime begun operations. The course consisted of instruction in the duties of platoon commanders, including the tactical handling of the platoon and technical instruction in handling of infantry weapons. British instructors were used

for: Stokes mortar, sniping and scouting, bayonet and musketry. French instructors were used in: Tactics, grenades, automatic rifles, 37-mm. guns, machine guns and field fortification.

4. The following French and British schools gave instruction to American officers. Courses varied from two to seven weeks in length. The aerial schools of our Allies which were used are covered in * * * report of the chief of air service.

French

Motor Transport Service Training School . . . Meaux
Engineer School . . . . Versailles
Artillery School. . . . . Fontainebleau
Trench Artillery School . . . . Bourges
School of Defense against Avions. . . . . . Arnouville-les-Gonesse

British

Fourth and Fifth Army Infantry Schools
Army Scouting Observation and Sniping Schools)
Army Trench Mortar Schools   ) of the
Heavy Artillery Schools   ) 5
Royal Field Artillery Schools   ) British Armies
Corps Gas Schools of several British Corps
Corps Bombing and Light Trench Mortar Schools
  of several British Corps
G. H. Q. Small Arms School (Lewis Gun) - Le Touquet
G. H. Q. Small Arms School (Machine Gun) - Camiers
Physical and Bayonet Training School - St-Pol
Depot Special Brigade (Gas Projecting School) - Helfaut
Antiaircraft Gunnery School - Steenwerck

5. American Schools: The school system proposed for the American Expeditionary Forces, was put into operation as promptly as preparation of sites, assembly of instructors and preparation of curriculum would permit. Some minor modifications and changes were made in the project as time went on in order to prevent duplication of work or when conditions necessitated. As a whole, however, the project was carried out as planned, and was functioning smoothly and efficiently when we had practically two million men in France. Without any question, all of our schools played a prominent part in fitting our officers and men to become efficient leaders and instructors and in producing the necessary cooperation between all arms and services by which only success could be realized.

6. The courses in all of our schools were entirely too short for efficiency but, under the circumstances, they constituted a reasonable compromise between the demand for haste in all our preparations and what was desirable.

7. At the beginning a large number of British and French instructors were used in our schools. Our plans provided that students who were found fitted for duty as instructors would after graduating from the schools be sent to the front for a tour of duty from where they would be brought back as needed, fresh from front line experience, for duty as instructors. These officers were necessarily of a very high standard and were in constant demand for duty as staff officers as our staffs expanded or new ones created. Many also became casualties. As the war progressed, however, we were able to approximate more and more to our original scheme and replace French and British instructors with our own. At the time of the Armistice, very few officers of the Allied armies were still being used as instructors at our schools. * * *

(a) Army Schools.

8. During the period of preliminary study of the school project, reconnaissances had been made with the aid of French staff officers, for suitable sites for both our army and I Corps Schools, the organization of which it was desired to begin without delay.

9. The city of Langres, Department of Haute-Marne, was found to satisfy the requirements set forth in paragraph 1 (subparagraph C) of school project, as a site for the army schools. This was an old fortress town and was an important French garrison town in prewar days. There were a large number of barracks in the city itself and in the vicinity which the French Government offered for our use. The General Headquarters of the A. E. F. were located at Chaumont only 22 miles away. If located at Langres the Training Section, General Staff, would be able to maintain close relations and officers from General Headquarters could readily visit the schools in order to give lectures or witness demonstrations. This site was approved and here was developed a large center of the military educational activities of the A. E. F., comprising the greater part of the schools composing the army schools. General Orders No. 46, dated October 10, 1917, directed the organization of the group of army schools and designated Major General (then Brigadier General) James W. McAndrew as Commandant. The schools began operations with the opening of the first course at the General Staff College on November 28, 1917.

10. A center of artillery studies and an army intelligence school were later added to the list of army schools as given in the original school project and were organized at Langres. No army aeronautical schools were organized and all army artillery schools except the army antiaircraft schools were placed under the direct supervision of the chief of artillery and located at points where more facilities were available for the instruction and care of student personnel.

* * * * * *

12. Staff College: The first director of the staff college was Brigadier General A. W. Bjornstad. He was assisted by several French and British instructors who had had wide experience in staff duty. Seventy-five officers were ordered to the first course of whom forty-two were graduated and recommended for general staff duty with troops. In all four courses of there months each were held. 534 officers were graduated and recommended for staff duty out of a total of 770 officers enrolled. A number of the officers enrolled and who completed part of a course had to be relieved before graduating on account of the urgent need of staff officers at various times.

13. Classes were continuously increased in size to meet the constantly growing demands for graduates. The class intended to begin January 1, 1919, was to contain 500 students. As rapidly as our own officers became available and competent, the foreign instructors were relieved and our own substituted. When the college ceased operations on January 1, 1919, all instructors were American except one Englishman and one Frenchman.

14. School of the Line: The purpose of the army school of the line was to give tactical instruction in the use of all arms and services in combination to include the regiment and to give instruction in how to issue proper orders. The students were officers of shorter previous military training than the students of the staff college. The courses as planned were to be for three months but it was not always practicable to keep the students for that length of time.

15. The first class was composed of 52 officers largely captains of the reserve corps who had just arrived from the United States. The line school had four sessions and graduated 488 officers.

16. The first classes at the staff college were composed largely of regular officers who had had sufficient prior tactical training. In view of the limited number of

these, beginning with the third course the line school was used as a feeder for the staff college and the 100 graduates who stood highest at the end of that course were detailed to attend the next class at the general staff college.

17. Several special courses for field officers were given as opportunity offered, the first course beginning July 16, 1918. In all six courses of two weeks each were held and a total of 476 field officers received instruction. These special courses were given to teach officers recent developments in tactics, the proper coordinating of the use of the different infantry weapons and the proper use of accompanying guns and tanks. The course was planned for field officers arriving with advance detachments from the United States and for field officers and senior captains of divisions in training.

18. Center of Information for General Officers: While this was provided in the original school project, it was possible to assemble officers for only two courses. The purpose of the center of information was to give general officers and colonels the benefit to be derived from witnessing demonstrations which were held in the various army schools; also by means of lectures and conferences to put before them the latest tactical lessons that had been learned.

19. The first course was conducted by the instructor personnel of the line school and took place between January 20, 1918 and January 31, 1918. It was attended by seven officers. Student personnel was not available for another course until November 1918 when a class of eighteen officers was ordered to report on November 20, 1918. The director of the general staff college prepared the course which was to be for one month. All members of the class were relieved and assigned to other duty before completion of the course. No other classes were started.

20. Candidates Schools: The schools for candidates for commissions in the infantry, engineer corps and signal corps were started as a part of the army schools at Langres; for candidates for commissions in field artillery as a part of the artillery school at Saumur, and for candidates for heavy artillery at first at Mailly-le-Camp at army heavy artillery school and later at the Saumur Artillery School.

21. The capacity of these schools as originally planned, however, was not sufficient to meet the ever increasing demands. Our wastage in officers was enormous from the beginning. The S. O. S. absorbed great numbers, so did all the staffs; when active operations began the casualties among platoon and company commanders were exceedingly heavy and sickness claimed many more. All the surplus officers sent over from the United States, those promoted from the ranks of the divisions as a result of schooling and examinations in the United States and the product of our candidates schools were all absorbed. Early last fall we were facing a serious shortage in officers only to be met efficiently by a tremendous expansion of our candidates schools.

22. A new infantry candidates school was opened at La Valbonne where accommodations for the increased student and instructor personnel could be obtained and the infantry candidates school at Langres was gradually being transferred to the new and enlarged school. By January 1, 1919, it was planned to have 22,000 candidates under instruction at La Valbonne, and to graduate classes containing between five and six thousand every month. At the same time plans were made to graduate 800 candidates per month from the Artillery School at Saumur, 400 engineer candidates per month from the engineer school at Langres, and 200 signal candidates from the signal school at Langres.

23. The total number of candidates graduated from candidates schools in France were: Infantry 6,895, Artillery (including both field and heavy) 3,393, Engineers 1,332, Signal Corps 365, a total of 11,985. The courses in all of the candidates schools were three months but several of the courses in the infantry, signal and engineer schools were reduced in order to meet the urgent demand for officers.

* * * * * *

(b) Corps Schools.

25. Corps schools were organized by these headquarters but the original project contemplated that each corps center of instruction would be under the direct control of the corps commander. The I Corps Schools were operated for some time in this way, but it was soon found that corps headquarters were going to be on the move too much to exercise efficient supervision of the corps schools, so the I Corps Schools reverted to control of training section. The others were never released to corps control.

26. The I Corps Schools began operations at Gondrecourt, Department of Meuse, on October 16, 1917. The plant and schools of the 1st Division in the vicinity of that town were taken over. The II Corps Schools were opened at Chatillon-sur-Seine on February 4, 1918, and the III Corps Schools at Clamecy on September 2, 1918. In all 13,916 officers and 21,330 noncommissioned officers were graduated from the various courses in our corps schools.

27. Courses were at first of five weeks duration but were early shortened to four weeks. No cavalry school was organized at any of the corps schools as there was no necessity for this school. Classes at the sanitary schools were found to be too small to warrant separate schools for each corps so sanitary school of I Corps Schools was discontinued in March 1918 and of II Corps Schools in April 1918, and all students given instruction at the army sanitary school at Langres. The artillery sections of the corps schools were also discontinued in June 1918, because of a lack of material and as it involved a duplication of work which was being satisfactorily performed at artillery organization and training centers and at Saumur. The aeronautical sections of the corps schools were consolidated in May 1918, at the II Corps Schools. In June 1918, the field officers classes were discontinued at the corps schools and instruction to field officers was given in special courses at the army school of the line.

28. Two special courses for the instruction of field officers were given at the II Corps Schools in February and March 1919. These courses were devised primarily to provide efficient supervision of the instruction in musketry which was planned for the latter part of March, April and part of May. 133 field officers completed the course of instruction at these two special courses.

* * * * * *

(c) Artillery Schools.

30. Army Center of Artillery Studies: Details are given in * * * report of the chief of artillery. * * *

31. The fourth course began May 12. The course has been enthusiastically received by its students, both of the artillery and infantry, as well as of other services. It has done much to promote mutual understanding between the infantry and the artillery. Its subject matter should be included in the future educational system in the United States. * * *

32. Saumur Artillery School: Details are given in * * * report of the chief of artillery.

33. After its initial use to train officers newly graduated from the training camps in the United States, the school was devoted to soldier candidates for the artillery coming from organizations in the A. E. F. It has effectively filled a very important function. * * *

34. Valdahon Artillery School: See also * * * report of the chief of artillery. * * * The school afforded a refresher course of four weeks to battery officers of field artillery. In addition, a certain number of field officers of artillery and infantry were included in each class. Much stress was laid on the tactical employment of artil-

lery, particularly the battery and battalion. To add realism to this phase of the work, a battalion of infantry was included in the troops assigned to the school, and a field officer of infantry placed on the school staff.

35. Three courses were held at Valdahon, at the end of which it became necessary to vacate this camp.

36. This school was virtually a combination of the artillery sections of the corps schools as originally contemplated. The I and II Corps Artillery Schools were actually organized. The former had four courses, from December 3, 1917, to June 15, 1918. The II Corps Artillery School had one course.

37. Difficulties were encountered in the operation of the corps artillery schools, due to the lack of terrain for firing ranges and unnecessary overhead in the instruction staff. With the augmented troop arrivals in the summer of 1918, these two schools were discontinued and the staffs sent to training camps, where they were urgently needed.

38. The location of the corps artillery schools with schools of other arms, particularly those of the infantry, and later the placing of infantry troops at a detached artillery school are believed to be the first systematic efforts in our service actually to use infantry in artillery schools. This should be continued in our home schools. The most desirable form is to place corresponding schools of the infantry and artillery side by side. If this is not feasible, infantry troops should be stationed at the artillery school for use by it. * * *

39. Heavy Artillery School: For the training of officers assigned to railway and tractor artillery in artillery subjects; and for the training of artillery soldiers in the work of artillery specialists.

40. This school was established at Mailly-le-Camp, Aube, by G. O. 51, A. E. F., October 29, 1917, * * * It was under the direct supervision of G. H. Q. In April 1918 the chief of artillery was given the immediate supervision of this school by G. O. 64, G. H. Q., A. E. F., 1918. The name of the school was changed from the Army Heavy Artillery School, A. E. F., to Heavy Artillery School, A. E. F., by G. O. 93, G. H. Q., A. E. F., June 11, 1918. In June the school was moved to Angers in order to provide for the increased personnel. There were eight regular courses, with a total of 1071 graduates. * * *

41. Army Antiaircraft School: For the training of officers and soldiers assigned to the anitaircraft service. The organization of this school was provided for by G. O. 46, H. A. E. F., October 10, 1917. * * * As at first organized it contained but one section, the artillery. This section was located at Arnouville-les-Gonesse, Seine-et-Oise, and began work September 26, 1917, and continued until November 11, 1918. A total of 240 officers and 5,000 men passed through this school.

42. Later as the troops arrived in France, the machine gun section was organized at Langres, and later moved to Perrancey, about four kilometers due west of Langres. * * *

43. The work of training began in April 1918, and continued until November 1918. A total of five battalions of antiaircraft machine guns were sent through this section. In addition, an infantry machine gun battalion was given a course in aerial firing, as well as about two hundred officers and noncommissioned officers from the heavy artillery.

44. About the same time there was added the searchlight section to care for the training of the personnel assigned to antiaircraft service. This section was located at Champigney, about three kilometers north of Langres. An advanced subsection was established at Colombey-les-Belles to which searchlight units were sent to receive their final training under actual conditions of service. * * *

45. On April 8, 1918 * * * the army antiaircraft school was placed under the commandant of the army schools at Langres and remained hereuntil the last. * * *

46. Trench Artillery Center: For the training of officers and soldiers assigned to the service of trench artillery, and for the organization and equipment, repair and main-

tenance of material. General Orders No. 46, H. A. E. F., October 10, 1917, announced the establishment of the army trench mortar school * * * In April, 1918, the name of the school was changed to army trench artillery school, A. E. F., and was placed under the commandant, army schools (G. O. 54, G. H. Q., A. E. F., 1918). The school was located at Fort de la Bonnelle, about 3 1/2 kilometers S. W. of Langres, where it remained until about September 10, 1918, when it was moved to Vitrey, Haute-Saone, about 40 kilometers east of Langres.

47. Because of the increase in the number of units of trench artillery to be trained, and further in view of the need for additional space for infantry candidates at Langres, advantage was taken of this last move to change the school to the trench artillery center. (G. O. 152, G. H. Q. A. E. F., 1918). The functions of the center were to provide for the organization and training of units of divisional and corps trench artillery; for the training of officers and soldier specialists of trench artillery, and for the development and test of trench artillery material. All divisional and corps trench artillery units were passed through this center. * * *

48. Tractor Artillery School: The instruction of selected officers and soldiers from organizations assigned to heavy tractor artillery was initiated at Mailly-le-Camp by General Coe in October 1917 to provide for a trained personnel to handle the French material then being supplied the 51st Regiment. The plant was small and the facilities inadequate. To meet this situation a number of officers and soldiers were sent to the French tractor schools near Vincennes in the latter part of January 1918 * * * The officers were sent to Camp de St-Maur; the soldiers to Le Tremblay, Dourdan, Boulogne and later to Sathonay.

49. In May 1918 the tractor artillery school for American officers was established at Camp de St-Maur near Vincennes * * * This school moved to Gien, Loiret, in August 1918. The establishment of O. and T. Center Number 5 at Anglouem, Charente, * * * enabled us to take care of the instruction of the soldiers who before this had been sent to the French schools. * * *

50. Heavy Artillery Candidates School: General Orders No. 32, G. H. Q., A. E. F., February 18, 1918, established at Mailly-le-Camp a school for candidates for commission in the heavy artillery. The school was made a part of the then army heavy artillery school, but in March 1918 was detached therefrom and transferred to and incorporated in the new Saumur Artillery School at Saumur. (G. O. 45, G. H. Q., A. E. F., 1918). Candidates for commission in the railway, tractor, antiaircraft and trench artillery passed through this school. Upon graduation they were required to take a course at the school which operated for the branch to which assigned. * * *

(d) Aviation Schools.

51. For aviation schools see Report of Chief of Air Service, * * * The report of the II Corps Aeronautical school is a part of report of II Corps schools * * *

(e) Miscellaneous Schools.

52. Motor Transport School 1, Decize. The purpose of this school was the instruction of officer and soldier personnel of the A. E. F. in the maintenance and operation of motor vehicles and motor trains. * * * School had a capacity of 500 students and began operations in July 1918. On March 1, 1919, the school was transferred to the educational subsection of training section and devoted to vocational training as a part of the educational program of the A. E. F.

53. The various courses given, length of each course, number of classes and number of graduates are shown below:

OFFICERS

Courses	1st Course Started	Length of Course	Number Classes	No. Students Graduated
Field Service	August 26, 1918	6 weeks	5	225
Motorcycle	August 26, 1918	3 weeks	1	3

ENLISTED MEN

Courses	1st Course Started	Length of Course	Number Classes	No. Students Graduated
Field Service	August 26, 1918	6 weeks	5	325
Park Service	Nov. 4, 1918	6 weeks	3	39
N. C. O.	August 14, 1918	2 weeks	14	1068
Mechanics	August 12, 1918	6 weeks	5	98
Oxy-Acetylene	Oct. 26, 1918	6 weeks	3	29
Drivers	July 22, 1918	2 weeks	15	1193
Motorcycle	July 22, 1918	3 weeks	10	349

* * * * * *

54. A. E. F. Gas Defense School: This school was located at Hanlon Field, 2 miles east of Chaumont. The purpose of the school was to instruct officers in gas warfare so that they would be competent to train troops in defensive measures against gas. Gas non-commissioned officers were given instruction at army and corps gas schools.

55. The length of the course was six days and 22 classes graduated. The first course began June 9, 1918, and school ceased operations November 24, 1918. Officers of the chemical warfare service were given special courses to fit them for their duties.

* * *

56. Chaplains School: This school was under the direct supervision of the Senior Chaplain, A. E. F., and was located at Lauplande near Le Mans. It operated from October 1, 1918 to February 1, 1919, and was in fact a replacement depot. Instruction was given concerning the equipment of chaplains and their duties in the field, especially in connection with burials and graves registration. The length of time any chaplain was under instruction depended on the needs of organizations, some remaining only one day while in other cases several weeks were spent at the school.

57. A similar school and replacement depot was operated from June 1 to September 30, 1918, at Neuilly-sur-Suize, near Chaumont, the character of instruction being the same as at the Le Mans school later.

58. Military Policy Corps Training Depot, Autun: This depot was established at Autun under the provisions of Par. 4, G. O. 150, A. E. F., September 5, 1918, for the purpose of training all personnel before being sent to military police units. The amount of training given individuals varied but averaged from two to three weeks. The capacity of the depot was 42 student officers and 1,000 soldiers. A school for the training of candidates for commission in the military police corps was operated in connection with this depot, but this course was discontinued on completion of the course that was being conducted at the time of the Armistice.

59. Interallied Schools: Each of the following interallied schools instructed a number of officers in the special subjects indicated.

Allied Road Traffic School, Rozoy-en-Brie
Interallied Center of Instruction for Tanks, near Fontainebleau
Interallied school for regulating officers, St-Dizier

60. American E. F. Bandmasters and Musicians School, Chaumont: This school was established at Chaumont under the provisions of Bulletin 84, A. E. F., October 28, 1918. The purposes of the school were:
(a) The training of bandmasters
(b) The training of musicians in the study of certain instruments.

The course for bandmasters was 8 weeks and for musicians 12 weeks. * * *

C-in-C Rept. File: Fldr. 263: Report

Educational and Vocational Training

July 7, 1919.

From: R. I. Rees, Brigadier-General, General Staff

To: A. C. of S., G-5

[Extract]

1. The educational work in the American Expeditionary Forces was organized under authority contained in Paragraph 449, Army Regulations and Section 27 of the National Defense Act of June 3, 1916 which reads as follows:

> In addition to military training, soldiers while in the active service shall hereafter be given the opportunity to study and receive instructions upon educational lines of such character as to increase their military efficiency and enable them to return to civil life better equipped for industrial, commercial, and general business occupations. Civilian teachers may be employed to aid the army officers in giving such instruction, and part of this instruction may consist of vocational education either in agriculture or the mechanic arts. The Secretary of War, with the approval of the President, shall prescribe rules and regulations for conducting the instruction herein provided for, and the Secretary of War shall have the power at all times to suspend, increase, or decrease the amount of such instruction offered as may in his judgment be consistent with the requirements of military instruction and service of the soldiers.

2. Prior to the army taking over the control of the educational work the Army Educational Commission of the Y. M. C. A. accomplished good results prior to the Armistice in the conduct of voluntary classes, the principal subjects undertaken being instruction in French, in the causes and progress of the war, in the history and ideals of the leading nations involved, in mathematics and to a smaller extent other subjects for which there was a demand. General Orders No. 192, G. H. Q., A. E. F., dated October 31, 1918 have official recognition to the educational scheme and defined the functions of the Army Educational Commission in its relation to the army. This order provided solely for the establishment of post schools and for instruction in more elementary subjects. This order was amended by General Orders No. 9, G. H. Q., A. E. F., dated January 13, 1919, establishing a more complete system of nonmilitary education and defined more succintly the duties of the Army Educational Commission of the Y. M. C. A. in its relation to the work and placing the control of all education in G-5, G. H. Q. General Orders No. 30, G. H. Q., A. E. F., February 13, 1919, in connection with G. O. No. 9 established a complete system of education for the American Expedi-

tionary Forces. Under provisions of these orders the following educational organizations were established:
1. Post Schools
2. Divisional Education Centers
3. American E. F. University, Beaune (Cote d'Or)
4. American E. F. Art Training Center, Bellevue, Paris
5. French and British Universities
6. Mechanical Trade Schools
7. Agricultural Institutes
   Business Institutes
   Citizenship Institutes
   Educational Extension Lecture Courses
8. Educational work for convalescents in hospitals

Under this organization endeavor was made as far as possible to parallel the army work to our educational system in the United States; the post schools supplying elementary education, the divisional educational centers being equivalent roughly to high schools and vocational training schools including the mechanical trade schools, the American E. F. University to under-graduate college work and graduate work for the technical professions and the French and British Universities for postgraduate work.

3. The formal educational work in the A. E. F. began January 2 with the post schools. All other organizations were put in operation as rapidly as possible and all were functioning by the first week in March. All educational work in the A. E. F. was placed on a voluntary basis for officers and soldiers with the exception that illiterates and non-English speaking soldiers were required to attend the post schools. The illiterates, however, were generally so eager to learn to read and write our language that the success in teaching illiterates is among the substantial results of the educational system; many organizations which came to France with a high percentage of illiterates returned entirely literate. The post schools generally dealt with elementary and secondary instruction, but some in the enthusiasm for educational training went far beyond this.

4. The divisional educational centers were naturally grouped in accordance with the subjects taught into academic and vocational. Along academic lines all subjects ordinarily taught in high school were given in these centers and even here advanced work was undertaken. The vocational schools in these centers were normally grouped about the organization in the division or section which had the equipment necessary to teach the subjects.

5. In order to meet the demand fully for educational training a number of special schools were organized. To supplement the more advanced work in agriculture given at the College of Agriculture at the University at Beaune, the American E. F. Farm School was established at Allerey and the entrants in that school were not called upon for any academic requirements of entrance, the appeal being made to farmer soldiers throughout the A. E. F. and the courses given were entirely practical. One of the extraordinary developments in the demand for learning in the American Expeditionary Forces was in fine and applied arts. In order to meet this demand the American E. F. Art Training Center at Bellevue, Paris, was established where exceptional work was done in painting, sculpture, architecture, city and town planning and interior decoration. Allied to this work was the organization in 14 base hospitals and convalescent camps of interesting educational work for convalescents in drawing, art and Allied subjects. Also there were entered more advanced students in art a detachment for study in the famous Ataliers of Paris, such as La Loux, Julian, and Jaussely. All these undertakings were in addition to the College of Fine and Applied Arts at the American E. F. University.

6. Realizing that the educational system could not within the exigencies of the military service reach all soldiers in the A. E. F. a correspondence school for exten-

sion courses was organized at the American E. F. University and very successful work has accomplished. The organization of the services of supply had developed fully equipped construction and repair plants offering ideal equipment and organization for training in mechanical trades. With the approval of the Commanding General, S. O. S., mechanical trade schools were established at seven of these centers with most successful results.

7. The American E. F. University at Beaune (Cote d'Or), organized under great pressure in the short space of three weeks, was a completely equipped university with 11 distinct colleges. The aim of this university was to be so organized as to meet whatever demand for higher training students entering called for and it is believed that this standard was attained and that no soldier student entering was unable to pursure courses of study desired by him.

8. University work in French and British Universities was successful beyond all expectations. In French universities it seemed that the foreign language involved might present an insuperable obstacle, but the result of three and one-half months of study demonstrates that the officers and soldiers who were fortunate to secure the detail as students not only were able to master the French language but were able early in the term to receive great benefit from the regular courses offered at each university. There have been examples of brilliant work done by our American students as attested by the university authorities and there has been almost without exception a concrete valuable accomplishment on the part of every student in attendance. Not the least valuable in this unique experience of American officers and soldiers has been their close contact with the French and British people. Through this contact there had grown up a fine understanding of the ideals, character and home life of the French and British citizen, and conversely, we have been able to present to the French and British educators and the people in the university towns a fine example of our young American citizen. The benefit it is believed has been entirely mutual.

9. In view of the unstable conditions existing throughout this entire educational effort in the A. E. F., due to the rapid repatriation of our soldiers and the resulting constant movement of troops, one of the most important branches in the educational work was that of field institute short courses and educational extension lectures. Reports indicate that at least half of the full strength of the American Expeditionary Forces was reached by this means. The object of these institutes and lecture courses was to bring vitally before the soldier the fundamental principles of occupation and employment, and perhaps most important of all, to present to him in a striking manner his duties and responsibilities as a citizen of the United States. There were therefore organized institute teams which operated in all points in the A. E. F., giving intensive instruction in business, trades and engineering, agriculture, occupational guidance and citizenship. One hundred and fifty-seven lecturers covered a wider field embracing in addition to the subjects already noted, history, art, teaching, geography, industry, foreign relations, industrial conditions and all other vital questions of the day.

10. In connection with all the educational work undertaken there was organized educational tours having for their object intimate personal contact on the part of the student with the basic facts of the history of France, a personal view of the great art treasures, an intimate study of geological formations and mineralogy, and familiarity with existing business, factory and commercial methods. It will be seen from the above that every effort has been made to give to the student the peculiar advantages attendant upon study in a foreign country.

Organization

11. The American E. F. educational system was organized and controlled by the 5th Section of the General Staff, G. H. Q. As the scheme developed it was found that any system not under complete army control would not be able to meet the demands of this important problem. Without detracting in any way from the valuable work already accomplished by the Army Educational Commission of the Y. M. C. A., operating under the guidance of G-5, it was deemed best to take over this commission and the entire personnel operating under its supervision. On April 15, 1919 the Y. M. C. A. completely severed its connection with the educational work in the army and all of its members performing educational duties were taken over by the army and placed in government control. The organization per se was not greatly disturbed. The commission became the educational corps commission and it with the members thus employed became the Educational Corps, A. E. F. This corps was composed of competent educators almost without exception from educational work in the United States. The total membership of this organization was 457. The advantage of this change was immediately apparent in the closer organization and in the better control under military authority of this excellent body of men.

Text Books

12. The Army Educational Commission, Y. M. C. A., particularly Dr. John Erskine, Chairman of that commission, took early action to secure from the United States an adequate supply of text books. These were purchased by the Y. M. C.A. for sale to the officers and soldiers of the A. E. F. With the increasing control which the army exercised over educational matters it seemed only just that the Y. M. C. A. should be relieved of the cost of these text books and that they should be taken over by the army and issued for use of the student soldiers. The army therefore purchased the text books from the Y. M. C. A. and they were used in all the schools organized to the great immediate advantage of the students, and of lasting value to the army in that they are now being shipped to the United States for use in educational work in the permanent establishment.

13. In connection with the use of books in educational work, it is a pleasure to testify to the valuable assistance rendered by the American Library Association in providing reference libraries for all post and divisional schools. A notable achievement on the part of this association was the installation in an incredibly short time of a complete library of 30,000 volumes at the American E. F. University at Beaune (Cote d'Or) and the most efficient administration of this library by representatives of that association with assistant supplied by the army. No demand has been made upon the American Library Association for assistance which was not met by them with the fullest cooperation and complete fulfillment.

Cost

14. Request by the Commander-in-Chief upon the War Department for authority to assume complete responsibility for the educational program resulted in an allotment by the Secretary of War of $3,000,000 to carry on the educational work. The estimate for this allotment was based upon the payment of salaries for members of the educational corps, for purchases of supplies not obtainable upon requisition, for supplies already available in the A. E. F., which included purchases of text books and the printing of educational material. The largest item of expenditure was the purchase from the Y. M. C. A. of the text books ordered by them furnished from the United States. The next item of importance is that of salaries for the 457 members of the educational corps.

The total cost of the educational program in the A. E. F. is as follows:

Text Books	$1,156,646.69
Salaries Educational Corps	318,720.86
Emergency Purchases	6,184.07
Supplies not obtainable on requisition	18,450.42
Traveling expenses, members educational Corps	24,000.00
Total	$1,524,002.04

As has already been noted the large item of expenditure was for text books. Arrangements have been made for the shipment of these books to the United States for future use in the permanent military establishment.

Summary of Attendance

15. The following statement of attendance upon schools is based upon reports actually received at G. H. Q., A. E. F. In view of the rapid movement of troops since January 1 many organizations, including several divisions after having established schools and having them well in operation, left France for the United States without rendering reports. The figures given, therefore are not complete but are conservative because no estimates have been attempted for attendance at schools in organizations from which reports were never received. The figures, however, are valuable as indicating the actual known accomplishments in education in the American Expeditionary Forces.

Post Schools	181,475		
Divisional Educational Centers	27,250		
A. E. F. University, (including Allerey)	8,528		
A. E. F. Art Training Center	367		
Mechanical Trade Schools	4,144		
French Universities	6,300		
British Universities	1,956	230,020	
Farmers Institutes	300,000		
Business Institutes	160,000		
Citizen Institutes	230,000		
Educational Lectures	750,000	1,440,000	
TOTAL			1,670,020

16. This report gives a brief survey of the work accomplished in education in the American Expeditionary Forces. * * *

Conclusion

17. It is believed that the above report indicates the value of the educational work in the American Expeditionary Forces. It is also believed that the educational scheme put in operation in the A. E. F. demonstrates that a combined military and educational program can be carried out in the army without detriment to military training and without doubt to the advantage of the individual soldier undertaking the work, and the mental training received by the soldier as a student in such an educational system can have but one result: That of making him a better soldier. It is submitted that a combined military and educational training system should be adopted as the training policy for our permanent military establishment.

R. I. REES,
Brigadier General, General Staff,
Educational Subsection, G-5.

C-in-C Rept. File: Fldr. 247: Report

Depot Division Training

1. Due to the necessity for combat divisions the original project of two replacement divisions for each corps was not carried out. Six divisions, the 39th, 40th, 41st, 76th, 83d, and 85th were designated as Depot Divisions. All except the 41st and 83d ceased operating as Depot Divisions after a short period, so that the main work of training of replacements and specialists was performed by two divisions.

2. The 41st Division organized the 1st Depot Division at St-Aignan---Noyers for use as a base and training depot under the provisions of G. O. 9, A. E. F., January 15, 1918. Total replacements handled by this depot, 295,666. This depot handled replacements for infantry, machine gun, supply train, ammunition train and specialists of all kinds. Signal and Medical Corps replacements were also handled here part of the time.

3. The 83d Division organized the 2d Depot Division at Le Mans July 8, 1918. Replacements for infantry, machine gun and supply train were forwarded from this depot. Total number of replacements handled, 193,221.

4. 1st Depot Division, St-Aignan. The instruction was divided into six weekly periods, the first period being devoted largely to elementary work. Each weekly period provided for more advanced training up to the sixth. Immediately upon arrival troops were classified by district instruction officers into three sections, according to their degree of proficiency. Class 3, the least proficient, began with the first period, class 2 with the third period, and class 1, the most proficient, with the fifth period.

5. The schedule of infantry instruction provided for:
Road March
Infantry Drill, school of soldier, squad and company
Infantry in attack (platoon and company)
Bayonet Training
Position, sighting and aiming drill
Antigas training
Bombing instruction
Musketry, target designation, range finding, fire discipline,
    direction, distribution and control
Physical training
Messages, saluting and military courtesy
First Aid Training.

6. During the road march instruction was given in march discipline, hygiene of march, road rules, care of feet, fitting of packs. Antigas training was made a feature of all drills. Special instruction was given to men who possessed special qualifications for and to those who had had any former training in handling 37-mm. gun, Stokes mortar, automatic rifle, grenade and as buglers. Special schedules were followed by machine gunners including pistol practice, throwing grenades, barrage dirlls, setting up barrage battery positions and handling the battery as a unit. Target practice was made an important feature for infantry as soon as man became proficient in position and aiming drills.

7. In the area occupied by 1st Depot Division there were constructed·
10 rifle ranges, total   163 targets
7 pistol ranges, total   45   "
7 machine gun (1,000 in) ranges, total 87   "
2 machine gun 600 yds. ranges, total   18   "
3 37-mm. and Stokes mortar ranges, one of 750, one 1,000 and one 1,500 meters.

8. The following schools were operated by the 1st Depot Division:
School for Mess Sergeants, Cooks and Bakers
- Length of Course: 6 weeks
  - Mess Sergeants 6 "
  - Cooks 4 "
  - Bakers 4 "

School for Company and Regimental Clerks
- Length of Course: 1 month

School for Company and Battery Mechanics
- Length of Course: 1 month

School for Infantry Pioneers
- Length of Course: 1 month

School for Musicians and Buglers
- No definite length of course.

School for Saddlers, Horseshoers, Stable Sergeants, Drivers and Packers
- Length of Course: 1 month

School for Chauffeurs and Auto Mechanics
- Length of Course: 1 month

School for Signallers
- Length of Course: Telegrapher, telephone and radio operators 6 weeks

Ordnance School
- Length of Course 1 month

Three cavalry training troops:
No definite length of training.

9. In addition to the foregoing, schools for officers, noncommissioned officers, and where practicable for privates were conducted at least one hour, four nights per week.

10. 2d Depot Division, Le Mans. The general system of classification and assignment of replacements to appropriate periods of instruction was similar to that at 1st Depot Division. The terrain in the region occupied by 2d Depot Division was more favorable than that occupied by the 1st for the construction of target ranges so this important feature was developed to the greatest possible extent. Six ranges were constructed with a total capacity of 760 rifle and 100 machine-gun targets. Approximately 175,000 men received instruction in rifle practice on these ranges. The system of instruction followed in this character of training at 2d Depot Division was later adopted for instruction of entire A. E. F. in rifle practice.

11. The system of grouping, character of instruction, schools operated and requirements before replacements could go forward follow:

(a) The 2d Replacement Depot (83d Division) began to operate on July 8, 1918.
(b) TRAINING AND SPECIAL INSTRUCTION:

Grouping A

Direction: District Commanders (Senior officer in each geographical area).

Personnel: Platoon replacements, including riflemen, bombers, rifle grenadiers and automatic riflemen.

Training Units: Rifle companies of division.

GENERAL INSTRUCTION:

Instructors: Training Cadres (not less than two (2) officers and 50 other ranks per company).

Time: Three weeks.

Instruction: School of soldier; squad, platoon and company drill, close and extended order; combat formations; musketry; bayonet; hand and rifle grenade; automatic rifle; antigas; personal and trench hygiene and first aid; military courtesy and regulations; physical training; games.

SPECIAL INSTRUCTION:

School	Duration of Course
Noncommissioned Officers	4 weeks, carried on with general instruction

Grouping B

Direction: Division Machine Gun Officer.

Personnel: Machine Gunners.

Training Units: Machine Gun companies of division.

GENERAL INSTRUCTION:

Instructors: Battalion and Company Commanders. Training Cadres not less than 2 officers and 35 other ranks per company.

Time: Three weeks.

Instruction: Antigas; nomenclature, operation and mechanism of gun; stripping and assembling; position, aiming, loading and firing; physical training; hand bombing; mechanism of and position, aiming and firing with the pistol; platoon and company drill, rough ground; target designation; ground cover, emplacements; packing, training animals; dismounted gun drill.

SPECIAL INSTRUCTION:

School	Duration of Course
Noncommissioned Officers.	4 weeks, carried on with general instruction.

Grouping C

Direction:

Personnel: Military specialists.

Training Units: Military Specialists Battalion.

GENERAL INSTRUCTION:

Instructors: Battalion Commanding Officer Training Cadre.

Time: Three weeks.

Instruction: School of soldier; musketry (to include rifle fire); antigas; military courtesy and regulations; physical training; personal and trench hygiene and first aid; care of arms, clothing and equipment.

SPECIAL INSTRUCTION:

School	Duration of Course
Stokes Mortar	3 weeks
One Pounder Gun	3 weeks
Pioneers, Sappers and company mechanics	3 weeks
Liaison Signallers (including telegraph operators, telephone operators, radio operators and runners)	6 weeks each for telegraph, telephone and radio oper.; 3 weeks for runners
Intelligence (including	
Observers	
Scouts	3 weeks
Snipers)	3 weeks
Military Police (including	3 weeks
P. M. Military Police,	4 weeks
Intelligence Police and	
Mounted Orderlies)	

Grouping D

Direction:
Personnel: Non-military specialists.
Training Units: Non-military specialists company.
GENERAL INSTRUCTION:
Instructors: Company Commanding Officer Training Cadre.
Time: Three weeks.
Instruction: Antigas; nomenclature and use of rifle; range practice; personal hygiene and sanitation, first aid; care of arms, clothing and equipment.
SPECIAL INSTRUCTION:

School	Duration of Course
Cooks and Bakers (including	
Cooks	6 weeks
Bakers	4 weeks
Mess Sergeants	4 weeks
Horse Transports (including	
Stable Sergeants	4 weeks
Saddlers	4 weeks
Horse Shoers	4 weeks
Drivers	4 weeks
Wagoners, mechanics	2 weeks
Motor Transports (including	
Drivers	3 weeks
Chauffeurs	3 weeks
Mechanics	3 weeks
Motorcyclists	3 weeks
Office Personnel (including	
Company and regimental clerks	4 weeks
Stenographers, typists and statisticians	3 weeks
Ordnance Repair	-------

Grouping E

Direction: Division Surgeon.
Personnel: Sanitary Personnel.
Training Units: Sanitary Train.
GENERAL INSTRUCTION:
Instructors: Commissioned Officers, Sanitary Train.
Time: Three Weeks.
Instruction: School of the soldier, squad and detachment; organization and function of the medical department; sanitary formations in combat; transportation of sick and injured; first aid; care of gas casualties, orthopedic appliance; personal and military hygiene, sanitation; construction of shelters for aid stations, etc.; elementary anatomy and physiology.

(c) Training Memorandum No. 3, Hq. 2d Replacement Depot, provided for the following tests before men were forwarded as replacements:

    2. No replacements will be sent forward who do not fulfill the following requirements:

      (a) All soldiers must speak and understand plain orders given in English.

      (b) All soldiers must be physically fit and must pass, before entraining, a venereal examination.

      (c) No men will go forward without adequate gas training as determined by the Division Gas Officer.

(d) All men will be properly equipped according to Equipment Manual for Service in Europe and Special Regulations and Special Orders as prescribed from time to time.

(e) All replacements must have completed prescribed rifle training.

(d) Training Memorandum No. 5, Hq. 2d Replacement Depot, provided for the following training for men not up to the required standard:

Training is based on a minimum schedule of three weeks - the fourth included if possible. Replacements, upon the time of assignment to the school, will be graded and placed in their appropriate period of instruction under the direction of the several unit commanders. Advance will be made at such time as the individual has satisfactorily completed the instruction in the period to which assigned. Further, men found incompetent for line duty will be relegated to headquarters or supply units and eventually assigned to duty on S. O. S. work. Par. 6 Training Memorandum No. 3, states that

6. Soldiers who cannot speak and understand orders given in English will either be assigned at once to the Supply Units of the several commands or, if no vacancy exists, their names will be reported to the Statistical Office, these Headquarters, for disposition.

(e) Six target ranges were maintained as follows:

Target Ranges existent time of 2d Depot Division.

Range No. 1, Chateau d'Hermitage: 100 targets each at 200, 300 and 500 yards range.

Range No. 2, Monce-en-Belin: 100 targets each at 200, 300, 500, 600 and 800 yards range.

Range No. 3, La Bazoge: 175 targets each at 200 and 300 yards range.

Range No. 4, St-Jean du Bois: 160 targets each at 200 and 300 yards range.

Range No. 5, Belgian Camp: 200 targets each at 200 and 300 and 500 yards. 125 targets at 600 yards.

Range No. 6, Mayet - M. G. Range: 100 targets each at 200, 300 and 500 yards.

(f) ARRIVALS AND DEPARTURES - July 1918 to December 1918, incl.

	ARRIVED						
	July	Aug.	Sept.	Oct.	Nov.	Dec.	Total
Infantry from U. S.	—	7000	5503	31123	47270	5800	96696
Machine Gun from U. S.	—	571	—	2494	3261	53	6379
Casuals and Evacuations from outside area	79	347	4822	14308	18800	7245	45601
Totals	79	7918	10325	47925	69331	13098	148676
	DEPARTED						
Infantry to Combat	2203	3575	6652	10320	31458	11290	65498
Machine Gun to Combat	70	1255	397	338	3150	78	5288
Forwarded to Blois and Regulating Station	—	31	3403	525	379	54	4392
Medical Replacements	—	—	—	—	262	15	277
Miscellaneous Detached	—	642	531	—	1090	273	2536
Casuals and Evacuations outside area	76	52	196	11441	10212	9285	31256
Total	2349	5555	11179	22624	46551	20995	109247

(g) Men of divisions which were skeletonized began to pass through the 2d Replacement Depot on October 21, 1918. The following divisions, and parts of divisions, were handled by the 2d Replacement Depot:

  31st Division
  34th "
  38th "
  84th "
  86th "
  4th Pioneer Infantry
  55th " "
  57th " "

----

www.ingramcontent.com/pod-product-compliance
Lightning Source LLC
Chambersburg PA
CBHW060333010526
44117CB00017B/2817